Elaine Hedges: A Tribute

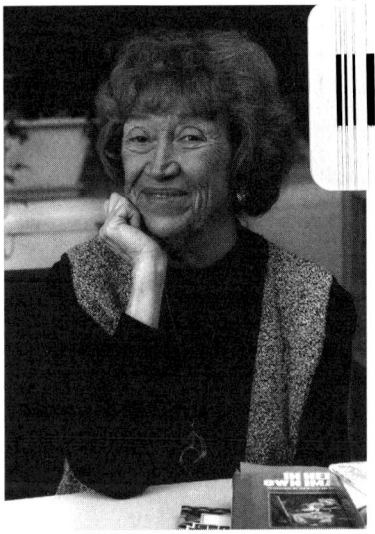

1927–1997

Elaine Hedges, recently retired and in her prime as an innovative scholar, died unexpectedly on June 5, 1997. In December she had also been ill. Then, weakened with anemia, she was pleased to edit this issue, for it was "something to do" while she was recovering. We did not know then that this would be the last of a long series of gifted and generous contributions she had made to The Feminist Press. Elaine participated in the Press's founding; served on its early reprints committee, as well as its more recent Publications and Policies Committee; brought us our all-time bestseller *The Yellow Wall-Paper;* edited *Ripening: Selected Work* and, with Ingrid Wendt, edited *In Her Own Image: Women Working in the Arts.* She was our most energetic and trusted reader, advisor, and mentor for twenty-seven years.

Elaine was also my friend and, in spirit, though we never talked about it, my sister. We did talk about how wonderful were our times together, how much pain and joy we shared.

We stopped the issue as it was going to press in order to dedicate it to Elaine and to print selections from a few of the many tributes we and the Towson faculty have received. We plan to collaborate with the National Center for Curriculum Transformation at Towson State University to produce a pamphlet honoring Elaine Hedges. Send tributes to The Feminist Press by July 30. For more information about a memorial service to be held at Towson State University in September 1997, call Sara Coulter at (410) 830-2334.

— *Florence Howe, The Graduate School, CUNY, and The Feminist Press*

"Elaine, Elaine, the blessing of you in my life: 'Joy, courage, strength, perspicacity, defiance.'"

—*Tillie Olsen*

"It has been a privilege to work with Elaine Hedges for the last twenty-five years in the English department, in the women's studies program, and in curriculum transformation projects. The excellence of her own work and the excellence that she enabled others to achieve are enduring testimony to her genius and generosity."

—*Sara Coulter, Towson State University*

"Elaine's passion and focus shone in her writing, her actions, and her conversation. Her leadership not only shaped an academic discipline worldwide, but it also shaped generations of students and devoted colleagues worldwide."

—*Annette Chappell, Towson State University*

"At some distant point when the great noises of our century have faded, those few notions which truly served to dignify and free humanity in profound ways should be clearly audible. Elaine Hedges' voice will be heard, and her untiring work in establishing women's studies will be understood and valued as something that transformed human experience in her time and for the future."

—*Dan Jones, Towson State University*

"Elaine's wonderful combination of intellectual rigor and imagination illuminated new worlds for everyone who knew her. But it's her interest and delight in life that I'll remember, and miss, the most."

—*Jan Wilkotz, Towson State University*

"I will remember Elaine as a friend, colleague, feminist, scholar: a woman who taught me how to teach as we developed and team-taught the introduction to women's studies at Towson State University. Over the years (almost twenty-five) we laughed a lot and talked a lot—I will miss our discussions of books, feminism, the classroom."

—*Judy Beris, Towson State University*

"Resolute, unflinching, and productive for women to the end, Elaine was an exceptional person. I'll miss her courage, which strengthened me, but also I'll miss her laughter; it was the deep laughter of one who knew—and loved—life."

—*Jo-Ann Pilardi, Towson State University*

"My first teaching position was at what was then Towson State College. Last fall I sought Elaine out to hug her and to thank her for being all she represented to me then. Much of the eager patience and studied optimism that I try to maintain comes from what I learned being around Elaine during those years, with her quiet strength and clarity of direction."

—*Johnnella E. Butler, University of Washington, Seattle*

"At a critical time in my own career, puzzling how to balance parenting, poetry, and scholarship with a sense of identity and some kind of future, I was blessed with Elaine's courageous example—believing in me, urging me on to important feminist discoveries. I shall always be grateful."

—*Ingrid Wendt, poet and coeditor of* In Her Own Image

"'I've pulled off most of the paper, so you can't put me back.' Elaine Hedges helped bring *The Yellow Wall-Paper* out from the obscurity in which it was walled up. Her work on curriculum transformation, on the *Heath Anthology of American Literature*, on women's verbal and visual arts all served to strip off more paper to make sure that none of us can be 'put back.' I think she saw herself as a foot soldier in our struggle, but, if so, she was that rare one who made it to the eighth rank and became a queen!"

—*Lillian S. Robinson, East Carolina University*

"Elaine Hedges was a pioneer in women's studies and feminist criticism, and an architect—continuously, until she died—of the curriculum transformation movement. Everything she wrote, every book she edited, has been groundbreaking and valuable to other scholars, to other teachers. I find it almost impossible to single out one aspect of her legacy for comment: I have used all of it, the work on quilts, the marvelously edited collection on Meridel Le Sueur, the unique anthology on women in the arts, the essays on curricular change. She was superb, too, at nurturing and bringing to useful life the work of others. I am grateful for her extraordinary legacy, and immensely sad to lose her unassuming and generous presence."

—*Deborah S. Rosenfelt, University of Maryland, College Park*

"I always think of Elaine as a quilter, the one piecing together the patches by bringing people together and showing how one layer fits into the next one."

—*Eileen Borris, Howard University*

"Elaine's retrospective of the last three decades in her introduction to this issue of the *Quarterly*, 'Looking Back,' takes on the character of a personal memoir of a life spent in women's studies. She took part in the early struggles, she fought for change at the heart of the academy, she contributed greatly to its achievements, and has left us with a clear agenda for future action."

—*Dorothy O. Helly, Hunter College and the Graduate School, CUNY*

"Much like the narrator of Charlotte Perkins Gilman's The Yellow Wall-Paper who tears down the restricting bars of the wallpaper confining her to her patriarchal world, Elaine Hedges tore down restrictions of the literary canon in the 1970s and brought Gilman's landmark story to The Feminist Press and national attention. Her contributions to Gilman studies, feminist scholarship, American literature, and quilting can never be 'put back.' But I am indebted to Elaine for more than her academic accomplishments. A truly generous colleague, Elaine taught me valuable lessons about sisterhood and integrity, which I carry on today."

—*Catherine J. Golden, Skidmore College*

"Elaine Hedges nurtured, mentored, and inspired generations of women scholars with energy, patience, insight, and love. It was a pleasure and a privilege to coedit the 1994 book *Listening to Silences* with her. I miss her wisdom. I miss her voice. I miss her warm encouragement and support. Her commitment to 'matters of real importance,' to borrow a phrase from Charlotte Perkins Gilman, never flagged. Her generosity as a colleague and as a friend knew no bounds."

—*Shelley Fisher Fishkin, University of Texas, Austin*

"Elaine Hedges was a great American feminist, as practical and beautiful as the quilts she loved so much—shrewd and kind and so hardworking—a pioneer."

—*Jane Marcus, City College and the Graduate School, CUNY*

"We are forever in debt to Elaine Hedges for her great contribution to the definition of women's studies and to the recovery of literature by United States women: stunning legacies letting us memorialize her by carrying them on."

—*Carol Kessler, Pennsylvania State University*

"Elaine Hedges, with her intelligent thought and articulate writing, built the bridge between quilts and the academy."

—*Shelly Zegart, Kentucky Quilt Project, Inc.*

"I first met Elaine in 1989 when she came to give a few lectures. I found her easy to get along with, and she did not demand personal comfort. She didn't mind riding on the back of my husband's bicycle in order to come to my apartment. We had a wonderful time together. Elaine will always live in my heart as a distinguished scholar and a wonderful friend."

—*Tao Jie, Peking University*

"I thought I should write about Elaine as a forerunner, an innovative and important figure, but I found myself writing instead these sentences: I'd had a gift now laden with sorrow—a holiday in Baltimore spent with Elaine just a few days before she died. We went to the aquarium; we wept at the Holocaust Museum; we posed for photos with Eleanor at the Roosevelt Memorial; and we shared stories. I have gleaned only pleasure from knowing Elaine. I am diminished by her death."

—*Blanche H. Gelfant, Dartmouth College*

Contents

Personal Narratives: Teachers, Students, Administrators

Pedagogy

Editorial

Looking Back, Moving Forward

Looking Back, *Elaine Hedges*

I began working in women's studies in the late 1960s, first trying to persuade recalcitrant members of my department to approve a single course on women writers, while joining with other faculty and students to agitate for child care, an affirmative action office, a women's center, and the creation of women-centered courses in other departments. Then came planning interdisciplinary women's studies courses and eventually persuading the administration to approve a program. Like so many others who were creating women's studies at the time, I was full of hope, even exhilaration. I also wondered: Would this radical challenge to the academy, to the traditional construction and dissemination of knowledge and to entrenched gender and race discrimination, succeed or fail? Would it gain momentum or falter in its effort to create significant change? Today, a quarter century later, although we have learned to rein in some of our utopian dreams, we can point to remarkable achievement: women's studies is a presence in the vast majority of colleges and universities in the United States, and it is a worldwide movement as well.

Figures tell only part of the story, but they are revealing. In the United States women's studies has grown from two programs and ten or so courses in 1969–70 to over 600 programs and countless thousands of courses in higher education. There are over 400 undergraduate minors offered, over 200 B.A.s, and about 140 graduate-level certificates or degrees. Internationally, at least fifty countries have women's studies programs, and many others have established women's centers and research institutes. Behind these figures is an extraordinary history of struggle and achievement by millions of students, staff, faculty, administrators, community activists, and others, both within and outside the academy. It is a history that still needs to be written. This issue is a step toward such a history. It contains a selection of articles reprinted from the pages of *Women's Studies Quarterly,* [1] from the journal's inception in 1972 to today, as well as several previously unpublished essays. It is thus both a retrospective and a celebration of a quarter century of reporting on women's studies in a publication that has devoted itself consistently to such reporting.

From its beginnings in 1972, the *Quarterly* has grown as women's studies itself has grown, expanding from four to sixteen pages, then to thirty-two, and, since 1980, producing double issues, including thematic ones, which now run well over 200 pages. In choosing among the wealth of material available to create this issue, we have had, of necessity, to be selective. Much on which the *Quarterly* reported has had to be omitted, or only briefly alluded to, including materials on grass-roots activism and women's studies in communities and in elementary and secondary schools; legal issues pertaining to education, including Title IX and affirmative action; book reviews and bibliographies that introduced readers to the new scholarship in the field; information about foundation grants, jobs, publications, and conferences. We have instead focused on the history of women's studies in colleges and universities in the United States and, more briefly, on the growth of women's studies internationally—the two areas on which the *Quarterly* has itself primarily focused.

This two-part issue begins, then, by looking back. Part 1, the retrospective, includes reprinted essays from the *Quarterly*'s twenty-five–year history, arranged in eight thematic sections. Its opening sections consider the ideological origins of women's studies and its institutionalization in higher education, including closeups of the formation of a dozen representative programs. Following this are sections on major educational developments that have contributed to or resulted from the growth of women's studies: feminist pedagogy, women's studies' critiques of the traditional disciplines, the curriculum transformation movement, and the formation of national organizations, especially the National Women's Studies Association (NWSA), which was created to support and extend women's studies work. The issue then contains, in a section entitled "Groundbreakers," key documents or events in the history of women's studies. The final section of part 1 contains excerpts from national reports on women's studies in nine countries to represent what is by now a global movement. Part 2, consisting of three original essays, moves forward, exploring some of the major opportunities and challenges facing women's studies in the years ahead.

The explosive growth of women's studies in the 1970s as a new academic field is chronicled in the first two sections of part 1. The selections from Florence Howe's editorials and articles, which regularly tracked and interpreted that growth, report the steady increases in the numbers of courses and programs, in structured minors and majors, and in the establishment of some of the earliest graduate programs, research centers, commissions and caucuses within academic professional organizations, journals, presses, and conferences. The closeups of specific programs flesh out these statistics with stories of the obstacles confronted, strategies used, and successes achieved—as well as the defeats experienced—by groups of women as they engaged with often resistant institutional politics and structures to establish programs. They show women's studies developing through a combination of freestanding interdisciplinary courses and departmental ones, the evolution of some programs into departments with their own budgets and faculty lines, and the marginal survival of others that lacked even basic essentials, such as office space. They also testify to the exhilaration of engaging in radical, pioneering work, and the exhaustion of doing such work on top of the regular demands of one's job, as well as the risks involved, especially for younger, untenured faculty. Not least, they show women struggling with the conflicts between feminist principles and institutional practices: the efforts to maintain ties to the activist student and community groups, which helped inspire and shape many of the earliest programs, to retain egalitarian decision- and work-sharing collective structures in the face of institutional pressures for hierarchical ones, and to preserve the original political emphasis and radical vision of women's studies while creating strong academic programs.

Such tensions and conflicts, as well as others, many of which women's studies continues to struggle with today, are explored in other pieces in the opening section as well. As early as 1973, as Deborah Rosenfelt's report on the Sacramento conference makes clear, there were tensions over charges of racism, class bias, and heterosexual bias in women's studies, and rifts between socialist and cultural feminists, separatists and nonseparatists, activists and academics. Gloria T. [Akasha] Hull's 1982 essay underscores the need for a strong Black feminist presence in women's studies, and Barbara Macdonald's, later in that decade, argues forcefully against ageism in women's studies— the neglect, stereotyping, and devaluation of the experiences and contributions of older women. Such dissenting and corrective voices have, from the beginning, been an essential part of the ongoing process through which women's studies has become more consciously inclusive.

Many of the personal narratives by students, teachers, and administrators, which comprise the third section of part 1, give further voice, at once eloquent and troubled, to the fundamental tension between feminist principles and institutional realities. If, in the 1970s, women faculty were a minority group in higher education and largely confined to the lower academic ranks (the Cornell University women's studies program closeup notes that Cornell's faculty was 93 percent male in 1975), women administrators were an even smaller minority. Three pioneers—a dean of students, a trustee, and the director of an academic women's center—graphically describe their efforts, as early feminist administrators, to enter the academy and, ideally, to change its policies and practices. Their essays describe their varying degrees of success and failure as "token women," and their strategies for survival—strategies often still necessary today, despite increased numbers of feminists in administrative positions in higher education. In other essays graduate students who are women of color describe their struggles with racism in the academy, and teachers write of their struggles with the anger, despair, and sense of alienation that students in women's studies courses are likely to experience at some stage of their new learning—the ironic price of women's studies' success in its critique of sexism. Other essays also testify to the creative strategies of teachers in helping students overcome such despair, and the increased self-esteem, identification with others, and expanded life goals that students positively report acquiring from their women's studies courses.

Creative teaching strategies are explored in the section on pedagogy. From the beginning women's studies practitioners were keenly aware of the need to change not only course content but also classroom procedures, not only what but also how we teach. The selections chosen reveal feminist faculty, within the relatively autonomous space of their classrooms, inventing diverse, unorthodox, and exciting teaching strategies in order to address specific student populations and to connect course material to the realities of students' lives. Refusing to divorce academic from nonacademic learning or the mind from the body and the emotions, insisting on the validity of personal experience, encouraging cooperation rather than competition in the classroom, sharing authority, respecting difference—these and other goals of feminist education are vividly demonstrated in the teaching practices the essays describe, from "bragging" to song to the creative use of the physical space of the classroom itself. As Michele Russell advises in her essay, "Black-Eyed Blues Connection," feminists must "use everything" in their teaching.

The brochure we created at my university in 1973 to advertise our women's studies program began by noting "what had long been true— that women were absent from history books, often misrepresented by male writers, an enigma to psychologists and sociologists, and of concern to anthropologists only if they were from primitive cultures." The statement describes the male-centered curriculum that women's studies challenges. Since the 1970s this challenge has been embodied in formal critiques of the disciplines—of their ways of selecting, constructing, and organizing knowledge to the exclusion, misrepresentation, or marginalization of women. Over the decades such critiques have been powerful instruments in advancing women's studies' work, and, to varying degrees, in effecting change within the disciplines themselves. We include a sampling of such critiques by feminist scholars in science, sociology, religion, and art. From the ways in which science has been a chilly climate for women to the omission of women artists from standard art history texts to the devaluation of women's paid and unpaid work, these critiques reveal the distortions inherent in the traditional curriculum—what it chooses to investigate, make known, and value. Such critiques, as Judith Plaskow says in her review of women's studies scholarship in religion, give women critical tools for questioning destructive ideologies. In addition, by offering new models, paradigms, and values, such critiques demonstrate the ways in which including women—their lives, history, achievements, and perspectives—can significantly alter, even radically transform, both what we know and why we know it.

The radical alteration, or transformation, of the entire curriculum of higher education that is implicit in the discipline critiques became an explicit goal of women's studies by the late 1970s as a result both of the growing body of feminist scholarship in the disciplines and of the recognition that, despite its successes, women's studies reaches only a limited number of students through the courses it offers, whether departmental or interdisciplinary. The closeup of San Diego's very extensive women's studies program in this issue noted that, in 1978, it reached only 6 percent of the student body, and although percentages at many schools are much higher today, it is still the case that women's studies and the traditional curriculum move along parallel but not converging paths. The movement to "integrate," "balance," "mainstream," or, as it is currently called, "transform" the entire curriculum has grown steadily since the 1970s; by now there have been over 200 formal projects, on individual campuses and through consortia, with one entire state (New Jersey) committed to an ongoing, statewide effort. Such projects are designed to introduce non–women's studies faculty to the new feminist scholarship for the purpose of transforming their courses. Early fears, discussed by Betty Schmitz in her essay, that curriculum transformation work would dilute women's studies or threaten its autonomy within the university, have proven unfounded, and on many campuses transformation work has strengthened women's studies. Recent projects have also become more inclusive, emphasizing the interrelationships of gender with race, ethnicity, and class, and including multicultural and international perspectives as well.

By the mid-1970s, given the growth of women's studies, it was apparent to many that a national organization was needed to facilitate the sharing of information and strategies, to increase the visibility of women's studies, and to augment its effectiveness. The NWSA was founded in 1977, and from then until 1982 the *Quarterly* was its official journal, regularly reporting on its annual meetings and other activities. The organization defined its purpose as encouraging nonsexist, nonracist education in both traditional and nontraditional educational settings, and members established caucuses for third world, lesbian, student, and staff groups, as well as for Pre-K–12. The articles in this issue show the NWSA as it struggled to define itself and its constituencies and to build coalitions in its early years, including the conference in 1979 at Storrs, Connecticut, on racism, at which the powerful speeches by Adrienne Rich and Audre Lorde reprinted here were delivered.

Such speeches might well be called "groundbreakers," the title we give to the next section in part 1, to describe some defining moments and events in the history of women's studies. Tillie Olsen's reading lists, 216 titles in all, published in the *Quarterly* from 1972 to 1974, were a groundbreaker for untold numbers of academic women, who eagerly circulated and used these rich lists of fiction, autobiography, biography, and poetry by women, most of whom were obscure and outside the official literary canon, many of whom were immigrant and working class, to help create some of the earliest women's studies courses. The Berkshire Conference on the History of Women, created in 1972 and quickly established as the major organization for feminist historians, was another groundbreaker, with its commitment to a "new" history that challenged traditional "political" history. So, too, was the Houston conference in 1978, the first federally mandated national women's conference, convened as part of International Women's Year. At that conference, ten months after the founding meeting of NWSA, women's studies delegates joined with others representing states and women's organizations to adopt a National Plan of Action addressing such issues as the ERA, reproductive freedom, welfare, and the needs of women of color and older women. A resolution on sexual preference was the most highly charged and controversial at the Houston conference, proof of Toni McNaron's assertion, in her essay "Finding and Studying Lesbian Culture," of the need for a lesbian history that would dispel harmful myths and stereotypes.

The two other pieces in this section—"Advice from a Chinese Revolutionary [Feminist]" and "Books That Changed Our Lives"— bring us voices from, respectively, 1942 and 1990. Ting Ling's brief but deeply moving talk to Chinese revolutionary women, reprinted in the *Quarterly* in 1976, brings us wisdom and advice we can still benefit from a half century later: the need for strong determination and aspiration. "Books that Changed Our Lives" is a retrospective, within this retrospective issue, and returns us to women's studies' early days in this country. At a meeting of the Modern Language Association in 1990 twelve women's studies practitioners recalled their "liberating books" from 1970. The list included works by Simone de Beauvoir, Gwendolyn Brooks, Dorothy Bryant, Rebecca Harding Davis, W. E. B. Du Bois, Zora Neale Hurston, Kate Millett, Robin Morgan, Tillie Olsen, and Virginia Woolf—some of the many works that invigorated and inspired women in the 1970s, or, to paraphrase Ting Ling, that strengthened our determination and aspiration.

Having looked back, we look ahead to the challenges, problems, and opportunities facing women's studies in the immediate future. Some of the most important of these challenges and concerns are examined in part 2 of this issue by Judith A. Allen, Ann B. Shtier, and Florence Howe, and in the second part of this editorial by Dorothy O. Helly. They include the need for a clearer definition and understanding of interdisciplinarity—especially as graduate programs are now developing to train the next generation of women's studies teachers and scholars—and institutionalization, the organizational forms necessary for women's studies' continued survival. I will mention a few other issues here, especially with reference to undergraduate programs.

Throughout higher education, tightened budgets have meant, and will continue to mean, fewer tenured positions and a growing reliance on part-time faculty—a situation with which women's studies is already too familiar. As Judith Allen notes in her essay, the majority of women's studies programs have no direct faculty lines. Meanwhile, the increased use of part-time faculty exacerbates problems that women's studies has struggled with from the start: curricular instability because of faculty turnover and the exploitation of part-time faculty, who are underpaid and overworked.

In addition, as higher education becomes more market oriented, women's studies programs will need to justify themselves in terms of students' job and career prospects. Programs can increase their emphasis on job counseling and on internships (already required by some undergraduate women's studies programs and a way of reconnecting women's studies to the community). They can also address the curricula of preprofessional and professional schools and programs, especially schools of education, social work, and public health, where women are the majority of the students. Curriculum transformation efforts also need to be directed toward these areas, which have been largely neglected. Despite reduced foundation support, on which it has heavily depended, curriculum transformation work within the traditional disciplines must continue if women's studies is to effect the profound educational change it has always envisioned. In addition, the current movement to redefine general education and core curriculum requirements in undergraduate education is providing opportunities to introduce courses and perspectives on gender, race, ethnicity, and class that have the potential of reaching large numbers of students outside women's studies courses, although the problems implicit in such courses—from diluted content to indifferent students—are often formidable.

For their continued health and growth, programs need to create stronger coalitions with Black and ethnic studies and with programs in gay/lesbian or queer studies, postcolonial studies, and cultural studies. Programs in gender studies present a special challenge: In some institutions they may threaten to subsume women's studies, making the study of women less visible or central; in others, they are a way of introducing women's studies into otherwise resistant settings.

Beyond this, as the recent convening of a national conference of program directors attests, programs are realizing their need for more effective communication with one another, both regionally and nationally, in order to share information about jobs, curricula, and program structures. And, not least, they are recognizing the need for strong and concerted *advocacy,* to correct misinformation and counter resistance both inside and outside the academy.

Moving Forward, *Dorothy O. Helly*

In examining the question of the future of women's studies, the issues that arise involve institutionalization—training scholars who will train the next generation—and institutional organization, programs versus departments and the active pursuit of interdisciplinarity. These issues involve undergraduate as well as graduate education and how we do women's studies research. This twenty-fifth anniversary issue of the *Quarterly* continues what has been a longtime effort to think through not only the diverse ways women's studies and feminist scholarship have affected disciplines, fields, and areas of study but also the problems and possible solutions proposed to ensure an ongoing place for this growing field. Essays by Judith A. Allen, Ann B. Shteir, and Florence Howe look to the present and future of women's studies. They reexamine women's studies in relationship to the women's movement and institutional organization and women's studies as a truly interdisciplinary pursuit; they also survey the evolving approaches to graduate work and Ph.D.s in women's studies; and they make comparisons with development of this expanding field around the globe.

One of the most pressing issues for women's studies as it looks forward to a new century, and the beginning of a new millennium, is the working out of interdisciplinarity and how to achieve it. The exciting news is that Ph.D. programs in women's studies are not only a reality but growing, increasing the urgency of working out how to train the scholars who will become the leaders of the next twenty-five years. There are pressing questions that involve not only how we will differentiate between research done for a freestanding women's studies degree and research that is informed by women's studies and feminist theory but also how this work continues to take place in the established disciplines. As the history of canonization in the disciplines has been exposed over the last twenty-five years, scholars have come to understand some of the struggles within disciplines that have taken place throughout the last century over how to construct basic concepts and methodology. Feminist scholars have demystified and critically assessed the existing disciplines, including how the factors of gender and race have been systematically excluded from basic disciplinary frameworks. This process has given scholars in women's studies the leverage to articulate their own theories and methods, while calling upon the traditional disciplines to become more inclusive if they are to continue to contribute to the knowledge base.

A working definition of women's studies research goes something like this: to examine women's experiences, past and present, placing women at the center of inquiry in order to find which theories and methods will enable the researcher to solve the problem posed. This kind of women-centered research by feminist scholars in the disciplines has already reshaped the disciplinary questions they ask. In the process it has often led faculty trained in one discipline to look beyond it for answers to their new questions. The issue for women's studies Ph.D. programs is how to use those disciplinary and interdisciplinary insights and the theory suggested by them to help train new scholars to do the interdisciplinary research that will increasingly define women's studies.

Embedded in the project to educate new women's studies Ph.D.s is the question of whether faculty trained in specific disciplines but informed by feminist questions can imagine their way into the next phase of women's studies scholarship. Equally, can students eager to be part of the next generation in women's studies learn from the processes by which their mentors expanded their own knowledge bases to aid in expanding it for themselves? Both students and those who train them must draw on the hard-won theoretical and methodological insights that have characterized ongoing feminist scholarship over the past twenty-five years. Asking women-centered questions within conceptual frameworks that did not originally allow for such questions has brought forth many new kinds of methodologies; Ph.D. programs will sharpen the debates about how to further refine and rethink these methodologies.

As yet, according to sociologist Lynn Goodstein,[2] who has been working on research connected with this problem, interdisciplinarity in the training of new women's studies Ph.D.s may be more talked about than practiced. Judith A. Allen raises the same issue. As Goodstein puts it, "Interdisciplinarity has become a buzzword: What does it mean? How would we know it if we saw it?" Goodstein's research addresses how faculty and students in existing women's studies doctoral programs are debating the question as it shapes program requirements, examinations, courses, and dissertation design. Other fields with interdisciplinary frameworks have been dealing with these problems: American studies, Black studies, criminology, and communications are examples. These interdisciplinary pursuits arrived on the academic scene about the same time as did women's studies, the late 1960s and early 1970s, and since then ethnic and area studies have joined them. Communications, for example, like Black studies, was granted almost immediate departmental status. Yet it, too, was a field formed by scholars with diverse disciplinary training brought together with a unifying vision of how they wanted to carve out a new interdisciplinary field. It is worth noting that the politics of institutionalization presented fewer obstacles to departments of communications than to organizational proposals that made gender and race their focus. It is wise, as we reassess where we have come from and where we want to go, not to forget that past, for it is no less relevant today.

Judith A. Allen's essay is directly concerned with those institutional and interdisciplinary issues critical to the survival and growth of the field. A native of Australia, Allen brings to women's studies in the United States both the distance of different origins and the knowledge of working on the spot. Her essay is a plea for those intense discussions within women's studies, at the undergraduate as well as at the graduate level, which she sees as critical to developing the range of interdisciplinary core courses needed to establish women's studies' claim to a distinct "domain of expertise." She examines the development of women's studies in the United States through the participation of faculty within the traditional disciplines, full-time professors joining with part-time instructors and students with whom they have shared a new vision of scholarship. But, for Allen, nostalgia about the kind of cooperation that marked the beginnings of women's studies in the academy may cloud our eyes to the fiscal and institutional realities in a university world of downsizing and "steady state" in contemporary "hard times." Allen's is a provocative essay, for she calls upon women's studies to look again at its institutional and scholarly aims and raises for redefinition what has been meant by saying that women's studies is the "academic arm" of the women's movement. Her solution is departmental status, and she gives her reasons. Allen calls for a tighter cross-national definition of the field of women's studies to make it a player in the competition for major grants, and tells us that we may be in a good position to end run our institutions to secure potential alumnae donors who feel they were deprived of a chance to learn women's studies in their day.

Pertinent to the ongoing debate about institutionalization and organizational structure is Ann Shteir's essay, which points to the growth of Ph.D. programs in women's studies in the United States and Canada in the 1990s as significant for the future of the field and as a symbolic mark of the visible achievements of a quarter century of work. She concentrates on programs that identify with the label "women's studies," opening the need for future discussion about the development of gender studies.

Like Allen, Shteir raises questions central to examining the success of women's studies as an interdisciplinary project. She reports on the key issues being raised by the scholars who are training doctoral students as well as by the students themselves: What should constitute the "core courses"? What should the comprehensive examination cover? Should doctoral programs include a professional development component? and, What should be the relationship between Ph.D. training and women-centered activism? Shteir outlines the several forms graduate women's studies training currently take for master's degrees as well as doctoral programs. Not surprisingly, the multiple origins of these programs account for the multiple structures that exist.

Shteir's report alerts us to how different institutions and faculty have mixed interdisciplinary and discipline-based components. Institutions offer both intellectual and practical reasons for this mix. Prime among ongoing debates are field definition and the extent to which graduate programs in women's studies should be linked to a grounding in one or more traditional disciplines. The question of how to pursue interdisciplinary research, raised by Lynne Goodstein and Judith Allen, underpins such discussions. The larger question is whether a new generation of women's studies scholars will emerge equipped to meet the challenge of continued intellectual growth and institutional survival. It is a challenge earlier generations of scholars in women's studies have worked on for twenty-five years.

Shteir also reports on the collaborative models of graduate training, based on working with specific disciplines on the one hand and with institutional consortia on the other. There is tragic irony, if not farce, when, as a result of discipline collaboration, the admissions requirements for consortial programs preclude students with a women's studies undergraduate degree. Shteir also explores the interinstitutional consortium model, where collaborating institutions—with undergraduate women's studies programs and no expectations of offering a women's studies Ph.D. in the near future—seek to introduce graduate-level work in the field. A similar approach within institutions has led to graduate-level minors, concentrations, and certificates in women's studies. Some of these models, of course, may prove to be interim arrangements if faculty decide to create instead full-fledged doctoral programs in women's studies. Shteir's essay raises questions critical to the development of graduate-level programs, building on the theme raised by Allen about the need for women's studies to work out "its domain of expertise."

Florence Howe's essay takes up some of these same threads, offering useful comparative insights on women's studies around the world. Her remarks should also be placed within the framework of the excerpts from the national reports included in the retrospective section of this collection. These reports from around the globe offer us a window on the creation of women's studies programs formed in the 1970s, 1980s, and 1990s in Europe (the Netherlands and Germany), Russia, Latin America and the Caribbean (Argentina and the West Indies), Africa (South Africa and Uganda), and Asia (Korea and India). This array shows both striking similarities and significant differences from the pattern of development—varied as it is—in the United States. In Western Europe, those working to establish women's studies in the 1970s also struggled with issues of institutionalization versus autonomy. There, choices were made to house women's studies in independent centers, especially when finding a place within traditional university structures took too much time and energy. Some doctoral programs did slowly develop, usually supported by interinstitutional cooperation. Patterns emerged: Women's studies research was pursued outside the university or only nominally attached to it, while teaching inside the university was largely within the frameworks of traditional disciplines. Howe points to how critical these different institutional patterns are to understanding what is happening in women's studies around the world. In some countries the struggle for women's studies, both as research institutes and as a teaching area within universities, has involved battles with governments, the prime funders of university systems. In Russia, however, where women's studies only emerged in the 1990s, post-glasnost scholars have had to make clear the difference between traditional social research on women, which was characterized by biological determinism and undertaken to solve some problem about women's relation to the state, and a new feminist approach that, as Anastasia Posadskaya recounts in her national report, sees gender as "a dimension of all spheres of social life." The Russian situation underlines the need to remember how women's studies in the United States went hand in hand with a larger women's movement and why the implications of that relationship need to be reexamined.

In Argentina women's studies developed in independent research centers located outside the university system and was aimed at post-graduate professionals. When some of these professionals realigned themselves inside the university, they established women's studies as a specialized postgraduate course of study. Within this context of professional practice, the interrelationship between theory and methodology and the application of women's studies to the design of social policies became a self-conscious agenda. Institutionalization of women's studies as interdisciplinary programs within the university through the master's level followed. At the University of the West Indies such questions also underlay decisions in the 1980s to create a Center for Women's/Gender Studies to coordinate regional campuses. The prior existence of a Center for Women and Development Studies committed to women's studies teaching, research, and community outreach offered a model on which to base this university structure.

In South Africa a women's studies center was initiated in the 1980s at the University of South Africa (UNISA). In addition, various university departments around the country offered courses informed by a gender analysis. Faculty resistance in traditional departments, however, prevented the development of undergraduate programs. For that reason, the first women's studies courses were offered at the master's level. The relationship between women's movements and academic women's studies in South Africa was shaped by apartheid. White women involved in political groups in the 1970s played a part in the development of women's studies in the 1980s. Some Black women, active at the grass-roots level from the late 1970s, also brought their politically developed feminism into teaching departments in the 1980s, helping to fight the battles needed to get women's studies courses taught. Finally, women in exile with access to international feminist movements on the one hand and involved in national liberation movements on the other returned home in the early 1990s to join in creating a "new South African feminism" in which it is hoped women's studies can be further institutionalized. Meanwhile, in East Africa, in Uganda, the relationship between a women's movement and academic women's studies has been closely correlated. The UN Decade for Women and the Nairobi conference in 1985 generated a proposal to establish academic women's studies, adopted in 1991 at the master's level. In Uganda the emphasis has been on the training of government workers who are, in the words of Victoria Mariam Mwaka, "gender-sensitive persons committed to development activities." Since the mid-1990s it has been developing an undergraduate and a doctoral program.

In Korea academic women's studies has been in existence since the mid-1970s; before the mid-1980s Korea had master's courses, and, by the mid-1990s, doctoral courses. Researchers in various fields at Ewha Womans University came together to write the first Korean textbook in women's studies by 1977. In a reversal of the pattern in other countries, women's studies then produced students who became leaders in a women's movement. Women's studies research also provided the theoretical framework for legislation on sexual violence as a social issue. Because women's studies has raised questions about sexuality and marital relationships, conventional academics have challenged feminist scholars to defend their work. Such scholars have found that this criticism has its uses, for it raises for visible, public discussion the very questions women's studies seeks to ask. In India, where in December 1994 Howe delivered the lecture on which her essay is based, women's studies, as in Korea, has been hailed as making academic social science more responsive to what Vina Mazumdar terms "the crucial questions of the day." Also, as in Korea, women's studies in India dates to the mid-1970s and has developed into a national women's movement. Along the way, in 1986, the parliament in India called for "education for women's equality" through curriculum revision. This was, as Vina Mazumdar reports, an achievement won by the women's movement, which consistently viewed women's studies as generating important "questioning and dissent" in the face of "revivalist, fundamentalist, and chauvinistic movements." The elimination of women's subordination, resistance to men's control over women's minds and bodies, has been called for by feminists as a human right. This reaffirmation of women's studies as the academic arm of the women's movement in India is worth examining, just as a redefinition of this formulation comes under scrutiny in the United States.

In her essay, Howe refers to women's studies' desire, from the beginning of its entry into the academy, to shape institutional politics, to challenge disciplinary elitism and exclusivity. Women's studies in the United States in the 1970s struggled with the complexities of how to situate itself within the departmentally structured university, where territoriality and competitiveness constituted "politics as usual." Feminist scholars were aware that the university mirrored the hierarchical structures of corporate life, which increasingly characterized the business world of the late nineteenth and early twentieth centuries, a time when many institutions of higher education were either created or restructured themselves. Corporate politics were never based on inclusion and cooperation—the approaches taken by feminists who reached across the traditional boundaries of full-time and part-time faculty and faculty-student relationships in forming women's studies. Today we face the question of how to assess those efforts: Were they simply ways of making a virtue out of marginality in the university structure or were they a meaningful effort to shape new and radical academic structures? For many faculty and students, women's studies programs offered an ideological haven in an unfriendly institutional environment. We also need to remember that there was little leverage from the margins, and early women's studies programs, like women in the paid workforce in the face of industrialization, took what was offered because they wanted to survive. Feminist faculty, however, did manage to infiltrate the male corridors of power enough to see occasional differences in "politics as usual," though these gains were rarely institutionalized and depended on the presence of particular women in particular administrative places. The process was exhilarating, but it also proved to be exhausting, as attested to by many of the essays reprinted in part 1 of this issue. The question of the structure of women's studies within the academy is now raised anew, as the survival as well as the expansion of women's studies becomes a burning institutional issue. Women's studies budgets, allocated at the pleasure of a supervisory administrator, remain weak reeds in the current fiscal storms. Courses and faculty in women's studies have no inherent institutional clout in the battles of downsizing. Judith Allen asks us to think anew about our options. Serious discussion of these issues is not new, but we must turn to these issues again with a sober assessment of our current goals.

From Howe's essay, we hear of J. P. Naik as the "father of women's studies in India," so called because he "believed in the significance of research as a strategy for change." From her extensive travels around the world visiting women's studies as it is practiced internationally and from her own thirty years of participation in innumerable international conferences, Howe reminds us of the direct relationship that has existed between women's studies and women's movements. Her own emphasis has always been on the role of education as a "human right" in this process of change. Out of the personal and professional experiences of feminists has come a greater understanding of gender inequality. And, she points out, a raised consciousness has not only been the consequence but also the cause of activism. Howe explains how different university structures around the world incorporate different ways of bringing women's studies into male-dominant and traditional structures of university life, and places into perspective the reasons why some women's studies programs outside the United States have developed first at the graduate level, directly connected to continuing professional education.

Howe acknowledges that the trend in the United States over the past twenty-five years has been for women's studies and the women's movement to grow farther apart, and she speculates about this. She also points to the slowness of universities both here and abroad to transform their traditional curriculum to include gender, as reported in the retrospective pieces republished in part 1. She is aware that the institutional fragility of women's studies may result from too much dependence on the voluntary labor of feminist faculty. Yet, through it all, the past twenty-five years have seen an extraordinary growth of feminist theory and a growing understanding of what women's studies offers as an intellectual enterprise. Most importantly, Howe reminds us that we are in peril if we do not remember and explore the meaning of our history. We have to remember that we have only begun to find ways to change the various patriarchal structures of the world, not only of the university, and that this goal—worldwide transformation—will take all our efforts for the foreseeable future.

NOTES

1. Although the title *Women's Studies Quarterly* is used throughout this editorial, several of the pieces reprinted in part 1 of this issue were published under the journal's first title, *Women's Studies Newsletter* (1972–81). For a brief history of the transformation of the journal, see Florence Howe, "The First Ten Years Are the Easiest" and "Chronology" in *Index to the First Ten*

    Years, 1972–82 (New York: The Feminist Press at The City University of New York, 1984).

2. A faculty member at Penn State University, Goodstein was a visiting scholar at Arizona State University, Tempe, in spring of 1997, when we had a telephone conversation on this issue.

Elaine Hedges *is emerita professor of English and former director of women's studies at Towson State University, Maryland. She is an editor of the* Heath Anthology of American Literature *and author of* Hearts and Hands: Women, Quilts and American Society *as well as numerous other books and articles on American literature and women writers.*

Dorothy O. Helly *is professor of history and women's studies at Hunter College and The Graduate School, The City University of New York. She is coauthor of the Hunter College Women's Studies Collective text* Women's Realities, Women's Choices: An Introduction to Women's Studies, *author of* Livingstone's Legacy: Horace Waller and Victorian Mythmaking, *and coeditor of* Gendered Domains: Rethinking Public and Private in Women's History.

A Note from the Editors: For part 1 of this issue, we have consciously chosen to preserve the original style of each essay, including punctuation, capitalization, and method of citation. We have also preserved all biographical notes as originally published. The few minor editorial alterations that have been made, either to clarify a reference or allusion or to alert the reader to a contributor's new name, are enclosed in square brackets. All excerpting of the essays is marked by ellipses. The original date of publication for each essay is reflected on the table of contents (in parentheses) and also at the start of each new essay. For those interested in reading these essays as originally published, or for those seeking other essays, back issues of the *Quarterly* are still available. To order a back issue or to subscribe to *Women's Studies Quarterly,* please contact The Feminist Press, 311 East 94th Street, New York, N.Y. 10128.

    Every effort was made to secure publication consent from the contributors whose work is included. Unfortunately, a handful of contributors remained out of reach; we invite those contributors to contact The Feminist Press. We also welcome readers' responses to this issue. We hope to begin gathering material for the thirtieth anniversary issue and appreciate your input, suggestions, and comments.

"Looking Back" copyright © 1997 by Elaine Hedges.
"Moving Forward" copyright © 1997 by Dorothy O. Helly.

The First Ten Years Are the Easiest

Florence Howe   *Selections, 1975–82*

Structure and Staffing of Programs (Spring 1975)

. . . After six years, women's studies courses are taught on over 900 campuses; on 112 campuses women's studies courses have been organized into "programs." In general, such programs have profited from the free university movement: they have not imagined that they could effect change simply by setting a good example in their own separate little corner of the campus. Rather, programs have operated from the premise that total separatism is counter-productive. To effect change, one needs at least two bases of power and a great deal of energy: first, among a broad student constituency that insists upon a women's studies program for its needs: second, among the university's own personnel that can forcefully press not only for resources necessary to the continuation of the women's studies program, but for change in the wider institution.

Thus, for some years now, pioneers organizing women's studies programs have used terms like "networks" or "interdepartmental" to describe the organizational structure best suited to accomplish complex goals. Early models were provided by SUNY/Buffalo and SUNY/Old Westbury where, inside an American Studies Program, feminist faculty taught some women's studies courses themselves, and invited others on their campuses to join them in offering others. At California State University/Sacramento the model became a program that had at its center several positions controlled by a Women's Studies Committee, which was in turn made up of tenured and nontenured faculty members from a sizable number of departments in the humanities and social sciences. These faculty members also taught women's studies courses. At the University of Pittsburgh, still another variety of network was proposed and (partly) instituted: the creation of five new positions—for faculty members to be hired half-time in traditional departments, half-time in women's studies. Three of those faculty were hired in 1972—in English, history, and psychology—and one of them, the coordinator Mary Louise Briscoe, was awarded tenure this year in the English department. But the other two lines remain unfilled.

Professor Briscoe's tenure decision is one bright spot in an otherwise dreary season of tenure decisions. Given the tendency of institutions to place nontenured faculty into the coordinator's spot in women's studies, the question of tenure will remain a consequential one for some time to come. The problems are obvious: an individual willing to divide her time between her discipline and women's studies cannot, it is alleged, be "serious" about her discipline. Indeed, she may not have the time or inclination to do traditional scholarly research and writing. She may instead be designing new courses, involving herself in acquiring the skills and knowledge of a second discipline. Or she may be engaged in ground-breaking scholarship that lies outside the traditional or her original disciplinary purview. We can all cite examples here: the young literary medievalist from Harvard who, in her first years of teaching, began to publish scholarly essays on nineteenth century women's medical history and literature; and long lists of literature teachers who have taken a year or more to read research in sociology and history in order to develop women's studies courses. The key question, then, becomes who is qualified to judge the teaching as well as scholarly productivity of such people, let alone their contribution to the campus and community? Traditional departments and committees on tenure will tend, understandably, to view women's studies faculty through their own discipline-tinted glasses. And at this point, there are no other procedures for tenure.

Obviously, then, one might counter, the route to go is the departmental one: argue on the campus for a Department of Women's Studies that will solve not only the problem of tenure (and thus continuity), but also the associated problems of budget, control of the curriculum, majors, and so forth. Some women's studies programs seem to be making that choice: see, for example, South Florida State University's report ("Administering a Women's Studies Program") in the Summer 1974 issue of the *Women's Studies Newsletter*. Such a decision may temporarily solve some of the more exacerbating problems described by women's studies programs reporting in this issue on their futures. But it also may create an organism vulnerable both to isolation and to excision. It is, in other words, more difficult to isolate and excise a network than a department, particularly in its early stages or when its faculty size and constituency among the student body are relatively small.

But the future of women's studies is not only a matter of short-range survival and growth. As important is its long-range ability to change educational patterns, not only on campuses but in other classrooms. Educational history suggests that departments tend to narrow rather than broaden the areas of concern with which they might have begun:

certainly, their chief aim becomes to acquire majors, rather than to effect change in the institution more generally. While it is no doubt important to educate women's studies majors, and while I would support the growth of graduate women's studies programs, it is as important, I believe, to reach those students in general education courses in such departments as history, English, psychology, and sociology. Theoretically at least—and I am willing to admit that theory is often easier than practice—it is the network, not the department, that is best able to promote such change.

First, the network or "program" is not a department: it cannot be accused, therefore, of nondepartmental protocol; its business is to effect change, not to enlarge its fiefdom. Second, feminists with appointments in two worlds, once they are tenured, should make of primary concern the changing of courses in their disciplinary departments. As I shall suggest in a later essay, the future of women's studies lies not only in developing a strong curriculum inside the program, but also in organizing other programs for the retooling of elementary and secondary school teachers, as well as of college and university faculty.

If I do not favor the departmental route, what advice can I offer to programs hard-pressed for budget and tiring of the battle simply to maintain what they have gained? Keeping in mind that advice is easier to give than to receive, I shall make two suggestions. On some campuses I have visited this year, and from some correspondence I have had, it seems clear that some feminists are simply tired. Perhaps, therefore, we need to remind ourselves of several old lessons: no one can sustain the energy movements require without periods of rest—or at least distance—from them; and the corollary—when people inside movements grow tired, they stop extending themselves to other people. Thus, tiredness may cause the network to tighten or harden into a clique. Programs should have sufficient leadership among their constituency so that organized periods of rest and study are possible for them. A second piece of advice follows in part from the first. Some feminists find that more restorative than a holiday is a visit to another campus or to a women's studies conference. What we need often are opportunities to exchange views and experiences with other feminists. Women's studies faculty and students have had relatively few opportunities to discuss such institutional problems as I have noted here. We have not had enough of such meetings locally or regionally, and we have had none nationally, at least in part because we've been too busy with our own campus concerns.

I think that we need the support now of a national network of women's studies programs, perhaps joined together in an association

capable of organizing such conferences and effecting rapid communication among us. For example, we need to talk about strategies for
dealing with the question of tenure for women's studies faculty. If traditional departmental tenure is impossible, and if we do not want to
turn women's studies into a separate department, what other structures might possibly meet our needs? We need to talk about funding,
about curriculum, and about other matters of concern not only to
women's studies but to a developing body of scholars engaged in interdisciplinary study, scholarship, and teaching. . . .

New Curricular Focus in Women's Studies Programs (Winter 1976)

In a year during which we have read each week of cutbacks in some college or university system, it is heartening to be able to report that the
growth of women's studies has continued at least at its previous rate. No
programs have been lost. We seem to have reached no plateau—the
growth is still accelerating slightly. While in the previous 18 months
(from the summer of 1973 until December 1974) 37 new programs were
announced, in the past 12 months, 40 new programs have appeared.
Perhaps more important than the continued rise in the number of programs is their new character. Two trends are observable here: a sharp rise
in the number of minor- or degree-granting programs has reversed the
percentages of last year—two-thirds of programs now offer minors or
degrees; and a concommitant formalizing of the curriculum has occurred
within those programs. Perhaps as interesting is the fact that programs
have begun to structure curriculum in terms of careers for students.

Women's studies courses and programs began, five or six years ago,
in order to compensate for the male-centered and -biased curriculum.
Most programs still offer courses arranged broadly, to cover as many
disciplinary areas as possible, and, in addition, to open up new interdisciplinary ones. Majors in women's studies, from the beginning, saw
themselves as attending a mini-college within a college. The main question became what could you do with it?

I remember feeling very hard-pressed by students who wanted to
know what kinds of jobs they could get with a women's studies major.
"The same kinds you'd get with an English or history major," I said, and
then went on to explain the limits of a B.A. But there was a measure of
discomfort in my response, not only because I thought women's studies ought to do more for students than English or history, but because
I knew there was something wrong with the conception of curriculum
as smorgasbord. It is not enough for students to discover that, in all
areas of knowledge and life, sexism has ruled; and that we will all have

to work for the next hundred years to undo and restore and revise and transform knowledge and change the conditions under which we live. It is essential that they be prepared to do one specific part of this work, and that means educating them in some depth in that part, and with the necessary tools they need for that work.

For several reasons, formalizing the curriculum is now possible. First, the acceptance of women's studies as a legitimate *area of study*—as a minor or for the B.A. degree or for graduate degrees—demands focus, since it is impossible to study an entire area. Second, students have asked for more order and less repetition in the courses they are taking. Third, the work of researchers has continued to accelerate and thus to push curriculum developers (sometimes they are the same persons) to develop a series of courses in women and U.S. history, for example, not simply the introductory survey.

Right now, formalizing is clearest among programs granting the B.A. A number of programs, including the one at Old Westbury, have chosen to focus on several "streams" or "concentrations"—for example, on women and the workforce; on publishing and journalism; and on revision of the high school curriculum. The most novel new program is Ohio State University's, in which the curriculum has been organized into seven "major modules" designed around clusters of related disciplines, or, in one case, around literature as a single focus. The most complex proposal comes from one of the oldest programs—at San Francisco State University—where students have been able for four years now to construct their own B.A. programs "with a focus on women." Now the program's planners are proposing a coherent "major" with a specific vocational intent. Students will be required to organize their courses with a theme in mind—for example, Women's Health Studies. Or they may choose to combine work in women's studies with a traditional discipline, perhaps to prepare for graduate school. Vocational fields mentioned in the San Francisco document are "counseling, media, administration, public relations, public health," in addition to the more general claim that the program will prepare students for "any vocational skill, with emphasis on and expertise in women's or sex-role issues." . . .

Fact Sheet on Women's Studies Programs in 1977 (Fall 1977), *Compiled by Florence Howe and Frances Kelley*

1. There are now 276 women's studies programs on college and university campuses in the United States. The growth rate of these programs in the last 18 months was 80 percent.
2. Women's studies programs can be found in the District of Columbia

and in all but nine of the 50 states. Those states without programs are Alaska, Idaho, Louisiana, Maine, Mississippi, North Dakota, Rhode Island, West Virginia, and Wyoming.

3. The state with the largest number of programs continues to be California, with 48 programs. Other states with significant numbers of programs include New York (38), Illinois (21), and Michigan (17).

4. Three-quarters of all women's studies programs can be found in public colleges and universities; one-quarter on private campuses. More than half of them (56 percent) are to be found in public four-year colleges and universities; 24 percent in private four-year colleges and universities; and 20 percent at public two-year colleges. There are no programs at private two-year colleges.

5. The largest area of growth is in the public two-year college. Of the 127 new programs, 40 percent are in the two-year community college, exactly twice the general percentage of two-year women's studies programs in the total 276 programs. Eleven of the new two-year programs are in California, and six are in Illinois. In general, the states with the largest numbers of new programs are California (16), Michigan (12), Illinois and New York (11 each), and Minnesota (10).

6. Slightly more than half (51 percent) of all programs offer a structured curriculum leading to the completion of a minor, certificate, or degree. Six programs (all located in California) offer the Associate of Arts degree; 56 programs, the B.A.; 16 programs, the M.A.; and 2 (SUNY/Binghamton and Union Graduate School), the Ph.D.

7. A number of mature programs have, in 1977, instituted the B.A. degree: Barnard College, the University of California at Berkeley, California State University at Sonoma, the University of Georgia, SUNY/Albany, the University of South Carolina.

8. Four older programs have instituted both the B.A. and the M.A. degrees: the University of Maryland, the University of Alabama, California State University at Long Beach, and SUNY/ Binghamton.

9. Four older programs have recently established certificates or minors and B.A.'s: the University of Nebraska, SUNY/ Stony Brook, Towson State University, and the University of Georgia.

10. Cornell University, with one of the two oldest programs in the country, begun in 1969, has just established a graduate minor, the first in the country.

"But What *IS* a Women's Studies Program?" (Fall 1978)

In several respects a Women's Studies Program is more difficult to define today than it was eight or nine years ago, when there were two of them—at San Diego State University and Cornell. Those two programs had a couple of characteristics in common: They were campus-based, academic programs that offered courses for credit to undergraduates. They had been begun by faculty and students conscious of the "political" statement inherent in announcing that a group of courses had become a "program."

Even a glance at the same two programs in 1978 suggests the current complexities. San Diego's program thinks of itself as a "department," and, in the university's terms, is moving to become one. It is also one of the 92 programs across the country that offers a minor or a certificate/minor to undergraduates. Cornell's program now offers not only the equally ubiquitous major, but also a unique minor that supplements a broad variety of *graduate* degrees.

Thus the original definition has been augmented by the presence of graduate programs, and, even more dramatically, by the rapid emergence of degree-granting programs. For the first time this year, more than half (163 or 54 percent) of the 301 Women's Studies Programs offer either minors, majors, or graduate degrees. And 40 of these programs offer two or more combinations of these degrees. A new program at Case Western Reserve, for example, offers the B.A., the M.A., and the Ph.D. in women's studies through American studies.

Especially to students in degree-granting programs (80 offer the B.A.; 21 the M.A.; and 5 the Ph.D. or equivalent) a Women's Studies Program says, here is a coherent body of knowledge that will prepare you to do the world's work, including scholarly work. The breadth and depth of that new body of knowledge, as we know in 1978, are not easily controllable or even definable. Degree-granting programs have begun to shape their courses around disciplines (women's history, for example) or professions (counseling and therapy) or themes and institutions (marriage and the family; employment policies and technology).

Even while qualifying specialists for the working world, the women's studies curriculum still has the quality of the eclectic smorgasbord, a sip and a taste here and there of refreshment sturdy enough to help students survive in and even right the intellectual imbalance of a mainstream diet. And of course most of the remaining 138 (or 46 percent) of Women's Studies Programs offer a body of "electives," supplementing the male-focused curriculum.

In addition to degree-granting and non–degree-granting programs, the Women's Studies Program list, making its fifth appearance in these pages, now includes four consortial programs: the Claremont Colleges (in southern California); the Five Colleges (in western Massachusetts); the Graduate Theological Union (in the Bay Area); and the Great Lakes Colleges Association (in Ohio, Indiana, and Michigan). Another, the Associated Colleges of the Midwest, is in formation. Probably these should be listed separately in the future, since they may offer no courses for credit directly, and, like some graduate programs, they may not be campus-based. In our next issue, we plan to list separately the score of new Women's Studies Research Centers or Institutes in existence or formation, some of which also offer courses or degrees.

The First Ten Years Are the Easiest (Index to the First Ten Years, 1972–82)

No one living during the early nineteen-seventies would have described the period as "easy." There was the War Against Vietnam, and the unfinished War on Poverty; feminism was still a laughing matter on the outside and a painful, sometimes a wrenching experience from the inside; and Women's Studies was hardly a name. But the period was also exciting if one enjoyed intellectual discoveries, if one wanted to see with fresh vision, and if one had the energy for new beginnings. It was a time for founding new institutions: thousands of women's organizations, most of them local and ephemeral, but a significant number still in place and growing from national to international; thousands of newsletters, journals, and presses, many of them also ephemeral, or now collapsed, but a significant number of them growing and reaching new audiences.

If we look only at national organizations and publications, the list of those institutions surviving the decade is impressive: the Commission on the Status of Women in the Modern Language Association as representative of a host of similar bodies inside professional associations; the Project on the Education and Status of Women at the American Association of Colleges; the Committee on Women at the American Council on Education; Sociologists for Women in Society; the Women's Caucus for the Modern Languages; the National Women's Studies Association; the Berkshire Woman's History Conference; the National Council for Research on Women; *Women's Studies: An Interdisciplinary Journal; Feminist Studies; SIGNS: A Journal of Women in Culture and Society; Frontiers; Women and Literature; the Women's Studies Quarterly; Ms. Magazine;* The Feminist Press.

Many of these institutions have had tenth birthdays, or will be having them shortly. And most would agree that in the decade before us the challenges threaten to overwhelm as they once invited and propelled us forward. It is more difficult to sustain than to start an institution; it is more difficult still to build when roots are shallow and the structures tall. Our achievements are not to be minimized, for these institutions build and are built upon by the hundreds of Women's Studies Programs and the thousands of women's studies courses now in existence. In 1972, there were 112 programs and about 5,000 courses; in 1982, the *Quarterly* reported 452 programs and an estimated 20,000 to 30,000 courses. The growth during the period from 1980 to 1982 may still surprise those who are not aware of the pace of change in Women's Studies. More than one-quarter of the 452 Women's Studies Programs currently in operation are less than three years old. Less than a quarter of them are ten years old. All Women's Studies Programs now have to do more than invent new courses, find faculty and funds, and satisfy students. Many of them have built significant structures on shallow roots with surprising ease.

What are these roots we didn't have to begin with, and that we must grow if we are to sustain our efforts through not only the next decade but others to come? One of the roots is money: The *Index* has no entries under "money," or "funding" and only two under "foundations." Women's Studies Programs, and most of the institutions named above, were initiated with little or no money, and have survived through inventiveness; volunteerism; the generosity of feminists; and the far-sightedness of several rooted institutions, including some colleges and universities. But Women's Studies and the feminist organizations and institutions that surround it have only recently begun to consider the development of funding bases in which to root the future development of the field.

Other roots as important as solid budgets include networks that sustain and support as well as transmit information easily and effectively. In no other area can one demonstrate more clearly the axiom we use as title: to begin the network has been easier than to sustain it. To effect communication a decade ago, we published *Female Studies I, II*, and *III*, even before the *Women's Studies Newsletter*, the antecedent of the *Quarterly*, was begun in 1972. These monographs, filled with course syllabi, bibliographies, and brief, encouraging essays about teaching the courses that were to be called "Women's Studies," were ordered by a few hundred people, many of whom heard about them at the annual meetings of their professional associations. The small network was self-sustaining: if you came to an annual meeting, you might join it instantly, and if that professional association had a caucus or a commission, you might become a name on a membership list and thus receive an informal communication or two through the year. But the groups, separated often by discipline, remained small enough for people to know each other's research and teaching interests. A few interdisciplinary conferences—at the University of Pennsylvania, for example, at the University of Pittsburgh, and at Sacramento State University, all before May 1973, as well as the first Berkshire Women's History Conference—allowed the major pioneers in each discipline to meet and to feel firsthand the attraction of interdisciplinary scholarship. We are still not clear about the size of the spurt forward in numbers after 1973, but we do know of the burgeoning of Women's Studies Programs, even as we also know of the doubling of the percentage of women earning doctorates during the seventies. In the eighties, there are more of us in the professions, as there are more of us in Women's Studies. It is not surprising that the slim networks with which we began have not managed to keep pace with the growth. How can under-budgeted institutions begin to communicate effectively not only with those who were around at the start, but with the geometrically progressive growth of those who have entered since the decade began?

And it is not only size and the lack of resources that hamper effective communication through networks. It is also the burden of the information itself, the growing lists of interested individuals not only in the United States but around the world, the bulk of knowledge, the plethora of books and journal articles, the volume of research-in-progress, the news about jobs, conferences, institutes, fellowships, grants, and of course the continued founding of new institutions. Who is doing research on widowhood? What are the latest statistics about mothers of small children in the workforce? Where are there fellowships in Women's Studies at the doctorate level? How might one find people interested in attending a summer institute on Women and Health? Who would be interested in a new journal or a new book? One can't mail to *everyone.* One can't write to all the existing institution to ask several questions. As the movement has grown, as its resources have multiplied, so has it become as difficult to know who has the information one needs, as to know how best to disperse the information one has.

One particular segment of this growing body of information might form still another layer of the missing roots of Women's Studies. Like hard budgets and technologically competent communication networks, we need to transform the body of scholarship about women's history into public history. I use the focus on history here analogically, symbolically. For one might make the same statement about the psychology of women, about literature by women, about the quilts women have created, or the social movements they have spearheaded. Though the numbers of Women's Studies classrooms and the students filling them have increased through the years, there are countless other classrooms beyond, and, in addition, there is the vastness of the world beyond the classroom, of what we might call the "mass" consciousness. How long has it taken for the Freudian concept of "penis-envy" to control the imagination of half-educated readers of popular magazines? Can one expect that revolutionary concepts spawned by Women's Studies—not only about "breast-envy" or "womb-envy"—be transmitted in fewer than fifty years? The essential idea with which Women's Studies began is, in fact, being hotly debated within its own walls: whether "nature" or "nurture" is responsible for women's "difference," and whether there is a "basic" difference at all between men and women, beyond the anatomically obvious one. Can one account for the "difference" by reading women's history as the history of oppression and survival, suffering and heroism, defeat and victory? Does the reading of women's history change the reading of public history? Can we begin through *human* history to read the possibilities for the future—more profoundly than we can now, once we see the interconnections between women and men, and the institutions they have created both separately and together?

As scholars in forthcoming issues of the *Quarterly* debate these questions, we expect them also to take into account the history of women's education in the century before ours, to seek the rooted wisdom with which to take the next steps, to anticipate the next spurt forward. The mass consciousness formed by the women's movement and the media's interpretation moved us in the seventies; in the eighties, we are on our own, and with decades of work to come. It is urgent, therefore, that we feel connected, not only to each other in the present, but to the thousands of others in the past: individuals, organizations, periodicals, and presses who preceded us. How did they manage to survive for more than eighty years? How did they incorporate their past as they continued to move forward? We need to comprehend these roots deep within feminist communities, then incorporate and extend them as well. . . .

We know the energy of Women's Studies has not yet "peaked," nor has it wavered from its original commitment to the strategy of change. In the eighties, we see the new national Women's Studies movements in India, Japan, Canada, and elsewhere around the globe joining forces with each other and with United States practitioners. We see ahead new forms of sharing curricular resources, publishing arrangements, and even faculty exchanges so as to facilitate a new vision of women's education built on the new scholarship about women . . .

Evaluation: Reflections of a Program Consultant

Nancy Porter   *Fall 1977*

When Florence Howe was in Portland last winter on her Advisory Council project to review women's studies programs, she made the distinction between a review and an evaluation: a review seeks information that can be quantified, an evaluation presupposes a standard against which a program may be judged.

Had I been more than just casually aware of the distinction last spring when, with another woman, I set out under the auspices of the Northwest Women Studies Association (NWWSA) to review a local community college's women's studies offerings, I might have "done" differently. I am not sure, however, which is one reason for sharing with other women's studies people an account of my first experience as a "program consultant" (as you will note, terminology and practice both become confused) and some reflections on what it was like to be a consultant whose work was in turn reviewed. As women's studies goes about developing and implementing models for program assessment, for internal (self-study) and external (review or evaluation) purposes, some aspects of my experience may serve as an alert to problems in the process that I do not believe are only semantic. The following, it should be understood, presents background material considered useful. Observations and interpretations are my own and may not represent the views of anyone else involved, including my co-consultant. The report itself is the property of the reviewed institution.

An official request for help in conducting this community college's review of its Women's Studies Program was made to the Northwest Women Studies Association in February 1976. . . . The administration wanted at least two consultants to come from colleges into which their students transferred. Of the three faculty who were finally chosen, one had to cancel at the last minute. The team thus consisted of two NWWSA members: Gisela Taber (at that time Director of Women's Studies at Lower Columbia Community College, Washington) and I (teacher of women's studies at Portland State University in Oregon).

The Procedure

The review was conducted in May 1976 and consisted of a day-and-a-half campus visitation during which the team was asked to consider ten areas of evaluation worked out jointly by the college's administration and women's studies teachers:

Objectives of the Program
Student and Community Needs
Teaching Methods
Working Conditions (Including Space Allocation)
Hiring Practices (Qualifications and Interviewing)
Structure of Women's Studies
Grievance Procedures (Faculty and Student)
Relationship with Administration
Transfer Credit
Future of Program

The schedule of the day on campus was established by the college and included: an hour of orientation and organization with administration and the voluntary women's studies coordinator; two hours of meeting with a self-selected group of students and staff (past, present, potential); an hour-and-a-half meeting over lunch with the women's studies teachers; and an hour meeting with the two administrative officers immediately responsible for the program. The previous afternoon I had observed the class about which there was a question of granting credit transferable to four-year institutions. We had been scheduled to write our report with a college administrative representative. Needless to say, we were not prepared to do so. We spent the time sifting through our various impressions, a process that intermittently occupied the next two months.

Why so long, particularly since we were compensated for only our day and a half on campus? A series of unscheduled crises in our respective work lives hampered us, but, for me at least, other factors were operating, the nature and implications of which I did not fully understand.

Gisela Taber and I met once and consulted by phone a number of times as we worked out what we wanted to say and how to say it. The only model of a review by a women's studies person we had in hand was an "evaluation" conducted by J. J. Wilson (of Sonoma State University, California) for a university in the region. The document proved useful, for organization of materials and for philosophy. In her report Wilson emphasized that she did not wish to impose on the visited program

either her experiences fashioned in her own different setting or her
ideas of what women's studies is supposed to be. Wilson noted the
rarity of evaluating a program when it was running "smoothly." "Most
evaluations are done under the gun," she wrote, "and observations
cannot but be tainted by such a crisis atmosphere."

Difficult to Find the One "True" Image

Gisela Taber and I faced writing a report about a program that had
been in hot water at various times in its four-year history. Although the
review was deemed a "normal" evaluation of a new program, we felt
the presence of past crises and present uneasiness. Moreover, our visitation spawned a considerable amount of data, much of it conflicting,
most of it "soft" (opinion), too little of it anchored in documentation.
We did not have much written material to work from: course descriptions and syllabi (in a few instances there was conflict between the
approved course description and the actual syllabus), an outdated
description of hiring procedures and qualifications (which made it difficult to ascertain practice), but nothing in writing about program
objectives, and no statistical information about class enrollments and
program size, except as had been incidental to the preliminary correspondence. Faced with the dramatically conflicting points of view we
heard expressed by each interviewed group on most issues (areas to
be evaluated), we decided we could not judge the "truth" in each case
or choose the one "true" image of the program.

We thought, though, that we could produce a document that would
promote trust among the groups and facilitate the process of self-study
on the part of the college. To this end we tried to reflect back to the
institution as accurately as possible what we had heard, from what we
hoped was our "impartial" perspective. We also decided to offer recommendations based largely, we thought, on "input" gathered from
the various individuals and groups who had told us what changes they
wished to see in curriculum and organization. We stipulated that the
recommendations were but suggestions to be discussed, modified,
adopted, or discarded as seemed best to the people involved. The
report ran 34 pages, including appendices, and was critical directly
and by implication of some of the practices of administrators and
teachers alike.

The official reaction to our report came from the administration:
"excellent . . . thorough and unbiased," a demonstration of the
Association's commitment to women's studies in the Northwest, a

"good jumping-off point" for the college to complete its own review, the letters read.

Objections of the Women's Studies Faculty

The women's studies faculty, on the other hand, although allowing that the report was "objective" and that it "legitimatized" women's studies as a subject area in the eyes of the administration, found a number of faults with both process and product, which I determined when I sought out the group's reactions. (By this time, Gisela Taber had left the area for a new job in Washington, D.C.) Some of their unhappiness was directed at the reviewing conditions, with the recommendation that "next time" the Association should dictate some of the terms of a good review. Under this heading they felt that the group had been given inadequate lead-time to prepare for the review (difficult because so much of the operation of the program outside teaching is voluntary labor, but they wished at least to collect student course evaluations from previous terms); that too few of us had done the reviewing; and that the review team shared an "academic" bias which was not informed about or overly sympathetic to the self-educational objectives of their community college view of women's studies. They also felt our sample of opinion had been small and random, controlled by who had turned up that day, a vocal group of women students and faculty/staff who felt their various needs were not being met by the program.

With respect to the written report, the women's studies group was distressed by the hedged and ambiguous language of some of the recommendations. They wished we had accompanied our "objective" narration with a "subjective" commentary. They had hoped we would air the report with them, for clarification of difficult points and interpretation of some of the views reflected, before we wrote the final draft. Above all, the women's studies teachers feared that the proportion of negative to positive "input" reflected served to create a negative impression of the program. As the coordinator said in the post-report session I had with some of the group: "You made it sound as though we weren't doing anything right."

They Hoped to Be Rescued

I began to have some of the same thoughts about our report. Why had we gotten such different reactions? I comforted my shock for a while by reasoning that women's studies, after all, was just a small part of the male administrators' job; for the women involved in the teaching, the program was a vital part of their political, social, intellectual lives: hence criticism directed toward them would hurt more. Disquieted equally by other analyses I could come up with, I began to resent the women's studies faculty. The resentment, which was the feeling of a difficult effort unappreciated for its difficulty, became my clue to look deeper, which brought me back initially to rereading the report.

From this distance, it seems that our goal of providing information for self-study that would satisfy everyone was not realizable in a public document, at this time and in that situation. In the first place, we made 28 recommendations, far too many for any one person or group to assimilate. The sheer number seemed to suggest much was wrong that needed attention. In the second place, although we liberally claimed to have based our recommendations largely on the college's own "input," some of the recommendations to promote accountability on the parts of students, faculty, and administration were drawn directly from our own experiences and implied, in some instances, "standards" against which the program's curriculum and operations had been judged. Despite J. J. Wilson's warning, we had used our experiences and, I am willing to say, our professional sense of women's studies as markers, knowing no other way to chart the waters. In the third place, although we encountered and in turn assumed good will all around for strategic purposes, the waters rippled with submerged currents.

I talked yet again with one of the community college's women's studies group in private conversation. "What was it you wanted?" I asked, hoping I was not sounding like a petulantly baffled Freud. After a pause came the answer, "I'd hoped you would rescue us."

My respondent understood sadly that the expectation of rescue was unrealistic, and that it had never been articulated in the review process. With the statement, however, for which I was grateful, several other issues became clear. I believe I knew all along that the women's studies teachers wanted to be rescued, even that the administration wanted to be rescued—after all, the review had been precipitated by a series of conflicts between administration and women's studies faculty—but suppressed the knowledge in the name of impartiality. Also, I began to see that much had been taken for granted in the interview with the women's studies faculty, particularly that the reviewers would know what the program wanted to do and why, without having it spelled out, simply because we were all women's studies people together.

Although our report included a statement recognizing the vulnerability of all parties in the evaluation—reviewers and reviewed alike— I believe that I, at any rate, let the desirability of being acceptably

"objective" outweigh and suppress my understanding of the nature of
the vulnerability the women's studies people experienced with respect
both to their own institution and to us as reviewers. They wanted their
hard-earned version of women's studies defended as valid for them
and their institution; and suggestions for change must have appeared
very much like conditions of acceptability in the women's studies
"profession," not guides for helping them better accomplish the educational goals specific to their setting and resources. The administration,
of course, undoubtedly felt that some of their notions of academic
standards and control had been vindicated.

The Need to Develop Guidelines

I worry about the establishment of a hierarchy of judgment, in which
some programs will be deemed acceptable (and hence funded) by
appearing more academically evolved, while others will be denied vital
support, or asked to change direction, because they appear less so.
Development of "professionalism" in women's studies, of which reviews
and evaluations are one evidence, raises some serious problems. In
future years, we will decide what constitute good conditions for reviews
and evaluations, what kinds of information are usefully collected, and
what models we need to develop. In that regard, clearly the "review" I
participated in should have been more professional in the sense of
valid: factual data should have been prepared in advance; program
objectives should have been defined (preferably in writing); teacher
and course evaluations should have been gathered from all classes;
more classes should have been visited; and assumptions that were inac-
curate should not have been made. However, I think it unrealistic to
suppose that conflicts around women's studies are unique, for, as J. J.
Wilson suggested, that is often the context in which evaluations and
reviews are conducted. In light of this, I think we need to develop
guidelines for how to evaluate in politically charged situations.

There is, however, a larger question. The essential impetus behind
women's studies is educational, not academic. Women's studies'
educational goals are not necessarily, certainly not exclusively, academic,
even in four-year institutions. For economic and other reasons, more
and more women are entering community colleges. Before community
colleges are judged, much work needs to be done to find out what is
going on in them and why; and the first step might well be the collection of many self-evaluations from many different kinds of institutions.

The "Bridge" between Black Studies and Women's Studies: Black Women's Studies

Gloria T. [Akasha] Hull   **Summer 1982**

This is a very full, a very suggestive topic. Thinking about it raises for me many issues—personal, political, philosophical, pedagogical—some of which I will touch upon in as coherent a fashion as their variety and complexity allow. I will look, first, at Black women's studies as a "bridge" and give a brief history of its evolution. Then I want to say something about women's studies and Black studies (mostly the latter) in relation to Black women's studies, and conclude with a statement on the activity and institutional situation of Black women's studies.

The "partnership" of Black studies and women's studies produces Black women's studies, a new area of work which is gradually being seen for the unique and important discipline that it is—a field which is not totally identifiable with either Black studies or women's studies, but one which those two areas should encompass. I probably need not point out here what is widely known: that Black women's studies arose, in part, in response to the neglect and mistreatment of Black women (as scholarly subjects—and as teachers and students) by both Black studies and women's studies. Beyond this,

> the inception of Black women's studies can be directly traced to three significant political movements of the twentieth century. These are the struggles for Black liberation and women's liberation, which themselves fostered the growth of Black and women's studies, and the more recent Black feminist movement, which is just beginning to show its strength. Black feminism has made a space for Black women's studies to exist and, through its commitment to all Black women, will provide the basis for its survival.
>
> The history of all of these movements is unique, yet interconnected. The Black movements of the 1950s '60s, and '70s brought about unprecedented social and political change, not only in the lives of Black people, but for all Americans. The early women's movements gained inspiration from the Black movement as well as an impetus

to organize autonomously. . . . Black women were a part of that early women's movement, as were working-class women of all races. However, for many reasons—including the increasing involvement of single, middle-class white women (who often had the most time to devote to political work), the divisive campaigns of the white-male media, and the movement's serious inability to deal with racism— the women's movement became largely and apparently white.

The effect that this had upon the nascent field of women's studies was predictably disastrous. Women's studies courses, usually taught in universities, which could be considered elite institutions just by virtue of the populations they served, focused almost exclusively upon the lives of white women. Black studies, which was much too often male-dominated, also ignored Black women. Here is what a Black woman wrote about her independent efforts to study Black women writers in the early 1970s: "At this point I am doing a lot of reading on my own of Black women writers ever since I discovered Zora Neale Hurston. *I've had two Black Lit courses and in neither were any women writers discussed.* So now I'm doing a lot of independent research since the Schomburg Collection is so close." (Italics ours.)

Because of white women's racism and Black men's sexism, there was no room in either area for a serious consideration of the lives of Black women. And even when they have considered Black women, white women usually have not had the capacity to analyze racial politics and Black culture, and Black men have remained blind or resistant to the implications of sexual politics in Black women's lives.

Only a Black *and* feminist analysis can sufficiently comprehend the materials of Black women's studies; and only a creative Black feminist perspective will enable the field to expand. [. . .] [1]

From the outset, it has been apparent that Black women as a group are the most capable of conceptualizing Black skin and female gender *together*—first, in the same body, and then, in the same idea, theory, course, article or paper, or whatever. What this reflects is (1) that Black women represent the "natural child" (if you will) of the "partnership," and (2) that it has been Black women researchers and teachers who have assumed the responsibility for and taken the lead in doing this work—or, to recall a trenchant folk tale, it has been Afro-American women who have taken up the load cast down in the middle of the road by everybody else.

With regard to Black women, white women's studies has come from its chequered past to a present state of critical evolution. Some of the old forms of oppression—such as complacent ignorance and hollow, exploitative tokenism—are still evident. And now that there is a greater consciousness in white women's circles about Third World women and racism, there is still a need to be on guard against new modes of negativity—for example, racist behavior which proceeds from incomplete personal sensitivity (i.e., still not *really* knowing or *really* caring who Black women are) or which results from going through "correct" antiracist form without true substance. I won't go into further detail on this aspect of the topic. There are white women here who can speak for themselves and who will, I am sure, recognize in a spirit of truth and accountability the racism of women's studies and outline what is being done about it.

However, I *would* like to talk briefly about the relationship of Black studies to Black women's studies—in certain respects, a question which more deeply concerns me, especially here at this National Council for Black Studies Conference, where the issue can be appropriately and, I hope, profitably raised. You will note what is obvious: that there were to have been no Black men on this panel[2]—which might suggest that this women's studies business, Black or white, is perceived as "women's work"; and, in ways which I am assertive about, it is. Yet, things are not so simple. Black studies programs and faculty are predominantly male. These (Black) men run the program and do the teaching. They are the other half of the equation whose *active* commitment is needed to bring about this "long overdue" union.

The commitment can and must proceed in a number of different, though related, directions. Probably the most basic and far-reaching is the responsibility to provide courses which fully include Black women— a Black Revolutionary Thought course, for instance, which studies Angela Davis as well as Frederick Douglass and Malcolm X; Harlem Renaissance literature courses which do not overlook Georgia Douglas Johnson and Angelina Grimké; discussions of the Civil Rights movement which do not start and stop with Rosa Parks on the Montgomery bus but give due credit to Ella Jo Baker, Fannie Lou Hamer, and Queen Mother Moore. Even more important and, yes, harder than this, is for male Black studies faculty to struggle with the self-scrutiny and reeducation which will enable them to approach Black women from a nonsexist perspective—to be able not just to say, but to see and analyze, *all* the reasons why Black women bottom out the economic scale, or to hear without Nathan Hare's defensive hostility what it is that Ntozake Shange was saying in *For Colored Girls*. . . . This kind of opened consciousness would be a first step from which many good things could follow—relative to staffing, teaching, enrollment (Black female students significantly outnumber Black male students in Black studies programs), collateral activities, campus alliances with women's groups, everything. Perhaps the very male-identified logos for the Council itself might even be redesigned. Later today, there is a session on "New Fields in Black Studies." If Black women's studies were to be thought of as such an area, just as a strategical means of rethinking and integrating Black women into Black Studies where they should be, this would be one program of action which would, in the language of the Conference brochure, "[help] meet the new challenges of the 1980s and beyond."

I indicated earlier that Black women's studies originated as a kind of "compensatory" response (to use sociological jargon)—but this was only part of the story. The other part is the value and pleasure of the work in and of itself. The book I edited with Patricia Bell Scott and Barbara Smith, *All the Women Are White, All the Blacks Are Men, But Some of Us Are Brave* (Old Westbury, N.Y.: The Feminist Press, 1981), was made possible by, and grew out of, the necessary research and teaching on Black women which was being spontaneously and lovingly done in a variety of disciplines all across the country. Some of this work includes using slave narratives by Black women to extend our concept of slavery, honoring the valor or of Black church women, discussing seriously and positively the experience of Black lesbians, compiling bibliographies of writers and musicians, and so on. Since *But Some of Us Are Brave* went to press, other books, dissertations, and articles continue to attest to the growth of the field.

It would be ideal if we could see Black women's studies within the context of colleges and universities as being not dependent on women's studies, Black studies, or straight disciplinary departments for its well-being, but existing as an autonomous academic entity making coalitions with all three. Realistically, however, institutional support will have to come from these already established units. This will be possible only in proportion to the elimination of racism, sexism, and elitism. Then all of us—in Black studies, women's studies, Black women's studies—can begin to form a genuine and lasting partnership.

NOTES

1. These paragraphs on the evolution of Black women's studies are taken from the Introduction to *All the Women Are White, All the Blacks Are Men, But Some of Us Are Brave: Black Women's Studies,* ed. Hull, Scott, and Smith (Old Westbury, N.Y.: The Feminist Press, 1981), pp. xx-xxi.
2. At the last minute, Charles Henry substituted for Margaret Wilkerson.

Gloria T. Hull is Associate Professor of English at the University of Delaware.

Staying the Course:
The Necessity for Remaining
True to a Radical Vision

Ann Froines   *Summer 1983*

The five goals listed below were initially presented at a conference for women's studies program administrators on "Women in the Curriculum," sponsored by the New England Women's Studies Association held at Wellesley College on October 23, 1982 and at a faculty workshop for the "Toward a Balanced Curriculum" project at Wheaton College, held on January 27, 1983.

With all the debate going on concerning the issues raised by efforts to integrate or "mainstream" women's studies into the liberal arts curriculum, it is appropriate to reiterate the original radical values and goals of the movement for women's studies in higher education. Not all of these values and goals are priorities for every Women's Studies Program, of course; but a large number of programs, including those with solid institutional support, are attempting to implement, in a variety of ways, some of these goals. They have shaped our program development efforts at the University of Massachusetts/Boston.

1. Women's studies must remain student-oriented as it develops its own identity and theory. We need to provide a space in the classroom for women to engage in consciousness raising as well as the more traditional learning. And feminist students need a healthy, supportive atmosphere for further intellectual development. Women's studies pedagogy emphasizes that *how* material is taught is as important as *what* is taught.
2. Women's studies should remain activist in the campus setting, working for the empowerment of women on campus, through support for affirmative action and the elimination of sexual harassment. By undertaking joint projects with Afro-American and ethnic studies programs, women's studies can promote solidarity among campus groups and programs with common experience of discrimination and invisibility.
3. Women's studies needs to maintain and renew its connections with

the women's liberation movement in the society as a whole. We ought to make ourselves available on a regular basis to do research inspired by the needs of women's organizations—research, for example, on the problems of older women in our society, or on technological developments in clerical work, or lesbian history, or the feminization of poverty. I mention these topics because the excellent work that has been carried out by women's studies practitioners in all these areas has already been utilized by social change organizations. We need to continue to view women's studies as the intellectual arm of the women's movement.

4. Women's studies must continue its efforts to reflect the diversity of women in the United States and the perspectives of women throughout the world, particularly those in the developing countries. We have much work to do within women's studies to establish a basis of equality and dignity among all women—including women of color, lesbians, and disabled women—so that real communication is possible. And projects to integrate women into the curriculum face the same challenge: who are the women being integrated?

5. Independent women's studies programs and departments should encourage, shelter, and support scholarly work that is really critical of antifeminist and antifemale research and publications. "Scholarship" continues to be published in all of the disciplines which helps to perpetuate the oppression of women or indulges in "blaming the victim."

. . . The efforts to implement its broader goals—to understand the relationship between education and social change—is, as Marilyn Boxer writes in the conclusion of her comprehensive review, "For and About Women: The Theory and Practice of Women's Studies in the United States" (*SIGNS* 7:3 [Spring 1982]), both "the greatest promise of women's studies and its most enduring problem." We might also see it as a necessity. For while it is certainly a struggle to remain true to a radical vision, without a common vision there is little that unites us. And there is also a pragmatic or strategic necessity as well. If our roots are neither strongly entwined with the women's liberation movement— broadly defined as women organizing to improve their lives in all areas—nor nourished by joint educational activities and mutual advocacy with the movement, then women's studies can be more easily and neatly trimmed by the shears of cost-cutting educational bureaucrats. Furthermore, attacks on women's studies by conservative and right-wing groups outside the university must be countered by support from progressive citizens and women's groups outside the university. We need, then, to make those connections real.

To increase our unity and remain on course, we need a shared vision of the society we would like to live in, and a common approach to the task of creating that society. Only out of debates and discussions about the goals of women's studies can this vision emerge. It is in this spirit that these remarks are offered.

Outside the Sisterhood: Ageism in Women's Studies

Barbara Macdonald   *Spring/Summer 1989*

This article originated as a keynote address to the June, 1985 annual conference of the National Women's Studies Association.

I have not come here out of the National Women's Studies Association's spontaneous commitment to and concern about ageism. I am here after a four-year fight, after other old women along with me wrote to the NWSA planning committee and demanded that ageism be addressed at a plenary session. We insisted that NWSA confront the question of how it is possible that the last thirty years of women's lives have been ignored in women's studies. This morning I have twenty minutes to speak to that topic.

I am not going to talk to you today about organizing. Old women do organize. That organizing ranges from a lobby watch of 132 women in a Detroit housing project to protect themselves from male violence, to the Older Women's League of 12,000 women throughout the United States who work to make legislative changes that affect the economic oppression of old women. But today I want to talk about what is *not* there, because until we see how invisible the lives of old women are, and why, we cannot even begin the kind of radical change that the challenge of feminism demands.

From the beginning of this wave of the women's movement, from the beginning of women's studies, the message has gone out to those of us over sixty that your "Sisterhood" does not include us, that those of you who are younger see us as men see us—that is, as women who used to be women but aren't any more. You do not see us in our present lives, you do not identify with our issues, you exploit us, you patronize us, you stereotype us. Mainly you ignore us.

Has it never occurred to younger women activists as you organize around "women's" issues that old women are raped, that old women are battered, that old women are poor, that old women perform unpaid work in the home and out of the home, that old women are

47

exploited by male medical practitioners, that old women are in jail, are political prisoners, that old women have to deal with racism, classism, homophobia, anti-Semitism? I open your feminist publications and not once have I read of any group of younger women enraged or marching or organizing legal support because of anything that happened to an old women. I have to read the L.A. *Times* or *Ageing International* to find out what's happening to the women of my generation, and the news is not good. I have to read these papers to find out that worldwide, old women are the poorest of the poor, or that in this country old women are the largest adult poverty group, or that 44 percent of old Black women are poor, or about the battering of old women, about the conditions in public housing for the elderly in which almost all of the residents are women, or that old women in nursing homes are serving as guinea pigs for experimental drugs—a practice forbidden years ago for prison inmates.

But activists are not alone in their ageism. Has it never occurred to those of you in women's studies, as you ignore the meaning and the politics of the lives of women beyond our reproductive years, that this is male thinking? Has it never occurred to you as you build feminist theory that ageism is a central feminist issue?

I look at the indexes of your recent texts—on women and economics, on women and unpaid work, women and psychology, images of women in literature, on Black women, on working-class women, on women and violence—and I find nothing under "old" or "aging."

Read those books used in women's studies as an old women reads them. They discuss the socialization of little girls from the moment of birth, the struggles of women through adulthood—and it turns out that "adulthood" ends with menopause, or with some attention to the woman in her fifties who is a displaced homemaker. Well, just try being an eighty-five-year-old Black woman in a shantytown in L.A., just trying to cross the street, when a government economic index has just valued your life at only $236 in the courts (in contrast to $328,475 for a thirty-four-year-old white man)—try that for a displaced homemaker. But we are not women to you; we are not adults. We are as invisible and as irrelevant in your classrooms as we are in a hostile male world—a world where we fight not only the same oppressions younger women do, but the oppression of ageism as well, and all without the support of the women's movement.

Meanwhile, as the numbers of old women rapidly increase, the young women you taught five years ago are now in the helping professions as geriatricians and social workers because the jobs are there. They still call themselves feminists but, lacking any kind of feminist analysis of women's aging from your classrooms, they are defining old women as needy, simple-minded, and helpless— definitions that correlate conveniently with the services and salaries they have in mind. All this week on this campus, workshops on aging have been going on, under the auspices of the Institute on Aging. Because ageism is not addressed, these workshops will do nothing to end the oppression of old women and will do much that contributes to that oppression, and women's studies has not done its homework sufficiently on its own ageism so that it can begin to effect change in the academic community to stop it.

But it is worse than that. For you yourselves—activists and academicians—do not hesitate to exploit us. We take in the fact that you come to us for "oral histories," for your own agendas, to learn *your* feminist or lesbian or working-class or ethnic histories, with not the slightest interest in our present struggles as old women. You come to fill in some much-needed data for a thesis, or to justify a grant for some "service" for old women that imitates the mainstream and which you plan to direct, or you come to get material for a biography of our friends and lovers. But you come not as equals, not with any knowledge of who we are, what our issues may be. You come to old women who have been serving young women for a lifetime and ask to be served one more time, and then you cover up your embarrassment as you depart by saying that you felt as though we were your grandmother or your mother or your aunt. And no one in the sisterhood criticizes you for such acts.

But let me say it to you clearly: We are not your mothers, your grandmothers, or your aunts. And we will never build a true women's movement until we can organize together as equals, woman to woman, without the burden of these family roles.

Mother. Grandmother. Aunt. It should come as no surprise to us that ageism has its roots in patriarchal family. But here I encounter a problem. In the four years it took to get NWSA to address ageism, feminism has moved from a position in which we recognized that family is a building block of patriarchy, the place where sexist hierarchical roles are learned, where the socialization of girls takes place, the unit by which women are colonized, manipulated, controlled, and punished for infraction—from that basic tenet of feminist theory, both mainstream and radical feminists have moved back to a position of reaffirming the family. Mainstream feminists are buying the notion that as long as a woman has a "career," family is a safe and wholesome place to be. Radical feminists have affirmed family as the source of our cultures—as a way of understanding our strengths and our oppression as Black, Jewish, Hispanic, Asian-American, Native American, working-class women. This return to family is reflected in our writings, where less and less is father seen as oppressor, but more as another family member, oppressed by white male imperialism. *(And, believe me, he is.)*

It will be for future feminist historians to explain how it was that in our return to family we never questioned its contradictions to our earlier feminist theory. Not that we can't contradict our own feminist beliefs—they aren't written in concrete—just that we never acknowledged the contradiction.

Nor can history fail to note that our return to family coincides with a reactionary administration's push back to family values, any more than it can ignore that our lesbian baby boom coincides with Reagan's baby boom to save the Gross National Product.

If we are to understand ageism, we have no choice but to bring family again under the lens of a feminist politic. In the past we examined the father as oppressor, we examined his oppression of the mother and the daughters, in great detail we examined the mother as oppressor of the daughters, but what has never come under the feminist lens is the daughters' oppression of the mother— that woman who by definition is older than we are.

The source of your ageism, the reason you see older women as there to serve you, comes from family. It was in patriarchal family that you learned that mother is there to serve you, her child, that serving you is her purpose in life. This is not woman's definition of motherhood. This is man's definition of motherhood, a male myth enforced in family and which you still believe—to your peril and mine. It infantilizes you and it erases me.

This myth of motherhood is not a white American phenomenon. Barbara Christian in her book *Black Feminist Criticism* points out how this myth is uncovered in the fiction of Alice Walker writing about Afro-American life and by Buchi Emecheta writing about Ibuza life. And nowhere, I believe, is it as bad as in white imperialist culture. This myth is summed up by the Ibuza saying: *The joy of being a mother is the joy of giving all to your children.* It is internalized by the young mother, but then internalized and perpetuated by her daughters. So that even when—as in Emecheta's *The Joys of Motherhood*—the mother has come to some insight, her daughter continues to see her as existing only for self-sacrifice.

The old woman is at the other end of that motherhood myth. She has no personhood, no desires or value of her own. She must not fight for her own issues—if she fights at all, it must be for "future generations." Her greatest joy is seen as giving all to her grandchildren. And to the extent that she no longer directly serves a man—can no longer produce his children, is no longer sexually desirable to men—she is erased more completely as grandmother than she was as mother.

It is for these reasons, because of everything you learned in family, that you, as feminists, can continue to see the older woman as a nonperson. It is for these reasons that you believe our lives as old women are not important and that we exist only to serve you.

We have all been so infantilized in family we have never made ourselves, as daughters, accountable as oppressors of the mothers, and we should know only too well that the failure to acknowledge the oppressor in ourselves results in confused thinking and a contradictory image of those we oppress. Thus you who are younger see us as either submissive and childlike or as possessing some unidentified vague wisdom. As having more "soul" than you or as being overemotional and slightly crazy. As weak and helpless or as a pillar of strength. As "cute" and funny or as boring. As sickly sweet or dominating and difficult. You pity us, or you ignore us until you are made aware of your ageism and then you want to honor us. I don't know which is worse. None of these images has anything to do with who we are; they are the projections of the oppressor.

I want to close by giving three very recent examples of ageism in some of our best writing as feminists. These are writers whose work I admire. But the ageism in their writing will be passed on through women's studies to other young women if it is left on the shelves unexamined, and I am not willing any longer to leave it there. *These writers are no more ageist that the entire women's community.* They have not personally failed me; they, like all the rest of us, have been failed by the women's movement.

In the novel *Triangles,* by Ruth Geller, we use our living grandmother as a character, and we make her the comic relief. We show her photograph on the back cover, with a blurb making her the subject of laughter—most of what is funny is that she is not in on the joke. And yet the sisterhood publishes this book, reviews it, and is silent.

In *Between Women,* edited by Sarah Ruddick, Louise DeSalvo, and Carol Ascher, we bring together a fine collection of essays on the relationship of the biographer to the famous women whose lives they have chosen to write about. But believing in the myth of motherhood, many of these biographers, not satisfied with status by association with these strong famous women of the past and present (such as Virginia Woolf and Simone de Beauvoir), proceed to turn their subjects, most of whom chose not to have children, into their mothers. This is no equal association between women. This is ageism, and as though these women had not given enough, the biographers (women in their fifties) in page after page ask to be mothered, nurtured, and have their lives blessed by their subjects. And still the sisterhood reviews this book, finds nothing offensive about it, and is silent.

In her essay, *Half of a Map*, Sandy Boucher, in speaking of old women who have been helpful to her, writes: "I would be *them* one day, and if I could be . . . as generous of myself as they were, then I could be proud to be old." Apart from the intolerable patronizing, only a male myth of motherhood makes this feminist think my pride in being old consists in my generosity to younger women. And still the sisterhood is silent.

I have to say of women's studies that when you make the lives of women over sixties invisible, when you see us as your mothers and fail to examine your oppressive attitudes, you are letting the parameters of women's studies be defined by men—by the man in your own heads. But more than that. In the consciousness raising of the late 1960s and 1970s, in the contribution made to feminist theory that grew out of those years, in the development of women's studies that followed, we planned curriculum with an entire piece omitted—that of age and the oppression of ageism. We cannot now patch up those structures in twenty minutes to cover the gaps of our ignorance. We have no choice but to go back once again, as we have had to do before, cover old ground in new ways, and rebuild this time with a wholeness that includes all women and all the years of our lives.

Barbara Macdonald *is a coauthor, with Cynthia Rich, of* Look Me in the Eye: Old Women, Aging and Ageism. *This article also appeared in* Calyx: A Journal of Art and Literature by Women *9, nos. 2 and 3 (Winter 1986): 20–25, and in* Sojourner: The Women's Forum, *August 1985.*

What Happened at Sacramento

Deborah Rosenfelt   **Fall 1973**

It is conceivable that truly feminist oriented women's studies programs (and individual feminists themselves) might have to consider withdrawing from the movement should mindless, political factionalism based on simplistic versions of class analysis ultimately prevail at this conference or in the movement nationally. . . . We can shape the future for ourselves as women but we must decide soon whether it is to be a diverse and flexible future based on a female culture which tolerates a wide range of differences or a narrow and ideologically or sexually inhibiting one which simply finds women emulating male models, i.e., practicing sexism in reverse.

—Joan Hoff Wilson, opening speech, May 26, 1973

Until very late and only under heavy pressure there was at the conference little space for political struggle. Instead, the assumption has been . . . that we are all women and therefore are united in sisterhood. We believe, however, that among us political differences do exist—differences in race, class, sexuality. We further believe that solidarity among us as sisters will be the result of (1) a clear identification of our differences, (2) a confrontation in anger and pain as well as in care of those differences, and (3) a struggle together around those differences.
. . . We feel restricted by the emphasis on the form of Women's Studies, i.e., the exclusion of our differences in race, class, and sexuality.

—Memorandum from the workshops and caucuses on Class, Race, Lesbianism, Heterosexual Bias, and Ethnic Studies

There it is—the cleavage in purpose and ideology that ran like a crack in the earth through the activities of the Women's Conference at Sacramento in May, appropriately called "Women's Studies and Feminism: Survival in the 1970s." The conference brought together—so to speak—some 700 women from throughout the western states for three long days of speeches, workshops, programs—and confrontations. So the work of the conference was carried out, really, on two levels: the usual conference activities of meeting, talking, listening, exchanging information and ideas; and that other, more complex, more difficult business of coping with this polarization of attitude and ideology.

After a multi-media presentation Friday night, the conference opened officially Saturday morning with doughnuts and coffee and three addresses by Joan Hoff Wilson and Kirsten Amundsen of Sacramento and Florence Howe of SUNY/Old Westbury. Wilson analyzed the sexism inherent in the attitudes of three groups which might (unfortunately) help shape the future: the "old" radical male left, male social scientists, and male writers of science fiction. Women and women's studies, she suggested, could provide alternatives to the sexist visions of such men, through the creation of a female culture with female values, free of the confrontation politics that marked the movements of the sixties. Amundsen spoke of the pain and conflict that many of those in the women's movement have suffered as their commitment to feminism has grown. She asked, Was it worth it? and answered in the affirmative with statistics suggesting the educative value of women's studies in changing women's attitudes about themselves, their capacities and expectations; and with economic data showing how far we still have to go. We cannot turn back now, she said; we cannot reject the discoveries about ourselves and our status that we have made; the revolution in our minds is irreversible. Howe described the work of re-education that must be done in the public schools, and reminded us that women's studies, far from being a purely academic endeavor, is and must be inherently political: it must live or die with the women's movement itself, and it is openly committed to changing people's lives.

The workshops that occupied the mornings and afternoons of the next three days were planned primarily to deal with tactics and strategies for organizing programs—funding, control, leadership, structure, community education; and with feminist teaching—curriculum, materials, classroom techniques. Many of these workshops, unfortunately, were overcrowded. Some 200 women, for example, came to the workshop on Feminist Teaching: Developing Courses to Create a Female Culture, and spent valuable time deciding how to handle the overflow. (The crowding could have been anticipated, since there were only five workshops scheduled concurrently at any one time.) Finally this group broke down into smaller working units on the basis of area of interest—not entirely a satisfactory solution for those who wanted to hear about other fields, and not always curative of the size problem: there were fifty at the "small" group discussion on literature. Still, these workshops gave us a chance to add to our bibliographies and our stock of ideas about teaching and organizing, to renew old contacts and make new ones, to air our frustrations and share our successes.

The conference planners had also included workshops on a Feminist View of the Class Struggle, and on Ethnic Studies and Women's Studies: Cooperation or Conflict. And for Sunday they had scheduled a Gay Women's Caucus and an Ethnic Women's Caucus. The large and well-organized contingent from San Diego, together with women from San Jose State and San Francisco State, organized in addition an ongoing session on Heterosexual Bias within the women's movement, and initiated a workshop on Racism in the Women's Movement, retitled by the conference planners A Feminist Perspective on Race. It was participants of these workshops and caucuses who produced the memorandum excerpted earlier, accusing the conference planners of heterosexual bias, class bias, and racism, ostensibly manifested in some of the following ways: (1) the original omission of workshops on lesbianism and heterosexual bias and the lack of social events except as planned by lesbian women on their own; (2) the requirement of a $4.00 registration fee for all participants rather than a sliding fee based on capacity to pay (the San Diego women refused to pay the fee, offering instead $25.00 for the group of twenty-six); insufficient free housing and inadequate provision of food for those who could not afford three days of restaurant prices; inadequate childcare facilities; and (3) too limited an effort to contact Third World women about the conference; a failure to integrate an analysis of racism into all aspects of the conference; the shift in focus implied in the change of name of the panel on racism; and the use of the term "Ethnic Women" instead of "Third World Women" in the program.

Not surprisingly, the conference planners reacted with pain and righteous indignation. They had, after all, planned workshops on all of these issues in advance, except the one on Heterosexual Bias; lesbians had been included in planning the program; the conference was well-attended by Third World women; and as to food, registration fees, and daycare, their own resources at the University were hardly unlimited.

But all these charges and countercharges may be viewed as symptoms of a deeper polarization in ideology. The battle lines had been drawn long before the conference, for the divisions which emerged there are those in the movement itself. The sorest of divisions are not, I think, between middle-class and working-class women, nor between Third World and white women, nor even between lesbian and straight women. These differences, except perhaps for sexuality, are determined by birth rather than by choice: one does not choose one's race or class. They must be acknowledged and explored, and their implications for the feminist movement understood. But because the differences themselves are incontrovertible—social fact rather than ideological construct—we must and often do accept them and examine them without the *Sturm und Drang*, the atmosphere of charge and countercharge, the personal vindictiveness and personal defensiveness, of grander ideological confrontations.

The deepest rift at the conference, and in the movement itself, is between the "socialist feminists" and the "cultural feminists," or, as conference lingo finally put it, between "Marxists" and "Matriarchs." There are lesbian women and straight women, Third World and white women, working-class and middle-class women in both camps. The socialist feminists, at their best, urge us to remember that a feminist analysis cannot ignore the oppressive dynamic of class, racism, sexism, capitalism, imperialism, and remind us to take account of struggles of national liberation in countries other than our own. The cultural feminists, at their best, urge the creation of a culture based on female talent, productivity, and value—in the arts, in myth, in historical interpretation, in the evolution of more humane life styles based on cooperation rather than male competitiveness. The cultural feminists see in the socialist feminists an unhealthy adherence to "male" analysis and "male" tactics, and a tendency to dwell on issues that divide women rather than unite them against the common enemy—men. The Marxists see in the Matriarchs a squishy tendency to retreat from the arena of political struggle into the hip safety of "doing your own thing." At their worst, the cultural feminists redbait; at *their* worst, the Marxists lay guilt trips about working-class consciousness and middle-class elitism on those who diverge from their views—and on themselves. There was plenty of the best and worst from both groups at the conference.

The two camps differ also on the desirability of confrontation itself; the Marxists welcome it, the cultural feminists wish that it would go away. Wilson's opening speech was, on one level, an attempt to forestall the confrontation she knew was coming. It was a defensive offense, which the San Diego contingent correctly interpreted as an attack on their politics, and an anticipation of their strategy—to place two or more women in each of the workshops to guide the discussion along "politically correct" lines: that is, to force the acknowledgment and discussion of differences in the areas of class, race, and sexuality—not in "society" in the abstract, but within the movement and at the conference itself. In a postscript to her speech, written after the conference had concluded, Wilson accuses these women of manipulating and controlling the workshops in an undemocratic, underhanded, and authoritarian way, rather than simply "facilitating" them. There is truth too in this charge; many of the women at the conference were never aware of the San Diego coalition's effort to pack and channel the sessions, and to that extent they were indeed the victims of manipulation.

Yet this group did provide a political analysis that might otherwise have been absent; a more democratic and more broadly-based planning procedure for the whole conference might have avoided the manipulation. Perhaps future conferences which are clearly regional in scope should be organized by a number of schools in the area. But no amount of careful planning will heal the deepest of ideological rifts within the movement—those choices that determine where we direct our energies and how we live our lives.

By the time Robin Morgan spoke on Saturday night, emotions were running high. An exponent of cultural feminism, Morgan envisioned completely autonomous women's studies programs, taught, run, and attended solely by women. She had frightened men out of her own classes, she said, by promising to give the women an automatic pass; the men, a grade on merit (an ironic smile) or an automatic F; she required no work from the women; from the men, a sixty-page paper and the establishment of a childcare center. Morgan attacked the "Marxists" directly; Marxism was useless as an approach to the problems of women, she asserted, and class analysis irrelevant and disruptive to the development of a women's movement. Catcalls and boos, whistles and cheers greeted her remarks.

This analysis, of course, is an oversimplification of the conflicts at the conference. There were other divisions along other lines. The separatists (some Marxists in the camp along with the cultural feminists) clashed with those who prefer not to give up on men entirely and who would prefer to see women's studies courses dispersed throughout the curriculum rather than centralized and perhaps isolated in a vacuum of our own making. Those who view courses and scholarly research in women's studies as valid contributions to the feminist struggle, and who see women's studies programs as important formulators of movement theory, clashed with those who view academic programs as inevitably middle class, elitist, and "academic" in the pejorative sense, and who argue that theory can emerge only out of active political struggle—preferably in an arena other than academia.

This latter clash came into sharpest focus Sunday night, when Rita Mae Brown spoke. Her message, and that of a succession of commentators afterward, was essentially a putdown of the "academics," an expression of the "off the campuses and into the streets" frame of mind. Then Tillie Olsen stood up, and questioned this implicit glorification of oppression and ignorance; herself a working-class woman, she said that the speakers were forgetting that women's studies could give

something we all need—knowledge. Again, cheers and whistles, catcalls and boos. At the request of the Sacramento women, Florence Howe chaired
the last formal session. A succession of women came to the micro-
phone to give their reactions to the conference: criticism, from some;
gratitude for the hard work of the conference planners from others;
pleas for the usefulness of both major ideologies within the movement
as a whole. There was one tense moment when Joan Wilson was asked
to answer the charges in the memorandum; some of the antagonisms
had become personalized. But if tense, the session was also cathartic,
and a mood of dialogue carried over into the final discussion in the
afternoon, under the trees.

And what of those—probably, after all, the majority—who came to
the conference unaligned with either of the major political camps?
What did they take away? Sadly, some left with a pox on both houses.
"To hell with all this," one woman said. "I'm going home to work on
my film." Many left with a mixture of weariness, frustration, pain,
ambivalence, and a curious optimism. The weariness and pain and
frustration arose from a sense that, no, we could not, with good will
and a smile, heal the deep divergences between us, nor synthesize
them in some glorious feminist utopia. Mutual tolerance is necessary,
but it has its limitations. The ambivalence was for the content of the
divergences themselves: the lines had been too clearly drawn to ignore,
but how could one commit oneself finally to either camp? Yet a false
objectivity can lead to impotence, and fence-sitting is uncomfortable.
Still, the conference forced us to reassess—and to keep reassessing—
our own attitudes and our own work; sometimes we get so bogged
down with the details of teaching and the day-to-day headaches of organizing and running our own programs that we lose sight of the larger
issues.

And the optimism? It came from the conviction that the movement—in spite of the polarization and the pain—is very much alive.
Feminism will survive in the 1970s, but the shape of its survival is still a
question mark.

Ms. Rosenfelt, *currently visiting writer-editor at The Feminist Press, teaches
women's studies and English at California State University, Long Beach.*

Closeups of Women's Studies Programs

Selections   *1973–83*

University of Washington (Fall 1973), *Julie E. Coryell and Mary L. Eysenbach*

Women Studies started at the University of Washington in 1970, the year of expansion of the war into Cambodia, the Kent State killings, and national demonstrations. In Washington, 1970 was also the year of the successful campaign for liberal abortion reforms, and at UW the beginning of agitation for university-sponsored child care facilities. Women had grown increasingly aware of the university's discrimination against them in employment and curriculum.

Three women initiated the first course. Innocently titled "Women 101," it surveyed the role of women in social history, psychology, literature, art, public media, work, sexuality, race, law. The course helped build interest in additional classes.

By fall 1970 the Dean of the College of Arts and Sciences convened a faculty and student advisory committee to investigate creation of a course of study. The committee chose the name "Women Studies," documented the nationwide growth of feminist studies, the extent of student interest at UW, and, supporting the evidence with excerpts from the Newman Report on Higher Education, proposed a plan for an undergraduate degree within General Studies, a flexible, interdisciplinary division of the College. The strength of the advisory committee's report lies in its vision for, in Gerda Lerner's words, making men *and* women the measure of human experience.

The College of Arts and Sciences has supported the Women Studies Program financially. Since spring 1972 we have had a half-time advisor, and since July, a half-time faculty director. Course instructors are paid through either departmental budgets or the General Studies budget, and we have had some funds for guest speakers. This year about thirty courses were offered with total enrollment varying between 150-350 per quarter. The undergraduate major requires at least five courses in Women Studies, 35 credits in a relevant department, and a senior thesis. Although no graduate programs are planned at present, some students can shape their work in graduate departments to fit their feminist interests.

Organizationally, Women Studies resembles several ethnic studies programs at UW. The committee warned against divisive competition between ethnic and women studies programs, for, while there is inevitable competition among such programs for funds from the university budget, there are also common interests, which Women Studies tries to emphasize. Although not every class in Women Studies is or will be relevant to Third World interests, the program as a whole must include wide cultural and historical perspectives.

Affirmative action, consciousness raising, career counseling, political action, academic change—how should the many feminist concerns be organized and where do women's studies fit? The answer developed at the University of Washington reflects the city and the university setting. Seattle has an active feminist community with a great variety of organizations ranging from official bodies to caucuses and coalitions. These include programs for political action, health care, abortion and birth control, rape relief, arts and crafts, educational reform, auto mechanics, affirmative action, child care, and legal services; lesbian groups; a feminist newspaper; and a feminist bookstore. Several feminist groups and women's caucuses meet at the university. The student government group, ASUW Women's Commission, prepared the thorough *Report on the Status of Women: Faculty, Staff and Students,* published in 1970. Since then they have filed class action suits, run consciousness raising groups for administrators, organized caucuses and survival classes from *pro se* law to physical self-defense. In 1971 a coalition of campus women's groups pressed for and won an Office of Equal Opportunity for Women. Black Women's Forum, Third World Women, and Las Chicanas are also active. The Division of Continuing Education operates a guidance center serving primarily older, out-of-college women and offers noncredit courses on issues relating to women and feminism. Finally, informal caucuses meet in some departments and academic areas.

In order not to duplicate work being done by others, people in the Women Studies Program have chosen to concentrate on developing the academic program of teaching and research on women. While this task cannot be accomplished in isolation from other feminist interests, neither can it be accomplished in subordination to them. This fact was recognized this winter when the interim advisory committee decided upon a permanent governing body of students, faculty, and staff chosen for their interest in the academic program.

Another conscious choice was to be an interdepartmental program rather than an independent department. This choice grew from committee members' conviction that the quality of teaching and research is better if faculty are clearly identified with and part of a regular department representing a cohesive discipline. The creation of an independent department could lead to isolation of its members from developments within their fields and also to isolation of the academic world from women's studies. Women's studies is a field of research which should contribute to the improvement of fundamental theory and methods of individual disciplines, and the results of this research should be available not only in specialized courses, but also in the regular courses of each discipline. The interdepartmental choice has worked well so far; it is not without problems for the future.

We recognize that we must look beyond the problems of immediate growth to the problems of long-range stability and survival, and that one key to success is for students to accept women's studies as a viable field. Many are genuinely motivated by stimulating, well-taught classes, but are diffident about choosing women's studies over a departmental major. Raising women's expectations and self-confidence can lead to new jobs, new research, and newly awakened courage to battle sexism in society, but traditional pressures for admission to graduate and professional schools, stereotypes of postgraduate work, and marriage still loom large on individuals' horizons.

Also important is that departments accept women's studies as a significant area of interest. Most of the faculty involved in women's studies are assistant professors whose promotion and tenure will depend on recommendations from their departments. How will predominantly male colleagues evaluate research and publications in women's studies? Will they be able to recognize quality, or will sexist prejudice bias their perceptions? Will they dismiss work on women as unimportant to the discipline? Will they take such work by its very subject to be evidence of the incompetence of the author? The past record of academe and the results of recent research on sexist bias in the identification of quality prohibit sanguine answers to these questions.

In addition to retaining faculty, the Women Studies Program needs new faculty members to balance the prevalence of graduate assistants' teaching. Will the hiring departments seriously examine job candidates able to contribute to women's studies or will they put traditional departmental needs first? In this era of budget cuts will women's studies courses be the first to go, or will high enrollments and student enthusiasm overcome the burden of tradition? Finally, where individual departments are reluctant to undertake these tasks, will the college administration allow departmental independence or put financial teeth into its commitment to an interdisciplinary program? Such problems are not unique to Women Studies; they explain the short life span of many interdisciplinary programs. Clearly, if we wish to age at all, much less age gracefully, we must make sure we win the right answers to these questions.

[*Note:* The Program for Women Studies at the University of Washington was approximately the second U.S. program to form. When the time came to name the program, then acting director Mary L. Eysenbach, chose not to include the apostrophe *s*, commenting, "The program is not exclusively by and for women."]

Portland State University (Spring 1975), *Nancy Porter with Julie Allen and Jean Maxwell*

In Three Voices

Nancy: When first we came to the isle of women's studies we were petted and made much of. That past—of *Female Studies VI*—seems almost a fiction.

Nancy's Mother: Perhaps the immediate past with its explosionof sensitizing, of sisterhood, the rage, the openness, the hopeful revisioning must now be succeeded by a period when we must think of the movement three years later in a different economic environment, a period of some disillusion, of rapid change, of realism—which forces us to try to understand where we are in the long struggle. The question may be now in 1975, "How do we retain the best of the past and maintain continuity in a time of recession and readjustment?"

Julie: I just came to the program last year. I didn't even know about *Female Studies VI*. I agree we need continuity and understanding, and I want futures, not just maintenance.

We remain funded as a student activity, still close to the ground. Our bid for legitimacy, a Certificate Proposal (equivalent to a minor), has taken all the hurdles up to the State Board. Approval there will be contingent, at least in part, upon assurance of academic funding from within the university (a modest prospect). Two great compromises: specification of a part-time faculty director (we still insist coordinator) made the proposal acceptable to the new university president (who has given the proposal much needed backing), and designation of part-time wage sections rather than any full-time equivalent women's studies faculty bought departmental acquiescence. Buckets of blood were shed over the issue of a coordinator. A number of students split off when the compromise was made. A number stayed, arguing that having the program funded as an academic part of the university was important for survival. In all the energetic to enervating debate of theory and strategy, few envisaged a time when we might need a coordinator to maintain continuity, to counter the attrition of regularly appointed faculty concerned (or happy) to teach women's classes, to rekindle student interest in collectivity, to negotiate with administration and budget people, to create new jobs in a no-growth time, to find new women to revitalize women's studies.

The above, undisguisedly, is Nancy sounding like a coordinator, unpaid, with a lot of responsibility and very little authority.

I was on leave during the coordinator crisis. Julie, Kathy, the various women who carried the program through are still fearful of a paid faculty coordinator, of what that could do to our collective sense of responsibility. Undergraduates and graduate students are vitally concerned with political organization. I am concerned to secure some positions for new people who will help us extend our offerings, expand, reassess, continue to build a program, an enclave in the university. Julie, a graduate student, and Kathy, an undergraduate, have offered this term a course called "Why Women's Studies?"—the first major rethinking of our introductory course since its inception. The class represents, I believe, one way the resources of the University can be used to meet a metropolitan community's needs. The class has drawn a heavier enrollment than any of our introductory courses in the past two years.

Julie: I really tire of the rhetorical approach. Kathy and I are eclectic. Two women who work in affirmative action in the county and in the Forestry Service asked us to explore with them practical issues of power and autonomy in their assignment with women. We see the reality of individual lives, of survival, the problem of women being pitted against each other for survival, the problem of a collective enclave in a competitive society, and the necessity of using competitive means for collective ends, with the effects second guessing have on the second guessers.
Nancy: Do you think our 'constituency' has changed? Are there fewer of us now who tend to see women's studies as coextensive with our own egos?
Julie: Not really, and that's not a good way to put it. We're pretty diverse in our needs and uses for the program. Somehow, though, we're all getting older.

And, I hope, wiser. Personally, I have felt over-identified with the program. Given the administration's predilection for dealing with one faculty member who represents continuity and commitment to the university, however, I have not honestly felt I had much choice, if we want the program to continue. The struggle for recognition and funding has taken its toll on all of us; but those of us who survive agree a new era may be dawning. It is difficult sometimes not to sound like Anne Moody at the end of *Coming of Age in Mississippi.*

State University of New York, Albany (Summer/Fall 1975), *Francine Frank and Joan Schulz*

Women's studies at the State University of New York at Albany began in the fall of 1971 with a course called Women in Modern Literature offered through the College of General Studies with the encouragement of that school and as a result of the efforts of faculty from the College of Arts and Sciences. The course was enthusiastically received by students, and it was praised highly in the student evaluations completed at the end of the semester. Many of these evaluations also recommended that more courses be offered in women's studies. Subsequently, the course was made a regular part of the offerings in the department of English and in the last two years has sustained multiple sections with high student enrollment each semester.

In the fall of 1972, the Albany chapter of the Caucus for Women's Rights at SUNY formed a subcommittee to develop a women's studies program. Working with interested faculty as well as with student groups, and with the support of the Women's Caucus, the Ad Hoc Committee on Women's Studies encouraged faculty in different departments to develop new courses, gained departmental acceptance of these courses and guided the official approval of them through the regular university committees. Such new courses as Women in European History, History of Women in the Americas, Women in Antiquity, Ethnography of Women, Twentieth Century Spanish Women Writers and Women in Education were put into the curriculum. Other courses were devised, to be given on an occasional basis, usually under the special topics format.

Currently, Women's Studies is a second field at SUNY/Albany. The undergraduate program does not include minors, but students are required to have a major and a second field. Second fields are more flexible than the traditional minor; they may be in any discipline in which a major is available, or they may consist of a coherent group of courses in various disciplines chosen by individual students and approved by their advisors. There are also a number of interdisciplinary second fields designed by the faculty, which are identified and described in the undergraduate bulletin. Women's Studies is included in this group, as is the recently established second field in Journalism.

Interdisciplinary second field programs fit into the framework of the bachelor's degree in interdisciplinary studies which the College of Arts and Sciences has offered since 1972. A brief description of this degree may help clarify the relationship. Interdisciplinary majors may be student-initiated or faculty-initiated. In the former, individual students design their own programs with an interdisciplinary concentration, following guidelines drawn up by the Interdepartmental Studies Committee. After obtaining the approval of two faculty sponsors, the students submit their proposals to the Committee for approval. Faculty-initiated programs are proposed by a group of interested faculty members from various departments and must also be approved by the Interdepartmental Studies Committee. They are structured along the lines of a regular major, but include courses taught in a number of departments. Usually, a faculty member is appointed as director of an approved program and allowed released time to carry out this work.

Although the interdisciplinary second fields do not require the approval of the Interdisciplinary Studies Committee, they have been developed in much the same fashion. In the case of Women's Studies, the program originated in an Ad Hoc Committee composed principally of interested faculty members. A director has been appointed and released from part of her teaching load to coordinate the program. At present, students wishing to major in women's studies may do so through the above-mentioned student-initiated interdisciplinary program. However, as there seems to be sufficient student and faculty interest to justify a major, the Women's Studies Committee will be developing a proposal for a faculty-initiated major.

It should be noted that, although they are based on existing courses in various departments, interdisciplinary programs are often instrumental in getting departments to establish new courses. Such interdisciplinary programs may also sponsor their own courses, and the Women's Studies Program at SUNY/Albany now offers one course, WSS 200, Perspectives on Women. A second introductory course is being planned: The Women's Rights Movement: Introduction to Feminism.

Administration. The directors of most interdisciplinary programs, including Women's Studies, are responsible to both the College of Arts and Sciences and to the dean of one of the divisions of the college. Thus, the director of Women's Studies reports to the dean of the Division of Humanities. This dual administrative structure has both advantages and disadvantages and may be modified in the future, once the vacant position of the dean of the College of Arts and Sciences has been filled.

Budget. There is currently no separate budget for Women's Studies. This is true of some, but not all, of the other interdisciplinary programs. A portion of the 1974–75 budget for the College of Arts and Sciences has been earmarked in principle for these programs. Disbursement of the funds, which include moderate amounts for temporary services and supplies and expenses, is decided upon by the program directors in consultation with the responsible person in the college office. The total for Women's Studies this year is $1,000, a major portion of which has been spent on a brochure explaining the program and in the hiring of lecturers in the Perspectives on Women course.

Faculty. The SUNY/Albany faculty includes an excellent group of women scholar-teachers who are also active feminists and interested in the Women's Studies Program. Twenty-one faculty members from 13 departments or programs have taught a course related to women's studies, expressed interest in developing a course or are contributing to the introductory course. At present there are no faculty members willing or interested in offering courses relevant to women's studies in the following important areas: biology, criminal justice, economics, psychology, social welfare, sociology.

Courses and enrollment. In the fall of 1974, 11 sections of nine courses were offered, with a total enrollment of 415. Most of the SUNY/Albany courses are open to students in other Albany area colleges through a cross-registration program, and SUNY/Albany students may enroll in certain courses at the other institutions.

Problems. The administrative structure of interdisciplinary programs at most institutions has certain inherent problems which are now classic and the Albany program is no exception. Among these are the following:

1. There is no budget for hiring faculty and the program can only exert very indirect influence on recruiting by departments if they and the administration are interested and supportive.

2. Participating faculty members may find their positions in their own departments weakened by their work in the program. This is especially true of a field like women's studies which is challenging some long cherished notions of traditional disciplines and where interested faculty tend to be younger, nontenured persons whose future at the institution will depend largely on the support of their departments. Partly because of such difficulties, the question of the desirability of departmental status for Women's

Studies has been raised often at many schools. For the present, as indicated earlier, the Women's Studies Committee has decided to propose a major within the interdisciplinary framework.

In spite of the difficult financial situation and the absence of new faculty lines, the Committee at Albany will continue to press for the use of some existing lines to hire faculty members who will fill the needs of the Women's Studies Program, as well as those of the relevant departments. Faculty members involved in the program believe they should be actively involved in the recruiting and screening procedures for such people. The evident and growing student interest in the program is a principal justification of this proposal. It is probably also the main reason the administration has been willing to support the program, even to a limited extent, thus far.

There is faculty and student enthusiasm, an excellent group of faculty and a good foundation for a strong program in women's studies at Albany. But it will be difficult to continue to develop and strengthen the program without additional financial support. Although the Women's Studies Committee realizes that there is little money for new programs, it hopes that some seed money may be made available to develop one or more "model" programs on SUNY campuses.

State University of New York, Buffalo (Summer/Fall 1975), *Women's Studies College*

This year, the Women's Studies College, one of the oldest women's studies programs in the country, was under constant attack by the university. So far we have waged a strong fight. We have successfully held our own, and may even have made some gains. Certainly, we have confronted some of the toughest issues of higher education: the nature of academic freedom; the plausibility of public education for and about women, the possibility of reverse discrimination; the relation of form to content. We want to share the experience of this year—the nature and the method of the university attack and of our counterattack— with as many women as possible. We hope that this article will contribute to building a strong national support network for women's studies programs and the women's movement.

Women's Studies College at SUNY/Buffalo is part of the Collegiate System that developed out of students' movements in the 1960s. The colleges were initially conceived to be experimental, innovative units, supplemental to departmental course offerings. In June 1974, when the original prospectus expired, a new prospectus was drawn up by the faculty senate to become effective in July 1974. The new prospectus aimed to eliminate courses and programs that countered traditional university education, and called on each existing College wishing to continue to draw up a new formal charter according to specified guidelines to be approved by a chartering committee and by the president by January 1, 1975.

After a series of discussions in the College during May 1975, we decided that women's studies should continue at SUNY/Buffalo. Our strategy for achieving this included writing a charter, going through the established procedures for rechartering and building mass support for the college. Since we had fundamental disagreements with the administration, we knew that only mass support could guarantee our future survival.

At this time, the issues we identified as difficult for the university to accept centered around the principle of collectivity. Our governing assembly, the decision-making body of the College, is made up primarily of students, and welcomes the participation of "community women." Faculty have no institutionalized authority; rather, they participate equally with other college members. Finally, we have two coordinators instead of one, and do not expect them to have advanced degrees.

Writing our charter took approximately six months. We always kept in mind our slogan, "The same—plus better." We discussed ways of writing that would meet the requirements of the administration without alienating our support. At the end of six months, we produced a charter with supporting documents, strategically directed to the administration, and yet not insulting to the integrity of our program.

The rechartering procedure called for a public hearing. From the beginning, we saw the public hearing as a vehicle for organizing a mass defense of the College as well as a forum for raising the issue of sexism throughout the university community. To our surprise, 350 people came to our hearing.

As we had anticipated, the chartering committee's questions focused on issues concerning collectivity. In addition, two central challenges to our College were posed: "Were we violating academic freedom by having a College which assumed that women were oppressed?"; "Were we violating academic freedom by offering some courses open only to women?" We took the offensive in response to those questions. Our concern was to move our supporters rather than convince our opponents. Our opponents' questions crudely implied we were unthinking imposters; this tactic, however, only helped build our support, since it is clear to most people at this university that we are seriously concerned about education of quality. We did not hedge on any issue central to our existence. For instance, we stated clearly the basic assumption of our program; that women are oppressed and that all courses in our curriculum must develop this focus. We then explained why this assumption is critical to the building of a strong program, and why this position does not represent a violation of academic freedom.

Although we heard from those in power that our public hearing hurt our case, after our hearing and the mass show of committed support, all administrative attacks focused on only one issue—the classes open only to women. We had forgotten what a powerful weapon the autonomous grouping of women is.

As soon as we realized that this was going to be the central issue, we began a re-evaluation of how essential our all-women courses are to our program. The administration and the chartering committee viewed the issue as a legal, political and/or moral issue—often jumping illogically from one to the other—and gave very little weight to our arguments that such courses were educationally sound for specific objectives. We know that this was a very serious issue on which emotions run very high. We discussed the issue fully in each of our classes, for it was apparent that we could only consider fighting for the right to offer some all-women courses if the majority of students considered it important. Only the pressures of numbers of people could force administrators to listen to our arguments about what might be educationally valid for our program. The vast majority of students voted to put up a strong fight should it be necessary.

The recommendation which came out of the university chartering committee to the president was that the Women's Studies College be chartered only if we adopt the principle of equal access to our courses for all. All other serious concerns about us had evaporated. This was the end of November, when there were only one and one-half weeks remaining before the end of the semester and the beginning of exams. We held two rallies to educate people about the issue, each attended by 350 people. At the first one we handed out petitions which called for the unconditional chartering of the college. At the second, five days later, people returned with nearly 4,000 signatures and we handed them in to the president. We also, at this time, demanded that the president meet with representatives from women's studies before making his decision about chartering. Our campaign for mass support had raised the issue of sexism throughout the university. We got moderately fair coverage in the student and administration newspapers, as well as in the Buffalo papers and on TV.

The rallies, newspaper articles and letters of support forced the administration to meet with us twice during the Christmas break. Since the administration sought legal counsel for the first meeting, we did so as well. We had the legal advice of two women lawyers who also helped prepare strategies for the negotiations. The lawyers were essential for consolidating the case for the legality of offering courses open only to women. Our arguments were complicated: basically they centered on the fact that Title IX allows for the establishment of affirmative action programs and that Women's Studies College is such a program. In our meeting with him, the president set aside the legal issues and moved to the content and objectives of our program. Though he began by describing our program as pointless counseling at best, before the end of the meeting we had established the framework necessary for considering women's studies essential to the university. In the second meeting the administration conceded that it is educationally valid to have classes open only to women.

The president's final statement expressed concern about our alleged violation of the principles of academic freedom and set forth the following conditions to our charter: (1) the exclusion of men from a Women's Studies College course will be justified only when such exclusion is clearly and directly related to the educational objectives of the course and necessary to the achievement of those objectives; (2) courses in which enrollment is limited to women should constitute only a small proportion of the total courses offered by Women's Studies College; (3) challenges or questions with regard to such exclusion will be heard via established academic channels and procedures. The president also stated that the College be reviewed for compliance after a period of eighteen months.

Women's Studies College accepted the president's conditions under protest. We have continued to function through the spring of 1975 but it is clear that the struggle is going to continue and the harassment might even increase. The administration continues to evidence concern about all-women classes. In spite of the fact that they conceded the principle, they are still attempting to prevent these courses from being offered. They are now reviewing each one and asking for justification. The course most severely queried is Women in Contemporary Society, our introductory course that has been offered for ten semesters and has had the highest enrollment in the College. The administration is aware that this course forms the basis for our program. It is also the course for which we can gather the most support. We are currently involved in crystallizing the educational justification for this and other such courses.

The attack on our program has taken another form: the cutting of our budget. This cut is particularly shocking to us, since we went through the chartering process expecting to maintain our program at its present level. While we have temporarily halted the proposed budget cut, we are not certain that we will be successful, since funds for women's studies and minority programs are being cut back across the country.

Postscript: We wrote this article three months ago, and now it strikes us as rather naive. For at the present time, the administration is threatening to end our program by August 15. The administration claims that the language of our charter commits us to "clustering" women together, thus allegedly violating basic principles of the university. It also claims that our expressed aim to develop education which meets the needs of women is exclusionary and illegal. Once more, the university is raising the issue of Title IX, suggesting that we have to do remedial work for men. We have presented, through regular academic channels, rationales for five of our all-women courses, and we have received unofficial word that they have all been accepted. The president has yet to comment. We hope that Women's Studies College and the women's movement are still strong enough to win this latest struggle.

Cornell University (Summer/Fall 1975), *Jennie Farley*

Origins. Cornell sponsored a conference on the status of women in January 1969. One outgrowth of that conference was a team taught course in the College of Human Ecology called The Evolution of Female Personality: History and Prospects. Offered in spring 1970, it is believed to have been the first interdisciplinary course on women offered for credit at a major university. In September 1970, a group of students, staff and faculty founded an experimental program called Female Studies. In July 1972, the program was re-named Women's Studies and accepted by the faculty of the College of Arts and Sciences for a four-year trial period. Thus, the Women's Studies Program at Cornell University is completing its third year in the College of Arts and Sciences. During 1975–1976, we will be evaluated by a faculty committee which will make recommendations about our future. To what extent are we reaching our aims in teaching, scholarship and service?

Enrollment. Since July 1972, we have offered 61 courses to more than 1,500 students, of whom about a fifth are men. We do not offer an official undergraduate major in women's studies, but students in the College of Arts and Sciences can design such a major themselves either as College Scholars or through the Independent Study Program. The Faculty Board is seeking to develop a minor at the graduate level so that candidates for the Ph.D. or the Master's degree can combine study in a traditional discipline with an interdisciplinary minor in women's studies. Most students in women's studies courses are undergraduates, but virtually all the courses have graduate students and extramural (staff and community) students as well. Minority women and men are well represented in women's studies. Our outreach activities include publication of a guide to persons seeking to return to study or to the job market after a period of retirement, workshops for teaching assistants and sponsorship of a weekly "Sandwich Seminar" which draws some 1,500 people each year.

Faculty. The program currently supports four assistant professors (jointly appointed with regular departments), a visiting assistant professor, eight to ten lecturers (hired on a one term, part-time basis) and an administrative aide.

Housing. Women's studies offices are located in a suite consisting of a library/conference room, three small offices and a coat closet, where, in fact, teaching assistants sometimes sit. In addition, we have regular use of an adjoining seminar room for 25 people.

Funding. Our operating budget (this year around $30,000) comes from the dean of the College of Arts and Sciences. It includes lines for partial support of the director, full support of the administrative aide and four lines for part-time lecturers. The president of the university granted women's studies support for jointly appointed assistant professors; the Affirmative Action Office supports another. We augment our funds by applying to the University Senate, the Cornell Center for International Studies, the Work-Study Program and the Office of the Dean of Students for support of additional personnel. In addition, we receive gifts from alumni and faculty.

Curriculum. Our courses have been mostly in the social sciences and humanities, with only one or two in the biology of sex differences. In fall 1974, the Faculty Board drew up a curriculum plan which called for core courses and advanced courses (in addition to Freshman Seminars and an introductory interdisciplinary course). This plan was presented to students for additions or corrections. The students registered in women's studies courses that term listed an additional 65 courses they would like to take.

Governance. Women's studies policy is set by the Faculty Board, composed of 14 members: faculty from four colleges of the fifteen at Cornell, elected representatives of the program lecturers and elected representatives of graduate and undergraduate students. Some 25 faculty, students and staff members serve on subcommittees of the board.

Problems. Women's studies faculty and students share concern that, in these times of tight budgets, the program will not be renewed. In a university where the faculty is 93 percent male, few voices are raised in favor of women's studies. We have solid support from a sympathetic dean, from concerned students and from Cornell's central administration. But money is short; departments are hurting; our fear is that women's studies will be squeezed out. We believe that in order to discover and systematize new knowledge in the various disciplines about women and men, we need an expanded program, not a contracted one.

Santa Ana College (Winter 1976), *Joanne McKim [Johanna Maybury]*

Santa Ana College (SAC), a two-year community college in southern California, is offering a unique program in women's studies. Beginning in the academic year 1975–1976, SAC is making a major in women's studies available. The program is designed to meet a comprehensive set of specific feminist objectives and goals. Accordingly, it is one of the first community colleges in the nation to adopt a *commitment* to feminism far more solid and long term than the typical patchwork "course-here-and-there" approach that most two-year colleges use in this subject area.

The focus of the program at SAC is to provide the theoretical background of feminism and analyze the existence of sexism and racism in a practical context, emphasizing particularly the realities women have to contend with to survive. Because SAC recognizes the importance of earning a living, women's studies majors are encouraged to combine women's studies with job training programs at the two-year level or select suitable electives in making a second major for the purpose of transferring to a professional school or a four-year institution granting the B.A. degree. The major at SAC requires 19 semester units for the A.A. degree.

This is a no-nonsense program, dealing with basic survival issues and covering ideological considerations. In general, the Women's Studies Program at SAC identifies these vital areas as: (1) *jobs*—seen in terms of training choices; hiring; discrimination; job security; retirement; the history of women's work inside and outside the home; the functioning of the economy, including an analysis of class distinctions; welfare and poverty; (2) *physical security*—viewed from an analysis of rape; forced sterilization; health care, including self-help examinations pregnancy, abortion, mastectomy; (3) *emotional well-being*—as affected by social pressures on identity, sexuality, sex roles, family organization; involving an analysis of therapy and needs for therapy; alcoholism and drug abuse; suicide; (4) *public policymaking*—as determined by community involvement and political action.

The Program emphasizes distinctive differences in cultural backgrounds, historical development and political patterns in the United States. For example, one very important course, the History of Women in the United States, specializes in the cross-cultural analysis of women, the family, women's work and women's roles in five historical settings: Anglo and European-based women, Chicanas, Black, Asian and Native American women. Students are encouraged to examine the ways women in each of the respective societies relate to each other and the relevant political and economic forces in each of the systems. Throughout, male-dominated institutions in the mainstream of society are analyzed. Their impact is judged, in large part, by the way they use women differently, often for the purpose of pitting one racial group of women against another.

The core courses in the curriculum are: Basic Feminism–Introduction to Women's Studies, Women and Work in the Twentieth Century, Women in U.S. History, Women in Cages—Women in Literature, Liberated Women—Women in Literature. Electives are offered in women's composition, feminist health, children's literature from a feminist perspective, psychology of aging, consciousness raising, assertiveness training, self-defense/offensive training, singles lifestyles, effective study and career planning. Additional electives being planned for adoption in the near future include the sociology of women, with a special focus on divorced and widowed women; the psychology of women; anthropology from a feminist viewpoint and women artists.

We urge students to choose courses that will develop or enhance skills that lead not only to fulfillment, but to *autonomy* as well. Nontraditional careers, such as forester, industrial hygienist, surgeon, electrician or television director, are emphasized as models of working women's lives. So are the general skills necessary to prepare women for these occupations. These skills include oral communications (speech, debate, acting), analytical thinking (logic, argumentative essays), creative expression (writing, art, theater) and the use of technical equipment (video, photographic materials, film making). Of course, mathematics and science courses are emphasized more heavily than in traditional programs.

At SAC we have a Women's Center on campus to meet the social and educational needs of students outside the classroom. Also, three facilities provide child care for student parents who need it. You may write for our brochure.

University of Pennsylvania (Winter 1976), *Elsa Greene*

In some respects, the Women's Studies Program at Penn is going very well. Our budget for next year has been doubled. The new money ensures that we can make long range plans for a flexible program which will serve diverse students' needs. We project that our fully developed curriculum will include an interdisciplinary introductory course, departmental courses, experimental seminars and interdisciplinary senior seminars. Although we will continue to encourage each women's studies major to design a program for herself which best suits her intellectual and vocational interests, we are concentrating on elaborating our curriculum in women's medicine, public policy and women's writing.

At the moment we have strongly established departmental courses and experimental seminars. For the fall semester (1975–1976), the Faculty of Arts and Sciences has offered 15 courses on women. This means that most students who opt for a traditional major can now study women as a part of their normal progress toward a degree. It also means that majors can count on the existence of a relatively wide array of permanent courses. Spring semester, in addition to department-based courses, we will offer a cluster of five thematically interrelated seminars on women. (Power is this year's topic.) These seminars will be open to majors and to others who want to do a minor in women's studies.

Besides increasing our cut of the University's budget, we are learning also how to influence the spending of other institutional resources. One of us spent a month last spring compiling a list of all the clubs, departments, learned societies and endowed lectureships on campus that have funds for bringing in outside speakers. We then sent a letter to every group asking them which of their programs for next year will be of special interest to women in order to: compile a calendar of women's studies events; and offer to advise them about possible women speakers if their planning for next year was not yet complete. The response has been gratifying. Most especially, we have now established our right to have at least half of the twenty thousand dollar major speaker fund allocated for women speakers.

Our happiest extracurricular accomplishment this past year was the founding of The Women's Cultural Trust. Seeking a way to provide visibility and support for craftswomen in Philadelphia, we incorporated ourselves as a "charitable trust" devoted to "the growth of women who are working to express the female experience." Technically governed by three trustees (a student, a craftswoman and the women's studies coordinator), the Trust operates a crafts gallery and a bookstore located near the center of the Penn campus. Since the crafts gallery opened in November 1974, it has displayed and sold the work of more than one hundred and twenty women potters, quilt makers, painters, graphic designers, weavers, banner makers, photographers, jewelry makers, clothes designers and toy makers. The bookstore stocks hard-to-find feminist periodicals and basic feminist paperbacks; it also orders and sells texts required for women's studies courses. The crafts gallery is beautiful—a psychic boon for the artists and their patrons, the bookstore is useful, and both have turned out to be economically successful. With its accumulated profits, the Trust has sponsored a poetry series and craft workshops; this coming year it will be able to award small grants to other groups in the metropolitan area who want to encourage the participation of women in the creation of our culture.

In spite of our budgetary, curricular and aesthetic gains, we have problems. For one, we are not yet completely over the difficulties of the transition from being an informal program governed by a committee of volunteers to being an institutionalized program with a paid two-person staff. Had we known two years ago what we know now about the process of selecting a coordinator, we might have managed better (that is, the first choice of the original women's studies planners proved unacceptable to the central administration, who hired a second candidate instead). Still, there seem to be real difficulties in maintaining a diversely representative group which can function effectively as a decision-making, work-sharing collective month after month after month within an institution where all but the paid staff must give most of their time to other, more pressing responsibilities. We have lowered our sights at present to a dean-appointed committee of eight faculty and four students who will plan curriculum, evaluate current courses and hire teachers for our experimental seminars.

Another perennial problem we face is how to mediate the conflict between the academic ideal of intellectual freedom and the feminist ideal of solidarity. Can we, should we, oppose nonfeminists or conservative feminists who want to teach courses about women? Should we allow a woman to speak on campus if some of us strongly disagree with her views? Can, should, an academic women's studies program exist primarily to serve the needs of feminists in the community? Who shall define what those needs are?

The Free Women's School, sponsored by our Women's Center, gives us one way of generating extended, open discussion about immediately critical conflicts. This fall, for example, a course called Feminist Ethics helped some of us to clarify issues concerning Jane Alpert's surrender and Susan Saxe's subsequent arrest in Philadelphia—events which have strongly affected the lives of many women in our community.

Our other hope for continuing to work effectively on the problems that confront us is the newly formed Greater Philadelphia Consortium for Women's Studies. The Consortium, with a membership of 13 schools in the area, sponsors forums, retreats and a metropolitan newsletter. It will also concentrate on facilitating the development of a national women's studies organization.

University of Virginia (Winter 1976), *Suzette A. Henke*

I have been teaching for the past three years as an assistant professor of English at the University of Virginia and am presently offering two courses in the field of women's studies: a lower division survey course on Images of Women in Literature, open to undergraduates of any specialty; and a more intense Special Topics seminar for English majors on Modern Women Authors.

Until now, only two other courses in women's studies have been available at the University: a course on Women in Hispanic Literature and a seminar on Women in Sociology, offered by the Spanish department and the sociology department, respectively. The history department has recently approved a first year colloquium on the topic of Women in History. And the psychology department is planning to offer a course on the Psychology of Sex Roles in the fall of 1976.

As in most universities, we are gradually beginning to build a network of women's studies courses: but progress is contingent on sometimes grudging and condescending decisions made course by course, department by department. Most departments will allow the introduction of one token course, sometimes even two. But for the most part, these courses are considered "faddish" and "unserious." And any suggestion of the initiation of an interdisciplinary Women's Studies Program meets with immediate scorn and protestations of impossibility.

The University of Virginia bears the burden of a peculiarly sexist history. It was the last state university in the United States to become coeducational and only did so at the instigation of a lawsuit. Most of the senior faculty were hired at a time when Virginia was an all-male "gentleman's" university. The transition to coeducation was difficult for administrators, faculty and students alike. Many, in fact, appear not to have made the transition.

Furthermore, the University of Virginia uses its long history as an all-male institution to justify the existence of a predominantly male faculty. Women constitute only about ten percent of the faculty in the College of Arts and Sciences: fifty out of five hundred. And the tenure statistics are even more astounding: only ten women hold tenure, in contrast to three hundred tenured males in the College.

Under these conditions, the resistance to a university-wide Women's Studies Program is enormous. The idea is almost unthinkable, although the university *does* support other interdisciplinary programs. Fraternities thrive. Football thrives. But women, as always, are consigned to the bottom of the administrative barrel.

This past year, a number of female instructors in the College of Arts and Sciences organized an Association of Women Faculty to provide a forum for discussion and for the future clarification of women's concerns at the University of Virginia. We hope, at least, to begin to establish some solidarity among women students and faculty at Virginia.

San Diego State University (Spring 1978), *Marilyn J. Boxer*

Despite hazards both external and internal, the Women's Studies Program at San Diego State University (SDSU) has now survived eight years, has been strengthened in the process, and has moved in new directions. Designated a "program" in 1970, it is in fact a functioning "department," thanks to two successive supportive deans.

Funded initially by the SDSU Foundation in a period of militant feminism, in 1974 Women's Studies was assimilated into the administrative structure of the College of Arts and Letters. In the California State University system, funding for academic programs is determined almost exclusively by student enrollment. Departmental status for women's studies, therefore, means that the resources generated by strong student interest are available for building the Women's Studies "Department." With a faculty allocation at present of 6.8 positions (plus .6 for administration), approximately 1000 students enrolled each semester (in Spring 1978, 1100), one full-time secretary, two half-time student assistants, eight offices, supplies and services expenses of over $2000, and the usual departmental share in audiovisual and library purchases and services, the women's studies annual budget approaches $150,000.

It is not only the size of the budget which distinguishes us. It is the fact that faculty are appointed to tenure-track positions designated as women's studies positions. We are evaluated for retention, tenure, and promotion solely on the quality of our research, teaching, and service in women's studies. Although at present such personnel decisions are made by an advisory committee of faculty tenured in other departments, as soon as three of us achieve tenure, Women's Studies will function as autonomously as any other department in the college.

The current tenure-track faculty include Pat Huckle in public policy and the law; Elyce Rotella in economics[1] and Barbara Watson in anthropology. I came as chair-person on a one-year appointment in 1974, and was given early tenure in 1977. I teach one course per term in history. In addition, eight positions are filled by temporary faculty, both full-time and part-time. Pamela Freundl serves as a full-time lecturer in psychology; Sandy Dijkstra, part-time, in literature; Renee Anspach and Sue Fisher, part-time, in sociology. Linda Mackey, Joyce Nower, and Carol Perkins, also part-time, regularly teach the introductory course.

In addition to the core curriculum taught by women's studies faculty, courses in specialized areas are occasionally offered by faculty in other departments. For example, a member of the Health Science Department has taught our course in Women's Sexuality approximately once every third semester. Next semester, a member of the Literature Department will teach a seminar on Doris Lessing. All such courses must be paid for out of the women's studies budget.

History of the Program

Women's Studies at SDSU, the first Women's Studies Program in the nation, has undergone a number of metamorphoses. At the urging of a committee of students, faculty, and community women, it was founded in 1970 by vote of the assembled faculty of the College of Arts and Letters. From the beginning the program was troubled by conflicts between campus and community and by deep divisions over political issues. Reflecting successive shifts in political orientation, the faculty and community persons involved also shifted several times. During the academic year 1973–74, and coincident with the beginning of a new university administration, the women's studies faculty decided to leave the campus and to concentrate their energies on community work.

Sensitive to the possible charges of an administrative takeover, the Women's Studies Faculty Advisory Committee then developed criteria for employment designed to recruit new faculty with professional training and academic credentials; with strong feminist commitments to students and the community; and with the ability to establish a stable program. After extensive recruitment, several new faculty were hired in the fall of 1974.

The shift from the primarily political emphasis of the early years to the strongly academic program of today reflects not only a revision in administrative policy and a turnover in faculty, but also a notable change in women's studies students. Unlike the students who agitated for women's studies courses and filled the first classes in the early

1970s, the majority today do not, at least initially, identify themselves as feminists. Only a minority of deeply committed radical feminist activists, and a very small group who identify themselves as socialist feminists, enter women's studies classes ready for advanced feminist analysis. Most, including some antifeminists, are just curious or looking for something new. Often, however, they emerge with a new consciousness, asserting on class evaluation forms that "this course has changed my life."

In the fall of 1974, 378 students enrolled in 12 women's studies classes; in the spring of 1978, 1100 registered in 28. While many of the courses are discipline-oriented (e.g., Women in American History, Women Writers, Psychology of Women), others, such as the Introduction to Women's Studies, or Contemporary Issues in the Liberation of Women, transcend the usual disciplinary boundaries. Our most innovative cross-disciplinary course, Sexism and the Social Sciences, was developed as a group project and uses the entire core faculty as guest lecturers and resource persons.

An 18-unit minor, developed in the fall of 1974, but available to students only since 1976–77, now enrolls about 80 students. Women's studies minors must take one of the overview courses, plus one course from each of the following groups: (1) the experiences of women in cultures or eras distinct from our own (historical and anthropological perspectives; (2) biological and sociological determinants of women's personality and behavior (psychology, sociology, sexuality); (3) artistic expressions by and about women (literature and the arts); and (4) the role of women in political and economic processes and the impact of public policies on women's lives (political science, public administration, economics, and education).

Students can take selected women's studies courses for credit for their majors in history, political science, public administration, American studies, European studies, and linguistics, or they may include a women's studies component of several courses in their interdisciplinary liberal studies and social science majors. After a year-long battle about the definition of women's studies as a "discipline," students can now include up to 24 units of women's studies as part of an individualized liberal studies major in three disciplines. We are thus able to serve those students whose educational goals and personal quests demand extensive involvement in our program; a smaller number whose vocational aims require some understanding of women; and an increasing population who choose a women's studies course out of curiosity about or frustration with sexism, because they need 3 units at 10 A.M. on MWF, or—as the majority report—because a friend recommended it as a meaningful learning experience.

Our success at satisfying student needs is demonstrated in college and university enrollment figures. Since Spring 1975 we have maintained the highest student-faculty ratio (SFR) in our college, and figures for the Fall 1977 term show us with an SFR of 28.9, far above the university-budgeted figure of 18.3 or our college average of 20.9, and the highest among 65 departments on the entire campus. Each time the college dean has increased our staffing, dozens of students have flocked to the new classes. While not happy about our overload—in an institution which assigns all full-time faculty four courses per semester—we recognize that strong enrollments remain our insurance in the face of the uncommitted and unconvinced powers which control the university system.

Profile of Women's Studies Students

Ninety percent of women's studies students are women, their ages ranging from 17 to 58. Surveys taken during the past three academic years show consistently that women's studies students are older than the average undergraduate: currently 39 percent are older than 22, and 12 percent are over 30. Fifteen percent of women's studies students are members of minority groups, slightly above the percentage of minority students (12 percent) in the student body population as a whole.

Like other students at this urban university, which draws heavily from working-class families, most women's studies students are employed. Typically, they work about 20 hours per week, though almost 15 percent work a full 40 hours. The four largest categories of employment are office clerk, sales clerk, waitress, and teaching assistant. More students enroll as seniors than in any earlier year, followed in diminishing order by juniors, sophomores, and freshpersons, perhaps reflecting the desire to take courses for personal interest after completing graduation requirements. Students come to us from every part of the campus, integrating women's studies with majors which range from ethnic studies to physics. The largest groups are concentrating in liberal studies (for the elementary education credential)—reflecting female students' propensity, despite the job market, to seek traditional women's work—and in psychology and business administration, the two most popular majors at SDSU.

In addition to academic courses, Women's Studies sponsors extracurricular activities that encourage a critical approach to both personal and vocational choices. Last November, with a $10,000 grant from the National Science Foundation, we organized a Workshop on Careers for Women in Science and Engineering, which gave two hundred students an opportunity to explore job options, training programs, problems, rewards, and lifestyles with forty successful women scientists and engineers. During "Women's Week" in 1975 and 1977, working with students and community groups, we focused on "resocialization" and "women's work."

Spurred by such activities in 1975, students formed the Feminist Union, choosing to open membership to students, staff, or faculty—women or men—who support feminist goals. Active in sponsoring such programs as a Susan B. Anthony birthday party and a reading by Tillie Olsen, Feminist Union members have in turn formed other groups: Sisters on Stage, a feminist guerrilla theater group now in its second extraordinarily successful year, and Science and Math Oriented Women. Other students, with Women's Studies advisors and support, have formed an Abortion Rights Coalition, Rape Task Force, Women's Resource Center, and, most recently, a Women's Studies Minors Association. Feminist students are now actively monitoring the student newspaper for sexist journalism, lobbying the campus security forces for better rape prevention measures, fighting the statewide administration over health service surcharges for gynecological care, publishing a newsletter, and somehow finding time to attend women's studies classes.

Women's Studies and General Education

Despite steady growth, our 1100 students represent only six percent of the student body, for the most part taking women's studies courses for elective credit. During the past three years, however, a new pattern of requirements for graduation has been devised which offers women's studies at SDSU a role in General Education (G.E.) for the first time. Our mission may now be expanded to include part of every student's education. While the new program imposes new limitations on students by requiring them to select 40 units from a relatively short list of mostly traditional courses, the list also includes as options eight women's studies courses.

In the second category of a three-stage G.E. program, students must select two from among thirteen social science courses designated "Foundations of Learning." Along with such courses as Principles of Economics, Introduction to Political Science, and Introductory Sociology, students may select the women's studies course, Sexism and the Social Sciences. At registration in the fall of 1977, when this course was offered for the first time, students filled both sections of 40 and asked for more. The enrollment of students primarily seeking units to fulfill graduation requirements will bring a new population into our compass—for example, the analysis of sexism in the new course elicited expressions of fear and hostility among some students this past fall. But it will also offer a new challenge to women's studies faculty: taken early in their college career, Sexism and the Social Sciences, "a feminist critique of conventional, biased concepts and modes of thought in disciplines dealing with human interactions," will, we hope, prepare students to challenge traditional interpretations and sexist instructors in subsequent courses.

Other women's studies courses accepted for the huge list of third-stage G.E. electives termed "Human Experience" include Women in Comparative Cultures, Socialization of Women, Psychology of Women, Women in History, Women in American History, Women Writers, Women and the Law, and Contemporary Issues in the Liberation of Women. Thus, while the redefinition of G.E. has in one regard proven reactionary, requiring a large concentration of ethnocentric studies in American and Western civilizations, it has provided women's studies with an opportunity to be included in a previously male-focused curriculum.

For the past two years we have focused our curriculum work on the development of General Education courses. Although 22 percent of our students indicated in a recent survey that they want a women's studies major, the faculty have been reluctant to undertake the enormous effort required to plan a major and guide it through the California State University system. We have two reservations. First, we question whether, given limited resources, we can serve student interests well with the highly specialized curriculum required for a major—as opposed to concentrating on survey courses of broad interest. Secondly, we worry also that the investment of time and energy in the development of the major would overburden our small faculty, most of whom face tenure decisions in the near future. At a recent meeting, we voted to delay proposal of a major until at least three of our faculty have been tenured. Women's studies faculty must publish or the program will perish.

NOTE

1. Rotella does hold a joint appointment but it is an unusual one: 60 percent women's studies, 40 percent economics, with Women's Studies designated her "home department" for purposes of committee service and personnel decisions.

George Washington University (Winter 1979), *Rosemary Beavers, Carol Bros, Patricia McDonough, Terry Savage, Lois West, and Phyllis M. Palmer*

From Students and Graduates, Rosemary Beavers, Carol Bros, Patricia McDonough, Terry Savage, and Lois West

The M.A. program in women's studies at George Washington University is undergoing dramatic changes in focus and structure. As students and graduates, we believe these changes raise questions about the quality of our Women's Studies Program, especially its lack of feminist focus and content.

A radical feminist believes that women are a distinct group, restricted by custom and law from complete participation in society. Moreover, feminists believe that women's lives—and the female experience—have worth and should be preserved. Therefore, feminists strive for equity, recognition of the importance of the female world, and fundamental change in the social order.

What is women's experience, both individual and collective? The curriculum known as women's studies attempts to answer that question. Women's studies should serve as a revolutionary force in a university, providing new ideas and methods for developing feminist consciousness. Women's studies should have a clearly stated point of view. Obviously each individual has her interest, but the inherently female experience that we share must be included. Women's studies must be taught from a feminist perspective, must use feminist research methods and feminist procedures to implement the program. Tillie Olsen has called this "coming to one's own voice."

Unlike the fifteen Women's Studies Programs described in Florence Howe's report, *Seven Years Later: Women's Studies Programs in 1976*, the Women's Studies Program at GWU was an outgrowth of an off-campus counseling course, Developing New Horizons for Women. The program was organized by the developer of that course, an administrator in the off-campus division of the university. This administrator recruited several interested faculty members to serve on an advisory committee to the Dean of the Graduate School. Thus, the program was created outside the feminist movement; furthermore, community feminists were not asked their views. In essence, the GWU Women's Studies Program was created in a vacuum.

The first students in the program were graduates of that same counseling course, Developing New Horizons for Women. By and large, these women had reared their families and were now interested in reentering the world of paid work. The content of the first group of courses reflected a basic lack of understanding about the nature of women's studies. In addition, few departments in the university were interested in expanding their course offerings to accommodate interested students.

By the spring of 1975, and despite the limitations described above, almost one hundred women had enrolled in the new graduate program. A new Dean appointed to head the Graduate School decided that the program needed a full-time academic director. After a six-month search, an academic feminist and activist was hired for the newly created position.

The new director, in her brief two-year tenure, began to recruit feminist students to the program and worked to expand the curriculum. In spite of this progress, personality and political conflicts developed between the director and members of the Women's Studies Committee. When the director's appointment came up for review, she was not rehired, despite prior reassurances from the Dean of the Graduate School. Vehement student protests against this action had no effect, and the director left in June 1977. . . .

After a two-month search, in which students were only superficially involved, an "Academic Coordinator" was selected to teach courses and advise students. This woman was painfully aware of her predecessor's fate (the alleged reason for the first director's dismissal was that she had failed to develop a coherent purpose and direction for the program). She spent the next nine months developing a new purpose and direction. Again, as when the program first developed, student and community feminists were not involved in discussion. In September 1978, the program's new direction was announced:

> The major goal is to provide a center to develop theory, research, and policy options in three areas of concern to women: family, education, and work. At the same time, the goal is to help students to develop as researchers and policy analysts in these three areas.
>
> The program seeks to attract students who are already working or who intend to work in governmental or organizational positions involving public policy issues relating to social equity for women.

Many of the problems of this Women's Studies Program reflect realities of George Washington University. Interested in maintaining solvency and overemphasizing profit-making, the university is unresponsive to students' needs and concerns. The GWU Graduate School offers degree programs which capitalize on the presence of government workers needing professional development. Such motivation for the expansion of graduate education has not been helpful to programs as they attempt to develop solid academic and research foci.

The Women's Studies Committee, charged with making curricular decisions, has followed the university's lead. The committee has not concerned itself with developing a solid interdisciplinary program; nor have most of its members been involved in teaching either women's studies courses in the program or courses on women in their own departments. They have been only peripherally involved in advising students and in contributing to the growth of the field of women's studies. When falling enrollments signaled some curricular problems in the Women's Studies Program, the committee sought to change the focus and hence the student constituency.

Students have no formal voice on the committee that administers the program. Even informally, the opinions and ideas of students are generally not solicited, and, when offered, have largely been ignored. We fear that studies in the humanities will not thrive under the new public policy program. . . .

From the Academic Coordinator, Phyllis M. Palmer

As the current Academic Coordinator of the graduate program in women's studies at George Washington University, I would like to consider two issues raised by the students' analysis. The first is the intellectual content of women studies. The second is the organizational issue of how programs have been, and can continue to be, established within the framework of collegiate institutions.

The first issue to develop is how feminism interacts with public policy, a speculation that has been raised but not explored by the students. It is an important question in general and must be answered for evaluation of the current GWU program in particular. Women's studies courses have quite successfully laid the groundwork (and more) for recovering women's private experiences. What we need to do now is to analyze how public institutions—legislatures, courts, corporations, educational institutions, and religious bodies—have shaped and limited these private experiences. As women's studies has revealed, part of women's oppression originates in dichotomizing private and public life. Both to confront that dichotomization and to examine the public forms it takes, we must undertake an examination of public sources of oppression and the links between private experiences and public behavior.

Studying public life and the formation and implementation of policy is more treacherous than studying private experience. It necessitates mastering the social science disciplines that were formulated as adjuncts to the developing bureaucratic orders of state and industry. These viewed human beings as machines, which operated according to discoverable principles of exactly the same sort that governed machines. Consequently, they divided humanity into component parts and then specialized in studying only the pertinent part—economic man, political man, social man, family man, physical man. (I use the term "man" advisedly, since the disciplines did not look at *women's* economic, political, social, and physical status.) The disciplines emphasized the split between various parts of people's lives and minds, and made it "unscientific" to look at persons as total human beings. The disciplines also were dependent on "objective" data: information could be quantified and calculated. For this reason, women's studies' attempt to critique dominant knowledge has required both interdisciplinary and supradisciplinary studies, as well as attention to those disciplines that still depend on nonquantitative data and that see humanity more completely, i.e., history, religion, philosophy, literature, and occasionally psychology and sociology.

This humanistic base for the development of feminist analysis, which must exist in all programs, constitutes the basis for the development of a critique of public behavior. We must especially confront the academic separation between subjective and objective knowledge which underlies the conflict we feel between private and public life. Since these dichotomies are fundamental paradigms of women's oppression and pervade both academic disciplines and academic structures, they must be confronted in all disciplines. Since a recovery of women's experience requires a holistic comprehension of public structures and intimate forms, women's studies entails an interdisciplinary investigation as well as one that breaks down the artificial lines between the university and those institutions and groups outside it. This is the purpose of a Women's Studies Program and emphasizes the study of public policy.

The second issue to be addressed is an organizational one: what are the proper setting, curriculum, student population, governance structure, and professional goals of a Women's Studies Program? Although Florence Howe's report *Seven Years Later* has provided a coherent summary for considering these questions, it describes a variety of possibilities dependent upon the particular campus and constituency. My remarks, therefore, are an assessment of the situation at GWU, intended to enlarge the discussion of what problems and possibilities exist for graduate training in women's studies.

The GWU program developed, like many others, because a handful of concerned women faculty used the prospect of substantial student demand to bargain for recognition and funding from skeptical administrators. The GWU faculty women were largely established professionals who were in the process of changing their traditional academic interests to more obviously political and feminist ones. The student demand was not from young undergraduates, who remain quiescent on most D.C. campuses, but from concerned and committed older women like the majority of women's studies majors and minors Howe found on the campuses she investigated.

The oddity of the GWU program is that it began as a *graduate* program within the Graduate School of Arts and Sciences. This was due to an institutional accident: the Graduate Dean was willing to give a trial to such a program, and most of the reentry women already had B.A. degrees.

While location in the Graduate School was fortuitous, starting as a graduate program entailed problems and questions that other women's studies graduate programs have, problems that are surfacing now in undergraduate programs as well. The most prominent was and is, "What responsibility does a graduate program have to offer professional skills and credentials comparable to those provided in other graduate-professional programs?"

The answer to this question at GWU has been that graduate students must be provided with the opportunity to develop skills for professional jobs, even if the degree does not (yet) have general recognition as a professional credential. Combining the goals of a substantial social critique with competence in particular areas of political activity and public interest, the program seeks to integrate a humanistic-feminist analysis of current theory and contemporary policy, with substantive knowledge and social science skills. The goal is to enable graduates to work effectively on the formulation and implementation of policies on the basis of a recognition of the uniqueness and worth of women's experiences.

As Howe notes in *Seven Years Later*, "The chief criticism of Women's Studies Programs raised generally by student majors [is] that programs lack curricular focus on job skills, field work, and credentials." Some of those students Howe surveyed who were interested in careers solved the problem by going on to graduate or professional schools, which offered recognized, conventional credentials. We would like, at the least, to provide a professional program that allows students to pursue work on women directly and that answers the needs all our students have: how to move from college to work and how to reconcile working for women with making a living.

As a final note and to clarify remaining points, the present Women's Studies Committee includes a philosopher, a religion professor, and an historian, all of whom are committed to the usefulness of their disciplines in the new focus on public policy. Second, while we have designed a program so that a terminal M.A. degree is a meaningful credential, many students have prepared for Ph.D. programs by doing a portion of the M.A. course work in the relevant academic discipline. Finally, the program has offered a coherent set of courses for Ph.D. candidates in other GWU schools and departments who want a women's studies minor. Currently students from education, psychology, American civilization, and history are choosing women's studies as a cognate field.

The women who established the graduate program at George Washington University were willing to take risks, giving much time and energy to the creation of the first university graduate degree program in women's studies in the United States. Without them, there would be no program now. They merit our appreciation. It is their effort that makes possible the program's extension into a new area: analysis of public policies affecting the lives of women. The need to train feminist policy analysts has been recognized by many in this university and elsewhere. The GWU program now has a policy focus, but one broad enough to accommodate a wide range of interests and ideologies.

Hunter College, City University of New York (Spring 1983), *Dorothy O. Helly*

I. 1971–1975. Hunter College was among the many colleges and universities in the United States where women's studies courses were developed by faculty in the early 1970s. The college is part of the City University of New York and currently has enrolled 17,000 students (the equivalent of 12,000 full-time students), three-quarters of whom are women. As was usual in the early 1970s, most of the faculty interested in women's studies were not tenured and some of the early participants did not stay for more than a year or two. Among them, however, were a few full-time and tenured faculty who formed an ongoing core, including Florence Denmark in psychology (who is now a past president of the American Psychological Association) and Francis Conant in anthropology. Another important member of this core, at that time untenured, was Sarah B. Pomeroy (who has since published major work on women in classical antiquity). Art historians who were with the group for a brief time were Ann Sutherland Harris (who with Linda Nochlin went on to organize the first major exhibit of women painters from 1550 to 1950) and Julia Keydel (now in filmmaking). The efforts of this group and those who aided them were directed at developing two interdisciplinary courses in women's studies. Under an "experimental course" category that then existed under the control of the college curriculum committee, women's studies courses could compete for authorization to exist each semester. The courses developed were "Images of Women in Literature and Art" and "Perspectives on Women in Biology, Psychology, and Anthropology." Pomeroy recalls hearing Sheila Tobias, instrumental in introducing "Female Studies" at Cornell University in 1969–70, speak at a women's political caucus in New York City in 1971 and being inspired as a result to bring women's studies courses to Hunter College. The faculty planning women's studies courses at Hunter also made use of the "Female Studies" series of syllabi and reading lists first compiled by Tobias and then by Florence Howe, as chair of the Commission of the Status of Women of the Modern Language Association. These course syllabi were published by the feminist press KNOW, Inc., and included a ten-course curriculum from San Diego State University, which had the first officially established Women's Studies Program in the United States. (See Marilyn J. Boxer's review essay, "For and About Women: The Theory and Practice of Women's Studies in the United States," *Signs* 7 [Spring 1982]: 661–95.)

The faculty involved at Hunter were told that in order to translate these experimental courses into regular offerings, they would have to gain the prior approval of each of the departments (disciplines) involved in the material taught. Women's studies faculty therefore faced the herculean task of convincing a great number of departmental curriculum committees that they should accept these courses and were warned by the incumbent provost (vice president for academic affairs) that he saw no way of allocating to an interdisciplinary program any budget, no way of supervising their faculty, and no way of simplifying their process of curriculum review.

In the midst of these difficulties, the faculty involved were encouraged by enthusiastic student support, in terms both of enrollment and of funds supplied one year by the student government for a lecture series on feminist topics. Others at the college were also encouraged to teach courses about women as departmental offerings, building up a base of interested faculty who would prove important at a later stage.

II. 1973–1976. The impasse was broken in 1975 as a result of a conjunction of factors. A new generation of energetic women students, the product of women's studies courses, was determined to create a women's studies major. They could now call upon a considerable number of faculty—both full time and part time—who had taught women's studies courses or departmental courses on women. This fairly large group had within it faculty who held strategic positions in the college governance structure, especially the college curriculum committee. These experienced hands could guide the proposal through appropriate channels and negotiate with college administrators. The crucial new factor, however, was the arrival of a new provost, who had worked with a new Women's Studies Program in his previous institution and saw no problem in finding solutions to budgetary and curriculum review questions.

As a result of this encouragement, an ad hoc group of students and faculty now worked out the curriculum for a women's studies major, including an introductory course and a senior seminar. Following a precedent set by Brooklyn College in the City University, a "collateral major" was proposed. This consisted of allowing students to complete a second major in women's studies (consisting of six courses) in addition to majoring in a traditional discipline (usually consisting of eight or nine courses).

III. 1976–1978. Once the program was approved, the provost arranged to place it under the administration of an academic dean and to allot it a budget. This consisted of one course release from teaching each term for its director, funds for faculty to teach the introductory course and senior seminar of the program, and the costs of a part-time secretary. The policy decisions of the program continued to be made by the self-constituted ad hoc group of students, faculty, and (library) staff who had brought it into existence. Subgroups shared the tasks of writing regulations and requirements for its administration, including the election of a coordinator, the first to be elected by this process being Sarah Pomeroy.

After a year of governance by this ad hoc group, the provost informed the program that it must conform to practices mandated by the university with regard to the composition and confidentiality of a committee that made personnel and budget decisions. This shift was made with reluctance, for it ended the more informal, if more chaotic, mode of governance in which everyone's word and vote carried equal weight.

IV. 1978–1979. One of the principal tasks of the new policy committee was to choose those who would teach the introductory course. It became apparent that reliance on the part-time faculty who had taught that course since the formal inception of the program in 1975 posed serious problems for the future of the program. Each instructor who taught the course organized it according to her primary disciplinary knowledge, supplemented by interdisciplinary information picked up through wide reading from the numerous reading lists and course syllabi now available. The course thus changed with each instructor and contained no standard range of topics. Hence, students who became majors had no specific body of knowledge on which to build. In addition, because these were times of fiscal stringency in the City University of New York, it was feared that budgetary cuts could wipe out the program by eliminating the funds needed to hire part-time faculty to teach it. Yet it was also clear that faculty carrying full-time teaching loads found it difficult to undertake the preparation of such a challenging interdisciplinary course along with their other course and committee work. They needed some guidance and some time.

The solution was a request to the college administration to sponsor—using outside funding at their disposal—a faculty development seminar in 1978–79, giving to ten faculty members one course released time for two semesters in return for a promise from their departments that they be allowed to teach thereafter one course a year for the Women's Studies Program. The supportive provost was convinced of the wisdom of such a seminar in part because he could find the funding for it at that time. Department chairs were persuaded to cooperate in releasing faculty to teach in the program after the seminar year by the promise of the allocation of the "head count" in the classroom (for budgetary purposes) to the department from which the faculty member was borrowed.

Faculty were offered, in addition to one course released time for each of two semesters to participate in the seminar, the chance to take part in organizing a uniform introductory course in women' studies, and to teach each other how to deal with topics that drew upon the other disciplines included and represented in the seminar. Ten faculty were selected out of the twenty-five (all women) who applied, and an eleventh member was added to administer the seminar. Modest funds were also provided to bring in people to discuss fields not represented by those in the seminar, and to tape and transcribe the discussions.

V. 1979–1982. A month or two into the faculty development seminar, it became clear that what was emerging as a syllabus for an Introduction to Women's Studies course was a topical organization so interdisciplinary in its contents that no textbook existed by which it could be taught. A group within the seminar proceeded to write a proposal to the National Endowment for the Humanities, outlining the progress already made by the seminar and suggesting the pioneering nature of a proposed textbook of this kind. To write it would take a great deal of time, but it would provide the first collaboratively written interdisciplinary text introducing women's studies and might provide a uniform basis for the further development of the field.

NEH funded the project, giving each participant in the writing of the text one more semester of one course released time (far less than was actually needed) and funds for reproducing drafts and paying three outside consultants to comment on the manuscript. In addition, it was possible to offer to share parts of the manuscript-in-progress with faculty throughout the country who wished to experiment with these sections in their courses. A description of the Hunter College Women's Studies Program, the faculty development seminar, and the textbook was presented at the National Women's Studies Association Convention held in May 1980 at Indiana University in Bloomington. An abbreviated version of this presentation is available in the issue of *Frontiers* which summarized that year's Convention.

Once the textbook project was underway, the authors decided to call themselves the "Hunter College Women's Studies Collective," and accepted an offer from Oxford University Press to publish the textbook in May 1983.

VI. 1982–1983. With this amount of experience behind them, the Women's Studies Program at Hunter College has already embarked on the next phase of introducing the new scholarship on women into the regular curriculum. The Policy Committee proposed the establishment of another faculty development seminar to bring together representatives from each of the departments offering introductory courses to ask them to consider the extent to which their course reflects information about and the perspective of women. Donna Shalala, the new president of Hunter College, who is committed to strategies for a feminist transformation of the academy, agreed to fund the seminar. A planning committee of three became responsible for running the seminar, but expected to call upon the other members of the Women's Studies Program to help launch this ambitious experiment. All workshop members are expected to consider the organization of the introductory courses in their departments, to compile a bibliography for the faculty who teach those courses, and to make a formal presentation to their departments at the end of their semester of work. In return, each is released from one course of teaching for that semester. As there are twenty-eight departments that will be involved in this process, half will be involved in each of two semesters. The first semester deals with the sciences and social sciences, and a college "Women in Science" lecture series is being sponsored to supplement its work. The funding for the project will include some clerical help and a small budget for bringing in some outside consultants and for reproducing the course outlines, bibliography, and conclusions of each participant in order to share this exercise as widely as possible with other colleges as well as within Hunter. It is not anticipated that the task of these workshops will be easy.

VII. Strategies for Institutional Change. In retrospect, it is possible to say that institutional change at Hunter College in terms of the discipline of women's studies depended on many factors which are difficult to predict. The timely presence of new administrators sympathetic to the program, the timely availability of funds which could be so allocated, and a climate of opinion in the academic community which made it possible to create a new program without large-scale, overt resistance were all crucial to success. But these opportunities could be taken advantage of only because of the prior and continued existence of people—students, faculty, and staff—who were committed to realizing a program in women's studies and willing to spend the significant amounts of time necessary to plan, organize, maneuver, and negotiate to bring it about

It is possible that the participation in the program of a core of full-time, tenured faculty was important for providing it with the appearance of solidity in the eyes of the rest of the academic community. The planning and carrying through of specific, highly visible projects in the name of the program has contributed to its acceptance as part of the regular curriculum of the college. The appeal of women's studies to large numbers of students has also been crucial, for it enabled the program to enlist the aid of traditional departments who benefited from allowing their faculty members to participate in the program. . . .

In 1983 the Women's Studies Program will move into new offices that will include a large conference room. There we can sponsor formal programs—films and talks in connection with current courses, panels, lectures, and workshops of topical interest—as well as informal get-togethers to celebrate women's studies prize winners or just to welcome a new semester. Students will be encouraged to look upon this space as a meeting place. Students taking women's studies courses need to talk to one another about the new view of the world they are absorbing, and to discuss problems this new perspective creates for them in other courses. Students can act as catalysts for introducing questions concerning women into the rest of the curriculum. Together with our faculty "mainstreaming" efforts, students' ability to raise women's issues in all their courses becomes the ultimate strategy for "mainstreaming" women into the entire college curriculum. Thus it is not one strategy or even two or three that we need to use; it is as many as we can put into operation as much of the time as possible.

NOTE

This paper was presented in a slightly different version at the International Conference on Research and Teaching Related to Women, arranged by the Simone de Beauvoir Institute of Concordia University, Montreal, July 26–August 4, 1982. The author is indebted to Sarah B. Pomeroy, coordinator of the Women's Studies Program, Hunter College of the City University of New York, for information about the earliest years of the program and for a keen editorial eye cast upon the final version.

Sarah Lawrence College (Summer 1983), *Judith Papachristou, Amy Swerdlow, and Gerda Lerner*

On Sunday, March 6, 1983, a champagne brunch was held to celebrate the tenth anniversary of the Women's History Program at Sarah Lawrence College. Originally intended as a small gathering for some twenty people, the celebration had to be expanded when it was learned that over 150 well-wishers—including many of the over fifty graduates of the Program—wanted to attend. The occasion was also used to honor Gerda Lerner, one of the founders of the Program with the inauguration of a scholarship in her name. . . .

Judith Papachristou

. . . Ten years ago, aided by a grant from the Rockefeller Foundation, Sarah Lawrence's M.A. Program in Women's History began. It is impossible to recount all of its history and accomplishments in a brief talk. In the past ten years, some of the most distinguished scholars and teachers of women's history came to work at Sarah Lawrence. This was the frontier of women's history: every course was a new course, an experiment in such new topics as Feminist Theory, Women in Classical

Greece and the Renaissance Women and Work, and The History of Afro-American Women. Within the College there evolved a strong support network of faculty and staff, the Women's Studies Steering Committee, which developed women's studies courses for graduate and undergraduate students.

The impact of the M.A. program very quickly moved far beyond the campus. Faculty and students reached out to share women's history with a larger community of women, offering in-service training for high school teachers in several Westchester towns, a course for employees of AT&T and a seminar in which community activists and students examined the subject of Women Organizing Women.

The M.A. program has also sponsored conferences and institutes that have had widespread impact: a Conference on Housework and Child Care for scholars, activists, students, and household workers; an institute for integrating women's history into the high school curriculum (cosponsored by the American Historical Association); an institute for national leaders of women's organizations (cosponsored by the Women's Action Alliance) which sparked the movement for a national Women's History Week. More recently, we have hosted conferences for women in our extended community on motherhood and on women's bodies, and this year we will grapple with issues of nuclear war and national security. Currently the M.A. program is participating with the Girls Club of New York in a model program that offers young women from disadvantaged backgrounds an opportunity to learn about the accomplishments of women like themselves in America's past.

Finally, I would like to say a few words about the most important component in the history of the M.A. program—our alumnae and students. During the past ten years, women of all classes, ages, and races, from all over the United States, and from Europe and Asia as well, have come to study here. Almost fifty have graduated from the program. Here at Sarah Lawrence they shared the excitement of inquiry and learning—they were and still are among the pioneers in women's history. Many of them have gone on to study for their doctorates at prestigious institutions. Today, fifteen are teaching women's history at the college level, three in high schools. Two are involved in academic administration; one is an elected member of the Vermont legislature; five are connected with publishing projects about women; one is impatiently waiting for her M.A. thesis to come off the press in book form. Many describe themselves as community activists.

We have indeed a great deal to be proud of and to celebrate together today. We also share a clear resolve—to continue the work and the tradition of the Sarah Lawrence program.

Amy Swerdlow

. . . When I came to Bronxville in 1972, I did not know nor could I have predicted, that the two remarkable and gifted codirectors of the Women's History Program would become the most important influences in my already long life. They became not only teachers and exemplars, but supportive mentors and later colleagues and friends. Nor did I, or my cohorts in those early years, know in advance that we were to become students of two women who themselves were becoming recognized pioneers of the new feminist scholarship, germinal thinkers in the field of women's history and militant leaders in the movement for women's equality within the historical profession. . . .

Those of us who are part of the Sarah Lawrence community know that Gerda Lerner was a presence to be reckoned with in her years here. She literally turned this campus on its ear, fighting to legitimize women's history as a field of study, planning and plotting to establish the M.A. program, energetically searching for the grant from the Rockefeller Foundation that launched it, and later struggling to preserve the program—arguing, cajoling, and even twisting arms on behalf of women and women's history.

Now Gerda Lerner has moved to larger, if not greener, fields. As Robinson-Edwards Professor of History at the University of Wisconsin, she is making a name for herself even at that venerable state university known for its liberals, radicals, mavericks, and outstanding scholars. Having introduced the first Ph.D. program in Women's History to that campus, she is using the same energy, commitment, ingenuity, and perseverance to find the grants to support it, to recruit talented students, and to cajole and coerce cooperation from colleagues. . . .

Gerda Lerner

. . . All of the women and most of the men at Sarah Lawrence college, in one form or another, were challenged and transformed by the questions that we raised—some sooner, some later. I think that that is the most important thing that women's studies is doing for our culture and for our educational system. It is impossible not to be transformed in your psyche if you are a woman, because what we are talking about is not just subject matter, a topic, a focus of inquiry, but a new angle of vision; it is a fundamental critique of all traditional knowledge as it has been handed down to us. No intellectual and no honest teacher can be unaffected when students of colleagues begin to raise questions which challenge tradition—when you are forced to ask yourself, "Is what I am teaching really about all of us, or am I teaching a small slice, or a small group? Am I leaving out important questions, important people, important ideas?"

I think it is this quality of transformation which gives women's history a very significant place in the intellectual life of everyone who comes in touch with it. I believe that women's history has a revolutionary value and potential that women's studies in other fields does not have, and the reason is that women's history also restores to women a sense of continuity. After all, we are, all of us, persons rooted in a continuum that goes from the past to the future, and our place in history is a deeply important personal matter—not just abstract knowledge. Where we stand, where our roots are, where we came from, who our models are, the heroes and heroines whose values we incorporate into our feelings—these matters are of the greatest significance in shaping the whole individual.

We have heard through the women's movement that women have suffered all kinds of discrimination. We know that, and we have been justly angered by the victimization of women throughout their historical existence. But I believe that nothing has been as damaging to women as five thousand years of systematic deprivation from access to knowledge and from participation in the formulation of the philosophies which explain the world to us and of the religions which shape our emotions and values. These philosophies and religions have been shaped by a small elite of men, who have systematically excluded *some* categories of men, starting with slaves, serfs, peasants, proletarians, colonials, and people of so-called minority races—but *all* women at all times. These groups have been excluded from making the cultural product by which the world is ordered and explained, and by which each individual formulates his or her vision of what the future might be. Gradually, one after another, these groups have entered into the system all but one: women. That is not a minor matter, nor is it a difference that we can ignore as we talk and lump together women and minorities. Women and minorities do not belong together in that way. Every minority group of any sort has women in it, but women are the majority, having always been at least half of the population. Yet women have been educationally deprived and have not participated in the making of abstract constructs which explain the world, the universe, and our relationship to one another.

For women the whole movement into intellectual liberation has only begun, because we had first to fight for access to the education that would enable us to see this. Sarah Lawrence College is a very special institution where a model experiment could take place and flourish. It is an institution that believes that you can combine analytical rigor and creativity, that you can combine tradition and breaking through the tradition, and that you can develop individual ways to find the form of your learning.

I'd like to say a little bit about what I and perhaps some of you might learn from the way in which these ten years have happened and the ingredients that made this program possible. First, we needed a vision, and our vision was to reclaim our history and heal the rift between abstract knowledge and practice, to create a community. We also needed a long-range perspective—because it was not always easy—to transform society as we transformed ourselves, and to understand and never let go of the understanding that women are uniquely situated so as to effect a nonviolent transformation, which is truly cultural revolution. We can do this because we are everywhere. We cannot be excised from any aspect of our society. We are in every class, in every rank of society, and while we are divided by differences of class and sometimes race, we have also certain things in common. If our consciousness is at a level where we can hold on to those things we have in common, then indeed we have that dynamic quality which transforms.

This program has been uncompromising in its commitment to rigorous scholarship. . . . Only the best kind of scholarship is good enough for women, because we have to undo a biased cultural product that is as old as civilization. You can't do that with rhetoric; you have to have good skills, and you have to have some knowledge of tradition. You have to have minds capable of analysis and creativity to critique without destructiveness. It takes a strong sense of our rootedness in sisterhood, and I think we have tried for that in this program. Scholarly results of work coming out of the courses in this program are astonishing. Some of the most influential essays in the field have come out of courses we have taught here, and students have done important work in their dissertations.

I think we are going to see a continued flourishing of the seed we have sown here. . . . We must not underestimate the power of the right ideas at the right time, firmly and strongly held. And so the students in the program now, and those of you who are students elsewhere, I wish you vision, perspective, community, and a strong dose of persistence. I thank all of you profoundly for your trust and love and support.

Teaching about Black Women Writers

Barbara Smith   Spring 1974

As a Black female who is also a graduate student in English, I have always felt outside the mainstream of Anglo-Saxon male consciousness which pervades the course materials I have been required to investigate. My long and deep involvement with Afro-American literature has been individually fulfilling, but I have never had a course in it nor gained the impression that white scholars view it as anything approaching valid art. Women's literature also strikes a responsive chord, but with both sets of non-mainstream writers there have been problems for me. I am not a Black male, but a female; I am not a white woman, but a Black one.

When I read that the poet-novelist Alice Walker was teaching a course in Black women writers at the University of Massachusetts in the fall of 1972, I was exhilarated. I had been trying to select a Black woman writer for a paper in a women's literature seminar, and I thought that sitting in on an entire course would give me just the inspiration I needed. The course was an inspiration indeed. Alice Walker's teaching is as poetic as her writing. In this course, she began with slave narratives and the early Black poets, Lucy Terry and Phillis Wheatley, and then launched into Margaret Walker's brilliant Civil War novel *Jubilee*.

In an interview, Alice Walker describes a similar course she taught at Wellesley the year before.

> When I first started teaching my course in black women writers at Wellesley (the first one, I think, ever), I was worried that Zora's [Zora Neale Hurston] use of black English of the twenties would throw some of the students off. It didn't. They loved it. They said it was like reading Thomas Hardy, only better. In that same course I taught Nella Larsen, Frances Watkins Harper (poetry and novel), Dorothy West, Ann Petry, Paule Marshall, etc. Also Kate Chopin and Virginia Woolf—not because they were black obviously, but because they were women and wrote, as the black women did, on the condition of humankind from the perspective of women. It is interesting to read Woolf's *A Room of One's Own* while reading the poetry of Phillis

Wheatley, to read Larsen's *Quicksand* along with *The Awakening*. The deep-throated voice of Sojourner Truth tends to drift across the room while you're reading. If you're not a feminist already, you become one (from *Interviews with Black Writers*, ed. John O'Brien; Liveright, New York, 1973).

Black women *and* Black women writers are inherently feminists because they are used to coping independently, to being practical about both external and internal situations and to seldom getting the pampering, chivalrous treatment that is the birthright of most white females.

When I began teaching at Emerson College in the fall of 1973, I was able to teach my own course in Black women writers. I did not attempt an historical approach, but focused primarily on novels. About half of my students were white women and half were Black students of both sexes. The few white males who signed up seemed taken aback at the course's focus and after a time hostile to it, although the class itself was the most open and human one I have yet conducted. Personal experiences, both the students' and my own, were an integral part of class discussions. For the first time I felt that my own identity and life experience directly connected me both to the teaching process and to the subject matter.

The students seemed to love the works I had chosen as much as I did, and one question we repeatedly explored was why they had never heard of these authors before. Both racism and sexism were obvious answers, but of the particular kinds that permeate literary and academic establishments. In the introduction to her extensive *Bibliography of Works Written by American Black Women* (see review in *Women's Studies Newsletter*, Winter 1974), Ora Williams describes the reactions she got when she told people about her project:

> My search for writings of American Black women has been given additional impetus by various reactions from my friends, co-workers, and teachers. Some colleagues engaged in teaching women's literature have not known works of Black women. Some have been excited about this bibliography indicating such a compilation is greatly needed. Others have reacted negatively with such statements as, "I really don't think you are going to find very much written," "Have 'they' written anything that is any good?" and, "I wouldn't go overboard with this women's lib thing." When discussions touched on the possibility of teaching a course in which emphasis would be on the literature by Black women, one response was, "Ha, ha. That will certainly be the most nothing course ever offered!"

As evidenced by Ora Williams' bibliography, interest in the academic exploration of Black women's unique experiences is growing. Mary Helen Washington of the University of Detroit has taught a course entitled "The Black Woman in History and Literature" for the past two years. Hortense E. Thornton at California State University in Sacramento is also teaching a course on "The Black Woman in Literature," using works by both female and male authors.

Because these writers have been largely overlooked, research in this area is particularly challenging and stimulating. Each teacher, critic, and student who approaches the works of Black women authors has something new and vital to add to a field that is just opening. I plan to teach another course next fall using many different works than in the first one and hope to have again a learning experience that transcends the remoteness and cultural myopia of the average classroom. If I am very lucky, another student may again hand me a note on the last day of class which says: "Thank you for opening my eyes."

Feminist Press Author Reveals Identity [as Harvard Dean]

Mary Howell, also known
as *Margaret Campbell*   *Winter 1976*

In 1972 I was appointed Associate Dean for Student Affairs at the Harvard Medical School, the first woman in the school's history to hold a position in the ranks of "high administration." I took this job because I want to believe that women physicians and medical students can make real contributions to the women's health movement, and because I *know* that we need the support, good sense and good politics of other feminists, working together to revolutionize our understanding of health and health care. I hoped to make connections between the two groups and to be a voice for change in the administration of the school. Now, three years later, I believe that I should no longer tolerate the pretense of that job.

The appointment was made in response to a request/demand by an active group of students and faculty (men and women both) for representation of women at the administrative level. The school's administrators have used me—by widely advertising my presence—to ward off complaints about their unwillingness to recognize the needs of the underrepresented in health affairs.

In fact, I have been permitted to play virtually no part in administrative decisions. I have been refused opportunities to sit on decision-making committees, have not been privy to policy deliberations— even for matters that concern students or are of special consequence for women—and have had essentially no access to other members of the administrative staff except for those in Student Affairs (and we are a ghetto of powerlessness, more so even than is the case in most student affairs offices).

Soon after I began to work at the job, these remarks were quoted in a school newspaper: "Howell said yesterday that she expects to 'act as a student advocate,' and simultaneously study the role of women in medicine and deal with 'women admissions and the conduct and evaluation of women students.'" A few days later, I received the following

message (typically, through a memorandum addressed to an inter-
mediary): "I am somewhat concerned at the breadth of responsibilities implied in the statement attributed to Dr. Howell by the *Harvard
Crimson . . .* Both Dr. (X) and I think it might be a good idea for you
to define Dr. Howell's responsibilities more specifically and in relation
to medical students. This should focus her efforts and make them
increasingly effective."

I have not been directly restrained in talking with students, a responsibility that I regard as of real and vital importance. It has also been
apparent, however, that no real effort was to be made to inform students
of the resources of my office, and in fact there have been maneuvers
to reduce student contact with the Office of Student Affairs. Student
Affairs Deans have also in the past three years had less and less opportunity to meet with faculty to discuss student concerns. We are presumed
to be student advocates, but in fact we are expected to *pacify* students.
Even "Office of Student Affairs" mail is opened and screened—and
not all is forwarded on to us.

On the basis of these three years of experience, I am skeptical about
the usefulness of "token" jobs. The problems that we are struggling
against, of disadvantage and deprivation of privilege, are not the problems of individuals. They will not be solved by the mere "elevation" of
individuals, unless those individuals are willing and able to speak and
act on behalf of the disadvantaged and deprived groups they represent.
We who come from those groups—defined by our sex, skin color, minority ethnicity, poverty or powerlessness as patients—are not helped, and
may even be hurt, by token appointments. Only when our representatives have real voice in policy decisions will real changes come about.
It is especially damaging to our cause when visible positions are filled
by persons who appear to be members of underrepresented groups
but who are in fact "honorary" white, middle class males, by their own
identification with the values of that empowered group. The same
effect is gained when a potentially strong representative voice advo-
cating change is lured into a "showcase" job and then silenced.

For myself personally, these three years have been a struggle to remain
"sane in an insane place." Some progress has been made on behalf of
women, largely because of a strong and growing coalition of women
and Third World students, employees and faculty. But working in the
midst of this administrative staff means working in an atmosphere of
dispassionate untrammeled exercise of power—where accountability
to students (for whom, presumably, a school exists), to the surrounding community (whose homes and lives are affected by the school's
activities) and to patients (for whom, presumably, the very institutions

of medicine exist) is negligible. The building itself is pervaded by a humorless, cold and unfriendly ambience. There is an effort, by the appointment of committees and delegates, to avoid responsibility for the consequences of decisions. And the strangled withholding of information, both the important and the trivial, from those whose fates are affected and those who seek to be their advocates, is both frustrating and alarming.

All of this can eventually infect anyone who works here and distort the vision. Vicious and habitual competition—among professionals whose jobs are as secure as any in our society—is a creeping mould that separates us, destroys trust and prohibits friendship and effective collaboration between us. It is especially saddening to see the hopes and dreams that some students bring to the school—of serving patients and of promoting health—falter and sometimes even wither and die. We who are faculty and administrators should draw sustenance from *their* vision and vigor—instead, they are put down, and told that "we don't do things that way." I want no more part of it.

I am returning to direct patient care because I believe that that is honorable and honest work. I know of no better way to work on behalf of women. But I have not retreated from the "larger" struggles of the women's health movement, nor have I moved very far away in space. If I can help, please call on me—I can still write, talk, share my home for meetings or retreats and offer my support and energy.

Making the Bridge between the Woman in Me Who's a Bitch, and the Woman in Me Who Is Sensitive and Tender . . . One Student's View of Women's Studies

Katie Herzfeld Singer   *Summer 1982*

Three and a half years ago, I entered the University of Michigan in Ann Arbor. Before the end of my second semester, I felt stagnated. I had stopped writing in my journal, the place where, since girlhood, I had been able to find my center. I had no questions for the books I'd been assigned to read; I was not in dialogue with other students or with my professors. Most disappointing of all, I was "succeeding" in this system. One of my favorite examples of this is that the night before a final exam in U.S. history, I studied the subject in *The Encyclopedia Britannica Junior*, since I hadn't read the assigned readings for the course, and I got a B+ on the exam.

I was frustrated then. My professor had not realized that I didn't think I understood U.S. history. And I felt very alienated in this community where dislike of school was readily acknowledged, but never challenged. None of my identities seemed connected to my education; I didn't sense any relationship between my classes, my dorm life, and my waitressing job. Discouraged, I dropped out of school.

I took a job as a chef's apprentice, which really delighted me. I could learn and support myself and work with people. I developed a routine for reading newspapers and magazines, I got back into my journal, and I befriended other dropouts. They were reading, too—feminist essays and fiction—and in our apartments, my feminist consciousness began.

Nine months after I left the University of Michigan, I visited Antioch College in Yellow Springs, Ohio. I noticed immediately that students, faculty, and staff were all on a first-name basis, and that this had something to do with the way people were learning. The education I had had in restaurants and apartments was validated. People were genuinely interested to hear about my experience, and I could even get credit for it. One of the classes I visited was a women's studies course called

Sexual Politics. The professor was late, and the class started without her. That excited me! These students knew that the license to learn was in themselves, not in the presence of a professor. The professor also recognized the students' authority, and once she did arrive, she allowed the students to continue to direct the class.

A connection began for me with women's studies—with a way of learning which invites cooperative interactions. Discussions in women's studies courses have helped me and my classmates explore our assumptions about women's roles, relationships between members of an academic community, the purposes of formal education, and our personal responsibility to create ideas and policies which reflect *our* realities: women's studies has been a tool for me to integrate my selves, and to feel connected to society.

I entered Antioch three months after my visit and enrolled in a course called Literature by Women of Southern Ohio. Along with my classmates, I studied oral testimonies, letters, and journals which had been published; conducted archival research; and did several oral histories. While maintaining the traditional value of rigorous scholarship, this course validated the learning that I had experienced in writing journals and letters, in sitting on Greyhound buses beside story-telling women, in my mother's kitchen. I could unfold myself in this class. . . .

I couldn't cram the night before in this course—first of all, because it had no tests, in the traditional sense, but also because I wanted what I could learn from these assignments.

The network which developed and the self-validation which I experienced in this women's literature course prepared me well for my first co-op. (At Antioch, work beyond the classroom—"co-op"—is required. Like course work, co-op experience is evaluated by the professor and/ or the job supervisor, and the student. There are no grades.) My co-op was in the Women's Studies Program of the Great Lakes Colleges Association (GLCA). Despite my student status, the committees I served on considered my ideas. . . .

Also at Antioch I have been studying dance with women who understand the tension in our bodies—the constrained anger and sexuality, fear and happiness. These teachers helped me become aware that I had sucked in my belly, centered myself there, and held tension particularly in my lower back—while dancing, while walking. Some of my classmates also have this tension. We've wondered about its connection to the corsets women were forced to wear during the Victorian era, and to the commercials and billboards we're constantly bombarded with, which tell us that a good woman is a skinny waist.

Last spring, my teacher told me to "make the bridge" between the lower and upper parts of my body, which I had conceived of as separate. Later she used the same phrase to help me integrate what she called "the woman in you who's a bitch, and the woman in you who is sensitive and tender." With this idea I've begun to accept and even to like my body, my shapes and changes, and to trust the signals my physical self gives to my mind and my heart. I have a developing appreciation for my womanliness, my biology, my intelligence, my emotions. I have begun to feel whole.

Still, there are divisions within me and between myself and other women. I have known the emptiness of being unable to communicate with my mother. I have felt the sharpness of a woman telling me before I left for this conference, "Have a good time, and tell them I think women's studies is stupid."

But I have tools now to help bridge such schisms. I have learned that I am my own best resource. I am beginning to be able to recognize and express my anger. I have learned from feminist analysis of sociology, oral history, archival material, and women's poetry and fiction that I am not the only woman who values journal writing, who is working to become comfortable with her body, who is struggling to understand our tradition without discrediting our foremothers. I have become more appreciative of the women around me—my relatives, my classmates, my teachers, women in my community—as resources for understanding our history, biology, and philosophy, and for creating more satisfying realities for ourselves.

Almost three years after swearing I'd never go back to school, I feel an intimate connection with my formal education. At the core of this connection are confidence and eagerness to explore what is possible in relationships between mothers and daughters, between women and men, between women of color and white women, between women who define their sexuality differently, between life-educated women and those who are also formally educated.

Right now my co-op is at the Open High School in Richmond, Virginia, where I teach courses in movement, literature by students, and short stories by women. I'm building new bridges in the process of my education.

And I'm aware of my responsibility to tell Florence Howe and Jane Hopkins, who said otherwise in their papers, that a first-year woman student is not a freshman.

NOTE

The following paper was originally presented as part of a panel on "The Meaning of Women's Studies" at a conference of the Virginia Women's Studies Association held on the campus of Randolph-Macon College on December 5, 1981. . . .

Personal Reflections
on Building a Women's Center
in a Women's College

Jane S. Gould   **Spring 1984**

Looking back, two things seem remarkable: First, on a personal level, it seems remarkable that I had the opportunity to be an administrative officer at an influential institution of higher education in a role that allowed me to be completely immersed in a major social revolution that touched on every aspect of women's lives. Second, despite the ongoing tensions between the principles of feminism and those of the institution, we were able to build a solid women's center which became an accepted feminist presence both on the Barnard-Columbia campus and in the larger community.

. . . In the fall of 1970, I welcomed the opportunity to meet with others at Barnard who believed, as I did, that colleges should acknowledge the major social revolution for women that was taking place outside the classroom. We were a mixed group—administrators, faculty, students, and alumnae—with different backgrounds and commitments, but with a shared conviction that Barnard should do more than it had always done. A "superior education" for women should offer more than admission to a still discriminatory, white-male tradition. We became an official task force, charged with considering an appropriate plan of action. We met with mounting excitement throughout the academic year under the charismatic leadership of Catharine Stimpson, then an assistant professor of English at Barnard. After months of discussion, we produced a report which became the basis for the establishment of the Barnard College Women's Center. Fortuitously, two of the Task Force members were alumnae trustees. With their influence, the income from a bequest left to the College by Helen Rogers Reid, Class of 1903, became seed money to start the Women's Center.

The Center opened in the fall of 1971. It was housed in a tiny room with a crumbling ceiling in the main old building behind the campus gates and, that first year, Catharine Stimpson, with one-third released time and the help of an administrative assistant, served as director. We were still a dream: underfinanced, understaffed, and with inadequate space and no clear focus. The high point of that year was a spirited panel discussion entitled "Is There Male Chauvinism at Columbia?" It turned out to be an evening of high comedy: A packed audience listened to such reputable Columbia figures as George Frankel, Eli Ginzberg, Seymour Melman, and President William McGiil, as they pontificated on an issue that they were obviously thinking about for the first time in their lives and, for the most part, without much understanding or conviction.

Within a few years, we enlarged our quarters, increased our staff to three full-time persons, and went from a budget of $16,000 to $125,000 in 1983. From 1975 on, about one-third of our budget came from outside gifts and grants, giving us an important degree of independence.

The first few years were critical ones: We were determined to build a structure which would be a permanent part of the College and which would also assure us a fair degree of autonomy. We had no models. Much time and energy were spent conceptualizing, defining, and, most important for our long-term survival and real strength, building bridges to other segments of the College. I became the director in 1972. Simultaneously, a small committee (composed primarily of members of the original Task Force) was appointed to develop a charter for the Center.

The charter took one year and nine drafts to complete and to receive College approval: Again, the time and patience—and mix of institutional realism with conviction—did pay off, hard though they were to sustain. It proved to be a flexible document, providing the underpinnings and general guidelines for operation and, at the same time, rooting the Center firmly within the context of the College. (The Center was defined as an administrative office with a director who reports to the President of the College.) "The Center's underlying aim," as stated in the charter, is to insure "that women can live and work in dignity, autonomy and equality." The charter acknowledged that the Women's Center would be expected to address the broad needs and aspirations of women and to serve as a physical and psychological meeting ground for women within and outside the academy. It encouraged the sharing of knowledge and experience and the development of ties among diverse groups of women. In addition, it encouraged the development of both academic and nonacademic programs and projects "which complement or coincide with Barnard's distinctive academic strengths in women's studies"—at a time when we had no women's studies program and but a handful of course offerings!

The Charter Committee struggled with the problem of how to give all constituencies a voice in setting policy. In the end, the Executive Committee was limited to members of the Barnard community: equal representation of students, faculty, administrators, and alumnae. Initially, there was no mention of men in the charter; but the one man serving on the Charter Committee, the dean of the College at that time, refused to give his approval until the following sentence was inserted: "The Center welcomes the cooperation of all—men and women—who are in sympathy with its aims."

From the beginning, the Women's Center was an enigma to the College. On the one hand, Barnard pioneered in setting up a women's center and in providing an operating budget which increased each year (and I know of no other women's college that has done this). At the same time, the College, like others with "special provisions" for women, regarded the Center as marginal and not part of its central mission. The College's ongoing concern about its public image, and its homophobia, so characteristic of women's colleges, have created tensions throughout the Center's existence. In addition, the College has demonstrated a distaste for emphasizing its commitment to *women*—except as students in a highly traditional curriculum—in any way that might offend segments of its constituencies, particularly contributors. These tensions have been exacerbated by the manner in which Barnard, like other academic institutions, has responded to the new conservative climate at the same time as feminists are insisting on making connections with what is happening to women in the larger political arena. Yet the College has undeniably made use of the Women's Center, on occasion, to demonstrate its commitment, open-mindedness, and good faith.

These contradictions between public posture and internal practice created an ambivalence that permeated the College community. Initially, many faculty, administrators, and students shied away from the Center, confusing it with a student lesbian group on campus. Even after numerous articles and reports on the Women's Center and its activities appeared in College and community media, the questions, "Why a women's center at a women's college?" or "Why does a women's center need its own voice?" kept coming up like a regular refrain. It is my guess that there are still many Barnard faculty who are tentative toward, if not hostile to women's studies, and who do not encourage their students to do research on women.

Barnard provides important optimal components for the education of women: a woman as its administrative head and a faculty and administration of more than fifty percent women; small classes and a faculty committed to teaching and to teaching women. Yet, like its sister colleges, Barnard often seems locked into its history. The deep-seated fear of being "lesser" than or "different" from a male college, or of being labeled a "lesbian school," are part of a heritage that is difficult to overcome. As late as 1979, at the Center's "Arden House Conference on Special Programs for Women in Higher Education" held for seventy representatives of women's programs in the northeast, we could see that remnants of these fears persisted among the prestigious women's colleges.

Recognizing and understanding this ambivalence and learning how to work with it have presented both a dilemma and a challenge. In the early days, we were often on the defensive, a position which demanded an excessive amount of time and energy. In retrospect, I can see that this position also forced us to think through each issue carefully, developing firm convictions earlier perhaps than we otherwise would have. Knowing that name-calling and baiting have been used throughout history to discredit, frighten, and divide women, we made a conscious and determined effort to keep this from happening to us. We stopped reacting and we worked even harder to be supportive of and sensitive to the needs and interests of lesbian and other minority groups; and we went to great lengths to include a diversity of women and women's thinking in all our programs, whether in a lecture on a "View of Women As Seen Through the Eyes of Christine de Pizan," a fifteenth-century woman of letters; in a film on *Women of Wounded Knee;* in a discussion of grass-roots organizing for battered women; in an analysis of the theological question "Is There a Feminist Understanding of Sin?" or in a workshop on "Perceptions of Black Women Writers." We learned that our programs must present perspectives that are directly related to the new thinking about women and to the particular experience of women from different races, class backgrounds, and sexual preferences.

In this spirit, we created the Reid Lectureship. In 1975, with additional money from the Estate of Helen Rogers Reid, Barnard '03, we designed a program to bring to Barnard each year one or, on occasion, two women who had distinguished themselves in their own fields and had shown some commitment to other women. We knew that it was important to invite women who might not be heard at Barnard under other circumstances, women from backgrounds traditionally underrepresented at Barnard. In fact, as we learned from minority students about their need for more role models, we established a rule that at least half of these lecturers would be women of color.

The full roster of Reid Lecturers reads: June Jordan and Alice Walker, Helen Rodriguez-Trias, Rhonda Copelon and Nancy Stearns, Ntozake Shange, Bella Abzug (the year she was fired from the President's

Advisory Committee on Women), Bernice Reagon, Mirra Komarovsky (the year of the Women s Center 10th anniversary celebration) and Toni Cade Bambara. The Lecturers were asked to share their personal perceptions and experiences as women, as well as their professional experiences as feminists, both at a public lecture and informally with small groups of students, alumnae, faculty, staff, and community people over a period of a day and a half. It became an outstanding annual event. June Jordan described the pain of being black at Barnard in the late fifties. Helen Rodriguez-Trias publicly defined, for the first time, the issue of sterilization abuse as it limits the lives of poor women. Rhonda Copelon and Nancy Stearns of the Center for Constitutional Rights described the historical role they played in the Supreme Court decision legalizing abortion. All of the Reid Lecturers added to our understanding of the commonalities and differences in women's lives.

My definition of feminism also insisted on linking feminism to social change and this, too, was reflected in Scholar and Feminist conferences, the Reid Lectureships, and a broad range of seminars, workshops, films, and lectures. Whenever possible, we looked at issues as they connected feminism with changing the larger society, whether in a talk by a Salvadorean woman on the situation of women in her tortured country, oppressed both by the Junta and by the macho men with whom they lived; a discussion of feminism, politics, and nuclear disarmament in Britain by a young Labor Party candidate; or an analysis by Barbara Ehrenreich of the ways in which multinational companies exploit women in third-world countries.

Still, we always threaded our way through the area of activism with care, mindful that the Center was also an administrative office of Barnard College. The Center as such did not take public activist positions: We did not picket, demonstrate, lobby, or take a public stand on an issue affecting women although, as individuals, we have always felt free to do what we felt was necessary. There was one notable exception, made with the full approval of President Jacquelyn Mattfeld: The Center chartered a bus and participated in the large ERA march in Washington in the summer of 1978.

But by no stretch of the imagination could the Women's Center be called neutral, or even representative of *all* women. We were, from the start, a strong advocate of women's rights, as borne out by our programs and by the advocacy role we took within the College. And although the Barnard administration was admittedly nervous about certain Women's Center programs, it was inconceivable that the College should attempt to regulate Center programs, as another prestigious, ivy-league college recently did. . . .

In retrospect, we can see that our very existence in the early seventies tapped into a great reservoir of feminist energy, which in turn helped to shape our identity. In a sense, it was like opening a floodgate; we were faced with an embarrassment of riches—idea, proposals, and offers to help on a wide range of projects and services designed to fill unmet and emerging needs. Some of these became early Women's Center projects and were continued only until other groups and institutions with larger resources stepped in to fill the gap. . . .

Other projects became an integral part of the Women's Center. Soon after receiving an announcement of the opening of the Center, Myra Josephs, Barnard '28, appeared on our doorstep with a pile of articles which she had been collecting for the past few years. Little did we know that this would become one of our major permanent projects. With a Ph.D. in chemistry which she had never fully used, Ms. Josephs had spent a lifetime thinking about the condition of women. In her regular volunteer job of scanning over 200 journals in the behavioral and social sciences for articles for the Institute of Rational Living, she began to see increasing numbers of articles on women. She became excited by what she saw and started to collect this material.

In 1973, we offered this material to the Barnard Library to form the nucleus for a women's library. To our surprise, the director of the Library turned down the idea, saying that he could not see "starting a new library for every fad that came along." Besides, he explained, the Barnard Library already had books on, by, and about women. We were dismayed, but his refusal resulted in the Women's Center's development of its own collection.

We called it The Birdie Goldsmith Art Resource Collection, in memory of Ms. Josephs's mother, an early feminist and suffragist. Ms. Josephs continued culling the literature and adding most of the significant articles on women from these journals until 1982 when she became ill and had to stop her work. In addition, she provided financial support to maintain the Collection. Today the Collection is the size of a small, special library collection with some 6,000 print items: books, articles, pamphlets, brochures, clippings, special issues of journals, and subscriptions to over seventy periodicals. Catalogued according to women's issues, it reflects the changes in the thinking of the women's movement over the past ten years. It is used by scholars, researchers, journalists, and activists from all over the world.

We learned quickly that, as women's consciousness was being raised, no women's center could ignore the constant demand for individual referrals on a whole range of personal services—health, employment, therapy, and legal and other social services. Acknowledging the urgency of these needs, but that we had neither the time nor the staff to do referrals well, we sought a closer relationship with the Women's Counseling Project, a small group of volunteers who had been working solely in this area since 1917. With our help, the Project moved from a small basement office at Columbia to Barnard in January 1978, and began a productive affiliation with the Women's Center and Barnard . . .

The single most important activity of the Women's Center has been the annual "Scholar and Feminist" conference. Starting in 1974, these conferences have come to be viewed as a unique experience in feminist inquiry, raising questions which are on the cutting edge of the new scholarship on women. The conferences are interdisciplinary and recognize the inextricable relationship between theory and practice, between scholarship and activism.

. . . The conference themes have paralleled, with such a logical progression, the growth, development, and tensions inherent in the new scholarship on women that, looking back, one can see a continuum which mirrors the issues that dominated feminist scholarship and the women's movement over the past ten years.

The first five conferences reflected the explosive expression of the women's movement in its universal reaction against patriarchal traditions, and stressed the connections and ties among *all* women. The search for commonalities of women's experience provided a unity of purpose and contributed to the emergence of women's studies as a new and important interdisciplinary field of scholarship. The first conference (1974) focused on the impact of feminism on the intellectual, professional, and personal lives of individual scholars. The second ("Toward New Criteria of Relevance," 1975) moved from the personal to a broader theoretical perspective, examining the impact of feminism on the research process in general. A high point of this conference was the late Joan Kelly's classic paper, "History and the Social Relations of the Sexes," which introduced the notion of "periodization." . . . Conference III ("The Search for Origins," 1976) went a step further and focused on the search for the historical, cultural, and psychological origins of women's oppression. Drawing on the perspective of anthropology and history of religion, Rayna Rapp gave a broad historical overview and Elaine Pagels presented a brilliant case study of early gnosticism, which showed the ideological and political exclusion of women in the establishment of the early church. Conference IV ("Connecting Theory, Practice and Values," 1977) explored the major contradictions between those conceptions of reality developed by feminist scholars and those accepted in traditional scholarship. Conference V ("Creating Feminist Works," 1978) looked at how individual feminists can break away from internalized sexism in their work. . . .

As the women's movement matured and became more diverse, and as feminist scholarship became more sophisticated, some basic concepts changed. Women's differences from men, originally seen as a source of oppression, were beginning to be viewed as a source of strength. Scholars and artists were moving away from the notion of "sameness" and toward an acknowledgment of "differences" among women, primarily differences of class, race, and sexual preference. The next five conferences reflected these developments as well as the fundamental changes in the larger political scene, most notably the emergence of the New Right and the backlash against women.

Conference VI ("The Future of Difference," 1979), drawing heavily on contemporary French feminist theories, explored those structures which organize and determine our concepts of sexual identity and difference among women and between women and men. Conference VII ("Class, Race and Sex: Exploring Contradictions, Affirming Connections," 1980) examined the way in which the primary institutions of power divide women along the lines of class, race, and sexual preference. . . . Conference VIII ("The Dynamics of Control," 1981) continued this dialogue in the context of the current political climate, and looked at the institutions and ideologies which control women's lives. Conference IX ("Towards a Politics of Sexuality," 1982) was undoubtedly and even unwittingly the most controversial conference of all. It addressed women's right to sexual pleasure and women's sexual autonomy, acknowledging that sexuality is simultaneously a domain of restrictions, repression, and danger, as well as of exploration, pleasure, and agency. . . . Conference X ("The Question of Technology," 1983) focused on the way technological change affects women's lives and expectations as a beginning in the development of a feminist analysis. . . .

As an administrative officer of the College, I saw my role as that of providing leadership and of being sure that the conferences maintained Barnard's commitment to excellence. I often walked a tightrope: If I were to have the trust of the feminist community, which was vital to the success of our programs, I had to make it very clear, that my role was not to control; yet the College made it equally clear, on several occasions, that I was responsible for everything that went on at the Women's Center. Should any conference or program evoke criticism from any important College constituency or be portrayed in the media in a way that did not meet the approval of the College, I was to be held fully accountable.

This, in effect, happened in the case of the "Diary" incident at the 1982 conference on sexuality. The planning meetings had been so stimulating and so full of new material and insights that members felt it was more like a study group than a planning committee. The committee decided to share this material with the conference participants in a publication to be called "Diary of a Conference on Sexuality." The committee decided to include background information on the organization of the conference; excerpts from the minutes of the planning committee meetings; a full description of each workshop, with suggested readings by workshop leaders; and a bibliography of readings used by the planning committee. The two artists on the committee assumed responsibility for producing the Diary, which would include some art work: contemporary and historical graphic material on sexuality. The Diary was to be distributed on the day of the conference to each conference registrant.

The Barnard administration saw the publication for the first time when it came off the press forty-eight hours before the conference. They regarded some of the graphics as so offensive and detrimental to Barnard that they removed the Diary from circulation, literally pulling copies from the registration packets. After negotiations, the College agreed to underwrite its reprinting, once all references to Barnard and to the Rubinstein Foundation (which had funded the first nine conferences) had been deleted. The revised Diary was mailed out to conference registrants several months after the conference.

The Diary incident—and the fear that the Rubinstein Foundation would withdraw its support (which it did), and the threat that the conference itself might be in jeopardy—provoked an outcry in the feminist community. In the months following the conference, there was an outpouring of letters from scholars and activists who had come to one or more of the conferences or participated as speakers, workshop leaders, or members of a planning committee. The letters stressed the importance and uniqueness of the conferences as a major arena for exchanging research and ideas, as a place where new ideas could be aired because the conferences were never fearful of controversy. It was clear from the outraged response from feminist scholars that these conferences occupy a central place in the broader community and, in a sense, belong to all who have shown their support these past ten years.

In these abbreviated observations and reflections, I have highlighted our major achievements. While they are significant, they nevertheless fell short of our original dream for Barnard. We saw the Women's Center as an initial response to the challenge of the women's movement, to be followed by other necessary components (most of which still do not exist at Barnard). We hoped to have a women's studies program; a research institute; an oral history program; a women's library and archive; a personal, educational, and vocational counseling center; and an adult education program for women. We hoped Barnard could be pointed to as a leader in the education of women, incorporating all the important issues of the women's movement and the new scholarship on women.

We believed then, as I believe now, that the only way in which a single-sex women's college can survive and retain its vitality is by actively acknowledging the important feminist truths that have emerged over the past twenty years. The legacy of the struggle for women's education demands that we keep changing, that we go beyond providing the "same" education that we always have. The Women's Center was and is an effort to hold the doors open for change. In a sense, it is only a beginning.

Jane S. Gould was a founding member of the Barnard College Women's Center and its director from 1972 to June 1983. . . .

Women Trustees
and Educational Equity

Jean E. Howard   *Fall 1984*

What role can governing boards play in furthering the goal of non-sexist education? I had an opportunity to think about this question repeatedly during the seven-year period, from 1974 to 1981, when I was a trustee of Brown University. The answer is not obvious, since boards of trustees are in general more conservative, ideologically, than the students and faculty of the institutions they serve, and their conservatism typically includes traditional attitudes toward sex roles and issues of gender. Even today, at least at Brown, the board of trustees is largely composed of people who are male, white, wealthy, and over fifty. It may be utopian to imagine that such boards will spontaneously and aggressively lobby for non-sexist educational practices or, just as important, will scrutinize their own attitudes and behaviors for sexist bias. Moreover, it is amazing how far removed from the day-to-day life of a campus a governing board can be. Trustees often come to campus two or three times a year from great distances, do not know in any intimate way what happens in the dorms and classrooms of the institutions they serve, and often rely for their information either on the administration or on their memories of what it was like to be a student there twenty, thirty, forty, or even fifty years previously. My point is that—whatever their ideological orientation—board members are often too removed from the actualities of higher education to provide informed leadership on many university problems.

And yet—boards cannot be ignored by those interested in promoting educational equity for students and non-sexist practices by the institution as a whole. Trustees exercise enormous power, though often that power is not readily visible to the university community as a whole. In what follows, I want to talk about some of the authority that trustees customarily exercise and about some of the routes that women trustees can take to insure that this power is used to promote sexual equity. By focusing on women trustees, I do not mean to imply that men do not or cannot care about these issues. Some do. But the composition of many boards is such that issues relating to gender are going to seem marginal to those people—most of them male—who constitute the powerful center of the group. And it is women who will therefore have to raise these issues and, in so doing, risk defining themselves as the marginal people men have always assumed them to be.

But, first, what do governing boards do that bears on the question of non-sexist education? Perhaps most central is the role trustees play in hiring and advising the president. Of course, in most institutions, trustees do not choose the president by themselves. Often faculty and sometimes students are involved. Nevertheless, trustees play a dominant role in this process, and it is hard to underestimate the importance of this power. Presidents have many obvious powers; they also set the tone of an institution, hire other administrators, and give faculties the cue as to what institutional priorities are. If the president is not sensitive to the needs of women—and has not clearly demonstrated his or her commitment to the goal of educational equity—then it is going to be very hard to make progress toward that goal under his or her administration. Therefore, it is vital that women trustees committed to educational equity be active on presidential search and review committees. They must insist that a demonstrable commitment to non-sexist education—and a sophisticated understanding of what that means, especially in colleges and universities with predominantly male faculties and male traditions—must be a primary, and not a secondary, criterion for the job of college president and, one would hope, for other administrative positions as well.

Second, governing boards play a large part in determining the financial course of an institution and in running its major funding campaigns. Again, trustees do not do this in isolation. Administrators make up yearly budgets, but trustees are vitally involved in major budget decisions and in the management of fund-raising campaigns. Obviously, how an institution spends its money is a good index of how committed it is to the goal of equitable education. Is there room in the budget to support a women's center? To upgrade women's athletic facilities? To raise the salary level of women faculty who, AAUP studies consistently reveal, earn less than similarly qualified and experienced male faculty? Faculty groups lobby for these priorities, but so must trustees who are interested in equitable education. Women trustees need to make sure that all financial decisions are made with full awareness of what the implications for women and for sexual equity will be. In the long run, such enlightened self-consciousness will leave the institution in a better position to solicit funds *from* women. Women who graduate from college these days are not becoming housewives. Increasingly, they have careers and money of their own. Are colleges and universities going to be able to attract regular and sizable contributions from these women? I would argue that it depends largely on how genuinely and how visibly these schools pay attention to women's concerns. Brown has just concluded a highly successful $158 million campaign, and women trustees were active in every aspect of that campaign, including the identification of funding objectives meant both to serve the needs of women on the campus and to attract the contributions of women alumnae. It is gratifying when good values and good business go together.

Making Links to the Campus

Another crucial way that women trustees can promote equitable education is to become sophisticated supporters of the ideas and programs of those *on the campus* who are working for that goal. I spoke earlier of the ignorance of trustees concerning contemporary campus life. The Brown of which I was a trustee in the late 1970s was not the same Brown at which I had been a student in the late 1960s, and trustee meetings could not, in a very satisfying way, put me in touch with this new Brown. What I gradually came to realize was that if I wanted to speak, on the board, about the needs of women on that particular campus, I had to be in touch with those women and on top of the specific initiatives they were undertaking to promote educational equity.

I do not mean that an outsider's perspective is not valuable, or that all issues concerning sexual equality should be discussed purely in terms of local conditions. But I am underscoring a fact of a trustee's existence—his or her occasionally ludicrous distance from the realities of a given campus' life. And I am suggesting that women trustees can sometimes best help the goal of equitable education, not by encouraging inappropriate initiatives from the board concerning matters better left to the faculty, but by being informed about what faculty and students and administrators are doing in this regard—and by supporting those efforts in ways that *are* appropriate: by, for example, lobbying the president on behalf of such efforts; by seeing that they receive adequate financial support; by working to see that such activities do not remain marginal and unacknowledged. The goal of achieving equity and of developing institutional practices free of sex bias is so difficult that those working toward this goal cannot afford to be separated from one another. Consequently, the wall surrounding the woman trustee, cutting her off from the rest of the campus community, needs to be broken down at every opportunity.

An Anomaly: Woman and Trustee

Links between women trustees and other campus women are important also because they help the woman trustee to remember that she is, indeed, both a trustee *and* a woman. Since trustees are so often male, it is easy for a woman trustee to feel, quite realistically, the intense marginality of her position, and to compensate either by assuming a male perspective on every issue or by ostentatiously separating herself from the kind of activist woman who makes many men in power uncomfortable.

Some women trustees actively acquiesce in their own marginalization: accepting assignments on powerless committees and never, never saying anything controversial. They deal with the tension of their role by adopting the style of the corporate wife: gracious, hard-working, and endlessly obliging. Other women trustees go for power and get on committees dealing with budget, investments, fund-raising, presidential searches, or trustee selection. But some women, in doing this, flee *any* association with even vaguely feminist issues and remain vociferously committed to the view that gender has no bearing on the major issues a trustee considers. As if there were no gender implications for every action and decision the board makes—from setting the spending priorities for a fund-raising campaign, to selecting a president, to choosing who will be honored on the platform at commencement. A woman trustee cannot be a very effective advocate for educational equity if she reflexively grabs for the role of deferential corporate wife, or if she deals with legitimate desires for power and acceptance by denying her own gender or by denying the complex ways in which educational institutions operate as ideological entities.

In finding a third alternative, the woman trustee may be aided by her alliances with other women on the campus—and on the board—who share her assumption that all institutional practices reflect assumptions about gender and that these practices must therefore be endlessly scrutinized and modified. There is a danger, of course, that in looking for support and alliances in the campus community at large, the woman trustee may affirm her identity as woman at the expense of her identity as trustee. But the pressures operating on a woman trustee make it much more probable, I think, that she will forget her gender than her position as trustee. It is prestigious to be a trustee and, in many contexts, it is quite plain that the "real" trustees are men. To be a woman and a trustee is therefore an anomaly—a paradox—and the easiest way to deal with the resulting tension may be to mimic male attitudes. I therefore truly believe that the woman trustee, to remain fully both, needs the support of campus women as much as they, in turn, need the power that she in her position can wield.

Finding and Informing New Trustees

Finally, if women trustees are to promote institutional change in regard to gender issues, they have to be concerned with that archetypal female issue: "reproduction"; that is, they need to seek out as new trustees people committed to the goal of equity. There is no point at which the institution will simply have "done enough" in this regard. To select new trustees wisely and to share with them quickly what one knows about the workings of the board are important tasks. Many women just learn how a board works—what the unwritten traditions are, where power really lies—when their terms end. This wastes human talent, and careful mentoring can help to stop it.

In conclusion, let me say that, for me, service on a board of trustees was one of those experiences that suddenly made very clear what it means to be "on the margins." To be young, female, an academic, and not very affluent made me an outsider. I think now that I did not handle that role as well as I might have. Made chairperson of a committee on the status of women, I did not consider what my own lack of power and experience might mean for the committee's own status or, in a larger sense, what it would mean to funnel women's issues into a single committee so that they could be "contained." Nor had I thoroughly come to terms with the paradox of being that double creature: a woman trustee. But to tell anecdotes about my personal experience is not the point and may lead to inattention to the underlying issues. If women trustees want to help make universities better places in which women can learn, teach, and lead, then they must first of all recognize the paradoxes of their own position and begin to deal creatively with them. That effort can never end because one can never stand cleanly outside the culture and the roles it inscribes for women to play. Yet from such efforts of self-consciousness come the energy and the courage to make fundamental changes in the institutions of which we are a part.

In short, boards of trustees and the women on them do have a part to play in furthering the goal of non-sexist education, and I have tried to sketch some aspects of that role. But to be a good advocate for institutional change, women trustees must themselves be self-scrutinizing and open to change. Otherwise they may perpetuate in practice what they in theory disdain. Such are the lures of power.

The Psychological Impact of a Women's Studies Course

Karen G. Howe   *Spring 1985*

Over the past fifteen years, there has been an effort by women's studies instructors at both high school and college levels to measure the impact of their courses on the students participating in them. There have been various motivations for these evaluation studies: in the earlier years they were necessary for justification of the women's studies courses; later they became important as assessments of the personal changes students were experiencing due to their course involvement. Since women's studies courses typically involve an integration of academic material with personal experience, there are often exciting and dramatic personal and attitudinal changes that occur in the students. Psychologists teaching Psychology of Women courses have been particularly interested in documenting and analyzing these changes. I have been teaching a Psychology of Women course for five years, and have been looking for a way to turn student reactions, such as, "This course changed my life," into quantifiable data. As other researchers have discovered, this is not easy. One area, however, that I have found to be a fruitful avenue to explore in documenting personal change in women's studies students is the change in students' perceptions of reality.

Methods Used to Study Change

First let me review some of the methods and problems involved in this type of research. One method of assessment that has been used is the interview with students in the course. Adamsky (1981) used this method, and reported personal changes such as increased self-esteem, expansion of life options and goals, identification with other women, and identification of one's own experiences as part of a larger social context. Brush et al. (1978) used interviews in conjunction with quantitative data but found that some of the important changes in self-confidence and self-concept only appeared in the interview format. Studies using quantitative approaches typically use questionnaires that are given to students during the first and last weeks of the course. They focus on changes occurring in the women's studies students, compared with a control group, usually a non–women's studies course taught by the same instructor. These studies vary in terms of their control groups, measurement techniques, and directions of their major findings. While most of them focus on self-esteem and self-concept, attitudes toward women, sex-role self descriptions, locus of control, and so on, their findings are varied. Some studies do find significant increases in self-esteem, changes in self-concepts, and greater liberality in attitudes about women in the women's studies students (Harris, 1981; Holleran, 1981; Ruble et al., 1975; Scott et al., 1977; Vedovato and Vaughter, 1980). Others, however, report little change (Borod, 1976), or the inability of the quantitative measures to pick up the changes that are noticed in interviews (Brush et al., 1978). In addition, change is sometimes also noted in control or comparison groups, which were usually other psychology courses taught by the same instructor (Canty, 1978). This could occur either because the instructor is "mainstreaming" some of the women's studies material, or because, as some researchers have found (e. g., Etaugh and Spandikow, 1981), college attendance itself produces some attitude changes. It is clear that there is a need for more sensitive and refined measurement techniques for this type of research.

In my own current research, I have been analyzing both quantitative and qualitative data and material to document personal changes in students participating in my Psychology of Women course. During the past two academic years, I gave a set of questionnaires to my Psychology of Women students and my Adolescent Psychology students, telling them it involved a survey of college students' attitudes on a number of current issues. The questionnaires that I used were the Attitudes Toward Women Scale (Spence and Helmreich, 1978), the Texas Social Self-Esteem Scale (Spence and Helmreich, 1978), the Personal Attributes Questionnaire (Spence and Helmreich, 1978), and the Attitudes about Reality Scale (Unger, 1983). Some interesting findings have emerged. My Psychology of Women students started off the semester with significantly higher scores concerning attitudes toward women than did my Adolescent Psychology students, indicating greater liberality regarding the rights and privileges of women in society. In fact, my students were already scoring so high on the scale that there wasn't any room for them to obtain higher scores as a possible result of taking the course. This is a common finding in studies evaluating women's studies courses; clearly there is a self-selection process operating so that students choosing to take women's studies courses already think in liberal terms regarding women, compared to the general student body. There was also a trend in the direction of increased self-esteem in the Psychology of Women students, but the most interesting finding to me was that there was a significant change in the Psychology of Women students' attitudes and perceptions about reality.

Measuring Change in Perceptions of Reality

The Attitudes About Reality scale is a new one developed by Rhoda Unger, and it taps the cognitive perspective that influences how people perceive the relationship between the individual and reality. High scorers on this scale believe that reality creates the person. According to Unger, they see reality as stable, deterministic, and irreversible. They have a belief in biological or intrapsychic causality rather than environmental causation, they see personal rather than social power as important, they believe that society works well, and they are generally content with the status quo. In contrast, people with low scores believe that reality is changeable and that it is influenced by cultural and historical definitions. They believe in environmental causality for social and personal phenomena, they are less content with the status quo, and are less likely to blame the individual who wishes to change that status quo.

Both Unger (1983) and I have found significant decreases in the scores of Psychology of Women students on this scale over the course of the semester, when compared with students in other psychology courses. This represents a change from the view that reality creates the person, to a view that the person creates reality. I found this a very interesting way to explain how the course material actually changes the cognitive perspective of the student. The cognitive changes that occur in a shift from higher to lower scores on the scale correspond to the progression of topics that are discussed in the course. We begin the course with discussion of the male bias in society and psychology, and criticisms of the biological and intrapsychic explanations of female development and personality in the early psychoanalytic theories of Sigmund Freud, Helene Deutsch, and Erik Erikson. We then focus on the theories and research that emphasize the environmental and social context factors influencing women's development: Karen Homey, Margaret Mead, Clara Thompson, socialization themes and factors, cultural influences, language, roles and role conflicts, experiences throughout the life cycle, and so on. In the course of discussing this material, the students experience a shift from the male interpretations of females that make up a good deal of psychology, to a more female-centered focus. It makes sense, then, that some of the students'

cognitive frameworks for viewing the world incorporate these themes
from the academic material.

   Another way to see this shift in the students' perceptions of reality
and the individual is through qualitative materials from the course—
various assignments, journals, and written comments. Many students
report that they develop a greater sense of control and optimism that
they can do something about their life situations, even though at the
same time they have become more aware of the presence of sexism in
their socialization and society. One of the most important themes here
is the students' realizations that what they have perceived as their
own individual problems are often not due to personal inadequacies
or inabilities, but are related to their status and experience as women
in a patriarchal society. This merging of the personal and the academic is similar to the "personal is political" theme that characterized
consciousness-raising groups in the past decade. The awareness of
these social forces affects the student's self-concept, her relations with
other women, and her view of reality. These themes are beautifully
integrated in the following statement by one of my students, a thirty-
four year old woman with three daughters of her own who was very
enthusiastic and eloquent about her experience in the Psychology of
Women course:

> My self-image has been elevated significantly. So many of us women
> think that we are the only ones whose lives are miserable because we
> have no place to go with our problems and our pain. This course pro-
> vided for me an outlet for my agony and my frustration. At the same
> time I developed a camaraderie with some of the other students in
> the class as well as with the instructor. A special kind of bonding took
> place among those students whose lives had been significantly
> affected by our socialization process, the male perspective, traditional
> expectations of women, or the motherhood mandate. To first have
> an opportunity to express oneself, then to have your problems
> acknowledged as a real, commonly shared problem is a relief. Out
> of this experience grows the idea that you are not alone, you are not
> crazy, you are not a bitch, but you are a real person with real feelings
> who is discovering that there is someone who cares about all of the
> bottled up feelings and frustrations. To be acknowledged as a credi-
> ble person is enough to boost one's self-esteem. But I think the
> course has given me more than a boost. It has given me courage.
> Courage to stand up for my rights; courage to disagree; courage to
> see myself as an equal with male authority figures; courage to take a
> stand on issues that I would have let slip by before; courage to with-
> stand male rejection; courage to strike up a conversation about

women's issues; courage to actively participate in a movement to bring about the changes needed for my three female children to live fulfilling, productive lives.

Women's Studies and Alienation

While many students comment in similar positive ways about their course experience, it clearly is not easy for students in the Psychology of Women course to change their views of themselves and their society. Many of the students experience anger and frustration as they become more aware of sexism and stereotyped views of women in society, psychology, and their own lives. For some of these students, class discussions and various written assignments and journals are sufficient for expressing their feelings and finding ways to effect change in their personal lives and relationships. Other students find the anger difficult to deal with and find that their new perspective alienates them from people not in the class. For example, one student wrote the following in her journal regarding this theme:

> I'm beginning to feel very isolated from a lot of people. All of a sudden sexism is everywhere and I'm disgusted by it. I'm very angry too. I have to fit in with the system somehow. But I don't know how I can when I don't agree with it. Some people aren't bothered by the issues we are. It always helps a lot if I can talk with someone who is into the class and feels in any way like I do. I love talking about this stuff. I feel very aware, saddened, and excited

Over the years I have been teaching the Psychology of Women course, I have observed a variety of ways in which such difficulties have been manifested. The class as a whole feels saddened and lost at the end of the semester; some students have trouble handing in the last piece of written work in the course, which will signify the end of the course experience; many students request a "Psychology of Women Part Two" so they can continue to explore the course issues; one semester some of the students met in the summer after the course ended to "finish" their integration of personal changes with course material.

A number of researchers (Morgan, 1978; Adamsky, 1981) have discussed the problem of potential alienation and conflicts arising from the student's participation in a women's studies course. The academic material in the course gives the class experience some of its power and force for the student, but often also conflicts with the instructor's ability to focus on and work with the personal dimensions of the course. Richardson (1980) has discussed the various conflicts involved in teaching Psychology of Women courses, and points out that while the cognitive/academic and emotional/personal dimensions of a women s studies course are theoretically integrated and complementary, often the focusing of time and energy on one of those areas leads to a lessening of focus on the other. As a result, the end of the class period or the semester arrives, the academic material was covered and mastered, but the subjective effects on the students may need more time for exploration.

In conclusion, then, two areas for further exploration and research in our efforts to document the psychological impact of women's studies courses are the changes in students' perceptions about reality, and techniques to aid the students in integrating these cognitive and personal changes into their lives.

NOTE
A version of this paper was presented at the National Women's Studies Association Conference, Douglass College, New Brunswick, New Jersey on 28 June 1984.

REFERENCES
Adamsky, C. Becoming a feminist: what is the process? Paper presented at the Eighth Annual National Conference on Feminist Psychology, Boston, March 1981.

Borod, J. The impact of women's studies courses on perceived sex differences, real and ideal self-perceptions and attitudes towards women's rights and roles. Ph.D. thesis, Case Western Reserve University, 1976.

Brush, L.R., A. Gold, and M. White. The paradox of intention and effect: a women's studies course. *Signs: Journal of Women in Culture and Society* 3 (1978): 876–84.

Canty, E. Effects of women's studies courses on women's attitudes and goals. Unpublished manuscript, 1978.

Etaugh, C., and D.B. Spandikow. Changing attitudes toward women: a longitudinal study of college students. *Psychology of Women Quarterly* 5 (1981): 591–94.

Harris, R.M. Changing women's self-perceptions: the impact of a psychology of women course. Paper presented at the Association for Women in Psychology Conference. Boston, March 1981.

Holleran, P.R. The progress of self-reported androgynous behavior in college women. Paper presented at the Eighth Annual National Conference of the Association for Women in Psychology, Boston, March 1981.

Morgan, E. On teaching women's studies. *University of Michigan Papers in Women's Studies*. Ann Arbor: Women's Studies Program, 1978, pp. 27–34.

Richardson, M.R. Sources of tension in teaching the psychology of women. *Psychology of Women Quarterly* 7 (1982): 45–54.

Ruble, D.N., J.A. Croke, I. Frieze, and J. Parsons. A field study of sex-role attitude change in college women. *Journal of Applied Social Psychology* 5 (1975): 110–17.

Scott, R., A. Richards, and M. Wade. Women's studies as change agent. *Psychology of Women Quarterly* 1 (1977): 377–79.

Spence, J.T. and R.L. Helmreich. *Masculinity and femininity: their psychological dimensions, correlates, and antecedents.* Austin, Tex: University of Texas Press, 1978.

Unger, R. Measuring attitudes about reality: implications for feminists. Paper presented at the First Annual New Jersey Conference on Women. Douglass College, New Brunswick, New Jersey, June 1983.

Vedovato, S. and R. Vaughter. Psychology of women courses changing sexist and sex-typed attitudes. *Psycology of Women Quarterly* 4 (1980): 587–90.

Karen G. Howe *is Assistant Professor of Psychology at Trenton State College.*

Dual Citizenship: [An Interview with] Women of Color in Graduate School

Ann Withorn   *Spring/Summer 1986*

Women of color face special challenges in graduate school in regard to personal survival and to finding support for their research. Six members of the planning group for this issue of the Women's Studies Quarterly, *Elba Caraballo, Marian Darlington-Hope, Michelle Foster, Margo Okazawa-Rey, Emily Steele, and Miren Uriarte, are graduate students as well as full-time faculty members. In this discussion, they explain the barriers women of color encounter as they try to earn the degrees minimally necessary for security, and therefore influence, within and outside the academy. I organized, taped, and transcribed the original discussion and distributed it to the participants. At a subsequent meeting, reactions to and expansions on the transcription were made; this final version was reviewed and approved by each participant.*

Caraballo: As a woman of color you are highly visible. Faculty will notice if you don't go to class, while they won't miss another white face.

Okazawa-Rey: When white students argue with faculty, that's "intellectual discourse." Yet when we argue with them, it is "going off," being "touchy" about race or gender issues. After two semesters you get characterized as always bringing up race or gender or what-have-you. . . . Or you get labelled argumentative, in general, and they dismiss you for that.

Steele: You also have to be very careful not to let them think you are too smart. In retrospect, one of the biggest mistakes I made was to let them know I was a faculty member somewhere else, and not just one of their dumb, dependent graduate students. Because then you become a threat— my god, you're a colleague!

Uriarte: Your fellow students don't know what to do with you, either. They don't even know enough about what you are doing to even discuss it. So they give icy stares when you bring up something that matters to *you.* Maybe they just don't want to know something which would make them look ignorant.

Caraballo: The idea for a lot of people is, "If you take your degree seriously," everything else stops. You have no business being on a board, or being involved in the community. For white students, who may come from all over the country to do graduate work, that is one thing. But it's another if you live here and you are going to live here after you get your degree.

There is also an assumption made by white students and faculty alike, that all people of color have a clique, that we feel close to all faculty members and students of color. It's just not true. We get caught in a double bind, because we are women and want to be nurturing especially to men of color in these situations. So even though I might think it, I don't want to oppose a black man, for example, in front of all those white people who will just use my words against all of us. I want to deal with him in some supportive way. And we have no role models for doing this and getting what we need, too.

Darlington-Hope: Many of the women professors seem to think that they have to be tougher, so any sign of understanding is seen as weakness. For me personally, I don't have any what you would call "relationships" with white men in any aspect of my life (the last one I knew was my doctor). So I always experience some sort of block when dealing with predominantly white male professors—they are like a foreign entity. It's not that I am intimidated, I just don't have any idea of who they are. But I do have some experiences with white women which could lead me to know something about them, but these women faculty members, by and large, don't act like any white women I have ever known, so I am still confused.

Foster: And the faculty of color are under the same presures as we are —so they have to make choices. I know how difficult it may be for them to vouch for students of color, especially given what they have already had to go through to get where they are.

Uriarte: Institutions are also more willing to accept people of color who are not as progressive, who are not activists. If you come with politics, in your intellectual work as well as in your outside activity, it is even harder for them to accept you.

Okazawa-Rey: The things I am interested in come from my life, from the lives of people in my community. They are questions I really want to have answered. So they are not just trendy questions; they don't go away. In addition, we are not supposed to have any feelings about our research, we are supposed to think about it objectively, and to base our ideas on what other people have said.

Steele: When I say anything interesting in a paper the professor always writes, "Who said this?" I want to answer, "Me, I said it. Isn't it brilliant?"

Uriarte: When I write I don't use the big words, but self-consciously try to explain the concept instead of naming it, in order to be accessible. But do you know how many times I have gotten back the response in the margins: "The word for this is . . ." as if I didn't know? Or they say, "This must be a problem of language," when I have made a deliberate choice to be clear.

The worst thing, for them, is not to know where your ideas come from. What they really mean, I think, is "Which white men did we get our ideas from?" because obviously they could not have come from us, or our community.

Steele: But when you read other white male students' papers, all you see are *their* impressions. And the very same faculty who say that you don't know anything will label their work "original thinking."

Okazawa-Rey: The question is, how do you try to prove something important when they don't recognize it even exists?

Coping Strategies

Foster: I use the term "disinvestment." To survive, I have to disinvest from that school. I go, I take classes, I do as little as possible there. They may try to put me down for it, for not being "involved enough," of course, but it's the price I have to pay for my sanity.

You have to play the game that they play. Like statistics. I took their big time statistics courses and made A's. I didn't exactly think about it, but when I was on the Admissions Committee I saw that they looked at every minority applicant and wanted to know how well they did in statistics. And I realized that that was their assessment for minority students —that if we had the "quantitative ability," then we could do it.

Steele: But it works both ways, too. When I was on the Admissions Committee they wanted to admit a woman of color who obviously had writing problems that were going to give her trouble. But they didn't care if they admitted her and she failed; they could just say, "See, we tried."

Uriarte: The way I have dealt with it is to be just stubbornly focused on what I am doing. I try to get my rewards outside, to get support from others who will appreciate my work. But the insecurity is always there. I write something and I have to get at least ten people to say that it is OK before I think it is good. I am afraid someone will say that my interests are "folkloric and exotic," and not something relevant to "real" sociology. I have to keep reminding myself that the word "minority" is imposed from the outside. I have to fight constantly against internalizing attitudes of the "majority," if I am going to be able to write at all.

Foster: I have two sets of sounds, the way I say things naturally and the way they want me to sound. I always have a hard time writing because I have learned enough now to know that I have to make it sound the way they want it to sound.

Caraballo: One way to do it is to learn how to get your thoughts across in their language. It was hard, but I have learned to translate "You jerk" into "I'm afraid I disagree with you," while still standing my ground.

Foster: For me, it is becoming more subdued. It is not easy for me not to be emotional, but I'm becoming able to go totally flat, emotionless, when I disagree with something. I look like I am dead. I have found that it throws people.

Darlington-Hope: I was in a class where the white woman faculty member said something so racist that I thought I was either going to jump on the table or kill her. The rage was such that I couldn't speak coherently. *Uriarte:* I have had to walk out of classes because what was going on was insulting. I have been in situations where I would either have to scream or leave.

Darlington-Hope: There are also real differences among the students of color. Some of us have really bought the idea of pleasing them. For example, one woman of color in our class obviously wants to be a legend in her own time. She's speaking everywhere; she's buying into it all. She's serving on all the right committees, impressing the right people. I cannot be that kind of student anyway. I'm a mother with two children and I don't have the time to do all that stuff—hanging out, going to all the colloquiums, sitting around asking faculty what they think.

Caraballo: But it works the other way, too. I was one of those students who did everything I needed to do right away to establish my credibility. For me it was a way to "hit the ground running" in order to convince them that they had to listen to me. So I got put into that position of model student, they put me on all these committees—I was on their minority affairs *and* admissions committees. First of all, for a very brief moment I was flattered, but that died soon because very quickly I realized that they really didn't want to know what I thought; they just wanted me to sit there and be quiet unless I agreed with them, or needed to say something to help them stay out of trouble over minority issues.

But I decided to stay because, if one of us wasn't there, they would sit there and make all these outrageous decisions. I came into the Admission Committee with a huge bag and took notes on everything they said. When they were saying stupid things about an applicant of color I would say, "Wait a minute, wait a minute," and go to my notes and show them an example of a white male with the same low grade, or low score, and about whom they had said, "Oh, he can overcome that." I would even show them who said it. That's a lot of work, but I felt it was important.

Finding Support

Foster: One of the big problems is that there is hardly anyone in graduate school who believes in mentoring. There is only one faculty member I know of at my school who will actually sit down with you and work with you, instead of just saying, "It isn't right, do it again." Do *what* again?

Steele: But there are some faculty who give you real support. By that I mean that they respect me and make me work, but give me room to do what I want. With one woman, for example, my gut feeling was that she respected me for myself, she repeated what I had said to her, not what she wanted to hear, for example. She really listened. She was also one of the only ones who acknowledged my other life away from the school.

Caraballo: Support means really respecting you. It means really teaching by listening and trying to combine and compare your ideas and their ideas, not judging them. It is not telling you to leave your ideas at the door. It is not saying, "That is interesting, but," which is very discounting. Instead, it is explaining how their view differs, not how it is better. It is accepting your idea of what is real and helping you present that in the best way. It is really engaging you in a respectful way.

Steele: I also get support from my students, especially as I work harder not to reproduce what is being done to me in graduate school. I'll be damned if I am going to do to someone else what has been done to me. Most important is to help students disagree with me, and to see a multitude of points of view. Then I feel like I am doing something right. That gives me enormous support.

Caraballo: It is interesting that all of the things we see as giving us support are active—staying involved in the community, teaching—and they are exactly what the institutions try to keep us from doing. This means that we are under a lot of special pressure.

An example of this was my experience in trying to set up a group to give me support for doing the dissertation. I was the only woman of color in a group of six women and I had a lot of hopes for the group, but I had to stop going. I felt like my role there was to give them support, but they couldn't give any to me.

It is almost like liberal white people think they have so much power that they can't offer me honest support as an equal, because they will inevitably patronize or oppress me, so they do nothing. It makes it very hard to find anyone to trust to read what I write for my dissertation. My sisters aren't in my field; they would fall asleep from boredom. I'm honestly thinking of my father, despite all the father-daughter issues, just because I can't honestly think of anyone I trust to read my stuff. It makes it hard to write, even though I think of myself as a decent writer. I'm paralyzed. My soul will go down in black and white and I need someone I feel comfortable enough with to give it to who will not come back as paternalistic or oppressive, but will come back as caring and respectful of who I am. And I can't identify a soul.

Foster: All of my support has come from my family, especially my immediate family—my son. My grandparents are the grounding points I use, because they support me and think it is good I am doing this, but if I don't it is OK, too. I am still me and they love me, with or without the degree.

Uriarte: It is hard to hear and accept support. We need to find people we really trust and let them tell us our work is good, and believe it. I realize that I some times want the very people I don't like to say I am good, and that is all backwards.

Okazawa-Rey: I would just be very pleased if I could get concrete help with my work. I don't need the emotional stuff from them. But I do need help with the ideas, with resources—that is real support to me, but I don't get much of that either.

Hopes for Change

Okazawa-Rey: When I first started graduate school I was much more idealistic. I wanted to become a better teacher; I wanted to know more about who I was teaching. Since then I have become more pragmatic. I am getting the degree because it is going to help me do what I want to do, period. My main hope now is that the degree will really give me some credibility, authority, and some power.

I also wanted to go to school to learn how to speak the language. I now see even more clearly that it is really important to be bilingual and bicultural, in other words, not to give up my language and my culture but to make use of the parts that fit my purposes.

I realize also that I like being at this elite institution where I am not supposed to be. I am proud of myself in some funny way. That feeling is confusing but if I admit to it, it allows me to get rid of some of my negativity.

Caraballo: It is like dual citizenship. We know that we are accepted by our community and, if we make it in these institutions, no matter how begrudgingly, then we have the potential to be accepted in both worlds. So even if they treat us as the exceptions, we know we have something they don't have—the ability to operate in both arenas. That is part of the threat we pose if they can't get us to betray ourselves, and it is harder and harder to make us do that as there are more and more of us.

Okazawa-Rey: The responsibility is on us to keep supporting the students of color who follow us. It is not really a burden, although sometimes it feels like it. Really it gives me energy. It's kind of a connection back home. It is like a reward, it feels good to be a resource—to work out strategies to beat them.

Steele: I don't mind working hard, as long as I see the reason for it. If these people at the top are like this, then I wonder what that means for me. All I can do is to try to change the model for learning and teaching where I work so that all this bad stuff is not perpetually reproduced.

Uriarte: What I aim to do, in part, is to get a respectful fear into people about what they can do and cannot do as white people. I want to show them that there are times where, no matter what they do or know, this is not enough and they have to recognize it. This is very difficult for people to accept. How can I tell them they cannot always help?

Foster: White people (I guess you might call them liberal or left, I just see them as white) always try to put race under class, and to say that it is really not race that divides us but class that unites us, no matter what I think. Or white feminists do the same thing about women's issues—we ar really all more alike as women than we are different because of race. But you can't do that; if you do, you are not listening to me. And if you don't listen to me, then I won't talk to you.

Postscript

Two concrete results have already come out of this conversation. The first was a decision by the women in the group interviewed to continue to meet together and give support and concrete advice to each other. The second was that this interview inspired some white feminist faculty in the Boston area to begin discussing how to stop the bad patterns, how to listen, and how to become more clear about both their limits and their obligations.

Elba Caraballo *and **Miren Uriarte** are Cuban and Puerto Rican, respectively;* ***Michelle Foster, Marian Darlington-Hope,*** *and **Emily Steele** are black;* ***Margo Okazawa-Rey*** *is a black Japanese American. All are in Ph.D. or ED.D. programs in elite private institutions in the Boston area, in which women of color are rarities. All but Caraballo are also mothers.* ***Ann Withorn*** *is a white Associate Professor of Social Policy at CPCS, where she teaches about a wide range of social welfare issues.*

Bragging about Bragging

Susan Koppelman Cornillon
[Susan Koppelman]   **Summer 1973**

One of the most important functions of women's studies is to establish an understanding of the crippling effects on our egos and self-esteem of our second-class status. I have developed a technique that I use in my women's studies classes that offers one approach to this task. My course, called "The Problems and Potential of Women," meets once a week for a three hour session and is limited to fifteen people.

The first night we go around the room and each woman talks a little about herself and about why she's taking the course. We try to begin knowing each other. I talk about how we women don't really think very much of ourselves, how we settle for less because we don't think we deserve more; how it is that we measure ourselves against Them instead of Them against us. I describe the traits that Gordon Allport discusses in *The Nature of Prejudice* in the chapter "Traits Due to Victimization."

Then apparently changing the subject, I ask my students to free associate about the word "bragging." They come up with negative associations reflecting liberal popular psychologizing, such as "people who brag are insecure; they are expressing their need for approval"; or pious moralizing about "people who aren't humble, self-centeredness, etc." I ask them if they can think of when it might be appropriate to brag about themselves. They answer no.

A quick glance at my notes and another apparent change in direction. We begin to talk about how bad the current job market is. I explain that when the market is bad, it's worst of all for women; that women are the last hired, the first laid off, the worst paid, the slowest to be promoted. I pass out a breakdown of U.S. Bureau of Labor Statistics.

Finally, we talk about the job interview situation. Again, those who have been through it are encouraged to share their experiences. I tell them mine. "If you're married, you won't be a stable employee. Your husband might be transferred," or "We won't waste our money training a single girl. You'll just get married and quit," or "What? A young married [woman]? No thanks! You'll be pregnant and leaving just about the time you learn the job." Ad nauseum.

Then we do a little role-playing. I describe a job that sounds interesting to the class. In fact, together we create the fantasy job. Then we help each woman invent her own vita, her own work history. I grant each a B.A. with some kind of honor and all of them equivalent work experiences. One might have been a waterfront director at a summer camp for six years; another a director of volunteer workers at a home for the elderly. They're each given both an experience in administration and supervisory activities that involve contact with people, as well as experience as a typist, cashier, etc.

That leads to my role of Mr. Lecherous Interviewer. I say to each, "Well, Missy, I have here the dossiers for twelve girls, each apparently well qualified. Tell me why the chick I choose should be you; what makes you special; what makes you think that you can do this job?"

I sit back and let my eyes wander speculatively, judgmentally, up and down her torso while she flounders for words. Finally she stammers something like, "You'll just have to figure that out," or "If they're so much better, I guess there's not much sense taking up your time." The best anyone has come up with is: "Well, I really want the job a lot and I'll do my very best." They don't know how to identify, let alone maximize the presentation, of their assets. They don't know how to brag. After each one has tried and fumbled, we talk about selling ourselves on the basis of abilities and accomplishments instead of on the basis of measurements and face. I point out the similarities between accenting your "good features" with make-up, or a small waist with a wide belt, and conceptualizing about your executive experience and abilities. Most of them know how to brag already about physical matters.

Having returned to our discussion of bragging, we read from Hogie Wyckoff's essay, "Radical Psychiatry in Women's Groups":

> We can become familiar with what insidiously keeps women down; not only the obvious overt male supremacy which we are all aware of and struggling against but also oppression which has been internalized . . . It is the incorporation of all the values which keep women subordinate (telling her she mustn't outdo men, etc.) . . . This oppression can be easily illustrated by using a technique we call "bragging." (*The Radical Therapist*, ed. Jerome Agel, Ballantine p.b., N.Y., 1971, p. 185)

I suggest to the group that we take a fifteen minute break and return, each prepared to brag. I ask each one to tell us something that she has done, accomplished or developed in herself, something that she is responsible for and proud of.

The first night it took fifteen women one hour and forty minutes after the break to get all the way around the group. It took them that long to find something about themselves that they could say. One woman in that class, very witty, dean's list, law school oriented, after much anguish, twisting her hair and turning in her chair, said, "Well, one thing I do know: I have beautiful boobs."

The majority of the other "brags" weren't that depressing, but almost all of them reflected the judgment of significant others in the lives of these women, and most of those significant others were fathers, boyfriends, and male teachers. None of the brags reflected personal assessments. None had resulted from self-initiated action or self-determined goals. Most frequently, they bragged about disciplined personality traits springing from an internalization of "feminine" ideals.

Afterwards we returned to the topic of women's low self-esteem. I'd quoted studies and statistics, famous writers, scholars and feminists, all sorts of provocative fictional and poetic material. They had been unaffected by and personally indifferent to the concepts, the information I was trying to turn them on to. I now returned to it, after the bragging session, and they leaped on the ideas, they hungered for the explanations. I had made existentially real for them that concept of low self-esteem.

Each week after that we spend fifteen minutes at the beginning of each session bragging about something that has happened within the past week. Sometimes the whole group decides not to take time to brag, but even then some woman may burst out with a brag. We are always delighted. We try to relate the brags to the course concepts. We begin to carry these concepts into our lives.

In midquarter, I don't come to class one night until an hour late. Instead, I contact one of the students, ask her to meet me and give her an envelope containing copies of the following instructions:

1. Separate into small groups of three or four.
2. BRAG.
3. Relate each brag to the women's movement. How does what you bragged about relate to your identity as a woman? How does it relate to all women living in a sexist society?
4. Can you turn your brag around, reverse it so that you are complaining about a problem? Relate this to being a woman in a sexist society.
5. Can you develop a generalized feminist analysis? What does each woman's triumph, achievement, self-esteem have to do with the other members?

6. Having developed a report together, choose a reporter to share the conclusions of your group with the rest of the class.

Time: one hour

After an hour, I come to class, the group reunites, and we begin to share experiences. We find women taking control of their lives; women breaking through and beyond internalized "feminine" self-images; women feeling powerful and independent; women establishing goals for themselves that grow out of their own desires and self-knowledge and that are not dependent on other's expectations of or desires for them. Self-fulfillment and self-development replace self-sacrifice. Brags about achievements begin to replace brags about attributes. Instead of "I am proud of myself because I am such a good listener," we hear, "I am proud of myself because I finally got up the nerve to take the GRE's and I know I did well," or "I told that bastard to get his hands off of me and I didn't apologize or worry about hurting his feelings."

At the end of the quarter—we have our final bragging session during a twelve hour marathon project presentation we have instead of a final exam. By now brags begin to include: "I designed a powerflow chart for the University administration and figured out what to do to get money for a women's self-defense course"; and "We held a meeting to plan an all-Ohio Women's Coalition Weekend for next fall, we figured out how to manage and structure it for two hundred people." Or "I wrote up a prospectus for the book I want to do on American women artists and sent it to a publisher." It was important when one woman bragged that she had masturbated to orgasm—the first in her life—after five years of marriage—and "wasn't going to fake a damn thing ever again."

For fear of misrepresenting myself and my class, let me add that the experience is never totally successful. I don't manage to reach all of my students, even in a class that small. Those students who are not reached are not necessarily unchanged because the technique is at fault, however. Some of them, I'm afraid, sign up because it is a pass/fail course and they think it will be easy. I try to avoid this by insisting on a personal interview with each student before she is permitted to register—but sometimes I miss them. However many opt out after the interview when they realize how much work will be required. And then there is the student who takes the course as part of a general self-improvement program that also includes transcendental meditation, modern dance, health foods, and yoga—as well as "The Problems and Potential of Women." Her final brag had to do with having risen above anger and general earthly cares. And, too, there are those occasional students who listen, participate, but decide that the changes will be too hard to make, the struggles too great.

Although the bragging experience is only a small part of what happens in this course, I think it is a valuable technique for beginning to solve two of our most important classroom problems. How do we help our students make existentially significant connections between their intellectual experiences in the classroom and the rest of their lives? And how do we help our students move from a sharing of individual feelings, concerns, and experiences to generalized principles and abstract social analysis?

White Woman, Black Women: Inventing an Adequate Pedagogy

Nancy Hoffman   *Winter/Spring 1977*

For Barbara Smith

As a white woman teaching literature written by black women for some years now, my experience has begun to make sense, to add up to some principles and some observations which may be useful to other teachers. I teach older, urban students who are or will become human service workers. We do little by way of formal literary criticism; we read literature to learn about American values, about problems of race and class, to understand the choices of characters, and to reflect on our own lives. Particularly because students work in intercultural settings, we use the classroom to approximate as much as it can the diversity students encounter on their jobs. Nearly sixty percent of our students are women, and I teach black novels and poetry by women because that is where you find portraits of strong, independent women; that is also where you find good literature unencumbered by the burden of prior critical judgment. I teach literature by whites in my courses as well. I myself am in the midst of a research project on an aspect of the history of relationships between black and white women, so I learn from my teaching.

I most frequently teach five novels which span the past fifty years, and with *The Invisible Man* (1952), tell about a world largely absent from the work of Hemingway, Faulkner, Fitzgerald, Mailer, Bellow, Malamud, or even James Baldwin. Absent as well from Christina Stead, Agnes Smedley, Kate Chopin, or Kate Millet. These novels are Zora Neale Hurston's *Their Eyes Were Watching God* (1937), Ann Petry's *The Street* (1946), Margaret Walker's *Jubilee* (1967), Toni Morrison's *The Bluest Eye* (1974), and most recently Alice Walker's *Meridian* (1976). (I note for the record that unlike white classics which are always in print, *Their Eyes Were Watching Cod, The Bluest Eye,* and *The Street* are out of print—unavailable to students except in libraries, or through Xeroxes.) These novels, particularly the recent ones by Morrison and Walker, carry on the tradition of the philosophical novel, a tradition which has been notably weak in America. The black woman's philosophical problem

might be phrased as a question: How do I invent an identity for myself
in a society which prefers to behave as though I do not exist? From
Toni Morrison:

> And she had nothing to fall back on; not maleness, not whiteness,
> not lady hood, not anything. And out of the profound desolation of
> her reality, she may very well have invented herself.

From the final chapter of *Meridian* called "Release": the narrator,
and then the black man, Truman, observe the black woman Meridian:

> She was strong enough to go and owned nothing to pack. She had dis-
> carded her cap, and the soft wool of her newly grown hair framed her
> thin, resolute face. His first thought was of Lazarus, but then he tried
> to recall someone less passive, who had raised himself without help.
>   It still was amazing to him how deeply Meridian allowed an idea—
> no matter where it came from—to penetrate her life.
>   "I hate to think of you always alone."
>   "But that is my value," said Meridian.

I mention the problem of inventing an identity to suggest the magni-
tude and significance of themes in black women's writing, and thus
the *importance of teaching it,* and *teaching it well,* not just to students like
mine, but to people at Wellesley and in Iowa as well.

There are two principles for whites who would teach about black
women. First, do your research and class preparation more thoroughly
than you would for teaching about your own female tradition or the
majority white male Anglo-American one. You must be able to gener-
alize about black women's culture when appropriate, and you will
probably feel ill at ease when doing so. Second, be prepared to play
dual and conflicting roles; only sometimes will your own anti-racism
and your solidarity with other women protect you from representing
the group oppressing black women. You must face interpreting literature in which white women like yourself (not society as a whole or, as
in the poem which I discuss, a no good white "cracker" man) inflict
pain on black women. You may be helping black women experience
anger and sadness directed in part at you.

Here is Alice Walker's brief poem, "Revolutionary Petunias." It's not
a difficult poem for a white woman to teach, because it permits the
teacher to be comfortably anti-racist. I'm going to explicate it much
as one would in a graduate school classroom; the poem demands in
part knowledge *from* graduate school.

REVOLUTIONARY PETUNIAS

Sammy Lou of Rue
sent to his reward
the exact creature who
murdered her husband,
using a cultivator's hoe
with verve and skill;
and laughed fit to kill
in disbelief
at the angry, militant
pictures of herself
the Sonneteers quickly drew;
not any of them people that
she knew.
A backwoods woman
her house was papered with
funeral home calendars and
faces appropriate for a Mississippi
Sunday School. She raised a George,
a Martha, a Jackie and a Kennedy. Also
a John Wesley Junior.
"Always respect the word of God,"
she said on her way to she didn't
know where, except it would be by
electric chair, and she continued
"Don't yall forgit to water
my purple petunias."

The poem shows that literary convention crosses lines of race, sex, and culture. Its title, "Revolutionary Petunias," is, of all things, an oxymoron, or an epigrammatic combination of contradictory terms. Although usually oxymorons are expressions of personal, private contradiction—mute cry, pleasing pain—the idea is potentially explosive and political. A puzzle like "revolutionary petunias" demands synthesis. When Walker contrasts Sammy Lou with the sonneteers, the word "sonneteers" carries further Walker's play with Renaissance convention. Walker associates the sonneteers with falseness; their sugar-coated phrases are easy art. Truth comes writ plain, as *some* of the sonneteers themselves also know. To translate the convention into the political world some four hundred years later, the bards of the civil rights movement, caught up in a rhetoric of martyrdom (as standard as the rhetoric of love), make an *ideologically* correct interpretation of Sammy Lou's nonpolitical act of anger. As Walker herself tells us in *Interviews With Black*

Writers, these "cultural visionaries" misconstrue the power of the unself-conscious rebel. They don't see Sammy Lou because she is "incorrect."

Once the self-conscious reformers are undercut, however, we are left with Sammy Lou herself and the need for research that graduate school usually ignores. The poem becomes for whites obscure and for many blacks uncomfortable. Even with Walker's own commentary on the poem, most whites do not know what to make of that catalogue of Americana—funeral home calendars, children named for Jackie Kennedy. I've been trying to escape, say black students, two syllable names which belong to maids; the naive, depressing habit of blacks to admire and imitate the ruling class, to honor *our* children with *their* names; and the narrow minded religiosity which dreams of death and judgment day.

Here is where I as teacher must know enough of American culture to explain that Sammy Lou is probably a sharecropper, that with her lethal hoe she chops cotton for a white man; that funeral home calendars usually have religious pictures on them, and that old fashioned black folks who believe in Martin Luther King and the American presidency often grace their children with famous names. From Walker's article, "In Search of Our Mother's Gardens" (*Ms.*), I learned that Walker places the creativity of Southern black women in their miraculous, colorful flower beds, and from *Interviews With Black Writers,* that Walker's own mother brought her a stalk of her old purple petunia bush when Walker's daughter was born. Are these details different from those a black teacher would supply? I think not. Could a black teacher explain these without research? Probably so. But if I could spend four or five years learning to understand Renaissance poetic convention, I can learn about black culture as well. It is far more accessible.

Perhaps I say the obvious, but there are white teachers who teach only Maya Angelou's *I Know Why the Caged Bird Sings* because they say they don't understand other black writers. (Personally, I think they like Angelou's self-portrait as the misunderstood bright girl who read Shakespeare in Arkansas. She confirms *their* values, and the value of high culture.) How did I find out about funeral home calendars and names like Martha and John Wesley? I happen to have worked in black Mississippi, but there are some perfectly obvious ways to get the same information. There are black bars, churches, restaurants. There is Atlanta, and most of Washington, D.C. There are black radio and TV stations, magazines and newspapers. (I could have found out all I needed to know from reading our local *Bay State Banner.*) There is a major field called black history. Then I could have asked Barbara Smith what she thought about my reading of the poem. (If you have no black person to ask, you might as well put down your book and start working on an affirmative action plan.)

But once the obscurity of the poem vanishes, the interpretation of its meaning remains. Here is where I always feel tense, reluctant to be the vehicle through which Walker exhorts black women to see their flower-loving, conservative, religious mothers in a different light. With her godliness, her willing relation to death, her so-called counter-revolutionary love of beauty, Sammy Lou exalts a certain kind of ordinary private self-definition which implicitly criticizes black militancy. I grit my teeth, and say so, and say at the same time Walker's broader point— "revolutions will have need of beauty"—which she quotes from Camus.

If my anxiety in interpreting "Revolutionary Petunias" is somewhat diffused by blacks and whites sharing a common enemy—the "cracker" Sammy Lou killed—let me turn to a passage from *Meridian* where I am positioned as the enemy by virtue of my *white* womanhood. It's a funny, bittersweet passage which dismisses white women and mythologizes the power, verve, and daring of black women. In this passage I am more than a vehicle through whom black women's experience of oppression is laid bare and interpreted; I am the direct source of oppression as well. Under circumstances which I know are a source of humiliation and anger for many of my black female friends, a black man—Truman—has just rejected Meridian in favor of a white, Northern woman. Naive young Southern civil rights worker, this is Meridian's first encounter with such a possibility. She is "bewildered" by his preference. "It went against everything she had been taught to expect."

> For she realized what she had been taught was that nobody wanted white girls except their empty-headed, effeminate counterparts— white boys—whom her mother assured her smelled (in the mouth) of boiled corn and (in the body) of thirty-nine percent glue. As far back as she could remember it seemed something understood: that while white men would climb on black women old enough to be their mothers—"for the experience"—white women were considered sexless, contemptible and ridiculous by all. . . .
>
> Who would dream, in her home town, of kissing a white girl? Who would want to? What were they good for? What did they do? They only seemed to hang about laughing, after school, until when they were sixteen or seventeen they got married. Their pictures appeared in the society column, you saw them pregnant a couple of times. Then you were no longer able to recognize them as girls you once "knew." They sank into permanent oblivion. One never heard of them doing anything that was interesting.

On the other hand, black women were always imitating Harriet
Tubman—escaping to become something unheard of. Outrageous.
One of her sister's friends had become, somehow, a sergeant in the
army and knew everything there was to know about enemy installa-
tions and radio equipment. A couple of girls her brothers knew had
gone away broke and come back, years later, as a doctor and a school-
teacher. Two other girls went away married to men and returned
home married to each other. . . .
    But even in more conventional things, black women struck out for
the unknown. They left home scared, poor black girls and came back
(some of them) successful secretaries and typists (this seemed amazing
to everyone, that there should be firms in Atlanta and other large cities
that would hire black secretaries). They returned, their hair bleached
auburn or streaked with silver, or perhaps they wore a wig. . . .
    Then there were simply the good-time girls who came home full
of bawdy stories of their exploits in the big city: one watched them
seduce the local men with dazzling ease, some used to be lovers and
might be still. In their cheap, loud clothing, their newly repaired
teeth, their flashy cars, their too-gold shimmering watches and
pendants—they were still a success. They commanded attention.
They deserved admiration. Only the rejects—not of men, but of
experience, adventure—fell into the domestic morass that even the
most intelligent white girls appeared to destined for. There seemed
nothing about white women that was enviable. Perhaps one might
covet a length of hair, if it swung long and particularly fine. But that
was all. And hair was dead matter that continued—only if oiled—
to shine.

Although Walker makes no causal links between her dismissal of
white women and the mythologizing of black women, there is a strongly
competitive sexual-political dynamic in the portraits. Walker takes over
"ownership" of the conventions with which black women are stereotyped by whites. She celebrates the usual litany of evils: outrageous
drama; wit and strength; independence; sexual liberty; a love for
adventure and risk. In order to exalt black women, she renders white
women impotent and lifeless. Here are a few of the most volatile, dehumanizing perversions of American racism and sexism, because, no
matter how skewed the contrast between black and white women, its
occasion is true. Truman, like other black men, for whatever reason,
prefers white women. He is a stock character in James Baldwin, in
Imamu Baraka, in Ralph Ellison where his rejection of black women
is rarely discussed. To make matters more complicated, Walker follows
this tour de force with a portrait of a second stock character—the

sugar daddy. He is Meridian's employer, an aging black professor with "a limp old penis" and "a veritable swamp fog of bad breath." While claiming to protect black women from white men, he pursues her around his desk and bribes her with presents. No wonder Walker needs to mythologize black women, paint them larger than life.

I have read this passage from *Meridian* five times this Fall to various classes; each time, despite the humor, my own feeling of tension is almost unbearable, the complexity of my own response difficult to sort out. And I listen for students' responses: surprise at the portrait of white women; silence at the portrait of white men who climb on top of black women old enough to be their mothers; startled but sympathetic laughter at the portrait of daring, outrageous black women. The passage has power to shock us. It shocks black women because they didn't think anyone would dare to say what they have always known; it shocks white women because they have never been asked to think from a black woman's vantage point about white women who choose black men. And if they are feminists used to critiquing white *male* portraits of women—the standard approach in "images of women" courses— they have never experienced such a radical denial of the commonality *between* women before. To Meridian, white women are "others," opposites, the "not me."

For these remarks to be useful, I mustn't dwell on *Meridian's* particular plot and characters. However, in each of the other four novels I mentioned at the outset, similar powerful issues are raised, and the teacher of black literature—no matter what her own color—must confront them. Here are the observations that I make in class—

First, I say that I do not respond to black women stereotyping white women as angrily as I do to *men* stereotyping all women. While the acts are equally distressing morally, politically they are different. White men have power to invoke their stereotypes to discriminate against women; black women have no power to invoke. *I*, a white woman, may freely discount Meridian's stereotype of me; it is inconsequential except as it fends off her own bitterness and anger.

Second, I say something about the sad domination of race over personal relations between black and white women. The burden of history—plantation mistress, mammy and slave; white lady, maid; menial worker, boss—has politicized friendships—despite feminism. This is a situation which white women must treat in a particular way: any feminist politics must continually account for the interests of black women, and individual white women should, of course, nurture their personal friendships with black women. Inevitably, however, white women must accept a certain mistrust from black women.

These first two observations are mainly directed at white students, many of whom care, for the best feminist reasons, about black women. The third observation concerns the key issue which divides black and white women—black men. Relationships either explode or go silent on the subject. My judgment as a white woman is to permit that division, to fix an arbitrary boundary. Although I have black friends who will criticize black male behavior in my presence, I refuse to do so in class. I "explain" *Meridian's* Truman and other black male characters at a distance: there are unemployment statistics; social policies which exploit or ignore black men; competing theories of the history of the black family. I know these, and cite them. But Truman, as his name suggests, has a set of familiar male problems; black women, I believe, should be free to sort out these problems privately, to test a black feminist viewpoint beyond the hearing of white women. Even the common simplistic formulation of the problem is too volatile and overwhelming for me to handle: white racism has robbed the black male of his manhood; how can a black woman criticize him, or watch out for interests which are hers alone? This silence, I should add, contradicts my usual feminist pedagogy, teaching that combines personal, literary, and political perspectives.

My fourth observation returns us to the vitality of literature by black women and the theme with which I began—the "other side" of black woman's double oppression which I call the magnificence of inventing yourself. In her own growth, Meridian, like other black women characters, passes through two stages of development. She first tries to define herself by converting the oppressor's stereotype to her own use. Then she learns that she, in Toni Morrison's language, must raise herself actively, that she has nothing to fall back on. She, unlike Lazarus, hasn't God's help; invisible to most, outside of history, she has a special freedom. Black women present a challenge and a model for us all.

Would a black teacher make the same observations? Probably not. She would be less worried than I about relations between blacks and whites and more worried about the integrity of black culture, I suspect. She would simply have a good laugh at or ignore the pallid, useless white women of Walker's *Meridian*; and she would, of course, not share my fear that in my admiration for black women writers, I am like those of whom I am always suspicious—people who feel alive and healthily self-critical only *outside* of their own culture. Still I teach from my own identity, and with my own problems visible. I'm fully alive to the complexity of reader-writer relations in the classroom, the potentiality for hurt and misunderstanding and awakening. And the students deserve the best writers we can offer.

Black-Eyed Blues Connection: Teaching Black Women II

Michele Russell   *Winter/Spring 1977*

In the first half of this essay (Fall 1976, vol. IV, No. 4) the author described the Wayne County Community College classroom at the downtown YWCA in Detroit, her students, her role as teacher, and the ways in which she took "one subject at a time" and encouraged "storytelling." In a subsequent issue, we will publish her annotated bibliography.

Give political value to daily life. Take aspects of what they already celebrate and enrich its meaning so they see their spontaneous tastes in a larger way than before. This means they will see themselves with new significance. It also imposes the responsibility of selectivity on the teacher. Embrace that. Apply your own political acumen to the myriad survival mechanisms that colonization and domestication breed into subject peoples. Remind them of the choices they make all the time.

No life-area is too trivial for political analysis. Note that a number of black women, myself included, have begun choosing long dresses for daily wear. In one class session, discussion begins with the remark that they're more "comfortable" in this mode. What does comfort consist of? For those who are heavy, it means anything not physically constricting. For working mothers, comfort means "easy to iron." For the budget conscious, "easy to make." For some of the young women in class, comfort is attached to the added respect this mode of dress elicits from brothers they pass on the street. For a Muslim grandmother, cleanliness and modesty are signified. For her daughter, also in the Nation, Africa is being invoked. The general principle which emerges is that this particular form of cover allows us greater freedom of expression and movement.

Don't stop here. Go from their bodies to their heads. A casual remark about wearing wigs can (and should) develop into a discussion of Frantz Fanon's essay, "Algeria Unveiled," in which he analyzes the role of protective coverings, adornment, camouflage, as tactical survival modes for women in the self-defensive stage of a movement. Help them to recall the stages of consciousness they've all experienced in relation to their own hair. When did they start to regard "straightening" or "doing" hair as "processing" it? When did they stop? Why? If some women in the class still change their hair texture, does that mean their *minds* are processed too? Read Malcolm on the subject. How do they feel about Alelia Walker in this context: the first black woman in America to become a millionaire for producing and marketing hair straighteners and skin bleaches. Take them as far as memory and material allow. Normally, there will be at least three generations of social experience personally represented in community college classes. Try to work with it all.

Go beyond what is represented in class. Recall all the ways, historically, that black women in America have used physical disguise for political purposes. Begin with Ellen Craft, escaping from a Georgia plantation to Boston in 1848, passing as a white man. Talk about the contradictory impact of miscegenation on their thinking and action. Then connect this to class members' public demeanor: the variations they choose and the purposes at work. What uniforms do they consciously adopt? Focus on motive as well as image; make intent as important as affect, a way to judge results.

Be able to speak in tongues. Idiom, the medium through which ideas are communicated and organic links of association established (i.e., community) must be in black women's own tradition. When black women "speak," "give a reading" or "sound" a situation, a whole history of using language as a weapon is invoked. Rooted in slave folk wisdom which says "Don't say no more with your mouth than your back can stand," our vocalizing is directly linked to a willingness to meet hostilities head-on and persevere. Take the following description of a black woman "specifying" by Zora Neale Hurston, for example:

> Big Sweet came to my notice within the first week that I arrived. . . . I heard somebody, a woman's voice "specifying" up this line of houses from where I lived and asked who it was. "Dat's Big Sweet" my landlady told me. "She got her foot up on somebody. Ain't she specifying?"
> She was really giving the particulars. She was giving a reading, a word borrowed from the fortunetellers. She was giving her opponent lurid data and bringing him up to date on his ancestry, his looks, smell, gait, clothes, and his route through Hell in the hereafter. My landlady went outside where nearly everybody else of the four or five hundred people on the "job" were to listen to the reading. Big Sweet broke the news to him, in one of her mildest bulletins that his pa was

a double humpted camel and his ma was a grass-gut cow, but even
so, he tore her wide open in the act of getting born, and so on and
so forth. He was a bitch's baby out of a buzzard egg.
My landlady explained to me what was meant by "putting your
foot up" on a person. If you are sufficiently armed—enough to stand
off a panzer division—and know what to do with your weapons after
you get 'em, it is all right to go to the house of your enemy, put one
foot up on his steps, rest one elbow on your knee and play in the family. That is another way of saying play the dozens, which also is a way
of saying low-rate your enemy's ancestors and him, down to the present moment for reference, and then go into his future as far as your
imagination leads you. But if you have no faith in your personal
courage and confidence in your arsenal, don't try it. It is a risky pleasure. So then I had a measure of this Big Sweet.
   "Hurt who?" Mrs. Bertha snorted at my fears. "Big Sweet? Humph!
Tain't a man, woman nor child on this job going to tackle Big Sweet.
If God send her a pistol she'll send him a man. She can handle a
knife with anybody. She'll join hands and cut a duet. Dat Cracker
Quarters Boss wears two pistols round his waist and goes for bad, but
be won't break a breath with Big Sweet lessen he got his pistol in his
hand. Cause if be start anything with her, he won't never get a chance
to draw it. She ain't mean. She don't bother nobody. She just don't
stand for no foolishness, dat's all."

Talking bad. Is it still going on? Some class members do it all the
time. All know women who do. Some, with a concern for manners,
find the activity embarrassing. One woman observes that it's getting
harder and harder these days to find targets worthy of such invention.
Another, bringing the prior comments together, says there's too little
audience for the energy it takes. Whatever our particular attitudes, we
all recognize in Big Sweet a pistol-packin' mamma, conjure woman,
voice of Judgment and reservoir of ancestral memory—all of which
are the bases of a fighting tradition also personified in Harriet
Tubman, Marie Leveau, Sojourner Truth, Ericka Huggins. Discover
the continuities in their words, acts and the deeds done in their name.
Emphasize how they transformed personal anger into political
weapons, enlarged personal grudges to encompass a people's outrage.
When words failed, remember how Aunt Jemima's most famous
recipe, ground glass plantation pancakes, made the masters choke.
   Take the blues. Study it as a coded language of resistance. In
response to questions from class members about whether feminism
has ever had anything to do with black women, play Ma Rainey singing,
"I won't be your dog no more." Remind them of our constant com-

plaints about being treated as a "meal-ticket woman," our frustration
at baking powder men losing their risables and of going hungry for
days. Know the ways in which Peaches are Strange Fruit. Introduce
them to a depression era Bessie Jackson responding humorously, but
resolutely, to our options for feeding ourselves when that period's dias-
pora forced us onto city streets. Two songs, written in 1930 and 1935,
document our determination to be treated with the dignity of workers, no matter how we labored. They testify to daily struggles over the
conditions of our labor, the urge to control turf and hours. The first
is "Tricks Ain't Walkin No More." She says:

> *Sometimes I'm up, sometimes I'm down*
> *I cain't make my livin around this town*
> *Cause Tricks ain't walkin, Tricks ain't walkin no more.*
>
> *I got to make my livin, don't care where I go.*
>
> *I need some shoes on my feet, clothes on my back*
> *That's why I'm walkin these streets all dressed in black*
> *But Tricks ain't walkin, Tricks ain't walkin no more.*
> *And I see four or five good tricks standin in front of my door.*
>
> *I got a store on the corner, sellin stuff cheap*
> *I got a market cross the street where I sell my meat*
> *But Tricks ain't walkin, Tricks ain't walkin no more*
> *And if you think I'm lyin, follow me to my door.*

By 1935, when they got to her door, they found she'd gone into a new
business. The address was the same, but the commodity had changed.
She sang:

> *When you come to my house, come down behind the jail*
> *I got a sign on my door, Bar-B-Que for Sale*
> *I'm talkin bout my Bar-B-Que*
> *The only thing I sell*
> *And if you want my meat, you can come to my house at twelve.*

Bring the idiomatic articulation of black women's feminism up to date
by sharing stories of the first time we all *heard* what Aretha was asking us
to *think* about, instead of just dancing to it. Let Esther Philips speak on
how she's *justified* and find out if class members feel the same way.
Be able to translate ideological shorthand into terms organic to
black women's popular culture. Let the concept of internationalism
be introduced. But approach it from the standpoint of a South African
Miriam Makeba, an Alabama-born Big Mama Thornton or a Caribbean

Nina Simone all singing Bob Dylan's "I Shall Be Released." Concentrate the discussion on each woman's roots, her place of national origin. Reflect on the history behind the special emphasis each woman gives to phrases such as: "every distance is not near," "I remember every face of every man who put me here," "inside these walls." Ask: What kinds of jails are they in? And what happens when we start acting to effect our own release? Devote one class session to a debate over whether it is an antagonistic contradiction for black women to use Bob Dylan's music as an expressive vehicle. Explore the limits of nationalism in this way.

The whole world is ours to appropriate, not just five states in the South, or one dark continent. Treat the meaning of this statement through Nina Simone's re-creation of Pirate Jenny. Play the music. Know the history it comes out of and the changes rung: from *The Beggar's Opera,* through Brecht and Weil's *Threepenny Opera,* to the Caribbean and Southern situations everywhere that Simone takes as her reference point. Know the political history involved and the international community of the oppressed she exhorts to rise. Particularly notice the cleaning woman's role. Recall the rebellions of the 1960s, when Nina Simone was performing this song. We all lived through the rebellions, but how did we relate to them? At what point did class members begin associating Detroit with Algeria, Watts with Lesotho, the Mississippi with the Mekong Delta, Amerika with Germany? Share your own experience and growth.

Use everything. Especially, use the physical space of the classroom to illustrate the effects of environment on consciousness. The size and design of the desks, for example. They are wooden, with one-sided stationary writing arms attached. The embodiment of a poor school. Small. Unyielding. Thirty years old. Most of the black women are ample-bodied. When the desks were new and built for 12-year-old seventh grade bodies, some class members may have sat in them for the first time. Now, sitting there for one hour—not to mention trying to concentrate and work—is a contortionist's miracle, or a stoic's. It feels like getting left back.

With desks as a starting point for thinking about our youth in school, class members are prompted to recall the mental state such seats encouraged. They cite awkwardness, restlessness and furtive embarrassment. When they took away our full-top desks with interior compartments, we remember how *exposed* we felt, unable to hide anything not spitballs, notes, nor scarred knees, prominent between too-short hand-me-down dresses and scuffed shoes. They remember the belligerence which was all the protection we were allowed.

We talk about all the unnecessary, but deliberate, ways the educational process is made uncomfortable for the poor. Most women in class hate to read aloud. So we relive how they were taught to read, the pain involved in individual, stand-up recitation. The foil one was for a teacher's scapegoating ridicule. The peer pressure to make mistakes. We look back on how good reading came to mean proper elocution to our teachers: particularly elderly black spinsters, also in the church.

We remember that one reason many of us stopped going to school was that it became an invasion of privacy. Not like church, which was only once a week, an event you could get up for. School was every day, among strangers, whether you felt like it or not, even if you ran out of clean clothes for the ritual. Showing up was the hardest part. After that, it was just a series of games.

Then, of course, someone inevitably says, "But here we are, back again." Is that a joke on us? Is it still a game? What are we trying to do differently this time around? To answer those questions, have women devise their own criteria for evaluating the educational process they engage in with you.

Be concrete. In every way possible, take a materialist approach to the issue of black women's structural place in America. Focus attention on the building where we are learning our history. Notice who's still scrubbing the floors. In response to class members who pin their hopes for the future on "new careers," pose the following questions: How is a nurse's aide different from a maid? What physical spaces are the majority of us still locked into as black women who must take jobs in the subsistence and state sectors of the economy? Do we ever get to do more than clean up other people's messes, be we executive secretaries, social workers, police officers, or wives? Within what confines do we live and work?

Reflect on the culture of the stoop, the storefront, the doorway, the housing project, the rooming house bathroom, the bank-teller's cage, the corner grocery store, the bus, hotels and motels, school, hospital and corporate corridors, and waiting rooms everywhere. What constraints do they impose?

If we conclude that most of our lives are spent as social servants, and state dependents, what blend of sex, race, and class consciousness does that produce? To cut quickly to the core of unity in experience, read the words of Johnny Tillmon, founder of the National Welfare Rights Organization in Watts, 1965:

I'm a woman. I'm a black woman. I'm a poor woman. I'm a fat woman. I'm a middle-aged woman. And I'm on welfare.

In this country, if you're any one of those things—poor, black, fat, female, middle-aged, on welfare—you count less as a human being. If you're all of those things, you don't count at all. Except as a statistic. I am a statistic. I am 45 years old. I have raised six children. I grew up in Arkansas and I worked there for fifteen years in a laundry, making about $20 or $30 a week, picking cotton on the side for carfare. I moved to California in 1959 and worked in a laundry there for nearly four years. In 1963, I got too sick to work anymore. My husband and I had split up. Friends helped me to go on welfare.

They didn't call it welfare. They called it AFDC—Aid to Families with Dependent Children. Each month I get $363 for my kids and me. I pay $128 a month rent; $30 for utilities, which include gas, electricity, and water; $120 for food and nonedible household essentials; $50 for school lunches for the three children in junior and senior high school who are not eligible for reduced-cost meal programs. This leaves $5 per person a month for everything else—clothing, shoes, recreation, incidental personal expenses and transportation. This check allows $1 a month for transportation for me but none for my children. That's how we live.

Welfare is all about dependency. It is the most prejudiced institution in this country, even more than marriage, which it tries to imitate.

The truth is that AFDC is like a super-sexist marriage. You trade in a man for *the* man. But you can't divorce him if he treats you bad. He can divorce you, of course, cut you off anything he wants. But in that case, *he* keeps the kids, not you.

The man runs everything. In ordinary marriage, sex is supposed to be for your husband. On AFDC, you're not supposed to have any sex at all. You give up control of your own body. It's a condition of aid. You may even have to agree to get your tubes tied so you can never have more children, just to avoid being cut off welfare.

The man, the welfare system, controls your money. He tells you what to buy, what not to buy, where to buy it, and how much things cost. If things—rent, for instance—really cost more than he says they do, it's just too bad for you. You've just got to make your money stretch.

The man can break into your home any time he wants to and poke into your things. You've got no right to protest. You've got no right to privacy. Like I said, welfare's a super-sexist marriage.

Discuss what it means to live like that. What lines of force and power in society does it imply? A significant percentage of black women have had direct experience with welfare, either as children or mothers. In discussing "how it happened to them," all become aware of how every woman in class is just one step away from that bottom line. A separation; a work injury; layoffs; a prolonged illness; a child's disability could put them on those rolls. It is a sobering realization, breaking through some of the superior attitudes even black women have internalized about AFDC recipients.

What other work do we do and how does it shape our thinking? Compare Maggie Holmes, domestic; Alice Washington, shoe factory order-filler; Diane Wilson, process clerk from Studs Terkel's *Working*. Study what women just like those in class say about themselves. Although, as with everything, a whole course could be devoted just to analyzing the content, process and consciousness of black women's jobs, be satisfied in this survey to personify history so it becomes recognizable and immediate; something they participate in.

Have a dream. The conclusion to be drawn from any study of our history in America is that the balance of power is not on our side, while the burden of justice is. This can be an overwhelming insight, particularly in times of economic stagnation, physical deterioration and organizational confusion. Therefore, it is important to balance any discussion of the material circumstances of black women's lives with some attention to the realm of their dreams.

In all other areas of life, we can talk about struggle, organization, sabotage, survival, even tactical and strategic victory. However, only in dream are liberation and judgment at the center of vision. That is where we do all the things in imagination that our awareness demands but our situation does not yet permit. In dream, we seek the place in the sun that society denies us. And here, as in everything, a continuum of consciousness will be represented.

At their most fetishistic, black women's spiritual dreams are embodied in the culture of numbers, signs and gambling. In every poor community, holy water, herb, astrology and dream book shops are for women what poolrooms, pawnshops and bars are for men. Places to hang on, hoping for a hit. As Etheridge Knight has observed in *Black Voices from Prison*, "It is as common to hear a mother say, 'I gotta get my number in today' with the same concern and sometimes in the same breath as she says 'I gotta feed the baby.'. . . In some homes the dream book is as familiar and treated with as much reverence as the Bible." In many homes, dream books produce more tangible results.

The most progressive expression of our dreams, however, in which mass liberation takes precedence over individual relief, and planning replaces luck, is occasionally articulated in literature. Sarah Wright provides such an example in *This Child's Gonna Live*. In that story of a black family desperately trying to hold onto its territorial birthright and each other in depression Maryland, the most fundamental religiosity of poor black people is re-created, its naturalism released. The landscape is made to hold our suffering and signify our fate. Particularly in the person of Mariah Upshur, the faith of the oppressed which helps us to fight on long after a cause seems lost is complemented by a belief that righteousness can make you invincible. Colloquially speaking, all that's needed is for God to send the sufferers a pretty day. Then, children will be cured of worms, and land thieves will be driven from the community, the wind will be calm for the oystermen, the newly planted rye will hold and a future will be possible in a land of "slowing-up roads" and death. That is, if we're deserving. What does "deserving" mean? Discuss Richard Wright's approach to this subject in "Bright and Morning Star."

Relate the fundamental hopes and values of Mariah Upshur's dream to other belief systems through which people have been able to attain freedom. The concrete experience of people "moving mountains" is communicated by the story of Tachai in the People's Republic of China. The triumph of vision, perseverance and organization over brute force to regain land is demonstrated in Vietnam and Cuba. Spell out the commonalities in all liberation struggles in this age which vanquish the moneychangers. Find examples in our own history where beginnings have been made of this kind. Make the Word become Flesh, so the new day that's dawning belongs to you and me.

As teachers, we should be able to explore all these things and more without resorting to conventional ideological labels. This is the basic, introductory course. Once the experiential base of the class-in-itself is richly felt and understood, theoretical threads can be woven between W. E. B. Du Bois, Zora Neale Hurston and Frantz Fanon. Then bridges can be built connecting the lives of ghettoized women of every color and nationality. In the third series of courses, great individuals can be put in historical perspective; organized movements can be studied. In the fourth stage, movements, themselves, may arise. Political possibilities for action then flow from an understanding conditioned by life on the block, but not bound by it. And the beginnings of a class-for-itself may take shape. But the first step, and the most fundamental, should be the goal of the first course: recognizing our*selves* in history.

Brief, A-mazing Movements: Dealing with Despair in the Women's Studies Classroom

Cheri Register **Fall 1979**

Women's studies majors at the University of Minnesota are required to take two quarters of a course called Women's Studies Seminar some time in their junior or senior year. While the theme of the seminar varies from quarter to quarter, its underlying purpose is constant: "to allow students to direct knowledge and methodology gained from courses and experience toward topics of an interdisciplinary nature with a focus on women." The variant that I taught in the fall of 1978 was called Feminist Learning: The University and Beyond. Its intent was to help students become conscious of the learning process and shift their focus from content to method, from *what* to *how and why*. It is a difficult transition to make, particularly in a university where passive lecture courses are the norm. The lack of tangible subject matter can be troubling, and it takes time to get used to the teacher's function, which is not to pass on information, but to guide, provoke, and challenge, often from the sidelines.

For their first lengthy assignment, I asked students to prepare an oral report on the impact of feminism on a particular discipline or area of inquiry. Many of our majors are double majors who seldom get an opportunity to tie together the two strands of their education. I expected the students to be excited about fresh approaches feminist scholarship offers to other disciplines. I did not expect the recitation of horrors that brought the class to the brink of despair. Students presented reports about male medical researchers who do research on women and keep their results secret; about men intent on preserving a clublike atmosphere in the professions; and about male psychotherapists who imprison women in mental institutions for failing to conform to society's notions of femininity. Much of the evidence offered by the students was either speculative or outdated, but the class had its own horror stories to tell. An image emerged of a vast male conspiracy with an irresistible momentum, motivated by a conscious, deliberate evil.

Midway through the assignment, I collected the class journals and was overwhelmed by the emotions invested in them: anger, frustration, disillusion, despair. Many of the students elaborated on the horrors recited in class, while others expressed concern about how the course was going. One wrote that all this "wallowing in negatives" was paralyzing her. Another was bored: "You can almost predict when the groans are going to start." I thought about intervening and clarifying the assignment, but it didn't seem fair to invalidate the reports already given and offer extra guidance to those yet to come. I also suspected that this venting of anger was necessary and that the assignment was probably premature. I decided to hold off and then put the anger to some pedagogical use.

When the reports had all been given, I set aside a period to "summarize and synthesize"—an ongoing responsibility I had assigned myself. I said that I had been overwhelmed by the anger and frustration and was disappointed that so few reports had mentioned signs of change attributable to feminism. I offered some possible explanations for what had happened:

1. On the first day of class, we had talked about personal reasons for becoming a women's studies major. Though one of the benefits extolled was the sense of community in women's studies classes, in this particular class of sixteen, some students were transparently hostile to each other, while others seemed alienated. In fumbling for a common bond, the students hit upon their shared anger toward male supremacy. To become "us," they focused on "them."

2. Some students equated radicalism with intense anger; thus, they demonstrated their political stance by being angry.

3. Some students apparently felt unsure of their commitment to women's studies and feminism, and worried that their interest might decline as their initial fervor waned. The recitation of horrors helped them sustain an emotional pitch on which their faith in the sincerity of their feminism depended.

I also wanted to put this anger into a wider perspective, to see it as part of a process, and to offer some assurance that it could be disciplined without stopping the process. I described my own development as a feminist scholar during the past ten years of changes in women's studies and the women's movement. I sketched this development also in a graph [see *Women's Studies Quarterly* 8, no. 4 (Fall 1979): 8], identifying four stages and assigning them alliterative titles and catch phrases.

Compensating is a time of discovery, and the emotional graph represents a "plateau" of excitement. Learning that the cotton gin *might* have been invented by Catherine Greene is cause for rejoicing. We amass information about powerful queens and "first-women-who" and use it eagerly as a defense against arguments that women are by nature inferior. I called this "the Pope Joan Syndrome" to point up a fallacy inherent in it: because we do not yet question male-defined standards, the ultimate symbol of achievement is a woman who disguises herself as a man and proves her worth in an all-male arena. The supply of eminent women is limited, however, and we soon wonder why there aren't more of them. Thus begins the slide into what the seminar students named "The Pit."

In our search for heroines, we encounter examples of failure, as well as success, and attribute it to discriminatory barriers, which we identify one by one. Soon enough it becomes apparent that discrimination is the rule, part of a huge system of oppression which pits men against women. This is a terrifying realization, but an essential one. The mode of consciousness raising that has the most indelible effect begins with a *lowering*: we descend into "The Pit," immerse ourselves in oppression, and "speak bitterness" to bolster our determination to climb back out on the other side. At the nadir on the emotional graph, we are indeed "wallowing in negatives," convinced that oppression is all-pervasive and irresistible. When we examine women's experience, we see only victimization. Yet we haven't forgotten all those exceptional heroines, and we begin to wonder how they resisted. Buoyed on our remembrance of them, we pull ourselves up to that first little "pinnacle" on the graph. From there, we discern a pattern in the oppression—one that we can possibly undo.

This leads to a new phase of discovery. What about women who haven't made it on male terms, but haven't succumbed to victimization either? What more is there to female experience? What have women done on their own terms? The transition from *Criticizing* to *Collecting and Constructing* involves a crucial change in perspective. Previously, we have viewed women through masculine lenses or at least in relation to men, as the objects of oppression. Now women become the subjects of our inquiry, as we examine women's experience *through women's eyes* and *from a feminist perspective*—that is, with a consciousness of oppression and the need for change understood. We discover a female culture— several variants of it, in fact—in which women have been the *creators* of behavioral norms, values, social structures, and artifacts. This is very exhilarating and propels us upwards. There are "pitfalls" along the way, however: among others, an isolationism that admits the existence of oppression but neglects the task of undoing it to avoid being tainted by it; and a neo-feminine romanticism that simply glories in nurturance and needlework and forgets oppression altogether. If we keep moving beyond these pitfalls, we begin to wonder what the world would be like if the female culture were the dominant culture. What form would female norms take if extended to humanity-at-large?

We are now on the brink of "The Abyss," ready to ask all the crucial questions: Where is "there"? Where does the center of human experience lie? What acts are worthy of remembrance and emulation? How does a work of art communicate? What is power and what are its uses? The answers lie on the other side, in an ideal world where women can serve as definers of truth and knowledge, where women's vision counts as a central perspective. To make the leap, we need to address the nature-nurture question and resolve the public-private split. We especially need to distinguish those aspects of female culture which are born of oppression from those which would be created even in its absence. Otherwise, we risk falling into the current that sweeps us back to where we began: we might argue female superiority along the same lines as the old anatomy-is-destiny doctrine, or we might be content with an illusory counterculture that poses no threat to the dominant male culture, or we might simply "value" our condition and forget why we undertook this process in the first place. Despite the dangers, I ended the graph with an arrow pointing optimistically upward and onward.

To show how women's studies has followed this process, I used examples from several disciplines. Rather than do that here, I would like to ask readers to trace their disciplines through the model and let me know whether it fits. . . .

As additional guideposts, I mentioned publications that had played a transitional role. Between *Compensating* and *Criticizing,* I put Linda Nochlin's "Why Are There No Great Women Artists?" (in Gornick and Moran, *Woman in Sexist Society,* 1971); and between *Criticizing* and *Collecting,* Carroll Smith-Rosenberg's "The Female World of Love and Ritual" (*Signs* 1:1, 1975). I saw attempts at *Conceiving* in Mary Daly's *Beyond God the Father*—particularly in the concept of "naming" and the exhortation to establish a new center "on the boundary" of patriarchy—and in Adrienne Rich's poetry, which strives for a "common language."

The initial response of my seminar class to the model was quite subdued: a few requests for clarification and some cautiously worded skepticism. One woman expressed concern that the graph might be used competitively, to put down people perceived to be at a "lower stage of development." I was grateful to have that danger pointed out, since the greatest risk I see in developmental models is their tendency to become reified. This model is meant only as a conceptual framework, an attempt to understand graphically a process that many of us have

gone or are going through. It is not a prescription for future generations of feminists, who must chart their own course. . . .

Despite the subdued discussion that first day, it was soon apparent
that "Cheri's model" or "that thing on the board" had made some difference. In class and in their journals, students reported that it gave them
hope of overcoming their despair, a vision of better things to come, and
a sense of direction. One woman, for example, resolved to stop dwelling
on the irrelevance of political science to women and start working on
devising a feminist political theory. This pleased me, naturally, but I
was even more gratified when the class suggested improvements in the
model itself, based on their experience. We decided that development
is not unidirectional, but that you can move back and forth at random
or at will. Each time you move or slip back toward "The Pit," you bring
along new insights from the *Collecting and Constructing* stage that give
you a new perception of the pattern of oppression. Since development
is cumulative, no stage is to be avoided. It might even be worthwhile
to lower yourself into the negatives now and then, to regain the impetus for overcoming the pitfalls on the way up. We also agreed that it is
possible to be in several stages at once, with reference to different
aspects of experience. The static, linear configuration of the graph
could be very misleading, and it would be better to visualize it in three
dimensions and in constant motion.

Our most nagging question about the process was, "How will we ever
make the leap without plunging into the abyss?" This threatened a new
despair, until someone had sense enough to ask, "Is it necessarily a
leap?" An answer was suggested on the last day of the quarter, when a
team of students conducted a class on Adrienne Rich's feminism and
its implications for feminist learning. In her poem "From a Survivor,
" we read:

> . . . *the leap*
> *we talked, too late, of making*
> *which I live now*
> *not as a leap*
> *but a succession of brief, amazing movements*
>
> *each one making possible the next*

Maybe the seminar has even been one of them.

Cheri Register *is Assistant Professor of Women's Studies at the University of
Minnesota.*

What Is Feminist Pedagogy?

Carolyn M. Shrewsbury   *Fall/Winter 1993*

Feminist pedagogy is a theory about the teaching/learning process that guides our choice of classroom practices by providing criteria to evaluate specific educational strategies and techniques in terms of the desired course goals or outcomes. These evaluative criteria include the extent to which a community of learners is empowered to act responsibly toward one another and the subject matter and to apply that learning to social action.

Feminist pedagogy begins with a vision of what education might be like but frequently is not. This is a vision of the classroom as a liberatory environment in which we, teacher-student and student-teacher, act as subjects, not objects. Feminist pedagogy is engaged teaching/learning—engaged with self in a continuing reflective process; engaged actively with the material being studied; engaged with others in a struggle to get beyond our sexism and racism and classism and homophobia and other destructive hatreds and to work together to enhance our knowledge; engaged with the community, with traditional organizations, and with movements for social change.

The concept of a liberatory environment suggests a new way to be with one another in the classroom. A classroom characterized as persons connected in a net of relationships with people who care about each other's learning as well as their own is very different from a classroom that is seen as comprised of teacher and students. One goal of the liberatory classroom is that members learn to respect each other's differences rather than fear them. Such a perspective is ecological and holistic. The classroom becomes an important place to connect to our roots, our past, and to envision the future. It is a place to utilize and develop all of our talents and abilities, to develop excellence that is not limited to the few. The classroom becomes a place in which integrity is not only possible but normal. The web of interrelationships in the classroom is seen to stretch to the local, regional, and global communities and, potentially, even beyond the boundaries of our earth.

Such a classroom builds on the experiences of the participants. We move on to seeing our experiences in different lights, to relating our experiences to other or new evidence, to thinking about our experiences in different ways. Under those circumstances we can integrate our new learning and modify our past understandings. But we remain grounded in our experiences, maintaining the sense of ourselves as subjects.

The vision includes a participatory, democratic process in which at least some power is shared. Learners develop independence. The classroom becomes a model of ways for people to work together to accomplish mutual or shared goals, and to help each other reach individual goals. Students are able to take risks in such a classroom. This is an active classroom, where the joy and excitement as well as the hard work of learning provide the kind of positive feedback that magnifies the effort put into learning. At its simplest level, feminist pedagogy is concerned with gender justice and overcoming oppressions. It recognizes the genderedness of all social relations and consequently of all societal institutions and structures. Thus, fundamental to a feminist perspective is a commitment to growth, to renewal, to life. The vision itself must continue to evolve.

In a feminist classroom, students integrate the skills of critical thinking with respect for and ability to work with others. Feminist pedagogy strives to help student and teacher learn to think in new ways, especially ways that enhance the integrity and wholeness of the person and the person's connections with others (Minnich, Rutenberg). Critical thinking, then, is not an abstracted analysis but a reflective process firmly grounded in the experiences of the everyday. It requires continuous questioning and making assumptions explicit, but it does so in a dialogue aimed not at disproving another person's perspective, nor destroying the validity of another's perspective, but at a mutual exploration of explications of diverse experiences.

The vision of a feminist classroom includes an erotic dimension,

> an assertion of an empowered creative energy, the sharing of intellectual discovery, which as [Audre] Lorde says, "forms a bridge between the sharers which can be the basis of understanding much of what is not shared between them," a lessening of difference (Allen),

or difference used in a creative way, to spark increased understanding of the many dimensions of life, of incongruities or paradoxes, the complexities inherent in seemingly simple things.

Feminist pedagogy ultimately seeks a transformation of the academy and points toward steps, however small, that we can all take in each of our classrooms to facilitate that transformation. Three concepts, commmunity, empowerment, and leadership, are central to these steps and provide a way of organizing our exploration into the meaning of feminist pedagogy.

The Theory: Empowerment

Of the three central concepts, empowerment has been the most frequently discussed, in part because of the early ties between feminist pedagogy and Paulo Friere's work in dialogical education. Feminist pedagogy includes a recognition of the power implications of traditional schooling and of the limitations of traditional meanings of the concept of power that embody relations of domination.

By focusing on empowerment, feminist pedagogy embodies a concept of power as energy, capacity, and potential rather than as domination. This is an image of power as the glue holding a community together, giving the people the opportunity "to act, to move, to change conditions, for the benefit of the whole population" (Lane). Under traditional conceptions of power as domination, justice requires that limits be placed on power and that a balance of power be achieved in order to mitigate the results of domination. Under conceptions of power as capability, the goal is to increase the power of all actors, not to limit the power of some.

Thus, a view of power as creative community energy would suggest that strategies be developed to counteract unequal power arrangements. Such strategies recognize the potentiality for changing traditional unequal relationships. Our classrooms need not always reflect an equality of power, but they must reflect movements in that direction.

This conception of power recognizes that people need power, both as a way to maintain a sense of self and as a way to accomplish ends (Janeway). Power can be used to enhance both autonomy and mutuality. To be empowered is to be able to "claim an education" as Adrienne Rich urges us. To be empowered is to recognize our abilities to act to create a more humane social order. To be empowered is to be able to engage in significant learning. To be empowered is to be able to connect with others in mutually productive ways.

To accomplish the empowerment of all, feminist pedagogy employs classroom strategies that: 1) enhance the students' opportunities and abilities to develop their thinking about the goals and objectives they wish and need to accomplish individually and collectively, 2) develop the students' independence (from formal instructors) as learners, 3) enhance the stake that everyone has in the success of a course and thereby make clear the responsibility of all members of the class for the learning of all, 4) develop skills of planning, negotiating, evaluating, and decision making, 5) reinforce or enhance the self-esteem of class members by the implicit recognition that they are sufficiently competent to play a role in course development and are able to be change agents, 6) expand the students' understanding of the subject matter of the course and of the joy and difficulty of intense intellectual activity as they actively consider learning goals and sequences.

Empowering strategies allow students to find their own voices, to discover the power of authenticity. At the same time, they enable individuals to find communion with others and to discover ways to act on their understanding. Empowering classrooms are places to practice visions of a feminist world, confronting differences to enrich all of us rather than to belittle some of us. Empowering pedagogy does not dissolve the authority or the power of the instructor. It does move from power as domination to power as creative energy. In such a system the teacher's knowledge and experience is recognized and is used with the students to increase the legitimate power of all. Empowering pedagogy takes seriously the goal of lifelong learning by consciously developing teaching/learning skills as well as by providing an informational subject base. It accepts the antihegemonic potential of liberatory education and provides a model of interrelationships that can be incorporated into a developing vision of a world in which hierarchical oppressive relationships are exchanged for autonomy within a community that celebrates difference.

The Theory: Community

"Theories of power," Nancy Hartsock tells us, "are implicitly theories of community." And likewise, our decisions about what we image as community influence the ways in which we construct systems of power.

But, to talk about community, one needs to reexamine the gendered nature of traditional classrooms. The work of Carol Gilligan on moral development provides insights for reconceptualizing community. Gilligan identifies differences in the moral development of boys and girls and the moral conceptions of men and women. One consequence is

the contrast between a self defined through separation and a self
delineated through connection, between a self measured against
an abstract ideal of perfection and a self assessed through the
particular activities of care.

Women seek to build connections. They seek to maintain connections that have been built. Relationships are more than a set of
interactions among people. They are the web of existence. For men,
the importance of separation results in the creation of rules as the
web of existence. Relationships with individual people are less
important than the fabric of rules.

These disparate visions in their tension reflect the paradoxical
truths of human experience—that we know ourselves as separate
only insofar as we live in connection with others, and that we
experience relationships only insofar as we differentiate other
from self (Gilligan).

The tragedy is that men in power have built a society that in its
public aspects reflects only the morality of rights side of the tension.

Within the classroom, too, the morality of rights is dominant. By
and large, students participate in our classes as individuals, taking
little responsibility for the class as a whole. The classroom has a set
of rules about fairness and equity but little consideration of differences in need. The rights of others in the classroom are respected, but little compassion and care is structured into the
classroom.

At the core of feminist pedagogy is a re-imaging of the classroom
as a community of learners where there is both autonomy of self
and mutuality with others that is congruent with the developmental
needs of both women and men. There are many advantages to
creating such a classroom. Learning is enhanced in such environments (see Nelsen, Schmuck in Bar-Tal and Saxe, Torney-Purta,
Johnson and Johnson, Schniedewind). Further, as Hannah Arendt
noted, power arises from the collective self-confidence in a people's
capacity to act and effect their fate. Empowerment is only possible
when there is a sense of mutuality.

Decision making when there is a community of mutuality rather
than a community of isolated individuals can take place by consensus as well as by formalized decision rules. Creativity is enhanced by the consensus process for "something emerges as a
desirable outcome, even though no member of the group thought

about it in advance" (Thayer). Differences and diversity in a community of mutuality can be recognized and seen as a source of creative energy (Lorde, Nelsen).

The personal can be recognized as political in a classroom with some sense of mutual community. Students may find connections with themselves, their individual and collective pasts, with others, and with the future. In such a classroom there is a need and desire to move learning beyond the walls of the classroom. Theory can be extended to action, and action can come back to inform theory and that can lead again to action.

For too long community has been seen as either the polar opposite of autonomy or as the rather weak conception of an aggregate of individuals together because of some shared formality like geographic boundaries. Feminist pedagogy includes teaching strategies that are based on a reconceptualization of community with a richness that includes the autonomy and individuality of members who share a sense of relationship and connectedness with each other.

The Theory: Leadership

Leadership in its liberatory aspect as an active element of praxis is the third crucial concept in feminist pedagogy. Leadership is the embodiment of our ability and our willingness to act on our beliefs. Florence Howe illustrated this in noting that

> a leader is someone who knows how to control her life, and who has a vision of possibilities for other lives apart from her own, for her community, for other women, for example, and who works to make that *vision* visible to others, to share it, without trampling on other persons, but engaging them, enabling them to work for that vision as well.

Feminist pedagogy focuses on the development of leadership. For example, students who take part in developing goals and objectives for a course learn planning and negotiating skills. They also learn how to develop an understanding of, and an ability to articulate, their needs. They learn how to find connections between their needs and the needs of others. They learn about groups and about the different leadership tasks in groups and take different leadership roles throughout the course period. As students struggle with evaluation methods, they learn how to evaluate actions and the connection between objectives and achievement. When things aren't working in the classroom, they learn how to analyze the problem and how to find alternatives. And the skill of the students as leaders helps all of this work more smoothly and effectively. Leadership is a special form of empowerment that empowers others.

The feminist teacher is above all a role model of a leader. S/he has helped members of the class develop a community, a sense of shared purpose, a set of skills for accomplishing that purpose, and the leadership skills so that teacher and students may jointly proceed on those tasks. There is a dynamic between leadership and followership, and effective leaders under the more modern sense of leadership are also effective followers. Between the two is a morality based upon responsibility. Individuals are responsible for their acts within the context in which they have freedom to act. They have responsibility arising out of the relationships they have with those with whom they share a community. The students' and teacher's joint responsibility for the successful conclusion of a class emphasizes the moral nature of leadership and followership activities. This is a very different perception of the classroom than that where teachers have responsibility for teaching and students for learning with the implication that each is at least partially independent. It emphasizes the moral nature of choices within a community and the necessity for agency by community members.

Leadership then is logically and intuitively connected to community and empowerment by providing the active mechanism for achieving the empowered community and for that community to continue to be effective within the broader world. It suggests that change does not take place magically but by the active exercise of agency, whether directed at ourselves or at structures.

Feminist pedagogy does not assume that all classrooms are alike. Indeed, it suggests how classrooms might differ depending, for example, on the initial competence of students (see Schniedewind, this issue). It does not automatically preclude any technique or approach. It does indicate the relationship that specific techniques have to educational goals. It is not limited to any specific subject matter but it does include a reflexive element that increases the feminist scholarship component involved in the teaching/learning of any subject matter. It has close ties with other liberatory pedagogies, but it cannot be subsumed under other pedagogical approaches. It is transformative, helping us revision the educational enterprise. But it can also be phased into a traditional teaching approach or another alternative pedagogical approach. It is not all or nothing, although practitioners find that taking one step makes the next step logically compelling. It is a crucial component of a feminist revolution.

BIBLIOGRAPHY

Allen, Carolyn. "Feminist Teachers: The Power of the Personal." *Working Paper Series* 3 (1981). Women's Studies Research Center, University of Wisconsin.

Bar-Tal, Daniel, and Saxe, Leonard, eds. *Social Psychology of Education: Theory and Research.* New York: Hemisphere Publishing, 1978.

Freire, Paulo. *Pedagogy of the Oppressed.* New York: Seabury Press, 1968.

————. *Education for Critical Consciousness.* New York: Seabury Press, 1973.

Gilligan, Carol. *In a Different Voice: Psychological Theory and Women's Development.* Cambridge, Mass.: Harvard University Press, 1982.

Hartsock, Nancy. *Money, Sex, and Power: Toward a Feminist Historical Materialism.* New York: Longman, 1983.

Howe, Florence. "New Teaching Strategies for a New Generation of Students." *Women's Studies Quarterly* 11, no. 2 (1983): 7–11.

Janeway, Elizabeth. *Powers of the Weak.* New York: Knopf, 1980.

Johnson, Roger T., and Johnson, David W. *Cooperative Learning: The Power of Positive Goal Interdependence.* Paper, n.d.

Lane, Ann M. "The Feminism of Hannah Arendt." *Democracy* 3, no. 3 (1983): 107–17.

Minnich, Elizabeth Kamarck. "Friends and Critics: The Feminist Academy." In *Toward a Feminist Transformation of the Academy,* edited by Beth Reed, pp. 1–11. Ann Arbor, Mich.: Great Lakes College Association Women's Studies Program, 1978.

Nelsen, Randle W. "Reading, Writing, and Relationships: Toward Overcoming the Hidden Curriculum of Gender, Ethnicity, and Socio-economic Class." *Interchange* 12, nos. 2–3 (1981): 229–42.

Rich, Adrienne. *On Lies, Secrets, and Silence.* New York: W. W. Norton, 1979.

Rutenberg, Taly. "Learning Women's Studies." In *Theories of Women's Studies,* edited by Gloria Bowles and Renate Duelli-Klein. Berkeley: Women's Studies Department, University of California, 1980.

Schniedewind, Nancy. "Cooperatively-Structured Learning: Implications for Feminist Pedagogy." *Journal of Thought* 20, no. 3 (Fall 1985): 74–87.

Thayer, Frederick C. *An End to Hierarchy and Competition Administration in the Post-Affluent World.* 2nd ed. New York: New Viewpoints (Franklin Watts, dist.), 1981.

Torney-Purta, Judith. "Psychological Perspectives on Enhancing Civic Education through the Education of Teachers." *Journal of Teacher Education* 34, no. 6 (November–December 1983): 30–34.

Carolyn M. Shrewsbury *is Professor of Political Science and an associated faculty with the women's studies program at Mankato State University.*

Affective Teaching for Our Lives: Singing in the Feminist Theory Classroom

Marjorie Pryse   *Spring/Summer 1994*

> Singing is best, it gives right joy to speech.
> Six years I squandered, studying to teach,
> Expounding language. Singing it is better,
> Teaching the joy of the song, not teaching the letter.
>
> — Genevieve Taggard, "Definition of Song," 1935

Although I had already planned to write about why I use a lot of music in the feminist theory classroom before I read Genevieve Taggard's poem, I have included a discussion of the poem within this essay because it helps me explain what I mean by affective teaching. Genevieve Taggard wrote protest poetry during the 1930s, considered herself a socialist, and proposes in this and other poems that emotion connects political work and poetry — indeed, that "singing it is better," that, without an affective component, people do not "learn" to appreciate either art or politics. As I understand her poem, she serves as a mentor for the feminist teacher trying to convey the power of socialist (and other) feminist theory. Her poem gives me one way of describing how I came to use music in the feminist theory course, what affect I am trying to effect, and what particular songs might work for others.

1

I began to teach affectively as a way of solving the fundamental problem many of us encounter in the women's studies classroom, namely, that we cannot predict how students are going to respond to feminism. "Six years I squandered, studying to teach, expounding language." We may choose texts and topics with care, present course content with attention to feminist pedagogy, and encourage

"Definition of Song" from *Collected Poems 1913–1988* by Genevieve Taggard. Copyright ©1938 by Harper & Row Publishers, Inc., renewed 1966. Reprinted by permission of Marcia D. Liles.

discussion from various points of view and still receive student evaluations that run the gamut from "This course made me feel uncomfortable" and "This teacher is too radical" to "Everyone should be required to take this course" and "This course changed my life." While changing students' lives, or at least their minds, remains an ideal goal, I at least have struggled for a more concrete version of that goal, one that creates a pedagogical paradigm I can then adopt as a guide for choosing texts, creating writing assignments, and constructing a teaching presence in the classroom. Because students are often careful to distance themselves intellectually from feminism and to defend themselves against the social contradictions it reveals or, alternatively, to "become feminists" for the duration of the course in which they expect to receive a grade, I have tried to rely less on how students respond consciously to feminism, something over which I have no control because I have no way of assessing their capacity and motivation for challenging attitudes they may have brought with them into the course, and more on my own response. In short, I have come to view my own classroom practice as the way I construct feminist subjectivity, "in" myself and "for" my students, and I have turned to affective teaching as a way of communicating that subjectivity. I have concluded that "singing it is better, / Teaching the joy of the song," while also "teaching the letter." Listening to feminist songs with students in my feminist theory course "gives right joy" to feminist speech, and it portrays the feminist subject as someone who feels and relates as well as analyzes and critiques.

The construction of feminist subjects articulates difference, offers experience of shared struggle within difference, and creates the classroom as an interdisciplinary space, in which interdisciplinarity moves beyond incorporating the usual mix of literature, history, sociology, psychology, economics, politics, and popular culture to include an epistemological fluidity, a way of knowing that creates a bridge between cognitive and affective apprehension. Such a way of knowing postulates that students do not really learn unless they experience nonverbal change, one that becomes difficult to find the words to describe—and, therefore, may be less subject to intellectualized defenses and socialized attitudes, to internalized sexism, racism, and homophobia. Teachers in the women's studies classroom have learned that "encouraging" students to challenge internalized attitudes usually requires charging the atmosphere, making efforts to increase the level of student discomfort as a way of moving beyond the limitations of a purely cognitive apprehension of difference. And some of us may hope to convey that the articulation of differences among women creates a set of goals which may be "shared," or held "in common," and which fall within the universe of "feminisms" or of what bell hooks has termed "feminist movement," in which the word *feminist* in the phrase "toward a feminist-centered classroom" (to paraphrase Adrienne Rich) becomes an adjective, not a noun.

In trying to create the classroom as a place for the construction of feminist subjectivity and an interdisciplinary and fluid epistemology, the only subject I can reasonably try to construct is myself. In other words, because I cannot know how students are responding or what they are thinking or how their own historical positions situate their motivation to engage in feminist analysis, instead of trying to "teach" students how to become feminist subjects, I focus instead on creating a model in the classroom, which for all practical purposes must be "me." Thus, although the historically situated person I am does indeed walk into the classroom, I take as part of my pedagogy in that space the task of constructing the teacher anew as feminist subject. In that space I "embody" feminisms. When I take class time to discuss with students their or my own expressions of sexism, racism, classism, or homophobia, I become a subject who engages in feminist process. When I struggle to make small groups work, I commit "myself" to collaborative feminism. When I ask students to engage in personal reflection and self-disclosure, "I" am moving them toward feminist reflection and analysis. When I bring women's music into the classroom, I am disclosing "as" a feminist subject: this is how I love, this is what moves me, this helps me feel what I think, this "shows" passionate care.

Sometimes I have difficulty helping students make the distinction between the feminist subject I am trying to construct in the classroom and my own personal history. The classroom does not become for me a place for self-disclosure in a specific sense, and part of constructing the feminist subject involves helping students make the distinction between "who I am" in the classroom and whether or not I have children, am married, or grew up middle-class. When I was asked the direct question by a male student in my Introduction to Women's Studies class about a year ago, "Are you a lesbian?" I hesitated for a few moments, reflected on the pedagogical consequences of ducking (did I want to convey that the feminist subject is evasive, easily intimidated, or closeted?), recognized the opportunism in the student's question, then answered yes. Later, listening to students imagine out loud how they might have responded had they been in my position, and exploring with them the power dynamics of the male student in the women's studies classroom (this particular student acknowledged that he "wouldn't dream" of asking any of his male or presumed-heterosexual professors such a question), I also drew the line at further questions. The women's studies course is not an examination of the instructor's life. On the other hand, I also understood why many students revealed during this discussion that they had pondered this and many other questions about "me" during the course: the commitment to constructing the feminist subject in the classroom also means behaving toward students in ways that will *disclose* feminist self without tying that self too narrowly to any single person's historical position or life experiences.

Trying to embody the one, to "be the body," who invites students to think about feminist subjectivity also reconstructs who "I" am: every interaction with students becomes an intervention in their lives and development; to this extent they are "mine" for a time and in a place that are historically contingent, and "mine" *only if* students engage in (re)search that becomes historically, analytically, and subjectively self-reflexive at the same time that they are trying to "discover" me, their "model" (for better or worse, it's their luck of the draw) of the feminist subject. Finding me "out" becomes one way of exploring what it might mean to find themselves out: hence, a benign view of the irrepressible question "Are you (or is my women's studies instructor) a lesbian?"

Genevieve Taggard writes:

> And of all forms of song surely the least
> Is solo. Only lark in the east
> Can say—what no other lone singer can say—
> The glory, the glory of the arriving ray.

I believe that, as women's studies teachers, we sometimes cast ourselves in the role of Taggard's lark; we want to be witness to those moments of expanding consciousness, of radicalizing thought, of the "dawn" of feminist analysis. When we come to our senses we may worry that students are "telling us what they think we want to hear" and that reports of the dawn are premature. It is seductive but probably mistaken to take as our measure of success in the classroom any individual student's feminist "transformation"; Taggard reminds us to look to a chorus, not the solo voice, for evidence of feminist movement:

> Singing is the work of many voices.
> Only so when choral mass rejoices
> Is the lock sprung on human isolation
> And all the many welded into one.

As I read Taggard's poem, she is confirming the necessity for feminisms to be plural. Although I may construct the feminist teacher-subject as the architect of a particular configuration of readings, discussions, and assignments that may enable students from a variety of subject positions to engage in feminist work, if I cannot elicit "singing" in my students, each with each and as a group, then, no matter how vocally they individually assert their feminism, such assertions do not create a "choral mass." To explain this in different words, if students, especially in the feminist theory course, which articulates seemingly contradictory approaches and reveals the "difference within" feminism, do not have any affective experience of working together, feminist theory indeed comes to seem a solo endeavor and feminism either the stance of a singly privileged position or of mutually exclusive positions. The construction of feminist subjectivity includes a sense of shared struggle; the struggle may be easier to convey than the shared experience, particularly within an emphasis on difference. Affective knowing can offer some experience in common, without muting the power of the articulation of difference.

2

Affective learning becomes the nonverbal, unarticulated, experiential "ground" upon which we construct the terms of historical and contemporary debate within feminist theory. And in order to create cumulative opportunities for students to discover for themselves that feminist theory is a process they have already become engaged in, that it informs their choices and explains their conditions, I have come to view art, and more specifically song, as a resource for creating an affective dimension within the classroom which is diverse enough to allow for a wide range of student response. Music becomes a refrain for our readings and discussions of feminist theory as well as a vehicle through which I can demonstrate that the feminist subject loves. I choose one or two songs to play in the classroom each week which emerge from or illustrate particular aspects of theory. Sometimes we comment on the lyrics or the music; more often we do not. But the singing voice enters the classroom, changes the tonal register, offers external confirmation that the theory we are trying to understand emerges from other women's experiences narrated in song, and creates an alternative, for the space of three minutes or so, to cognitive response. I intend the frequent presence of music as this affective "refrain" to have a cumulative power; without saying so, I hope to convey an integration between cognitive and affective modes of apprehension and analysis as a way of enhancing students' appreciation of feminist theory in their lives.

I myself have not been much of a listener to songs in my own life. I have always enjoyed music, especially women's music, but would not consider myself avid or expert. It would not surprise me, however, if students were to conclude the opposite from the way I have brought music into the women's studies classroom. This is what I mean when I say that being positioned as the instructor gives me the opportunity to construct feminist subjectivity, and even my own "best" self, but perhaps with any consistency only within the classroom, my "work" place. Having made this confession, I will list some of the songs I have used and the contexts in which I have located them, and I encourage readers of this essay to extend the list.

"Glad to Be a Woman," written by Elizabeth (Betsy) Rose and sung by Meg Christian, captures the optimism of the women's liberation movement of the 1970s; I use it in opening classes in the theory course, which begins with the history of nineteenth- and twentieth-century feminism (*Meg/Cris at Carnegie Hall*, Olivia Records, 1983). Other music of historical interest is "The Work of the Women," "Bread and Roses," and "Anthem" ("Women unite, liberation is our right"), sung by the Womenfolk Song Project in 1975. I take my cuts from an original recording copyrighted by Educational Activities in Freeport, New York; if you have an older feminist friend who has kept old records, you might find it in her collection. Another song I use early in the course, more readily available, is the energetic, passionate "You Bet (I Sing Love Songs)," by Holly Near (*Imagine My Surprise*, Redwood Records, 1978). In introducing these and other songs, I usually say that they express a feeling or an energy that characterized 1970s feminism for some women.

As we read about and try to understand the numerous forms that feminist theory has taken and points of critique each brings to bear, I identify and play additional songs for students. When we discuss liberal feminism, for example, I play "Free to Be You and Me" and "William's Doll" (as sung by Marlo Thomas and Friends on the 1972 album *Free to Be You and Me*, Bell Records). A few remember hearing these songs as children, and, because some of the students in the course are preparing to become elementary school teachers, "William's Doll" in particular elicits anecdotes about sex-role socialization from their own school experiences or the classroom observations that form part of their Teacher Education coursework.

With the entire range of women's music to choose from in order to illustrate lesbian feminism, it is not difficult to select a few titles.

I choose songs that will reflect the emotional power of lesbian feminism, that will counteract stereotypes about lesbian sexuality, and/or that will offer a response to homophobia. I have used Cris Williamson's "Sweet Darlin' Woman" (*Meg/Cris at Carnegie Hall*), Holly Near's "Imagine My Surprise" and "Fight Back," Alix Dobkin's "Talking Lesbian" (*Lavender Jane*, Dobkin, 1975), and Meg Christian's "Leaping Lesbians" (*Face the Music*, Olivia, 1977). Because we arrive at lesbian feminism fairly early in the theory course and because, unless students have a chance to confront and articulate their own homophobia, they will not be able to move *beyond* affective response to arrive at any cognitive understanding of and appreciation for the contributions of lesbian feminism, bringing women's music into the classroom gives students a different way of "hearing" what lesbian feminist theory has contributed.

When we discuss class issues and socialist feminism, I play "Bread and Roses" or Holly Near's "Mountain Song/Kentucky Woman." In joining class issues with global feminism, I play "More Than a Paycheck," sung by Sweet Honey in the Rock (*"We All . . . Everyone of Us,"* Flying Fish Records, 1983). Nina Simone's "To Be Young, Gifted, and Black" (*Songs of the Poets*, RCA, 1976) captures some of the early strength of black empowerment in the wake of the civil rights movement and, like Rose's "Glad to Be a Woman," is exuberant, conveys a sense of worth to listeners who are black and female, and brings politics into music directed at a specific audience.

Genevieve Taggard wrote in 1935:

> Body sings best when feet beat out the time.
> Translated song, order of bold rhyme, —
> Swing the great stanza on the pavement, — use
> The public street for publishing good news.

All of the music I bring into the feminist theory classroom takes as its premise the close relationship between song and the public street, and I understand this to include the relationship between feminist theory and feminist political action, the way the student can know she is singing feminism when she sees what her feet are doing. I hope, by playing music for students, to "translate" the power of feminist theory into song, and the songs they hear do indeed bring theory into the "order of bold rhyme" and "swing the great stanza on the pavement."

Deepest of all, essential to the song
Is common good, grave motive of the throng;
Well-spring of affirmation in accord
Beneath the chanting utterance, the word.

Not all of the music I use is affirming or boldly challenging in its tone. My colleague, Jennifer Scanlon, introduced me to the lyrics of Sabía, and we both play for our students *"La Andina"* (Andean Woman) and *"Madre Campesina"* (Peasant Mother), offering students English translations as well as copies of the Spanish lyrics (*Live! En Vivo!,* Flying Fish Records, 1989). The somber tone of these songs recognizes class struggle and portrays the material conditions of the lives of women who struggle for survival for themselves and for their children. I write the names of the women Holly Near has memorialized on the board (and students read them aloud) as we listen to her song about the "disappeared" women in Chile and Argentina in *"Hay Una Mujer Desaparecida."* And when we talk about the long-term psychological effects of domestic violence, I play for them Pat Humphries's "Jamie" (*Same Rain,* Moving Forward Music, 1992) and Tracy Chapman's "Behind the Wall" (*Tracy Chapman,* Elektra/Asylum Records, 1988).

One challenge for 1990s feminism, and for the women's studies classroom, is to build coalitions among groups that are keenly aware of their differences and do not necessarily recognize any common language but which do understand the need for collective responses to injustice, discrimination, patriarchy, capitalism, and imperialism. I know that, no matter how persuasive are the theorists we have read and discussed and no matter how clear I ask students to be in explaining the terms of different feminisms, after the course is over some students will still refuse to engage in feminist analysis and, if they identify with any particular theory, will continue to be most comfortable with notions of liberal feminism and individual rights. I bring in music to make one final attempt to convey the spirit of collective action, even for students who remain unmoved by the letter.

In the course's final moments I ask students who have already learned how they differ positionally as well as theoretically to push back their desks and stand in a semicircle, as if members of a chorus. In Introduction to Women's Studies, I invite students to join Holly Near in "Singing for Our Lives." In the feminist theory course, I choose Pat Humphries's a cappella "Never Turning Back"; the lyrics of this song encourage students to "walk proudly," "sing loudly," "love boldly," "reach across our borders," and "keep on moving forward."

As the verses progress, students sing more loudly. Last spring, when the students stood to sing, their bodies moved. When they became aware that they had an audience outside the classroom, they sang with particular energy, and when their song ended so did their introduction to feminist theory.

Before they began I had asked them to think, while they sang, about the way each verse of the song addresses a particular aspect of feminist theory, and, whether or not they did so, I had constructed the possibility of bringing together affective and cognitive meaning. What I hoped they learned, although I did not say so, is that feminist movement is a form of song—it is political poetry—and that, whatever the differences that proudly divide feminist (re)sisters, in that pride and collective recognition of difference there is also the core of a reconstructive love: for self, for women, for workers, for "others," for politics.

I cannot assess whether feminism dawned in that classroom, but singing happened, and bodies of different class, racial, national, regional, and sexual orientations moved in a group. That moment is an example of "what I mean" in the classroom, or what it means to construct feminist subjectivity: predictably free of external interruptions other than the distractions each of us brings to the space or the conflicts we create for one another, anyone there is free to construct a sense of collective struggle across differences, and, no doubt because I am assigned to instruct the class, I take the initiative to seize that freedom.

> Song is not static—joy becomes a dance.
> In step, vast unison, in step advance.
> This is the life of song: that it mean, and move,
> And state the massive power of our love.

Genevieve Taggard was a socialist, a protester, and a poet who wrote about women's lives. In "Definition of Song" she becomes a feminist teacher. Perhaps I have brought song into the theory classroom to make certain that theory also "mean, and move,/And state the massive power of our love."

Marjorie Pryse is Professor of Women's Studies at State University of New York College at Plattsburgh. She is co-editor, with Judith Fetterley, of American Women Regionalists, 1850–1910: A Norton Anthology *(1992).*

Women's Studies and Science

Anne Fausto-Sterling   **Winter 1980**

The following paper was originally a talk delivered at the Research Conference on Educational Environments and the Undergraduate Woman, sponsored by HERS, New England, at Wellesley College last year [1979].

One manifestation of the rigid division of sex roles in our society is the fact that relatively few women are scientists, especially physical scientists and mathematicians. My interest in addressing the subject of women and the science curriculum stems from my desire to change this situation, to allow equal access of men and women into science. The college curriculum is only a small part of this problem. The different socialization of girls and boys, especially with regard to mathematical ability and career aspirations, starts early. We each have our own personal stories to tell in this regard. Mine is from the fifth grade when I had my "doctor-nurse" argument with my teacher. He insisted that I had not meant it when I had said I wanted to be a doctor, that I really intended to become a nurse. In the process of arguing indignantly with him, I learned a great deal about the outside world. The point, of course, is that many things shape the development of boys and girls well before they enter college. These include early socialization, the lack or presence of female role models, and the role of peer pressure.[1]

In the past decade, many people have tried to root out from textbooks those elements which make it particularly difficult for women to relate to the curricular material. A great deal of important and necessary work has been done, some of which deals with the science curriculum. In mathematics and the physical sciences there are several general problems. The first is the omission of women from the textbooks. Consider, for example, a physics textbook which takes its workbook examples from problems observed on a construction site. Usually there are no women construction workers dropping their two-pound hammers from a height of thirty feet in order to find out the force with which they will hit the ground. A subcategory of the use of sex-stereotyped problems is the introduction of the incompetent female who needs male help to figure out the answer. The fact is that problems are usually designed around situations more familiar to men—working on a construction site, throwing a beer can out of a moving car, and so forth. Textbooks could contain examples and problems which come from many areas of our culture, including those with which women are more familiar. For example, what female doesn't know how carefully milk has to be watched so that it doesn't boil over? What physical and chemical lessons can be drawn from this observation?

In addition to the problem of "invisibility," we must still be on the lookout for the use of curricular material which is degrading or offensive to women. An example of this is a handout used in a mathematics class at Brown University in the very recent past. The instructor believed that students would find it clever and amusing. It is a table full of mathematical puns about one pretty little Polly Nomial. The gist of the story is that little Polly ventures out on her own, with the result that she is raped by a vulgar fraction named Curly Pi who approaches her with his power series extrapolated. (Although the word "rape" is never used, the interpretation is unmistakable.) The moral of the fable is that little Polly Nomial should never have wandered out in the first place. Needless to say, some of the women in the classroom where this handout was used felt angry, frightened, and hurt.

I believe that changing the design of textbooks so that they better reflect the multiple aspects of our culture is very important. However, there is an aspect to this approach which makes me uncomfortable. Suppose you have an old tumble-down brick wall in your yard. The first thing you want to do is to try chipping out the rotten cement and repairing the wall with freshly mixed concrete. This may in fact solve your problem, but whether or not it does depends on how rotten the wall is. At some point it may be necessary to ask if it isn't better to tear down the entire structure and build a new wall. We have come through a period in our examination of the curriculum of chipping out the rotten cement (or at least pointing to its presence), and we must now enter into a period in which we stop looking at the cement chips and ask some basic questions about the whole wall. I will address three topics: the hierarchical structure of science itself and science teaching in particular; a cultural view of scientific work as solitary rather than communal; and the emphasis in modern science on analysis, i.e., breaking the whole into its component parts, rather than on synthesis, the ability to abstract a whole from the many pieces.

Modern science is hierarchical in structure.[2] Generally research is done by a scientist who obtains a grant in her or his name and then employs a variety of underlings—postdoctoral fellows, technicians, dishwashers, and others—to aid in the work. Our society is in general hierarchical, and women are found more frequently on the lower rungs of the ladder. This is as true in a research laboratory as in the Senate. I would like to raise the following question (for which I have no clear answer): would more women participate in science if it were not so organized? Hierarchy in the classroom translates into the expert who stands before the class and delivers lectures, offering as revealed knowledge the "facts" and "laws" of science.

The format of the science classroom is quite different from that of the literature classroom (which for one thing has many more women in it). It is typical at Brown, for instance, that science teachers lecture through the pre–final-examination reading period, rather than assign reading intended to give an overview to the course. This happens much less frequently in humanities courses. In literature courses the raw material—novels, short stories, drama, poetry—is made directly available to the student, who is encouraged to read and judge it directly for herself or himself. This could be true of science teaching as well. Courses could be conducted by discussion and teacher-guided examination of the issues and processes of science (the so-called "facts" being learned as a side benefit). The expert with revealed knowledge could become an especially well-informed co-explorer with the students. I suggest that this is an avenue which the science curriculum will have to take in order to change the sex composition of the students who study it.

One way to break out of the fact-teaching syndrome is to discuss the historical development of a concept which we now hold to be "the truth." For instance, in one of my courses I teach students what biologists currently understand of the cellular events involved in fertilization. I could do this in either of two ways: (1) I could present the modern "facts" and leave it at that, or (2) I could offer some historical insight into the evolution of ideas about fertilization. The latter approach involves teaching about a scientific process, while the former simply involves stuffing information into the students' heads. Similar approaches to teaching chemistry, physics, and mathematics are surely possible.

If hierarchy forms one end of a spectrum, then communally planned and shared endeavor forms the other. Consider the following reflection from the Nobel Prize–winning physicist Yukawa: "At middle school I was relatively fond of mathematics, the reason being that one could solve a problem by oneself, without relation to other people."[3] If, in fact, this perception about mathematics, as currently taught, is correct, then it might not be surprising that some basic emotional needs felt by a majority of women are not met by the study of mathematics. We are all aware of the stereotype of the maladjusted computer freak who works late into the night, brilliant but lonely, and most of us do not envision that as a way to live.

Here again, we need to ask whether mathematics must be the sort of individualistic field that it is today. In my upper-level experimental embryology course, by contrast, students work cooperatively on their take-home exams, and the results are often quite exciting. Why, in the teaching of mathematics, can't problems be solved by teams of students? Why can't cooperative endeavor rather than individual prowess be stressed? There is no reason except that our entire educational system is geared to emphasize the successful individual and to weed out the "failures." Certainly the lack of emphasis on personal interactions in the sciences plays an important role in keeping women out of the area. And the remedy for this aspect of the problem is nothing short of a revolution in our views about education.

In an article entitled "Feminine Intellect and the Demands of Science,"[4] Eleanor Maccoby discusses the differences and similarities in intellectual skills between women and men. This article, written by a person whose authority is widely accepted, even by feminists, contains some remarkable assumptions about the nature of scientific thinking and work. Here I will deal with one of them—the question of analytical thinking. The summary of the article states that women "think less analytically [than men] and so are less original." What is striking is the equation of the words "analytical" and "original," an equation which I think accurately reflects the views of most American scientists. In the body of the paper, Maccoby quotes the 1963 studies of Kagan and his associates, who gave boys and girls an array of pictures showing people and objects in various situations. Each child was asked to put together the pictures that seemed to belong in the same group. Girls were more likely to group, for example, a picture of a doctor, a nurse, and a wheelchair, because they are all associated with the care of sick people. Boys were more likely to group pictures which had some detail in common—for example, all pictures of people who had their right arm raised. Kagan named the former grouping "functional," and the latter "analytical." I ask you to decide which was more original, and which made more sense. It is a complicated question to answer, but it is certainly not at all obvious that the abilities of the girls made them less suited to scientific work than those of the boys.

If, instead of using Kagan's term "functional," we suggest that the girls he tested had a greater ability to synthesize a whole from existing parts, the entire subject appears in a new light. Yukawa, the physicist mentioned earlier, in discussing current trends of modern physics, remarked: "I do not deny that further . . . abstraction on our part may be necessary when we go deeper . . . in pursuit of nature. Nevertheless, I feel very uneasy about the fact that this one-sided trend to abstraction lacks something which is very important to creative thinking. However far we go away from the world of daily life, abstraction cannot work by itself, but has to be accompanied by intuition or imagination."[5] I am suggesting, by drawing together these rather different sources, that the fact that modern science, particularly in North America, places greater value on analytic than on synthetic skills needs to be questioned. Without entering into the argument of why girls and boys develop different skills, we can certainly see that the structure of science gives greater value to male-held abilities. What we need *not* do is accept this view of science as axiomatic.

What does all of this have to do with women's studies? The first decade of women's studies has been more or less in the "cement-patching" mode. In examining a survey of several hundred women's studies courses across the country, I found only one which dealt exclusively with scientific subject matter—a course on female biology. This is not surprising since it has never been clear to anyone of what a course on female linear algebra would consist. In general in the past ten years women's studies has served the purpose of providing female students with a place to feel comfortable and a way to fill in the obvious gaps in knowledge discovered in our primarily male institutions. However, with at least ten years of experience behind us, and a whole new generation of intellectuals being trained in broad interdisciplinary skills, women's studies is beginning to expand the borders of human knowledge to such an extent that in certain areas our old constructs must be abandoned. I can describe this on a personal level by indicating the connections I have made in discussing my interest in biological aspects of the development of gender identity with associates studying semiotics, or the theories of the French structuralists, such as Lacan. Women's studies of the coming decade will mean a breakdown of the traditional divisions and categories of knowledge. In the sciences, it can mean that we begin to question the basic cultural assumptions about what science is and how it should be pursued.

I've covered a lot of ground in this discussion. Let me summarize my train of thought and offer a conclusion. It is part of my moral framework that men and women should participate equally in all aspects of our society. In our culture scientific endeavors are primarily carried out by men, and the question I have addressed is what can be done to change that. Leaving aside the well-documented socialization process that shapes girls into women well before they enter college, I have narrowed the question in order to look at what might be different in our college science curriculum. The answers that I came up with have surprised me because they expanded from what I thought was a limited narrow question into rather global answers. I have ended up arguing that we must call into question the basic function of our educational system; change the hierarchical structure of science itself, turning it into a more communal endeavor; and critically examine some of the basic philosophical assumptions of Western science.

My conclusions may seem overwhelming and discouraging, but I don't feel that way. It might be useful to end by sharing the broad context out of which my thinking grows. I do not see the elimination of constrictive sex roles as something which can happen separately from a large number of other very profound and far-reaching changes in our society. When I think about women and science, I have to fight a strong feeling that in order to tackle the topic I must first write a treatise on world revolution (something I am *not* about to do).

In order to break out of the dilemma, I have to remember what I have come to understand—through many years of political activity—about how individuals effect social change. Our society is composed of intricate interconnecting networks. A particular social structure has many contributing factors, some of which we view as root causes, and some of which we understand to be superstructures. However, root causes and superstructures feed back and forth between one another in such a complex fashion that one is left with the impression that everything must be changed simultaneously. Let me give a concrete example: women's struggle to earn equal pay for equal work. The root cause for an unequal pay system lies in the profit motive: the owners of capital will pay the least amount possible in order to produce. The superstructure supporting and supported by this system includes all of the stereotypes about women and sex roles. Stereotypes provide justification for paying women less; they also keep women and men divided, making it less likely that they will struggle in a united way against the profit motive which is causing them to be underpaid in the first place. How does one break into this cycle? The answer is: in many ways and at many different levels. One way, for example, is through the fight for the Equal Rights Amendment, which will provide important tools for reaching the goal of equal pay. There is also the struggle to change the ideology of sexism—to rewrite the textbooks with boy nurses and girl doctors. And, of course, there are the more conventional kinds of class struggle—unionization drives, for example. In order to achieve equal pay for equal work, many issues must be attacked, on many levels, often all at once. Each of us, as a participant in political struggle, must choose where we can be most effective. Even if it is in only a small part of the arena, we can do whatever is individually possible, understanding how it fits into the larger picture.

During certain historical periods change happens slowly. It occurs through the daily accumulation of modifications made by limited struggles. These small changes, however, set the stage for periods when larger qualitative shifts are possible. Right now our struggles consist of redesigning a course here; fighting to hire a female scientist there; encouraging more women to think more broadly and to respect the skills they already have, while developing the ones they don't yet have. But out of these small changes will grow larger ones. And if the results are as widespread as some of us wish, they will be part of a revolutionary change in our way of viewing the world.

NOTES

A number of the ideas in this paper were stimulated and developed through discussions with Elizabeth Weed, Christina Crosby, and Karen Romer, and by a talk given at Brown by Walter Massey.

1. A recent article by L. Fox, D. Tobin, and L. Brody, "Sex-Role Socialization and Achievement in Mathematics," in M. Wittig and A. Petersen, eds., *Sex-Related Differences in Cognitive Functioning* (New York: Academic Press, 1979), considers how a number of these factors relate to women's ability to pursue careers in mathematics and the physical sciences.
2. See, for example, J. R. Cole and S. Cole, *Social Stratification in Science* (Chicago: University of Chicago Press, 1973).
3. H. Yukawa, *Creativity and Intuition: A Physicist Looks at East and West* (Tokyo: Kodansha International Ltd., 1973).
4. Eleanor Maccoby, "Feminine Intellect and the Demands of Science," *Impact of Science on Society* 20 (1970): 13–28.
5. Yukawa, *Creativity and Intuition.*

GENERAL BIBLIOGRAPHY

There is a brand-new, excellently thorough bibliography about women in science, from which I have taken most of the background reading I did while developing these ideas:

Henifin, M. "Bibliography: Women, Science and Health." In R. Hubbard, M. Henifin, and B. Fried, eds., *Women Look at Biology Looking at Women.* New York: Schenkman, 1979.

Anne Fausto-Sterling is Associate Professor of Biology and Medicine at Brown University.

Reconceptualizing Introductory Sociology: Two Course Outlines

Nona Y. Glazer   *Fall/Winter 1986*

Many scholars and educators who are involved in the curriculum integration movement seem to assume that "feminist scholarship" is a nonproblematic concept. They assume, too, that the theoretical differences between various feminist approaches can be resolved through the use of an eclectic method that draws equally and fairly from each approach.[1] I challenge both assumptions, arguing for the use of a unified theoretical perspective rather than an eclectic one. Furthermore, I argue specifically for the use of a socialist-feminist perspective and against the use of a liberal pluralist approach; for I believe that without a coherent and critical framework, the criticisms of both radical and socialist-feminist scholarship will be co-opted or dampened by the dominant liberal outlook that is so prevalent in higher education in the United States.

Feminist scholarship is neither a homogeneous body of knowledge nor one whose theoretical conflicts can be treated as of only minor significance for either political understanding or political action.[2] A reminder of the diverse historical roots of each feminist approach in the women's movement may be helpful.[3] These approaches may be roughly categorized as *liberal, radical,* and *socialist.* The women's rights movement of the National Organization for Women, the drive for the Equal Rights Amendment, and presidential panels and commissions are the sources for various types of contemporary *liberal feminist* analysis. Liberal feminist scholars, taking capitalism and the U.S. political system for granted as inevitable or desirable, usually focus on ways in which women are denied access to opportunities in capitalist society that are open to men. Liberal feminism examines the legal, organizational, and psychological status and roles (including responsibilities the women, but not men, carry) that bar women from the formal and informal access that gives men their chance at occupational and political success.

The radical liberation movement, with roots in both liberal political activity and the New Left, is the source of *radical feminism's* analysis and its variations. Radical feminist analysis views male domination as the source of women's oppression and examines the many ways that men subordinate women through male control of language, female sexuality, female reproduction, the organization of knowledge, and other cultural elements. The emphasis is on understanding the cultural content of male control of women's sexuality, childbearing capabilities, self-conception, relations with other women, and women's culture. Hence, there is a concern with language, meaning, myth, text, song, spirituality, philosophy; furthermore, there is a critique and a rejection of the organization of contemporary daily life. Radical feminists reject access to what men have, preferring to aim for women's control over their own lives and for a social world rebuilt to recognize femaleness, female culture, and female values as legitimate. Ultimately, radical feminism looks to a reconstruction of the meaning of gender, to the disappearance of male and female as categories used to oppress. Radical feminists also often reject any reliance on the state to change the condition of women, seeing the state as just one more instance of a male-dominated domain.

The Marxist-feminist/socialist-feminist liberation movement, with roots in both the Old and the New Left, was the major source for *socialist-feminist* analysis. This approach starts with a premise that it is the organization of the political economy that dominates social relationships and social existence today. Ideology and social relations of class, race, and gender are the focus of study, to be understood historically. Capitalism, the capitalist state, and male domination are exploitative of most men as well as women. Sometimes, however, the state may be used by women to reduce the impact of exploitation and oppression. There is a concern with women's work both in the home (as housekeeper, wife, and mother) and in the workplace outside it, and with the ways in which capitalism itself is changing and, in turn, changes daily life. Class struggle and class conflict, how ideologies are used by ruling classes to justify their subordination of other classes, and how women of different classes accept justifying ideologies are all of central concern.

The breakdown of feminist theories into three major categories necessarily obscures subtle differences within each category and may even leave out some branches of feminist thought, though probably none that has developed a singular theoretical analysis.[4] Indeed, some liberal feminists may find the categories puzzling or resent the view that there are distinct and contradictory alternatives rather than an overarching eclectic approach. However, both radical feminists and Marxist/socialist feminists have recognized these three categories since the beginnings of the current women's movement, though many variations have developed within each category since the late 1960s. Thus, some liberal feminists have grown increasingly critical of capitalism; some radical feminists have moved toward the analysis of texts, and others toward intensified explorations of sexuality; some socialist feminists have built dual systems theories, giving patriarchy and capitalism equal weight in women's oppression, while others have treated patriarchy as an historically specific ideological component, second to the power of capitalism in women's oppression. In spite of variations, an awareness of the three main categories of feminist scholarship points to some fundamental and unresolvable theoretical and political differences that make "curriculum integration" a project calling for much reflection about *what* scholarship is to be integrated, and what, if any, reinterpretations must be made of social factors in addition to gender.

I will present two course outlines, each of which relies on women's studies scholarship. The contrast between them is in their approaches to theory. The first outline takes a liberal pluralist view of knowledge, an eclectic approach to theory. This approach to knowledge means, ultimately, a liberal feminist understanding of women, society, and social change. The second outline takes a different view of knowledge. It begins with the assumption that it is necessary to select a single, unified, theoretical perspective to guide our understanding. Most important, the approaches differ in their views of theory. The eclectic approach willingly combines diverse explanations, using them simultaneously, and overlooking the fact that they rest on diverse and incompatible paradigms. This eclectic approach created two illusions: that established social science is being "rethought' and that eclecticism has great tolerance for theoretical and political analyses of all persuasions. Actually, this is what Marcuse calls "repressive tolerance." Since the eclectic approach presents research findings outside the theoretical context within which the research was developed, all manner of critical views of social life, especially of capitalism, are lost.

The focus here is on sociology. However, the issues are important to any social scientist who thinks that bringing feminist scholarship into established courses will hasten women's emancipation.[5]

The Limits of Liberal Pluralist Knowing

Every theory or mini-explanation rests on a paradigm, a set of interdependent assumptions underlying the content of the theory. These assumptions concern the units to be studied, the processes by which stability and change occur, what human nature is, and the role of people as agents of social change. They also include understandings of the relation between society and the individual, and answers to the question of whether social science can establish universal, panhistorical theories or only ones that are historical and specific to particular societies.

I believe that the socialist-feminist paradigm gives us the most adequate beginnings for curriculum integration. It combines a focus on subordination as defined by gender with a recognition of the interconnections between gender and other forms of subordination—by class, race, sexuality, age—rather than seeing each as autonomous, and it takes an historical approach to gender issues rather than searching for universal generalizations. Very important for feminism and other social movements for the oppressed, the socialist-feminist paradigm posits human action as critical for social change.[6]

In contrast, the liberal pluralist approach to knowledge has weaknesses that do not make it desirable as a framework for curriculum integration, including the following:

1. The dominant paradigms of the "established curriculum" (the term I use to refer to typical curricula outside of women's studies courses) are compatible with only one version of feminism, the liberal feminist approach. For example, established sociology curricula share with liberal feminism important elements of a view of social life. Courses are infused with assumptions about the "naturalness" of social life as presently organized, the desirability of order and consensus in contrast to struggle and conflict, the relative autonomy of social institutions, and the critical importance of impersonal social forces in shaping social life. Individual opportunity and rights are conceptualized as more important than the rights of collectivities of people, e.g., than of classes, race and ethnic groups, women, or workers. Human nature is seen either as competitive or—even when human behavior is viewed as essentially plastic—at least not incompatible with competitive behavior. Social rewards are assumed to be distributed on the basis of merit, though admittedly, some people start with different advantages than others by an accident of birth or because of prejudice or poverty. Moreover, though liberal feminism certainly questions such advantages when they manifest themselves as sex discrimination, it criticizes other forms of domination only mildly. It takes a fundamentally benign view of capitalism, just as most sociological analyses do. Some liberal feminists, no doubt, would like to eliminate the harsher aspects of capitalism. For example, liberal feminists may support retraining programs for women who lose jobs because of plant closure, and they support "comparable worth." Also, many lib-

eral feminists may deplore the cutbacks in social welfare entitlements that affect women especially. Nonetheless, liberal feminists support capitalism, implicitly accepting vast class differences in access to political power, status, and material benefits.

2. Liberal feminists adopt an eclectic approach to curriculum integration rather than explicitly selecting a single theoretical perspective. An eclectic pluralist approach draws upon all varieties of theories to explain phenomena that are themselves conceptualized as in or of different domains. The pluralist approach to knowledge assumes that competing theories reflect not just alternative perspectives but the fact that social life is divisible into different domains. Each domain (e.g., the gender division of labor, occupational structures, fertility, health care systems) is conceived as autonomous or semi-autonomous or subject to study "as if" that were the case. Given an assumed loose connection between domains, it makes perfect sense to approach each domain with a distinctly different paradigm and to ignore contradictions between those paradigms. In this way, for example, a radical feminist analysis of sexual harassment can be accepted, *in part*, as an approach to one aspect of a "domain." However, its fundamental challenges are defused by its being treated as theoretically adequate for only that domain of sexuality. Similarly, some socialist-feminist analyses can be included in a liberal pluralist approach; for example, an analysis of women's problems in paid and unpaid work can be seen as germane to structural aspects of occupations. However, a socialist-feminist analytical approach is often used side by side with a "social roles" approach without any appreciation of how the assumptions underlying these contradict each other. Socialist feminism is thus defused as a major critique of capitalist society by being presented as relevant to only a specific aspect of employment. Radical feminism and socialist feminism are reduced to being two among many diverse ways of thinking about the domains of social life rather than being confronted seriously as theoretical challenges to liberal social philosophy and liberal feminism.

What does this mean? It means that liberal feminist thought can be used to reshape the curriculum while giving the appearance that "all views are being used." It means that it is easy to depoliticize the contributions of both radical feminism and socialist feminism.

3. The commonality among feminist scholars is a commitment to female emancipation gained by individual and/or collective efforts. However, the visions of emancipation differ markedly from one approach to another. The three major feminist perspectives make quite different assumptions, which direct their adherents to quite dif-

ferent questions about women's oppression. For example, the view that people are inherently self-aggrandizing and selfish leads to a different interpretation of how human action can reshape society than does a view of people as highly malleable or inherently caring. The first might especially encourage individual endeavors, and the second might emphasize collective action. The assumptions of the three feminist perspectives cannot be simply placed side by side, that is, be "integrated," because they contradict each other. Hence, one approach must be chosen to transform an introductory sociology course in a coherent way.

4. The commitment to female emancipation conflicts with most sociological theories of the establishment, and at the macro level, fits only with the Marxist political economy perspective. This is the only one committed explicitly to a struggle against social oppression. The Marxist political economy paradigm, however, is likely to be absent from most established curricula because it challenges the most powerful of American social relations, capitalism. . . .

Two outlines follow, illustrating the difference between taking a traditional liberal pluralist approach to knowledge and curriculum change and taking a Marxist political economy approach. Each outline represents only a fraction of a course, a section emphasizing unpaid work. Each includes some materials on paid work for contrasting analyses. Both outlines use feminist scholarship to alter the traditional sociological presentation of *work*. The first accepts the basic liberal perspective of sociology, placing feminist scholarship within that framework and taking an eclectic approach. In the second, a critical view is taken of the cultural and political domination of capitalism, not only of male domination. This leads to reconceptualizing *work* itself and to asking questions about gender relations, racism, and capitalism. This reconceptualization derives from a rich Marxist-feminist scholarship that has developed over the last fifteen years and also from my own research about women's unpaid work outside the household. Research from other perspectives is used but is also reinterpreted within a socialist-feminist analysis.

Course Outline 1: Liberal Pluralist Approach

In the first outline, the course is organized around the traditional sociological view of society as divided into a set of "institutions." Typically, introductory sociology books devote a half or more of the text to exploring, one by one, each of these institutions. [For the course outlines, see the complete text of this essay in *Women's Studies Quarterly* 14, nos. 3 & 4 (Fall/Winter 1986).]

The outline uses a liberal pluralist approach to feminist scholarship. Feminist scholarship has changed the curriculum by recognizing that women's unpaid labor appears in all social institutions. However, the outline maintains the established sociological perspective. Social institutions are treated as discrete entities. Most sociologists consider these institutions to be *interdependent,* sometimes overlapping and shaped in various ways by each other. Yet, both introductory sociology textbooks and the traditional organizational format of sociology curricula divide society into these domains. As I have noted earlier, this supports the view of society as composed of autonomous or semi-autonomous domains. In turn, this implies that political action may change one without others, e.g., that sexism can be eliminated while racism is left untouched. Each institution appears equally important in this approach to curriculum integration in spite of substantial revisions to recognize women's experiences.

Contrast this with a curriculum that does not recognize feminist scholarship. If the concept of women's unpaid work were recognized, it would likely be limited to "The Family." Even women's paid work would probably not appear in "The Economy," since before feminist scholarship, the studies rarely researched women's paid employment. Men's employment experiences were emphasized, or the economy was treated as gender-blind. Although some of women's work as volunteers might have been considered under "The Polity," recognition of the varieties of unpaid female labor did not come about until the emergence of feminist scholarship in the 1960s.

This first outline does not include a bibliography because, given the liberal pluralist approach to knowledge, most of the bibliography presented in the second outline could be used. My main purpose is, of course, to emphasize how the conceptualization of the two outlines differs. The second outline reorganizes thinking about women's work in such a way as to transform the very questions asked and that is what the transformation of curriculum through feminist scholarship ought to entail. . . .

Course Outline 2: A Socialist-Feminist Approach

In the second outline, I use a Marxist political economy framework as a means of integrating feminist scholarship. I do use research from each of the feminist perspectives, but I locate it *within* a Marxist framework. I do not present a bit of each within its own framework, as in the interests of a pluralist tradition of knowledge. Instead, I reinterpret studies of women's work that use such concepts as social role, role overload, changing roles. What I would not do is present the various scholarships as a cafeteria offering, nor would I pretend that each should be allowed to "stand on its own." A virtue of the second outline is that it approaches unpaid work by redefining topics. These redefinitions provide a specific view of how such phenomena as the family, the economy, politics, human action, and personal troubles are related to each other. The outline as presented below would serve best as a guide to instructors.

Certain issues commonly discussed as sociology of work are left out deliberately: these include "worker satisfaction" as an interest of managers in their attempts to increase productivity; the informal as contrasted to the formal structure of the work situation; changes in the work process from a management perspective. Studies of these and other topics could be integrated into a course to demonstrate the class-based similarities that may cross gender. . . .

Summary

I urge feminists to consider the importance of presenting a unified theoretical understanding of any topic that we want to *transform* by using feminist scholarship. I have discussed why I think such a unified understanding is crucial for maintaining a critical feminist perspective, and I have pointed out ways in which a liberal pluralist view of knowledge can depoliticize feminism. I believe that it is important to give students an interpretation of the social world that supports their being politically active. Students in my classes frequently ask: "So what do we do?" I do not suggest they join this or that organization, or in other ways tell them what to do. Instead, I advise them to examine the assumptions underlying their interpretations of the social world: What are they assuming about human nature, about human action, about how social relations change, and so on? I suggest that they evaluate the reasonableness of the assumptions that they make explicit. Then, I suggest that they work out what their assumptions imply about an ideal social world, and, once they have ascertained the implications, decide whether they still accept their assumptions. For all of us, these tasks become more possible with a unified and critical theoretical view than with a *potpourri* of disconnected, contradictory explanations.

NOTES

1. This viewpoint is demonstrated in a recent journal issue devoted entirely to curriculum integration. Only one among the many articles (including those by leaders of the movement) acknowledges differing viewpoints/

theories among feminists. Marian Lowe and Margaret Lowe Benston note that radical feminist and Marxist/socialist-feminist scholarship have been the most challenging to mainstream scholarship, and the least acceptable in the liberal academy. See Lowe and Benston, "The Uneasy Alliance of Feminism and Academia," *Women's Studies International Forum* 7, no. 3 (1984): 177–83.

2. For an expanded treatment of each of the three major frameworks covered in the discussion . . . and of the theoretical and practical implications of their use in curriculum integration, see forthcoming, Nona Y. Glazer, "What Does It Mean to Integrate the Curriculum? Issues for a Feminist Sociology," *Signs* 12, no. 1 (Fall 1986).

3. For discussions of the three categories of feminism as distinct approaches beginning in the late 1960s, see Judith Hole and Ellen Levine, *Rebirth of Feminism* (New York: Quadrangle, 1971); Maren Lockwood Carden, *The New Feminist Movement* (New York: Russell Sage, 1974); Sara Evans, *Personal Politics* (New York: Vintage Books, 1979).

4. For excellent discussions of the philosophical assumptions of each of the three major frameworks and some of their variants, see Alison M. Jagger, *Feminist Politics and Human Nature* (Totowa, N.J.: Rowman & Allanheld, 1983).

5. My argument for theoretical coherence and against "eclecticism" is specific to attempts to integrate feminist scholarship in introductory courses. It does not apply to women's studies courses, which I believe to be the appropriate arenas for our theoretical debates. In teaching women's studies courses, it is possible to discuss the three major categories of feminism in detail. One does not pretend, however, that such presentations provide an "integrated" view of gender. Curriculum transformation does not simply entail adding material on women to the curriculum; rather, it entails changing established curricula that are permeated by assumptions that go well beyond ones about gender and determining how to make use of feminist scholarship, given its various and competing assumptions.

6. Radical feminism, too, is threatened by the liberal pluralist approach to knowledge. I think that the liberal pluralist approach is limited by its idealist philosophical conception of social life, its often ahistorical view of women and men, its romanticizing of historically determined female characteristics (that are common, unfortunately, among subordinated peoples), and its distrust of rational theorizing.

Nona Y. Glazer is Professor of Sociology and Women's Studies at Portland State University. This essay was developed originally when the author was a National Fellow in the Faculty Development Program, supported by the Andrew W. Mellon Foundation at Wellesley College Center for Research on Women. Portions of the essay were presented at the Northwest Women's Studies Association Conference, Bellingham, Washington, April 1984.

We Are Also Your Sisters: The Development of Women's Studies in Religion

Judith Plaskow   *Spring/Summer 1993*

Women's studies in religion has been a bit of a stepsister within women's studies. The suspicion on the part of many intellectuals in our secular culture that anyone interested in religion must be a reactionary has served to marginalize and delegitimize feminist work in religion. While feminists can study and make use of other patriarchal ideologies, such as psychoanalytic theory, without automatically being seen as in collusion with them, the same trust — and interest — has not been extended to feminist work in religion. This suspicion of the field is unfortunate for at least three reasons: (1) religion plays a key role in the dynamics of women's oppression (as well as women's liberation), and understanding these dynamics is a central task of women's studies; (2) women's studies in religion is a well-established, vital, and exciting field; and (3) to a greater extent than is the case with many other areas of women's studies, feminists in religion maintain strong links to women outside the academy.

Probably few people in women's studies would disagree with the first contention — that religion plays a central role in the dynamics of women's oppression. Even restricting ourselves to the contemporary scene, one has only to look at the abortion debate in the United States, the impact on women of the rise of the religious right all over the world, or the long arm of the Catholic church's opposition to birth control, to see the power of religion in enforcing traditional roles. The messages the world's religions have sent women are for the most part entirely in line with dominant cultural injunctions. But religion adds to these injunctions the message that they are God's commands or part of the structure of the universe. It thus serves as an important vehicle for the internalization of cultural codes and at the same time makes them more rigid and difficult to alter.

It seems that for many people in women's studies, the negative impact of religion on women constitutes a good reason to simply dismiss it. But for feminists in religious studies, awareness of this

impact—which, in any event, is only one aspect of religion—
represents not the end of study but the beginning. It becomes important not only to understand the complexities of the relationship
between religion and culture but to *change* the world's religions and
the ways they function in women's lives.

Connections between feminist critique and social change have
been evident in all areas of women's studies in religion from its beginnings. In the classroom, feminist teachers of religion have helped
students to understand the ways religious attitudes affect them,
whether or not students perceive themselves as influenced by
religion. Seeing the direct line, for example, between the church
fathers' attitudes toward women's sexuality and the treatment of rape
victims in U.S. courtrooms gives students new insights into the dynamics of sexism. But women's studies in religion does not simply
set out these connections. It also gives students the critical tools for
questioning destructive religious ideologies and rooting out their
damaging effects in the students' own lives. The many women who
have learned to accept abuse as part of their God-given fate, for example, need specific tools for reinterpreting the Bible in ways that affirm their right to self-determination, tools that women's studies in
religion can offer (Thistlethwaite 1985). Moreover, feminist critiques
of religion can offer women positive understandings of spirituality
and new ways of looking at the sacred, the world, and themselves from
a woman-centered perspective. It can help women claim the power
to name themselves and their own experiences in the context of a
political/religious discourse rooted in visions of a new social order.

In terms of scholarly work, feminist critiques of religion always
have contained within them visions of religious change. When
Valerie Saiving argued in 1960 that all theology had been written
from the perspective of male experience, she held out the hope that
a theology rooted in female experience would offer a different understanding of central religious teachings. When in 1968, Mary Daly
published *The Church and the Second Sex,* the second wave's first book-
length critique of religious sexism, she concluded with "modest
proposals" for the eradication of sexual discrimination in the Catholic church. When in *Beyond God the Father* (1973) Daly completely
repudiated the church and her former optimism, she left Christianity,
but not religion, behind. Rosemary Radford Ruether's important in-
dictment of the dualisms embedded in the Christian worldview
(1972) envisioned women as the spokespersons for a "new humanity arising out of the reconciliation of spirit and body."

This combination of critique and alternative vision is also evident in professional organizing in the field. In 1971 a women's caucus was established by women in the American Academy of Religion (AAR) and the Society for Biblical Literature (SBL), and in 1972 the AAR Working Group on Women and Religion met for the first time. The many women and men who crowded into a small room to hear Mary Daly read "Theology After the Demise of God the Father" (Plaskow and Romero 1974) shared a profound sense of excitement, a conviction that we would end up revolutionizing the study of religion and religion itself. By 1975 the Women and Religion Section was upgraded from a working group to a major program unit of the AAR, and was drawing large crowds to its sessions. Seventeen years later, there is also a flourishing Women in the Biblical World program unit in the SBL, and the AAR Section not only remains well attended but has generated a number of new working groups that are exploring emerging areas in the field.

It would be an exaggeration to say that these developments in women's studies in religion have permeated or transformed the discipline, but AAR meetings provide ample evidence that they have had a significant impact. While the Women and Religion Section was founded partly to create a space on the program for women's studies work, papers in this area are now sufficiently common that it is frequently necessary to choose among several being given at the same time. Moreover, the fact that these papers are integrated throughout the program means that scholars in religion who would never come to the women's section are being exposed to work in women's studies in the context of their own disciplinary groups. This "mainstreaming" has freed the women's section to remain at the cutting edge, setting up interdisciplinary panels or panels on feminist issues that do not fit within the boundaries of established subdisciplines.

From Critique to Construction

The work in women's studies in religion produced in this context over this period has been enormously rich, complex, and diverse, but it is also possible to discern within the diversity certain patterns of development. Like feminist work in many disciplines, feminist studies in religion have gone through three stages that are at once consecutive and overlapping. Initially, the preponderance of works in the field focused on the analysis and critique of male texts, institutions, and traditions. Then, without critical work being abandoned, there was a gradual shift toward recovering women's history within and outside of patriarchal traditions. Most recently, there has been a burgeoning of constructive writing focusing on the reform or transformation of existing traditions and the creation of new ones. The first step on the path toward feminist analysis of religion consisted simply in *noticing* the persistent misogyny of prominent religious authors. When I was a graduate student in the late 1960s, there was scarcely a theologian we studied who did not have something dreadful to say about women. Karl Barth argued that women are "ontologically subordinate to men." The great radical Dietrich Bonhoeffer, writing a wedding sermon from the prison where he had been sent by the Nazis, said that "the wife is to be subject to her husband . . . The place where God has put the wife is the husband's home." Ancient authors expressed essentially the same views, only with more virulence and disgust.

While scholars in other areas of women's studies tend to identify this naming of women's oppression with the essence of women's studies in religion, in fact it is simply the first moment in the genesis of the discipline. Since, as I learned from my fellow graduate students, it is easy enough to trivialize such passages or dismiss them as mere "personal prejudice," the real feminist work in religion began as scholars made connections between specific misogynist comments and the deeper structures of a religious tradition—as they turned to analyzing the texts, images, institutions, and structures that sustain and constitute women's oppression. Thus Rosemary Radford Ruether explored the connections between the church fathers' misogyny and the hierarchical dualisms that pervade their worldview (1974). Mary Daly pointed out the ways fundamental Christian symbols—God the father, or the godfather, as she called him, Yahweh and son—reinforce women's oppression (1973). Nancy A. Falk explored the roots of the disparagement of women in early Buddhist texts (1974). I described the connections between women's legal disabilities within Judaism and the fundamental presuppositions of the legal system (1983). Rosemary Radford Ruether's early collection of essays, *Religion and Sexism* (1974), though focusing mainly on Christianity, is an excellent example of this phase of exploring and critiquing male images of women.

While critiques of religion constituted a higher percentage of feminist writing fifteen years ago, time has not lessened the need for such work but has seen it extended into new areas. As the 1983 date of my essay indicates, the critique of Judaism trailed behind work on Christianity. In terms of the Christian tradition, scholars have now taken up themes—the relation between Christianity and abuse, for example—that were neglected earlier (Brown and Bohn 1989; Thistlethwaite 1985). Moreover, as women of color and other women from oppressed groups have entered religious studies in still small, but increasing, numbers, recent work has paid more attention to the relationship between sexism and other forms of oppression, both within the Christian tradition and within feminist work itself. Rosemary Radford Ruether was always concerned with the interstructuring of sexism, racism, and anti-Semitism in Christian history (1975), but many other critiques focused more narrowly on sexism. Now, Clarice J. Martin has argued—and of course her argument applies to every area—that feminist critical interpretation of the New Testament needs to attend to race and class, as well as to gender (1990). Ada Maria Isasi-Diaz and Yolanda Tarango have described the intersection of sexism, ethnic prejudice, and racism in the experience of Hispanic women (1988). Jacquelyn Grant has criticized feminist theologians who claim to speak from women's experience but who ignore the experience of black women (1989), and I have described the phenomenon of anti-Judaism in Christian feminist writing (1991).

At the same time that such critical work continues (and needs to continue), feminist scholars in religion increasingly have shifted their focus to recovering the religious lives of women. In doing so, they concur with Elisabeth Schüssler Fiorenza's argument that accepting male texts as accurate depictions of women's reality constitutes a form of collusion with patriarchy insofar as it acquiesces in the erasure of women's experiences (1983). Whatever religions have said *about* women, women have also been *actors* in religious life and have found meaning and sometimes power in their religious traditions. Two early collections that began to explore the terrain of women's religious experiences are Rosemary Radford Ruether and Eleanor McLaughlin's *Women of Spirit* (1979) and Nancy A. Falk and Rita M. Gross's *Unspoken Worlds* (1980). *Women of Spirit* is interesting because it covers much the same ground as *Religion and Sexism,* but from the perspective of women's activity rather than men's attitudes. The essays in *Unspoken Worlds* use anthropology to open up the rich variety of women's religious lives in non-Western cultures. But these collections represent only a small fraction of the work that has been done on women's history. To mention just a few resources specifically in religious studies—leaving aside the vast material in other fields—there have been studies of individual women (e.g., Brown 1991) and collections of women's writings (e.g., Umansky and Ashton 1992), studies of particular periods of religious history or facets of women's religious lives (e.g., Fiorenza 1983), studies of women in marginal and heretical groups (e.g., Pagels 1979), and an increasingly voluminous literature on women's relationships to goddess worship (e.g., Bar-stow 1983). This work has been important for more than the information it has uncovered. Feminist work on women's spirituality, on women's participation in major religious movements, and on women's activities in marginal and heretical groups, has raised fundamental questions about the formation of canons and the reliability of sacred texts, about the processes of defining orthodoxy and heresy, and about the importance of power relationships in the definition of "normative" tradition. Bernadette Brooten's work on the evidence for women's leadership in the ancient synagogue, for example, raises important questions about the hegemony of rabbinic Judaism, and the extent to which rabbinic documents are a reliable guide to ancient Jewish practice (1982). Elaine Pagel's work on women in Christian Gnostic groups (1979) raises the question of how particular movements come to be defined as heretical, and whether women's participation might be one of the factors that elicit this label. Carol P. Christ, drawing together a number of studies of women's religious participation, argues that the development of patriarchal religion was neither an accident nor a sociological necessity, but that at key points in the development of the Christian tradition, female images and power were actively suppressed (Christ 1987a, chap. 3). Thus the recovery of women's history does not simply add information to existing frameworks but challenges basic paradigms (Christ 1987b) in such a way as to reconfigure the history of religions.

Beyond the critique of patriarchal traditions or even the recovery of women's history, the last decade has seen a great flowering of constructive work in women and religion. Attempts to create religious symbols, ideas, and rituals empowering to women have been so far-reaching and various that it is difficult even to begin to characterize them. Early efforts to reinterpret biblical texts positively, or to find a woman-defined spirituality in dreams or in literature (Christ and Plaskow 1979) have blossomed into wide-ranging explorations of the sacred, the self, and the world, undertaken from the perspectives of many women's experiences. The difference between the two widely used teaching anthologies published a decade apart is indicative of the changes that have taken place in the field. When Carol P. Christ and I put together *Womanspirit Rising* in 1979, we felt we had included portions of most of the major constructive feminist works then available. The collections contained no writing by women of color or out lesbians, a serious deficiency we should have corrected, by soliciting new work, but a deficiency that reflected the field at the time. On the other hand, when we edited *Weaving the Visions* in 1989, we had to sift through huge amounts of material, making difficult choices about what to include and what to leave out. By then, there was a great deal of serious work by women of color, by lesbians, and by women bringing the resources of diverse religious traditions to bear on a range of feminist issues. This new writing had changed our understanding of the field and of women's experience, forcing us to find new organizational and theoretical frameworks for structuring the volume.

This phase of development has brought new arguments and divisions among feminist scholars in religion, as women have positioned themselves differently in terms of religious and other loyalties. At the same time, there has been a great deal of cross-fertilization among women in oppressed groups, among those with different religious commitments, and among those who define themselves as in or outside of established traditions. The division in early discussions of the gender of God, for example, between those who sought to introduce female imagery into traditional God-language and those who wanted to speak of the Goddess (Christ and Plaskow 1979) has become a much larger conversation about the reconceptualization of the sacred. Goddess thealogy (e.g., Starhawk 1979; Christ 1987a) has had a profound impact on the naming of ultimate reality by feminists within traditional religions (e.g., Ruether 1983; Plaskow 1990), and feminists across traditional/post-traditional lines have been speaking of a God present in every aspect of creation (e.g., Starhawk 1979; Christ 1987; Heyward 1984; Harrison 1985; Cannon 1988). Scholars working in non-Western traditions also have brought their concepts of ultimacy to bear on feminist discussions of the sacred (Klein 1985; Brock et al. 1990).

Discussion of the nature of the self also has expanded enormously, and along lines consonant with a larger feminist discourse. Issues of diversity and multiple allegiances are increasingly central to conversation among women in religion (Russell, Kwok, Isasi-Diaz, and Cannon 1988; Brock et al. 1987; Sandars et al. 1989; Isasi-Diaz et al. 1992). Scholars in the field have sought to formulate an understanding of the self as relational and at the same time deal with the divisions of race, class, and sexual orientation that mark the academy as much as the larger society (Williams 1985). The attempt to grapple with these issues also has meant that women increasingly have linked the feminist transformation of religion with specific problems of social justice, such as racism, nuclearism, ecological crisis, and violence against women (Christ and Plaskow 1989, pt. 4; Andolsen et al. 1985; Harrison 1985).

Issues of Audience and Connections
with Women's Studies

I have been writing here about the development of academic women's studies in religion. Part of the liveliness of the field, however, is due to its connections with communities of women outside the academy. On the one hand, women around the country are seeking to develop a woman-centered spirituality based on practices as diverse as tarot reading and Goddess worship. On the other hand, many women are working within established traditions to expand the roles available to women, create new liturgy, press congregations to deal with new family constellations, and so on. Many academic women in religion have strong connections with one or more of these strands in a developing women's spirituality; some are ordained, some are active members of congregations or women's spirituality groups of various kinds.

These connections may well be one reason for the suspicions about feminist work in religion: feminists in religion are seen as religious, and therefore apolitical, conservative, or strange. It seems to me, however, that, at the same time one certainly does not need to be religious to study religion, this relationship with the grassroots is one of the great strengths of women's studies in religion. It means that many women working in the area are involved in real communities of accountability and testing. While initially, all women's studies grew out of the women's movement, this relationship has become more attenuated with time, as women's studies has become more professionalized and debates and theory in some academic fields have grown more abstract. While professionalization and abstraction certainly are not absent from women's studies in religion, feminists in religious studies have effectively maintained the connections with the grassroots that characterized women's studies at the beginning.

Links to a wider community have made feminist work in religion distinctive, at the same time that such work has benefited from larger conversations and debates within women's studies. Religious studies is a multidisciplinary field. In making use of literary, social scientific, philosophical, and historical methods as their specialties and interests demand, feminist scholars in religion have brought the issues and tools of other disciplines into their own work, and then shaped them into vehicles for institutional change. Sophisticated literary analyses of biblical texts (e.g., Trible 1978) are addressed not simply to scholarly audiences but to the millions of women whose self-understandings are shaped by biblical paradigms. Feminist work on prehistory is used as a starting point for reimaging a female-centered religious symbolism and practice (e.g., Christ 1991)—but also for creating such symbolism and practice in actual communities of women. Academic work thus feeds practice, and practice leads to deeper and more grounded analysis.

The opportunity to bring ideas to the test also gives a sharpness and immediacy to the theoretical debates that women's studies in religion shares with other areas of women's studies. Animating themes in feminist circles, like the nature and reconceptualization of female sexuality, have received major attention in religious studies (e.g., Heyward 1984 and 1989; Harrison 1983 and 1985). Feminist work in religion has used the language of postmodernism and debated its appropriateness (Welch 1985; Davaney 1987; Christ 1989). But often the terms of these debates are reshaped after experimentation in community. For example, the distinction between liberal and radical feminism is important in religion, but its limits are also clear. Feminists in the field have offered competing visions of the nature and scope of a feminist reshaping of religion and have seen these both lived out and rendered more complex by women struggling with their religious traditions. The debate between an essentialist and social constructionist understanding of women's nature and roles becomes very concrete in the context of the creation of new rituals. What events in their lives should and do women want to celebrate and ritualize, and what assumptions about women's nature and roles are embedded in different responses to this question? (Christ and Plaskow 1979 and Plaskow and Christ 1989 reflect both these debates.)

The importance of these links to particular communities is nowhere clearer than in the discussions of difference that increasingly have claimed the attention of women in the field. Women of color in religion, like women of color in other disciplines, have criticized the hegemonic assumptions of white, middle-class feminist discourse (e.g., Grant 1989) and have begun to articulate a vision of religious transformation that emerges out of their own experiences and reflects the concerns of their communities (Williams 1989; Sandars et al. 1989; Isasi-Diaz et al. 1992; Brock et al. 1987). Indeed, the most striking development in the last decade has been the chorus of different voices that has emerged in religious studies, calling for a theology, ethics, and biblical interpretation that have as their goal the liberation of all women (e.g., Brock 1988; Chung 1990; Weems 1988). Of course, there have been parallel developments in other areas of women's studies. But because of the importance of religion in the black community in the United States and in many Third World com-

munities, this work on difference often stands in an immediate relationship to particular contexts of struggle. Thus *womanists* in religious studies have adopted Alice Walker's term in preference to
feminist partly because it names their own difference and partly because it is immediately understood by black church women for whom
the word *feminist* connotes white, middle-class concerns (Gilkes 1989).
Mujeristas have spoken about theology as a communal process entered into with Hispanic women committed to the struggle for justice
in church and society (Isasi-Diaz and Tarango 1988). Feminist work
in religion, then, belongs to the larger universe of feminist discourse,
but brings a subject matter and angle of vision that make an important contribution to women's studies.

Implications for Teaching

These links to a wider community also have a number of implications for the teaching of women's studies in religion. On the college
level, some students to whom religion is important shy away from
courses in this area because they are afraid to apply feminist insights
to this aspect of their lives. By the same token, however, precisely
because many students have religious loyalties and commitments,
critical reflection on religious attitudes toward women and women's
religious roles can have an especially profound impact on their attitudes and self-perceptions.

The teaching of women's studies in religion, moreover, takes place
in seminaries as well as in undergraduate and graduate programs.
On this level, faculty are dealing with students who, as ministers of
congregations, will shape people's understandings of self and God,
deal with family problems and crises, and act as role models for both
children and adults. Clearly, then, it is crucial that such students be
helped to think critically about the relationship of religion to specific
forms of oppression and about the ways in which they can create
change in their own communities.

In terms of the informal educational channels I have mentioned,
there are many ad hoc groups of women who meet to discuss literature in women's studies in religion and to reflect on its relationship
to their lives and religious institutions. Women scholars in religious
studies often have opportunities to teach or interact with such
groups. Work in this field is thus an excellent vehicle for generating and sharing feminist strategies and ideas with women who are
not enrolled in formal educational programs but who are hungry
for new ways of looking at the world and concerned to make concrete changes in the organizations that affect their lives. In all these

ways and on all these levels, women's studies in religion is a powerful vehicle for individual and social change.

REFERENCES

Andolsen, Barbara Hilkert, Christine Gudorf, and Mary Pellauer, eds. *Wom-
en's Consciousness, Women's Conscience: A Reader in Feminist Ethics*. Minneapolis:
Winston Press, 1985.

Barstow, Anne L. "The Prehistoric Goddess." In *The Book of the Goddess*, edited
by Carl Olsen. New York: Crossroad, 1983.

Brock, Rita Nakashima. *Journeys by Heart: A Christology of Erotic Power*. New
York: Crossroad, 1988.

Brock, Rita Nakashima, Yasuko Morihara Grosjean, Patria Agustin, Kwok
Pui-lan, Soon-Hwa Sun, and Naomi Southard. "Asian Women Theologians
Respond to American Feminism." Special section. *Journal of Feminist Studies
in Religion* 3, no. 2 (Fall 1987):103–150.

Brock, Rita Nakashima, Paula M. Cooey, Sheila Greeve Davaney, Rita M.
Gross, Anna C. Klein, and Rosemary Radford Ruether. "The Questions
that Won't Go Away: A Dialogue about Women in Buddhism and Christianity." *Journal of Feminist Studies in Religion* 6, no. 2 (Fall 1990):87–120.

Brooten, Bernadette J. *Women Leaders in the Ancient Synagogue*. Chico, Calif.:
Scholars Press, 1982.

Brown, Joanne Carlson, and Carole R. Bohn, eds. *Christianity, Patriarchy, and
Abuse*. New York: The Pilgrim Press, 1989.

Brown, Karen McCarthy. *Mama Lola: A Voudou Priestess in Brooklyn*. Berkeley:
University of California Press, 1991.

Cannon, Katie Geneva. *Black Womanist Ethics*. Atlanta: Scholars Press, 1988.

Christ, Carol P. *Laughter of Aphrodite: Reflections on a Journey to the Goddess*.
San Francisco: Harper & Row, 1987a.

_____. "Toward a Paradigm Shift in the Academy and Religious Studies."
In *The Impact of Feminist Research in the Academy*, edited by Christie Farnham. Bloomington: Indiana University Press, 1987b.

_____. "Embodied Thinking: Reflections on Feminist Theological Method."
Journal of Feminist Studies in Religion 5, no. 1 (Spring 1989):7–15.

_____. "Mircea Eliade and the Feminist Paradigm Shift." *Journal of Feminist
Studies in Religion* 7, no. 2 (Fall 1991):75–94.

Christ, Carol P., and Judith Plaskow, eds. *Womanspirit Rising: A Feminist Reader
in Religion*. San Francisco: Harper & Row, 1979.

Chung, Hyun Kyung. *Struggle to Be Sun Again: Introducing Asian Women's Theology*. Maryknoll, N.Y.: Orbis Books, 1990.

Daly, Mary. *The Church and the Second Sex*. New York: Harper & Row, 1968.

_____. *Beyond God the Father*. Boston: Beacon Press, 1973.

_____. "Theology after the Demise of God the Father." In *Women and Religion*,
revised ed., edited by Judith Plaskow and Joan Arnold Romero. Missoula,
Mont.: American Academy of Religion and Scholars Press, 1974.

Davaney, Sheila Greeve. "Problems with Feminist Theory: Historicity and the Search for Sure Foundations." In _Embodied Love: Sensuality and Relationship as Feminist Values_, edited by Paula Cooey, Sharon Farmer, and Mary Ellen Ross. San Francisco: Harper & Row, 1987.

Falk, Nancy A. "An Image of Woman in Old Buddhist Literature: The Daughters of Māra." In _Women and Religion_. See Daly 1974.

Falk, Nancy A., and Rita M. Gross. _Unspoken Worlds: Women's Religious Lives in Non-Western Cultures_. San Francisco: Harper & Row, 1980.

Fiorenza, Elisabeth Schüssler. _In Memory of Her: A Feminist Theological Reconstruction of Christian Origins_. New York: Crossroad, 1983.

Gilkes, Cheryl Townsend, respondent. "Christian Ethics and Theology in Womanist Perspective." _Journal of Feminist Studies in Religion_ 5, no. 2 (Fall 1989):105–109.

Grant, Jacquelyn. _White Woman's Christ and Black Woman's Jesus_. Atlanta: Scholars Press, 1989.

Harrison, Beverly Wildung. _Our Right to Choose: Toward a New Ethic of Abortion_. Boston: Beacon Press, 1983.

_____. _Making the Connections: Essays in Feminist Social Ethics_, edited by Carol S. Robb. Boston: Beacon Press, 1985.

Heyward, Carter. _Our Passion for Justice: Images of Power, Sexuality, and Liberation_. New York: The Pilgrim Press, 1984.

_____. _Touching Our Strength: The Erotic as Power and the Love of God_. San Francisco: Harper & Row, 1989.

Isasi-Diaz, Ada Maria, and Yolanda Tarango. _Hispanic Women: Prophetic Voice in the Church_. San Francisco: Harper & Row, 1988.

Isasi-Diaz, Ada Maria, Elena Olazagasti-Segovia, Sandra Mangual-Rodriguez, Maria Antoinetta Berriozábal, Daisy Machado, Lordes Arguelles, and Raven-Anne Rivero. "_Mujeristas_: Who We Are and What We Are About." _Journal of Feminist Studies in Religion_ 8, no. 1 (Spring 1992):105–125.

Klein, Anne C. "Nondualism and the Great Bliss Queen." _Journal of Feminist Studies in Religion_ 1, no. 1 (Spring 1985):73–98.

Martin, Clarice J. "Womanist Interpretation of the New Testament." _Journal of Feminist Studies in Religion_ 6, no. 2 (Fall 1990):41–61.

Pagels, Elaine. "What Became of God the Mother?" In _Womanspirit Rising_. See Christ and Plaskow 1979.

Plaskow, Judith. _Standing Again at Sinai: Judaism from a Feminist Perspective_. San Francisco: Harper & Row, 1990.

_____. "Feminist Anti-Judaism and the Christian God." _Journal of Feminist Studies in Religion_ 7, no. 2 (Fall 1991):99–108.

_____. "The Right Question is Theological." In _On Being a Jewish Feminist_, edited by Susannah Heschel. New York: Schocken Books, 1983.

Plaskow, Judith, and Carol P. Christ. _Weaving the Visions: New Patterns in Feminist Spirituality_. San Francisco: Harper & Row, 1989.

Ruether, Rosemary Radford. _Religion and Sexism_. New York: Simon and Schuster, 1974.

_____. _New Woman New Earth: Sexist Ideologies and Human Liberation_. New York: Seabury Press, 1975.

_____. "Motherearth and the Megamachine." In *Womanspirit Rising. See* Christ and Plaskow 1979.

_____. *Sexism and God-Talk: Toward a Feminist Theology.* Boston: Beacon Press, 1983.

Ruether, Rosemary Radford, and Eleanor McLaughlin. *Women of Spirit: Female Leadership in the Jewish and Christian Traditions.* New York: Simon and Schuster, 1979.

Russell, Letty, Kwok Pui-lan, Ada Maria Isasi-Diaz, and Katie Geneva Cannon, eds. *Inheriting Our Mothers' Gardens: Feminist Theology in Third World Perspective.* Philadelphia: Westminster Press, 1988.

Saiving, Valerie. "The Human Situation: A Feminine View." In *Womanspirit Rising. See* Christ and Plaskow 1979.

Starhawk. *The Spiral Dance: A Rebirth of the Ancient Religion of the Great Goddess.* San Francisco: Harper & Row, 1979.

Thistlethwaite, Susan. "Every Two Minutes: Battered Women and Feminist Interpretation." In *Feminist Interpretation of the Bible,* edited by Letty M. Russell. Philadelphia: The Westminster Press, 1985.

Trible, Phyllis. *God the Rhetoric of Sexuality.* Philadelphia: Fortress Press, 1978.

Umansky, Ellen M., and Dianne Ashton. *Four Centuries of Jewish Women's Spirituality.* Boston: Beacon Press, 1992.

Weems, Renita. *Just a Sister Away: A Womanist Vision of Women's Relationships in the Bible.* San Diego: LuraMedia, 1988.

Welch, Sharon. *Communities of Resistance and Solidarity.* Maryknoll, N.Y.: Orbis Books, 1985.

Williams, Delores. "Women's Oppression and Life-Line Politics in Black Women's Religious Narratives." *Journal of Feminist Studies in Religion* 1, no. 2 (Fall 1985):59–71.

_____. "Womanist Theology." In *Weaving the Visions. See* Plaskow and Christ 1989.

***Judith Plaskow** is Professor of Religious Studies at Manhattan College. She is author of* Standing Again at Sinai: Judaism from a Feminist Perspective, *coeditor of* Womanspirit Rising: A Feminist Reader in Religion *and* Weaving the Visions: New Patterns in Feminist Spirituality, *and cofounder and coeditor of the* Journal of Feminist Studies in Religion.

Feminist Art History and the Academy: Where Are We Now?

Norma Broude and
Mary D. Garrard   *Spring/Summer 1987*

. . . Because ours has been a conservative discipline, art historical feminist scholarship has yet to receive the kind of acceptance and recognition that feminist scholarship has been accorded in other fields. In contrast to both history and literature, for example, where lively dialogues between feminists and others in the field are commonplace, feminist work in art history is rarely reviewed, rebutted, or even acknowledged in print. The field of literature is additive tolerant: The traditional literary canon may be hotly defended, but the MLA admits all comers to its plethora of sessions, whose numbers are multiplied to accommodate a variety of points of view. A smaller discipline, art history has been monolithic, slower to accept sweeping new ideas and methods, perhaps because it fears it can be transformed totally. Very few feminist art historians hold academic positions in the major Ph.D.-granting institutions, a situation that has effectively limited the capability of feminist scholarship in art history to grow and perpetuate itself in the normal academic manner. Things are changing in other fields: At Princeton, for example, recent appointments have included Elaine Showalter and Sandra Gilbert in English literature and Natalie Davis in history. But in the male-dominated art departments of Princeton, Harvard, and other Ivy League universities, the once reprehensible Marxists and the still controversial but currently voguish semioticists are now happily accommodated, and the feminist viewpoint is still not represented.

It is worth noting that the first shots of feminist revisionism were fired as early in art history as in any discipline. In 1971, nearly simultaneously with the publication of Kate Millett's earthshaking *Sexual Politics*, art historian Linda Nochlin published an article that was to become the cornerstone of feminist art history, entitled (with deceptive innocence), "Why Have There Been No Great Women Artists?"[1] Nochlin's question was not *her* question but *their* question, the one that had commonly been used by defenders of the patriarchal art world to fend off women's demands for equality within that world. While acknowledging that there were no female equivalents for Michelangelo or Rembrandt, Nochlin pointed out that women had lacked the educational experiences essential to the creation of art: early encouragement and apprenticeship, classical studies and access to the nude model, which from the sixteenth through the early twentieth centuries was the foundation of the artist's development. Women's past exclusion from the hallowed circles of Great Art was thus a result of institutional bias, and not of gender deficiency.

. . . [O]ne of the most significant ideas of feminist art history appeared in its *Ur*-text: the revelation that artistic geniuses were not born but made, and that their makers were men, the direct beneficiaries of this apparently "natural" order. The feminist reappraisal of the myth of artistic genius was extended by Carol Duncan (in a 1975 article called "When Greatness Is a Box of Wheaties"), who exposed acerbically the extent to which "greatness" has been a totally male-defined concept.[2] . . .

The other revelation in Nochlin's 1971 article, less emphasized by the author but much more influential upon subsequent scholarship, was the suggestion that women might have been artists in greater numbers than previously supposed. She cited by name a handful of "the small band of heroic women, who, throughout the ages, despite obstacles, have achieved pre-eminence, if not the pinnacles of grandeur": Lavinia Fontana, Artemisia Gentileschi, Angelica Kauffmann, Mary Cassatt, Käthe Kollwitz, and more, concluding her essay with a long look at Rosa Bonheur. With this stroke, Nochlin opened the way for the rediscovery and reinstatement of countless women artists, whose names were no longer familiar (thanks to . . . nineteenth-century male critics and scholars, who had systematically written women out of their art histories[4]). . . .

So large has the basic issue of the neglect of women artists loomed, both in the public and scholarly consciousness, that far less attention has been paid to the equally vigorous and parallel development of feminist theory in art history and to the feminist critique of male art history. . . .

Meanwhile, feminist art historians took up the analysis of misogynous stereotypes and distortions found both in male art and in art history itself. Nochlin, again, had provided the keynote, in a memorable College Art Association (CAA) paper of 1972 (published in 1973), a hilariously incisive exploration of erotic imagery in art as exclusively focused on the female body to satisfy exclusively male needs, and of the crude reflection in such art of the power relationship between the sexes.[14] This piece was closely followed, in 1973, by Carol Duncan's fuller examination of the female nude in avant-garde painting of the early twentieth century. Duncan defined, in an essay with important implications for social history as well as art history, the close correspondence between the brute assertion of virility and power (over women) on the part of artists like Kirchner and Picasso and the pressures of the contemporary suffragist movement that threatened masculine supremacy.[15] Duncan's article offered a model for the analysis of the interactive relation of art and society, as well as the wry recognition that "vanguard" or progressive art might in fact reflect regressive and reactionary social values. However, the danger of characterizing all images of women in male art as sexist was implied in a CAA paper given by Norma Broude in 1975 (published in 1977), in which Broude demonstrated that the description of Degas as "misogynist" by his art critic contemporaries resulted from their own sex-biased expectations, founded in masculine concepts of conventional female beauty which blinded the writers (and later art historians) to Degas's atypically sympathetic images of women as independent and sometimes vibrantly intellectual figures.[16] Similarly, in 1982 Svetlana Alpers pointed to images of women by Vermeer that reflect a deeper acknowledgment of female humanity than was common in the seventeenth century. [17]

A different line of exploration was taken up by those who raised the question of whether there might be a separate female aesthetic. (Elaine Showalter has characterized this line as "gynocritics," the study of female creativity, contrasting it with the "feminist critique" of men's writing.[18]) Among the first writers to look at art from this viewpoint were art historian–critic Lucy Lippard and artist Judy Chicago (1973), who focused upon contemporary, largely abstract art to express the view that "there is a definite and pervasive women's imagery based on women's biological and social experience" whose prevalent images are a central focus, ovoid and circular forms, boxes, overlapping flowers, webs (Chicago), and a preference for a uniform density or overall texture, repetition, layers, sensuous tactility, and looseness of handling (Lippard).[19] This bold embracing of a correlation between the female body and women's imagery in art struck many as excessively reductionist and limiting. a form of biological determinism that women were trying to escape. . . .

If there has developed no consensus on whether women's art has betrayed, or must betray, gender-distinguished formal tendencies, feminist artists and scholars alike have agreed that women's art *can* be productively directed toward the expression of female values. The leading spokeswomen in the creation and definition of feminist art have been artists Miriam Schapiro and Judy Chicago, whose writings no less than their own artistic projects, beginning with their joint creation, *Womanhouse* (1972), and continuing in such independent ventures as Chicago's *Dinner Party* (1979) and Schapiro's "collaborations" with women's traditional art and her "femmages," have served to educate all women in the arts in their rich female artistic heritage.[21] While Chicago has celebrated the great women of history—Elizabeth I, Mary Wollstonecraft, Virginia Woolf—*(The Dinner Party)* or archetypal female experience *(The Birth Project)*, Schapiro has championed and embraced in her own art the anonymous women, particularly of nineteenth-century America, who produced the quilts and other needlework of domestic use and private exchange, objects whose style and values gave art another level of meaning.

Art historical reevaluation of the female craft traditions accompanied the artistic reorientation of taste. In an important *FAJ* article of 1973 ("Quilts, the Great American Art"), Patricia Mainardi defended quilting and other needle arts as universal *female* genres, which offered qualities equivalent to those of the "fine" arts—formal complexity and beauty, personal expression, social and communal meaning—and she questioned the devaluation of textile arts, their subordination to the fine arts and their exclusion from art history.[22] The relation between the "high" and "low" arts was explored in the context of modern painting by Broude, who in an article of 1980 reexamined the modernist theoretical tenet that abstract art, because of its significant content, was superior to the decorative craft traditions by which it was sometimes inspired.[23] Contrasting the efforts of Matisse and Kandinsky to discredit (even as they exploited) folk art and craft with Miriam Schapiro's deliberately created dialogue with women's folk and craft traditions, Broude pointed out that feminist art, by virtue of its political and social content, could never be "merely decorative." . . .

By the mid-1970s, some art historians began to discover a female expressive sensibility in representational art of the past. Frima Fox Hofrichter, in 1975, showed that seventeenth-century Dutch painter Judith Leyster had, in a painting called *The Proposition*, countered and critiqued the traditional pictorial theme of the female procurer by presenting a woman unreceptive to her masculine propositioner.[25] Around the same time, Ruth Iskin and Susan Yeh, working independently, initiated a feminist reexamination of Cassatt's female images.[26] In a review of the 1976 *Women Artists* exhibition (1977), Mary Garrard challenged the Harris-Nochlin position that women artists had more in common with male contemporaries than with other women, observing that while this might be true in the realm of style, the disparity of social experience between the sexes suggested that women's different vision of the world might be discerned if their art were examined iconographically.[27] In two studies of themes treated by seventeenth-century painter Artemisia Gentileschi (1980 and 1982), Garrard presented evidence of a major female artist's replacement of female stereotypes with credible, assertive, and even heroic images of women.[28] These iconographic, or (in Showalter's term) gynocritical approaches to women's art paralleled in theory the first feminist studies of women writers, namely, Patricia Meyer Spacks's *The Female Imagination* (1975) and Ellen Moers's *Literary Women* (1976), and they parallel in date the ongoing gynocritical analyses of Sandra Gilbert, Susan Gubar, Annette Kolodny, and others. . . .

The belief that a feminist perspective can lead to the reformulation of the entire history of art has by now permeated our field, and we ourselves, along with Eleanor Tufts and Alessandra Comini, have been perhaps the most vocal proponents of this position. The call for reconceptualization of the discipline was heralded in an article by Garrard ("Feminism: Has It Changed Art History?" *Heresies,* Winter 1977–78). Comini, in a CAA convocation address that was subsequently published (1980), and Tufts, both in lectures and in writing (1981), have each advocated the reinvigoration of traditional art history through the inclusion of women.[33] In an anthology published in 1982 (Broude and Garrard, *Feminism and Art History: Questioning the Litany*), we gathered what seemed to us the most significant art historical essays and articles that had been written—studies that, taken collectively, sketch the new form that an art history shaped by feminist insight might have. . . . In the early 1980s, the feminist call grew louder for the inclusion of women artists in the art history textbooks—Janson, Gardner, Hartt— a demand that several publishers have now begun to heed.[34] In our own view, however, the addition of women artists to a history that remains in every other respect the *same* history is cosmetic and insufficient. Since the early 1980s, we have projected the writing of a new, thoroughly revisionist art history textbook, inclusive of the achievements but also the *values* of women, that reconsiders the narrow hierarchies of art history and places the attainments of men in a broader perspective. . . .

In many of these new directions, as we have seen, art historians have paralleled investigations carried on in other fields, particularly in literature and history, but with major differences that should be pointed out. As a discipline, art history is more aesthetically oriented than history and more historically oriented than literary criticism. Art history is further distinguished from literary scholarship in the sense that it takes far less time to see, even to absorb an inage, than it does to read a poem, a short story, or a book. This relative swiftness of perception permits art historians to deal with a wider variety of images and has directed the natural course of an art historical investigation toward breadth of scope and toward the analysis of the relationships between works of art rather than to the analysis of a single text. In this, art history is closer to history, which is also more concerned with the interaction between forces and events than solely with the events themselves. From this broader perspective ensues the desire to discover pattern, sequence, and development within a series of images, a concern that distinguished in particular the earlier stages of our discipline.

Structural analysis of this kind, in fact, has always been the basis of art history, if by it we mean analyzing to discover invisible relationships that underlie surface phenomena (i.e., the disparate works of art of a period). It is perhaps for this reason that many art historians have for many decades been confused by structuralism as a "new" methodology, because, like Molière's gentleman who did not know that he was speaking prose, we have been doing structuralist analysis all along. Our concern with patterns of style development, for example, goes back to Wölfflin in the nineteenth century. The earliest art historical studies of the medieval cathedral were efforts to sort out stylistic differences among the Romanesque regional schools (Arthur Kingsley Porter) or to analyze changes in style and structure from Romanesque to Gothic (Henry Focillon, Erwin Panofsky). What historians might have expected to see done first—e.g., the social and economic analyses of Gothic architecture by writers like Henry Kraus and Georges Duby—has come late in art history.[36] Structuralism was the hallmark of our discipline in its infancy and recent efforts to "modernize" art history by exploring the special relevance of semiotics, structuralism's visual stepchild, appear to many, by contrast, to be narrow and simplistic.

As in other disciplines, today's semioticists in art history are often more concerned with developing theories than with understanding works of art. Elaine Showalter has pointed to the proliferation of new methodologies in literature and has suggested some possible reasons for this phenomenon which are equally applicable, in our view, to art history. She writes:

> The new sciences of text based on linguistics, computers, genetic structuralism, deconstructionism, neoformalism and deformalism, affective stylistics, and psychoaesthetics, have offered literary critics

the opportunity to demonstrate that the work they do is as manly and aggressive as nuclear physics—not intuitive, expressive, and feminine, but strenuous, rigorous, impersonal, and virile.[37]

The elevation of this new "literary science," she further observes, is leading to the establishment of

a two-tiered system of "higher" and "lower" criticism, the "higher" concerned with the "scientific" problems of form and structure, the "lower" concerned with the "humanistic" problems of content and interpretation. And these levels, it seems to me, are now taking on subtle gender identities and assuming sexual polarity.[38]

We can only agree with this assessment, and can point in our field to a similar tendency, fostered by the newer, more "advanced" methodologies, for terminology to drown out content. . . . [O]ur period is not the first in the twentieth century to see this phenomenon: a formalist disregard for content emerging just when feminists are becoming sensitized to the sexist meanings, both covert and overt, of "universal" icons of "great art." . . . Is there a connection, we might . . . ask, between the contemporaneous emergence of the formalist dialectic in the writings of such art critics as Roger Fry and Clive Bell and the suffragist movement in the years before the First World War, and the present-day emergence, promotion, and survival of structuralism and semiotics in the academy—both functioning as an unconscious means of combatting feminist scholarship and sensibility that stress content and interpretation? . . .

In the early 1970s, the burning issue that faced feminist art historians was whether or not there had been women artists of merit (there have); in the mid-1970s, the question was whether there was a unique female expressive sensibility (there is); in the late 1970s, the issue was how much a feminist perspective might alter the shape of history itself (quite a lot). In the early 1980s, an old question has surfaced to become the center of feminist debate: whether feminist scholars should remain separate from or try to alter the mainstream. We take exception to the direction of thinking among feminist literary critics who see a growing separatism as the wave of the future. This position is supported by Showalter, who succinctly defines its premise:

I do not think that feminist criticism can find a usable past in the androcentric critical tradition. It has more to learn from women's studies than from English studies, more to learn from international

feminist theory than from another seminar on the masters. It must
find its own subject, its own system, its own theory, and its own voice.[41]

There is much sense and promise for feminist scholars in this point of
view. Yet is feminist scholarship our only goal? In the spirit of interdisciplinary dialogue, we dissent from this view, for we feel that women
now have a larger responsibility and opportunity. Let us employ an opti-
cal metaphor. In the past, the world was viewed through a single lens,
a lens that was male. Now, we humans have begun to take into account
that we have two eyes—one male, the other female. But these two eyes
continue to see separately, because the collective brain has not yet
begun to integrate their individual perspectives. In the future, it is to
be hoped, humans may be able to apply our integrating faculty, and to
have a new, whole, three-dimensional vision of history and culture.

For if as feminists we dismiss the entire legacy of the patriarchy as
tainted, we dismiss a significant portion of our own history as well,
because we ignore not only the contributions women have made to
culture, but also the reflection of those specifically female elements
within male culture. A case in point is ancient Greece, whose art and
myth reveal the survival of matrifocal values, and in their juxtaposition
with the ascendant patriarchal ideals, reflect a cultural balance between
masculine and feminine that the Greeks themselves respected and preserved—though traditional historians have more frequently seen fit to
emphasize only Greece's masculinist traditions. It is a mistake, in our
view, for feminists to equate all of received culture with patriarchy. For
even though the political and social institutions of Western civilization
since ca. 3000 B.C. have indeed been patriarchal, our literary and
artistic traditions have reflected a more equitable balance between
masculine and feminine elements.

Given the purposes of art and humanistic studies, it is not surprising that this should be so. A distinction made long ago by art historian
Erwin Panofsky is still relevant: "The ideal aim of science," he wrote,
"would seem to be something like mastery, that of the humanities
something like wisdom."[42] Within cultural history, it has been the arts
and humanities that have sustained our species' memory, affirming its
association with the earth and with nature, and celebrating its rituals,
traditions, contradictions, and beliefs. By contrast, the more masculinist disciplines of the applied sciences have had as their purpose
not only the understanding of man's relation to the earth, but also
the controlling, and, perhaps ultimately and inadvertently, the
destruction of it. We feminist women must not relinquish our share
of that larger whole, the central humanist tradition of Western cul-

ture. Born into one sex, socialized and educated in the ways of the other, and armed for the first time with an educated consciousness of culture's acute need for its female component, women can ill afford to retreat into specialized one-sex concerns at a time in history when females may be uniquely equipped to assist our transition to genuine human universality.

Retrospective judgment suggests that at each of the theoretical crossroads feminists have faced, their bolder instincts have turned out to be the right ones. And the bolder claim at this juncture, we feel, is not separatist but centrist. We part somewhat in this regard from Susan Gubar, who said, commenting on Princeton's new literary appointments, "it means a commitment on the part of the institution and the department to a fairly radical way of looking at the world."[43] Let us suggest, instead, that it is a commitment, at long last, to a *normal* way of looking at the world. For if we persist in defining ourselves as radical, we will remain forever on the distaff side. The core of the liberal arts is now ours to grasp—let us not be so modest.

NOTES

1. Nochlin, "Why Have There Been No Great Women Artists?" *Art News* 69 no. 9 (January 1971): 22–39, 67–71, reprinted in *Art and Sexual Politics*, ed. Thomas B. Hess and Elizabeth C. Baker (New York: Collier Books, 1973), pp. 1–39.

2. Duncan, "When Greatness Is a Box of Wheaties," *Artforum* 14 (October 1975): 60–64. Also important is Lisa Vogel, "Fine Arts and Feminism: The Awakening Consciousness," *Feminist Studies* 11, no. 1 (1974): 3–37.

. . . . . .

4. See M. D. Garrard, review of Laura M. Ragg, *The Women Artists of Bologna*, in *Women's Art Journal* 1 (Fall 1980/Winter 1981): 58–64.

. . . . . .

14. Nochlin, "Eroticism and Female Imagery in Nineteenth Century Art," in *Woman as Sex Object: Studies in Erotic Art, 1730–1970*, ed. Thomas B. Hess and Linda Nochlin, *Art News Annual* 38 (New York: Newsweek, 1973).

15. Duncan, "Virility and Domination in Early Twentieth Century Vanguard Painting," *Artforum* 12 (December 1973): 30–39, revised and reprinted in *Feminism and Art History [:Questioning the Litany*, eds. Norma Broude and Mary D. Garrard (New York: Harper & Row, 1982)] pp. 293–313. For a related discussion of the gender limitations displayed in Picasso's art, see Broude, "Picasso: Artist of the Century (Late Nineteenth)," *Arts Magazine* 55 (October 1980): 84–86.

16. Broude, "Degas' 'Misogyny,'" *The Art Bulletin* 59 (March 1977): 97–107; in Broude and Garrard, *Feminism and Art History*, pp. 247–69.

17. Alpers, "Art History and Its Exclusions: The Example of Dutch Art," in Broude and Garrard, *Feminism and Art History*, pp. 183–99.

18. Showalter, "Toward a Feminist Poetics," in *The New Feminist Criticism: Essays on Women, Literature, and Theory*, ed. E. Showalter (New York: Pantheon. 1985), p. 128.

19. Lippard, writing in *Women Choose Women*, an exhibition organized by Women in the Arts. The New York Cultural Center, New York, January 12–February 18, 1973. Chicago's views were expressed in her teaching, and later in *Through the Flower: My Struggle as a Woman Artist* (New York: Doubleday, 1975). A selection of Lippard's prolific, thoughtful criticism is reprinted in *From the Center: Feminist Essays on Women's Art* (New York: E. P. Dutton, 1976). In 1972, Pat Mainardi argued against the existence of a separate feminist sensibility and in favor of the female artist's freedom to be "sensitive and delicate or strong and bold," as male artists are free to be ("A Feminine Sensibility?—Two Views," *FAJ* 1, no. 1 [April 1972]: 4). A similar stand was taken by women artists whose response to Nochlin appeared as "Eight Women Reply: Why Have There Been No Great Women Artists?" *Art News* 69, no. 9 (January 1971): 40–45. See also Cindy Nemser. "Stereotypes and Women Artists," *FAJ* 1, no. 1 (April 1972), reprinted in Loeb, *Feminist Collage*, pp. 156–66, and Ruth Iskin, "Sexual Imagery in Art—Male and Female," *Womanspace Journal* 1, no. 1 (1973).

. . . . . .

21. See Schapiro, "The Education of Women as Artists: Project Womanhouse," *Art Journal* (Spring 1972), reprinted in Loeb, Feminist Collage, pp. 247–53; and Arlene Raven, "Feminist Education: A Vision of Community and Women's Culture," *Ms.* (May 1975), reprinted in Loeb, *Feminist Collage*, pp. 254–59.

22. Mainardi, "Quilts: The Great American Art," *FAJ* 2, no. 1 (Winter 1973): 1, 18–23; and in Broude and Garrard, *Feminism and Art History*, pp. 331–46. See also Rachel Maines, "Fancy Work: The Archaeology of Lives," in Loeb, *Feminist Collage*, pp. 78–82; C. K. Dewhurst, B. MacDowell, and M. MacDowell, *Artists in Aprons: Folk Art by American Women* (New York: E. P. Dutton, 1979), and Anthea Callen, *Women Artists of the Arts and Crafts Movement*, 1870–1914 (New York: Pantheon, 1979).

23. Norma Broude, "Miriam Schapiro and 'Femmage': Reflections on the Conflict between Decoration and Abstraction in Twentieth-Century Art," *Arts Magazine* (February 1980): 83–87; reprinted in Gouma-Peterson, *Miriam Schapiro: A Retrospective*, pp. 32–38, and in Broude and Garrard, *Feminism and Art History*, 315–29.

. . . . . .

25. Hofrichter, "Judith Leyster's *Proposition*—Between Virtue and Vice," FAJ (Fall 1975): 22–26, reprinted in Broude and Garrard, *Feminism and Art History*, pp.173–81.

26. Iskin, "Cassatt and her Oeuvre from a Feminist Perspective," *Womenspace Journal* 1, no. 2 (1973): Susan Yeh, "Mary Cassatt's Images of Women," *Art Journal* 36 (Summer 1976): 359–63.

27. Garrard, " 'Women Artists' in Los Angeles," *The Burlington Magazine* (July 1977): 531–32.

28. Garrard, "Artemisia Gentieschi's *Self Portrait as the Allegory of Painting,* " *Art Bulletin* 62 (March 1980): 97–112: and Garrard, "Artemisia and Susanna," in Broude and Garrard. *Feminism and Art History,* pp. 147–71. An iconographic approach was earlier used by Madlyn Kahr to uncover persistent stereotypes of women in male artists' treatment of the Delilah theme (Madlyn M. Kahr, "Delilah" *Art Bulletin* 54 [September 1972]:282–99, reprinted in Broude and Garrard, *Feminism and Art History,* pp. 121–45).
......

33. Tufts, "Beyond Gardner, Gombrich, and Janson: Toward a Total Art History," *Arts Magazine* 55 (March 1981): 150–54; Comini, "Art History, Revisionism, and Some Holy Cows," *Arts Magazine* (June 1980): 96–100.

34. The 1980 edition of Helen Gardner's *Art through the Ages* includes the work of seven women artists; the 1985 edition of Frederick Hartt's *Art: A History of Painting, Sculpture, Architecture* includes some twenty-three, with several others mentioned, and the phenomenon of women artists directly addressed.
......

36. Kraus, *Gold Was the Mortar: The Economics of Cathedral Building* (London and Boston: Routledge & Kegan Paul, 1979); Duby, *The Age of the Cathedrals: Art and Society, 980–1420* (Chicago: University of Chicago Press, 1981: first French ed. 1966–67). Heinrich Wölfflin's *Principles of Art History: The Problem of the Development of Style in Later Art* was first published in 1915.

37. Showalter, *Feminist Criticism,* p. 140.

38. Ibid.
......

41. Showalter, *Feminist Criticism,* p. 247.

42. Panofsky, *Meaning in the Visual Arts* (Garden City, N. Y.: Doubleday/ Anchor Books, 1955), p. 25.

43. Gubar, in "Princeton Fostering Women's Studies," *New York Times,* 15 June 1985.

Norma Broude *is Professor of Art History at American University, Washington D.C. A specialist in nineteenth-century French and Italian painting, she is editor of* Seurat in Perspective *(Prentice Hall, 1978), coeditor with Mary D. Garrard of* Feminism and Art History *(Harper & Row, 1982), and author of* The Macchiaioli: Italian Painters of the Nineteenth Century *(Yale University Press, 1987). Broude was the first affirmative action officer of the Women's Caucus for Art and is currently a member of its Advisory Board.* **Mary D. Garrard** *is Professor of Art History and Chair of the Art Department at American University, Washington, D.C. She collaborated with Norma Broude to produce* Feminism and Art History *(1982). Her recently completed book on the seventeenth-century Italian painter Artemisia Gentileschi will be published (1988) by Princeton University Press. Garrard was the second national president of the Women's Caucus for Art (1974–76), and she has served on the board of directors of the College Art Association (1976–80).*

Integrating Women's Studies into the Curriculum

Myra Dinnerstein, Sheryl O'Donnell, and Patricia MacCorquodale   *Spring 1982*

. . . From the outset, women's studies has had a transformative goal: the changing of materials and courses of study so that all phases of education, from kindergarten through graduate and professional schools, will accurately reflect the lives and concerns of women as well as men. . . . Incorporation of women's studies materials into the traditional curriculum, however, has been slow, indirect, and usually accomplished when women's studies professors themselves integrate their materials on women into their non-women's studies courses. A women's history specialist might include such topics as "Childbirth" or "Women's Legal Status" in a survey of American history. A professor of the anthropology of women could include *Woman, Culture and Society* among required readings for a seminar on cultural anthropology. But few professors outside of women's studies specialties incorporate the new research on women into their courses. It is still possible to take a college degree in any one of our universities and never learn that women create culture, or that their volunteer work in church and civic groups affects the economy, or that the least studied forms of political action seem most congenial to women's lives. If the purpose of women's studies is to transform liberal education by integrating female experiences into all descriptions and analyses of human behavior, we must define strategies by which women's studies programs might affect the entire academy.

Concerned about the best ways to increase the numbers of students reached by women's studies courses, and moved by the need to provide all students with an education that reflects the experiences of both sexes, women's studies scholars and teachers have begun a new movement to integrate women's studies into the traditional curriculum. This strategy has been called by a variety of names, most popularly "mainstreaming," but it has as its goal the reshaping of course content and curricular design. It should be distinguished from the compensatory approach to curriculum reform. To "add women and stir" is not enough and is, in some cases, misleading. A special unit on women's suffrage in a history or political science course which includes no other material on women may give students the erroneous impression that women are important only when they have entered the public sphere. The "exceptional women"—those who left the private sphere of home and children, where most women have spent their lives—are presented as worthies, while the majority of women are ignored because their actions may not be understood as "public" and are therefore not viewed as significant or political. Integrating women into the curriculum requires a whole new way of viewing and describing human activity, not just a supplementary gesture. Thus, "mainstreaming" is both a broadening of course content and a transformation of the principles of curricular selection and organization. . . .

Description of Curriculum Integration Projects

College administrators who are interested in supporting the integration of women's studies into the curriculum now have a variety of approaches from which to choose. A number of universities, including California State at Hayward and the University of Arizona, have used their women's studies programs to extend the new scholarship on women throughout their curricula. Other schools utilize faculty who are teaching courses on women's studies or whose major research is focused on women. Still others look for leadership to administrators who have themselves been pioneers in women's studies. Some schools, eager to bring the results of new research on women to their campuses, are limited by having small numbers of women's studies faculty and by encountering resistance to new programs in a time of declining financial resources and tight budgets.

Small liberal arts colleges like Wheaton and Guilford seek to involve the entire faculty in their integration efforts, while large state universities like Montana State and the University of Arizona concentrate on professors who teach large, introductory-level undergraduate courses. Projects seeking to transform disciplines—for example, The Feminist Press's project to transform introductory American literature courses—involve participants from universities throughout the country; while such coalitions as the Great Lakes Colleges Association, the Wellesley Faculty Development program, and the Georgia State Project deal with faculty from a number of colleges within their region.

Most of the projects represented at the SIROW Conference [(Southwest Institute for Research on Women)] are new mainstreaming efforts, although several colleges, notably Stephens and Guilford, started their activities in the early 1970s. Strategies for mainstreaming range from campus faculty development projects to conferences to institutes and seminars. Using a faculty development model which includes as a major component the opportunity for independent research or reading, most of the projects described at the SIROW Conference help faculty acquaint themselves with the new scholarship on women so that they can then initiate curricular change.

At some institutions, notably Montana State, the University of North Dakota, and Wheaton, projects were initiated by faculty members, who conducted research studies of three kinds: content analyses of textbooks (e.g., "Treatment of Women in Anthropology Texts"); surveys/questionnaires (e.g., "Women Students' Success in Agricultural Engineering"); and literature reviews (e.g., "Women in the History of Mathematics"). They then used the results to modify their courses.

Mainstreaming projects often supplement independent faculty research with seminars or workshops, visiting scholars, and resources supplied by the project staff: articles, books, bibliographies, and review essays. Two of the SIROW participants held conferences. The Georgia State conference, "A Fabric of Our Own Making: Southern Scholars on Women," presented the new scholarship on women in order to stimulate new ideas for research and course development. The Sixteen-College Informal Coalition, a consortium of independent colleges—primarily women's colleges—held a conference to study the integration of women's studies into the liberal arts curriculum and the role women's colleges might play in that effort.

Courses, summer institutes, and workshops proved helpful to several schools. California State University at Hayward granted twelve faculty members two credits of released time to attend a semester-long faculty development course team-taught by two women's studies faculty and featuring lectures, readings, and independent projects. Summer institutes for faculty are a major part of the integration project at Lewis and Clark College, the Great Lakes Colleges Association program, and The Feminist Press's project on American literature. Wheaton sponsored a two-day conference for the entire faculty, administraitors, and student leaders at the beginning of its project, and a one-week interdisciplinary workshop to introduce faculty to the new scholarship about women.

Several projects include the creation of "products" as an important part of their strategies. The Feminist Press's project on "Reconstructing American Literature" will produce a volume of syllabi, bibliographies, and related materials, plus brief essays on courses which have begun to be changed, and a new anthology of American literature which significantly increases the inclusion of women and minority writers. Both Montana State and the University of North Dakota required participants to prepare written accounts of their research and revised curricula for possible publication. Selected papers and slides from the art exhibit will be made available to those who attended the conference at Georgia State.

The most important product resulting from the faculty development programs, however, was a changed curriculum, passing on to students an enlarged and corrected picture of social reality.

Role of Administrators

College and university administrators who see the logic of including women in the curriculum have asked: "What can I do? The curriculum is a faculty prerogative." Our conference participants indicated that administrative support was important to virtually every effort to effect curricular change. In fact, one of the most striking features of curriculum reform reported by SIROW Conference participants was the extent to which administrators served as leaders in the development of integrated curricula on their campuses. Many of the seventeen program representatives described how administrators, including presidents, provosts, and assistant deans, played a key role in initiating projects to integrate the new scholarship on women—some by contacting funding agencies or writing grant proposals, others by supporting the efforts of women's studies faculty.

Administrators' support was often prompted by a vision of how the new scholarship on women would fulfill their institutions' commitments to liberal education. Presidents of women's colleges questioned whether their unique responsibility to women students was being met by the traditional curricula. Liberal arts deans wondered whether their schools' definition of a well-rounded education could possibly meet the changing needs of both sexes. Provosts of religious schools felt that their traditional commitment to justice and truth needed to be implemented through the inclusion of women in the curriculum. . . .

SIROW Conference participants listed several ways that administrators emphasizing institutional commitment to the pursuit of knowledge created support for curriculum integration projects:

1. *Building upon an Existing Women's Studies Program or Faculty.* Administrators find that integration projects have been most successful where they have been built around a core of women's studies faculty whose presence (1) provides the campus with local expertise, lessening dependence on outside scholars; and (2) provides a critical

perspective on current research that helps to prevent the cosmetic "add women and stir" approach. On campuses without formal women's studies programs, administrators have been able to encourage curriculum integration by bringing women's studies faculty together and by providing interdisciplinary forums at which the rest of the faculty can be introduced to their work.

Needless to say, support of women's studies faculty, who have been integrating material on women into their courses for years, is important to the process of curriculum change. Women's studies faculty are experts on both women's studies and integration, having created concepts and theories that are used to organize and make sense of the new data on women. They have written innovative materials, revised textbooks, unearthed examples and illustrations, and conducted new research to complete the view of human behavior traditionally offered in their disciplines. Most administrators find these faculty members a logical group to work with on the initiation of curriculum change efforts, though on some campuses administrators have initiated programs aimed at changing the entire core curriculum without focusing specifically on women's studies faculty.

2. Public Recognition and Publicity of the Projects' Efforts. Public administrative support has increased the legitimacy and visibility of curriculum integration. Presidents', deans', and provosts' written and verbal reports on college activities have provided a forum for acknowledging the importance of the new scholarship and teaching about women. Mentioning such projects to opinion leaders outside the university— legislators, religious officials, funding officers, community groups, civic organizations, and alumni/ae—also assigns them value. Administration-sponsored events (lectures, kick-off dinners, women's history weeks) and participation in scholarly conferences have lent weight and authority to mainstreaming projects.

3. University-Wide Support of Interdisciplinary Efforts. Administrative encouragement of interdisciplinary efforts to review, modify, and develop the curriculum has helped to correct narrow views of the academic disciplines as isolated entities. Administrators who have worked to create institutional structures allowing for interdisciplinary courses and team-teaching have been especially helpful to women's studies scholars, because the new research on women is, by definition, interdisciplinary.

4. Renewed Institutional Commitment to Teaching and Curriculum Integration. Administrative support would indicate to the faculty that participation in curriculum integration and awareness of the new scholarship on women are important activities to be seriously considered in tenure and promotion decisions and in the allocation of merit funds. Released time to develop materials or to attend faculty development seminars may be necessary to allow faculty members the time and information required to revise course syllabi. SIROW Conference participants proposed that administrators sponsor teaching awards to instructors who integrate materials on women into their courses.

   5. Financial Support for Integrating Curriculum within a National Framework of Faculty Development. Colleges and universities with ongoing faculty development projects have committed at least a portion of their funding to the new scholarship on women. Money for consortial workshops, attendance at professional women's studies meetings, visiting scholars, and outside consultants has been particularly important for linking the integration projects into the national network of scholars engaged in curriculum revision. Funds for books, journals, films, and other materials that can be used by a large number of faculty are essential.

   The sensitive issue of the extent to which administrators should exercise their power to influence curriculum content evokes questions about academic freedom in the classroom and faculty autonomy. To mitigate tensions, successful administrators formed alliances with interested groups such as women's studies faculty or curriculum committees so that revisions were made through regular institutional procedures. Skilled administrators were those who saw to it that faculty initiated and directed curricular integration while offering them moral, financial, and institutional support.

Funding Prospects: Past and Present

Funding by government and private agencies has been a key factor in promoting projects to integrate women's studies into the curriculum. Several project directors noted the availability of federal grants and foundation monies as crucial to their undertaking their projects when they did. Fifteen of the seventeen projects represented at the SIROW Conference have received some form of external support from such agencies as the Fund for the Improvement of Postsecondary Education, the National Endowment for the Humanities, and the Women's Educational Equity Act. Four private foundations—the Carnegie Corporation, the Ford Foundation, the Andrew W. Mellon Foundation, and the Lilly Endowment—have also funded projects. The significance of funding as a factor in promoting curriculum integration may be skewed by the fact that extensive programs with outside funding were more likely to attract the attention of SIROW Conference organizers than were small programs funded by deans and provosts.

Given the declining availability of outside funding opportunities, new ways to fund curriculum revision must be found. Projects will need internal funds to support their work and will increasingly have to offer faculty supports and incentives that can be provided by the institutions themselves, such as released time, summer stipends, book grants, and faculty development grants. General faculty development programs can make certain that some of their funds are specifically earmarked for changing the core curriculum rather than producing advanced-level courses. Standing college committees can focus their energies on devising strategies for integrating materials on women into the curriculum. Alumnae gifts are a potential source of funding which may have been previously neglected. Three of the projects at the SIROW Conference had received funding from alumnae specifically to support the integration of women's studies into the curriculum.

Benefits of Women's Studies Integration to Colleges and Universities

The experience of the 357 women's studies programs now in existence, as well as the seventeen integration projects represented at the SIROW Conference, suggests that efforts to integrate women's studies into the curriculum offer many benefits to colleges and universities in addition to those occurring in the classroom:

1. The curriculum reflects the experiences of both sexes and therefore provides an accurate picture of social reality.
2. The process of integrating women's studies provides an occasion for a thorough review and critique of an entire college curriculum to assess how it is meeting the needs of its students and whether or not it reflects and incorporates advances in research.
3. Interdisciplinary networks for communication, research, and teaching offer intellectual stimulation and increase the interaction of colleagues.
4. A curriculum that responds to the interests of women and minorities is an attractive inducement in recruiting and retaining students, especially the growing numbers of returning women students enrolled in continuing education and evening courses.
5. Increased faculty publication results from involvement in new areas of research and teaching.
6. Women's studies integration provides an impetus for strengthening library holdings and for organizing materials on women in special collections and archives.

7. For women's colleges, efforts to integrate women's studies provide an opportunity to rethink and revitalize their unique mission.

8. For all liberal arts institutions, efforts to integrate women's studies provide the opportunity to review and expand their commitment to the open-minded pursuit of truth.

. . . . . .

Myra Dinnerstein, *head of Women's Studies and director of the Southwest Institute for Research on Women (SIROW) at the University of Arizona, is director of the project on "Integrating Women's Studies into the Curriculum."* **Patricia MacCorquodale,** *Assistant Professor of Sociology at the University of Arizona, is chair of the executive planning and evaluation committees for this project.* **Sheryl Rae O'Donnell** *is director of the "Project for Curricular and Instructional Development in Women's Studies" at the University of North Dakota, where she is an Assistant Professor of English.*

Women's Studies and Projects to Transform the Curriculum: A Current Status Report

Betty Schmitz   **Fall 1983**

The idea that the impact of women's studies should be extended to the general curriculum through formalized faculty and curriculum development programs appears to be catching on. Sixty colleges and universities sent representatives to the Wheaton College Conference on "Moving Toward a Balanced Curriculum," held on June 22–24, 1983, to learn from such established projects as the ones at Wheaton, Smith, Montana State University, the University of Maine/Orono, and the University of Arizona how to incorporate the new scholarship on women into the liberal arts curriculum.[1] Columbia University, whose incoming freshman class is 44 percent female, has appointed a Co-education Coordinator whose responsibilities include exploring ways of balancing the university's curriculum in order to ensure that it responds to the needs of women students. Spelman College is proposing a curriculum development project in Black women's studies to incorporate the study of Black women throughout its curriculum and at selected institutions in the Atlanta area.[2] Antioch College is looking at curriculum integration as one component of the total reorganization of the disciplines. Yale University has received a grant from the National Endowment for the Humanities to support the revision of ten courses in the general curriculum and the development of ten new women's studies courses. In addition to these new initiatives, there are currently 42 "established" projects with resources and materials to assist other campuses in initiating curricular change.[3]

Why is this curriculum integration craze sweeping the country? Why, after more than a decade of resistance to women's studies, are college administrators embracing the concept of using feminist research to transform the curriculum? What are the motives that compel faculty to participate in such efforts? Is it that, as many women's studies faculty fear, these projects offer a diluted and sanitized version of women's studies and represent an attempt on the part of the institution to abolish or curb women's studies programs and cut back on woman-centered spaces within the academy?

As I survey the number and scope of projects, I am struck both by the diversity of their goals and by the political reasons for their inception.[4] In many cases, campus feminists, after dogged but unsuccessful attempts to create a formal Women's Studies Program, seized an opportunity that presented itself to influence an existing curriculum or faculty development program. As Elizabeth Arch of Lewis and Clark College put it at the second Plenary Session of the National Women's Studies Association Convention at Ohio State in June:

> We grabbed the opportunity that the National Endowment for the Humanities grant presented and used it to establish a larger women's studies presence on campus by introducing individual willing faculty members in many departments to the new scholarship on women through a faculty development seminar. The hope was that a larger presence would create a more favorable context in which women's studies could be taken seriously at this institution for the first time.[5]

Seventeen faculty members participated in a month-long seminar with feminist scholars and used the insights gained from this seminar to revise courses taught in the core freshman general studies program. More importantly, this core group of faculty now constitutes a Women's Interest Group that has been instrumental in building "gender balancing" of the college's curriculum into the academic planning process.

Similarly, the project directed by Janice Harris at the University of Wyoming took advantage of the general education reform process to increase the presence of feminist scholarship in the curriculum. By holding a retreat for general education committee members and departmental representatives to introduce them to the new scholarship on women, women's studies faculty have influenced the process by which courses get approved for the new core: the general education committee now reviews all course proposals for the inclusion of the study of women and minorities.

At other institutions, administrative leadership has been the impetus for revision of the general curriculum. Lorna Edmundson, the newly appointed Co-education Coordinator at Columbia University, points to the initiative of the Dean of Columbia College, Robert Pollack, as a critical factor in the institution's move to reevaluate its curriculum. Pollack convened a series of meetings for department heads to consider how both the content and the methodology of courses would have to change once women were sitting in the classes.

One of the first steps in preparing for the new student body was to make more visible the 24 existing women's studies courses and appoint a Committee on Gender Studies to review the general curriculum and make recommendations for change. Revisions in the core curriculum have already occurred. The Contemporary Civilization course now includes the status of women as a standard topic. At Wheaton College, as President Alice Emerson observed in her opening remarks at the Wheaton Conference, "balancing the curriculum" became a compelling institutional mission because of "a critical mass of people who cared"— including herself and former Provost Ruth Schmidt—and who recognized that their belief that women matter had to be reflected in the college curriculum.

With the growth and expansion of these projects comes the concern, expressed repeatedly at both the Wheaton Conference and the NWSA [(National Women's Studies Association)] Convention, to conceptualize the relationship between women's studies and projects to transform the general curriculum. Much of the discussion about "autonomy" and "integration" has unfortunately conveyed the idea that we are two separate groups of people—the women's studies faculty and the "integrationists." It is not that simple. Margo Culley began her talk on Women's Studies/Black Studies at the Wheaton Conference with an impassioned defense of "living on the margin" because it is only there that truly radical work can occur. She then dramatically flipped over the pages in front of her: "But that's not what I've been asked to speak to you about today. 'Balancing the Curriculum' . . . ," she began. This is the schizophrenic nature of the work we are doing, and many of us are wearing both hats within our institutions. Nearly one-half of the projects listed in the Wellesley College Directory of Projects [*Ed. note:* see *Women's Studies Quarterly* XI:2 (Summer 1983): 23–29] are run by women's studies or other women's program staff. Many of the curriculum integration projects have in fact begun as efforts to help women's studies survive within an institution by increasing the base of support and developing advocacy groups among senior faculty. At the University of North Dakota, after more than a decade of offering the usual selection of women's studies courses in the humanities and social sciences, there is now, as a direct result of the curriculum integration project, a self-designed minor through the Honors College, an Introduction to Women's Studies course that fulfills general studies requirements, and released time for a Coordinator of Women's Studies. The University of Utah project, initiated under the auspices of the Northern Rockies Program on Women in the Curriculum, created a larger advocacy base for women's studies, and this new support and visibility constituted one factor in ensuring continuing funding after termination of the operations budget had been threatened. Almost all of the campus-based curriculum integration projects that have provided resources to faculty for course development have created new women's studies courses as part of the effort.

Yet we must acknowledge that there are cases in which "mainstreaming" has been used as a rationale to eliminate or curb women's studies. A Coordinator of Women's Studies at a community college in Oregon was given as a rationale for the nonrenewal of her contract that the college had made a commitment to integrating women's studies throughout the curriculum and would hire someone with different expertise and skills than hers to direct this effort. In other cases, administrators who have become fascinated by the concept of curriculum integration at one of the several conferences devoted to this topic, but who have failed to realize the extent of the revolution being contemplated, have expected women's studies faculty to begin educating their recalcitrant colleagues, even though there may be no line budget for women's studies. In many cases, the women's studies faculty do *not* control the funds for these projects and have not been consulted during the planning phases. It is more than ironic that after many bitter and unsuccessful tenure struggles, women's studies faculty are now being asked to embrace the opportunity to educate their tenured colleagues who receive handsome stipends for work that often replicates feminist scholarship of a decade ago. A larger question is the extent to which feminist pedagogy can survive in the "integrated classroom" and the degree to which, in the words of Helene Wenzel, the "changer" becomes the "changed." (Helene Wenzel spoke on "The Changer or the Changed? Feminism in the Universities" at another NWSA Convention session, called "Whatever Happened to Autonomous Women's Studies?")

One part of the debate centers around whether an established Women's Studies Program should focus its resources on nurturing the best feminist and radical teaching and scholarship or engage in an effort to transform the institution's curriculum. Panelists offered differing opinion during the Plenary Session at the NWSA Convention. Gloria Bowles set the stage for discussion by summarizing the concerns of autonomous women's studies programs: What do integrationists mean by integration? For whose benefit is the balance in the curriculum? Will the radical perspective of women's studies be lost in the process?

As an argument against mainstreaming, Johnnella Butler pointed to the fact that since women's studies has not been sufficiently generative

nor inclusive it cannot take the lead because we don't yet have sufficient information about *all* women. "The mainstream is sick and dying.
We must be about *replacing* the mainstream."

Marian Lowe observed that some integration is imperative at this
moment to counteract the growing body of antifeminist scholarship
triggered by reaction to feminist gains. "At this point integration's
main successes may come in slowing down the inroads on the few gains
we have made." She urged, however, that not too much effort be
placed in this arena, for only a social revolution will result in the full
acceptance of feminist scholarship in academe. Most of our effort must
be toward ensuring spaces where alternative visions for the future can
be nurtured. And this, Lowe believes, may mean rejecting available
funds for mainstreaming.

Peggy McIntosh rejected the "either-or" conceptualization of the
issue and identified five factors that have contributed the mistaken
impression that women's studies and projects to transform the curriculum are in competition with one another: (1) publicity; (2) funding sources; (3) terminology; (4) administrators' misconception that
one must be better than the other; and (5) perceived loyalty to the
disciplines. She urged that we continue to explore ways of extending
women's studies as far as possible within our institutions. She too,
however, was cautionary: we must take "the most inclusive version of
women's studies into the curriculum and remember that the heart of
feminist thought must be done within woman-centered spaces within
institutions."

What emerged from the two conferences was a sense that there is
a way, in Peggy McIntosh's words, "to weave the work together," to
ensure that these efforts are strong and mutually enhancing. From my
own perspective, I see women's studies and curriculum integration as
two points on a continuum. Projects to incorporate feminist scholarship into the general curriculum gain their strength and lifeblood
from the radical thinking done in women's studies. The work of those
of us introducing new faculty to feminist research is, by pushing against
the mainstream, making a place for more radical thinking within the
academy. I invite further discussion of this question through the
Readers' Speakout in the *Quarterly*.

NOTES

1. The Wheaton College Conference Proceedings, *Toward a Balanced
   Curriculum*, will be published by Alfred Schenkman Publishers in November
   1983. The book will include panels and presentations of the conference,
   abstracts of projects at participating institutions, and other resources for

integrating the study of women into the liberal arts curriculum. . . .
2. The Women's Research and Resource Center at Spelman College was also
   the site of a workshop on Black women's studies for faculty in Black colleges,
   sponsored by the Wellesley College Center for Research on Women under
   a two-year grant from the Fund for the Improvement of Postsecondary
   Education, codirected by Patricia Bell Scott, Gloria T. Hull, and Barbara
   Smith.
3. See "Directory of Projects: Transforming the Liberal Arts Curriculum
   through Incorporation of the New Scholarship on Women," compiled by
   Peggy McIntosh with Katherine Stanis and Barbara Kneubuhl, *Women's
   Studies Quarterly* XI:2 (Summer 1983): 23–29. A listing of resources and
   materials from established projects will be available in October 1983 for
   $3.00 from Betty Schmitz, Clearinghouse for Curriculum Integration
   Projects, Montana State University, Bozeman, MT 59717. The Wellesley
   College Center for Research on Women continues to provide matching
   funds to institutions around the country for consultants to assist in developing local projects. Contact Peggy McIntosh, Faculty Development
   Program, Center for Research on Women, Wellesley College, Wellesley
   MA 02181.
4. Marilyn Schuster and Susan Van Dyne classify institutional models for
   curriculum integration as "top-down" (initiated through administrative
   directive), "piggy-back" (developed to target an existing program or series
   of courses), and "bottom-up" or "collaborative" (initiated by faculty to maximize all internal resources through a network model). See their forthcoming essay on "Transforming the Curriculum: The Changing Classroom.
   Changing the Institution," Working Paper Series, Wellesley College Center
   for Research on Women, Wellesley, MA 02181.
5. Papers from the NWSA Plenary Session "Envisioning the Future of Women's
   Studies: Autonomy / Integration / Transformation / Revolution will appear
   in a special issue edited by Gloria Bowles for the *Women's Studies
   International Quarterly.*

Betty Schmitz, *director of the Project on Women in the Curriculum at Montana
State University, will be writing a regular column for the* Women's Studies
Quarterly *on curriculum integration projects and issues. She is the author of
a forthcoming book to be published in June 1984 by The Feminist Press, tentatively entitled* How to Integrate Women's Studies into the Curriculum.

Designing an Inclusive Curriculum: Bringing All Women into the Core

Elizabeth Higginbotham   *Spring/Summer 1990*

To be successful, transforming the curriculum involves three inter-related tasks. The first is to gain information about the diversity of the female experience. The second task is to decide how to teach this new material, a process that typically involves reconceptualizing one's discipline in light of a race-, class-, and gender-based analysis. Often this means learning to move typically marginal groups into the core of the curriculum. Furthermore, efforts can be made to present issues on people of color in their complexity, rather than in stereotypic ways. The third task is to structure classroom dynamics that ensure a safe atmosphere to support learning for *all* the students. This paper will discuss each of these tasks. It begins with a critique of the traditional curriculum in light of its treatment of people of color.

Marginal in the Traditional Curriculum

When I consistently see many bright and respected scholars failing to take steps to bring women of color into their teaching and re-search, I look for social structural explanations. A sociological per-spective can help us to understand the roots of racist thinking and the many forms it takes in traditional disciplines and women's stud-ies. This approach is more productive than blaming these schol-ars—or simply attacking them as racists. The search for the social structural roots of the marginalization of people of color in schol-arship and education takes me back to my early schooling.

As a Black person in a society dominated by whites, I was always an outsider—a status that Patricia Hill Collins (1986) argues has advantages and costs. I was cognizant even as a young child that the experiences of Black people were missing in what I was taught in elementary school. This pattern was later replicated in junior high and high school, then in college, and later in graduate school.

But while I had been critical all along, not until I entered graduate school could I debate with others about the content of courses.

Throughout my whole educational career, agents of the dominant group attempted to teach me the "place" of Black people in the world. What was actively communicated to me was that Black people and other people of color are on the periphery of society. They are marginal. I learned that what happens to people of color has little relevance for members of the dominant group and for mainstream thinking.

Early in school, when we were studying the original thirteen North American colonies, I was exposed to the myths about who we were and are as a nation. One of the first lessons was that America is a land that people entered in search of freedom—religious freedom, the freedom to work as independent farmers, freedom from the privileged nobility and the hierarchical stratification of Europe, and freedom from the rapid industrialization of Europe. Colonists, and later white immigrants, wanted change in their lives, and they took the risk to begin life anew in this budding but already glorious nation. The fact that they were seeking their "freedom" while enslaving others (principally Native Americans and Africans) was not viewed as a contradictory activity, but just "one of those things" the United States had to do to build a great and prosperous nation.

New York, where I grew up and received much of my education, prided itself on being a progressive state, and required schools to devote time to the Negro experience (as it was called). We discussed slavery in the South, and during Negro History Week we learned about Harriet Tubman, Booker T. Washington, Frederick Douglass, and George Washington Carver. We were explicitly taught that Black people did not share the same history as whites. African people had been forced to come to North America against their will, and instead of finding freedom, they had had to work as slaves.

The experiences of Afro-Americans never informed the standard characterizations of the society: even the slave experience of Africans and Afro-Americans did not alter the image that America was a land in which people found freedom. As a student, I had to master the myths and accept them as part of my socialization into the political system. I also learned that the information I accumulated about Black people—and later other people of color—was nice to know for "cultural enrichment." Exposure to the experiences of Afro-Americans, Puerto Ricans, and others was useful to develop tolerance for difference and make us better citizens, but this information was never meant to identify concepts, to develop perspec-tives, or to generate images or theories about the society as a whole.

I was in school to learn the experiences of the dominant group (which was also very male, as well as white and affluent)—and that would be the basis for an understanding of the system. If I learned that, I could go to college and perhaps do more interesting work than my parents did.

In spite of the intended message, it was hard for me to under-stand why the experiences of Black people were not incorporated into our images of who we are as a nation. At the time there was no mention of Asian Americans, Chicanos, or Native Americans. But I came to understand the practice. Whatever happened to Black people was an exception to the rule—we were a deviant case—just like using "i" before "e" except after "c." Since the experiences of Black people did not have to be included in our search for the truth, they were not the material from which theories and frame-works were derived.

As I reflect on my early educational experiences, I see that the messages I received as a child, an adolescent, and an adult blamed the victim. For example, we were taught that the African people who "came" to America were not civilized; therefore, they could not pursue the American dream as initial settlers and white immi-grants had been able to do. The lack of Black participation in main-stream American society was attributed to lesser abilities, defective cultures, lack of motivation, and so forth. To make a "victim-blaming" attribution, teachers did not actually have to say that Black Americans were lazy, ignorant, or savage—although that would surely do the trick. Instead, victim-blaming was subtly encouraged in classes where images of America as the land of freedom and opportunity were juxtaposed with the Black experience, without any reconciling of the contradictions through a structural expla-nation. Students then relied on prevailing myths and stereotypes to explain the Black "anomaly."

As a young Black girl, I found these messages problematic, and throughout my life I have sought answers to questions about the experiences of Black people at different historic moments. As a scholar, I still struggle with how best to use the knowledge I have gained. Thus, I approach the issue of curriculum integration with a fundamental critique of the traditional curriculum. I did not be-gin by discovering that women were missing from the curriculum—instead I have always perceived schools as foreign institutions. The information taught in schools was alien to me, to my family, to my neighborhood, and in a certain respect to the city, New York, in which I lived. Yet, in order to move to the next educational level and succeed in society, I had to master this information and pass tests. In my view, you were smart if you could pass the tests, but you had to look elsewhere for information to help you survive in the real world.

Today's wave of curriculum reforms presents an opportunity to restructure education, to alter the environment which was alien to me and many others. Such a remedy would include in the curriculum all the people in the classroom and the nation. Instead of focusing solely on the experiences of dominant group members, faculty members would teach students to use and value many different experiences in order to develop conceptions of life in this country and around the world.

I began by discussing my early experiences, because these experiences are common to many. Although we learn these lessons as members of either privileged or oppressed groups, they are similar lessons. If we are clear about the origins of practices that exclude people of color, we can dispense with blaming ourselves and each other for the difficulties we face in trying to change the curriculum. We are swimming upstream against the intellectual racism that flows through American ideology. The *disregard* for the experiences of Black people and other people of color is part of the American creed. To create a multicultural curriculum we must "unlearn" the ideology which marginalizes all but a tiny elite of American citizens.

Curriculum transformation has the potential for changing our traditional visions of education in American society. Yet, it can also replicate old biases. This is especially likely to occur in situations where the integration process is envisioned as a minor tune-up to an educational system that is fundamentally solid. From my perspective, however, our curriculum needs a major overhaul. It needs much more than the addition of women. It must incorporate the men who are omitted—especially working-class men and men of color. Elizabeth Minnich (1990) reminds us that fundamental change is not possible unless we first understand why these groups were excluded. Enlightened by such a critique, we can decide how we want to change and what we will teach. We can then select the path that leads to a restructuring of the curriculum toward inclusiveness across many dimensions of human experience.

Curriculum Change Starts with Faculty Development

Integrating the diversity among women into the curriculum is difficult. Most faculty members are just learning about women through recent exposure to feminist scholarship; few of them are knowledgeable about and at ease with material on women of color. This is understandable. No one mentioned women of color when most contemporary college faculty pursued their degrees, yet the lack of correct information is a major contributor to the limited and inadequate treatment of women of color in courses and in research projects.

As the products of educational experiences that relegated people of color and women to the margins of their fields, faculty members need to compensate for the institutionalized biases in the educational system. They can work to eliminate this bias by gaining familiarity with the historical and contemporary experiences of racial-ethnic groups, the working class, middle-class women, and other groups traditionally restricted to the margins. The first step is to acknowledge one's lack of exposure to these histories.

Structural difficulties make learning new information about women and people of color problematic. It is often hard for faculty members to compensate for the gaps in their knowledge when they are faced with heavy teaching responsibilities and the pressure to publish. College administrators can encourage efforts with release time, financial support for workshops and institutes, and the like. Even without such resources, faculty members can develop long- and short-term strategies—for example, by organizing seminars to explore the new scholarship. All that is needed is a commitment and a shared reading list.

Another difficulty is the interdisciplinary nature of women's studies. Most faculty members are trained to research a specific discipline. Fortunately, over the years, more resources and tools have become available to help navigate this interdisciplinary field. The Center for Research on Women at Memphis State University has been a pioneer in this area; other research centers and curriculum projects have produced bibliographies, collections of syllabi, essays, and resources to assist with curriculum change. Some resources specifically include race, class, and gender as dimensions of analysis.

Institutionalized racism and sexism are structured into both the commercial and academic publishing markets, thus making it more

difficult for scholars studying women and people of color to publish their work. Women's studies centers have initiated projects to
help faculty identify relevant citations and locate new research and
the development of women's studies and racial-ethnic studies journals has helped a great deal, but structural barriers persist that
impede access to research on certain populations, particularly
women of color, working-class women, and women in the southern
and western regions of this nation. Thus, the very resources college
faculty need about women of color are difficult to locate.

Learning to identify myth and misinformation about people of
color is a critical task in course and curriculum revision. It is a
process that alters teaching content and classroom dynamics. For
example, with new knowledge faculty members can teach students
in ways that appreciate human diversity. Faculty members will also
be better prepared to interrupt and challenge racist, sexist, class-
bias, and homophobic remarks made in the classroom.

My own areas of specialization have given me information on the
experiences of different racial and ethnic groups in this society. I
often forget that everyone is not familiar with how most of the
Southwest became part of the United States; with the Chinese Exclusion Act of 1882; with the implications of the Immigration Act
of 1924 for people of color; with the internment of Japanese-
American citizens during World War II; and with the fact that
Puerto Ricans are citizens, not immigrants, and cannot be considered undocumented workers. One has to remember that most
dominant-group faculty and students are not nearly as familiar with
these histories as are students who belong to specific ethnic and
racial-ethnic groups. The history of oppression is part of the oral
traditions in ethnic and racial-ethnic communities as well as religious groups. Afro-American, Latino, Asian American, and Native
American students enter our classrooms with at least a partial
awareness of the historic struggles of their people. They frequently
feel alienated in educational settings where their teachers and other
students relate to them without any awareness of their group's history. For example, a faculty member or a student who talks about
how Japanese Americans have *always* done well in this country denies the reality that racism has severely marred the lives of both
Japanese immigrants and Japanese Americans. For much of this
century Japanese aliens were denied the opportunity to become
citizens. During World War II they were removed from the West
Coast and placed in internment camps, primarily because Anglos

resented their economic success. Non-Japanese American faculty and students may be unaware of this history. The lack of correct information on the part of faculty members has consequences for what happens in the classroom: to the Japanese American student, Anglo ignorance of these issues is symptomatic of the persistent denial that racism is an issue for this group (Wong, 1985).

With new information, faculty can challenge myths and begin to interrupt racism in the classroom. The mastering of new information is a key ingredient in combatting the feelings of powerlessness many faculty members experience in the face of the racist and sexist attitudes of their students. Once we acknowledge our lack of information, we can use the many resources available to learn about the experiences of women, people of color, working-class people, and other traditionally marginalized groups.

What Do I Do with New Information?

A key issue faced by faculty is finding a "place" for working-class women, Black women, and other women of color in the curriculum. How do we challenge established practices of marginalizing these populations and truly develop a different educational process? How do we weave this new information on women and specifically women of color into a course on the family, the labor market, the sociology of education, the introduction to political science, and so forth? This is where many faculty learn by trial and error.

Revising the content of one's course requires the clarification of personal goals and educational aims (Andersen, 1987). This is not an issue that faculty approach lightly. One cannot introduce a reading or a lecture where minority women are covered and then merely assume that the goal has been achieved. Curriculum transformation requires much more. Yet, as we move toward that goal, our individual educational philosophy and commitment to our discipline will play a key role in how we resolve these issues.

It is common practice to begin initial integration efforts with one or two lectures on women of color. Faculty who stop at that level of inclusion find that their course is not transformed and that this addition has little impact on students. In fact, this approach can generate new problems. An instructor who performs the obligatory lecture often encounters opposition from students. For example, a Black woman colleague of mine taught a traditional course on the family and included a unit on the Black family. A few vocal students were quick to remind her that they had signed up for a course on the family, not the "Black family." Had she incorporated material on the Black family in every unit throughout the course, the "Black family" would not have appeared to be anomalous, but an integral part of the study of the family.

Yet, this additive approach is problematic. If faculty introduce material on Black women or women of color as interesting variations on womanhood, such actions indicate that readings and lecture materials on these populations are not part of the "core" knowledge covered in the class. Students can tolerate a certain amount of cultural enrichment, but if this material exceeds more than one or two lectures, they lose their patience because they think the instructor is deviating from the core. This reaction can be avoided if material on white working-class women, Black women, and other women of color (as well as men of color and working-class people) is integrated throughout the course. The diversity of experiences should be presented as knowledge that students are responsible for learning and will be evaluated for covering.

Approaches that keep women of color on the margins or peripheral to the course materials fail to address critical issues of racism, sexism, and classism. Faculty who use such approaches tend to introduce material on white middle-class people as the norm, and then later ask for a discussion on the variations found among working-class whites and people of color. This approach does a great deal to foster ideas that blame the victim. Students may even use such discussions as opportunities to verbalize the racism they have learned from the media and other sources. Such interactions tend to polarize a class, and then the faculty member has an additional battle to wage.

In sociology, where attention is given to norms, ideal types, and the like, women of color are often incorporated as deviant cases. Peripheral treatments of groups are obvious to students; furthermore, these approaches complement students' previous learning about racial-ethnic groups. Often when an instructor is about to begin the one obligatory lecture on the Black family, the Black woman, Latinas, working-class women in the labor market, or whomever, a student will ask the question all the students want answered, "Are we going to be tested on this?" This also tends to happen when a guest speaker who is a racial minority or a female is invited to class. Students may listen politely but not feel compelled to write anything down or remember what was said.

Students carry old lessons into the classroom. They have already learned that what happens to people of color (or to women) does not count. This has been evident in their learning prior to college and continues in most college courses. Learning about different groups is treated as cultural enrichment, not as a part of the basic scholarship of a field. These are essentially correct impressions on the part of students. The core material is still about affluent white men; the historical experiences, social conditions, and scholarly contributions of people of color and women are marginal to the disciplines.

Beyond a Universal Model of Gender. In many curriculum integration efforts in social science teaching, the marginalization of women of color takes two forms. Women of color are addressed either as tangents to the "generic" woman or as the "exceptional" woman of color. In the first case, African American, Asian American, and Native American women and Latinas are present, but their experiences are not critical to the development of theory or paradigms. This teaching strategy is often linked with the view that gender relations are the foundation for universal experiences. Within this framework, other sources of inequality, particularly race and class, might be acknowledged, but they are clearly less important than gender. As a result, scholarship on women of color in both women's studies and curriculum integration efforts is marginalized (Baca Zinn et al., 1986). Faculty tend to rely upon the experiences of white, middle-class, heterosexual Americans as the norm and view all others as merely exceptions to the rule.

Sandra Morgen (1986) is very critical of this universalist stance. She identifies how looking at the experiences of women of color expands our understanding of critical issues for women and gives a feminist perspective greater depth. Morgen examines how we can develop deeper appreciations of motherhood, the feminization of poverty, and women and resistance by examining the historical and current situations of women of color.

With regard to motherhood, Morgen identifies the way that most white, middle-class feminist scholars see the nuclear family as normative. In a discussion of Dinnerstein's *Mermaid and the Minotaur* (1976), Adrienne Rich's *Of Woman Born* (1976), and Nancy Chodorow's (1978) *The Reproduction of Mothering*, Morgen argues that much feminist scholarship about "the" family

> presumes that working women are a relatively recent phenomenon, and that working mothers are even newer, and that the nor-

mative family is mom, dad and the kids, and that mothers live with their children and are the primary, if not near exclusive force in their socialization. These assumptions are problematic when explaining the historical and contemporary experiences of many poor and working-class women, and of many women of color. These women have as a group been in the labor force for a much longer period of time, and in situations like slavery, sharecropping, domestic work or unregulated industrial production that did not allow for the kind of full-time motherhood, or the specific mother-child relations which are presumed in Chodorow, Dinnerstein, and Rich (Morgen, 1986, p. 12).

The impact of racial oppression on the mothering behavior of women of color in the 19th century is a theme in the work of Bonnie Thornton Dill (1988). She describes how racial oppression not only shaped the productive roles of African American, Latina, and Asian immigrant women, but also influenced the reproductive labor of these women. Dill's and Morgen's works demonstrate that much can be gained by using the experiences of women of color to develop new theories about women's experiences. Such approaches sharply contrast with those that fit the experiences of women of different classes and races into a universal model.

Morgen (1986) also describes how an analysis of the feminization of poverty can be informed by looking at the circumstances of women who are not new to poverty. She is joined by other scholars who have discovered that not all women are a husband away from poverty. While many middle-class white women experience a significant decline in their social status when they sever their attachment to a middle-class white male, many working-class women and women of color find themselves attached to men and still poor (Burnham, 1987). Their poverty is not only a gender issue but is related to a legacy of class and racial discrimination (Higginbotham, 1987).

We can also see beyond approaches which focus on women as victims by learning how working-class women and women of color resist class and racial oppression (Morgen, 1986). Rather than a continuum from accommodation to rebellion, Morgen sees diverse personal and protracted struggles against oppression. These women actively resist the limitations placed on their lives by gender, class, and racial oppression. Denied access to many public spheres, they do not protest by voting or writing letters to congressmen; instead, they are involved in grassroots organizing, efforts to improve public schools and other neighborhood institutions, jobs actions, and the like. Morgen's book (co-edited with Ann Bookman) *Women and the Politics of Empowerment* (1988) incorporates much of the new research on women and resistance, research which is primarily on working-class women. Rich examples of resistance are also found in the new scholarship on women in domestic work (Clark-Lewis, 1985; Rollins, 1985).

If we abandon the practice of keeping working-class women and women of color on the margins in our teaching and our research, and seek ways to incorporate the diversity of women's experiences, we are more likely to involve students and challenge their racist assumptions. We can also move students beyond seeing women of color and working-class women as victims.

Addressing the Lives of Ordinary Women of Color. A second way that women of color are introduced into the curriculum is by a brief look at a few "exceptional" examples. This method is very common in history and the social sciences, where "exceptional" Black women such as Sojourner Truth, Harriet Tubman, Ida B. Wells, and Mary McLeod Bethune are discussed. In contrast to marginal treatments of women of color, described above, where the population of women of color is seen as an undifferentiated mass, this approach holds up a few models—non-victims—for admiration. In the case of Black women, this is often done under the guise that racism has not been terribly difficult for them. The subtle message to students is that if successful Black women could achieve in the face of obstacles, other Black women failed to attain the same heights because of faulty culture, lack of motivation, and other individual deficits. A faculty member might not intend to reinforce the individualistic lessons of the American ideology, but students interpret the material in this way because it is a common theme in our history. The "exceptions" approach fails to depict the larger social system in which the struggles of women of color, whether successful or not, take place.

In "The Politics of Black Women's Studies," by Barbara Smith and Gloria Hull, which is the introductory essay in *But Some of Us Are Brave: Black Women's Studies,* the authors warn of this practice:

> A descriptive approach to the lives of Black women, a "great Black women" in history or literature approach, or any traditional male identified approach will not result in intellectually groundbreaking or politically transforming work. We cannot

change our lives by teaching solely about "exceptions" to the
ravages of white-male oppression. Only through exploring the
experiences of supposedly "ordinary" Black women whose "un-
exceptional" actions enabled us and the race to survive, will we
be able to begin to develop an overview and analytic framework
for understanding the lives of Afro-American women (1982,
pp. xxi–xxii).

To do otherwise is to deceive ourselves. The experiences of a few
exceptional Black women, as typically portrayed in the classroom,
serve to deny the reality of oppressive structures. This approach
does not help students develop an appreciation for the role of race,
class, and gender in people's lives. As we attempt to bring women
of color out of the margins, we must be prepared to challenge students' tendency to romanticize a few heroines.

These two practices, teaching about women of color as tangents
to the "generic" woman and examining the lives of exceptional
women of color, work to justify and perpetuate the marginalization
of women of color in women's studies scholarship. Approaches such
as these retard the field of women's studies and complicate the task
of integrating women into the high school and college curricula.
While these approaches might represent a step or phase in the
process of changing the curriculum, we must also remain clear on
the larger goals and objectives of curriculum transformation. As
pointed out earlier, each step in transformation brings its own set
of problems and contradictions into the classroom. If we are not
clear about our ultimate goal, we may become discouraged and
retreat before new problems. In the end, we seek a curriculum that
teaches an awareness and appreciation of the diversity of human
experiences as well as the commonality of the human condition.

If a course is structured around the dominant group experience
and people of color are marginalized, faculty members lose the opportunity to critically address social structure—that is, the ways in
which the institutions of society shape our options and influence
our behavior. Transforming the curriculum requires explicit discussions of the roles of gender, race, and class in shaping the lives
of everybody. This is accomplished by exploring the diversity of the
experiences of men and women in the United States and around
the world. For example, being female means privileges and the ac-
companying restrictions of dependency for some women, while for
others it means poverty and the burden of supporting themselves
and dependents.

Within this framework, no norm or modal case is taken for granted. If one teaches the sociology of the American family, it is with an eye on examining the diversity of family forms and lives. In family studies, only a minority of today's families fit the supposed norm of the 1950s and 1960s, of a full-time-employed father and a mother at home with the children. Therefore, it is easier and more accurate to look at the variations of family forms and discuss which factors obstruct or support specific types of family structures. Faculty members might even find that students, who are well aware of the variety of families, might be motivated to explore the factors behind this diversity. This perspective is the core of a recent textbook about the sociology of the family, *Diversity in American Families*, by Maxine Baca Zinn and D. Stanley Eitzen (1987). The book, which elaborates how race and class, major structures of inequality, affect specific family forms, is well received by students because it does not hold up any single type as the norm by which all other families are judged.

Racism, Diversity, and Classroom Dynamics

Racism is a pervasive classroom problem that has to be addressed. One approach is to inform students that racism often takes the form of misinformation about racial-ethnic groups. Discussions of how misinformation is systematically taught in the schools and the media, and in informal ways from friends, parents, and the like, may relieve individual students from feeling guilty for holding racist notions. Students should be encouraged to think critically about the information they get regarding their own group and others' groups, so that they will learn to question broad generalizations like "All whites are middle class" and "All Blacks are poor." Information that sheds light on the diversity within a group is more likely to be correct.

Students should be encouraged to think critically about information that devalues or dehumanizes members of specific groups. For example, any idea that some people (usually Blacks, Latinos, or Native Americans) are more comfortable with hunger, poverty, and the like than other groups (usually white Americans) implies that the former are "less than human." Any information that students received which has the effect of dehumanizing a group can be identified as racist and therefore not a fact of the social world.

These are just a few ideas to help faculty think about combatting racism in the classroom. Correct information and changing teaching methods will do a great deal to challenge the racism embedded in our educational system—where there are a limited number of legitimate lines of inquiry and where "inquirers are only allowed to ask certain questions" (Spelman, 1982, p. 15).

The manner in which material on "new" populations is introduced into a classroom can either challenge students' racism or confirm it. Faculty members often interpret students' resistance to material about racial-ethnic groups as a lack of interest in the unique experiences of Afro-Americans, Asian Americans, and other groups. Indeed, students might have little specific interest in these unique experiences, but they can learn the value of a race, class, and gender analysis. As they enhance these skills, they may begin to grasp how structural barriers that shape life options for people of color may also affect their own lives.

How faculty develop an appreciation of diversity will depend upon where they teach. The institutional setting is a key ingredient. An approach might work very well in one setting and then fail miserably in another. If one's institution accepts the challenge of curriculum change, there may be structural supports which would be lacking in an institution that has reconfirmed its commitment to the traditional curriculum. Faculty members must consider the specific agendas and resources of their college or university and gauge their actions accordingly.

A plan for action should also be informed by the racial, class, and ethnic backgrounds of the students and other faculty, as well as by the gender composition of the classrooms and the institution's geographic location. An instructor can teach the same course in different institutions and experience very different classroom dynamics (Chow, 1985). Faculty in homogeneous liberal colleges where there are few people of color and the working-class students are very quiet may need to use methods which differ from those who teach in public institutions with more heterogeneous student bodies.

For example, when teaching an undergraduate urban sociology course at Columbia University, I used the urban environment to challenge students' stereotypes and misinformation. I took my entire class on a walking tour of Harlem, the Black community down the hill from Columbia. On the tour they could see middle-class housing, both single-family dwellings and apartment complexes, as well as stable working-class housing and deteriorating housing. They could also see Harlem's cultural institutions, such as libraries, churches, community centers, and the like. This tour worked wonders in shaking up the unquestioned "fact" that Harlem is a slum. It also opened students up to questioning other "facts" about the world that they had so readily accepted. A walking tour of a Black community is not an option for faculty located in a small college town who may face students with the same stereotypic notions. Such faculty will have to develop different resources, such as films, speakers, and reading materials that capture the lives of human beings living in Black communities. (One resource is Bettylou Valentine's (1978) *Hustling and Other Hard Work,* a report of five years of field research that challenges standard misinformation and communicates the ways that human beings struggle to survive.)

Plans for curriculum changes are also shaped by the interpersonal dynamics in the courses you teach. Do you depend solely upon the lecture or do you encourage discussions? Do all your students participate in discussions? Is your class a chilly one for women? (Hall, 1982). Do your Black students and other students of color participate in the classroom discussions? (Moses, 1989). Are the people of color in your classes likely to challenge stereotypic or racist comments made by white students? In general, are you pleased with the classroom atmosphere?

Many faculty members who bring a central perspective on women into the classroom find that they abandon their dependency on lectures, which helps to promote lively discussions in class. Yet, this is not a smooth path. Some students, especially those who have enjoyed privilege, might be the most vocal, while students from traditionally disadvantaged populations are more likely to remain silent. It is also possible for students from the majority group to be silent in the face of shifting expectations on them as students. There can be many reasons for students' silence, Vicky Spelman (1982) reminds us. It can reflect a lack of concern; fears, especially about saying the wrong thing; lack of knowledge about the material; or even resistance to the material. Spelman encourages faculty to carefully address the conditions under which discussions take place. We must take precautions to insure that we develop an atmosphere where all class members are full participants.

The routes individual faculty members take to enhance classroom dynamics will vary widely, but there can be some goals we all share. Part of the task of the college instructor is to create an environment where there can be an honest and open exchange about the material and where students can do what they are rarely asked to do—learn from each other.

Conclusion

Curriculum transformation is a challenge in which all faculty can participate. As we pursue short- and long-term goals it is important to be mindful of the several tasks involved in the process: securing information, integrating material into our teaching, and establishing a supportive classroom. Do not become discouraged by the slow progress. Establishing support for faculty can be critical in the success of projects. Join with other colleagues in learning new materials and experimenting in the classroom. The presence of support groups can help faculty members reflect on their progress and motivate them to take new risks. Faculty who accept this new challenge may find a rejuvenated interest in teaching their students.

REFERENCES

Andersen, Margaret. 1987. "Curriculum Change in Higher Education." *Signs: Journal of Women and Culture in Society* 12 (Winter): 222–54.

Andersen, Margaret. 1988. "Moving Our Minds: Studying Women of Color and Reconstructing Sociology." *Teaching Sociology* 16 (April): 123–32.

Baca Zinn, Maxine, Lynn Weber Cannon, Elizabeth Higginbotham, and Bonnie Thornton Dill. 1986. "On the Costs of Exclusionary Practices in Women's Studies." *Signs: Journal of Women and Culture in Society* 11 (Winter): 290–303.

Baca Zinn, Maxine, and D. Stanley Eitzen. 1987. *Diversity in American Families.* New York: Harper and Row.

Bookman, Ann, and Sandra Morgen, eds. 1988. *Women and the Politics of Empowerment.* Philadelphia: Temple University Press.

Burnham, Linda. 1986. "Has Poverty Been Feminized in Black America?" In *For Crying Out Loud: Women and Poverty in the United States,* ed. Ann Withorn and Rochelle Lefkowitz. New York: Pilgrim Press. Pp. 69–83.

Chow, Esther Ngan-Ling. 1985. "Teaching Sex and Gender in Sociology: Incorporating the Perspective of Women of Color." *Teaching Sociology* 12 (April): 299–311.

Clark-Lewis, Elizabeth. 1985. " 'This Work Had A End': The Transition from Live-in to Day Work." Southern Women: The Intersection of Race, Class and Gender, Working Paper #2. Center for Research on Women, Memphis State University.

Collins, Patricia Hill. 1986. "Learning from the Outsider Within: The Sociological Significance of Black Feminist Thought." *Social Problems* 33 (December): S14–32.

Dill, Bonnie Thornton. 1988. "Our Mothers' Grief: Racial-Ethnic Women and the Maintenance of Families." *Journal of Family History* 13: 412–31.

Hall, Robert M. 1982. "The Classroom Climate: A Chilly One for Women?" Project on the Status and Education of Women, Association of American Colleges, Washington, D.C.

Higginbotham, Elizabeth. 1986. "We Were Never on a Pedestal: Women of Color Continue to Struggle with Poverty, Racism and Sexism." In *For Crying Out Loud: Women and Poverty in the United States*, ed. Ann Withorn and Rochelle Lefkowitz. New York: Pilgrim Press. Pp. 97–109.

Hull, Gloria T., Patricia Bell Scott, and Barbara Smith. 1982. *But Some of Us Are Brave: Black Women's Studies*. Old Westbury, N.Y.: Feminist Press.

Minnich, Elizabeth Kamarck. 1990. *Transforming Knowledge*. Philadelphia: Temple University Press.

Morgen, Sandra. 1986. "To See Ourselves, To See Our Sisters: The Challenge of Re-envisioning Curriculum Change." A Publication from the Research Clearinghouse and Curriculum Integration Project, Memphis State University, Center for Research on Women.

Moses, Yolanda T. 1989. "Black Women in Academe: Issues and Strategies," Project on the Status and Education of Women, Association of American Colleges, Washington, D.C.

Rollins, Judith. 1985. *Between Women: Domestics and Their Employers*. Philadelphia: Temple University Press.

Spelman, Vicky. 1982. "Combatting the Marginalization of Black Women in the Classroom." *Women's Studies Quarterly* 10 (Summer): 15–16.

Valentine, Bettylou. 1978. *Hustling and Other Hard Work*. New York: Free Press.

Wong, Eugene F. 1985. "Asian American Middleman Minority Theory: The Framework for an American Myth." *Journal of Ethnic Studies* 13 (Spring): 51–88.

Elizabeth Higginbotham is Associate Professor of Sociology and Social Work at Memphis State University and Publications Director at the Center for Research on Women. She has been working in curriculum change and also conducting comparative research on professional and managerial women. Professor Higginbotham is author of a forthcoming book, Too Much to Ask: The Cost of Black Female Success.

This is a revision of a paper originally published as part of the Memphis State University Center for Research on Women's Research Clearinghouse and Curriculum Integration Project. The author would like to acknowledge the suggestions of Lynn Weber Cannon, Angela Ginorio, and Kenneth Goings.

The Case for a National
Women's Studies Association

Elsa Greene   *Winter 1976*

Thinking wishfully, the case for a national women's studies association is very straightforward: Most of us who are committed to the study of women are short on time, energy and money. By organizing ourselves, we could make our work easier and more effective.

Since 1973, when Catharine Stimpson first suggested the formation of a national association, there has been widespread consensus about a few basic functions that such an organization might serve. First, we clearly need a nationwide communications network. Learning administrative tactics through trial and error is expensive. We would benefit from prompt reporting on our strategic failures and successes. Not only might we sometimes avoid repeating each other's mistakes, we might also use up-to-date information about successes elsewhere to strengthen the case for funding similar—or unique—projects of our own. It is ironic that as women fighting to undo institutionalized ignorance about ourselves, we have neglected to learn thoroughly enough about each other's accomplishments.

We need to know what is happening month by month around the country, and we also need ready access to central files on curricula, existing programs and research projects—proposed and in progress. One national resource center would spare us the impersonal drudgery of form letter interchanges about our programs; it would facilitate instead less voluminous and more purposeful correspondence among us.

In addition to conserving our resources, an all-inclusive women's studies network would increase our power. We would gain informal power simply by being in touch with each other—transmitting insights, encouragement, job gossip, advice—rather than working in isolated groups. (As Elaine Reuben pointed out during a conference held last spring at Indiana University, traditional educational administrators are forever keeping each other up on recent developments. To deal with them effectively, we need comparable information from our kind.) A national association would also give us the formal means to legitimate ourselves through national policy statements, and it would give us the power to mobilize support for individuals and programs that are forced into especially drastic struggles for survival.

The potential benefits of a national association seem indisputable enough so that I almost wonder why I am sitting here three years after Stimpson's piece writing yet another essay stating once again the case for a still nonexistent organization. If an association is self-evidently desirable, why haven't we formed one up to now? Partly most of us have been overloaded taking care of our own immediate needs. Partly we have managed to meet each other in women's sections at the conventions of traditional professional associations, at feminist conferences and at regional conferences on women's studies. Partly we have gotten by with subscriptions to the *Women's Studies Newsletter*—letting a few women supply the money and energy for our only national publication. But mainly we don't have an association yet because no one has been willing to face the practical political issues involved in translating the idea of a national organization into a reality.

Carol Lafazan's notes on a recent discussion sponsored by Brooklyn College list several of the problems we would need to confront in the process of creating a national organization. For one: "There is great political diversity among women's studies programs. Will all programs be willing to support all other programs?" The vision of our association mobilizing on behalf of threatened sisters fades. Should we require a referendum on each imperiled group before committing our resources to their struggle? Should we limit membership to only those with whom the rest of us would be prepared to stand in the event of a crisis? (Both of the above questions are premised on the possibly optimistic assumption that in our diversity we will be able to arrive at a national structure that will accommodate us long enough to put our supportiveness to the test.)

A second problem is related to the first: "We must guard against becoming a traditional 'professional' organization. We should be clear about what the powers and functions of this organization will be." How do we fight for our survival without trapping ourselves in a codified, self-perpetuating fortress? How do we gain the visibility and influence of a strong association without becoming a token ghetto of feminists surrounded by an unaltered patriarchal monolith? Too much associating exclusively with each other, and—as Florence Howe has warned— we could go the way of the home economics profession which has many students, moderate status and no power to affect the general curriculum.

One last illustrative difficulty: "We should guard against unequal distribution of power. Students, faculty and staff women must be equally involved at all levels of the organization." Granting for the moment that we will be imaginative enough to devise an effective national structure which accommodates ideological differences and minimizes power differences among students, faculty and staff women, how do we establish regional power equity? How do we make sure that small programs are not dominated by large ones? Shall we vote as programs? As individuals? Shall we vote at all? And are community women to be excluded from the association?

Thinking realistically, perhaps the benefits of remaining unassociated or of gathering in small, spontaneous local groups outweigh the value of a national organization. But no. We do need current information about each other, access to comprehensive academic resources and the power of mutual support. All three requirements are best fulfilled by a national association. The national structure would in no way supercede existing regional and local groups such as the Western States Women's Studies Association and the Greater Philadelphia Consortium for Women's Studies. In fact, better communication nationally should facilitate the growth of regional associations—groups whose functions would not be in conflict with the services of the national organization. Implementing a national association will be a strenuous challenge. Let's get on with it.

The women at San Jose State University have begun to plan a national conference which will result in the formation of a national women's studies association. In putting together a design for a viable, equitable meeting, they have been handicapped by the nonexistence of a national communications network. (The principle of collective decision making will be impossible to honor until we have a mechanism for contacting all of the women who have a stake in what is being decided.) Not being able to consult everyone, the San Jose women have had to make difficult choices—not about the eventual structure or function of the association but about the process that will lead up to the meeting at which the association will take shape.

Tentatively, the San Jose proposal calls for widely participatory planning activities based in women's studies programs across the nation to be followed by a small, working meeting of representatives from each existing program. That the first national women's studies conference should be invitational will raise some outcries that the San Jose design is elitist. But invitations will go to programs, not to individuals, and hopefully the conference will be able to pay travel expenses for at least one representative from each school. Thus, women from all regions will be able to participate in the proceedings regardless of their institutional budgets.

As more and more women hear about the proposed meeting at San Jose, they are contributing ideas and offering to take part in the planning. Regional women's studies conferences are deliberating the issues. We should be clear as we proceed that the primary question before us is not whether to have a national network but what kind of network we want to have. Those few of us who live in cities—or have long distance telephone and travel funds—will keep in touch. Somehow the *Women's Studies Newsletter* will continue. But only a national association can ensure an equitable distribution of knowledge, power and responsibility among us all.

Planning a National Women's Studies Association

Elsa Greene and Elaine Reuben   *Spring 1976*

On Saturday, March 20, thirty women came together in Philadelphia to begin laying the groundwork for a National Women's Studies Association and to plan for a national founding convention at which the Association will be launched. After two days of intense and high energy discussion, the group agreed in principle on a working paper which proposes a shape for the Association; they also created and approved an outline for a three-day, representational convention to be held in mid-November at San Jose State University.

In response to a proposal for a nation-wide conference on women's studies initiated by women at San Jose State in the summer of 1975, the Ford Foundation offered to fund a national planning meeting at the University of Pennsylvania. As San Jose had asked, the original grant was meant to cover costs for "six or seven" regional representatives. However, the conveners of the meeting—Marilyn Fleener and Sybil Weir of San Jose; Elsa Greene and Eileen Warburton of Pennsylvania— decided to go back to Ford for enough money so that 30 representatives could attend. Greene's letter to the Foundation explained that to provide sufficiently varied regional representation and to include some women who are directly in control of national women's studies resources, it would be necessary to assemble "ten predesignated [regional] representatives, plus ten additional representatives to be selected [by lot] from among nominees submitted by interested programs in each geographical area," plus ten representatives-at-large, e.g., women's studies journal editors, officers of funding agencies and two of the meeting conveners. The letter continued: "This design . . . will ensure that planning for the nation-wide meeting will be truly national from its inception. It will also establish our commitment to democratic process—a commitment which is basic to the ideals of those developing women's studies programs across the country."

Ford appropriated additional money and the conveners proceeded, with some trepidation, to implement their proposal. Eileen Warburton made up ten regions by drawing lines on a map so that approximately

15 programs would be included in each area. Sybil Weir and Elsa Greene chose initial regional representatives from among those who had volunteered help in response to the circulation of the San Jose proposal. Since neither one knew more than a few of the correspondents, they were free to be random about the particular individuals they selected. They did, however, choose so that a wide variety of programs, including those at community colleges, would be included.

The conveners asked each predesignated representative to contact all of the programs and individuals in that region who might be interested in contributing ideas and nominating an additional representative to the Philadelphia meeting. Numerous problems arose: The "regions" turned out to be awkwardly arbitrary; time pressure, out-dated mailing addresses, vacation schedules and budgetary pressures compounded the difficulties of regional communication. Among those contacted, third world women were underrepresented. A number of committed individuals volunteered to attend the meeting at their own expense and were dissuaded in the name of maintaining regional balance. Each woman who was to be present came to realize that a hundred others could as well have come in her place.

Despite complications, when the 30 representatives finally assembled in Philadelphia—from Henniker, Missoula, Cincinnati, Miami, St. Louis, Albuquerque, Brooklyn, Pittsburgh and Pomona—they did, indeed, reflect much of the diversity of women's studies. Each report given at the opening session on Saturday night focused on the particular concerns of each region. But the results of a poll of those who could not attend showed two dominant ideas nation-wide: an insistence that any planning for a conference or an association be inclusive and flexible; and a serious mandate to begin the task.

On Sunday morning, the representatives struggled to clarify the tensions among the interests of regions, programs and individuals who might be served by a women's studies association. The group also began to define a focus for an association which would be inclusive without diminishing the organization's identity as a body specifically committed to feminist education.

By Monday afternoon, the planners arrived at virtual consensus on a design for the National Association—one which mediates some of the tensions among our diverse interests and reflects our concern for inclusive, democratic process. All of the quotations and paraphrases that follow are taken from rough drafts generated during workshops and approved in principle at Monday's plenary session. They are offered here as a beginning—to invite critical comments and suggestions for revisions. A coherent, elaborated, amended draft of the working paper will be printed up and circulated well in advance of the national convention. . . .

The Association

Purpose. "As a national women's studies organization our aim is to provide and encourage nonsexist, nonracist feminist education in traditional and nontraditional areas of education."

Program. Activities to implement the overall purpose will include: communications (perhaps through a bimonthly newsletter, a quarterly journal and annual conferences); strategies for changing traditional curricula, programs and institutional practices (disseminated through a national index of curriculum resources and program information); advocacy; research; legal and moral support; outreach; self-evaluation; and links with other groups supportive of our goals.

Membership. Voting membership will be available to 1) individuals and 2) programs, educational institutions and projects concerned with feminist education and/or services and having a policy committee. Nonvoting corresponding membership will be open to affiliate groups.

Dues. Depending on income, individual dues will range from $1 to $50; program dues will range from $5 to $100. The newsletter of the Association will be sent to all dues-paying members.

Governance and Structure. The following is an interim plan for at least two years, but not more than four years. It represents an attempt to "work both regionally and nationally" and to include programs' interests and the interests of those not connected with academic, credit-granting programs.

"The membership will make policy; the Coordinating Council will implement policy; the staff will carry it out." National governance will be carried out by a Coordinating Council to be elected annually (or for two-year terms) by the membership. Each of 12 regions will elect two representatives to the Council. These persons must represent two different constituencies of the members of this Association within that region. "We expect that at least four of the elected members of the Coordinating Council will consist of third world women. In the event that this does not occur, a national election will be held among third world women in the Association." Also, if among elected members of the Coordinating Council, "there is not a person to voice the special concerns of lesbian women, the council will establish a mechanism for election of such a person by the entire membership." The Coordinating Council will elect two conveners from among themselves; meet twice a year in addition to the annual meeting; hire staff for a national office; decide the location of the national office; set the agenda for the annual national convention; be responsible for implementing the functions of the organization.

The annual convention will set priorities for the Association and make significant policy decisions. Voting delegates to the convention will include three persons (from different constituencies) per dues-paying program and ten regionally-elected delegates from members not affiliated with programs who have paid dues and who come from clearly identifiable categories of the regional membership (such as women's studies faculty out of work; students who are graduates of programs; community project people not in member programs; high school or elementary school teachers; others).

The Founding Conference

The planning group agreed that revision and ratification of the proposal for a National Association should constitute a major part of the agenda for the first national meeting. Since a representational voting structure for the Association cannot go into effect prior to its approval at the founding conference, the planners devised a one-time method for selecting delegates to that meeting.

Regions and Delegates. "A goal of the first National Conference is to bring into being officially recognized regions—the formal organization of which will permit the development of informational and supportive networks.

"Preliminary to this first National Conference . . . most of the potential regions are not yet clearly defined by existing organizations, although regional affinities are acknowledged both by tradition and informal network.

"Therefore, the [Workshop] on Regions and Delegates has drawn up 12 temporary regions to be used for the purpose of selecting by lottery the 144 special (students, primary-elementary-secondary teachers, minority women) and 156 at-large delegates who will participate in conjunction with the approximately 200 [delegates] representing the existing programs identified preliminary to the national planning conference. Each program is to be represented by one delegate . . . who may be a student, staff person, faculty member or administrator."

Feminist Travel Pool. Every delegate to the meeting at San Jose will be assessed an equal amount for travel costs, wherever she/he happens to live. The common fund will cover travel expenses for everyone.

Conference Agenda. Mornings of the three-day meeting will be given to work on the National Association. The afternoon program will consist of workshops on issues concerning women's studies development—one day on curriculum, one on administration and one on funding. Time and space will be provided throughout the three days for meetings of special interest groups and for spontaneous workshops and caucuses. In addition to elected delegates, some foreign observers may be invited to attend the proceedings. . . .

Writing It All Down: An Overview of the Second NWSA Convention

Catharine R. Stimpson   **Summer 1980**

Few conventions about education have either much cheer or tenderness. Those of the National Women's Studies Association do. In this, too, NWSA is unusual. One of the many good events at the 1980 Convention at Indiana University in Bloomington was a workshop that Frances Doughty of the National Gay Task Force gave. She used letters, photographs, and other archival remnants to portray a "lesbian friendship group," women who were either friends or lovers for thirty years. The audience touched its past with blissful curiosity. Then Doughty told a story about a famous member of the group: Janet Flanner, the writer. Shortly before her death, someone asked Flanner if she had any messages for the next generation. "Write it all down," Flanner answered, "Write it all down."

Throughout the NWSA Convention, people were, if unknowingly, obeying Flanner's command. Many of the approximately 1,500 participants were keeping notebooks, journals, diaries, or their technological equivalents: photographs and tapes. It rained consistently in Bloomington from May 16 to 20. People who walked or jogged around the campus returned to their rooms with shoes or sneakers squelching. Recording events, codifying time, was almost as common an experience as being wet.

The sense of history was collective as well as personal. Significantly, this was the *second* NWSA national gathering, tangible proof that the organization could survive, a phenomenon that some observers might not have predicted, given NWSA's vulnerabilities. Structurally, it is a convoluted compound of caucuses, taskforces, committees, assemblies, and a national office. Financially, it is still fragile, particularly given the desire to respond to diverse constituencies. Neither birth, nor blood, nor age, nor specific occupation, nor geography unites its members. A cause does. Morally and politically, NWSA is hugely ambitious. The 1980 theme was "Educating for Change," but the change for which NWSA stands is nothing less than a series of transformations of public and private lives. That such a group could endure was cause for celebration and a sense of reassurance.

Having a past eased some things. At the first session of the 1980 Delegate Assembly, in a wood-paneled hall with chandeliers and crimson curtains, the Convention Coordinators spoke of their good fortune in having previous work on which to build. In 1979, the Assembly had passed scores of disparate, often unwieldy, resolutions. In 1980, NWSA members or delegates who wished to propose a recommendation or resolution were required to present its cost and a method of implementation as well.

The Convention self-consciously recognized that the women's movement to which NWSA adheres has its own past, too. A panel at the opening session was called "*Sexual Politics:* Ten Years Later." The 1979 meeting had occurred thirty years after the publication of another central feminist text: Simone de Beauvoir's *The Second Sex.* When Millett and de Beauvoir were writing their books, many of the Convention participants were adults, but many were unborn, babies, in primary school, or high schoolers. (Of the 796 people who filled out demographic data cards, 351 said they were between 25 and 34 years of age.) Women's studies, in brief, now has a multitude of unequally stored memory banks. Ironically, despite the fact that several Convention sessions took up the theme of "Mothers and Daughters," there were few, if any, mechanisms through which the memory banks in the NWSA itself might have been systematically tapped. Generations of work within the movement were only erratically drawn upon.

More often, two linked, subterranean feelings appeared to emerge, disappear, and then re-emerge. The first was some skepticism about the good faith of women in positions of authority, who both were and were not comparative old-timers in women's studies. NWSA must never embody the principle of blind obedience, of a bland stupor of the will. On the contrary, NWSA must persistently challenge authorities. At the panel at the opening session, Elizabeth Janeway lucidly outlined the process through which women reject weakness and come into their own strength. They begin, she said, with "mistrust . . . disbelief . . . a refusal to accept orthodox myth, dictionary definitions, and standard explanations." They move next to a sharing of disbelief, and then, finally, to action. There they cease to be "*angst*-ridden victims and become members of a movement.". . .

The second feeling was some grumbling about Convention arrangements. Some participants grumped about registration lines, food, the campus bus service, the telephones. A little like dependent daughters who want perfect mothers, they tended to confuse a Convention and an organization with a home. They also were indifferent to the extraordinary efforts of the people who put on the Indiana hootenanny/

celebration/campus camp/chautauqua/academic gathering. Indiana University volunteers alone had labored for a total of 3,320 hours. If they had been paid at the new minimum wage rate, they would have earned about $10,000.

However, the Convention mood was mostly sturdy, spirited, and supportive. Because Indiana University is vast, an environment that embraces both bucolic lushness and high-rise buildings, living spaces and meeting places tended to be far away from each other. Good feelings, then, had to sustain themselves without relying on an excess of proximity. People were also energetic. The Convention program listed about 250 sessions, 40 meetings, 12 special events, sports and exercise classes, art exhibits, films, parties, and dances. Either "cornucopia" or "collage" would have been an appropriate metaphor for the schedule.

The quantity of events reflected the number of ends the Convention was to realize. First, it was to give people a chance to exchange pragmatic information, facts about a lot of things. Many sessions and workshops concerned building a women's center, or conducting a class, or writing a grant proposal, or devising a political strategy. Second, the Convention was to be a scholarly forum. For better or worse, NWSA has yet to find an alternative to the academic paper as a scholarly medium. . . .

Despite an occasional session on Islam, Cuba, or cross-cultural feminism, the focus of scholars tended to be the United States. Once again, women's studies veered toward the provincial. Fortunately, some of the most sophisticated papers defied such a pattern and showed the influence of contemporary European theories. Oddly, there was little history. Bloomington seemed to swerve away from one of the most fertile of women's studies enterprises. Brooding about this, one of the most promising young historians of women wondered if it was an accident, or if scholars in general were not saving their papers for their disciplinary meetings and historians in particular for the Berkshire Conference.

Some of the greatest intellectual excitement appeared in two fields that have been historic antagonists: science and religion. The potential tensions between them for feminist scholars have yet to be articulated, let alone resolved. In part, the meetings about science were explosive deconstructions of dominant theories about the secular world. People asked how a patriarchal society might have shaped scientific inquiry and practice, and how, in turn, scientific theories about nature might have "produced sexist understandings." In contrast, the meetings about religion were, in part, controversial, conflicting reconstructions of pictures of a sacred world. Feminist theologicians disagreed about the usefulness of patriarchal traditions, and about the truth of certain female traditions. Hovering over both academic and nonacademic gatherings was a mythic presence, the figure of a goddess and her surrogates, which some worship but others find weird. For example, Sally Gearhart, after a reading of her fiction, casually remarked, "those into the craft, I mean witchcraft," and another woman advanced the claims of a "theosophic" approach to feminism and to life.

Still another purpose of the Convention was to assess NWSA's structure and guiding principles, laws, and decisions. Once again, the relationship between NWSA and the United States Agency for International Development became a volatile test question for both internal governance and official morality. I cannot pretend to have a full understanding of the drama, but it seemed to provoke an argument about the relative powers of the Delegate Assembly and the Coordinating Council. In 1979, the Assembly had passed two resolutions (8 and 48) that had severed any connections between NWSA and AID. Later, the Council had concluded that because the resolutions were in some conflict with the NWSA Constitution, they could not be acted upon. In 1980, some Assembly members said that the Council had to be more responsive to Assembly decisions; that the Council could only set aside Assembly resolutions if they were patently, plainly unconstitutional.

The issue also involved NWSA's commitment to politics other than those of the women's movement. Nearly all, if not all, of the people at the Bloomington Convention would agree that feminism is inseparable from other movements for social justice, in America and elsewhere. However, they might disagree about the necessity of banning AID as a Convention exhibitor, or as a source of travel money that might bring Third World women to America to the NWSA or that might send NWSA representatives abroad. Ultimately, the Third World Caucus offered a resolution that suggested that AID involvement with NWSA violated that section of the NWSA Constitution that pledged the organization's support of the well-being of Third World women. The resolution also asked NWSA to study AID and to suspend any link with it until that research was completed and discussed.

It was important that the Third World Caucus should play such a role. The actual number of Third World women at the Convention was small. Of the 796 people who handed in the demographic data cards, 23 said they were Black; 17 Hispanic; 15 Native American; 9 Asian. Yet the Third World was a strong, palpable force. The Delegate Assembly happily learned that a "woman of color" would be a Coordinator of the 1981 Convention, at the University of Connecticut at Storrs, and that central themes would be race, racism, and the contributions of Black women.

Less happily, the Convention still showed the entanglements of feminism and racism. During a workshop about the chances of "sisterhood" between Black and white women, one of about 20 formal sessions on Third World matters, a Black woman asked if white women were prepared to let Black women lead them. She was never fully, honestly answered. At the same place, a white woman called for a "humanistic feminism." She said that "hu" was "hue," and that we were all women of color. Her pun insensitively ignored the years of effort within feminism to acknowledge the reality of differences among women, the consequences of race and class and sexual preference. Calmly, with patient courtesy, a Black woman told her that she could not so hastily wipe out the centuries of history that had forged the Black woman's collective experience. One evening, a play about Calamity Jane, who was a racist even according to the play's author, proved a torment for many in the audience.

A fourth and final purpose of Bloomington was to offer women a place in which to cultivate common ground. An NWSA meeting initiates and deepens conversations, friendships, and romances. It lets a woman who might be thought to be impolitic, impolite, and freakish in her home community see human images similar to her own. She is no longer a solitary feminist or opponent of nuclear energy or lesbian. She has colleagues and peers. The Convention is both exhilarating and a profound relief.

Organized around the idea of change, the Convention participants displayed their own signs of change. The phrase "women of color" entered the language of many. The substitution of "wimmin" for "women" attracted some. Lesbians were a vigorous, vital group, but more men seemed to be wearing badges in Bloomington than in Lawrence, Kansas, and little boys lived in the dormitories and rode elevators that otherwise forbade men to be in them after 10 P.M. One cannot have the comfort of illusions about the degree of change that NWSA has brought about in the world beyond its gatherings. We are still marginal, if illegitimately so, to many educational institutions and projects. We must still devour our dreams for sustenance. We still have our contradictions, unexamined actions, and bouts of pettiness. Yet we do educate. We do dream. Despite our frailties, we are energetic and alive. Bloomington was a part of the process of the creation of our history, even as other organizations, which may ignore or mock us, slouch toward obsolescence.

Catharine R. Stimpson *is Professor of English at Douglass College, Rutgers University.*

Encounter with American Feminism: A Muslim Woman's View of Two Conferences

Leila Ahmed   *Summer 1980*

April 1980. The Barnard Conference. "The Scholar and the Feminist"—my first direct as opposed to page-mediated encounter with American feminism. And then it came home to me: how simple the one-dimensional experience of reading: how easy, ordered, and amenable to order it makes things seem—coherent and amenable to coherence. Sitting in that hall, listening to papers that often clearly drew on the rhetorical strategies of an oral tradition, quite different from those in scholarly writing, even in that feminist scholarship self-consciously dismantling the rigidities of tradition; being aware of the responses of a highly—and diversely—responsive audience; straining to catch verbal shortcuts; sometimes clearly missing nuances that relied on a depth of American experience: all this makes it impossible to respond to the conference as a coherent event—not because *it* was incoherent, obviously, but precisely because there was such a sense of vitality, ferment, such a richness and general manifoldness to it—and a sense too of the manifoldness of feminist stances in America.

My own interest being Third World women, I attended the workshop on "Class and Race Issues in Women's Studies." Angela Jorge, treating the topic experientially, described experiences of the Black Hispanic community and related them to Puerto Rican culture, and Florence Howe then outlined relevant developments in women's studies. Offered concurrently was "Perspectives on the Black and Hispanic Family," and, another I was sorry to miss, "Defining the Erotic" from a lesbian perspective.

Of course it is only in the academy, formally, that the discussion of such topics, relations between women, the erotic between women, is new. Women have been discussing such topics among themselves down through the ages, discussing them at least in that vast array of non-verbal ways that we have of "discussing" things (gestural language being only the most obvious). I have a particularly vivid sense of this because in the society in which I grew up—in Cairo—elaborate understandings, "statements" about how women related to women, were never made verbally but were signaled in an infinite number of ways: by silence sometimes, or by the kind of language with which we surround a subject. My sense too is that much of what was thus conveyed was oblivious to, disregarding of, even running counter to the dominant culture. Thus, it remained inarticulate, "hidden," not dangerous. *Then the NWSA Second National Convention at Bloomington.* Here too I headed for sessions on Third World women. "Teaching about African Women": Brenda Berrian (University of Pittsburgh) showed that comparisons could be made between women in Africa and Third World women in America by looking at women in parallel situations—moving from rural to urban settings. Susan Rogers (University of Minnesota) shared outlines of her courses, notably "Comparative Study of Women: Women in Liberation Struggles, China, Cuba, Mozambique, Guinea Bissau." In another session, "Women and Development: Third World," Suresht R. Bald (University of California/Santa Cruz), not focusing on particular societies but aiming at a theoretical overview, analyzed consequences of political change for women in terms of a grid of variables (types of revolution, nature of struggle, ensuing economies, cultural matrices). Irene Thompson (University of Florida) spoke on women in China.

American interest in Third World women. Well, one thing had become clear to me, reading through women's studies materials and attending the conferences: I wasn't a Third World woman, or didn't count—was invisible. "Third World women" I now came to understand, could mean one of three things: first, it could mean minority women in the United States; second, it could mean Puerto Rican or African women (but with an excluding notion of Africa, a funny-shaped shrunken continent—no Egypt, Morocco, Sudan); third, it could mean a Third World that had achieved visibility through revolution, as in China or Cuba.

The women who seem to be excluded by these definitions are the Muslim women of the Third World—these are most particularly the invisible ones. When we are seen, it is always as Other, although no culture is more directly continuous with the Judeo-Christian than the Islamic, no part of the world closer to the (older) Western world. We all know that Jerusalem is sacred to Christian, Jew, Muslim. But do we allow ourselves to become aware of the cultural implications of this? That if one could lay the blueprints of cultural ideologies one over the other—Christianity, Judaism, Islam—the lines would most often merge? Is it this submerged resemblance, I wonder, this mirroring back in different cultural idiom of all the inbuilt injustices to women institutionalized in their own societies, internalized in themselves, that makes it so necessary for us to be Other—makes difficult, such an uneasy thing, this looking at Islam?

One session at the NWSA Convention did focus on Islam; the room was packed. The session itself I found bizarre. "Islam and Feminism": no dearth of topics to which a session with such a title might address itself— from the law-reforms relating to marital life that "conservative" Muslim feminists are fighting for, piecemeal, against entrenched resistance, to the stance of radical feminists who see Islamic ideology as fundamentally inimical to women, believe that no mere reform can be adequate, and see resolution only in radical social change and the rejection of that ideology. Expecting the panel to address topics within that spectrum, I was wholly nonplussed to find that the general thrust of the presentation was the mind-boggling assertion that Islam was a feminist religion.

The panelists were three Muslim women. The first began by pointing out that Muslim women had had rights (to own property) only recently gained by Western women—thus attempting to establish that the Muslim world hasn't always been backward compared to the West. But from then on the claims made for Islam and what a generally nice "feminist" religion it was seemed to me to grow more and more absurd. Divorce, they said, had had to be bitterly fought for in the West; in Islam it has always been available. (Available for men, they should have said, since it deprives women of their children and can deprive them of shelter. Divorce is still bitterly fought for, for women—in those countries where Islam is not too implacable even to permit a fight.)

Panelists also said that in Islam women and men are equal. But women inherit half what men do; two women must testify for every one man; men can have four wives—the list of inequities is interminable. They said Islam was a feminist religion because it banned the murder of girl-infants and, in permitting four wives, it was actually being restrictive, previous custom allowing more. All this is standard Muslim apologetics that we Muslims grew up with. What's always left out when we hear "how it improved the condition of women" is that it improved it *in Arabia*. How can I, how can any Egyptian with any notion of Egypt's pre-Islamic history, regard as anything but, for women, constrictive and disastrous in terms of lost rights and freedoms, the coming of monotheisms, the conquest of Egypt by the Arabs, and its Islamicization? And yet all this is not to deny Islam's vision of dignity, justice, and equality for all, though this vision has not been realized in the letter of its laws. . . .

Leila Ahmed studied English at Cambridge University and is a teacher and writer.

Disobedience Is What NWSA Is Potentially About

Adrienne Rich   **Fall 1981**

For those of you who are unaware of it, I want to start with the fact that the advance coverage of this Convention by the Hartford *Courant* on May 19, 1981, was headlined "Lesbian Housing Available for Women's Conference at UConn" and focused entirely on the arrangements for a "lesbian section" of the dormitory, where "between 60 and 75 women" would by request be lodged. Heavy emphasis was laid on alleged difficulties between lesbians and heterosexual women last year in Bloomington, and the issue of "segregated" housing. There was no mention whatsoever of racism as the theme of the Convention.

I feel it is important to start by analyzing this. It is, first of all, a deliberate erasure of our declared purpose here. The National Women's Studies Association chose, as a part of the feminist movement rather than as a dutiful daughter of academia, to address the estrangement, ignorance, fear, anger, and disempowerment created by the institutional racism which saturates all our lives. Many of us have come here in a mixture of hope and fear, hope and anger, hope and determination. Many, it may be assumed, have stayed away: some for lack of money, some for lack of hope, some for lack of determination, some for lack of caring. But these meetings have a purpose, and this purpose, visibly stated in NWSA's literature, has been wiped out by the local press.

It should be obvious to us by now that this kind of erasure serves and supports the racism of the larger society. Over and over in the past, women have met or tried to meet across barriers of color and lines of privilege, only to have those efforts erased in the historical record and the academic curriculum. We thus lack transformational models and the evidence that what we are trying to do has a history with its own mistakes and advances, from which we could learn. Even more, the woman of color herself has been obliterated from the record. To quote from the title of a forthcoming collection edited by Patricia Bell Scott, Barbara Smith, and Gloria Hull: *All the Women Are White, All the Blacks Are Men, But Some of Us Are Brave: Black Women's Studies.*[1] How simple, then, for the Hartford *Courant* to erase the issue of racism, in a state where the Ku Klux Klan openly marches, by playing on a different string of bigotry and fear—the New Right's vocal antifeminism and homophobia. How easy, as well, for these tactics to touch the strings both of homophobia and of racism in the enclave of Women's Studies itself, where lesbians are still feared and women of color are still ignored.

It would be very easy—given the demands of the task NWSA has set itself here—for us to lose our hard-won threads of connectedness and purpose, to focus, as the media intend us to do, on *their* choice of agenda for us. But we don't have to do this. We can choose to see the connections between what is being floodlighted, targeted, on the one hand, and what is being rendered invisible, on the other. White feminists and lesbians are not, on the whole, immediately identifiable: we have to be pointed out. Women of color are, on the whole, identifiable, but they aren't supposed to be here anyway, so their presence, and whatever we have in common as women, must be erased from the record. White women who seem to be crossing the lines drawn for us by the white fathers must be targeted so we can be ordered back behind those lines; the white community must understand that these women are not acting like their fathers' daughters. Women of color who are found in the wrong place as defined at any given time by the white fathers will receive their retribution unseen—if they are beaten, raped, insulted, harassed, mutilated, murdered, these events will go unreported, unpunished, unconnected, and white women are not even supposed to know they occur, let alone identify with the sufferings endured.

There is a word which has been resounding in my head for several months, since I first read it on the cover of the Southern lesbian/feminist journal *Feminary*: that word is DISOBEDIENCE. (The latest issue of *Feminary* is devoted to that theme.) And in thinking about this week of meetings of NWSA, it has seemed to me that disobedience is what NWSA is potentially about, in choosing to build a conference around women's response to racism. The question now facing Women's Studies, it seems to me, is the extent to which she has, in the past decade, matured into the dutiful daughter of the white, patriarchal university—a daughter who threw tantrums and played the tomboy when she was younger but who has now learned to wear a dress and speak and act almost as nicely as Daddy wants her to; and the extent to which Women's Studies will remember that her mother was not Athena, but the Women's Liberation Movement, a grassroots political movement with roots in the Civil Rights Movement of the 1960s; a movement blazing with lesbian energy, whose earliest journals had names like "It Ain't Me, Babe," "No More Fun and Games," "Off Our Backs," "Up From Under," and "The Furies." In other words, how disobedient will Women's Studies be in the 1980s: how will this Association address the racism, misogyny, homophobia, of the university, and of the corporate society in which it is embedded; and how will white feminist scholars and teachers and students practice disobedience to patriarchy?

In that same issue of *Feminary* Minnie Bruce Pratt writes the following in an essay on "Rebellion":

> I did not understand until years after I had left home that the heroes
> I worshipped for their individual willful pursuit of the honorable
> right were men who were doing this for their rights, for the rights of
> white men; that it was very true that the War had been fought for
> states' rights, but that this was the same as fighting it for slavery, since
> at issue was the right of the white men who ran the Southern states
> to maintain their rule over black men and women, and white women
> too; that some were kind, thoughtful, gallant, even principled men
> in their way, but they were not going to give up control of that state.
> I did not see until years later that while I admired those dead heroes,
> the living men around me were miserable; that the heroes had
> fought not for change but for the right to keep things the way they
> were; that, in fact, every war that I knew of that had ever been fought
> was between two sets of men, each wanting to run things their way. I
> understood finally that I had fantasized about the Great Rebellion
> because I wanted some vicarious motion, change, control of my life,
> but that this was a delusive daydream, one that white people of the
> old Confederacy have been caught in since before the War, the day-
> dream, the romance of rebellion, the breaking out of the nightmare
> of slavery, race hatred, economic differences, sex differences; that
> this was a romance because the act of rebellion satisfied the need for
> change while the values which were defended, those of white male
> supremacy, remained the same. I understood years later that I was
> fascinated by Jackson and Lee and Stuart because I was confined in
> my life as a white woman, as a girl; that they satisfied in me the great
> need to move, to rebel, to change, without my having to change at
> all; that their obsession with will attracted me because I was allowed
> a will only in regard to those "below" me, black men and women, and
> later, children. I was not encouraged to consider using my will against
> those white men who determined how things were. Such a use of the
> will was never discussed in my home; the will that was valued was the
> will of the dead heroes, the will for things to remain the same. I
> understood years later that my mother and grandmothers and great-
> grandmothers had been heroines, in one way, and had used their will

to grit their teeth and endure, to walk through the ruins, blood, and mess left by men. I understood finally that this heroic will to endure is still not the same as the will to change, the true rebellion.

And at the end of the essay, Pratt writes:

> After the February 2d anti-Klan march in Greensboro I wore my bright yellow button that says "Stop the Klan!" around Fayettesville. And at 7-Elevens and at garage sales, white men would stop me and look at it and smile and say, ever so politely, "Why, I belong to the Klan" (whether they actually did or not was, of course, irrelevant), and then become violently abusive when I refused to accept this as a joke. I had crossed their line between white and black; I had, to them, repudiated whiteness and joined with the others. I had never had this sort of reaction to any women's buttons I had worn, but I realized that they had literally not been radical enough—they had been "Pass the ERA" buttons. If I had worn a button that read "Support Lesbian Mothers," I'm sure the abuse would have been intense, because I would have absolutely crossed the line they have drawn between man's world and woman's world.[2]

To understand where as white women we have been situated in the overall system of oppression which also oppresses us, is crucial knowledge if we are serious about our lives. Pratt's essay is really about the difference between true and false rebellion. False rebellion is to varying degrees in varying places acceptable to the white fathers. True rebellion is something that, with each step we take, cuts us further off from identification with racist patriarchy, which has rewarded us for our loyalty and which will punish us for becoming disloyal. It does not matter how we change our names or what music we listen to, or whether we celebrate Christmas or Chanukah or the Solstice, or how many books by women we teach —so long as we can identify only with white women, we are still connected to that system of objectification and callousness and cruelty called racism. And that system is not simply a "patriarchal mindfuck," an idea, which the feminist can assume she has tossed out along with "mankind" and God the Father. It is a material reality of the flesh and nerves; and our relation to it as white feminists is a complex function. As the Black writer/activist Michele Russell writes, in her "Open Letter to the Academy," addressing white women in the university:

> Your oppression and exploitation have been more cleverly masked than ours, more delicately elaborated. The techniques, refined. You

were rewarded in minor ways for docile and active complicity in our dehumanization. At base, the risk of your complete alienation from the system of white male rule that also exploited you was too great to run. The perpetuation of the race depended upon your reproductive capacity: your willingness to bear and rear succeeding generations of oppressors. While your reproductive function has been the only reason for your relative protection in the colonizing process, ours, on the contrary, has sharpened the knife colonialism applies to our throats and wombs. Witness government-sanctioned mass sterilization in Puerto Rico, New York, and Brazil.

And in thinking of the issue of enforced sterilization, we must also inevitably think of the issue of NWSA's position on the presence of, and funding by, agencies such as A.I.D. Russell continues, still addressing white women scholars:

I draw on these discrepancies in our condition not to assign blame or to suggest that you are blind to the implications of this process. We also know that history is full of examples of white women rejecting the cultural and economic blackmail that kept you in service. You walked out on your jobs: in the home, in mills and mines, in heavy manufacturing, in bureaucracies. Occasionally, small minorities succeeded in creating artistic and intellectual communities that sustained elements of a culture independent of the dominant commodity relations of bourgeois society. But on balance, that history—the one of your resistance—is still to be discovered and amplified by this generation. All of you. That is why you are important.

The central question, of course, is "What version of civilization will you construct?" What stories will you tell each other and leave for future generations? What truths will consistently inform your plot? How will you define yourselves in relation to the central patterns of domination in the world, and how will you align on the side of freedom? How rigorously will you face your own past with all its warts?[3]

Only as white women begin to understand both our obedience and complicity, *and* our rebellions, do we begin to have the tools for an ongoing response to racism which is neither circular rhetorical, nor resentful. White women's antiracism, and lesbianism, have both been profound refusals to obey.

It seems to me that the word "guilt" has arisen too often in discussions such as these. Women of color in their anger are charged with provoking guilt in white women; white women accuse each other of provoking guilt; it is guilt, endlessly, that is supposed to stand between white women and disobedience, white women and true rebellion. I have come to wonder if guilt, with its attendant connotations of being emotionally overwhelmed and bullied or paralyzed, is not more a form of defensive resentment or self-protection than an authentic response to the past and its warts. Guilt does not move, guilt does not look you in the eye, guilt does not speak a personal language. I would like to ask every white woman who feels that her guilt is being provoked in discussions of racism to consider what uses she has for this guilt and how it uses her; and to decide for herself if a guilt-ridden feminism, a guilt-ridden rebellion, sounds like a viable way of life.

Each of us needs to know that no other white woman has any competitive monopoly on understanding racism. Each of us needs other white women as allies in meeting the immense rush of forces which are stirred up at the mention of something we are not supposed even to think about, or are supposed to think about only in the terms the fathers have taught us. Only then can we come to some notion of what our docility and complicity have meant, how we as victims of objectification have also objectified other women, what rewards we have reaped from our obedience, and what our present and future responsibility must be.

Finally, I want to say something about my personal understanding of racism. For a long time, particularly in the 1960s, I had to believe that, though white, I was not a carrier of racism. If, as a political choice, I was actively engaged in teaching Black and Puerto Rican and Asian freshmen instead of white graduate-school poets; if I joined in the fight for Open Admissions at the City University; if a kind of nobility and heroism my spirit craved had become opened to me through King's *Letter from Birmingham Jail,* Baldwin's essays, the letters of George Jackson; if the words of Frantz Fanon and Malcolm X felt cathartic and cleansing to me, why did those words also feel accusing and menacing? What in me felt accused or threatened, even while something else in me felt those words as a lifeline of sanity?

The white male Left offered no answers. The racists were all "out there": the pigs, the rednecks, the reactionary bourgeois professors, Nelson Rockefeller, the "Jewish" landlords. The racists were my parents, my Southern family, not those whites who marched singing "We Shall Overcome," and certainly not anyone white who had worked in the early days with SNCC or traveled to Mississippi. Credentials were important: particularly a Black lover, a Black child; as if they could solve, once and for all, the problem of how and when, if ever, the white person stopped thinking racist thoughts or seeing in racist patterns;

became washed clean, as it were; became "part of the solution instead of the problem." There was a very "born-again" spirit among white antiracist activists in the 1960s—as if we could discard our pasts, as if we must, having once seen the political light, have no fear or hatred of darkness anywhere in our souls.

I speak of that period because it has been part of the history I have needed to face rigorously, in particular as a feminist committed to the struggle of all women for liberation. I think we need to get rid of the useless baggage that says that by opposing racist violence, by doing antiracist work, or by becoming feminists, white women somehow cease to carry racism within us.

As Chris South writes, "The roots may be in the patriarchy but they've grown into us." What *was* true for me was that in growing into feminism and coming out as a lesbian I found a sense of personal and collective history and identity, affirmed by the words of white women who had struggled in the past for justice and freedom *as women*: the Grimké sisters, Anthony, Schreiner, Goldman, Gilman, Woolf, to name a few. Feminism became a political and spiritual base from which I could move to examine rather than try to hide my own racism, recognize that I have antiracist work to do continuously within myself. Increasingly, the writings of contemporary lesbian and feminist women of color have moved and challenged me to push my horizons further, examine with fresh eyes the world I thought I knew and took for granted. There is an inner tension and dynamic I need to be constantly checking, between my beliefs and standards for myself, and how I still think and act as a daughter of white patriarchy. If I say that I am trying to recognize and change in myself certain failures to see or hear, certain kinds of arrogance, ignorance, passivity, which have to do with living in a white skin, that is, which have to do with racism, I can say this as a woman committed to the love of women, including love for myself.

NOTES

1. *Ed. note:* To appear in November, published by The Feminist Press.
2. Minnie Bruce Pratt, "Rebellion," *Feminary* II: 1 and 2 (1981): 6–20.
3. Michele Russell, "An Open Letter to the Academy," in Bunch et al., eds., *Building Feminist Theory: Essays from Quest, A Feminist Quarterly* (New York and London: Longman, 1981), pp. 101–10.

Adrienne Rich's newest book. A Wild Patience Has Taken Me This Far: Poems 1978–81, *will be published in November by W. W. Norton.*

Copyright © 1981 by Adrienne Rich. Reprinted by permission of W. W. Norton and Company, Inc.

The Uses of Anger

Audre Lorde   **Fall 1981**

Racism. The belief in the inherent superiority of one race over all others and thereby the right to dominance, manifest and implied.

Women respond to racism. My response to racism is anger. I have lived with that anger, on that anger, beneath that anger, on top of that anger, ignoring that anger, feeding upon that anger, learning to use that anger before it laid my visions to waste, for most of my life. Once I did it in silence, afraid of the weight of that anger. My fear of that anger taught me nothing. Your fear of that anger will teach you nothing, also.

Women responding to racism means women responding to anger, the anger of exclusion, of unquestioned privilege, of racial distortions, of silence, ill-use, stereotyping, defensiveness, misnaming, betrayal, and coopting.

My anger is a response to racist attitudes, to the actions and presumptions that arise out of those attitudes. If in your dealings with other women your actions have reflected those attitudes, then my anger and your attendant fears, perhaps, are spotlights that can be used for your growth in the same way I have had to use learning to express anger for my growth. But for corrective surgery, not guilt. Guilt and defensiveness are bricks in a wall against which we will all perish, for they serve none of our futures.

Because I do not want this to become a theoretical discussion, I am going to give a few examples of interchanges between women that I hope will illustrate the points I am trying to make. In the interest of time, I am going to cut them short. I want you to know that there were many more.

For example:

• I speak out of a direct and particular anger at a particular academic conference, and a white woman comes up and says, "Tell me how you feel but don't say it too harshly or I cannot hear you." But is it my manner that keeps her from hearing, or the message that her life may change?

• The Women's Studies Program of a southern university invites a Black woman to read following a week-long forum on Black and white women. "What has this week given to you?" I ask. The most vocal white woman says, "I think I've gotten a lot. I feel Black women really understand me a lot better now; they have a better idea of where I'm coming from." As if understanding her lay at the core of the racist problem. These are the bricks that go into the walls against which we will bash our consciousness, unless we recognize that they can be taken apart.

• After fifteen years of a women's movement which professes to address the life concerns and possible futures of all women, I still hear, on campus after campus, "How can we address the issues of racism? No women of Color attended." Or, the other side of that statement, "We have no one in our department equipped to teach their work." In other words, racism is a Black women's problem, a problem of women of Color, and only we can discuss it.

• After I have read from my work entitled "Poems for Women in Rage" a white woman asks me, "Are you going to do anything with how we can deal directly with *our* anger? I feel it's so important." I ask, "How do you use *your* rage?" And then I have to turn away from the blank look in her eyes, before she can invite me to participate in her own annihilation. Because I do not exist to feel her anger for her.

• White women are beginning to examine their relationships to Black women, yet often I hear you wanting only to deal with the little colored children across the roads of childhood, the beloved nurse-maid, the occasional second-grade classmate; those tender memories of what was once mysterious and intriguing or neutral. You avoid the childhood assumptions formed by the raucous laughter at Rastus and Oatmeal, the acute message of your mommy's handkerchief spread upon the park bench because I had just been sitting there, the indelible and dehumanizing portraits of Amos and Andy and your Daddy's humorous bedtime stories.

I wheel my two-year-old daughter in a shopping cart through a super-market in Eastchester in 1967 and a little white girl riding past in her mother's cart calls out excitedly, "Oh look, Mommy, a baby maid!" And your mother shushes you, but she does not correct you. And so, fifteen years later, at a conference on racism, you can still find that story humorous. But I hear your laughter is full of terror and dis-ease.

• At an international cultural gathering of women, a well-known white American woman poet interrupts the reading of the work of women of Color to read her own poem, and then dashes off to an "important panel."

• Do women in the academy truly want a dialogue about racism? It will require recognizing the needs and the living contexts of other women. When an academic woman says, for instance, "I can't afford it," she may mean she is making a choice about how to spend her available money. But when a woman on welfare says, "I can't afford it," she means she is surviving on an amount of money that was barely subsistence in 1972, and she often does not have enough to eat. Yet the National Women's Studies Association here in 1981 holds a Convention in which it commits itself to responding to racism, yet refuses to waive the registration fee for poor women and women of Color who wished to present and conduct workshops. This has made it impossible for many women of Color—for instance, Wilmette Brown, of Black Women for Wages for Housework—to participate in this Convention. And so I ask again: Is this to be merely another situation of the academy discussing life within the closed circuits of the academy?

To all the white women here who recognize these attitudes as familiar, but most of all, to all my sisters of Color who live and survive thousands of such encounters—to my sisters of Color who like me still tremble their rage under harness, or who sometimes question the expression of our rage as useless and disruptive (the two most popular accusations), I want to speak about anger, my anger, and what I have learned from my travels through its dominions.

Everything can be used, except what is wasteful. You will need to remember this, when you are accused of destruction.

Every woman has a well-stocked arsenal of anger potentially useful against those oppressions, personal and institutional, which brought that anger into being. Focused with precision it can become a powerful source of energy serving progress and change. And when I speak of change, I do not mean a simple switch of positions or a temporary lessening of tensions, nor the ability to smile or feel good. I am speaking of a basic and radical alteration in all those assumptions underlining our lives.

I have seen situations where white women hear a racist remark, resent what has been said, become filled with fury, and remain silent, because they are afraid. That unexpressed anger lies within them like an undetonated device, usually to be hurled at the first woman of Color who talks about racism.

But anger expressed and translated into action in the service of our vision and our future is a liberating and strengthening act of clarification, for it is in the painful process of this translation that we identify who are our allies with whom we have grave differences, and who are our genuine enemies.

Anger is loaded with information and energy. When I speak of women of Color, I do not only mean Black women. We are also Asian American, Caribbean, Chicana, Latina, Hispanic, Native American, and we have a right to each of our names. The woman of Color who charges me with rendering her invisible by assuming that her struggles with racism are identical with my own has something to tell me that I had better learn from, lest we both waste ourselves fighting the truths between us. If I participate, knowingly or otherwise, in my sister's oppression and she calls me on it, to answer her anger with my own only blankets the substance of our exchange with reaction. It wastes energy I need to join with her. And yes, it is very difficult to stand still and to listen to another woman's voice delineate an agony I do not share, or even one in which I myself may have participated.

We speak in this place removed from the more blatant reminders of our embattlement as women. This need not blind us to the size and complexities of the forces mounting against us and all that is most human within our environment. We are not here as women examining racism in a political and social vacuum. We operate in the teeth of a system for whom racism and sexism are primary, established, and necessary props of profit. Women responding to racism is a topic so dangerous that when the local media attempt to discredit this Convention they choose to focus upon the provision of Lesbian housing as a diversionary device—as if the Hartford *Courant* dare not mention the topic chosen for discussion here, racism, lest it become apparent that women are in fact attempting to examine and to alter all the repressive conditions of our lives.

Mainstream communication does not want women, particularly white women, responding to racism. It wants racism to be accepted as an immutable given in the fabric of existence, like evening time or the common cold.

So we are working in a context of opposition and threat, the cause of which is certainly not the angers which lie between us, but rather that virulent hatred leveled against all women, people of Color, Lesbians and gay men, poor people—against all of us who are seeking to examine the particulars of our lives as we resist our oppressions, moving toward coalition and effective action.

Any discussion among women about racism must include the recognition and the use of anger. It must be direct and creative, because it is crucial. We cannot allow our fear of anger to deflect us nor to seduce us into settling for anything less than the hard work of excavating honesty; we must quite serious about the choice of this topic and the angers entwined within it, because, rest assured, our opponents are quite serious about their hatred of us and of what we are trying to do here.

And while we scrutinize the often painful face of each other's anger, please remember that it is not our anger which makes me caution you to lock your doors at night, and not to wander the streets of Hartford alone. It is the hatred which lurks in those streets, that urge to destroy us all if we truly work for change rather than merely indulge in our academic rhetoric.

This hatred and our anger are very different. Hatred is the fury of those who do not share our goals, and its object is death and destruction. Anger is the grief of distortions between peers, and its object is change. But our time is getting shorter. We have been raised to view any difference other than sex as a reason for destruction, and for Black women and white women to face each other's angers without denial or immobilization or silence or guilt is in itself a heretical and generative idea. It implies peers meeting upon a common basis to examine difference, and to alter those distortions which history has created around difference. For it is those distortions which separate us. And we must ask ourselves: Who profits from all this?

Women of Color in America have grown up within a symphony of anguish at being silenced, at being unchosen, at knowing that when we survive, it is in spite of a whole world out there that takes for granted our lack of humanness, that hates our very existence, outside of its service. And I say "symphony" rather than "cacophony" because we have had to learn to orchestrate those furies so that they do not tear us apart. We have had to learn to move through them and use them for strength and force and insight within our daily lives. Those of us who did not learn this difficult lesson did not survive. And part of my anger is always libation for my fallen sisters.

Anger is an appropriate reaction to racist attitudes, as is fury when the actions arising from those attitudes do not change. To those women here who fear the anger of women of Color more than their own unscrutinized racist attitudes, I ask: Is our anger more threatening than the woman-hatred that tinges all the aspects of our lives?

It is not the anger of other women that will destroy us, but our refusals to stand still, to listen to its rhythms, to learn within it, to move beyond the manner of presentation to the substance, to tap that anger as an important source of empowerment.

I cannot hide my anger to spare you guilt, nor hurt feelings, nor answering anger; for to do so insults and trivializes all our efforts. Guilt is not a response to anger; it is a response to one's own actions or lack of action. If it leads to change then it can be useful, since it becomes no longer guilt but the beginning of knowledge. Yet all too often, guilt is just another name for impotence, for defensiveness destructive of communication; it becomes a device to protect ignorance and the continuation of things the way they are, the ultimate protection for changelessness.

Most women have not developed tools for facing anger constructively. CR [consciousness-raising] groups in the past, largely white, dealt with how to express anger, usually at the world of men. And these groups were made up of white women who shared the terms of their oppressions. There was usually little attempt to articulate the genuine differences between women, such as those of race, color, class, and sexual identity. There was no apparent need at that time to examine the contradictions of self, woman, as oppressor. There was work on expressing anger, but very little on anger directed against each other. No tools were developed to deal with other women's anger except to avoid it, deflect it, or flee from it under a blanket of guilt.

I have no creative use for guilt, yours or my own. Guilt is only another way of avoiding informed action, of buying time out of the pressing need to make clear choices, out of the approaching storm that can feed the earth as well as bend the trees. If I speak to you in anger, at least I have spoken to you; I have not put a gun to your head and shot you down in the street; I have not looked at your bleeding sister's body and asked. "What did she do to deserve it?" This was the reaction of two white women to Mary Church Terrell's telling of the lynching of a pregnant Black woman whose baby was then torn from her body. That was in 1921, and Alice Paul had just refused to publicly endorse the enforcement of the Nineteenth Amendment for all women—excluding the women of Color who had worked to help bring about that amendment.

The angers between women will not kill us if we can articulate them with precision, if we listen to the content of what is said with at least as much intensity as we defend ourselves from the manner of saying. Anger is a source of empowerment we must not fear to tap for energy rather than guilt. When we turn from anger we turn from insight, saying we will accept only the designs already known, those deadly and safely familiar. I have tried to learn my anger's usefulness to me, as well as its limitations.

For women raised to fear, too often anger threatens annihilation. In the male construct of brute force, we were taught that our lives depended upon the good will of patriarchal power. The anger of others was to be avoided at all costs, because there was nothing to be learned from it but pain, a judgment that we had been bad girls, come up lacking, not done what we were supposed to do. And if we accept our powerlessness, then of course any anger can destroy us.

But the strength of women lies in recognizing differences between us as creative, and in standing to those distortions which we inherited without blame but which are now ours to alter. The angers of women can transform differences through insight into power. For anger between peers births change, not destruction, and the discomfort and sense of loss it often causes is not fatal, but a sign of growth.

My response to racism is anger. That anger has eaten clefts into my living only when it remained unspoken, useless to anyone. It has also served me in classrooms without light or learning, where the work and history of Black women was less than a vapor. It has served me as fire in the ice zone of uncomprehending eyes of white women who see in my experience and the experience of my people only new reasons for fear or guilt. And my anger is no excuse for not dealing with your blindness, no reason to withdraw from the results of your own actions.

When women of Color speak out of the anger that laces so many of our contacts with white women, we are often told that we are "creating a mood of hopelessness," "preventing white women from getting past guilt," or "standing in the way of trusting communication and action." All these quotes come directly from letters to me from members of this organization within the last two years. One woman wrote, "Because you are Black and Lesbian, you seem to speak with the moral authority of suffering." Yes, I am Black and Lesbian, and what you hear in my voice is fury, not suffering. Anger, not moral authority. There is a difference.

To turn aside from the anger of Black women with excuses or the pretexts of intimidation, is to award no one power—it is merely another way of preserving racial blindness, the power of unaddressed privilege, unbreached, intact. For guilt is only yet another form of objectification. Oppressed peoples are always being asked to stretch a little more, to bridge the gap between blindness and humanity. Black women are expected to use our anger only in the service of other people's salvation, other people's learning. But that time is over. My anger has meant pain to me but it has also meant survival, and before I give it up I'm going to be sure that there is something at least as powerful to replace it on the road to clarity.

What woman here is so enamoured of her own oppression, her own oppressed status, that she cannot see her heelprint upon another woman's face? What woman's terms of oppression have become precious and necessary as a ticket into the fold of the righteous, away from the cold winds of self-scrutiny?

I am a Lesbian woman of Color whose children eat regularly because I work in a university. If their full bellies make me fail to recognize my commonality with a woman of Color whose children do not eat because she cannot find work, or who has no children because her insides are rotted from home abortions and sterilization; if I fail to recognize the Lesbian who chooses not to have children, the woman who remains closeted because her homophobic community is her only life support, the woman who chooses silence instead of another death, the woman who is terrified lest my anger trigger the explosion of hers; if I fail to recognize them as other faces of myself, then I am contributing not only to each of their oppressions but also to my own, and the anger which stands between us then must be used for clarity and mutual empowerment, not for evasion by guilt or for further separation. I am not free while any woman is unfree, even when her shackles are very different from my own. And I am not free as long as one person of Color remains chained. Nor is any one of you.

I speak here as a woman of Color who is not bent upon destruction, but upon survival. No woman is responsible for altering the psyche of her oppressor, even when that psyche is embodied in another woman. I have suckled the wolf's lip of anger and I have used it for illumination, laughter, protection, fire in places where there was no light, no food, no sisters, no quarter. We are not goddesses or matriarchs or edifices of divine forgiveness; we are not fiery fingers of judgment or instruments of flagellation; we are women always forced back upon our woman's power. We have learned to use anger as we have learned to use the dead flesh of animals; and bruised, battered, and changing, we have survived and grown and, in Angela Wilson's words, we *are* moving on. With or without uncolored women. We use whatever strengths we have fought for, including anger, to help define and fashion a world where all our sisters can grow, where our children can love, and where the power of touching and meeting another woman's difference and wonder will eventually transcend the need for destruction.

For it is not the anger of Black women which is dripping down over this globe like a diseased liquid. It is not my anger that launches rockets, spends over sixty thousand dollars a second on missiles and other agents of war and death, pushes opera singers off rooftops, slaughters children in cities, stockpiles nerve gas and chemical bombs, sodomizes our daughters and our earth. It is not the anger of Black women which corrodes into blind, dehumanizing power, bent upon the annihilation of us all unless we meet it with what we have, our power to examine and to redefine the terms upon which we will live and work; our power to envision and to reconstruct, anger by painful anger, stone upon heavy stone, a future of pollinating difference and the earth to support our choices.

We welcome all women who can meet us, face to face, beyond objectification and beyond guilt.

Audre Lorde's *Chosen Poems and her "bio-myth-ography" entitled* I've Been Standing on This Street Corner a Hell of a Long Time *will be out in 1982.*

Copyright © 1981 by Audre Lorde. Reprinted by permission of the Charlotte Sheedy Literary Agency.

Tillie Olsen's Reading Lists I–IV

Tillie Olsen   *1972–74*

Tillie Olsen's Reading List I (Winter 1972)

Tillie Olsen is well-known as the author of Tell Me A Riddle, *a volume of stories about the lives of working-class women and men used frequently in women's studies courses. She is also a self-taught scholar and teacher who has offered to share her reading lists with the* Newsletter. *In future issues, we will print lists on such themes as "mothering," "growing up," aging, "the hard work of women." We begin here with a list called "A Spectrum."*

A Spectrum

Novels

Story of An African Farm by Olive Schreiner
Middlemarch by George Eliot
The Mill on the Floss by George Eliot
The Awakening by Kate Chopin
To the Lighthouse by *Virginia Woolf*
Cement by F. Gladkov
Daughter of Earth by Agnes Smedley
The Man Who Loved Children by Christina Stead
The Dollmaker by Harriette Arnow
Ultima Thule by H. H. Richardson
Time of Man by Elizabeth Madox Roberts
Put Off Thy Shoes by Ethel Voynich

Stories

"The Revolt of Mother," in *Best Stories of Mary Wilkins Freeman*
"A Jury of Her Peers," by Susan Glaspell in *U.S. Stories*
     ed. by Martha Foley
"Nor-Bibi's Crime" by Vera Inber in *Short Stories of Russia Today*
"Wagner Matinee," in Willa Cather's *Youth and the Bright Medusa*

"Old Mortality" and the Old Order stories, in Katherine Anne Porter's
   The Collected Stories
"Prelude," "At the Bay," and "Six Years After," in Katherine
   Mansfield's *Collected Stories*
"Babushka Farnham," in Dorothy Canfield Fisher's *Fables for Parents*
"The Bed Quilt," in Dorothy Canfield Fisher's *Vermont Lives*
"Story of an Hour," in Kate Chopin's *Collected Works*
"Between Men," in Doris Lessing's *A Man and Two Women*
"The Yellow Wallpaper" by Charlotte Perkins Gilman (shortly to be
   reprinted by The Feminist Press)
"The Darling" by Anton Chekhov
"The Sky is Gray," in Ernest Gaines' *Bloodline*

Lives

Eighty Years or More by Elizabeth Cady Stanton
A Mortal Flower by Han Suyin

Literature

A Room of One's Own by Virginia Woolf
Thinking About Women by Mary Ellman

Tillie Olsen's Reading List II (Spring 1973)

Women: A List Out of Which to Read

. . . MOST WOMEN'S LIVES: lives, history, realities largely absent from
literature (read as balancer, corrective, of prevalent images of women
as protected, passive, parasitic, decorative, narcissistic, primarily sex
object, "the other," etc.). Each entry should be read with the following
in mind. 1) The hard and essential work of women, in and out of the
home ("no work was too hard, no labour too strenuous to exclude us").
2) Limitations, denials imposed; exclusions and restrictions in no way
necessitated by biological or economic circumstances. 3) How human
capacities born in women—intellect, organization, art, invention,
vision, sense of justice, beauty, etc.—denied scope and development,
nevertheless struggled to express themselves and function. . . .

p [and pb] = paperback	h = hardcover	op = out of print
d = drama	f = fiction	b = bio. or autobiog.

Four 100-Year-Old Women (read, preferably, as a cluster, and with 1), 2), 3) above in mind.)

Grandmother Brown: Her First Hundred Years (1827–1927),
   ed. Harriet Connor Brown. b/op
Mountain Wolf Woman, Sister of Crashing Thunder: Autobiography of a Winnebago Indian, ed. Nancy O. Lurie. b/p
Autobiography of Mother Jones, ed. Mary Field Parton. b/p
The Autobiography of Miss Jane Pitman, by Ernest Gaines. f/p

Fiction

Alcott, Louisa May, "Transcendental Wild Oats," in Bronson Alcott, *Fruitlands,* comp. by Clara Endicott Sears. b/op
Cather, Willa. *My Antonia.* f/p
Childress, Alice. *Wedding Band.* d/p
Dinesen, Isak, "Sorrow-acres," in *Winter's Tales.* f/p
Ellis, Katherine. *Life of an Ordinary Woman.* b/op
Fisher, Dorothy Canfield, "Ann Story," in *A Harvest of Stories.* f/h
Glasgow, Ellen. *Barren Ground; Vein of Iron* f/p
Greenberg, Joanne. *In This Sign.* f/p
Hansberry, Lorraine. *Raisin in the Sun.* d/p
Hughes, Mary Gray, "The Thousand Springs," in *The Thousand Springs.* f/p
Le Sueur, Meridel, "The Annunciation," in *The Annunciation.* f/op
Lewis, Janet. *The Wife of Martin Guerre.* b/p
Mansfield, Katherine, "The Woman at the Store," in *The Short Stories of Katherine Mansfield.* f/p
Marriott, Alice. *Ten Grandmothers.* b/h
Murray, Pauli. *Proud Shoes.* f/h
Petry, Ann. *Street.* f/p
Porter, Katherine Anne, "The Jilting of Granny Weatherall," in *The Old Order.* f/p
Walker, Alice. *The Third Life of Grange Copeland.* f/p
Walker, Margaret. *Jubilee.* f/p
Wilder, Laura Ingalls. Children's series, including *By the Shores of Silver Lake—These Happy Golden Years.* f/p
Woolf, Virginia, "Memories of a Working Women's Guild," in *The Captain's Death Bed.* b/h
Wright, Sarah. *This Child's Gonna Live.* f/p

Slaveys, Servants, Servers

Anderson, Barbara. *Southbound.* f/h

Chekhov, Anton, "A Sleepyhead," in *The Short Stories of Anton Chekhov.* f/h

Childress, Alice. *Like One of the Family: Conversations from a Domestic's Life.* b/h

Emerson, Ralph Waldo, "Mary Moody Emerson," in *Lectures and Biographical Sketches,* will have to represent the lives of countless unmarried girls and women spent in the hardest kind of service, whenever and wherever needed by any family branches. b/h

Hellman, Lillian, "Sophronia" in *An Unfinished Woman.* b/p

Hurst, Fanny. *Lummox.* f/op

Mansfield, Katherine, "The Child Who Was Tired," "Life of Ma Parker," and "The Tiredness of Rosabel," in *The Short Stories of Katherine Mansfield.* f/p

Parker, Dorothy, "Clothe the Naked," in *Collected Stories.* f/h

Porter, Katherine Anne, Hatsy in "Holiday," *Collected Stories.* f/p

Powell, Margaret. *Below Stairs.* b/p

Myth Dispellers

Peretz, Isaac Laeb, "She Women," in *Stories and Pictures.* f/op

Reyher, Rebecca H. *Zulu Woman.* b/p

Some Women in Works by Men

Agee, James. *Let Us Now Praise Famous Men.* b/p

Chekhov, Anton, "In the Ravine" and "Peasants," in *Seven Short Novels.* f/p

Clarke, Adam. *Memoires of the Wesley Family.* (Susannah Wesley, mother of John and eleven other children—a marvelous example of 3) above.) b/op

DuBois, W. E. B, Josie in "On the Meaning of Progress," *The Souls of Black Folk.* b/p

Gorky, Maxim, Gorky's grandmother in *Childhood.* f/p

———. *Mother.* f/p

Hardy, Thomas. *Tess of the D'Urbervilles.* f/p

Lawrence, D. H. *Sons and Lovers,* especially Part I. f/p

O'Casey, Sean. *Collected Plays;* "Mrs. Cassidy Takes A Holiday," in *Inishfallen Fare Thee Well.* d/p b/p

Rolvaag, O.E. *Giants in the Earth.* f/p
Sinclair, Upton. *The Jungle.* f/p
Wright, Richard, "Bright and Morning Star," in *Uncle Tom's Children.* f/p
Zola, Emile. *L'Assommoir; Germinal,* (Section I, part 2). f/p

Tillie Olsen's Reading List III (Summer 1973)

MOTHERING AND WIFEHOOD: Mothering (as distinguished from
Motherhood) and Wifehood are rarely a major or even minor part of
literature, although women have always been defined by them, and
they are the major part of most women's lives. Women's courses do not
know, or do not understand, the necessity of including the relatively few
works that tell something of what mothering and/or wifehood mean.

I. These titles repeated from the two previous listings are essential
reading, preferably as a cluster.
Arnow, Harriet, *The Dollmaker* (pb).
Brown, Harriet, *Grandmother Brown, Her First Hundred Years* (biog., op).
Richardson, H. H., *Ultima Thule* (op).
Stead, Christina, *The Man Who Loved Children* (pb).
Woolf, Virginia, *To The Lighthouse* (pb)
Wright, Sarah, *This Child's Gonna Live* (pb).

Stories:

Cather, Willa, "Wagner Matinee" in *Troll Garden.*
Gaines, Ernest, "The Sky Is Gray" in *Bloodline* (pb).
Mansfield, Katherine, "Six Years After" in *The Short Stories of
Katherine Mansfield.*

II.
Colette, *My Mother's House* (pb) and other glimpses of Sido in
Earthly Paradise (pb).
Fisher, Dorothy Canfield, *Fables for Parents,* especially
"The Forgotten Mother" (op).
Lessing, Doris, the section, "Free Women II," in *The Golden Notebook*
(pb).
Paley, Grace, *The Little Disturbances of Man* (op but soon
to be reprinted in pb).
Schreiner, Olive, *From Man to Man* (op).
Struther Jan, "Three Stockings" in *Mrs. Miniver* (op).

III. Add to the Agee, Gorky, Lawrence, O'Casey (*Juno and the Paycock, Plough and the Stars*), Wright, titles in "Some Women in Works by Men" in Reading List II, Henry Roth's *Call It Sleep* (pb); that Jewish mother should be contrasted with Phillip Roth's Sophie in *Portnoy's Complaint* (pb).

IV. The conflict, mother/writer, is written of in Storm Jameson's autobiography, *Journey to the North,* and in letters in *Life and Letters of Harriet Beecher Stowe,* Annie Fields, ed. (op).

Tillie Olsen's Reading List IV (Winter 1974)

A List Out of Which to Read, Extend Range, Comprehension

* =a classic of its kind and essential reading
\# = only part of the book is concerned with these years
j = merits adult attention, although usually classified as children's book
t = written by young women (thirty or under)

Forms and Formings: The Younger Years

These books are listed in their own kind of order, arranged in a spectrum by the period of time they cover, or in clusters for special reasons.

The Younger Years: A Spectrum of Girlhoods

* Charlotte Bronte. *Jane Eyre* pb/f/t
* George Eliot. *Mill On the Floss.* pb/f
* Louisa May Alcott. *Little Women.* pb/f/j/t
* Benjamin A. Botkin. "Jenny Proctor's Story" in *Lay My Burden Down: A Folk History of Slavery.* pb/b
* Olive Schreiner. *Story of An African Farm.* pb/f/t
* Sarah Grand. *The Beth Book.* op/f
* Elizabeth Cady Stanton. *Eighty Years or More.* #/pb/b |
* Nancy Lurie, ed. *Mountain Wolf Woman.* #/pb/b
* Laura Ingalls Wilder. *Little House in the Big Woods* to *These Happy Golden Years.* (Pioneer Series) pb/b/j
* Mary Johnston. *Hagar.* op/f
* Agnes Smedley. *Daughter of Earth.* pb/f/t
* Vera Brittain. *Testimony of Youth.* op/b
* Catherine Cookson. *Our Kate.* #/b/pb
* Olivia. *Olivia.* op/b

* Elizabeth Maddox Roberts. *Time of Man.* op/f
* Katherine Anne Porter. "The Grave," and Miranda in "Old Order"
   in *Leaning Tower and Other Stories.* pb/f
* Dawn Powell. *My Home Is Far Away.* op/f
* James Agee. Young Emma and Ivy in *Let Us Now
   Praise Famous Men.* pb/b
* Christina Stead. *The Man Who Loved Children* (patriarchy). pb/f
* Lore Segal. *Other People's Houses.* op/f
* Paule Marshall. *Brown Girl, Brown Stones.* pb/f
* Toni Morrison. *The Bluest Eye.* pb/f
* Alix Kate Shulman. *Memoirs of an Ex-Prom Queen.* #/pb/f
* *A trilogy of the 1950s, preferably read as a cluster:*
   * Sylvia Plath. *The Bell Jar.* pb/f/t
   * Hannah Green (Joanna Greenberg). *I Never Promised You a
      Rose Garden.* pb/f/t
   Barbara Probst Solomon. *The Beat of Life.* op/f/t
H. C. Brown. *Grandmother Brown: Her First Hundred Years.* #/op/b
Zdena Berger. *Tell Me Another Morning* (girlhood in Auschwitz). op/f
Jeanette Everly. *Bonnie Jo, Go Home* (a pregnant teenager). pb/f/j

Girlhood Labor (in addition to unpaid, necessary household labor)

Dorothy Sterling. *Freedom Train: the Life of Harriet Tubman.* b/pb/j
Herman Melville. "Paradise of Bachelors and Tartarus of Maids"
   in *Complete Stories.* h/f
Rebecca Harding Davis. *Margaret Howth.* op/f
Elizabeth Stuart Phelps. *The Silent Partner.* f/op
Elizabeth Stuart Phelps. "28th of January" in *Sixteen For One.* f/op
Ida Pruitt. *Daughter of Han.* pb/b
Lucy Larcom. *New England Girlhood.* h/b; *An Idyl of Work.* h/p
Emile Zola. Seventeen-year old Catherine in *Germinal.* pb/f
W. E. B. Dubois. Josie in "On the Meaning of Progress" in *The Souls
   of Black Folk.* pb/essay
Katherine Mansfield. "The Child Who Was Tired" in *Short Stories.* h/f
Anton Chekhov. "Sleepyhead" in *Best Known Works.* pb/f
Honwana, L. B. "Dina" in *We Killed Mangy Dog and Other Stories
   of Mozambique.* op/f

Also see Cookson, Powell, Yezierska, Holland, Wilde, Smedley, Brönte,
Moody and Varney. Begin counting the numberless and nameless "little maids" and slaves or slaveys who populate fiction of the past.

Childhoods

* Dorothy Canfield. *Understood Betsy.* pb/f/j
George Madden Martin. *Emmy Lou: Her Book and Heart.* op/f/j
* Ruth Holland. *Mill Child.* pb/f/j
* Katherine Mansfield. "The Doll's House," "Prelude," and "At the
  Bay" in *Short Stories.* pb/f

Dawnings, Flowerings, Strivings, Sexuality

* May Sinclair. *Mary Olivier.* op/f
* Dorothy Richardson. "Honeycomb," *Pilgrimage, Vol. 1.* h/f
*Colette. *Claudine.* h/f; *Ripening Seed.* h/f
Rosamond Lehmann. *Dusty Answer.* op/f
Rosamond Lehmann. *Invitation to the Waltz.* op/f
Emily Carr. *The Book of Small Growing Pains.* pb/b
Anzia Yezierska. *Arrogant Beggar* (an immigrant girl). op/f
* Henry Handel Richardson. *Growing Pains.* op/f;
  The End of a Childhood. op/f
* Isabel Bolton Miller. *Under Gemini.* op/b; *Days of My Youth.* op/f
* Jessamyn West. Her girl self in *Hide and Seek.* h/b;
  Cress Delahanty. pb/f/j
Josephine Johnson. *Now in November.* op/f; "I Was 16," in
  Winter Orchard, and Other Stories. op/f
Jo Sinclair. *The Changelings.* op/b
* Doris Lessing. *Martha Quest.* pb/f
* Hannah Green. *The Dead of the House.* pb/f
* Carson McCullers. *The Heart Is a Lonely Hunter.* pb/f
Carson McCullers. *Member of the Wedding.* pb/f
Violet LeDuc. "The Golden Button" in *The Woman with
  the Little Fox.* h/f
* Katherine Mansfield. "The Wind Blows" and "Garden Party" in
  Short Stories. hc/f
* Christina Stead. *Salzburg Tales.* op/f ; Teresa in *For Love Alone.* op/f
* Eudora Welty. "Livvie" in *Selected Stories.* pb/f
Dorothy Parker. "The Waltz" in *Collected Stories.* pb/f
* Betty Smith. *A Tree Grows in Brooklyn.* pb/f
Jean Stafford. "The Tea Time of Stout Hearted Ladies" in
  Best American Short Stories 1965. pb/f
Maxine Kumin. *Through Dooms of Love.* h/f
Lenore Marshall. *Hill Is Level.* op/f
Jane Mayhall. *Cousin to Human.* h/f

Maureen Howard. "Bridgeport Bus" in *Prize Stories 1962:*
  The O'Henry Awards. pb/f
* Alice Munro. *Lives of Girls and Women*. h/f;
  Dance of the Happy Shade. h/f
Blanche Boyd. *Nerves*. pb/f
Toni Cade Bambara. *Gorilla, My Love*. pb/f
Anne Moody. *Coming of Age in Mississippi*. pb/b
Joyce Varney. *Welsh Story*. h/b
Maya Angelou. *I Know Why the Caged Bird Sings*. pb/b

Writers About Themselves

* Ellen Glasgow. *The Woman Within*. #/op/b
Storm Jameson. *Journey to the North*. #/h/b
Zelda Fitzgerald. *Save Me the Waltz*. #/p/f; also see the first part
  of Nancy Milford's *Zelda*. pb/b
Henry Handel Richardson. *Myself When Young*. op/b

Appearance

Doris Lessing. "Notes for a Case History" in
  A Man and Two Women. pb/f

Rarities

Mary Webb. *Precious Bane*. op/f
Nancy Hale. *New England Girlhood*. pb/b
* Katherine Hathaway. *The Little Locksmith*. op/b

Rape, Brutality, Degradations, Prostitution

* Jean Rhys. *Good Morning, Midnight*. op/f
Dorothy Parker. "Mr. Durant" in *Collected Stories*. pb/f
Christina Stead. *The Puzzleheaded Girl*. op/f
Olive Schreiner. Bertie in *From Man to Man*. op/f
* Samuel Richardson. *Clarissa*. pb/f
* Nelson Algren. *Never Come Morning*. pb/f
John Reed. *Daughter of the Revolution*. op/f
Eudora Welty. "At the Landing" in *Wide Net, and Other Stories*. h/f
Katherine Mansfield. "The Little Governess" in
  Short Stories. pb/f
Patricia Griffith. "Nights at O'Rourkes" in *Prize Stories 1970* . pb/f

Bertolt Brecht. "The Infancide of Marie Farrar" in
  Selected Poems. pb/b

Assumption Girls Belong to Their Elders

Jean Stafford. "The Liberation" in *Stories.* pb/f
Nancy Hale. "Rich People" in *The Pattern of Perfection.* pb/f

Second Berkshire Conference on the History of Women

Mary Dunn   *Spring 1975*

The Berkshire Conference of Women Historians decided in 1972 to lend support to research in the history of women. The field was regarded with some suspicion by many historians who did not see it as legitimate, and insisted that it was a "fad" whose time would soon pass. Moreover, too many people doing research in the field were working in isolation; rarely does one history department employ more than one person working in the history of women. Professors Lois Banner and Mary Hartman made the first proposal for a conference which would assert our belief that the history of women is a legitimate field which can make major contributions to the understanding of the past. They agreed to organize a meeting and seek sponsorship from Douglass College. They worked on a shoe-string budget, and prepared for a small conference of 75 or, hopefully, 100 interested workers who would have an opportunity to talk together, share ideas and resources, and build enthusiasm. Advance registrations suggested bigger crowds than anticipated, and by conference's end nearly 600 had registered and many more had attended without registration. Clearly, this conference was greatly appreciated by historians of women.

At the following spring meeting (May 1973), basking in the Douglass success, the Berkshire Conference agreed that conferences on the history of women should be continued, and voted to undertake two more, one in fall 1974 and another in 1976. It was decided that we should employ a larger committee in order to spread the work load, which had been extraordinarily heavy for Banner and Hartman; that we would need financial support; and that we should again find sponsorship from an institution with special concern for women's education. Sponsorship was quickly settled. Several institutions offered, among them Radcliffe whose new Dean of Admissions, Alberta Arthurs, had attended the first conference at Douglass and wanted a second conference at Radcliffe.

The program committee[1] began to meet in the fall of 1973 in order to decide on the emphasis desired for the program. We advertised for proposals in newsletters, and we received hundreds of them. The completed program had 52 sessions—enough, we thought, to allow small groups to get together in the sessions and talk about their work. The emphasis was firmly placed on what we might call a "new" history, getting away from traditional political or biographical approaches. Instead, we wanted to display a variety of new and creative methods for dealing with a challenging historical problem—rediscovering the lives of a long-neglected and often silent majority. Attendance speaks for the continued need for such conferences and the attractiveness of the program. We thought we would have about 1,000 people; final registration was exactly 2,000; and still more people attended sessions without registering at all. This is roughly equivalent to the size of the annual conventions of the Organization of American Historians. We also attracted people from every generation: several high school groups registered, many undergraduate and graduate students, professional historians of all ages, and interested women from diverse groups. For example, we had a delegation from NOW, and a group of elderly retired nurses who were attracted by various sessions on women and medicine.

The committee met at the end of the conference to put together impressions, gossip, overheard remarks. It was our impression that the program was, overall, good history and well-received. A number of major research trends were recognized: women and the family; women's role in industrialization; the historian's new concern with the private spheres such as sexuality, health; women and the professions; women and social institutions, such as church, trade unions or schools. This program also highlighted the new methodological developments which are essential to women's history, such as demography, oral history, psychohistory. Many scholars reported finding greater interest in their research than they had expected and more historians engaged in active research than they knew existed. Therefore an important contribution of the conference was the opening of communication among scholars in new fields, which will help avoid duplication of research, foster cooperation, further exchanges of information, and offer opportunities to test hypotheses and interpretations.

The quality of sessions reported on ranged from "brilliant" to "dreadful," but the overwhelming majority of papers seem to have been good, solid work, and there were differing perceptions of success. One session was reported to have had a rather mediocre paper by a graduate student; but another committee member had been told by the student in question how much she had learned about how to shape her work, and how stimulating it had been to be involved in a session with mature scholars. Indeed, the mix of senior and junior historians learning from each other was a major asset of the conference. Senior historians could communicate their professional experience and set new work in a broad context; younger historians expressed their fresh enthusiasm for new methods and new topics.

What problems did arise; where might we like to improve in the future? First, the old problem of overly-long papers, which limit discussion and audience involvement. This problem is persistent in academic meetings, and the next program committee will have to grapple with it again. In fact, we might experiment much more with format, and encourage new ideas about presentation. Second, not all of the workshops were successful in sharing problems, ideas and information. The ones which worked best were linked to formal sessions, and/or ones for which the members had met to plan in advance. Third, although it was grand to have undergraduates on the program, it was, we now realize, patronizing to put them in a separate session. Since it is quite an innovation to include undergraduates in meetings of this kind at all, we won't apologize for not doing it in quite the right way the first time. Next time, however, we might advertise that we will consider undergraduate research, and if it is good put it in regular sessions. Fourth, the decentralization of the committee did produce some mix-ups, situations in which everyone thought someone else was taking responsibility. Slightly tighter organization might help avoid problems, but on the whole, the virtues of a democratic committee are more important than its faults. Fifth, we were a little cheese-paring in our budget. We should in particular have budgeted transportation funds for which graduate students and professors emeriti could apply. Sixth, it may have been a mistake to spread out through three days. Seventh, there has been comment about the role of men on the program, and particularly about some of the male commentators who attacked the legitimacy of the history of women and thereby challenged the premises of the conference. Men were welcomed on the program, but in future any historian (male or female) who is vehemently opposed to the validity of women's history ought not to be invited to *comment*. Comments, to be helpful, must work within some common assumptions of value, and not attack the entire enterprise. However, we might, at our next conference, arrange for debate on some topic like "Is women's history a separate story?" In the long run, the role of men in the program may be less important than their absence in the audience, which was most disappointing.

In sum, we would say that the conference meant many things to many people. An observant Radcliffe undergraduate, a reporter for

The Crimson, told me that she saw several interlocking groups: the historians, very professional; the feminists, very political; and the feminist historians. But we had more than that. We attracted many women who hoped that the past would help them understand the present and plan for the future; we had the jobless, who looked for an intellectual opening and maybe a job opening; we had an "old girls" group which enjoyed being the "movers and shakers," the senior historians at a meeting which recognized them as powerful perhaps for the first time; we had another group which was becoming socialized in the profession in a way that we hope was supportive and satisfying. All these, and many more, engaged in our enterprise. The effect was, we think, a declaration to the profession that the history of women is an important field for research and teaching, and that without it there can be no true understanding of the past.

NOTE

1. Louise Dalby, Skidmore College; Ellen Dubois, SUNY, Buffalo; Mary Maples Dunn, Bryn Mawr College; Linda Gordon, University of Massachusetts, Boston; Gwendolyn Evans Jensen, University of New Haven; Patricia King, Schlesinger Library, Radcliffe College; Sally Gregory Kohlstedt, Simmons College; Claudia Koonz, College of the Holy Cross; Catherine Prelinger, Yale University; Carroll Smith-Rosenberg, University of Pennsylvania; Barbara Rosenkrantz, Harvard University; Lillian Shiman, Nichols College; Barbara Sicherman, Radcliffe Institute; Kathryn Kish Sclar, University of California, Los Angeles; Martha Tolpin, Radcliffe Institute; Martha Vicinus, Indiana University.

Advice from a Chinese Revolutionary [Feminist]

Ting Ling **Summer 1976**

The following comes from a speech made by Ting Ling on the occasion of International Women's Day in 1942 to the women of Yenan, then the center of Communist insurgency in mainland China. . . .

First, don't allow yourself to become ill. Sometimes you may feel that an unregulated lifestyle is romantic, poetic and attractive. But it isn't appropriate for the present situation. No one cares about you more than you care about yourself. And nothing can be worse than to lose your health at this time. Good health is the most essential thing. Look after it and take tender care of yourself.

Secondly, keep yourself cheerful. Only by remaining cheerful can you have youthfulness, vitality and the ability to lead a full life, the reserve strength to endure the hardships of our situation, to have good future prospects and to have pleasure. I'm not talking about a mere contentment with life, but about the joy of struggling ahead and progressing. That's why, every day, we must do meaningful work, study, contribute something of ourselves to others. Loafing only makes our lives empty, weary and withered.

Thirdly, get into the habit of using your brain. Get rid of your aversion to deep thinking and your strong inclination to always follow the crowd. Think well about what you are about to say or do. Consider whether your action will actually be effective, whether or not it goes against your deepest convictions and whether or not you are willing to accept responsibility for it. If you act in this way, you will have no regrets; this is what is called a rational person. You will not be gypped or trapped by sweet words nor tempted by small gains. You will not fritter away your passion nor waste your life, and you will avoid worries.

Fourthly, have the determination to drive ahead to the end. Women who are fully aware of the present moment have to know how to shed every rose-colored fantasy. Our joy is a battle within a storm and not playing the harp under the moon or reciting poetry in front of a flower. Without strong determination, you will certainly quit half-way.

You will either be in a continual state of distress or will become corrupted. The strength of your endurance is cultivated through "constancy." Without a great aspiration it is impossible to resist greed and to avoid becoming a victim of comfort. Only those who work for all humankind, not just for themselves, have this kind of aspiration.

Finding and Studying Lesbian Culture

Toni McNaron   **Fall 1977**

On a Wednesday afternoon in the dead of winter, twelve lesbians met
to begin a six-week exploration of our culture. Our most immediate
and persistent awareness was lack of precedent; our sense of breaking
new ground added excitement and urgency to all our meetings. We
felt a deep frustration at how hard it is to "study" something for the
first time. Out of our experience together, we want to share what we
found, and, even more, our process. We hope this process may serve
as a model from which others can begin their investigations within
their own communities. By sharing method, we can evolve a fruitful
way to talk about lesbian culture, leaving behind the bankruptcy of
social science.

The group began as part of an aftercare program at Christopher
Street, a drug treatment center in Minneapolis, for lesbians and homo-
sexual men. I was asked by the staff if I would facilitate a study group
on some topic that might interest the women. Knowing my own dis-
satisfaction with how lesbians have been studied, and feeling a need
to focus the group on a topic about which neither I nor they were
experts, I chose the matrix of lesbian culture. For thirteen years, I have
taught English literature and later women's studies at the University
of Minnesota. Over those years, I have grown progressively more impa-
tient with the usual structures and goals of education. I wanted to see
if I could use my teaching skills in a setting where participants would
have no external reasons for staying with the group unless it addressed
genuine personal and intellectual needs.

The background of the group is varied. Though most have been
chemically dependent, women have worked with us who are not; we
are open to any lesbian wishing to study her culture. Our ages range
from 19 to 45; "formal" education extends from grade school through
a Ph.D., though most of the women attended some or all of a four-year
college. We come from the Midwest predominantly, though the South
and East are represented. As far as our sexual histories go, we include
born dykes, a recent divorcée, and several women who have realized
their lesbianism within the women's movement during the past two or

three years. We are white except for one Native American woman; several women express strong ethnic identification (Jewish, Scandinavian, southern).

As for class, I consciously delayed exploring that dimension until after the initial stages of our work/study. We wanted to see if any common factors could be identified as those of lesbian culture, regardless of socioeconomic and political differences. We have continued the group, however, and are even now, at several participants' request, discussing our class background. The group seems evenly divided between middle and lower or working class, though education has confused many of us working-class women, and decisions to live alternatively have caused downward mobility for some of the middle-class women. Once we've completed our work on class and its relationship to our being lesbians, we may well report our findings in a separate piece.

Design

Out of a personal conviction that our deepest notions of culture begin with and center on ourselves, our behavior, and our values, I brought to the opening session the idea of four concentric circles within which we might operate. We labeled each circle, beginning with "me" for the inner circle. The second rim was "you's" or lesbians immediately connected with us, our own special community, with whom we can check perceptions, feelings, questions. The circle beyond this group was "live they's" or lesbians living in other places, with whom we may come into contact at special moments (conferences, concerts, speeches). We have less direct ties with this group, a relatively more abstract relationship. Into this group we put women contributing to present lesbian culture, e.g., T. Grace Atkinson, Margie Adam, Jeannette Foster, Willie Tyson, Rita Mae Brown, May Sarton, Meg Christian, Adrienne Rich, Jane Rule, Alix Dobkin, Bertha Harris, Jean O'Leary. These women form a new circle because separation of space and more subtle factors make them less accessible. I can identify and connect with a poem of May Sarton's or a song of Alix Dobkin's, but I cannot really know why they made those pieces or what they feel or think about various issues surrounding lesbianism. We are linked, however, through a medium which defies geographical location and generational differences. These ties are significant because they widen my sense of concentric circles of lesbian life and because at certain moments the intensity of response cuts through the layers between us. I begin to feel echoes of my personal and communal life—I begin to feel expansive, part of a great web centering on me and stretching through time and across nationality and custom.

At the outermost circumference were the "dead they's"—lesbians from former times whose lives and thoughts have been preserved. Until recently, we have had perforce to know of such women from male, heterosexist publishers. Our discovery of them has thus been clouded. Women have now begun to publish materials on these lesbians which will be more trustworthy than older versions. Men's translations of Sappho's poetry, for example, are the ones to reach print, and though such men may have admired her, they have conveyed a skewed picture of her and her work. With Mary Bernard's translation, we finally have a woman's version of what Sappho was up to. To read Bernard and an earlier translation side by side enlivens the problem before us. Our group agreed that contemporary and future lesbian scholars must redo much that history has overlooked or misinterpreted. The prospect for at least several decades—of gently brushing away the dust of neglect and crud of denial—made us feel that special breath-holding which must accompany any archaeological dig. And the civilization we uncover will be our own, not some faraway, foreign example of quaint structures and residual mores.

Process

We began with ourselves, the "me" of the design, telling each other details from our lives which are pertinent to our being lesbians. We divided our autobiographies into two segments—one prior to age ten (before we had begun to menstruate or get caught up in the dating maze) and one from age ten to the present. Once we all had told our stories, we looked for common details and emerging patterns, and found the following connecting themes:

- a prevalent feeling of being isolated and lonely—an "outsider"—from childhood
- a sense of ourselves as different from those around us
- seeing ourselves as survivors, with a strong endurance factor, not to be kept down indefinitely
- a feeling that what we're getting just isn't enough
- a sense that we're very strong or very weak, dealing or hiding; we work hard for any balance in our daily lives
- a feeling that there are few places where or times when we can relax and play
- an inability to forget or avoid what we know (about self, others, the world)
- a feeling that the outdoors has been positive space for us
- a sense of having been tomboys for too long.

Our next step was for each of us to talk with at least one lesbian not in our group, until we found some point of similarity. From these conversations, we became surer of our initial perceptions. Some of us continue to connect stories with friends, believing that their agreement with and additions to our original list adds strength and depth to a consistent pattern of lesbian feelings and ideas. The next step has been to read and listen to "live they" stories/theories and see how often we find similar conditions and responses. The final step will be to read lives of, conditions for, and works by lesbians of the past, again looking for common experience. To the extent that such links can be made between my life, the lives of my friends, and lives of famous lesbians and/or their creations, I can feel less isolated and unique. I can understand that my perceptions are not shaped only by my particular circumstances and makeup . . .

Rationale

Why is such an awareness helpful? For the reasons that her history and culture are vital to any woman: without a sense that I go back further than my literal birth, I find it difficult to feel substantial or to resist strains on my energy and self-respect caused by attitudes toward me both as woman and as lesbian. Like heterosexual feminists, lesbians need to meet together for solidarity. Knowing that my story falls into a context of other, older stories (whether of accomplishment or horror) lets me believe in my ability to survive. To remain isolated from my own lesbian culture for one more day delays beyond all acceptable limits my coming into my own strength and power.

In sharing expectations we have when meeting another lesbian, we laughed as we agreed that such expectations could not possibly be met by a mere mortal dyke. As we tried to identify why we continue to express them, someone remarked that "even if a given lesbian falls short of my high expectations, she supports me just by existing in the world.". . .

Myths/Rituals

An entire session was devoted to current myths about lesbians, producing a predictable run-down of negative stereotypes held about us by the society in which we grow up, get educated, work, and try to live. Old angers surfaced at such a shoddy state of affairs, since we realized that all such myths are imposed from outside, that the best we can usually do is make satires or humor of what is intended to keep us depressed and frightened. In an attempt to translate anger into positive energy, we named those myths which have had the most severe impact on our lives.

For several, the myth that lesbians are not "real women" has weighed heavily on our growing up, forcing us to try out masculine roles in an attempt to fit society's view. A parallel version of this myth was one woman's sense that she was labeled "unable to get a man." This kept her from following her feelings, especially during high school, when she knew she was a lesbian but, in order to cope with her environment, withdrew from people who told her that she could change if she just tried to date boys.

The myth most often cited was that lesbians are sick "I thought I had to go get cured"; "I was chronically depressed and unable to cope, which made me feel irresponsible and pretty near to what the myth wanted me to feel—sick"; "Because I know unsympathetic people would see me as somehow unclean, diseased, I buy into their myth by hiding my lesbianism"; "I don't want to be limited to the society of lesbians, so I worry about saying who I am, since other people will think I'm weird and stay away." Two members talked of ways in which the myth of lesbians as child-molesters kept them from forming friendships or from showing affection to women; both said that because they accepted this myth, they denied their sexuality and with it all feelings, holding themselves rigid so as not to touch anyone or let anyone know they wanted to be touched.

In trying to see how such myths operate, we discussed internalizing negative stereotypes, a process which keeps us victims of the very system which fears us. Several women argued strongly that we must reverse this process, by refusing to absorb the dominant society's myths, by turning self-hatred outward, and by fighting back. For some, this has meant participating in lesbian/gay rights marches or action programs; for others, it involves saying out loud at work or in other nonlesbian settings that we are lesbians. For many, it has involved taking ourselves seriously enough to seek help in ending habits which keep energy depressed and our sense of self-worth silenced or weakened.

Finally, we focused on the stark truth that those externally imposed myths, which have tremendous power over us individually and as a culture, have been made up either to keep us incapacitated or to keep a homophobic society from examining its own problems with sexuality. Trying to think of indigenous myths, we felt sadness and anger because we could not list any. We talked of the function of myth and rituals, concluding that they exorcise, cleanse, and heal an individual member of a culture so that she can function more fully within her group. We affirmed the power of rituals to be tangible proof of our realities, the ability of participants to speak a reality into existence, to say "it is" because I name it and you recognize it. Lesbians need to design ritual structures allowing us to move from recognition of the oppressive culture to affirmation and confirmation and celebration of our own culture.

One of the most moving parts of our painful work came when we let ourselves know why we resist making rituals to heal us and convert us from victim to actor:

- In our fervor to reject negative, dead rituals within the inherited culture, we have rejected a deep need we have for live rituals.
- To design and participate in a ritual is to take ourselves seriously and to hold onto massive self-consciousness; this remains difficult for many lesbians, since it means taking responsibility for our own lives.
- There is something final about rituals because of their publicness and declarativeness; we are still fearful of being so final.
- To participate in a ritual is to call attention to ourselves, and for some of us that raises specters of punishment from outside and of guilt or confusion from inside.
- To participate in a culture's rituals is to declare a willingness to be accountable to that larger group. That's just plain scary.

We talked about ways to guard against a deadness which we legitimately reject many existing rituals. Flexibility, participation, and focus seem to be goals offering some assurance of vitality. In addition, we talked of continually changing lesbian rituals, so as to work against their becoming hollow.

Then we evolved an exciting list of moments in our lives as lesbians which deserve ritualization. They share a quality of being difficult times which can be made easier by group activity acknowledging a particular lesbian's struggle, and, most important, the commonness surrounding it in the lives of an entire culture:

- coming out
- losing our blood families
- creating intentional families
- leaving the church
- arriving as a new member of a community
- getting into relationships
- the sexual aspect of lesbian relationships
- the end of relationships

- aging as a dyke
- movement into and out of solitude.

These are more than mirrors of the dominant society's ceremonies, and in each instance we agreed that we have experienced them often, painfully, and with effort. It would have been healing and helpful if we could have attended a ritual built to acknowledge such moments. We didn't want to wait for someone else to address this need. After working together, we had a certain clarity about many aspects and problems of lesbian culture. We felt an impulse to nurture our culture as well as study it. Consequently, our work group planned and staged a massive Coming Out Ritual, held in the country on the first Sunday in May. This ritual celebrated women who had come out, ever; over two hundred women attended. . . .

What Next

Having spent concentrated time talking out these issues, we are now eager to try out our process with other lesbians. One way to ensure our future is by recording stories until they overlap and become legend. We also want to publish our process in lesbian journals, papers, newsletters, in the hope that others will organize similar work groups, discuss our infant model, and use it, possibly in modified form. If you then share your results with us, we can establish a network of lesbians engaged in direct cultural analysis. Eventually we can devise a tested and valid method to use in large-scale study of us.

The gains of such a process are immeasurable to those of us doing it and to lesbians who will follow us. What this generation of dykes could leave to our cultural posterity is a way to organize our chaotic, often painful experience into some body of data (hard and very soft) which would let lesbians five or fifty years from now build new layers from an already-articulated base. Such a system would offer lesbians and the (homophobic) society at large much-needed information about our history, our artifacts, and our day-to-day lives. For most of us, no such information existed, and we had the grim alternative of reading false, even destructive, things about ourselves in standard textbooks, or of remaining ignorant. At present, much is being published by individual lesbians and by clusters of lesbians. What is missing is a systematic analysis of us as a culture, and that is where we hope our work can be helpful. . . .

Copyright © 1977 by Toni McNaron.

The IWY Conference at Houston: Implications for Women's Studies

Elizabeth Baer and
Dora Janeway Odarenko   *Winter 1978*

. . . But for women who had also attended the four-day founding convention of the National Women's Studies Association in San Francisco
just ten months earlier, there was a familiar urgency of another sort:
could there be a new integration of race and class and sex? Once more
the endorsement of a program would affect the possibilities for widespread grass-roots coalition and the extent to which the priorities of
race, class, and lesbianism would be recognized. Just as women went
to San Francisco determined to strengthen ties between traditional
feminist education and the larger women's movement, so at Houston
an issue awaiting resolution was the actual breadth of the proposed
National Plan, which was being defended as the minimal National Plan
of Action for women of this country.

In Houston, as in San Francisco, the pressure of time was certainly
a reality, given an ambitious platform of twenty-six major issues, alpha-
betically arranged, debate on each of which, if allotted equal time,
could not exceed twenty-five minuses. Moreover, if the task of the
NWSA San Francisco Convention was considerable—four days for 500
delegates to approve a program—the scope of the Houston Conference
might have rendered it overwhelmingly impersonal—1,842 delegates,
plus 4,000 official special observers and guests, 15,000 registered
observers, 1,700 media people, and hundreds more who poured through
the large exhibit hall. But finally, in Houston as in San Francisco, it
would be the function of individual caucuses, preorganized or con-
solidated under the pressures of the occasion, to shape amendments
that were far more specific about needs of particular groups. . . . At
Houston, Disabled Women, Minority Women, Older Women, Rural
Women, and Welfare Women would be sufficiently insistent, the needs
of Pro-Plan notwithstanding, to refuse to table their objections until
the allotted time for new business in the last session; instead they wrote
out amendments in triplicate and, by standing in long lines at micro-

phones, succeeded in introducing amendments that were eventually
passed. In the same way, the resolutions on Education and on Rape
were amended.

"Wonder Woman" Not a Delegate

At the opening session in the Coliseum on Saturday morning,
Congresswoman Barbara Jordan of Texas, the keynote speaker, urged
women to accept the differences—economic, cultural, social, political, ideological—among themselves and to remember that "no one
person and no subgroup at this conference has the right answers.
"'Wonder Woman' is not a delegate." She insisted, "This conference
is one more effort on the part of women for total recognition and
total inclusion." Commissioner Liz Carpenter of Texas likewise identified "the faces and voices ignored and silenced too often by the decision makers." Naming one woman after another, each representing
a different kind of work, or a different class or race, she challenged
her audience with a variant of: "Would you deny this woman and
those like her their full rights as citizens of this great nation?" And
again and again she answered, "Not me!" . . . But among this diversity, there was no mention of lesbian women. Punctuating the partial
standing ovation that Carpenter received, there were shouts of "What
about the lesbians?"

From the tenor of the opening session, then, it seemed clear that
minority women were being acknowledged—rhetorically, if not through
the strength of the resolution concerning them. But it seemed equally
clear that, the Sexual Preference resolution notwithstanding, the rights
of lesbian women would have to be fought for yet once more.

Time to Support Women's Studies

On other fronts, the needs that were defined by NWSA in San Francisco
were ably represented. Early on Saturday evening, Amy Swerdlow, former associate director of the Master of Arts Program in Women's History
at Sarah Lawrence College, member of the *Women's Studies Newsletter*
Advisory Committee and The Feminist Press Reprints Advisory Board,
succeeded, despite strong antiamendment sentiment, in presenting a
significant addition to the Education resolution. Earlier a delegate had
called for the insertion of the words "and race" and "nonracist," respectively, within the phrases "sex-stereotyping" and "nonsexist counseling." Swerdlow's proposal was equally critical: in a list outlining
appropriate action through which state school systems can move
against sex and race stereotyping, Swerdlow amplified the phrase

"Review of books and curriculum" by adding: "The integration into the curriculum of programs of study that restore to women their history and their achievements and give them the knowledge and methods to reinterpret their life experiences." Swerdlow passionately urged her amendment: "Women's studies has supported the women's movement; now it's time for the movement to support women's studies!" Observers in the galleries, more alert than the delegates, erupted into shouts of "UP! UP!" indicating their insistence on a "Yes" vote. Whereas an earlier amendment, backed by Alabama, Indiana, Utah, and other conservative delegations (and proposing an emphasis in schools on handwriting, spelling, and the work ethic) had been defeated, this one was approved. Its passage, where others failed, demonstrated an exciting level of grass-roots support for women's studies; it illustrates as well the frequent and active participation of observers (and some members of the press) throughout the conference.

Coliseum Was Not the Only Forum

Nor was the Coliseum the only forum for discussions of women's studies at Houston. The Albert Thomas Convention Center, a five-minute walk from the Coliseum, housed hundreds of demonstration booths. The feminist presses and journals represented—Academy Press, *Coyote Howl*, Daughters, Inc., Diana Press, The Feminist Press, KNOW, Lollipop Power, Motherroot *Ms.*, *Northwest Matrix, Quest,* Radical Women Publications, Shameless Hussy Press, *Signs*, and others—reported brisk business and lingering discussions. A slide show of Judy Chicago's latest project, "The Dinner Party," ran continually, as did Lenore Weitzman's slide show on elementary textbooks. Representatives from various women's organizations ranging from Wages for Housework to WEAL to the National Women's Studies Association handed out free literature. . . .

Reflecting sensitivity to this need, the second floor of the Convention Center, named "Seneca Falls South" to indicate the historical continuity of the women's movement, was established, according to the program, to "reflect the energy and excitement which have been characteristic of the movement for more than 100 years." One could literally have spent the entire weekend here, participating in women's studies workshops, coordinated by Phyllis Palmer, of George Washington University, and the National Women's Studies Association. Or attending films, slide shows, lectures, and displays at the Women's Artspace. Or watching self-defense demonstrations, mime, poetry, concerts, and feminist comedy on the Seneca Falls Stage. . . .

In addition, there were Panels on the Arts; a Film Festival; and

Briefings from the Top: Distinguished Women in Government Lecture
Series. . . .

Meanwhile, Back in the Coliseum . . .

Over in the Coliseum, by Saturday evening, . . . Third World women
actually pushed through a substitute resolution which is far more specific about the needs, and oppressions, of each group than the proposed Minority Women Resolution; the substitute resolution was
movingly read, in turn, by a Native American woman, an Asian
American woman, an Hispanic woman, and a Black woman. When it
was passed, women joined hands and sang, amid some tears, "We Shall
Overcome."

Possibly the most highly charged resolution was that on Sexual
Preference. The ERA resolution—for many the high point of the
conference—passed overwhelmingly late Saturday night, but the
ensuing holiday mood and decision to adjourn until Sunday created
real worry for supporters of other resolutions on the list: would the
conference get to vote on all of these items and, if they did, would the
press still be there to cover them? For many lesbian women, the Saturday
sessions were a time of watching and assessment, with understandable
caution and doubts about the viability of IWY. After all, the Sexual
Preference resolution had not been part of the original Plan of Action,
but had been included only after thirty-four states adopted various
recommendations on sexual preference. As Betty Powell, Black lesbian
feminist activist, former Co-Chairperson of the National Gay Task Force
Board of Directors, tenured lecturer at Brooklyn College, explained
afterwards, "Were the heterosexual women here for us, too? Would
they rise to the occasion, standing up for the lesbian women as the lesbian women had been standing up for them? What would the process
be like, waiting in line at the mike, knowing there would be only a few
minutes to start an educational dialogue? How would their listeners
hear what they had to say?"

And so, Saturday at midnight, with shouts of "Sit down!" and
"Sellouts!" during the lengthy vote and revote on adjournment after
the passage of the ERA resolution, the lesbian presence and voice
strongly emerged. By Sunday morning, orange armbands were being
worn by lesbian women and their supporters. By Sunday afternoon,
hundreds of balloons stenciled "We Are Everywhere" were ready in the
corridors to be distributed during the resolution preceding Sexual
Preference—another outward and visible sign of months of extensive
preparation. One by one, they bobbed into view, filling the hall. In some
ways, the mood had lightened. Under the control of Anne Saunier, a

young NOW member from Ohio who was chair of the Sunday session, the agenda had been moving along briskly; the press was still there in force.

The resolution was read by Jean O'Leary, Co-Executive Director of the National Gay Task Force, IWY Commissioner from New York, and the only Commissioner to identify herself as a lesbian. The debate that followed, frequently forced back to order by Saunier, was probably the most lively and substantive of the conference. The opposing arguments were predictable: an affirmative vote would be "self-indulgent at this time," destroy the chances for ERA, split the movement by attaching to it a label that many had been struggling to dissociate themselves and the movement from. To this charge there were many logical replies: Betty Powell spoke of lesbian invisibility, which "like the invisibility of all minorities negatively perceived by society has for so long fostered only ignorance of our persons, our values, our actual life-styles, and also ignorance of the effect of legal, social, and economic discrimination upon our lives. We have all of us—Black, Brown, Red, Yellow, and White, old, young, imprisoned, and disabled—begun to see ourselves and each other more clearly. Clearest of all is the fact that the oppressions we suffer, as distinct and varied as they are, stem universally from the condition of simply being women in this world." Charlotte Bunch defined lesbianism as "more than sexual preference; it is a matter of civil rights, a life-style . . . the vote is for all women who are controlled by fear of being called a lesbian." And Betty Friedan, silencing the hall, turned the tide: "There is nothing in ERA to protect lesbians, and so we must allow them to be protected in their own civil rights."

Significant Energy for the Future

The rights of women in poverty were the final task of the day. With the passage of a strong amendment for welfare women—"Welfare First—We're Always Last," read their placards—the major work of the conference was over. Voting on a Women's Department and preliminary discussion of implementation remained for the last plenary session.

Significantly, then, the Houston conference confirmed the rights of a number of groups of women, and in so doing acknowledged their full membership in the movement. Far from splitting the conference or the movement, such actions may have healed it. The enormous joy that was perhaps the most keenly felt especially by lesbian women and minority women will provide significant energy for the future. For those watching national patterns, Houston left the women's movement far more alive than anyone, prior to Houston, had expected.

Books That Changed Our Lives

Fall/Winter 1991

Introduction

This discussion began as a way to celebrate the two decades of consciousness we've all lived through and to have a bit of fun doing it. We may still manage that bit of fun, but in the meantime we've all noticed a spate of critical journalism on the questions we took completely for granted as we began to write our essays: Can books change lives? Are they more powerful than film or television? And if they can change lives for the better—which is part of what we may be taking for granted here today—can they not also affect them for the worse? I am referring, of course, to books that sink below the common scale of degradation to levels of violence against women, and others, beyond even the visual media. Do we dare claim such revolting artifacts as responses to two decades of consciousness? As part of the backlash we've been threatening enough to incite? And if that's the case, what is our response to be?

I raise these questions not to cloud the session's celebratory joy but to remind us all that these two decades are only the beginning of a new century of struggle.

Florence Howe

These essays were first presented at the Modern Language Association Annual Meeting in Chicago in December, 1990. Panelists were instructed to write no more than two pages on the book or books that, twenty years ago, changed their lives.

Domna C. Stanton

One is not born, but rather becomes, a woman." If there is a phrase that inaugurated my life as a feminist, it is that one. But this one too: "... she is the incidental, the inessential. ... He is the Subject ... she is the Other." Of course, there was more, so much more in those thousand pages of French that I read for months in 1960 at Wellesley College, dazzled by Simone de Beauvoir's knowledge and frames of reference — philosophy and history; psychoanalysis, psychology, sociology, and anthropology; religion, mythology, and literature — pages and pages that again and again provided overwhelming evidence of women's oppression by the first sex. Above all, however, it was the existential message that inspired me in that first reading of *The Second Sex*: that being a woman was a historical situation, not an essence; that my capacity to create myself would only be limited by the anguish of freedom and the fear of taking responsibility for my life; and that I could indeed become the committed intellectual on behalf of women that de Beauvoir so empoweringly symbolized.

Ten years later, in the winter of 1970, when I taught my first course, Feminism and the Feminine in France, my rereading of *The Second Sex* provided a roadmap for the new feminist criticism: de Beauvoir's groundbreaking chapters on literary works by men, what we would later call "images of women criticism"; her powerful analyses of Freud and Engels; and her harsh discussion of women writers whose creativity had been stifled and ambition narrowed to dilletantism and amateurism.

I have reread *The Second Sex* with students many a time since then — most recently this semester. In that process, however, other strands and strains have become painfully visible: the text's androcentrism and sexism and contempt for feminists; its classist assumptions of intellectual and material privilege; its heterosexism; finally and most recently, its facile, and inherently racist, analogies between women and slaves.

I wonder, of course, why I did not see those strains in 1960 or 1970. Even more troubling, I wonder how a text so impure, so incorrect, my PC students say, could have so empowered me. I search the yellowed notes from those years — yes, I still have them — for signs that I had perceived the text's own complicity with the ideologies it condemned. And, yes, in 1975, scribbles in the margins and the corners and the backs of those first typed notes begin to outline objections and criticisms. Inevitably, reading all my subsequent class notes on *The Second Sex* becomes the record of the changes and lurches in feminist criticism over the past fifteen years. To be sure, de Beauvoir changed too. In a 1976 interview she recognized that she was no feminist in 1949, that she had been a token woman and was inured to living in a world where men are oppressors. "The main thing that [feminists] have taught me," she continued, "is vigilance . . . not to let anything pass, not even the most trivial things." But the interview was dotted with unvigilant blind spots, at least as I read it in 1982. Of course, no matter how vigilant or correct my/our discourse is today, it too has its blind spots, since we don't have the hindsight to see them.

Still, the poles of blindness and insight which we inhabit at one and the same time may not be the problem; perhaps utopianism is: the idea that *The Second Sex* could have been born full-blown from some place outside of the historical conjunction of gender and class and sexual and racial ideologies; and that unless its origin was pure, it could not radicalize, should not empower.

After these twenty years of women's studies, as we become "post-lapsarian" models for real and metaphorical daughters, we know this utopianism cannot be fruitful, however infantile our yearnings for the pure, all-knowing mother text may sometimes be. We do not need a sacred text that seals our conversion for life. We do need sister texts with which we can have heated debates, even decades of disagreements — imperfect, provisional models that inscribe the strengths and blind spots of the past and thus of our own struggles as we reread them.

A mirror of myselves in 1960, 1970, and 1980, *The Second Sex* still empowers me in 1990 — now with the knowledge that we are no less infected by the ideological air we breathe than de Beauvoir was in postwar Paris and yet that our feminist practices have made the crucial difference in us and among us.

I hope that, at the December Modern Language Association meeting in 2000, when Florence Howe sponsors yet another of these celebrations, I hope that a young feminist will take the podium to tell her story of — and with — *The Second Sex*. That story will surely contain the history of the coming decade of feminist theory and praxis, a history of blindness and insight that can continue, as de Beauvoir has for me, powerfully, even radically, to change our lives.

Domna C. Stanton is Professor of French and Women's Studies at the University of Michigan. Her publications include The Female Autograph: Theory and Practice of Autobiography from the Tenth to the Twentieth

Century *and* Women Writ, Women Writing: Gender, Discourse, and Difference in Seventeenth-Century France, forthcoming in 1992.

Lillian S. Robinson

At the University of Texas, where I am a visiting professor this year, all first-year graduate students in English are required to take an orientation seminar. Each week throughout the fall term different members of the department are invited to come in and lecture the new students about the approaches or methods that inform their own intellectual work. On Halloween, appropriately enough, Jane Marcus and I were accorded an hour and a half to introduce feminist criticism.

We began with an exercise where we went around the room asking students to name all the feminists they could think of, sorting the names they gave us into three columns: writers, critics, and Everybody Else, a category that included activists, social theorists, women in public life, and so on. With this extraordinary list as a literal and conceptual background, we launched into a discussion of the way that feminist criticism took its shape and its priorities from the feminist movement. In the women's room (where else?) after the presentation, Jane said to me, "I don't know. Last year I did this number by myself, and I told them there has *always* been a feminist criticism. Since Sappho anyway."

"Well," I replied, "That's the narrative for the odd-numbered years, and the one we just did is for the even-numbered years. And, of course, they are contradictory and both true."

But there is a third narrative we might have recounted. Also, needless to say, at variance with the others and also true. Which is that the first and the single indispensable work of feminist literary criticism is a slim volume by Virginia Woolf called *A Room of One's Own*.

In the 1978 preface to my first book, *Sex, Class, and Culture*, I tell the story of how I became a feminist critic, sitting up all night mesmerized by news of the Tet offensive and reading *A Room of One's Own*. Dissertation-blocked and Vietnam-obsessed though I was, I wanted to bring Woolf's arguments up to date. Some months later, in the fall of 1968 and as a private commemoration of the fortieth anniversary of the lectures that were to become *A Room of One's Own*, I wrote a long essay, the first piece of what has turned out to be my life's work. Provocatively, I called it, "Who's Afraid of A Room of One's Own?"

Although I believed that *A Room of One's Own* was one of the most beautiful books ever written, I felt it had flaws, particularly in its understanding of sex and class and the relation between them. I thought Woolf didn't know enough about politics — my kind of late-sixties style street-fighting anti-imperialist politics. But I thought I could help her out. Having been born on April 18, 1941, the day Virginia Woolf's body was found, I was all of twenty-seven years old. Since then I have read and reread *A Room of One's Own* a number of times. I do not believe in sacred texts. Much of my career has been spent, after all, thumbing my nose at canons. So I will not say that *A Room of One's Own* is my Bible. But if Melville could say that a whaling ship was his Harvard and his Yale, *A Room of One's Own* has certainly been my whaling ship — my pirate ship, my tugboat, and my spaceship as well.

At each stage of my evolution as a feminist critic, as I brought different social and literary problematics to bear on the project and explored the intersections of class, race, gender, and sexuality, as I contemplated the revolution of the word and the revolutions beyond that, I have found that Virginia Woolf has been there ahead of me. Not that she provided comprehensive answers that made my own efforts redundant. Rather, the much thumbed-through text showed that she had posed most of the hard questions and recorded the consequent search for answers with elegance. With elegance.

Whether the issue was class or color, war or empire, she offered neither blueprint nor roadmap but, rather, served simultaneously as forerunner, companion, and comrade in the struggle. In 1968 I set out, with all due respect and a whole lot of chutzpah, to teach Virginia Woolf a thing or two. Well, my recursive reading of *A Room of One's Own* over the past twenty-two years reveals that the old girl has certainly learned a lot!

Lillian S. Robinson is Visiting Scholar in Residence at the Harry Ransom Humanities Research Center, University of Texas at Austin. She is author of Sex, Class, and Culture *and* Monstrous Regiment, *and coauthor of* Feminist Scholarship: Kindling in the Groves of Academe.

Nellie McKay

Books have always been a part of my life. Of the hundreds (thousands?) I have read over more than forty years, which ones really changed my life? Perhaps many, for many different reasons.

So I begin my contribution to this tribute to books with my experiences with *The Night before Christmas*, which I "read" before I could read. That, of all the books read to me before I learned to read, might have set my course toward a career in reading books.

In my childhood home we read books. First my mother read and we listened, then, as we children learned to read, we took turns and read aloud. Television came to our house late. For a long time, in the evenings we read aloud to each other, graduating in time from the Dick and Jane and Spot books from which we learned to identify the written word (and seemed not to have suffered irreparable psychological damage) to "wholesome" novels like *Little Women*. But first there was *The Night before Christmas*. As a very young child, I really loved that Christmas favorite read to us each year. Soon I "learned" to read along before I learned the art of reading itself. I knew when the text on a page ended, and I would "read" with great aplomb. What fun that was! My parents too believed I read as I sat, book on narrow lap, and correctly turned the pages until the whole was done. And so for at least one Christmas season, when friends of my parents came to visit, I impressed them with my reading. Shamelessly, I admit, I loved my stage, although I soon realized the cost of my deception: I really had to learn to read!

On a more serious note, in spite of a heavy dose of books from as far back in my life as I can recall, two books stand out because the impact that they made on me some twenty years ago continues to reverberate inside of my consciousness. The first was W. E. B. DuBois's *The Souls of Black Folk*, which I read for the first time on Thanksgiving Day, 1969. I was a first-year graduate student then and read it on the advice of a friend. I had never read DuBois before; I had not known the power of the man or of his words. Having come of age in New York City during the violent 1960s and having "given up" Shakespeare to study American literature because I wanted to try to understand the meaning of America and American **RACISM**, spelled in bold capital letters, I had thought of myself as politically knowledgeable. And then I read *Souls of Black Folk*. It changed my worldview and the way I saw my life in relation to the world. DuBois's words continue to guide my intellectual thoughts.

And then there was Zora Neale Hurston's *Their Eyes Were Watching God*. If I had discovered the soul of my race in DuBois, it was from Hurston's masterpiece that I first understood the meaning of black femaleness and my true relationship to the world of white and black men and white women. Back in those dark days of the early 1970s, when Alice Walker was in search of all of our mothers's gardens—

from a photocopy of a photocopy, passed from black woman to black woman to black woman, because the book was not in print—I too discovered Janie and how she discovered herself. And suddenly I knew without a doubt that it was too late to turn back. I had come home to begin the search for myself.

Nellie McKay is Associate Professor of Afro-American Studies and English at the University of Wisconsin, Madison. Her publications include Jean Toomer, Artist: A Study of His Literary Life and Work *and an edited volume,* Critical Essays on Toni Morrison.

Catharine R. Stimpson

Does a single book change a life? Not by itself, for nothing exists in isolation. A lightning bolt needs a sky charged with electricity and a vulnerable ground. Nevertheless, some books are like bolts or, to change the metaphor, like blades cutting through the brain. For me, Gwendolyn Brooks's *Selected Poems* was such a knife, a blade of tempered steel, a handle studded with jewels of rhetoric, in a sheath of the finest leather.

I read the *Selected Poems* in the late 1960s while I was preparing the first course in black literature at Barnard College. The English department was staggering toward diversity. A few years later it would hire a black woman to teach the course. Domna Stanton was also at Barnard. Together, in the early 1970s, we would wear a path to the door of the dean of the faculty on a yearly pilgrimage to get the courses about women listed together on a page in the college catalog.

Obviously, Brooks was writing about black culture and history. Obviously, for a white woman, the *Selected Poems* was poetry about the Other. I learned, as one can, from poetry. Brooks gave me a complex voice, at once tough and elegant, forceful and funny. This complexity of voice was compatible with poems that were crucibles in which cultures met and fired each other: the ballad, the sonnet, the blues, the Western canon. Virgil walked through Bronzeville. I could then read "The Anniad." Brooks's voice warned me about my own eye. I was to see the Other clearly. I was not to be a voyeur, however, not to hide in a little booth at Benvenuti's, not swoop around as a lady from the Ladies' Betterment Society. To inoculate myself against the infection of voyeurism I was to regard my own world, to defamiliarize it, in Shlovsky's famous phrase. I could not fade

Into the shelter, the dear thick shelter
Of the familiar
Propitious haze.
(63)

Brooks carried the weightiest and sharpest of pain in her poetry.
She was, simultaneously, ironic and free. She praised a sensibility
that was not new to me but one that she cut out indelibly. The poem
"Langston Hughes" articulates this sensibility: Hughes

is merry glory.
Is saltatory.
Yet grips his right of twisting free.
(123)

Merry glory, salt, the right to twist free—for this I am indebted to
Gwendolyn Brooks.*

*Catharine R. Stimpson is University Professor at Rutgers University and
author of numerous publications, including* Where the Meanings Are:
Feminism and Cultural Spaces, *a selection of her essays.*

Meena Alexander

1970, the book that changed my life? The thought takes on accretions
like a monstrous piece of grit dropped into my head, a pearl of no
discernible shape, particolored, grossly illicit, and fills me with fear.
In 1970 I was nineteen years old. Raised in India and North Africa, I
had come to Britain as a graduate student to study English literature,
the culmination of a good colonial education. I swallowed up books,
bits and pieces of philosophy—Kant, Husserl, Wordsworth, Col-
eridge, all that stuff, all written by men. Suddenly one day in the
library—it was a summer's day with a clear sky, daffodils, peonies,
and the English oaks curving outside—I found myself blind.

I could see all right in a hazy sort of way. I simply could not read.
Near books, my sight twisted, sizzled, firing the alphabets of English
till they lost all discernible shape. Those letters I had taken such
pains to learn as a young child from a strict English tutor became
cloudy, misty, formless. It even seemed to me at moments that those

---

*I have quoted here from Gwendolyn Brooks's *Selected Poems* (1944; reprint, New
York: Harper and Row, 1963).

letters took on the swirling syllabic forms of my mother tongue Mala-
yalam, the language I could speak but not read, so absolute had been
my English education. In the time-honored tradition of the young
intellectual I was having a nervous breakdown, and for a month and
more I was effectively incapacitated in my duties as a graduate student. I went away into the countryside to rest, quite sick at heart.
Studying Wordsworth's "picture of the mind," I had lost my own.

Twenty years later, 1990. In my first novel *Nampally Road*, set in
Hyderabad, in India, I have the narrator teaching Wordsworth. But
there is trouble in the streets. She is pulled away to the scene of
trouble. People surround a police station. A woman is held there.
She has been raped by the police. The narrator enters, glimpses her
curled up in the muddy cell. The people set fire to the police station.
The old building constructed by the British starts to burn. Bit by bit
the narrator is drawn into the only world that endures for her, and
she struggles to build up a new, different picture of the mind, of the
female body, of shared labor, of practice in a postcolonial world. If I
can take the liberty of seeing beyond the end of the novel — the last
lines read "her mouth was healing slowly" — I would have this dena-
tured woman, this narrator, learn to listen to the other women's
language, read and write it, figure its syllables of pain, of endurance.
It is a task that many women in India, and indeed here, have taken
to themselves, to ourselves, figuring out bodily syllables of a female
speech, a female language, the once crossed out, the damaged, the
desecrated. We must spell out what bleeds, what burns, what is given
birth from our bodies. Else blindness, else books that pitch us to the
brink of various destructions.

As women who read and write, we must also be women who
publish, for publishing is the power to enter into visibility, to remake
the marginalized, to spell out the madness. "We fearfully ask on what
ground we ourselves stand," mused Mary Wollstonecraft in her great
novel *Maria*. To spell out our own ground, to make up spaces in
which to exist, we must learn to read and write, as if it were for the
first time, like the barred, banned creatures we are, like Rassundara
Devi, who in 1876 published the earliest autobiography in Bengali,
Amar Jiban. As a married women, held within the confines of domes-
ticity, she taught herself to read and write in secret, hiding a page
from a book in the kitchen, scratching out the alphabets on the sooty
wall.

And having said this now, my fear drifts away as mist might.
What seemed illicit, misshapen, grotesque, has become in the telling
part of a larger female story, a fabric of a hundred thousand strands,

growing and growing. I salute the perpetual making of books by women, books that will change our shared lives. At the tail end of the century I salute these very special decades of feminist publishing.

Meena Alexander is a poet and Associate Professor of English and Creative Writing at Hunter College, City University of New York. She is also author of the prose works Women in Romanticism: Mary Wollstonecraft, Dorothy Wordsworth, and Mary Shelley *(1989) and* Nampally Road *(1991).*

Robin Morgan

Undoubtedly *Sisterhood Is Powerful* is the book that changed my life. During the 1960s I was a political activist, a civil rights organizer in the North and South both, and an antiwar agitator. I worked as an editor in book publishing and was a published poet. But the earliest "women's liberation" caucuses in the then so-called New Left were my special joy, and when, by 1967, my own group decaucused as a ladies' auxiliary and became autonomous feminism's energy began to inform my life in earnest.

Because my whole women's consciousness-raising group was getting a bit bursitis-weary of lugging mimeographed position papers with us everywhere, it seemed a sensible and simple thing to combine my skills with my politics and compile an anthology.

Sensible, possibly; simple, no.

I had no idea how enormous the task would become, much less a clue about what it would do to my own consciousness. It was that task, more than anything else in those highly activist years, that drew me to radical feminism.

The anthology transformed my own life at least as much as it has the views of other women, literally thousands of whom have written or told me it wrought drastic shifts in their attitudes and daily realities. For me it caused an implosion.

When the book came out in 1970, the publisher feared that "this women's lib thing" had already peaked and there would be no audience for it. They were facing rather a shock. In fact, the early 1970s will always seem almost filmic to me—a montage of thought, emotion, and furious action. The logo I had designed for the cover—the women's symbol of a circle with a cross beneath and a fist rising in the center—became the international symbol for feminism. I suddenly faced a huge and growing pile of requests from women for me to lecture, organize, advise, and agitate around the country and, in fact, the world. I realized with a sense of irony how much we'd tried to do what we called "outreach" with our leaflets or how we'd begged the media for a shred of attention, and now a book had done it. And, however much willful dullards might accuse literature of being hopelessly elitist and old fashioned by Marshall McLuhan's standards, those first books from this wave of feminism in the United States had a staggering effect. With the royalties I formed the first feminist fund to churn monies back into the feminist movement—about eighty thousand dollars in the first five years alone. And I packed my bag and took to the road.

Today—twenty years and, for me, thirteen books later—*Sisterhood* still stands as a landmark. It also stands as that rare creature, a book steadily in print and selling. It's been translated into numerous languages, excerpted, quoted, used as a basic text in hundreds of women's studies courses, and hoarded—in yellowed, dog-eared shape— by hundreds of thousands of women. (And, according to seventeen unconnected letters in different languages over the two decades, it has been hurled at the heads of certain recalcitrant sexist men; given its size, this may have caused concussions, if not changed consciousness.) It gives me great delight that the book is still of such use to my sisters all these years later. Because that's what my intention was: to have it used as a tool, singing in women's hands and minds.

All unwittingly, I began the introduction to *Sisterhood* with the words "This book is an action." It was. Oh, it was.

Robin Morgan is an award-winning author who has published thirteen books — poetry, fiction, and nonfiction—including Sisterhood Is Powerful *and* Sisterhood Is Global. *She is Editor-in-Chief of* Ms. *magazine.*

Elaine Hedges

It's so difficult to choose just one book to celebrate from that eventful publishing year of 1970! I'll focus on one, but I want to mention, if only briefly, the great importance to me of several others as well.

By 1969 and 1970 I was active in the academic branch of the women's movement. I was a member of the newly formed Commission on the Status of Women of the Modern Language Association and of the MLA Women's Caucus, and I was working on my own campus for salary equity for women and for courses in that new phenomenon called women's studies. But I was also in intellectual and emotional transit and professionally in what had become for me a scholarly limbo. Not too long before, after much delay and only reluctantly, I had finished my doctoral dissertation on William Dean Howells; writing that dissertation had come to seem increasingly claustrophobic and irrelevant to what was going on in the rest of my life. I was reading widely in the literature that was emerging out of the women's movement, and among the books that importantly helped me define the new directions that my thinking was taking, books that helped catalyze and confirm those directions, I'd want especially to recall Kate Millett's *Sexual Politics* and also the wonderful anthologies that were then appearing — those inexpensive, and therefore so accessible, collections of early women's movement writings. These included, in 1970, Robin Morgan's *Sisterhood Is Powerful*, Leslie Tanner's *Voices from Women's Liberation, Liberation Now* (whose editors, in a fine feminist gesture, chose to omit their names from the title page), and, in 1971, Vivian Gornick and Barbara K. Moran's *Woman in a Sexist Society: Studies in Power and Powerlessness*. The personal essays, poems, scholarly studies, theoretical analyses, and radical manifestoes in those anthologies not only supplied me with a wealth of information and ideas but also gave me the invigorating sense of being part of a whole collectivity of women activists and scholars, all working, confidently and energetically, for change. And, not least, the anger that so many of the writers expressed as the extent of the oppression of women became increasingly clear encouraged and validated my own.

Millett's book, though, had a special impact. First of all, it was a doctoral dissertation, the likes of which I'd never read and certainly unlike the one I had so laboriously written. For someone who, like me, had entered the academy as a "dutiful daughter," Millett's willingness to take scholarly risks, to be so critical and so ambitious in the scope of her criticism, was both unsettling and exhilarating. It may be difficult today to appreciate the mystification that surrounded the canonical male writers in those long-ago years when I was in graduate school, but I still vividly remember the solemn and somewhat intimidating aura of classes devoted, for example, to reading the initiation theme in William Faulkner's "The Bear" — that story of a great white hunter — as a universal paradigm. And a form of that intimidation persisted into the 1960s, when any woman associated with radical political movements was likely to feel pressured into accepting as "liberated" the sexual views of those male authors, like D. H. Lawrence, Henry Miller, and Norman Mailer, whom Millett so vigorously dismantled. She may have engaged in some overkill, but hers was one of the earliest examples of revisionary reading, and I was ready for those readings — or for that critical approach — as I was for her crucial, central argument that relations between the sexes are political, involve issues of power. When, in 1973, I wrote the afterword to the Feminist Press edition of Charlotte Perkins Gilman's story "The Yellow Wallpaper"—the writing that marked my own beginnings as a feminist critic—my reading of that story, not as a clinical study of female pathology, as it had been read, but as a drama of sexual politics (a key phrase that I used in my interpretation) certainly owed a great deal to Millett.

What else mattered to me in 1970 about her book? Today, as critics, we aren't supposed to create what are called "totalizing" narratives to explain women's subordination, but in the happy innocence of the early 1970s I learned much from what Millett offered as her "systematic overview of patriarchy as a political institution." We had several such narratives in those days: Eva Figes's *Patriarchal Attitudes*, also published in 1970, was another, a book that swept through Western religion, philosophy, literature, science, and psychology from the Bible to Dr. Spock to chart the contours of patriarchal oppression. And, indeed, despite our present critical distrust of such narratives, those early ones still powerfully inhabit my imagination.

And then there was Freud. At a time when I was still struggling to disengage myself from the last in a series of psychiatrists, Millett's dismantling of that Olympian figure (also occurring, of course, in the anthologies I was simultaneously reading and in Figes) provided important intellectual and emotional support. What was my surprise, therefore, when I returned to *Sexual Politics* in order to prepare these remarks, to realize that the reader Millett addresses in her preface is "he." But that shadow of patriarchal thinking didn't cloud her pages for me, and *Sexual Politics* was very much one of my liberating books.

Elaine Hedges is Professor of English and Director of Women's Studies at Towson State University. She is coauthor of Hearts and Hands: The Influence of Women and Quilts on American Society *and an editor of* The Heath Anthology of American Literature.

Mary Anne Ferguson

I welcome a chance to acknowledge the major sources of my ideas for my textbook *Images of Women in Literature*. In 1970 the eight members of the Commission on the Status of Women were my consciousness-raising group. Just being invited by Florence Howe to join, not as an envelope stuffer, as I had suggested, but as a contributor to its first sessions at the Modern Language Association (MLA) meeting gave me a new sense of myself. Our exciting discussions inspired me to rethink from a feminist perspective everything I had ever read; the teaching experience of Florence and Elaine Hedges and the early theoretical work of Carol Ohmann and Elaine Showalter expanded my horizons. Mary Ellmann's *Thinking about Women* (1968) led me to organize my new insights around stereotypes. Jane O'Reilly's article "The Housewife's Moment of Truth" in the first issue of *Ms.* magazine made me realize with a "click" of recognition that the stereotypes were alive and well in American life and culture. My new consciousness about the unfairness of women's position in the profession and the injustice of their literary treatment made me very angry, and my students' anger when I taught my first course about "Images" made me search for at least *some* positive images. I had to create my own anthology if more than "one out of twelve" authors in it were to be women. The crucial insight I needed came in 1970 when Florence introduced me to Tillie Olsen's "Tell Me a Riddle."

As a lifelong reader, I had vicariously experienced writers' feelings; I put myself in their characters' places but always projected what I would feel in their circumstances. Somehow Tillie's writing enabled me to experience the pain of her characters as *they* felt it. I felt no separation between the world of the characters and my own; the intensity of the emotions I shared with them made me want to act, to do something to change the circumstances that caused such suffering. I identified strongly with Eva in "Tell Me a Riddle." For the first time I felt that being a woman was a denial of human aspiration and potential for altruism. But Tillie did not let me focus on being a woman as the only cause of that denial.

I came to see that other "circumstances" (Tillie's favorite word) — poverty, race, class, lack of education — were involved in the denial of humanity to the majority of the world's people. Tillie made me see that the humanism that I as a "WASP" liberal had believed in was a cloak for the perpetuation of power by those who had it, but she also prevented me from leaping to the conclusion that anything less than concern for all humanity could be the goal of feminism.

Reading Tillie not only clarified goals for me; it also reinforced my belief in the power of literature to bring about social change. In 1940 I wrote my master's thesis on Percy Shelley's belief that poetry is the unacknowledged legislator of the world; in 1970 in Tillie's writing I saw something of *how* literature subverts established power. Tillie blurs the distinctions among author, narrator, character, reader; she unifies dreams, songs, the future, the past, speech, thought. Her punctuation, spacing, italics, and repetition undo the boundary between prose and poetry. She turns a narrative of lived experience into an elegy for the unused talents and dreams of ordinary human beings. The feelings her work expresses and elicits release energy to hold on to goals and to act to try to fulfill them.

In 1990 I feel even more strongly grateful to Tillie than I did when she raised my consciousness in 1970. Over the years since the first commission forum, when I met her in person, she has become my friend and sister, a personal reward for our shared political goals. I am happy to have the opportunity to say so publicly.

Mary Anne Ferguson is Professor Emerita of English at the University of Massachusetts, Boston, and editor of Images of Women in Literature, *5th edition, 1991.*

Florence Howe

I read *Life in the Iron Mills* in a scrappy Xerox made from an 1861 issue of the *Atlantic* which Tillie Olsen had handed me late in the afternoon of a cold winter day in New York twenty years ago. I don't remember the month, but I remember the gray day and the caution: Don't read this at bedtime. I did, of course—too curious to wait until morning. It is, if you've never read it, a most disturbing book, and for me there were additional circumstances that kept me up until morning, weeping each time I turned to its pages. Consciousness is, as we all know now, so peculiar that it was only while writing this brief essay that I could say to myself that, of course, the novella that night stirred up my father's suicide and the waste of that life as well as the young Hugh's in Rebecca Harding Davis's fiction.

More than that, to go on for a moment with the personal: From that time forward I was to be a close colleague of Tillie and Jack Olsen, whose lives were also attached to *Life in the Iron Mills.* For the first time in my life I felt freed to tell these two people who I was, who I really was, still with pain and embarrassment left over from forty years of practicing silence. They loved me. They loved *me.* That in itself was an amazing experience. And I learned from them to think politically about class, to reenvision my life in terms of class, to take some pride in my roots. And, of course, for the first time in my life I began to consider the question of literature from the perspective of class, to ask whether there might not be working-class writers worth republishing, as well as such middle-class writers as Rebecca Harding Davis who were sensitive to working-class lives.

You know what happened next: The Feminist Press, founded in late 1970 with the idea of publishing nonsexist children's books and brief biographies, switched gears to focus on "lost" women writers. I began traveling to San Francisco to work with Tillie on the afterword to *Life in the Iron Mills*. Tillie responded to my query about working-class writers by offering Agnes Smedley's *Daughter of Earth* as well as a "reading list" published in several issues of *Women's Studies Quarterly* (then called *Women's Studies Newsletter*). The rest is history, including Elaine Hedges's edition of Charlotte Perkins Gilman's *The Yellow Wallpaper* and Alice Walker's of the work of Zora Neale Hurston.

And how did *Life in the Iron Mills* change my life? Formatively: I had to ask myself how it could have happened that so rare a piece of literature as that novella—and I use those words with all the awareness of twenty years of feminist literary theory—how so rare a piece of literature could have so completely disappeared from view. And I had to conclude, moreover, that it could not have been the only piece to disappear. What occurred to me as I was writing this piece is that never once did I feel like T. S. Eliot rediscovering John Donne. And how could I? For I am pleased to say that I knew in my bones even then that we were going to be many women rediscovering many women. Did I know that twenty years later we would be publishing twenty-six hundred years of women writing in India—one hundred forty writers out of a potential list ten times that size? No, I was not that prescient.

In the course of these twenty years I went from being full-time faculty member in writing and literature to being full-time publisher, especially of "lost" women writers. Just a month ago The Feminist Press was awarded a Special Citation by *Publishers' Weekly* for twenty years of such work. And if I am not around when some of you celebrate the conclusion of the next twenty years, perhaps you will remember this moment and cheer Tillie and Jack Olsen and Rebecca Harding Davis.

Florence Howe is Professor of English at City College, City University of New York, and Director of The Feminist Press.

Electa Arenal

I read through my pores, my ears, my loves. My life has changed the books I read, transformed the life of books, taken them off their pages. I stop living by the book. The book starts living by me.

Here are fragments . . .

Almost twenty years ago a good friend, seeing me in the throes of my first great passion for a woman (writer, translator), gave me *Woman in Sexist Society: Studies in Power and Powerlessness* (twenty-seven essays, two plays, and an oral quartet) collected and introduced by Vivian Gornick and Barbara K. Moran. The contents poured through me, took easily to my bloodstream, changed my mind, pointed out "the devious way in which society deals with its truths" (67).* My disloyalty to a civilization that wanted me *virgen o puta,* temptress, goddess, or child improved.

Woman in Sexist Society and dozens of books I skimmed, read parts of, had read and reread in memory—words, poems, periodicals—redirected my spirit, inspired what Hortense Spillers called "the release of the passionate dance of thought."

But I wonder. If the lessons we all learned a generation ago had taken in more of us, had taken us thoroughly enough, would we be here today in this (lecture) form? Do we continue always to question form—and authority?

Everyone in this room might get to speak her mind, after hearing the twelve of us give five minutes to "the book(s) that changed my life." We might be in a circle—or circles. We might share differently. I start saying, "We would not have . . .," I want to say, we will not let greed grow, growl in the desert, growl at our neighbors, growl across this land . . .

Is what Shulamith Firestone claimed still relevant—that "the myth of Emancipation [has] operated in each decade to defuse the frustrations of modern women?" (677).

Yesterday I spoke with the hotel chambermaid, a woman from Guerrero, Mexico, about my father's second wife, Macrina Rabadán, leader, peasant organizer from Guerrero. She said, "*La querían mucho. Decían—Ayuda mucho a la gente*" (She was loved. They said she helps people a lot). Twenty years ago my sister had exactly the same experience in another hotel in Chicago. I puzzle. We women don't "rob ourselves of ourselves and each other" (44) as much as we did twenty years ago, but the robber barons and generals are still in power. It's time we turned them into teenage mutant ninja turtles. We must not continue being terrorized by the idea of going beyond the pale.

Woman in Sexist Society helped explain why Betty Friedan's *Feminine*

---

*All quotations are from the New American Library edition (1972) of *Woman in Sexist Society.*

Mystique had been such a flop a few years earlier with my Barnard students. Barnard, like Bryn Mawr, was "a metaphor for the discrepancy between women's apparent freedom and their actual social and psychological entrapments" (599).

Backing her objection to the comparison of writing with giving birth and pregnancy—"a slur on the labor of art," she called it—Cynthia Ozick invoked Woolf, Babel, Dostoevski, Conrad, Dinesen, and Eliot (437). I forgave her enshrinements and breathed with relief. When people called my two children my best creation, I would bristle.

In the margins of some pages I'd written "*Eso digo yo*" (that's what I say) beside "cultivation precedes fruition"; "Art must belong to all human beings" (448); "The university must ask the right questions" (446). I'd just been asked by a department head: "*What* women writers?" Books like *Woman in Sexist Society* gave me and Marcia Welles the courage to continue searching for and putting together materials for a course on women writers of Spain and Latin America, which we did manage to get through recalcitrant committees, she at Barnard and I at Richmond College.

I'd been brought up with the woman question tucked into the program of the revolution. It was not until *Woman in Sexist Society* and *No More Masks!* and *The Yellow Wallpaper* and Sor Juane Inés de la Cruz had been reread and countless other women writers had been found together with consciousness-raising groups that I understood a new revolution was afoot.

Frederick Douglass had been childhood reading, but his voice resounded in a new way in Catharine Stimpson's sobering and prophetic historical study, a tracing of the nineteenth- and twentieth-century alliances and painful divisions between women's liberation and black civil rights movements, of what happens when "the vital self-interest of one group collides with that of another" (645).

What *is* our vital (self) interest?

The more we verbally reject the ivory tower, the more we seem to live in it. I'm on the thirtieth floor of the Swiss Grand, and you? Have not too many of us embraced the goals of Ozick's students and "settled down into a perpetual and phantom coziness" where "the obvious . . . is not permitted to thrust its scary beams?" (450).

I invoke Bobbye Ortiz, my political mother, who died last June—founder of Action for Women in Chile, a founder of the Women's International Resource Exchange (WIRE)—as a representative of the hundreds of unknown women who twenty years ago became involved in the tasks of feminist publishing.

I invoke the women who performed as witches at the 1969 founding meeting of the Chicago Women's Liberation Union.

I invoke Adrienne Rich, Audre Lorde, Mary Daly, and Judith
McDaniel, who at the 1977 MLA here in Chicago helped us to
intensify our efforts to "transform silence into language and action."

*Electa Arenal is Associate Professor of Spanish and Women's Studies at the
College of Staten Island, City University of New York, and coeditor of* Untold
Sisters: Hispanic Nuns in Their Own Words.

J. J. Wilson

I would like to speak about so many books, friendly and moving in
every sense, many of them published by our Feminist Press, but I've
had to be selective. As a principle of selection, and to avoid overlap, I
thought I would use my West Coast perspective. Tempting as it
would have been to talk about Tillie Olsen's raising of the humble
iron to metaphor, even symbol, I knew that might be in overlap
territory, as her writings and her advice about reading have influenced so many of us here.

Then I remembered an experience I had in the early 1970s, actually an experience of not getting to read a certain book, an experience
that changed my sense of what reading should and could be—not a
casual, promiscuous act but a tender and lasting transaction. Here's
the much abridged and perhaps by now mythologized story.

Somehow into my hands had come a paperback called *Ella Price's
Journal*, which I read in spite of the misleadingly seductive cover
because I was becoming aware of the power of the journal form to
chart our small but significant changes, especially for people not in
the literary mainstream. It conveyed, most convincingly, the struggles of a community college reentry student, a woman, to pay attention to her own changes and those of society in the 1960s. It worked.
Not my story exactly but that of many of the students I was coming
to know, and admire, in my own classrooms. The appeal was all the
more powerful because of my locality, the Bay Area, and, sure
enough, I discovered with some detective work that the author, like
Tillie Olsen, could be found in the telephone directory! So I called up
Dorothy Bryant on Stuart Street in Berkeley and asked her to come
read from her *Ella Price's Journal* at our very first feminist lecture
series entitled, all too provocatively, Pandora's Box. . . . She accepted
our invitation (only later telling me it was her first such performance), and, as she did not at that time drive, I had the privilege of

driving her to and fro. During the drive we became the friends we still are today, and, of course, the conversation turned to Dorothy's current work. To my delight it was a novel about an English teacher—alas, an anomaly in the publishing world—and Dorothy was having no response at all to the manuscript. I was yearning to read some more of "my" author's work, especially a story about someone in my new trade (this was in the early 1970s).

Dorothy agreed to let me read the manuscript and went into her house and got it for me that very night. I remember that it was quite heavy, in a picturesque carpetbag, and I was excited to meet a book *en déshabillé*, so to speak, and bore it proudly home—only to hear the telephone ringing insistently as I walked in the door, and there was Dorothy, having thought better of exposing her child to her chauffeur whom she did not really know she could trust. She asked me please to return it at my earliest convenience and not to look at it after all. . . . I promised to comply with the author's wishes, but, gee, it was tempting to sneak a look—a novel by Dorothy Bryant about an English teacher. Of course, I did eventually get to read it when she herself had published it as *Miss Giardino* in 1978 with her Ata Press. It was just the book I had hoped for—asking all the difficult questions about the teaching of writing, questions that still have not been answered.

What changed for me from this experience was that I realized for the first time that books were written by people, vulnerable people, who feared exposure to critics and yet were brave enough to offer it to us. What a good lesson when I had taken that whole process somewhat for granted before. And Dorothy gave me permission to tell this story about us both.

J. J. Wilson is Professor of English at Sonoma State University and coauthor of Women Artists: Recognition and Reappraisal from the Early Middle Ages to the Twentieth Century.

Susie Tharu

The late 1960s and early 1970s were a period of tremendous upheaval in India. In the cities almost every week people took to the streets protesting against food shortages, rising prices, continuing unemployment. University students protested against outmoded and irrelevant curricula and organized parallel classes. Many of the most gifted among them abandoned formal studies to join the important peasant movements that had emerged in several parts of the country for the first time after the 1940s.

I myself had just come back to India, having been at university in England between 1967 and 1969 during what must have been the most exciting years to be a student in Europe. Before that I had been at university in Uganda during the even more exciting final years of that country's struggle for independence from colonial rule. Those were full years. As full as anyone in their twenties could have asked for. And they were certainly years in which I grew and years in which many things changed the way I thought. I can cite people, experiences, ideas, and even events that affected me deeply, and many, many books that slipped in wedged themselves into the spaces of my life: Franz Fanon's *Wretched of the Earth*, Jomo Kenyatta's *Facing Mount Kenya*, Doris Lessing's *The Golden Notebook*, Karl Marx's *German Ideology*, Premchand's *Godan*, Rabindranath Tagore's *The Home and the World*, Mao Tse-tung's *On Contradiction*, Ananda Coomaraswamy's *Art and Swadeshi*. I could easily speak here today about one of these books, none of them feminist in any obvious sense of the term but each of them sharpening an understanding of exploitation, subordination, and power which was to help me grapple with my own experiences as a middle-class woman and identify closely with others whose oppression related to class, caste, or race.

But my life was not actually transformed by any of them in quite the same way as it was a decade later by an oral history book I worked on with four other women. Its title, *We Were Making History*, is a quotation from one of the women who had been part of a major peasant rebellion in Telangana in the 1940s. At the height of the movement peasant men and women had taken possession of, and were cultivating, large areas of land on which they had earlier worked as laborers bonded to feudal landlords. People's courts settled disputes, and newly trained medical volunteers, many of them women, moved from village to village. Students from the universities helped design the curricula and run evening schools in which local and global issues were discussed. Among the authors read out loud to them were Charles Dickens, Richard Wright, and Ding Ling. In the literature of the Indian socialist movement Telangana is spoken of as the Yenan of India.

What interested the five of us — two political scientists, two teachers of English literature, and a medical doctor — was that women were involved in large numbers in this and many other aspects of the movement. In fact, some of the people we spoke to said that often a third of the active support for the movement came from women. The book we set out to write was to be a record of women's involvement in the movement from a socialist-feminist point of view. Well-trained academics that we were, we made bibliographies and listed sources. Clearly this was going to be *our* book. It was going to answer the questions we were asking and tell the country and the world about the movement. It might be a good idea, one of us suggested, almost as an afterthought, if while we were about it we asked the women to tell us their life stories.

Little did we realize what that suggestion would lead to. For, as we got past the desk work and began talking to the women — and, more important, began learning how to listen to the women and find tools and concepts to understand and appreciate what they were saying — our project was transformed. Sessions commonly lasted eight or nine hours, and I listened, transfixed. No part of my formal education had ever demanded or required such intensity from me. Truly I had never before been addressed with such deep or challenging serious- ness. Imaged in the story of their lives and the shape of their strug- gles were both the everyday detail and the enormity of the task that faced us if societal institutions and knowledge were to be reimagined and redesigned to be accountable to people and not, as society today is, accountable to the state or industry (as contemporary education or medicine is); or to property (as the law is); or to some mystically etched nation (as the literary curriculum is). Without exaggeration, there was no subject in my life that I would handle without question again. The project that was being handed down to us was a lifetime project, perhaps more than a lifetime, but it was one to which I wanted to become equal.

Susie Tharu teaches in the Department of English Literature at the Central Institute of English and Foreign Languages in Hyderabad, India, and is coeditor of Women Writing in India: 600 B.C. to the Present.

National Reports on Women's Studies around the World

Selections

Fall/Winter 1994
and Spring/Summer 1996

Beginning in the late 1970s, reports on women's studies in India, several European countries, and the West Indies, for example, appeared in WSQ. In 1992, 1994, and 1996, WSQ published a series of national reports on women's Studies in thirty-eight countries. For a sense of the global life of women's studies we have selected short excerpts from nine of these reports. We chose the selections especially to illustrate the varieties of processes through which institutionalization has occurred, in general very slowly in the 1970s, and more rapidly in the 1990s. We chose them also to illuminate the various relationships between women's studies and the women's movements in each of these countries. All three of these international issues are still available.

1970s: The Netherlands (Spring/Summer 1996), *Willy Jansen*

Institutionalization

. . . From the early 1980s on, special units or departments were set up in women's studies. To meet the demand on the side of the students, the part-time and temporary staff of the early period expanded. A recent survey by the Dutch Association of Women's Studies shows that more than 260 different courses were taught in 1994–95. Eight universities offer more than five courses in women's studies, and four offer a degree based on a recognized three-year graduate program specializing in women's studies within the social sciences or the humanities. Some 200 women teach women's studies courses at the universities, and 300 do research, with an overlap of 150 who both teach and do research (Lasthuizen 1995).

With the financial support of the Dutch Ministry of Education, women's studies teachers and coordinators were appointed in almost all universities. A hard battle was fought to get tenured positions and professors. With the appointment of seventeen full professors in women's studies plus a number of professors in other disciplines actively devoted to women's studies, women's studies gained not only respectability but also the power to apply for funds within and outside the universities and to set up teaching and research programs. A professorate is needed to accept Ph.D. students and train them for a degree. Nationwide cooperation has made it possible to offer a full Ph.D. curriculum in women's studies at the Netherlands Research School of Women's Studies. During the spring of 1995 this research school was given official recognition by the Netherlands Royal Academy of Science. Between 1990 and 1994, thirty-nine women's studies theses (some interdisciplinary) were successfully defended.

At the eleven women's studies units with one or more chairs, academic work is combined with many other activities. Students can do applied research at the community level or on demand for women's groups. Information and gender assessment instruments are provided to policymakers (cf. van Lenning, Brouns, and de Bruijn 1995; Verloo and Heijmans 1995). Refresher courses are given for professional groups. Documentation centers have been set up, and these centers have cooperated to compose a Women's Thesaurus for retrieving information on women and women's studies. Lectures are given to the general public. Large interdisciplinary international and national conferences have been organized, and their results published. . . .

During the institutionalization process, units were confronted with the dilemma of integration versus autonomy. Again and again they found themselves in situations requiring a choice between equally undesirable alternatives. Integration would mean invisibility and becoming subject to automatic loss of positions resulting from the frequent reorganizations that plagued the universities. To choose autonomy for an emerging discipline in this setting carried the risk of being not strong enough to survive. This dilemma on the organizational level would repeat itself on the theoretical level and on the level of individual identity. What would serve the development of women's studies and its participants better: to support the teaching of women's studies in the disciplines or to create an independent institute for women's studies? to introduce a feminist perspective in the existing disciplinary theories or to develop interdisciplinary gender theories? to remain a psychologist, linguist, or anthropologist or to become a women's studies expert?

Most units continue to react to this dilemma by balancing somewhere between the two extremes and using the best of both. This careful balancing has been named a "double track policy." Experience has shown that organizationally a double track policy, despite the cost of tremendous amounts of time, energy, and knowledge, has definitely been essential to the survival of women's studies in the universities. This becomes all the more clear when the universities are compared with the vocational colleges. At these colleges the path of integration was chosen. Individual female staff members were very successful in integrating a women's and emancipatory perspective in existing study programs. Yet unfortunately, many of the courses disappeared when the staff member left. The professional colleges lacked recognizable units, headed by a chair, that could maintain and defend positions or programs, or keep records of women's studies courses taught and women staff interested in this topic. The tremendous input of women's work had little permanent effect and easily slipped out of sight and out of the collective memory. On the other hand, the few units who placed their emphasis on autonomy also have had a difficult time, as their student numbers are not sufficient to maintain a viable unit. Most students want to combine their interest in women's studies with work toward a regular degree. The fact that there is not yet a word for the professional practitioner of women's studies is indicative of the dilemma for students as well as for teachers of women's studies.

REFERENCES

. . . . . .
Lasthuizen, K. 1995. *Onderzoekers vrouwenstudies in Nederland. Een overzicht* (Scholars in women's studies in the Netherlands: A survey). Utrecht: Nederlands Genootschap Vrouwenstudies.
Lenning, A. van, M. Brouns, and J. de Bruijn. 1995. *Inzichten uit vrouwenstudies: Uitdagingen voor beleidmakers.* Ministerie van Sociale Zaken en Werkgelegenheid. Den Haag: VUGA.
. . . . . .
Verloo, M., and E. Heijmans. 1995. *Kwaliteit van onderzoek: Inzichten uit vrouwenstudies voor toegepast onderzoek.* Ministerie van Sociale Zaken en Werkgelegenheid. Den Haag: VUGA.

Willie Jansen is a professor of women's studies at the University of Nijmegen, Netherlands.

1970s: Germany (Spring/Summer 1996), *Tobe Levin*

Integrating Women's Studies Content

. . . Just as women themselves have encountered formidable gate-keepers, so too has women's studies been unwelcome. I have been discussing the general position of women in higher education. Turning now to the women's studies field, as of December 1993—according to the latest available figures (Bock 1995)—seventy-six women's studies positions had been assigned or planned at German universities and *Hochschulen* (college-level institutions) (excluding *Fachhochschulen* [colleges specializing in a limited number of disciplines]), all in the old German states plus Berlin and Brandenburg, and with the exception of one women's studies post in Potsdam, no plans are being made to increase representation in the field in the new states. Now, this number represents an even sadder situation once we note that, of ten thousand full professorships (C-4) in Germany, women's studies accounts for only eighteen, that is, 0.2 percent of the total (Bock 1993b:24), a figure that, in Ulla Bock's view, "reveals the low esteem in which the field is held in academia" (Bock 1993b:11).

In the seventies, the initial emphatic response of intellectual feminists led to a debate pitting institutionalization against autonomy. Some left the university altogether, founding independent institutions. Others began offering classes in the *Volkshochschulen* (VHS) (people's high schools or community colleges), well-attended non–degree-granting institutions for adult learners that charge nominal fees and are found even in villages; they offer a vast number of courses, including consciousness-raising groups for women and a broad range of feminist classes. These schools provide a particularly fertile ground for women's lifelong education. As for those who stayed in academia proper, Ute Gerhard notes that they could perform as feminist scholars only outside normal channels, without research grants or institutional backing. . . . Only toward the beginning of the eighties did the situation ease, with institutional acceptance beginning and, from the mid-eighties, allowing posts that integrate women's studies content to appear fairly secure, though still exceedingly rare. One of the most troubling challenges to conservative minds has been the claim of women's studies to boundary transgression, resisted with vehemence by the traditional, discipline-oriented institution. Of course, women staff in the middle ranks have been offering feminist perspectives on prescribed material or placing new items on the agenda. But their limited contracts and isolation have made this situation less than ideal, and arguments concerning it as a desirable option have accompanied the discussion of women's studies since the early 1970s. Scholars who want women's studies departments to anchor the gains of the field have been arguing with others for whom integration of feminist perspectives in all disciplines seems the better move. In fact, both strategies have been fruitfully employed. For instance, Bielefeld University's *Interdisciplinäre Forschungsgruppe Frauenförschung* (IFF)

[Interdisciplinary Research Group for Women's Studies], launched in 1983, became the first "department" that inaugurates and directs graduate research. In Dortmund the first graduate school for women's studies in sociology, financed by the *Deutsche Forschungsgemeinschaft* (German Research Association), began its three year cycle of fellowships in October 1992. Called "*Geschlechterverhältnis und sozialer Wandel.*

Handlungsspielräume und Definitionsmacht von Frauen" (Gender and the Transformation of Society: Parameters for Women's Action and Their Power to Define) the program supports eight doctoral candidates and one postdoctoral candidate with stipends awarded by the interinstitutional consortium behind the initiative—the Universities of Bielefeld, Bochum, Essen, and Dortmund. According to a 1992 press release, supporters expect the initiative to have a significant "resonance not only in the state but in the nation." The graduate school complements an already existing network of women's studies professorships in North Rhine–Westphalia, where feminist education minister Anke Brunn has assured that her state leads all others in this domain, with forty women's studies professorships (eleven C-4, twenty-eight C-3, one C-2, including those projected). To compare: Berlin has thirteen, Hesse six, Bremen and Lower Saxony five each; Baden-Württemberg and Rheinland-Pfalz two each; Saarland, Hamburg, and Brandenburg one each (Bock 1995).

Thus, despite formidable obstacles, recognition of women's studies is growing, if slowly. The DFG's (German Research Association) commission, for instance, has begun awarding fellowships and supporting projects. "Yes, scepticism still exists, with certain fields not yet having budged an inch," Gerhard concedes. Nonetheless, Gerhard's Lilac Chair in the department of social sciences in Frankfurt may serve as a model of interdisciplinarity and structural innovation: women can earn normal sociology degrees while choosing to study and be tested on specific women's studies themes (i.e., the diploma makes its owner a sociologist; the major, however, is in women's studies). . . .

REFERENCES

. . . . . .
Bock, Ulla. 1993b. "Die Zeit verändert die Knoten im Netz. Wege der Institutionalisierung von Frauenforschung an bundesdeutschen Hochschulen." In *Die Institutionalisierung von Frauenforschung und Frauenförderung in Deutschland, Europa, und den USA*, 3:66–83, edited by Universität of Mainz. Mainz: Interdisziplinärer Arbeitskreis Frauenforschung Mainz.
———. 1995. Telephone interview, 25 April.
. . . . . .

Tobe Levin joined the English department at the University of Maryland, European Division, and in 1986 began teaching U.S. minority women's literature and women's holocaust memoirs at J. W. Goethe University, Frankfurt am Main, Germany. A cofounder of WISE, she coedits the association's bilingual newsletter. . . .

1970s: India (Fall/Winter 1994), *Vina Mazumdar*

. . . By its very nature women's studies is interdisciplinary. Apart from that, women's studies is also a *critical* discipline. It is critical because it raises crucial questions about the way social theory has traditionally posed questions of analysis, and, by doing so, women's studies makes way for a broader and receptive social science, alive to the crucial questions of the day. Thus, the practitioners of women's studies ask: Why did women's historic roles in the discovery of agriculture, pottery, and textile production in India (and the world) remain hidden from the educated community for so long? Why has the massive infrastructure for agricultural research and development failed even to *see* women's contemporary roles and problems? Why has women's labor in the family remained outside the framework of any analysis of the production and reproduction of commodities and services and their valuation? And why have investigations into the caste-class-community nexus failed to examine its connections with controls over women's labor freedom and behavior?

Women's studies has been crucial in helping social science to broaden the notion of the "social," thus transcending the earlier narrow formulations. A crucial example in this respect is redefining old notions of "class." In the orthodox formulation "class" was often opposed to divisions of gender, caste, and ethnicity. In this reading class was seen as *the* central organizing principle of social analysis, in contrast to differences of gender, caste, and ethnicity, which were seen at best as transitory phenomena with the onset of modernization. As women's studies has shown, this analysis does considerable violence to the situation on the ground. Thus, class is not a "model" that can be "applied" to the real world; class is a real historical product. Women's studies practitioners argue that disposition of gender is crucial to an understanding of class differentiation. Historical, in opposition to formal, class analysis shows that class exists not in opposition to differences of gender, caste, and ethnicity but, rather, in and through them. The Indian theories of purity-pollution, or boundary maintenance between dominant and suppressed caste and tribal groups, also operate through greater controls on women. Such controls also prevent women and their children from acquiring any identity beyond the one of birth, defined by the family, caste/ethnicity, and class. In the final analysis women's studies has actually enriched our analysis of these central organizing social principles of our time and society. M. N. Srinivas, doyen of Indian sociology, describes women's studies as the "only significant development in Indian social science in the last two decades—a thrust from below."[3]

From its embryonic origins in the mid-1970s, women's studies has now become a national movement. The First National Conference on Women's Studies was convened in Bombay in 1981, and the response was overwhelming; the mandate given by that conference led to the establishment of the Indian Association for Women's Studies in 1982. The association's membership now includes 18 universities, 10 colleges, and 15 research institutes as well as more than 650 individuals, many of whom are from the academic profession. Since the association came into existence the University Grants Commission has drawn the attention of the universities to promote an understanding of women's issues through the teaching, research, and extension activities of various disciplines, and nearly forty universities have entered the field. The National Policy on Education (NPE), adopted by Parliament in 1986, for the first time prescribed a new "role" for the national educational system, of providing "education for women's equality," through the revision of curricula, the reorientation of teachers and planners, and direct involvement in women's empowerment.

It is important to remember that the National Policy on Education did not design women's studies but only accepted the demand of academic participants in the women's movement, voiced through a decade of struggle. The perspectives, ideology, and strategies adopted by the women's studies movement was thus not evolved by the government or the academic establishment but, rather, by the movement and its allies. The primary objectives of the movement have remained constant:

1. to *change* social perceptions, attitudes, values and structures that obstruct or deny gender equality as a value. Some of these are traditional and deep rooted in our past. But some are very new, ideas, institutions, and movements that manipulate old practices, norms, customs, and primordial loyalties of people to set the clock of social development back. Typical illustrations of such new wine in old bottles is the escalation of dowry and dowry-related violence, the spread of female infanticide and feticide, market propaganda that glamorizes women's role as primarily consumers, and communal and ethnic

movements that project protection of cultural or religious rights of a group at the cost of gender equality and women's freedoms;

2. to promote, activate, and support processes of reform of the education and communication systems, so that, instead of being a tool in the hands of reactionary movements, they play "an active interventionist role" against such attacks.

Women's studies, as viewed by the Indian women's movement, is meant to be a potent instrument, playing a deliberate and active role in the battle for people's minds and values now raging all over the world. A typical manifestation of this is a growing cynicism about education, and higher education in particular. The powers that be (the real manipulators are often hidden under the cover of international or national development strategies) would like to transform education from its original role as a value-generating process to one for skill transfer only. They would like to discourage questioning and dissent and the academic freedom to reanalyze the past and the present from more humanist perspectives. The same forces, however, quite often compromise with and even encourage the use of false history and selective cultural symbols by revivalist, fundamentalist, and chauvinistic movements. A common element in all these movements around the world, and definitely in India, is opposition to gender equality. The time has come to question the rationale behind such opposition.

The issue appears to me to be primarily one of conflict between the political, cultural, or communal identity of a group, on the one hand, and human rights, the future of civilization, and social transformation with a humane face, on the other. Gender equality, or elimination of women's subordination, by its very nature threatens all movements for the preservation of narrow group identities, which require control over women's minds and bodies. Women play a double role, of transmitting a sense of identity to future generations and of maintaining the cultural practices and values that are tied up with that sense of a group identity.

Similarly, forces that require keeping the majority of people in subordination as a passive group to be exploited or manipulated also need to control women and, through them, the rest of society. Unfortunately, many scientists have become willing instruments of such manipulation. Experiments in genetic engineering, or reproductive technology, diverting major investments to research and development for destructive weapons, and encouraging environmental destruction or mismanagement of natural resources are typical examples of the prostitution of scientific knowledge to serve vested interests.

The Indian women's movement has laid a special responsibility on women's studies to combat and counter such forces. Acceptance of this fighting role and the higher social responsibility that it entails necessarily influences women's studies' approach, methodology, organization, and operational perspectives. It is not possible for this struggle to be carried on by a small group. The objectives of women's studies cannot be achieved by a monopolistic attitude or by confining it to a discipline, a course, a program, or a degree. Still less can our objectives be realized by creating new institutions for this purpose.

There is a close parallel between women's studies and the women's movement as a whole: autonomy continues to be a battle cry of both. Yet a choice has to be made between seeking autonomy for autonomy's sake and taking on the far more difficult role of catalyst, to influence larger systems and movements. Autonomy, separation, can also lead to isolation, marginalization, and even alienation. Women's studies practitioners, when they confine their dialogue only to persons within the movement, do tend to develop jargons and terminologies of their own, which reduces their ability to communicate with others. Sometimes jargon also promotes a kind of hierarchy within the women's studies movement, between those who claim longer experience and greater theoretical rigor and new entrants who have the concern but not the experience. It has also been occasionally noticed that such pursuit of theoretical rigor within an autonomous framework encourages elitism and a drifting away from the burning concerns of the majority of women. If this trend succeeds, it would defeat the basic objectives of women's studies as the academic arm of the women's movement. . . .

NOTES

. . . . . .

3. Inaugural address, International Congress of Sociology, New Delhi, August 1986. Published in *Economic and Political Weekly* 22, no. 4 (24 January 1987).

Vina Mazumdar *is vice chairperson of the Centre for Women's Development Studies, of which she was founder director, 1980–91, in New Delhi. She has written widely on women's studies and the women's movement in India.*

1970s: Argentina (Fall/Winter 1994), *Gloria Bonder*

The Origins and Development of Women's Studies

. . . Women's research and studies programs emerged in the late 1970s and, to a certain extent, they remain outside the university system. It was during the dictatorship that NGOs such as the Women's Studies Center (CEM), and research centers such as the Center for Studies of State and Society (CEDES) and the Center for Population Studies (CENEP)[19] developed programs aimed as much at professionals as at students of the social sciences and humanities. With the return to democracy in 1983, many of these professionals returned to the university, though they generally maintained their affiliations to and continued to work within the private research sector.

In 1984, the first postgraduate seminars in women's studies were created in the faculty of psychology at the University of Buenos Aires. This initiative was carried out by members of CEM who returned to the universities via these courses. In 1987, also in the faculty of psychology, the first women's studies program in Argentina was established as a specialized interdisciplinary postgraduate course of study.[20] The principal aim of the program was to articulate objectives completely new to the traditional academic standards held in Argentina. The program set out to "provide a high level of academic development at the theoretical, methodological and technical levels applicable to research, teaching, and design of policies and social programs on women and gender issues."[21]It is a three-year program which includes an introduction to women's studies, and courses examining the family, education, health, and work. Seminars on the methodology of social research, placing emphasis on feminist investigation, and courses on strategic planning and the design of social policies from a gender perspective are also offered. In addition, students are required to obtain work experience in research centers, government bodies, social organizations, or other spheres which focus on women. Finally, periodic reflection groups are held in which students analyze the personal and professional implications of what they are learning.[22]

Two groups of students, all women, completed this program between 1987 and 1993, and a total of forty-eight graduates earned the title Specialist in Women's Studies.[23] The first group was comprised of graduates in social sciences and humanities, although some came from backgrounds in architecture, agriculture, and medicine. Almost all belonged to feminist organizations and/or had been active in the women's movement or political parties. With an average age of forty, almost all had had professional experience in their fields and, in some cases, also in women's issues. These characteristics profoundly affected the level of their participation in the courses and their ability to gain the most from their training and experiences.

The first crop of graduates is now working in the National Council of Women's Issues or as advisers to deputies, senators, and government administrators; as researchers and consultants to national and international bodies working on women's issues; or as university professors. In all cases they combine academic and professional work with feminist activism, though obviously the degree to which they participate in a more political sense varies in quality and quantity.

It is important to emphasize that this postgraduate program has, within the academic sphere, a highly complex and unusual central objective: to develop in these students an interest in and an ability to combine research and theoretical development with the practical means to design and implement policies and actions aimed at overcoming discrimination against women. In this sense it stands apart from other programs which simply "recycle" academic activity, with a women's studies perspective, and remain isolated from the problems and initiatives experienced in other spheres, such as the state, parliament, and social organizations.

Apart from this program out of seventy public and private universities, thirty-two offer some form of teaching, of varying degrees of complexity and types of organization, related to gender issues.[24] At the University of Rosario, for example, a master's degree in women's studies has recently been approved. Currently, there are three interdisciplinary programs: one in the Faculty of Philosophy and Literature at the University of Buenos Aires, another at the University of Lujan, and a third at the Catholic University of Córdoba. Other universities offer specific seminars and outreach programs, the majority addressing sociological and historical issues and, to a lesser extent, psychological themes. There are very few courses in literature, anthropology, economics, art, and, most notably, in the field of education itself. A little over half the academic initiatives related to women's studies include outreach programs such as conferences, workshops, or round table discussions. Some of these programs are for the university community itself, others for teachers from primary or secondary schools, and some programs attract people from the community who are interested in women's issues.

There are thirty-one academic centers in the country that conduct interdisciplinary research on such topics as women and work, health, identity, family, and sexuality. Very few institutions have publication programs beyond bulletins or edited papers. There are plans to produce one or more journals, but unfortunately these have not yet been established due to lack of finances. This limitation renders invisible to the academic community an expanding group of researchers and teachers that is building the field of women's studies. In fact, the vast majority of the research exists as reports which often do not even reach other colleagues within the same discipline.

NOTES

. . . . . .

19. CEM is the Centro de Estudios de la Mujer, founded in 1979. CEDES is the Centro do Estudios de Estado y Sociedad created in 1976, and CENEP is the Centro de Estudios de Población that has been developing its work since 1974.

20. Since 1990, the Faculty of Psychology at the University of Buenos Aires has offered the Introduction to Women's Studies as an optional course.

21. Bulletin No 2, 1992. Course of the Specialism of Women's Studies, Faculty of Psychology, University of Buenos Aires.

22. The inclusion of the reflection groups in the curriculum of a postgraduate program is an important innovation within traditional academic concepts and, as such, it has not been easy to gain its acceptance. This activity is crucial, however, because working within women's studies implies much more than the simple acquisition of knowledge. Indeed, it makes the professional and personal identities of the students and their concepts of reality problematic. Thus one can foresee that women's studies may stimulate anxieties and conflicts that the student may have difficulties overcoming individually. The reflection groups are linked to academic work in that the analysis of such conflicts is a very important step in learning and assimilating the material, which if excluded from the course structure would be lost.

23. In 1991 the same study plan was implemented, under agreement, at the University of Comahue in the south of the country. About twenty graduate students participate each year, all of them women. The majority are political activists, university professors, and professionals of note within the province.

24. Survey conducted by the National Program of Women's Equal Opportunities in Education (PRIOM), 1993.

. . . . . .

Gloria Bonder is director of the Women's Studies Interdisciplinary Postgraduate Course at the University of Buenos Aires and general coordinator of the National Programme for Women's Equal Opportunities in Education at the Ministry of Culture and Education.

1970s: Korea (Spring/Summer 1996), *Chang Pilwha*

Women's studies as an academic subject in Korea came into being in the middle of the 1970s. In the course of the last twenty years remarkable progress has been achieved. The first master's and Ph.D. courses in women's studies in Asia have been developed, and most of the more than one hundred universities and colleges in Korea have come to include various women's studies courses in their general curricula. . . .

One of the remarkable achievements of women's studies education is that it has produced many of the leaders in the women's movements. The rapid spread of women's studies across the nation is partly attributable to the availability of specialists. This, in turn, contributed to encouraging women's movements and produced practical results for Korean society. Those who benefited from the courses have put their skills into practice on what they have learned to identify as being in need of change. They have been instrumental in achieving legal reforms, such as the family law, the equal opportunity law, and the law on sexual violence. Particularly noteworthy is that women's studies research is responsible for raising the issue of sexual violence as a social issue and for providing a theoretical framework for legislating a special amendment in relation to sexual violence.

New organizations were created as a direct result of women's studies education, to activate the woman's movement with various emphases: a women's weekly paper, a women's hot line, a sexual violence relief center, and so on. Many of our graduates are currently working in the mass media and in publishing companies, leading public opinion on gender issues. In general, women's consciousness was raised across the board; women were voted in as trade union leaders, and some successful candidates began to appear in local governments, even though their proportion is still one of the lowest in the world.

Such educational efforts have contributed to building women's confidence. The remaining question is how this confidence can be kept up in reality. We have yet a long way to go to achieve equality of opportunity, and even further to enjoy practical equality with men. However, the goal is not simply to achieve equality with men; it is not our goal to excel like men in a war of aggression and greed, domineering, subjugating, and oppressing less powerful people who have fewer worldly possessions. If equality is a goal, it is in order to enable women as full members of society with equal rights and obligations to determine the course and direction that the society is taking. Women have to be empowered in order to make their own experiences and insights more meaningful to and useful for their society. . . .

Chang Pilwha *is associate professor of women's studies at Ewha Womans University, Republic of Korea, and director of the Asian Center for Women's Studies.*

1980s: West Indies (Fall/Winter 1994), *Rhoda E. Reddock*

The Institutionalization of Women's Studies

. . . The issue of exactly how this program was to fit into the very complicated and bureaucratic UWI [(University of West Indies)] structure was something that occupied the minds of WDS [(Women and Development Studies)] group members from the start. Indeed, this process could probably have been achieved much earlier had we been willing to overlook some of the realities of our situation. These were four in number. First, the University of the West Indies has three campuses in three different countries, each with its own concerns, culture, and ways of doing things. Additionally, there are eleven noncampus territories served by the UWI, each with its local university center. A very elaborate structure has developed to manage this complex structure at national and regional levels. Second, the University of Guyana has had a close working relationship with the UWI for a number of years, and the WDS group sought to maintain a very close working relationship with the Women's Studies group of the University of Guyana. Third, the membership of the WDS groups has always been broadly based, including staff from a range of disciplines and faculties as well as librarians, administrators, students, and nonuniversity persons. It was important, therefore, that the program continue to reflect this diversity of interest and facilitate the legitimate participation of all interested persons. Fourth, as with universities throughout the world, the UWI faced major financial constraints, and new demands on the budget were not being welcomed.

Issues in Institutionalization. One of the most long-standing issues of debate and discussion was whether the program should be incorporated into an existing faculty or whether it should be an independent interdisciplinary unit. From very early we were advised that our easiest possibility was to become a unit within the Faculty of Arts and General Studies, for the following reasons: (1) women's studies could fit easily within General Studies; (2) faculties already have budgets that could be applied to WDS activities; (3) there was already much interest among staff from this faculty; and (4) four of the first full-fledged courses were offered under the auspices of this faculty.

. . . On the other hand, it was argued that incorporation into an already existing faculty ran the risk of alienating members of other faculties and departments. Further, the major aim of women's studies, to challenge the basis of knowledge in all disciplines, would not be fulfilled. Moreover, it would be extremely difficult for students from one faculty to register for courses in another. Hence it became necessary, although much more difficult, to challenge the disciplinary divisions, which, after all, was at the center of women's studies. It was also argued that our structure could become a model for other interdisciplinary programs.

The proposal for institutionalization contained the following elements: An interdisciplinary Center for Women/Gender Studies is to be established with branches on each campus. In addition to the campus offices, a regional coordinating unit (presently located on the Mona campus) will exist to facilitate regional coordination. A professor/ director will be based in the regional coordinating unit and senior lecturers appointed to head each of the campus branches of the center. The responsibilities of the campus heads will include coordinating teaching, research, and outreach as well as administration of the program on that campus. A Campus Board of Studies is to be established, consisting of members of staff involved in teaching, research, and outreach in WDS/Gender Studies. This board is to define policy and programs at the campus level and contribute to the development of regional policy and programs. Members of the board with appointments in other faculties will report on relevant WDS/Gender Studies activities at those faculties' campus board meetings. A Regional Board of Studies, headed by the professor and regional coordinator and with campus and WAND [(Women and Development Unit)] representation, will develop overall policy and monitor programs on the three campuses. The Center is to have the ability to develop courses on its own in collaboration with various faculties and departments. It should have some degree of autonomy over its own courses and staff and shared responsibility for joint courses. The WDS groups are to continue to exist as voluntary advocacy and support groups on each campus. They would also be represented on the campus boards and regional boards to insure their continued participation in and contribution to the program.

Overall, the goals of the Center for Women and Development Studies are: to establish a multidisciplinary and interdisciplinary program of teaching, research, and outreach; to streamline and strengthen offerings at the undergraduate level; to develop graduate teaching and encourage graduate research; to develop nondegree teaching (e.g., certificate and diploma courses) through "distance education" to non-campus territories, a biennial certificate course, and special short courses for policymakers; to publish and disseminate research reports, books, and teaching materials relevant to the program; and to carry out fund-raising activities related to the development of the program.

Naming. Next to institutionalization, the issue that caused the most discussion and debate was the naming of the program. In its early conceptualization the program was perceived as Women and Development Studies, since Women's Studies alone did not attend to wider social, political, and economic issues facing Third World women especially. To some extent the word *development* also reflected the views of members anxious that the group name be moderate, not radical and feminist. For the government ministers of the region who endorsed the introduction of such a program around 1986–87, its name was seen as further evidence of their efforts to comply with United Nations' agreements "to integrate women into the development process."

At some point within the decade, the name of the program emerged as an issue. Some felt that the words *woman* and *women* were limiting, in that they give the impression that men are excluded, whereas *gender* included relations between women and men. Others felt also that to win the support of a largely male university hierarchy the word *gender* might be more acceptable. Those opposed to *gender*, argued that the area of studies had emerged out of a women's movement that had recognized the subordination and oppression of women and had worked to end women's invisibility. To remove the word *woman* from the title of the program would be a step backward. The Saint Augustine group suggested a compromise title, The Center for Women and Gender Studies, but, unfortunately, in my opinion, the other two campuses have chosen the name the Center for Gender and Development Studies. . . .

Rhoda E. Reddock *is senior lecturer and head of the Center for Gender and Development Studies at the University of the West Indies (UWI), St. Augustine Campus, Trinidad and Tobago. . . .*

1980s: South Africa (Spring/Summer 1996), *Debby Bonnin*

. . . In 1984 the University of South Africa opened its Women's Studies Center. Despite intense efforts by women academics, they were not allowed to offer a teaching program. The center offers a resource facility, produces a newsletter, runs various seminar series, and since 1995 has offered a Certificate Course in Law (run with private sponsorship). It hopes to offer an honors degree in 1997. In addition, numerous departments within many of the universities have offered courses on women and gender since the early 1980s. These courses cover a wide range, from "Women's Voices in Society," offered by the English department at the University of Natal, to "Women in Ancient Greek

Gynaecological Works," offered by the classics department at the University of Natal, to "Normative Theory: Feminism," offered by the politics department at the University of Stellenbosch, to "Nutrition During Pregnancy and Lactation" offered by the dietetics department at the University of Western Cape. Most courses are within the faculties of humanities and social sciences. The University of Natal and the University of the Western Cape offer the widest selection of courses. Overall, sociology seems to be the discipline that takes women's studies most seriously, and most of the universities list courses within their sociology departments (Budlender 1994). Given their status as the elite universities, it is interesting to observe that neither the University of Cape Town nor the University of Witwatersrand responded to the Budlender questionnaire.

In 1989 the first women's studies courses, a master's degree, and a one-semester undergraduate course in women's studies were offered at the University of Natal–Durban.[4] The following year, the Pietermaritzburg campus of the University of Natal offered an honors program in gender studies[5] and then an interdisciplinary undergraduate course. The introduction of these courses was preceded by a module[6] on feminism and philosophy, the favorable response to which encouraged the introduction of the honors course. An attempt to begin a women's studies course at the University of the North foundered in the face of resistance from other academic staff.[7] In 1995 the University of Western Cape (UWC) offered, for the first time, an honors and master's degree in women's studies. The University of Natal's courses differ from those of the Western Cape in that they are hosted by existing academic departments. The University of Transkei, University of Port Elizabeth, and University of Durban–Westville are discussing plans for women's and gender studies programs.

In 1991 the Women's Studies Network was formed in Natal. Meeting quarterly, it sought to involve women from the Pietermaritzburg and Durban campuses of Natal University, the University of Durban–Westville, and the University of Zululand's Ngoya and Umlazi campuses. In reality, however, only the first three universities were consistently involved. In 1993 a Black Women's Research Network formed a national organizational with regional structures, but it did not exist for very long. In 1996 the University of Cape Town plans to open a Gender Institute, which will provide nine-month-long research associateships for women from other African countries. In 1995 a limited pilot program is being run (EORP 1994). . . .

NOTES

......

4. Because of a lack of resources and the retirement of the coordinator this year (1995), the master's and the undergraduate courses have been suspended, and at this point no other staff member is prepared to take on the large, unpaid task of coordinating the program. As part of the general university restructuring, a small committee is in place to lobby for a gender school, which would encompass both women's studies and a new gender studies program. Currently, the university is supportive of this initiative and has appointed a full-time coordinator for a two-year period.
5. Because of a lack of resources the honors program is suspended for 1995.
6. *Module* refers to a smaller course within a semester; a module would consist of several lectures.
7. The issues that allegedly succeeded in scuttling the initiative at the University of the North were who is the coordinator of the program and why is she someone new to the university; what are the criteria for selecting her; why is the committee made up of only unmarried women (who are regarded as not having any direction, since they have no husbands to guide them). Untruthful rumors about the personal lives of the committee were also circulated, in an effort to discredit their integrity.

......

REFERENCES

......

Budlender, D. "Preliminary Report on Questionnaire to Universities." *Agenda Evaluation.* Unpublished Report.

......

Debby Bonnin is an industrial sociologist, who holds a joint post in the sociology department and the Centre for Industrial, Organizational, and Labour Studies at the University of Natal, Durban. She is a founding editor of Agenda, *a quarterly South African feminist journal, and is the convener of the women's studies working group for the South African Sociological Association.*

1990s: Russia (Fall/Winter 1994), *Anastasia Posadskaya*

Feminist Agenda for Women's Studies

Those who pose the question "Why women's studies?" would argue that under socialism we used to have quite a lot of research on the issues of women's reproductive health, on the combination of employment and motherhood, on working conditions, etc. Why can these works not be called "women's studies"? Isn't women's studies merely a fashionable Western name for any study involving women as object? One of the primary tasks of feminist scholarship in Russia was and still is to distinguish between traditional "research on women," which was mostly biodeterministic and instrumental, and women's studies as a research and educational field, which rejects biodeterminism as an explanation of differences between women and men in society and claims a noninstrumental approach when considering women's issues—which reveals gender as a dimension of all spheres of social life and which questions the methodology, methods, and results of traditional scholarship. The educational task of women's studies is to raise public consciousness of gender issues and to make them a part of the mainstream educational curriculum. Politically, the aim of women's studies is to provide the emerging women's movement with a comprehensive vision of the society and so to place women's concerns into a political agenda.

I am strongly convinced that the main dilemma of the development of women's studies in Russia is how to maintain the feminist agenda in women's studies when we have only a few feminist scholars and a weak independent women's movement. My answer to this dilemma is that *the work to develop women's studies under the current situation is not and cannot be "purely" academic work.* In fact, I believe that, to be feminist, it should never be purely academic. In order to achieve any visible success, a special comprehensive strategy should be worked out, including research, educational, institutional, and public activity. . . .

Has this feminist critique brought any practical results? One could say that, on paper, there have been some positive responses to this critique. As a result of recommendations suggested by a position paper on the state Program on Women, Maternity and Childhood, beginning in April 1991, fathers were also entitled to child care assistance. Fathers were also allowed other provisions in order "to combine work and fatherhood"; they may, for example, take their annual leave right after the birth of a child. Yet without additional support from the media and the state, very few fathers dare use these rights.

The critical storming of the Draft Law on the Protection of Family by feminists, after the law had passed the first hearings in Parliament, forced advocates to make some important changes. The notorious article entitling all women with children under fourteen years of age to work a shorter, thirty-five hour week was removed. Article 33, which states that, from the moment of conception, a child is under protection of the law, has been changed to apply only to a child after birth. In that way the challenge to abortion rights has been lifted. Other positive changes in the law should not be exaggerated, since they are merely improvements of a bad law, whereas a comprehensive policy for the advancement of women is unlikely to be adopted. Nevertheless, the gender analysis of current policy and law is a permanent and sharp subject in the agenda of women's studies in Russia.

Sociological and Methodological Issues

Crisis of Language. One of the first problems for feminist scholarship in Russia was the use of emancipation language. Words like *equality, solidarity,* and *socialism* (as well as any notion of "social") were marked as connected to the passing system and hence inappropriate for a new "democratic" discourse. Seemingly, the equality of women could not be placed on the agenda only because it was connected to the usage of Marxist methodology. A historical approach to the analysis of social phenomena, so crucial for women's studies, could be denied simply on the basis of its being Marxist.

Following many discussions among feminists, the decision was made to introduce into the Russian language the word *gender* in order to avoid harmful connotations and to create a situation in which people might be intrigued by the content of the unknown word. The introduction of the concept of "gender" permitted feminists to emphasize the differences between the biological and social elements in the construction of femininity and masculinity without any reference to other traditions, including Marxism. The use of the term *gender* was also helpful in avoiding criticism that we were "forgetting men." Finally, and especially important, the use of *gender* opened the space for Russian women's studies to join the global feminist debate, helping thus to overcome historic isolation as well as (unintended) pretensions of being "quite specific."

Gender studies (*gendernye issledovaniya*) is now a term widely used in academic circles. The research journal *Sociological Studies* opened a new section on gender studies under a subtitle, "Discussions," and translated several essays by Western scholars (Mariam Chamberlain, Susan Magaray, Denis Kandyoti, and Hilary Rose, in *Sociological Studies,* no. 6 [1992]). The Academy of Sciences has published a monograph entitled *Women and Social Policy (Gender Aspect),* which includes articles by scholars at the Center for Gender Studies. I am strongly convinced that the decision to use *gender* contributed to the academic recognition of women's studies as well as to women's studies' feminist content. . . .

Anastasia Posadskaya *is director of the first Center for Gender Studies in the former Soviet Union and Russia, and a founding member of the feminist group LOTOS (League for the Emancipation of Sexual Stereotypes). . . .*

1990s: Uganda (Spring/Summer 1996), *Victoria Miriam Mwaka*

. . . In July 1987, Makerere University held a donors' conference to solicit help for the rehabilitation and development of the university. At the donors' conference, the proposal to establish a women's studies department at Makerere was discussed. Most of the international donor agencies were aware of the existence of women's studies in other universities, supported the proposal, and pledged financial support. A university committee was set up with a mandate to establish a women's studies department in the faculty of social sciences. The curriculum was drawn up by experts from the United States, Zambia, and Zimbabwe. The department was inaugurated in May 1991, with a core staff of five and thirteen master of arts students. I had the honor of being appointed as the founder head (1990–95) of the new department. The department was expected to produce women and men who could work in the Ministry of Gender and Community Development as well as in other departments and such ministries as health, education, and agriculture, where women predominate and where the focus is on women as participants and beneficiaries (Mwaka 1994:110).

The women's studies department at Makerere University is the first of its kind in Uganda and, more generally, in East Africa. In keeping with Makerere's commitment to build for the future, and to diversify curriculum, the department offers interdisciplinary courses on women and development. The courses introduce key concepts in the analysis of gender relations in different political, economic, and social areas that are currently undergoing transformation, especially with regard to population, reproduction, health, education, family and kinship, rural and urban society, employment, income generation and resource distribution. On completion of the course, candidates are to be able to disseminate the new scholarship on women, stimulate critical approaches to established knowledge, develop practical skills and creative potential, and become role models and advocates for increased opportunities for all women.

As part of its activities, the department trains student leaders from different backgrounds, who might then serve in various ministries, departments, institutions, nongovernmental organizations, or international missions and who would facilitate the integration of women into higher decision making and influence policy decisions on gender issues. The department has worked to revitalize university education, bringing it closer to burning social, economic, and political issues, to working toward their solution, and to producing gender-sensitive persons committed to development activities. The causes, processes, and consequences of gender disparities have been investigated, analyzing structural, cultural, and attitudinal factors that disadvantage women. Men and women have been helped to understand, recognize, and acknowledge the multidimensional lives of women in society—through public lectures, seminars, and the mass media. The department has contributed to the global and national debates on the gender question by linking scholars with activists, extension/field workers, nongovernmental organizations, international concerns, and grass-roots women.

Between 1990 and 1995, the M.A. program enrolled fifty-four students, thirteen of whom have graduated. Six of these fifty-four were male. The male candidates are expected to become gender-literate and serve as sensitizers of other men on gender issues. In Uganda currently, the minister of gender and community development is female, while the permanent secretary and the minister of state for gender and community development are male.

REFERENCES
. . . . . .
Mwaka, V. M. 1994. *Women in Top Management in Uganda.* Association of Public Administration and Management Research Report. . . .
. . . . . .

Victoria Miriam Mwaka is professor of geography and the founder and head chairperson of the women's studies department at Makerere University. She has just been elected president of the International Women's Cross Cultural Exchange Organization and was honored to serve as the deputy chairperson of the Uganda Constituent Assembly from 1994 to 1995.

Strengthening Women's Studies in Hard Times: Feminism and Challenges of Institutional Adaptation

Judith A. Allen

Introduction

Probably, in a century from now, cultural historians will conclude that women's studies was one of the striking intellectual, pedagogical, and institutional innovations of the late twentieth century.[1] Its development as a field has been uneven, exemplifying preoccupations of its region, nation, state/province, city, and institution. Its presence is strongest in the United States, existing in some form in at least 530 universities and colleges by a 1989 estimate, which has been recently updated to 611.[2] Despite the strength of women's studies as a well-represented educational movement and cultural presence, typical models of U.S. women's studies render the field, perhaps paradoxically, *institutionally* fragile. This weakness shows in several key respects, especially striking compared to aspects of the field's development in countries such as the Netherlands, Australia, New Zealand, India, and Canada.[3] Such vulnerability marks several levels: resources, research profile, graduate study, faculty and staffing, autonomy in hiring and tenure/promotion recommendation, representations and evaluations of the field.

An analysis of some reasons for the relative institutional weakness of women's studies provides a basis upon which to identify useful strategies for strengthening the field. The need for attending to these issues—related not only to the field's survival into the next millennium but also to its defensible mission and objectives for its advancement and development—presses acutely on women's studies administrators and faculty. Many departments and programs are now confronting explicit structural downsizing or streamlining, Responsibility Center Management (RCM), erosion of state legislature investment in and subsidizing of higher education, and internal reconfiguration of material resources and institutional capital. Materially, the situation facing women's studies at century's end might be seen, unequivocally, as "hard times"—and times considerably tougher than those of the halcyon founding days of the 1970s, or so one spin on women's studies' narratives goes.[4]

The challenge of adapting to changed external circumstances is not always well met by the field, for reasons worth analysis and redress. Sometimes reasons for this reside in the realm of the political, discursive, or "ideological." In certain contexts the *modi operandi* of women's studies programs have exhibited the ostrichlike grip of what Sally Kitch characterizes as "totalitarian utopianism" within the strands of the feminist thought informing their governance and even their pedagogy.[5] These have, in turn, formed the basis of the critique-of–women's studies publishing industry, replete with fantastic exaggerations, incendiary rhetoric, and methodological gaucheries. Books and articles represented as "women's studies bashing" regrettably, but almost inevitably, have obstructed some important dialogues within a field of vast intellectual unevenness and diversity.[6]

Meanwhile the contiguous development of other interdisciplinary studies poses a different set of institutional and intellectual challenges for women's studies. These fields include cultural studies, critical theory, and various minority, ethnic, and sexualities studies. Such other fields bear upon women's studies' representation of itself in relation to them and upon characterizations made of women's studies.[7] Moreover, there are grounds to argue that, as a collectivity, the field of women's studies has been disturbingly transfixed, even beguiled, by the specter of "backlash," as proclaimed by Faludi's 1992 text.[8] The atrocities wreaked by the dark shadows of "backlash" have been lovingly rehearsed over and over at NWSA meetings as well as at more regional, professional venues, such as the Committee on Interinstitutional Cooperation (CIC) meetings of women's studies administrators from the Big Ten universities. This overengagement with a monolithically historicist "backlash" characterization of the 1980s and 1990s minimizes powerful counterevidence about the development of the field. In fact, over half of the women's studies programs and departments presently operating in U.S. universities and colleges have as their founding dates a year in the period of so-called "backlash."[9] Some explanations for women's studies practitioners' lively engagement with "backlash" link this engagement with the structural fragility of the field at a national level.

The case advanced here is that women's studies has everything to gain from careful analysis of its own institutional setting and from engaging both skillfully and more explicitly in institutional politics. In particular, its strengthening and survival in meaningful and effective forms entails revisiting certain institutional strategies, analyses, and rhetoric not much revised since the first debates on women's studies in the 1970s. Among these matters are the relative advantages and disadvantages entailed in the typical organization of the field in the format of *programs* in universities principally organized and governed through *departments* as the basic constituency of academic representation.[10]

Moreover, confronting the challenges of the moment involves a reconsideration of the field's *first* evaluation of several matters, including, in no particular order, fund-raising, donor relations, doctoral degree programs, development of interdisciplinary research missions, lobbying to have criteria of scholarly merit relevant to research in the field integrated into existing criteria deployed by endowments, foundations, and other sources of research funding, and the establishment of national standards for the field at every academic level.[11]

One of the most critical challenges may be a clear-eyed assessment of the case for establishing, at a national level, a professional organization dedicated to the advance of women's studies, comparable in scope and scale with other such organizations.[12] The professional needs of the field cannot be assessed or adequately provided for, moreover, without a preliminary and eventually a thoroughgoing interrogation of the founding catchphrase of women's studies as "the academic arm of the women's movement."[13] The evolution of debates on the sexual politics of knowledge engaged in by feminists scholars and teachers within the politicized cultural site of the academy justifies reservations about that founding slogan, if "arm" is taken to mean a mere limb of an elsewhere feminist body politic.

Some thoughts on the problems generated by the field's adherence to this slogan are explored as the departure point for discussing strategies that have proved effective in securing the favorable institutional reconfiguration of both resources and the value of women's studies. A particular focus on fund-raising, donor relations, and the building of resources for development and innovation is offered. These accounts are introduced with the objective of initiating fieldwide discussion, especially exchange of insights and advice, as a desirable routine feature of our professional culture.

Reconsidering the Field's Identity: "The Academic Arm of the Women's Movement"?

The designation of women's studies as "the academic arm of the women's movement" has various origin stories and several possible readings. For some it is the assertion of the connection between a feminist educational project *inside* the academy and feminist politics and constituencies of women *outside* the academy. For others it encapsulates the activist duties of academic feminists. Antiacademic positions within the academy made early women's studies practitioners vigilant about establishing structures of governance and pedagogy that countered the institution's hallmark hierarchy, competition, adversarialism, and sexism. Early practitioners believed that alternative, subversive structures could be developed inside the academy through a range of strategies, including resisting departmental status by having no appointed faculty within women's studies itself but instead declaring affiliates all over the campus as a kind of guerrilla force.[14]

Yet, for all the discussion of structure and process, the terms of the discussion did not include formally interrogating both the refused and the preferred structures in the light of theories of interdisciplinarity nor a detailed address of how universities were structured fiscally and conceptually. Julie Thompson Klein contends that, with regard to the rapid adoption of program status as the desired institutional form, key discussions were preempted:

> In the early 1970s, "women's studies" was a restricted choice from limited alternatives that were not of women's own design. A pattern for name and structure already existed, permitting women's studies to become established relatively quickly and obviating the need to fight more general battles about innovation and crossing disciplinary boundaries. Seldom, though, was there debate on whether that structure was the most appropriate one, let alone what the ideal structure might be.[15]

Participants involved in the founding of programs in the 1970s remember the situation differently: that they talked of nothing but structure. Arguably, that discussion took place within certain assumed parameters—ones that Klein's study of interdisciplinarity suggest would need to be scrutinized.[16] In any case, by the early 1990s, even with the program rather than department structure, the increasing specialization and sophistication of academic forms of feminist scholarship led some feminist critics to charge a loss of political edge, co-option, accommodation with a particularly stark patriarchal institution, or worse, the betrayal of nonacademic women.[17] This debate, as informed by the academic-arm slogan, does not explore the practical and institutional consequences of the expectation that women's studies will remain a marginal insider, poised near open windows and doors within the academic house.[18] The academic-arm model for women's studies affects research, faculty, degree offerings, professional organization, and resource allocation.

Research and Faculty Location

The *institutional* weakness and fragility of U.S. women's studies have many measures. In the first place, our field is not even ranked in national ratings of graduate study and research performance, such as the prestigious National Research Council. It is not a distinct field represented among those nominated as eligible to compete for major U.S. endowments and grants. Officers of national foundations report that they have no objection to women's studies becoming so, following a case being made, but they also report that no approach from professional leadership in the field comparable to that from the Modern Language Association, the American Historical Association, the American Political Science Association, and so forth has been forthcoming in pursuit of this objective.[19] Instead, feminist scholars, whether they are appointed to women's studies or not, apply for research grants and supervise doctoral dissertations via their disciplines of training.[20]

The National Women's Studies Association (NWSA) has announced no interdisciplinary research mission for the field nor has any other competing professional and scholarly organization undertaking to represent the field. The current mission of the NWSA does not specifically address women's studies as a site of academic research, per se, at all, undertaking rather "to further the social, political, and professional development of women's studies throughout the country and the world, at every educational level and in every educational setting . . . [as] a forum conducive to dialogue and collective action dedicated to feminist education and change."[21] This broad, multifaceted mission does not, unfortunately, convey a clear research rationale to funders of research in institutions of higher education.

Instead, as any feminist scholar knows, the women's caucuses, subfields, councils, or working parties within mainstream disciplines are the most significant sites for the articulation of feminist scholarly research missions.[22] In most cases the rationale is disciplinary. As Klein observes, resistance "to moving outside one's field of expertise was as strong in women's studies" as in other fields. Moreover, citation data "indicate that much of feminist scholarship retains a strongly disciplinary character."[23] Reviewing this data and the publication history of the key journals in the field, such as *Signs, Feminist Studies, Women's Studies International Forum, Women's Studies Quarterly, International Journal of Women's Studies,* Judith A. Allen and Sally L. Kitch contend that the frequent characterization of women's studies as a field of interdisciplinary research and teaching is little supported by available research evidence.[24]

The lack of genuinely interdisciplinary scholarship has some solid institutional explanations. Serious, systematic, and methodologically sound study of the professional field of women's studies is not *routinely* and *annually* undertaken on behalf of faculty members of the NWSA.[25] Some indicative glimpses of the constraints upon the field's capacity for autonomous, interdisciplinary research are provided by Diana Scully's recent analysis of data from the NWSA's commissioned study of backlash against women's studies programs. According to her sample of 276 returns (a 45 percent sample), two-thirds of faculty chairs and directors have their entire tenure line located in a disciplinary department. Moreover, 56 percent reported that there were no faculty lines located in women's studies.[26]

In research/teaching institutions, where each faculty member's research and scholarly activity undergo annual evaluation, the lack of tenure lines in over half the nation's women's studies units means that women's studies has no recognized "place at the table" in evaluation of faculty research equivalent to that recognized for the "tenure home" department. Research, then, by default, remains a matter of purely departmental prerogatives. This encourages women's studies' faculty research toward a carefully disciplinary orientation, especially if such faculty members are still to secure tenure and promotion. All of this amounts to powerful institutional brakes upon the development of interdisciplinary research missions and profiles within and for women's studies.

Curricula

Structural pressure toward monodisciplinary feminist research and scholarship also produces parallel pressures toward instructional monodisciplinarity as the essence of the actual curriculum that women's studies chooses to claim as its own. Analysts maintain that the curricula of the field typically advanced through programs offering a few topical courses, combined with a larger number of single-discipline courses cross-listed with women's studies, hardly match aspirations to thoroughgoing curricular and pedagogic interdisciplinarity.[27] Only a third of national women's studies units, according to Scully's sample, offer an undergraduate major.[28] This gives the educational enterprise of the majority, then, an air of electiveness, optionality, or even, in many cases, haphazardness.

For practical purposes, in most institutions, women's studies can offer its minors, or area certificates, only because gender-related courses exist within the ordinary offerings of discipline-centered departments. In most universities and colleges surveyed,[29] the fiscal credit for student interest in women's studies thereby accrues to the disciplinary department providing the courses students need to complete women's studies requirements. This amounts to a dependency relationship. At times, to obviate the lack of intellectual and pedagogical supervision of the actual education its students receive, women's studies programs have established review committees which select courses that meet women's studies requirements, replete with many associated problems.[30] Basically, programs function as clearing houses, or conduits, for students interested in the topic of women into department offerings. The institutional fragility of women's studies, then, reduces it to being a coordinator of curricular cross-listings, listers, and their enrollees. This, essentially service work, is effected with varying levels of efficiency and enthusiasm.

The ubiquitous cross-listing strategy can retard or defer developing the field's claimed curricular interdisciplinarity. It removes pressure for the unit to devise and design innovative, interdisciplinary, synthesizing courses with coherent interconnections to the kinds of programs of study that would be comparable to the majors and minors offered by disciplinary departments. Consequently, few women's studies programs pursue lively and challenging debates about theories of interdisciplinarity and the most desirable versions of interdisciplinarity for the field.[31]

Despite the continued assertion that a women's studies education is interdisciplinary, very few graduates with minors or majors to date received a substantially interdisciplinary education. Instead, they received a smorgasbord of disciplinary courses, which, when combined, do not constitute interdisciplinarity. Yet women's studies as a field retains the claim that its offerings to students *are* interdisciplinary. This claim has sometimes been made in the aggregative sense: that is, by adding together disciplinary courses "about women" (in an imaginary intellectual cocktail shaker), the result can be synthesized into an interdisciplinary outcome. I believe we must reject this claim, agreeing, as Jonathan Z. Smith contends, that students "cannot be expected to integrate anything the faculty can't or won't."[32] In short, the presumption that students somehow magically undertake "self-synthesis" is unwarranted, unsound, and frankly lethargic on the part of our field.

The lack of a full interdisciplinary curriculum of course offerings and degree programs *centered or located within* the women's studies unit that would be required for students to receive minors, majors, and other degrees has other consequences. The most serious of these are fiscal and structural. Lack of program teaching capacity mandates dispersing students out of the program into the discipline departments. Typically this has meant that only the smaller portion of required courses that "count" for students are offered by women's studies as a unit or site. Thus student enrollment levels within women's studies itself have not always justified the appointment of either any full or joint women's studies faculty lines, at least in public institutions, which, to some extent, match hiring with enrollment pressures. This is the situation of half of the universities offering women's studies courses in the United States today. Without the pressure of sizable student numbers, many administrations will not consider making new appointments in the women's studies area, especially if less expensive ways have been found to offer the few core or topical women's studies courses required.[33]

Graduate Degrees

A major consequence of the usual organization of U.S. women's studies in programs or centers rather than departments, when they are located within department-centered universities, is that, compared with other countries, graduate degree programs have been exceptional. The field does not have its own graduate students in most institutions offering graduate degrees. This does not mean, however, that women's studies does not contribute to graduate student education. On the contrary, women's studies' joint-appointed faculty are heavily represented in discipline departments, teaching graduate candidates course work and serving on dissertation committees. Moreover, they provide countless hours of advice, counseling, editing, and intellectual engagement. This contribution often amounts to "remedialism," updating or broadening disciplinary approaches, covertly educating the key departmental players affecting the candidates' progress, and even adding "exotic," diversifying, or unusual perspectives to business-as-usual intellectual frameworks for students' work. It is overwhelmingly a service role to structures determined by others.

Consequently, the field lacks an autonomous, balanced, and adequate mission for interdisciplinary *graduate* women's studies education. The underdevelopment of graduate education is connected with the underdeveloped state of interdisciplinary women's studies research. Moreover, the underdevelopment of both are connected to the lack of departments of women's studies with fully determined missions. For the cry always arises, particularly in response to the suggestion of doctoral degrees in the field, that there is no point: What jobs could graduates obtain? The implicit answer is that, of course, as we all know, no institution would ever employ anyone with a women's studies doctorate.

This a priori negativity about the significance of interdisciplinary doctoral degrees is an especially ominous indicator of our field's future vibrancy and viability. It is not a judgment articulated after a full and careful comparative study of academic and other employment prospects for holders of doctorates and master's degrees, especially in the humanities and social sciences. Such comparison actually generates important findings. In fact, one of the most significant growth areas in position postings during the past five years is for positions that wholly or partially call for gender-related expertise. Most postings indicate that this expertise could be satisfied through a range of academic paths, which could, in principle, include doctoral women's studies, were candidates actually available. Considerably more such academic postings exist than, say, for fields like anthropology, folklore, philosophy, French, Italian, German, Chinese, political theory, fine arts, linguistics, and many other fields.[34] Do we see any suggestion that these fields should be made to abandon doctoral programs? Do we see their practitioners voluntarily undertaking to rescind any claim to offer anything of sufficient graduate-level value to justify continuing doctoral work simply because jobs are not, for now at least, very plentiful?

As a matter of fact, the largest number of positions advertised in a single field are in English. This is not surprising, given that English is almost universally required for all undergraduates. But by no means do all, most, or many English doctorates obtain academic posts in their field or indeed in any academic field at all. This largest single group of doctorates on the market is produced in numbers way in excess of any registered demand. Do we thereby see drastic and systematic downsizing imposed on English doctoral intakes nationwide, organized in relation to the contours of the job market? No, we do not.[35] Why?

The most straightforward reason (beyond what we might call professional self-interest) is that, in most fields, doctoral study is the crucial activity of training new scholars and researchers to continue the field's research mission and especially to extend that mission into new domains. The doctorate is related first and foremost to knowledge generation and intellectual development: it is a key way in which the field lays its claim to its domain of expertise—its distinct contributions and insights to collective culture and to improvement or change in approaches.[36]

Doctoral-level research and training remains significant for all fields, including those currently without large academic job markets. Their doctoral degrees have neither been canceled nor rescinded by the universities conferring them. That is because the reasons for their foundation were not predicated on a guaranteed level of likely academic positions being available to its graduates. No field has ever been able to guarantee this.

To offer a doctorate is part of perceiving and representing one's field as a critical, enduring, generative field of knowledge, invaluable for the progress and improvement of human cultural understanding, whether with or without immediate practical or policy ramifications.[37] It is difficult to believe that women's studies faculty accept that this is true and valid for folklore but not for women's studies. Every time we permit our field to be represented as not needing to offer doctoral-level study, we are permitting it to be portrayed as without the significance and intellectual profundity of other fields. We announce that we do not take our field seriously, or at least not seriously enough intellectually, to warrant interdisciplinary doctoral degrees. By default, we make it reasonable for our institutions not to take us seriously enough to support or advocate doctoral-level development. More seriously, we are accepting a secondhand position for women's studies in initiating and influencing the direction of research and new knowledge. This permits the view of women's studies as merely a "teacherly," undergraduate enterprise in which the synthesis of other fields' scholarship is the curricular mission.

Consequently, women's studies is left relying on the wisdom of the traditional disciplines and on such disciplinary feminist scholarship as those disciplines permit to flourish. Hence, it is the disciplines that finally are choosing what the intellectual aegis, framework, and scholarly content of women's studies shall be. It is the disciplines that thereby control the training of all future women's studies faculty, rather than the field of women's studies itself. It is hard to imagine disciplines like history, archaeology, physics, or musicology permitting other disciplines to train their future faculty. The major result of all this is the training of feminist faculty to be much more identified with their discipline than with interdisciplinary women's studies. This amounts to a powerful professional socialization,[38] and, on most campuses, discipline-identified feminist scholars greatly outnumber any women's studies appointed faculty.

Other Loyalties and Identities

Such feminist faculty mainly identify with their own disciplinary department. There, in their "home base," they would insist on having autonomy over hiring, tenure, promotion, and related developmental activities. To the suggestion that women's studies needs the same self-determination over hiring, tenure, and promotion, however, discipline-based or discipline-identified feminist faculty can resist on grounds that they fear or resent the possibility of being "excluded" by such professionalization. Hence, feminist faculty located in disciplines who are teaching those courses for their departments that also meet women's studies students minor or major requirements are not usually or necessarily a source of agitation for faculty lines in interdisciplinary women's studies units. In some cases, such faculty have opposed such appointments taking place.

Opposition here is based on an understanding of women's studies that does not include a vision of reaching professional parity with other academic areas with course offerings—with a distinct mission and structure, including hiring autonomy. Instead, these faculty view women's studies primarily as a network and a source of institutional feminist support and identity for (usually select) feminist faculty located in departments. Undergraduate and graduate students' intellectual and interdisciplinary degree program needs are not on the radar of this understanding.

When pressed, some feminist scholars in discipline departments oppose interdisciplinary women's studies graduate degrees, with the preference that graduates continue to move only in the direction of their discipline. Feminists are by no means immune from disciplinary chauvinism. That women's studies organized in departments (or whatever quasi-departmental units can permit hiring, tenure, and promotion autonomy) represents only a small minority of nationwide units so far suggests, among other factors, the salience of often senior feminist scholar sentiment *against* the professionalization of the field along genuinely interdisciplinary lines.

Revisiting the Question of Department
Status for Women's Studies

In half of U.S. institutions some full or joint women's studies appointments have been made, generally during the past decade.[39] In most of these cases the number of lines is insufficient to warrant the move of women's studies to department status (or whatever institution-specific structure permits hiring, tenure, and promotion autonomy) with, thereby, enough critical mass to undertake the work of interdisciplinary professionals.[40] The result is an awkward limbo. It might best be characterized as semi-professionalized. The nation is full of saintly, martyred women's studies program directors desperately trying to enlist service contributions from affiliated faculty, beyond the small group of joint-appointed faculty. Why?

As a program, the work required for women's studies to be operational in the university or college can be at least the same as those falling to departments. Often, to compensate for insufficient faculty and staff resources, the burden is in fact much greater—advising, admissions, publicity and promotional work, hiring and evaluating teaching and graduate assistants, classes scheduling, visiting and local speaker programs, personnel committees, student administration, budget submissions, library liaison, and much more. Only two or three or four women's studies faculty to do it all and those same faculty having comparable responsibilities in their "home department" too often leads to demoralization for women's studies faculty.[41]

Furthermore, populist notions of governance were devised for women's studies in the 1970s, when the main, if not only, model for the field was the loose, voluntary program without faculty lines. This model generated the expectation of a large number of committees or consultative bodies, which decided everything related to women's studies in large, unstructured meetings that were highly focused on process.[42] With full-time, fully budgeted lines in their disciplinary departments, the "pioneers" have become the senior feminist faculty of the 1990s. Often enough, they have joined the ranks of provosts, deans, associate deans, and other university- and college/school–level administrators. Coping with a greatly increased service load in their department, they frequently no longer can, nor are willing or able to, contribute to sprawling, unstructured, collective meetings, since such contributions have no "value" or are rendered invisible in the assessment of service work. This gradual and perfectly understandable withdrawal happens at the very time that a condition of semiprofessionalism exists for their universities/colleges' women's studies programs with the appointment of at least some joint faculty lines and the offering of undergraduate majors, graduate minors, and other diversification of activities.

This changed situation—especially in half of U.S. institutions offering women's studies that now have at least some joint faculty appointments—intensifies the interest of women's studies program directors and joint-appointed faculty in considering alternative organizational arrangements. Legal obligations and liabilities accompany the inauguration of joint-appointed faculty. Tenure, promotions, salary justification, outside job offers, research grants and accounts administration, benefits packages for maternity, invalidity, disability, and early retirement are the tip of the iceberg of new responsibilities falling upon programs with new joint-appointed faculty. With little "local" experience for handling these duties correctly, interest in departmental structure—and the kinds of basic resources and information it can confer—increases among new faculty in women's studies units.

Moreover, women's studies' commitment to affirmative action and increasing the representation of people of color among both faculty and graduate candidates can amount to little more than exhortation when the field neither hires its own faculty nor recruits its own graduate students. Hence the representation of people of color within our field remains only at whatever level has been achieved by those conventional disciplinary departments presently determining the pool of faculty available to act as women's studies faculty and students in women's studies graduate courses. Obviously, by their actions within their disciplinary departments, the faculty members who act as women's studies faculty have worked conscientiously to enhance diversity in hiring, recruitment, and retention in their "home" department. This is not the same, however, as our field taking direct systemic responsibility for the racial, ethnic, regional, religious, cultural, and socioeconomic composition of our field's practitioners and clientele. Our field, then, reflects the same structural and cultural "whiteness" as the dominant departments through which it is generally constituted. As long as the program with neither full faculty lines nor graduate degrees remains the most typical form of women's studies organization in the United States, we need to be clear on this critical consequence: our field will continue to decline to take systemic power to combat institutional racism, ethnocentrism, heterosexism, and related cultural prejudices in recruitment of our faculty and students.

Revision, Recharacterization, and Professional Representation

All of these factors make "the academic arm of the women's movement" a rather fragile limb, an arm in a sling of institutional and identity-politics constraints. After three decades of work and development, our field should be better positioned to deal with the challenges of the next millennium. Instead of seeing feminists working inside the academy as women's studies practitioners accountable to a women's movement *outside,* it is high time to acknowledge the complex sexual politics of knowledge and institutions undertaken daily and career-long by women's studies professionals. Outside is inside. Women's studies practitioners are as much representative of the women's movement *inside* this particular cultural site as are feminists working elsewhere. We do not say that feminist judges, lawyers, and workers in various echelons of the criminal and civil justice systems are the "justice arm of the women's movement" or that other feminists are the "medical arm" or the "mass media arm" and so forth.

The formulation "academic arm of the women's movement" imperceptibly acquired negative associations—mainly, a loss of autonomy and right to devise context-sensitive strategies and analyses without the implicit obligation to "check in" or act with the approval of "central office." The women's movement always is positioned in a purer space, *outside* the blandishments of the corrupt academy with its long history of contributing to cultural misogyny and the subjugation of women.

Persistent debates have raged about the asserted obligation of women's studies scholars to ensure that all their work, writing, and other scholarly production is always accessible to less educated women outside the academy. Sometimes the rhetoric of this demand has been characterized as populist and anti-intellectual.[43] Certainly there has been a recurring conflict over the extent to which women's studies is obliged, as a field, to engage in outreach to women in the community, to intervene in women's movement political struggles, as if it were not, by definition, already doing so. The implication of this demand is that women's studies' work *inside* the academy is either not political or not political enough.[44]

Perhaps this special accountability demanded of women's studies derives from the possibility that, when originally coined as the academic arm, women's studies was not seen as serving or directly useful to most women or enough women, whereas feminist work in other institutions seemed more likely to make a constructive difference. The ethic among women's studies practitioners, that they should maintain a marginal relation to the institution, is part of this suspicion of the academy itself.[45] For all the insistence on the outreach mission, commentators question the extent and practical significance of these efforts.[46] Yet, as Sally L. Kitch reported on the process of dialogue with community women, especially over the departmentalization of women's studies, activists explicitly appreciated the distinctly *academic* contribution of feminist scholars, who provided expert testimony for policy reforms. Ironically, these nonacademic women were positive, arguably more positive about the distinct mission of academic feminists than some academic feminists.[47]

The pervasive view of women's studies as the academic arm of the women's movement was formulated before the powerful and significant feminist critiques of knowledges developed, particularly those critiques that have developed since the late 1970s. A reconceptualization is in order, and a recognition that the academic-arm metaphor may have outlived its usefulness, at least in some of the ways it is interpreted. We need ways to understand women's studies interventions into the academy as a powerful cultural site—the site productive of some of the world's cultures' most devastating phallocentric discourses—as a crucial form of cultural politics; a site that has made, and continues to make, momentous difference to women's experiences and gender relations. Above all, women's studies needs to be free to take its working context, the institution of higher education, the academy, seriously— deadly seriously. A critical corollary of taking the institution seriously is taking ourselves seriously as practitioner professionals in need of professional organization, representation, and advocacy. Women's studies needs a professional organization with a structure, mission, modus operandi, fiscal accountability, governance structure, and ongoing projects that communicate one simple message: that we take ourselves as seriously as a faculty profession as groups such as professional physicists, computer scientists, pathologists, criminologists, jurists, or scholars of interdisciplinary areas such as Asian studies, religious studies, or cognate fields.

Recent discussions among women's studies administrators both within and outside the auspices of the NWSA disclose some perplexing strategic problems in securing the professional needs of our field. Thorough analysis and strategic planning will be required in order to determine a prompt timetable for the establishment of fully professional representation of the field. One option under consideration is whether this can be achieved within an existing organization, such as the NWSA, subject to a determination of whether it is able or willing to undertake the fundamental revision of its mission, rationale, priorities, governance, fiscal procedures, and rules of accountability that would be necessary to serve this academic field's professional needs. Another option would be the establishment of a new organization in recognition of the new and discrete needs of the field and the inability or unwillingness of existing organizations to both meet these needs and also to retain their longer-standing, valuable, and perhaps preferred objectives. Presumably, time devoted to careful evaluation of conceivable alternatives will determine a consensus in our field about the best path toward meeting our professional needs.

Fiscal Realities

As we face the new century, women's studies departments and programs situated in both private and public institutions cannot ignore the centrality of securing resources and material support beyond that provided by their institutions. My own university, Indiana University, is not atypical in being a large state institution experiencing a drastic reduction in its operating budget provided by its state legislature. Currently, with only 21.6 percent state provided funds (compared with over 65 percent in 1980), such universities and colleges have been redescribing themselves as "state assisted" rather than "state funded," especially when compared with fully state-funded universities in Britain, Western Europe, Australia, New Zealand, and Canada. Recently, prestigious institutions like the University of Michigan have seen even more drastic reductions in state support. With only 10 percent of its operating budget now provided by the legislature, Michigan's executives have begun to quip that their university is merely "state located."[48]

Faced with significant resource challenges, two sources assume central importance in women's studies's survival: income generated by student enrollments in courses and as majors and as graduate candidates, and funds secured externally from alumnae/i, other donors, public endowments, and private foundations. The importance of energetic and innovative work on these sources of support is underscored by some key facts of institutional life in moments of declining state support.

One simple fact is that no academic unit or area of study, however well funded previously, is automatically judged entitled to a living or to continuity in a previously enjoyed standard of living if their operation is a "loss center" in income terms. This is often the fundamental precondition of so-called downsizing and other contraction strategies such as the amalgamation of two or more academic units into entities such as a department of interdisciplinary studies. Although administrations may be much more willing to take this punitive action against politically critical areas of study, such as women's studies, various ethnic and minority studies, and cultural studies, it is not *usually* action taken against these units if they are generating income and sources of support comparable to more mainstream areas, which can seem more secure in "hard times."

Interdisciplinarity Imperiled?

Another tendency in institutional responses to the curtailment of external funding is the adoption of a "steady-state" mentality, which stands to imperil interdisciplinary studies. Its rhetoric takes various forms, but the common message is "this is not a good time to invest in change." It tends to operate at a macroscopic or highly aggregated level, without taking account of vast differentials between academic units as to their income-generating potential with appropriate and planned institutional investment.

Part of the reason that financial crisis tends to accentuate this "macroscopic focus,"[49] which disadvantages women's studies, is because the culture of its inclusion in the first place was, to paraphrase how a dean and colleague recently put it, merely adding a chapter to the existing book without asking what that new chapter implied or impelled about the allocation of pages, words, and missions of the previously existing chapters.[50] His suggestion was that hard intellectual work must accompany the integration of academic innovations like women's studies. It could not just be grafted onto a steady-state or given institutional structure and expect to be effective without significant restructuring and without logical resource reconfiguration.

In the absence of such intellectual work and of resource and value reconfiguration, Klein argues that women's studies, like other interdisciplinary activities, can "fall victim to the academic equivalent of last hired, first fired . . . undermined by misinformation, bias, and easy generalizations."[51] As such a field, women's studies has an urgent mission in ensuring its survival: to challenge assumptions that work to privilege disciplinary work over interdisciplinary. For it is obvious that most academics do not understand even what interdisciplinarity is, usually confusing it with multidisciplinarity, that is to say, two or more intact disciplines collaborating.

What is missing in most discussions of interdisciplinary projects, like women's studies, is the work of *synthesis* in producing a new outcome. Klein uses geometric metaphors to highlight this problem. According to her, disciplinary work is conceptualized along the vertical axis of "depth." By contrast, interdisciplinary work occupies the horizontal axis of "breadth." The depth/breadth dichotomy misrepresents exactly how interdisciplinarity operates because it excludes the most critical and distinct dimension—synthesis. Klein writes:

> Synthesis connotes creation of an interdisciplinary outcome through a series of integrative actions. Synthesis does not derive simply from mastering a body of knowledge, applying a formula, or moving in a linear fashion from point A to point B. . . . Integrating knowledge is neither routine nor formulaic. It requires active triangulation of depth, breadth and synthesis. The discussion is incomplete if adequacy of disciplinary knowledge remains the primary focus.[52]

The problem for Klein and for evaluations of women's studies as a scholarly field is that as long as the existing meanings of "depth" and "rigor" remain unchallenged, their default meanings derive from disciplinarity. It is our task to challenge these meanings and recast them in relation to the interdisciplinary mission of our field. In common with other interdisciplinary fields, "depth" in women's studies scholarship "derives from competence in pertinent knowledges and approaches. Rigor derives from attention to the integrative process."[53]

Hence, the typical lack of institutional-level analysis of these dichotomies and their effects disadvantages women's studies along with other interdisciplinary studies in downsizing institutions. As commentators note, sentiments intellectually supportive of interdisciplinarity as the cutting edge are readily articulated but rarely matched with the requisite resources.[54]

Steady-state approaches to reduced state investment in higher education also tend to overlook the possibility that times of income crisis are *precisely* the moment to invest in innovation—to reallocate resources based on performance indicators, what people aged under twenty-five call "organizational morphing," within the slate of institutional changes necessitated by stagnant or declining budget allocations. The stupendous success of some administrations taking this latter view offer powerful contrast with the more typical "steady staters." The steady-state mentality can act as an enormous brake on the development of new interdisciplinary areas such as women's studies, various ethnic and minority studies, and cultural studies. Its rhetoric and conservative strategies descend upon us at the very point that, nationally, women's studies is increasingly making joint and full faculty appointments, implementing undergraduate majors, designing graduate degree programs, and extending research centers and institutes. In other words, now more than ever, the field needs critical institutional investment. If our central administrations were to remain the only prospect for resources, then the immediate to long-term prospects for our field would look bleak indeed. Only by ignoring this wider context could "backlash" be entertained as the global explanation for all instances of women's studies' "failure to thrive." Reasons for stagnation and decline in local examples of our field can be considerably more specific.

The moment of fiscal restraint and crisis-driven institutional change is not the moment to be marginal. To take the institution seriously in this moment is to envisage and execute strategies designed to make women's studies *integral* to the operations and culture of the university or college. The objective here is to ensure not only its survival but its innovative development. This pursuit of demarginalization implies change of varying proportions. In some contexts this may involve a huge shift, a complete rethinking of women's studies' relationships with all other academic units, with new, revised demands for accountability, efficiency, productivity, excellence, and self-support.[55] In others reconfiguring the position of women's studies toward greater centrality will be a more disaggregated enterprise.

Women's Studies as a "Profit Center"

In order to be able to achieve the developments and innovations we require for our field, women's studies administrators and faculty, like those in other university and college departments, are asked to demonstrate that women's studies can secure a significant portion of the resources needed to do so by means other than the traditional increase in the base budget of programs and departments. Attention to increasing the income secured by instructional effort is one critical prerequisite in most institutions for securing the faculty lines in women's studies needed to diversify degree offerings, develop credible graduate programs, and expand the research achievements and profile of the unit.

Women's studies is currently in no one, uniform place with regard to these challenges. For women's studies at Ohio State University for instance, where annual enrollments are over 3,000 of 52,000 total university enrollments and women's studies is the fourth largest undergraduate major in the college of humanities, fiscal downsizing stands to present little immediate threat.[56] Strenuous efforts to have women's studies courses made part of the general education curriculum have established its contributions as an integral part of the university. A nationally competitive Master of Arts in women's studies and the plans to develop a doctorate further integrate the field, supplying nearly thirty teaching assistants for women's studies courses.[57] This justified more joint appointments, which in turn provided the basis for the further exploration and development of an interdisciplinary research mission and evaluation criteria in faculty scholarly work. All this combined to enable the move to departmental status, formalized in October 1995.[58] The new department is currently hiring its first two full-time, fully budgeted positions, notwithstanding global downsizing.

For many women's studies programs, marginality has meant that women's studies has not become institutionally integral in ways comparable with Ohio State and those other women's studies units that have pursued comparable strategies. In order to alter marginality, a number of different and even novel strategies will be needed, especially given the difficult fiscal position of women's studies in many universities and colleges. These strategies include methods of increasing enrollment in course offerings through the women's studies program or center, thereby increasing paid credit hours taken by students within the women's studies unit itself. In cases where enrollments in women's studies are very small, imperiling the viability of the unit, especially where the unit has joint faculty lines with associated productivity measures and accountability, other strategies may be necessary. Here, strategies should maximize the credit hours and enrollments credited to women's studies and enlarge the course offerings and teaching capacity of the existing unit.

A key principle under these circumstances may be to consider ending the orthodoxy of a skeletal women's studies operation that forwards its students to the disciplines for their courses. Instead, units can establish ways to bring discipline-based faculty into the women's studies unit to teach its courses. Some deans have been willing to permit departments whose faculty teach in women's studies courses to count these as courses taught in the home department. Development of sufficient interdisciplinary courses *within* women's studies to enable students to complete majors, minors, and/or area certificates is essential. Only by meeting student demand for women's studies within women's studies as a fiscally accountable academic unit can we map the real demand and market for interdisciplinary women's studies.

A critical strategy for planning effective recruitment for increasing enrollments and, therefore, for income to support women's studies is to study past and present enrollees. Who are our students? What is their sex ratio, their race and ethnicity, their age group, their marital status, their place of residence or origin relative to other student cohorts and to other small programs and departments? What majors or other areas of study do typical women's studies students pursue? How closely do their choices match the expertise of the women's studies faculty available to instruct them? At what stage in their academic careers do they enroll in their first women's studies course? Which students among all enrollees seem most likely to do a minor, an area certificate, and/or a major once, or if, it should become available? What proportion of those students who do a major in women's studies are double majoring? What proportion of enrollees take only one women's studies course, and how does this compare with other small departments and programs and with school norms? What proportion of women's studies enrollees come from outside the school or college, or, put differently, to what extent can women's studies be a magnet for students universitywide?

Answers to questions like these can impact on a range of necessary activities, especially publicizing and promoting of offerings throughout the university and beyond it. Put simply, the larger the ratio of students to faculty, the more income the unit generates, justifying not only survival but, in the best case scenario, further investment, even in moments of financial downturn. One of the great strengths of our field that *can* emerge from such self-study is that it can attract large numbers of students, bringing new students into the school or college in which women's studies is located fiscally. Similarly, answers to the above questions can help shape the intellectual orientation of courses offered to such potential recruiting areas as the general education curriculum and also help assess the faculty expertise needed for a truly interdisciplinary array of course offerings.

With targeted strategies based on an overhaul of student requirements, on the study of statistical trends, and on an appraisal of universitywide policy and directions opportunities can be found to strengthen the performance of women's studies—to turn it into a profit or income center, fiscally speaking, thereby considerably fortifying its position in response to downsizing pressures.[59] This involves a more pragmatic view of our instructional enterprise than has been characteristic of our field or of other liberal arts and humanities.

Development Opportunities

The role of external donors, whether alumnae/i or not, can be of fundamental importance. Moreover, visible and generous donors' gifts can provide critical impetus, encouragement, incentive, or just plain pressure upon macroscopic, "steady-state" administrations. Such "bosses" would otherwise respond to proposals for, let us say, a named chair in women's studies unequivocally in the negative.

The example of the chair in women's studies is not chosen at random. In September 1996 the Indiana University Foundation announced a planned estate gift of $1 million to establish a full-time, fully budgeted chair in women's studies. The gift came from a woman alumna and her husband. This alumna became reengaged with the university through a feminist-inspired colloquium designed for potential women donors. She made the gift, in partnership with her husband, partly through reflecting on her own sense of deprivation in not having had access to women's studies. With a university policy of matching, dollar for dollar, any gift of $1 million or over, the funds for this chair eventually will be $2 million. The donors were absolutely clear in their stipulations: the chair was not to be a joint appointment, so characteristic in our field, but a full-time position budgetarily located within women's studies.

There are special possibilities and issues to attend to in order to achieve such funding and potential self-sufficiency. Regrettably, typical fund-raising entities and personnel on most campuses are unaware of these possibilities. Usual styles of fund-raising and donor relations can be worse than useless for our purposes, because they are relentlessly phallocentric and often downright sexist. Moreover, many of the rules about who may be approached as potential donors are stacked against a new interdisciplinary field without a long history of offering an undergraduate major and graduate degrees. Thus, if women's studies is to achieve significant external funding and a donor base, many of the standard conventions will need interrogation. Some may have to be broken; others declared simply inapplicable.

Several points about this gift speak more generally to strategies for gaining resources for women's studies and for critically evaluating fund-raising rules. First, the donor was not an alumna of women's studies. Structurally, she could not be.[60] Earlier discipline-based feminist faculty governing women's studies had not established an interdisciplinary major. Moreover, prior to 1992, the dean had appointed no faculty lines to facilitate the offering of a major within the program.

Second, the donor was not even an alumna of the College of Arts and Sciences, where women's studies is located. Instead, her training was in the School of Health, Physical Education, and Recreation. One of the golden rules established in fund-raising is the law of alumnae/i territory: you never go after other schools and departments' graduates. Given our unprofessionalized history, this is protocol that, if respected, would work to exclude women's studies from significant fund-raising—as it probably has so far.

There is no reason to think that Indiana University's Women's Studies Program was lucky enough to find the only such woman of means who could be a potential women's studies donor currently living in the United States. Most women's studies departments and programs probably have such women within the alumnae population of their university or college. But such women often have no means of access, no bridge to knowledge about women's studies, unless our field finds a way to build it. Moreover, such prospects can be guarded, territorially, by those who claim prior entitlement: the department of their major or the school of their enrollment and graduation. So we need, as a field, to devise effective strategies and local tactics. Frankly, we have to break some of the rules and work toward our own best interests as a field.

Third, and this is very significant: no one solicited this gift. The gift did not come through aggressive targeting, driven by competition, "schmoozing," and the tactics of mainstream fund-raising, which,

understandably, make many of us queasy. It came because, at some risk
to her own reputation within the foundation employing her, one
woman—Peg Zeglin Brand—changed the culture of the university's
relations to alumnae. She found a way to offer them enriching contact
with a wider university than they had known—one informed by feminist vision—and information about this *new* field of women's studies.[61]
This unsolicited gift came as an appreciative vote of confidence in the
social relevance and excellence of our field from one woman and her
partner's wish to see it expansive, effective, and able to push knowledge and research barriers to their limit. The reasons for the donors'
investment, as for many women's studies donors, are personal or
forged in pursuit of their understanding of their interests. This is
another way in which rules and traditional protocol do not serve us
well.

Moreover, such donors' investment in and expectations for women's
studies closely follow personal motivations. These donors want to be
turned to for advice and to exchange wisdom, news, and opinions.
This means that they want to be told the truth, the real truth, about
prospects for women's studies in the university or college in question
because they want to be able to help. Not for them is the other golden
rule of fund-raising: what I call the rule of "rah, rah, rah!" If, at other
universities and colleges, women's studies has department status, more
than ten faculty appointees, huge enrollments, research institutes, and
graduate offerings, but their alma mater does not, these donors want
to know why. They tend to be no more satisfied than women's studies
practitioners with the answer that seems nationally valid: the situation
of women's studies is such as is the dean's pleasure. These donors are
dedicated people who want a great deal more involvement than just
to send an annual check and to receive the perfect, pro forma, development officer–approved thank-you letter.

Conclusion

As the downturn in higher education increasingly generates the catchphrase of "targeted investment," the means exist for women's studies
to constitute itself, nationwide, as one of those targets. To achieve this
objective will take planning, professionalism, intellectual rigor, and an
unambiguous conviction that the academy is a critical site for feminist
intervention. It also will take collective will to deliver finally the interdisciplinary potential of our field, in both research and teaching, no
longer satisfied with lip service, tokenism, unreal loyalties, and uncom-
pensated, self-sacrificing service to existing structures in ways that do
not build our field. There are opportunities to radically change for the

better the institutional position of women's studies, to strengthen the
field in terms of whatever constitutes strength and distinction in different institutions. Sometimes these chances are right under our noses
in institutions that we have not had to, or been inclined to, take too
seriously.

The choice no longer remains not to enter our institutional politics
fully and effectively, unless of course we are so demoralized that we no
longer care if women's studies, or some plausible evolution from it,
survives into the next century. In order to be effective, we need a place
at the table from which to bargain, negotiate, and battle. The chair in
the corner, self-consciously marginal, is not giving us that effectivity.

NOTES
The observations and arguments advanced in this article are drawn from four
years experience as director of women's studies in a large state research/teach-
ing university and, so, are inflected by that particular university system. I
should like to thank the following people for their invaluable assistance in its
preparation, especially their discussion of key issues and debates with me, in
some cases, over a long period of time, for their concrete support for women's
studies in my working environment, and for their grace and generosity, especially over the points on which we may disagree: Harriet Adams, Peg Zeglin
Brand, Brian Carr, Laurel Cornell, Glenna Crooks, Laura Frader, Stephen
Garton, Carol Greenhouse, Elizabeth Grosz, Helen Hardacre, Dorothy O.
Helly, Julia Horne, Florence Howe, Sally L. Kitch, Dale Ellen Leff, Fedwa Malti-
Douglas, Karen Metelnick, Dottie Mortimore, Carol Pateman, Jean Person, M.
Jeanne Peterson, Janice A. Ramsay, Stephanie Sanders, Janet Smith, and
Jacqueline Zita. The shortcomings that remain, of course, are my own.
    1. Comprehensive analytical histories of the development of women's stud-
        ies are still to be written. Some note various dates in the late 1960s for the
        commencement of programs in their universities. For a useful overview,
        see Marilyn Boxer, "For and About Women: The Theory and Practice of
        Women's Studies," *Signs* 7, no. 3 (1982): 661–95. For valuable surveys and
        chronicles of the state of the field at particular moments, see Florence
        Howe and Carol Ahlum, "Women's Studies and Social Change," in
        Academic Women on the Move, ed. Alice Rossi (New York: Russell Sage
        Foundation, 1973); Florence Howe, *Seven Years Later: Women's Studies
        Programs in 1976* (Washington, D.C.: National Advisory Council on
        Women's Educational Programs, Department of Education, 1977);
        Florence Howe, "Breaking the Disciplines," in *Myths of Coeducation: Selected
        Essays, 1964–1983* (Bloomington: Indiana University Press, 1984, originally
        published 1978); Florence Howe and Paul Lauter, *The Impact of Women's
        Studies on the Campus and the Disciplines* (Old Westbury: State University of
        New York Press, 1980); Florence Howe, "Women's Studies and Curricular
        Change," in *Women in Academe: Progress and Prospects,* ed. Mariam
        Chamberlain (New York: Russell Sage Foundation, 1988); Catharine R.

Stimpson, "Women's Studies: An Overview," *University of Michigan Papers in Women's Studies,* vol. 2 (Ann Arbor: University of Michigan, 1978); Catharine R. Stimpson, "Feminist Criticism," in *Redrawing the Boundaries: The Transformation of English and American Literary Studies,* eds. Stephen Greenblatt and Giles Gunn (New York: Modern Language Association, 1992); Catharine R. Stimpson and Nina Kressner Cobb, *Women's Studies in the United States* (New York: Ford Foundation, 1986); Association of American Colleges, ed., *Liberal Learning and the Arts and Sciences Major: Reports from the Field,* 3 vols. (Washington, D.C.: Association of American Colleges and Universities, 1990–92); and Beverly Guy-Sheftall and Susan Heath, *Women's Studies: A Retrospective* (New York: Ford Foundation, 1995).

2. For a late 1980s estimate, see Caryn McTighe Musil and Ruby Sales, "Funding Women's Studies," in *Transforming the Curriculum: Ethnic Studies and Women's Studies,* eds. Johnella E. Butler and John C. Walter (Albany: State University of New York Press, 1991), 23. For a recent figure, see the 1997 women's studies program list included in this issue.

3. For accounts of the field's development in various countries, see Rosi Braidotti, "Women's Studies the University of Utrecht," *Women's Studies International Forum* 16 (July/August 1993): 311–25; Tao Jie, "Women's Studies in China," *Women's Studies Quarterly* 24 (Spring/Summer 1996): 351–64; Saskia Grotenhuis, "Women's Studies in the Netherlands: A Successful Institutionalization?" *Feminist Studies* 15 (Fall 1989): 525–40; Vina Mazumdar, "Women's Studies and the Women's Movement in India: An Overview," *Women's Studies Quarterly* 22 (Fall/Winter 1994): 42–55; and Peta Tancred, "Into the Third Decade of Canadian Women's Studies: A Glass Half-Empty or Half-Full?" *Women's Studies Quarterly* 22 (Fall/Winter 1994): 12–26.

4. See, for instance, Sylvia Walby, "'Backlash' in Historical Context," in *Making Connections: Women's Studies, Women's Movements, Women's Lives,* eds. Mary Kennedy, Cathy Lubelska, and Val Walsh (Washington, D.C.: Taylor and Francis, 1993); and Karla Mantilla, "NWSA Business (1994 NWSA Conference in Ames, Iowa)," *Off Our Backs* (August/September 1994): 14.

5. Sally L. Kitch, "Utopianism and Fundamentalism in Feminist Thought" (paper presented 20 April 1996 for the Feminism, Sexuality, and Culture Series, Women's Studies Program, Indiana University).

6. See, for instance, Katherine Roiphe, *The Morning After: Fear, Sex, and Feminism on College Campuses* (Boston: Little Brown and Co., 1993); Laura Wright, "Anti-Feminism: Generation X–Style," *The Minnesota Review* 41/42 (Fall 1994): 129–32; bell hooks, "Dissident Heat: Fire With Fire," in *Outlaw Culture: Resisting Representations* (New York: Routledge, 1992); Daphne Patai and Noretta Koertge, *Professing Feminism: Cautionary Tales from the Strange World of Women's Studies* (New York: Basic Books, 1994); Christa Hoff Sommers, *Who Stole Feminism? How Women Have Betrayed Women* (New York: Simon and Schuster, 1994); Rene Denfeld, *The New Victorians: A Young Woman's Challenge to the Old Feminist Order* (New York:

Warner Books, 1995); Camille Paglia, "The Nursery-School Campus: The Corruption of the Humanities in the U.S." in *Vamps and Tramps* (New York: Vintage, 1994); Camille Paglia, "The MIT Lecture: Crisis in the American Universities," in *Sex, Art, and American Culture* (New York: Vintage, 1992); and Melanie Morton, "Camille Paglia and the Anti-Feminist *Backlash*: Assessing Discursive Strategies," *Proceedings of the Second Berkeley Women and Language Conference*, 4–5 April 1992.

7. See, for instance, Ellen Rooney, "Discipline and Vanish: Feminism, the Resistance to Theory, and the Politics of Cultural Studies," *differences* 2, no. 3 (1990): 14.

8. See Susan Faludi, *Backlash: The Undeclared War Against American Women* (New York: Crown, 1991), especially pages 281–332.

9. These findings are from a questionnaire distributed at a pre-conference meeting at the National Women's Studies Association; Program Administrators Questionnaire, prepared by Judith A. Allen and Tiina Kirss, 6 June 1996.

10. For further discussion of this issue, see Judith A. Allen and Sally L. Kitch, "Disciplined by Disciplines?: The Need for an Interdisciplinary Mission in/for Women's Studies," *Feminist Studies* 24, no. 1.

11. The issue of "national standards" is a particularly critical one in current institutional politics, requiring, in the absence of a national-level response from our field, considerable creativity on the part of women's studies chairs and administrators. On the politics of national standards and research competitiveness for interdisciplinary fields, see Julie Thompson Klein, *Crossing Boundaries: Knowledge, Disciplinarities, and Interdisciplinarities* (Charlottesville: University Press of Virginia, 1996).

12. See Chela Sandoval, "Feminism and Racism: A Report on the 1981 National Women's Studies Association Conference," in *Making Face, Making Soul—Haciendo Caras: Creative Perspectives by Women of Color*, ed. Gloria Anzaldua (San Francisco: Aunt Lute Press, 1990) and "Speaking for Ourselves," *The Women's Review of Books* 8, February 1991, 27–30.

13. See Sandra Coyner, " Women's Studies," *NWSA Journal* 3, no. 3 (1991): 349, and Renate D. Klein, "Passion and Politics in Women's Studies in the Nineties," *Women's Studies International Forum* 14 (1991): 125–34.

14. Howe, *Seven Years Later*, 21.

15. Klein, *Crossing Boundaries*, 116.

16. These parameters include certain "founding assumptions" ably documented by Howe, *Seven Years Later*, including (1) that program status would permit women's studies to change the entire curriculum of the university (21); (2) that women's studies served also as a "vocational and human counseling center, a 're-entry' route to higher education, and a place to meet friends" (24); (3) unlike Black Studies, which hired its own faculty, women's studies would be constituted by existing faculty in the main and would not have hiring autonomy (25); and (4) the pedagogic focus was undergraduate, with graduate degrees a matter for future debate (38–39).

17. For a useful and exemplary exposition of this position, see Ellen Messer Davidow, "Know-How," in *(En)gendering Knowledge: Feminists in Academe,* eds. Joan E. Hartman and Ellen Messer-Davidow (Knoxville: The University of Tennessee Press, 1991).

18. Klein, *Crossing Boundaries,* 123.

19. David Jones, project officer, National Endowment for the Humanities, interview with author, 23 November 1993.

20. In the absence of women's studies being a recognized research field, with a distinct evaluative committee, the NEH 1997–98 awards for Fellowships for University Teachers indicate the extent to which feminist research is applied for and supported through disciplinary grids. Of a total of 106 awards, twelve were awarded to projects related to women, gender, and/or sexuality, and recipients included women's studies teaching faculty. The registered research fields of their proposed projects, however, were as follows: French literature, European history, philosophy, British literature, sociology, music history and criticism, anthropology, and American studies. The same applies to the many prominent feminist scholars who are recent recipients of MacArthur Foundation fellowships and grants, such as Posalind Pollack Petcessky and Susan McClary: the classification of their project and research field is strictly disciplinary. See "Current Announcements," National Endowment for the Humanities online site (http: www.neh.fed.us).

21. The current mission is set forth in the most recent conference program; National Women's Studies Association, *Borders/Crossings/Passages: Women Reinterpreting Development* (Seventeenth Annual Conference, Skidmore College, 12–16 June 1996), 8.

22. Examples of this kind of professional formation are found in the Modern Language Association (MLA), the nation's largest professional academic body. It has the subdivision "Division on Women's Studies in Language and Literature" as well as a "Committee on the Status of Women in the Profession" dating from 1969. Other organizations such as the American Historical Association, the Organization of American Historians, and the Social Science History Association have comparable divisions or subgroups, attending both to research and scholarly development and to professional representation.

23. Klein, *Crossing Boundaries,* 120–21.

24. Allen and Kitch, "Disciplined by Disciplines?"

25. At a recent conference of women's studies administrators entitled "The Next Twenty-five Years" (Arizona State University, Tempe, 12–14 February 1997), a panel discussion and meeting on professional organizational needs disclosed that the need for reliable, annually updated data on the state of departments, programs, faculty, and students was the highest priority on most participants' agenda. Nearly twenty years ago, Howe and Lauter, *The Impact of Women's Studies,* identified data and study of the field as critical; they hoped that the newly formed NWSA would be the professional body to undertake this work as a routine, annual matter on behalf of its members (19).

26. Diana Scully, "Overview of Women's Studies: Organization and Institutional Status in U.S. Higher Education," *NWSA Journal* 8 (Fall 1996): 123–24.
27. For a critique of the lack of synthesis in programs based principally upon monodisciplinary offerings, see Klein, *Crossing Boundaries*, 120.
28. Scully, "Overview of Women's Studies."
29. Ibid.
30. Problems here can include acrimony and contention, bitter feelings and "bad press" for women's studies faculty as "thought police" and arbiters of "political correctness" (especially on those campuses with high profiles in the so-called "culture wars"), and excessive time consumption, labor intensiveness, and inefficiency.
31. For an account of these debates, see Julie Thompson Klein, *Interdisciplinarity: History, Theory, and Practice* (Detroit: Wayne State University Press, 1990), especially pages 19–74.
32. Jonathan Z. Smith, quoted in Jerry Gaff, "Avoiding the Pitfalls of General Education," *Educational Review* 61, no. 4: 54–55, and cited by Klein, *Crossing Boundaries*, as "Smith's Iron Law" (214).
33. Examples of cost-saving measures that justify fewer appointments include increasing the supply of voluntary adjuncts or employing, by "soft money," graduate candidates as instructors, especially at the introductory level.
34. Judith A. Allen, Peg Zeglin Brand, Laurel Cornell, Carol Greenhouse, Fedwa Malti-Douglas, M. Jeanne Peterson, and Stephanie Sanders, "Enhancing Gender Studies," *Strategic Directions Charter Implementation Proposal* (Bloomington: Indiana University, 1996), Table 5.
35. This is not to say that institutions are not limiting intakes for fiscal reasons and due to other local factors, including some faculty feeling against training new doctorates in a poor job market. But the move is not global, systematic, nor externally imposed.
36. See Judith S. Glazer, *A Teaching Doctorate? The Doctor of Arts Degree, Then and Now* (Washington, D.C.: American Association of Higher Education, 1993); William G. Bowen, Neil L. Rudenstine, and Julie Ann Sosa, *In Pursuit of the Ph.D.* (Princeton, N.J.: Princeton University Press, 1992); and Betty D. Maxfield and Susan Henn, *Employment of Humanities Ph.D.'s: A Departure From Traditional Jobs* (Washington, D.C.: National Academy of the Sciences, 1980).
37. For discussion of these issues, see John Henry Newman, *The Idea of a University*, ed. Frank M. Turner (New Haven: Yale University Press, 1996); Bob Brecher, Otakar Fleischmann, and Jo Halliday, *The University in a Liberal State* (Brookfield, Mass.: Avebury Series in Philosophy, 1996); Mortimer R. Kadish, *Toward an Ethic of Higher Education* (Stanford, Calif.: Stanford University Press, 1991); Renate Simpson, *How the Ph.D. Came to Britain: A Century of Struggle for Postgraduate Education* (Guildford: Society for Research into Higher Education, 1983); and Pjotr Hesseling, *Frontiers of Learning: The Ph.D. Octopus* (Dordrecht, Netherlands: Foris Publications, 1986).

38. For a discussion of this process in universitywide terms, see Stephen Jay Kline, *Conceptual Foundations of Multidisciplinary Thinking* (Stanford, Calif.: Stanford University Press, 1995), 197–98.
39. Musil and Sales, "Funding Women's Studies," 22–23.
40. Many institutions have a "full-time equivalent" faculty-appointee formula as the basis for a case for departmentalization. The Indiana University–Bloomington campus chancellor reports a convention of a minimum of at least the equivalent of three full-time faculty, appointed full time or jointly within the existing unit, as a benchmark for department status.
41. For a recent discussion of these issues, see Alice Kessler Harris and Amy Swerdlow, "Pride and Paradox: Despite Success, Women's Studies Faces an Uncertain Future," *Chronicle of Higher Education*, 26 April 1996, p. 64. They describe women's studies as underfunded, staying above water only through the dedication of overworked and overcommitted faculty.
42. Howe, *Seven Years Later*, likened these meetings to community meetings with attendance in the fifteen institutions sampled ranging from ten to twenty-six (26–27). With a lack of budget, hiring, and staffing autonomy, internal governance was often the only site for agency (Howe and Lauter, *The Impact of Women's Studies*, [26–27].)
43. Gayatri Chakravorty Spivak, "In a Word: Interview," *differences* 1, no. 2 (1989): 124–56 and Gayatri Chakravorty Spivak, *Outside the Teaching Machine* (New York: Routledge, 1993).
44. This seems to be a prevalent view of commentators on the field. See, for instance, Davidow, "Know How," 290.
45. For a perceptive account and critique of this view, see Lynette McGrath, "An Ethical Justification of Women's Studies; or What's a Nice Girl Like You Doing in a Place Like This?" *Hypatia* 6 (Summer 1991): 137–52.
46. Klein, *Crossing Boundaries*, 118–19
47. Sally L. Kitch, "Becoming a Department: Issues of Organization and Institutional Status for Women's Studies" (unpublished lecture presented 18 April 1996 at Indiana University, Bloomington).
48. Kenneth Gros Louis, chancellor, Indiana University, meeting with department heads, Bloomington, Ind., 11 February 1997.
49. See Marilyn Frye, *The Politics of Reality: Essays in Feminist Theory* (Trumansburg: The Crossing Press, 1983), 8–12.
50. Donald Warren, dean, and Frances Stage, associate dean, Indiana University School of Education, interview with author, Bloomington, Ind., 3 December 1996.
51. Klein, *Crossing Boundaries*, 209.
52. Ibid., 212.
53. Ibid.
54. Ibid., 235–36.
55. Indiana University Board of Trustees, *Strategic Directions Charter* (Bloomington: Indiana University, 1996).
56. Judith A. Allen, *Women's Studies in the CIC: Report 1994–95* (Bloomington: Indiana University, 1996), Table 1.

57. Ibid., Table 3.
58. Kitch, "Becoming a Department."
59. At Indiana University, in the period from 1993–97, the College of Arts and Sciences underwent a disastrous decline in student credit hours (therefore fees), down by about one-fifth, as well as serious drops in majors and the number of reenrolling students. Yet, within that same period, women's studies increased its enrollments, hence student credit hours, without any increase in faculty costs or cost per credit hour, by a staggering 50 percent. This was largely a result of changing requirements from primarily cross-listings to a women's studies–centered array of interdisciplinary course offerings.
60. Women's studies at Indiana University will have alumnae/i after fall 1998; 1997–98 is the first year of conferring a new interdisciplinary major. Conventional wisdom has it that it will be at least ten and probably twenty or more years before the first cohort of graduates may include among them women and men who could contribute back to women's studies development.
61. The credit goes to Peg Zeglin Brand, a feminist philosopher and artist, jointly appointed to women's studies, philosophy, and the fund-raising Indiana University Foundation. Convinced that the usual approach of philanthropy and soliciting among alumnae/i was both sexist and phallocentric, Peg Brand insisted on a radical insight: women earn, acquire, and inherit wealth too, and they certainly invest it. In addition, they often play a critical role in determining the philanthropic destinations of both corporate and family resources—even when the nominal donor is a man. And donations can be sought in mixed-sex partnerships and devised in egalitarian ways not usually foregrounded in a development ethos oriented toward wealthy men.

***Judith A. Allen** is director of gender studies and professor of gender studies at Indiana University, Bloomington. She was formerly foundation chair of women's studies and director of the Australian Institute for Women's Research and Policy at Griffith University, Brisbane. She is author of numerous articles on feminist critiques of knowledge, feminist theory, and women's studies. Originally a historian, her books include* Sex and Secrets: Crimes Involving Australian Women Since 1880 *and* Rose Scott: Vision and Revision in Feminism, 1880–1925.

Copyright © 1997 by Judith A. Allen.

The Women's Studies Ph.D.:
A Report from the Field

Ann B. Shteir

Doctoral work in women's studies is, gloriously, in an expansionist mode. Across the United States and Canada, as well as in Europe, and globally, faculty at many universities are shaping—or struggling to shape—graduate opportunities for students. My essay is an overview of various North American programs that offer doctoral-level work in women's studies. Highlighting several types of program models, I focus on curricular features, history, and other aspects of program design. My capsule account draws upon program materials and follow-up conversations. I discuss only programs that designate themselves "women's studies." Taking self-definition as a separate issue in itself, I do not include here doctoral programs in gender studies; nomenclature in our field is shaped by complex features, including local university cultures and broader political climates.

Questions that inform my discussion include: Do programs see women's studies as a discipline in itself? What blend of interdisciplinary and discipline-based work do they require? How do they shape any core or foundational courses? Do doctoral programs call for comprehensive examinations, and how is that requirement organized? What professional development activities are offered? Is there a link to activism? This largely informational account will be useful, I hope, to colleagues who seek to establish doctoral programs of some kind in their own institutions.

Graduate work in women's studies at the master's level is widespread across the United States and Canada. Many universities offer M.A. degrees, or M.A. concentrations, or M.A. minors, or certificates in conjunction with M.A. degrees in a discipline.[1] Doctoral programs sometimes arise from existing M.A. programs. Ph.D. programs also may emerge as part of a package when creating a new graduate program or may trace their genesis to the establishment of research institutes. There is no one institutional recipe for establishing a program of doctoral work in women's studies.

As of this writing, the models for Ph.D. study are (1) an independent study program, (2) freestanding programs in women's studies, (3) interdepartmental and collaborative degrees, offered jointly with a discipline, (4) consortium arrangements, (5) graduate minors in conjunction with main field for Ph.D. work, and (6) certificate links.

Early Innovation: An Independent Study Program

The pioneer of doctoral opportunities in women's studies may well be the Union Institute. The Union Institute was established in the 1960s as a flexible, tutorial-based program for adult learners. Doctoral work, under the aegis of the College of Graduate Studies, dates back to 1970 and is rooted in individual program design and innovative program delivery; students design their own research concentration, work with affiliating faculty, and chair their own doctoral committees. Women's studies is one "area of emphasis" within the College of Graduate Studies, and students can receive a Ph.D. in multi/interdisciplinary studies "with an emphasis in women's studies."

There is no set curriculum in women's studies, and there are no core course requirements. All students attend an introductory institute colloquium, "peer day" meetings, and residential seminars. The "peer day" requirement calls for two students to meet to develop a course outline for a one-day event, which they then evaluate. Over the course of doctoral study, every student participates in three five-day residential seminars, which take place across the United States and also have taken place in England and Japan. Faculty propose the topics for these seminars, many of which focus on women's studies and feminist issues.

The program material describes the combination of flexibility and coherence as the heart of the institute's philosophy: "All doctoral work at The Union Institute rests on four cornerstones. It is interdisciplinary; it incorporates an awareness of its social impact; it fosters a mingling of theory and practice; and it includes formal considerations of personal growth." In line with these principles, all students serve in internships. Based on a proposal developed by the individual learner and a supervisor, the internship is a minimum of 500 hours and equivalent to three months of full-time study. The internship can take place anywhere. While the graduate program has its headquarters in Cincinnati, Ohio, other sites offer opportunities to students. The Union Institute Center for Women, located in Washington, D.C., aims to bring together scholars with community women.

The Union Institute brochure about its "doctoral program with an emphasis in women's studies" lists seventeen faculty members in women's studies from a wide range of disciplines. While faculty members are based at universities across the United States, they meet face to face and via teleconferencing. When students shape their women's studies doctoral committees, they call not only on program faculty but also on other scholars and activists who serve as adjunct faculty members and mentors; additionally, Union Institute graduates and current learners serve on committees.

Freestanding Doctoral Programs

The three North American universities that offer freestanding Ph.D.s in women's studies are Emory University, Clark University, and York University. Emory University began its Ph.D. program in 1991. There are thirty-four Ph.D. students currently working their way through program requirements, four of whom are finishing their dissertations and are now on the job market. Two students have completed doctoral work. Paula Greenfield Washington wrote a dissertation entitled "Charismatic Leadership, Gender, and Corporate Culture: A Study of Executive Officers and Their Senior Management Teams." She has a position at Emory teaching graduate and undergraduate courses on feminist theory and on women and leadership. Isa D. Williams wrote "Father/Daughter Relationship: An Investigation of the Socioeconomic Impact on Career Choice." She has a position at Agnes Scott College.

Students pursue doctoral work through the Emory Institute for Women's Studies, with a core women's studies graduate faculty of nine, and another sixty associated faculty, drawn from across the humanities and social sciences. Strictly a Ph.D. program, it aims to prepare students to be teachers and researchers in women's studies. The program prospectus describes the Ph.D. curriculum as focusing on the study of women, gender, and feminist theory "with an emphasis on grounding in a traditional discipline, interdisciplinary study, and comparative theoretical and empirical perspectives." Students design their own curriculum in close consultation with a faculty committee and are strongly encouraged to take a set of courses in the discipline most closely aligned with their individual interests. Coursework requirements call for all students to take a seminar in feminist theory, as well as an introductory course on feminist approaches with guest lecturers from the core faculty in various disciplines. Comprehensive examinations are based on reading lists developed with a faculty adviser. While there is no set bibliography, the exam contains a general section on feminist theory and the history of feminist thought and also a section based on the student's dissertation area.

The close connection of the Ph.D. program to the Emory Institute of Women's Studies facilitates student access to resources, which include a colloquium series and conferences. In addition the institute sponsors professional development activities for students, notably job and publishing workshops. All doctoral students at Emory are required to complete a week-long course for prospective teaching assistants; there is also a separate workshop on issues in teaching women's studies.

The freestanding, interdisciplinary graduate Women's Studies Program at Clark University, established in 1992, draws on Clark's tradition of curricular innovation. It, too, is strictly a doctoral-level program, and fifteen students are currently enrolled. (Students earn an M.A., but only en route to the doctorate.) The program's first Ph.D., Angela Bowen, will receive her degree in 1997 for her dissertation "Audre Lorde, Life and Politics"; she now has a tenure-track job at the University of California, Long Beach.

Clark University's prospectus phrases the goals of its Ph.D. program in this way, "to provide a foundation in women's studies as an integrated, cohesive discipline and, at the same time, to enable students to gain competence in focused segments of that discipline." The curriculum is organized as core courses in women's studies combined with courses in an interdisciplinary area. Core courses include a proseminar, a team-taught, cross-disciplinary course in the foundations of feminist inquiry and methodology, and a graduate research colloquium. Students also are expected to acquire "in-depth proficiency" by taking seminars and courses in one of three interdisciplinary areas: (1) geography, environment, and development; (2) language, literature, and the arts; and (3) history, psychology, and society. A student with other interdisciplinary interests may formulate a different program of study to complement the core courses. Clark's focus on "interdisciplinary areas" contrasts with Emory's "grounding in a traditional discipline."

Clark Ph.D. candidates are required to take an oral comprehensive examination before embarking on their dissertation proposal. Before this, they are required to write a qualifying master's paper. For the Ph.D. comprehensive exam a student selects three fields: one broadly interdisciplinary and two discipline based; these fields may be related to the dissertation topic but need not necessarily be. Students work with advisory committees to develop the three fields, and the exams are individually tailored. The format for comprehensive exams issues from the belief that, while women's studies has indeed become a discipline in itself, students can benefit from having some experience with the methods and philosophical cohesion of other disciplines.

The program prides itself on a climate of spirited interdisciplinary exchange. More than thirty faculty members teach regularly in women's studies, drawing on teaching and research expertise from across the humanities and from areas such as geography, the social sciences, and international development. The doctoral program at Clark grew out of an active and long-standing women's studies program, which itself forms part of a decade-old Women's Studies Consortium in Worcester, linked as well to Boston and Amherst area colleges, universities, and women's research centers. Graduate women's studies students at Clark are closely involved in program governance.

The Graduate Programme in Women's Studies at York University admitted its first students for M.A. and Ph.D. study in January 1992 and now numbers seventy students, thirty-seven of whom are pursuing doctoral work. A student will complete her doctoral requirements in 1997 and will be awarded the first women's studies Ph.D. in Canada.

The York doctoral program aims to embody interdisciplinarity, and does not require a discipline-based concentration apart from women's studies. Requirements for the Ph.D. in women's studies call for students to select from among five core half-courses before moving on to take a variety of elective and cross-listed courses. The core half-courses are women's history, women and culture, gender and public policy, feminist theory, and feminist methodology. The program faculty numbers sixty, drawn from the humanities, social sciences, fine arts, environmental studies, and the law school. (There is no linkage yet to the sciences—a notable curricular lack at York, as indeed at most other universities surveyed for this article.)

Ph.D. students in women's studies at York University are required to complete a comprehensive examination with written and oral components. Each student is responsible for a general field reading list and also for a specialization list that relates to, but is not too narrowly tied to, the dissertation topic. There has been considerable, sustained, and fruitful discussion about whether students should select readings for the general field list from titles proposed by the program or whether each student should tailor a reading list in consultation with a chosen comprehensive examination committee. Discussions link closely to issues of discipline formation in women's studies and concerns about canonicity. There are questions about breadth and also about possibilities of common ground: "How can we ensure that students engage with both the humanities and the social sciences, and also draw on other areas as they learn to produce new knowledge in Women's Studies? Are there some books and articles that we believe everyone would do well to know about by the time they finish their degrees?" (Shteir 1996, 7). At this point, students select titles for the general field section of the comprehensive examination from areas such as feminist classics, public policy, women's history, and feminist pedagogy. Students work closely with their comprehensive examination committee to define the issues and underlying questions that generate the choice of titles for their reading lists. Models for the comprehensive examination are currently under review.

The primary focus of York's doctoral program is feminist scholarship. While there is interest in developing a practicum or ways to bring together student research and community projects, no plans are yet in place. The program has a designated representative to the National Action Committee, a cross-Canada feminist umbrella group. York's Graduate Programme in Women's Studies works hard to create a vibrant culture for students. All students attend an annual seminar series in which faculty members present research, and topics of professional development for students are also discussed. The program has sponsored two conferences to date: "Celebrating Mary Wollstonecraft" and "Graduate Women's Studies: Visions and Realities." A collection of essays arising from the May 1995 York conference, *Graduate Women's Studies: Visions and Realities,* was recently published (Shteir 1996). Many students participate in activities organized by the Centre for Feminist Research. The program welcomes both full-time and part-time students, and course scheduling acknowledges the diverse realities of student lives.

York University, a large university with a history of interdisciplinarity and innovation, has been offering undergraduate women's studies courses since the early 1970s. Undergraduate women's studies programs in three liberal arts colleges, as well as feminist courses in many other areas, offer graduate students in women's studies opportunities for teaching assistantships. York University is currently consolidating the graduate program, undergraduate programs, the Centre for Feminist Research, the Nellie Langford Rowell Women's Studies Library, and the journal *Canadian Woman Studies/les cahiers de la femme* into an innovative pan-university School of Women's Studies.

Soon, the list of freestanding M.A. and Ph.D. programs will add the University of Washington; their proposal is currently under review by the graduate school. The University of Washington has set fall 1998 as their target date for enrolling the first students. They are formulating several options for students, including a master's degree, geared primarily to students whose goal is to enhance their professional careers; a Ph.D. for students who already have an M.A. or equivalent; and an M.A./Ph.D. for students holding a B.A. (or the equivalent). Plans currently being proposed call for M.A./Ph.D. students in women studies[2] to take foundational courses in feminist histories, theory, and methods. In addition, students would select a discipline of concentration or cognate field.

The proposal for a graduate program in women studies at the University of Washington developed out of twenty-five years of women studies teaching. A women studies program began there in 1971, and a B.A. degree in women studies has been offered since 1992. They also offer a graduate certificate in women studies (see the discussion of certificate programs below). The undergraduate women studies unit was recently approved for change in status from a program to a department. Ten tenure-track faculty members in women studies are the core complement for the undergraduate and graduate programs in women studies. While there are many other affiliate and adjunct faculty from departments across the College of Arts and Sciences, the core faculty for women studies is an important feature of this graduate proposal because it ensures that academic and administrative governance of the graduate program sits in the hands of faculty whose primary appointment, and hence primary time commitment, is to this unit.

Interdepartmental and Collaborative Models

The University of Michigan offers an interdepartmental Ph.D. that combines women's studies with a student-selected discipline. There are now eight students in joint doctoral programs in women's studies and psychology and in women's studies and English, and a proposal is underway for a joint degree in women's studies and history. The director of the women's studies program chairs an interdisciplinary doctoral committee, with a representative from each participating department. This committee oversees all stages of a student's work.

Joint doctoral students take a course on advanced research and three required courses in women's studies, choosing among courses in feminist theory, on approaches to feminist scholarship in the humanities and/or in the social sciences, or on women of color. They also take nine additional hours of women's studies and cross-listed courses. One part of the preliminary examination calls for building on research completed in the advanced research seminar and defending a revised seminar paper to a three-person committee approved by the interdisciplinary program committee. Each student is assigned a faculty adviser who is affiliated with both the women's studies program and the student's other department. Each doctoral student has access to a one-year teaching fellowship in women's studies.

Women's studies at the University of Michigan, dating back to the early 1970s, offers an undergraduate concentration and an energetic and varied range of programs, projects, and academic resources, including a journal edited by graduate students as a forum for feminist graduate research. More than forty faculty members, with research and teaching interests covering a broad disciplinary and interdisciplinary range, affiliate with women's studies. The women's studies program has a central emphasis on women of color and actively recruits students and faculty of color. It also offers a graduate certificate (see the discussion of certificate programs below).

At the University of Toronto, the Graduate Collaborative Program in Women's Studies, begun in 1994, calls on the resources of a large discipline-based university that has a long history of undergraduate offerings in women's studies. Nineteen graduate units from across the humanities, social sciences, and life sciences have agreed to collaborate to offer opportunity for M.A. and Ph.D. study. Students fulfill admission and degree requirements for both a "home" department and the Graduate Collaborative Women's Studies Program. The graduate degree carries a notation of specialization in women's studies. There currently are eighteen M.A. and twenty-nine Ph.D. students in this program.

The Graduate Collaborative Women's Studies Program offers one required core course on scholarly and theoretical approaches to women's studies. Entitled the Philosophical Foundations of Women's Studies, this course focuses on the philosophical questions raised by interdisciplinary women's studies scholarship and on the use of feminist methodologies in specific disciplines. Doctoral students also participate in a coordinated-research seminar, usually in the year they are preparing their dissertation proposal. Since this institutional model draws on courses taught through collaborating units, students have access to more than one hundred courses taught by more than ninety faculty members. The program director has referred to the "exceptional intellectual commitment of the faculty to Women's Studies as a scholarly and pedagogical field" (Armatage 1996, 12).

After a decade of discussion and lobbying, the University of Toronto model emerged as a solution to several institutional restrictions. A disadvantage is that students in the interdisciplinary Graduate Collaborative Program in Women's Studies must be admitted first into a discipline, satisfying admissions criteria there. This routing makes it difficult for undergraduate majors in women's studies at the University of Toronto to gain admission to their own graduate program. The collaborative program, however, may provide an advantageous mix of credentials for the student who specifically seeks a disciplinary base for future teaching.

The Consortium Model

Linkage among neighboring and neighborly institutions can offer opportunities to both faculty and students who want to pursue women's studies work at the doctoral level. The Graduate Consortium in Women's Studies at Radcliffe College does not itself award the Ph.D., but it offers courses that can be applied toward doctoral degrees at participating institutions. This creative design dates back to "a conversation among friends in 1988" and began formally in the 1992–93 academic year (Perry 1996, 18). Students from participating institutions receive credit at their own institution for their work in the Graduate Consortium. The consortium-participating institutions are Boston College, Brandeis University, Harvard Divinity School, Harvard Graduate School of Arts and Sciences, Harvard Graduate School of Education, Massachusetts Institute of Technology, Northeastern University, and Tufts University. While the program is open to all graduate students, it gives priority to doctoral students.

The Graduate Consortium has a multipronged mission: "graduate education, faculty development, research advancement, institutional change, and community-building" (Fall 1996, 8). Courses accepted by the consortium promote cross-disciplinary work by specifically drawing together faculty from different disciplinary locations. The team-teaching course model is preceded by collaborative course development and review. In 1995–96 three teaching teams were developed and taught these consortium courses: Narratives of Kinship in Industrializing Societies: Literary and Ethnographic Approaches; Gender, Representation, and Social Control; and Feminist Perspectives in Research: Interdisciplinary Practice in the Study of Gender. The teaching teams were made up of eight faculty members from seven disciplines. Enrollment was forty-three students, more than half of whom were in doctoral programs.

The consortium model has attracted the attention of women's studies practitioners at four Arizona universities working to establish a statewide Ph.D. These universities already work together; program administrators meet regularly, and the four programs jointly sponsor a yearly pedagogical workshop for faculty. Given the long timeline for initiating and implementing such matters within the state university system, it may well take until the next century for their vision to become a reality. They would like to start with a feminist "summer camp" for Ph.D. students, staffed with senior scholars in women's studies and including an interdisciplinary reading group.

Graduate Minors in Conjunction with Main Field for Ph.D. Work

Indiana University offers a Ph.D. minor in women's studies that draws on rich multidisciplinary faculty resources and builds on the university's long history of women's studies offerings. The Ph.D. minor consists of four courses from a list approved by the women's studies program. All students are required to take a graduate program course surveying contemporary research in women's studies in either the social and behavioral sciences or in the humanities. They have six core faculty and more than thirty-five affiliated graduate faculty. The program does not itself require an examination, but a Ph.D. minor adviser may be invited to attend a student's oral qualifying examination within their major field. Indiana University is working toward developing a doctoral program in gender studies to be offered through women's studies.

At the University of Minnesota, the Center for Advanced Feminist Studies (CAFS) provides opportunity for M.A. and Ph.D. students to pursue a graduate minor in feminist studies. The women's studies department is proposing a Ph.D. in feminist studies to the university; the review and approval processes are currently underway. The graduate minor combines interdisciplinary feminist work with competency in feminist method in a student's specific field of study. Doctoral students take a course on feminist research and writing in addition to the core course on feminist theory and method and eight credits of electives required for all CAFS graduate students. Formally affiliated with many departments, CAFS offers integrated interdisciplinary courses in discipline-based "home" departments. Admission is contingent on prior acceptance to a degree-granting department. Nearly seventy faculty members have graduate examining status, and a CAFS faculty adviser sits on a student's home department examining committee and mediates departmental requirements with the student's feminist scholarly direction. The Center for Advanced Feminist Studies developed out of the women's studies department at the University of Minnesota. As an interdisciplinary research unit, it sponsors many conferences, research projects, and colloquia, welcomes visiting scholars, and fosters the professional development of graduate students through teaching, internships, and other means.

Graduate Certificates

Graduate Certificates in women's studies are offered at many universities and serve several purposes. At Emory University, for example, Ph.D. students in programs other than doctoral women's studies also may work toward a certificate in women's studies. The certificate program draws upon women's studies graduate courses, along with other features of Emory's doctoral program. At the University of Washington, a graduate certificate in women studies was put in place in the early 1990s to offer students enrolled in a graduate program the opportunity to receive recognition for graduate-level courses taken on women's studies topics. It has served institutionally as a bridge for the establishment of a freestanding graduate program in women studies at the University of Washington. Courses on feminist theory and feminist method that began under the rubric of the graduate certificate in women studies will become foundational courses for their emergent graduate program.

The University of Michigan also offers a graduate certificate program, with forty-one students enrolled as of fall 1996. Based on fifteen credits of coursework, the graduate certificate can be combined with either a master's or doctoral degree. It combines required interdisciplinary women's studies courses with approved electives from other areas; strongly recommended is a course on women of color, such as Feminist Scholarship on Women of Color. All graduate women's studies certificate students pursue independent research with a faculty member; there are more than sixty-five affiliating faculty.

At the City University of New York the women's studies certificate program complements existing doctoral programs by offering students an additional specialization in women's studies. Once accepted into a doctoral program in The Graduate School, a student may apply for the certificate. Students take twelve credits of required and elective courses. The required proseminar in women's studies, for example, focuses on history and methodologies in women's studies and explores how feminist scholarship relates to traditional disciplinary paradigms.

Emerging Programs

Among emerging programs, or programs nearing formal establishment, the proposal for a Ph.D. in women's studies at the University of Iowa, stalled for some time because of internal university politics, received approval from the faculty senate in spring 1997. The proposal goes next to the Iowa State Board of Regents.

The Iowa proposal, drawn up in 1994, was initially for a Ph.D. in feminist studies. Many discussions about nomenclature of course preceded such a decision. Florence E. Babb, chair of Women's Studies, has reflected on the possibilities in this way:

Would it be a Ph.D. in Women's Studies, in line with the name of our [undergraduate] programme? Would it be Gender Studies to signal that we want to understand gender as a relationship and socially constructed?, or Feminist Theory to attract the "serious" students? We settled on Feminist Studies because it suggests our interest in taking a feminist perspective in any number of directions. . . . Moreover, we felt it signaled our political commitment to feminism as a movement as well as a scholarly philosophy. (Babb 1996, 42)

By the fall of 1995, however, the university administration persuaded the women's studies program to designate the proposed Ph.D. program "women's studies." The argument, accepted reluctantly, was that the name "women's studies" would be less alarming for the Iowa State Board of Regents than "feminist studies."

Plans for a Ph.D. program in women's studies at the University of Iowa build upon an undergraduate program that began in the early 1970s and eventually came to offer an undergraduate minor. There are six faculty joint appointments to their undergraduate program in women's studies. Because one university in Iowa has approved a B.A. in women's studies, and another an M.A., the planning committee at the University of Iowa made the strategic decision to go directly for a doctoral degree program.

The proposed University of Iowa Ph.D. curriculum calls for students to take core courses as well as courses in a "diversity" component. Designated core courses cover theory and research, the history of feminism, and feminist pedagogy. The women's studies committee is planning for a required practicum. They will require doctoral candidates to take part in a seminar for students writing dissertations. In addition, students will be required to take a cluster of courses in a single discipline; this is meant to give them methodological strength. The University of Iowa's emphasis on a cluster of disciplinary courses reflects a strong Ph.D. specialization in feminist anthropology, which is housed within the anthropology department. This degree gives students the latitude of a feminist program within a disciplinary department, while also providing grounding in the theory and method of a single field.

After twenty-five years of work, women's studies teachers at the University of Iowa want to see their hopes realized. Many questions, however, continue to preoccupy them with regard to an emergent Ph.D. program in women's studies. Florence E. Babb highlights some of these questions: "What admissions policy will encourage a diverse pool of applications for a very small number of openings? How can our faculty avoid burn-out when we have promised new core graduate courses, close advising of doctoral students, etc., and we are already exhausted before we begin? Can we maintain a commitment to both theory and practice, interdisciplinary scholarship and disciplinary strength?" (Babb 1996, 45).

Questions such as these have wider applicability within the community of graduate women's studies faculty and administrators. We know that women's studies' institution builders in the academy have learned to keep a sharp eye out for opportunities. Working from the margins toward the center, juggling administrative lines, following up on long-standing informal connections, women's studies faculty members have shown immense administrative creativity.

One strand in the history of many programs discussed here is that the impetus for graduate program development usually has come from faculty who focus on shaping a future for the next generation of women's studies students but who themselves were not trained in women's studies. We must seek out ways to offer program development for faculty. Are we organizing faculty development seminars that highlight not only pedagogy but also women's studies content? Among the graduate women's studies programs surveyed for this article, the Graduate Consortium in Women's Studies at Radcliffe notably emphasizes the value of its course offerings not only for graduate students but also toward faculty development for prospective teachers and for participating seminar leaders as well. If we are aiming to shape women's studies as a discipline and to train students who will take this new field into the future, then faculty, too, need to further develop and refine their tools.

Each new addition to the growing roster of doctoral configurations in women's studies sharpens the profile of women's studies as a field of study. We envisage possibilities and work with colleagues to make curriculum and governance real within the features of our academic home bases. In so doing—when we legitimize, institutionalize, professionalize, and credentialize women's studies—we act to define our often diverse understandings of this new area of knowledge. Certain questions continue to inform our planning: What are the benefits of a doctoral degree in women's studies? Will there be jobs enough for our students in academic, governmental, and public policy arenas? What work can we be doing at local, regional, and national levels to keep the climate for interdisciplinary and pioneering work fresh and receptive? How can we work, and work better together, to shape strong programs? These questions surely keep us young and active and thinking on our feminist feet. Let us celebrate the questions that we ask, along with our discomfort at answers that are too easy or too pat. Then let us move on to celebrate what we have accomplished to date and to work to shape agendas for doctoral programs in women's studies for the next decade as well as for the long-term future.

PROGRAMS DISCUSSED

Clark University, Women's Studies Program, 950 Main Street, Worcester, MA 01610-1477, Jody Emel, director; tel: (508) 793-7358; fax: (508) 793-7780; e-mail: jemel@vax.clarku.edu

City University of New York, Women's Studies Certificate Program, Room 40-04, Grace Building; postal address: 33 West 42nd Street, New York, NY 10036-8099, Electa Arenal, director; tel: (212) 642-2247; fax: (212) 642-1978; e-mail: esmall@email.gc.cuny.edu

Emory University, Institute for Women's Studies, 301 South Callaway Center, Atlanta, GA 30322, Robyn Fivush, director; tel: (404) 727-0096; fax: (404) 727-4659; e-mail: lloyd@emory.edu

Graduate Consortium in Women's Studies, Radcliffe College, 10 Garden Street, Cambridge, MA 02138, Renee Fall, coordinator; tel: (617) 496-3022; fax: (617) 496-0363; e-mail: GCWS@radcliffe.edu; http://www.radcliffe.edu. GCWS/

Indiana University, Women's Studies Program, Memorial Hall East 129, Bloomington, IN 47405-2201, Judith A. Allen, director; tel: (812) 855-0101; fax: (812) 855-4869; e-mail: wost@indiana.edu

The Union Institute, 440 East McMillan Street, Cincinnati, OH 45206-1947; tel: (513) 861-6400; fax: (513) 861-0779; e-mail: admissions@tui.edu; http://www.tui.edu

University of Arizona, Department of Women's Studies, Communication 108, P.O. Box 210025, Tucson, AZ 85721-0025, Judy Temple, director; tel: (520) 621-7338; fax: (520) 621-1533; e-mail: jtemple@ccit.arizona.edu

University of Iowa, Women's Studies Program, 202 Jefferson Bldg., Iowa City, IA 52242-1418, Florence E. Babb, chair; tel: (319) 335-0322; fax: (319) 335-0653

University of Michigan, Women's Studies Program, 234 West Engineering Bldg., Ann Arbor, MI 48109-1092, Sidonie Smith, director; tel: (313) 763-2047; fax: (313) 647-4943; e-mail: jmackey@umich.edu

University of Minnesota, Center for Advanced Feminist Studies, 496 Ford Hall, 224 Church Street S.E., Minneapolis, MN 55455, Helen Longino, director of graduate studies; tel: (612) 624-6310; fax: (612) 624-3573; e-mail: cafs@tc.umn.edu

University of Toronto, Graduate Collaborative Program in Women's Studies, 2 Sussex Avenue, Room 232, Toronto, Ontario, Canada, M5S 1J5, Kay Armatage, director; tel: (416) 978-3668; fax: (416) 978-5503; e-mail: grad.womenstudies@utoronto.ca; http:/www.utoronto.ca/womens

University of Washington, Women Studies, B110 Padelford, Box 354345, Seattle, WA 98195-4345, Shirley J. Yee, director; tel: (206) 543-6900; fax: (206) 685-9555

York University, Graduate Programme in Women's Studies, S718 Ross Building, 4700 Keele Street, North York, Ontario, Canada M3J 1P3, Ann B. Shteir, director; tel: (416) 736-5607; fax: (416) 650-8075; e-mail: gradwmst @yorku.ca

NOTES

1. The *Guide to Graduate Work in Women's Studies* prepared for the National Women's Studies Association by Karen Kidd and Ande Spencer was inevitably incomplete by its date of issue and did not include Canadian universities.
2. Although the field has almost universally adopted the apostrophe *s,* the University of Washington prefers "women studies." When the time came to name the program, then acting director Mary L. Eysenbach chose women studies, commenting, "the program is not exclusively by and for women; besides, we do not refer to Black's studies or Chicano's studies."

REFERENCES

Armatage, Kay. 1996. "Collaborating on Women's Studies: The University of Toronto Model." In Ann B. Shteir, ed., *Graduate Women's Studies: Visions and Realities,* pp. 10–17. North York, Ontario: Inanna Publications and Education, Inc.

Babb, Florence E. 1996. "Graduate Women's Studies in the Heartland: Breaking Ground for a Ph.D. Programme in Women's Studies at the University of Iowa." In Ann B. Shteir, ed., *Graduate Women's Studies: Visions and Realities,* pp. 41–45. North York, Ontario: Inanna Publications and Education, Inc.

Fall, Renee. 1996. "Graduate Consortium in Women's Studies at Radcliffe College, 1995–96 Annual Report." Radcliffe College, 22 July.

Kidd, Karen, and Ande Spencer, eds. 1994. *Guide to Graduate Work in Women's Studies,* second edition. College Park, MD: National Women's Studies Association.

Perry, Ruth. 1996. "Inventing a Feminist Institution: An Informal History of the Graduate Consortium in Women's Studies at Radcliffe." In Ann B. Shteir, ed., *Graduate Women's Studies: Visions and Realities,* pp. 18–25. North York, Ontario: Inanna Publications and Education, Inc.

Shteir, Ann B. 1996. "Making the Vision a Reality: York University's Graduate Programme in Women's Studies." In Ann B. Shteir, ed., *Graduate Women's Studies: Visions and Realities,* pp. 2–9. North York, Ontario: Inanna Publications and Education, Inc.

———, ed. 1996. *Graduate Women's Studies: Visions and Realities.* North York, Ontario: Inanna Publications and Education, Inc.

Ann B. Shteir *is associate professor of humanities and director of the Graduate Programme in Women's Studies at York University, Toronto, Canada. She edited* Graduate Women's Studies: Visions and Realities *and is the author* *of* Cultivating Women, Cultivating Science: Flora's Daughters and Botany in England, 1760 to 1860, *which was awarded the 1996 Joan Kelly Memorial Prize in Women's History.*

Copyright ©1997 by Ann B. Shteir.

"Promises to Keep": Trends in Women's Studies Worldwide

Florence Howe

In 1994 I was invited by Vina Mazumdar, emerita director of the Centre for Women's Development Studies in New Delhi, India, to give the annual J. P. Naik Memorial Lecture. J. P. Naik was the father of women's studies in India. He urged that educated women and men had "promises to keep," responsibilities to assure the education of others. He believed in the significance of research as a strategy for change, even when political power would seemingly silence all change. He dared Vina Mazumdar to open the center in the mid-1970s by saying, "Good work that needs to be done never gets held up for lack of resources, only for lack of determination." He was also fond of telling Vina Mazumdar that "men will never be liberated until women are liberated."

The essay that follows, revised for publication here in February 1997, is based on the lecture delivered in December 1994. The Centre for Women's Development Studies has published the original text of the lecture as a monograph.

I come to this topic from thirty years in women's studies in the United States, from fifty-two national reports on women's studies from individual countries, from my own travels to Japan, Korea, Argentina, Australia, India, and various countries in Europe, as well as from participation in a score of international conferences over the past fifteen years.[1] By now, women's studies in its various forms may be found in scores of countries on every continent, among thousands of scholar/activists, and millions of students. I believe that the development of women's studies as an arm of the worldwide women's movement is as important for the future of world peace as disarmament, and as important for the health of the planet's air, water, trees, and other resources as the ecology movement itself.

Education is a human right, and women as well as men need an education free of gender bias and containing an understanding of women's history and culture. We know that women who have had such education not only understand the world's fragility—that ethnic wars and the misuse of the planet's resources will destroy the world for generations to come—but also understand the power of women to change not only their own personal lives but the social order.

The connections between the women's movement and worldwide movements for peace have been evident not only in the last three decades but in the early years of this century, when peace and suffrage were twin goals that women's movement leaders discussed and worked to establish. In our time, I see as additional goals a woman's right to control her body, including the right to bear children as well as the right not to, and the right to equal opportunities in employment for equal pay, with provisions for childcare. Central to these goals and movements has been the rise of women's studies. It is not possible to ignore the body of knowledge now available even to those who would want to turn the clock back, to urge women to leave the workforce, for example, and care for a single child or possibly two, and ignore the world's turmoil. Indeed, what I see happening worldwide now is different: the march of feminist women into public office via politics.[2] And again, I see this connected to the worldwide study of history, and the energy released by knowledge about women that ends their invisibility—individually and collectively. As the American historian Mary Beard said fifty years ago, but as some of us understand today palpably, women have been a "force" in history.

I read the worldwide backlash against individual women, and against feminism in general, as evidence of the strength of this actual and potential force. Even the Republican right wing in the United States—ready to promote prayers in the schools and orphanages for indigent children of mothers under the age of eighteen or twenty—will not take a formal stand on the issue of abortion, since it affects women of all social classes. It remains to be seen whether women inside and outside the women's movement can rally to support indigent women and children as the Republican right moves to end what they are calling "the welfare state."

Trends in women's studies worldwide connect us despite regional and national differences, even despite significant differences in the forms of our educational institutions. These trends connect us even over time and space, as I was recently reminded by reading *Changing Lives*, a group of essays by Asian pioneers in women's studies.[3]

If one begins with the obvious question, Where did women's studies come from? there are striking commonalties. Again and again, I hear them embedded in the echoes of worldwide experiences. Characteristically, two types of "passages"—moments of awareness or a deepening in consciousness inspired by experience—move faculty into women's studies; both are visions from the rocks of inequality. The first I shall call personal, the second, intellectual or work related.

The personal passage into women's studies typically narrates a critical experience that makes visible the inequality between professional husband and professional wife. In an essay in *Changing Lives*, Li Xiaojiang, director of the Center for Women's Studies at Zhengzhou University and professor of Chinese literature and language, describes her life as a young girl, outachieving all the boys in her class, working hard at studies and sports and citizenry, and succeeding. But then, after gaining a significant academic position, she marries, has a child, and finds herself, unlike her husband, expected to do all the housework and child care, as well as her academic work, while he does only his academic work. How is she to deal with this? She writes most poignantly of her conflict—her love and her burden:

> As long as I was unwilling to part with my husband and family, I had to assume all the consequences. . . . I was forced to . . . carry a load which would be twice as much as that usually carried by a man.
> All modern women are doomed to fall into such a trap. Most are wallowing in it silently and in a docile manner. . . . But the question baffles me: why are women alone made to suffer in this manner?[4]

Li Xiaojiang eventually asks her husband to share some chores, but she goes on to the main point of consciousness for women's studies pioneers:

> In an age that boasts equality between the sexes, why do women lead a painfully laborious and depressing life? . . `. Despite the fact that women's inherent status and value have been completely obliterated by the writers of history and society, I harbor the hope that my academic studies may contribute to the rediscovery of that status and value.[5]

It is a painfully familiar story, with many variations. I have my own: back at the end of the 1960s, in Baltimore, Maryland, my former husband and I drove off in two directions each morning to our two different teaching jobs and drove back in the evening. One evening I forgot to pick up the laundry, and my husband charged me fiercely the next morning with negligence. I apologized and said I'd remember that evening. But all day long something troubled me about the morning's scene, even about my humble apology, for the laundry lay in *his* direction, not mine. Nevertheless, I picked up the laundry that evening, and presented it to him, with the following statement: "This is the last time I will pick up the laundry. It occurred to me today that the shop lies in your direction, not mine. You could pick up the laundry far more easily. Further, the laundry is yours, not mine—I wash mine by hand—and we both use the bed and bath linen. It's now your turn to deal with the laundry." Change hardly transpired overnight. For most of that year I bought new sheets and towels, for my husband wouldn't at first take the laundry in, and I kept my word.

The second passage to women's studies is an intellectual or work-related passage. My own came from several sources, one of which I will describe to you. In a 1968 study of sex-role stereotypes, male and female clinical psychologists were asked to check off on a bipolar scale of 132 items those that described the "healthy American male," the "healthy American female," and the "healthy American person." Years later, the findings are still shocking: the items checked for "male" and "person" were identical in every respect; those checked for "female" were entirely different. Thus, women were "religious"; men and persons were "not religious." Thus, men and persons were "rational" and "not emotional"; women were "irrational" and "emotional."[6]

I'll return again to *Changing Lives,* in which there are several examples of the ways intellectual effort has inspired consciousness. Sometimes these moments are painful. In one of them, at the end of her research project, when Malavikar Karlekar tells the sweepers who had been her subjects that "they had been of considerable help" to her, one of them responds: "You will write your book, but what will happen to us?"[7] In Korea, when Cho Hyoung presents a research proposal on poor urban women, a senior male sociologist remarks, "Why should a promising young sociologist like you spend so much time and energy on such trivial matters as women and poverty?" "Gradually," Cho Hyoung writes, she "became grateful to this man who had unintentionally prepared me to face the anti-feminist world."[8] It is, of course, not only an antifeminist world but often antireformist and antidemocratic, especially with regard to poor women or women of different races or ethnicities. These passages make wonderful stories—of blinders removed from vision, of what we have been calling re-visioning, and, of course, of idealism. These are features of women's studies worldwide.

So, in fact, I have begun with my conclusion. That though we in the West may have begun with the idea that women's studies, as an arm of the women's movement, was a strategy for changing education, it has, throughout the world, become far more than that. We've known that women's studies changes individual lives, but, and I am speaking for myself here, I have not before now understood how women's studies may turn academics and researchers into activists—that women's studies itself may galvanize a movement. At first this idea seemed strange to me, since I came to women's studies already an activist, with a decade of experience in the civil rights and antiwar movements. I had always thought of women's studies as growing out of movements. But, as I have seen, women's studies in some countries in Asia and Africa as well as in Eastern Europe has been a strategic force to energize and develop a nascent women's movement. In other words, a raised consciousness may be the cause as well as the consequence of activism.

The good news is that it is hard to find a country without some women's studies center or program just beginning, or of an age between one and twenty-five. When the planners of women's studies sessions came from the United States, Canada, and India to Copenhagen in 1980 for the United Nations' NGO (nongovernmental organization) Forum with a modest program of panels and roundtables, we hoped to be joined by perhaps fifty others; none of us expected the hundreds that flocked to major sessions and came as well to roundtables and announced their own programs. Fourteen hundred people from fifty-five countries registered in what, thanks to Vina Mazumdar's vision, became Women's Studies International: A Network and Educational Project of The Feminist Press. Joined by twenty-five women's studies programs from as many countries, Women's Studies International went on to organize panels and roundtables for Nairobi's NGO Forum in 1985 and for Beijing in 1995.

There we met with women's studies pioneers from China and Korea, from Latvia and Hungary, from Uganda, Ghana, and South Africa, from Peru and Argentina, from Turkey, Norway, Germany, France, and Russia.[9] It is difficult to think of a country without a women's studies center or an academic women's studies program of some sort. The spread of women's studies since 1985 and Nairobi has been especially rapid: we can count some ten African countries with women's studies projects or programs. Since the end of the Cold War, we can count programs in most of the countries of Eastern Europe. And, since the mid- to late 1980s, we can count mainland China, as well as Taiwan, Hong Kong, and Vietnam—all with some women's studies programs or centers. So the first trend is proliferation, the spread of women's studies worldwide, which, I have no doubt, will continue for many years to come.

These programs or centers, regardless of their geography and even their institutionalization, have three characteristics in common: they are research centered, formally or informally; they are teaching institutions, formally or informally; and they are centers of activism, again formally or informally. A fourth characteristic is not as universal as the other three, but it is growing in importance: publishing of journals or even books—again formally and independently, or informally, or through other channels. Often, one activity is more important than the others; often one activity leads the way to the others.

Significantly, I see the presence of research worldwide as more ubiquitous than teaching, which is, of course, where women's studies began in the United States. In India, Professor Naik urged the Indian Social Science Research Council (ISSRC) to study the status of women in India at a moment that coincided with the beginnings of the worldwide women's movement, following the UN meetings in Mexico City in 1975. Just as women's studies began in India with research on women, so in Russia did women's studies pioneers spend their first two years in research that challenged the newly established government's attempt to change laws regarding women's rights to education, employment, and even abortion.[10] Scandinavian women's studies centers report that they work on problems posed by politicians, bureaucrats, and other researchers, and are supported by government grants rather than the university.[11] And in the United States, Mariam K. Chamberlain at the Ford Foundation as early as the mid-1970s envisioned "centers for research on women" as adjuncts to the women's studies teaching programs on campus. There are now seventy-seven of these in the United States alone; some of them are on campuses, and one-third of them are separate nonprofit institutions like The Feminist Press in New York or the Center for Women Policy Studies in Washington, D.C., or the Centre for Women's Development Studies in New Delhi, or the Center for Women's Studies in Buenos Aires, Argentina.

In Argentina, in the late 1970s, when fascism ruled the universities as well as the nation, women's studies began in an independent NGO, composed chiefly of psychologists and other social scientists, with a program of action-oriented research.[12] In Africa the pattern for women's studies—in Botswana, Tanzania, and Nigeria, for example— begins with university faculty setting up a research group with an agenda that includes major social issues, seminars both for researchers and for dissemination, and a publishing program.[13] In Japan, where women's studies teaching is quite well established, research is now turning to a study of Japanese women, including minority women and the past two decades of feminism.[14]

Certain themes may be found in research programs worldwide. These include the need for better nationally and internationally gathered statistics and the need for more statistics-driven studies to galvanize the women's studies movement. Ubiquitous also is an emphasis on what is often called "participatory research"; the effort to design research that serves women, especially the least privileged, rather than uses them to benefit the researcher. With regard to this type of research, there are increased efforts to use research not only to effect education locally but to change public policies—to educate communities to politics and political activism. Increasingly researchers are turning to history, both the history of women in communities and nations and the history of the women's movement over the past century. Finally, there is worldwide concern about the human rights of women, and researchers are increasingly focused on violence against women in all its forms—in peace and during war. I see this renewed emphasis on human rights as one aspect of women's increasing participation in ecological struggles to preserve the trees of Africa or to provide clean water to the children of India.

As I turn to teaching, which is where my own work and the work of many women's studies pioneers in the United States began, I want to add at once that, even where there were no formal teaching programs—as in many of the independent centers that were founded off campus and outside the mainstream of university life—there were always seminars, public lectures, and the dissemination of research findings. Of course, these also teach. But worldwide, women's studies has built on research to create teaching programs, especially for college and university students, and even to create teaching programs for faculty, very often male faculty, who would not, on their own, find their way into the new research on women or into women's studies courses. And in some countries—the United States, Britain, New Zealand, and Argentina come quickly to mind—such teaching programs extend themselves into primary and secondary education and into the preparation of teachers.[15]

While undergraduate teaching programs have been women's studies' most visible form in the United States, such programs have not been exportable as such, simply because the U.S. organization of undergraduate education does not translate itself into other systems. There are now approximately 620 of these teaching programs in the United States, one-third of them offering some graduate degrees as well as undergraduate degrees. I should add that there is hardly a college in the United States that does not at least offer some courses in women's studies. (Courses are small units in the U.S. system; whereas programs or majors are what in most parts of the world would be called "courses."[16]) Almost all of the 1,800 four-year colleges and universities in the United States offer some women's studies courses;

one-third of these institutions offer programs, comparable to what one might think of as departments, but with some differences. Most of the larger programs are located in the 160 universities that offer graduate degrees as well as undergraduate degrees. The U.S. system of higher education incorporates additions to the curriculum in processes usually described as "difficult" or "complex" by those attempting to work through them. On the other hand, there is a process, and, in more than 2,000 two- and four-year colleges and universities, countless thousands of individual faculty members have been able to add countless women's studies courses to the curriculum. I remember a conversation with Vina Mazumdar many years ago, in which she said that such easy additions to the curriculum might just as easily be eliminated. Quite so, for when specialists capable of teaching such courses move from one campus to another, often the courses disappear with them, especially if there is not an organized program standing guard.

But what do women's studies programs teach? In the United States some single units—what we call courses—are arranged as interdisciplinary introductions to women's studies as an area of study. But the curriculum that follows may be disciplinary and may consist of courses in any one of fifteen or sixteen broad fields, disciplines, or interdisciplinary areas. They may range from a course called "U.S. Women Writers in the 19th Century" (cross-listed in English and women's studies) to "Women in Politics" (cross-listed in political science and women's studies) to "Women and the Family" (cross-listed, depending on emphasis, with history or sociology and women's studies), to "Women and Violence" to "Women in Developing Countries." And I am merely skimming the surface of the curriculum here. The important point is that, because of the U.S. educational structure, women's studies faculty have not thus far had to choose between "autonomy" or "integration," or between "separation" or "ghettoization" and "inclusion."

In India, as well as in most countries of the world, there are two or three strategies with which to create teaching programs, all of them difficult to achieve. Years ago Vina Mazumdar was hopeful about the institutional route through which questions on women could be appended to the degree examination in history, political science, and sociology, among other fields, thus forcing the inclusion of lectures on women through those fields. But few women's studies pioneers have been sanguine about introducing whole new degrees in women's studies into the university structure. There are at least two obstacles: the theorizing of women about such institutional strategies and, of course, an even more difficult obstacle, the patriarchal university.

I can name a few success stories, despite such obstacles and reservations. In India, for example, there are "courses" and "papers" on women, chiefly at postgraduate levels in selected departments—sociology in Bombay, political science and history in Delhi. While there are thirty-seven research units in India and twenty independent research centers, there are relatively few degree-granting teaching programs. My experience in Hyderabad, and even in Delhi, in 1994, convinced me that women's studies faculty were not especially interested in teaching programs, even at the graduate level, and were not thinking about the fact that, without teaching programs, there will not be subsequent generations of researchers in women's studies. And there seems to be no easy route—given the undergraduate system of education—to allow the adding of a new area of inquiry called women's studies.

On the other hand, in Argentina, for example, after a long hiatus outside university structures, Gloria Bonder and her colleagues in the independent Center for Women's Studies in Buenos Aires, were invited into the faculty of psychology at the University of Buenos Aires, and asked to establish an M.A. course in women's studies for practicing psychologists or others who wanted that degree. The faculty has now been invited to establish a second degree-granting program in women's studies, this one for health professionals.

One of the important elements in women's studies in the United States has been an emphasis on changing pedagogical practices in the classroom to encourage independent thinking and long-lasting integration of the content of the curriculum. In other words, feminist educators were especially aware that the passivity of women students in the classroom merely reflected and reinforced social conditioning. Much has been done to change this. When I was asked, however, to consult with Argentine educators devising a new graduate curriculum, and wanting some new pedagogical ideas, I was dismayed to learn that all of what we have been taking for granted in the United States since the mid-1970s seemed very "radical" to them.

Had I been preparing this paper a decade ago, I would have begun with activism. I would have said that the very first trend was a significant relationship between women's studies and women's movements. I would have said that women's studies has emerged and has continued to emerge from women's movements all over the world. In the United States, for example, one can date the women's movement from Betty Friedan's 1963 book, *The Feminine Mystique,* or from the founding of the National Organization for Women in 1966. While I began teaching courses in 1964 that eventually I came to see as women's studies courses, that phrase—"women's studies"—did not come into use until 1969 at the earliest, and it was somewhat later that women's studies named itself "the academic arm of the women's movement." I would say that all the programs founded before the mid-1980s—in India and Japan, in Argentina and elsewhere in Latin America, all over Western Europe, in Canada, Australia, and New Zealand, as well as in the United States—came out of women's movements.

On the other hand, programs founded since then, especially in Eastern Europe, Africa, and parts of Asia, *are—or are becoming—* women's movements. In some ways, this is interesting, baffling, exciting, and worrisome. It is interesting and exciting because, of course, those of us who have been in women's studies for twenty to thirty years know that one of the problems in India, in Canada, in parts of Europe, and in the United States is the widening separation between the women's movements and women's studies. Older women's studies programs share a trend that is potentially very dangerous: the split between the women's movement and women's studies, brought on in part by the development of highly specialized fields of scholarly inquiry and in part by what I can only call a "generation gap," differences between the activist pioneers who began women's studies and the young graduate students becoming instructors in the field. The new generation of scholar/teachers in the university often is as little aware of the history of the women's studies movement as their students. The research findings they teach, the theorizing they are often totally absorbed by, may be as remote from women's lives as the traditional male agenda has been for centuries. So, as a real trend, this is a significant worry for all of us in women's studies.

On the other hand, from reports of developing women's studies perspectives in Asian and African countries, one gets the impression of women's studies *as the women's movement,* or perhaps assuming leadership in, or teaching future leaders of, a nascent women's movement. Perhaps you understand at once why this worries me, especially in countries where all academics, researchers or teachers, would be a tiny minority of a specially privileged class: can these women's studies pioneers *be* or *become* a women's movement? In other places, for example, some countries of Latin America, women's studies practitioners have been viewed by members of some parts of the women's movement as out of touch with reality, like other academics.

Perhaps one way to begin to understand these trends is to consider what has happened in the world over the past decade. While some walls came down in Europe and in the Middle East, fiery nationalisms have begun to burn in their place and radical fundamentalisms to grow more boldly visible. Carnage and the religious right affect women even more adversely than they affect men. It is as though, since women have been traditionally the vessels of culture and the vehicles through which it is carried into the next generation, they must be the bloodiest and most brutalized victims of culture wars.

In certain environments, therefore, it is understandable that there is too much political turbulence or just plain danger for a women's movement to develop in ways that it did in the West, for example, or in India. Rather, scholars, some of them teachers as well, touched by the international movements now opened to them—as in Eastern Europe, China, parts of Africa, and the Middle East—have seized on women's studies as a relatively nonthreatening, even seemingly nonactivist form of women's movement. After all, seminars and publications are different from street demonstrations.

In some of these countries, these activists have decided to substitute the term "gender studies" for "women's studies" or "feminist studies," especially in Eastern Europe where the communists allegedly settled "the woman question" decades ago, and where the term is linked to the old order and hence anathema to the new. As Anastasia Posadskaya, formerly an economist at the Moscow Academy of Science and one of the pioneers of women's studies in Russia, tells the story, when she first mentioned "gender studies," which is what she and her colleagues determined to call their new program several years ago, she was inevitably asked, "What is this gender'?" There is no Russian word for "gender," and so she and her colleagues could describe their perspective—one we would call feminist or women's studies—under this new label "gender studies," which is how women's studies is known in Russia.[17]

Though my own experience in the United States could have told me that a publishing arm moved women's studies forward rapidly and coherently, and though I have long urged the establishment of feminist presses in many countries throughout the world, only this past year have I come to the conclusion that publishing needs to be named as the fourth essential arm of women's studies. In some ways, we've all known this: take the publications program of the women's studies unit of the Shrimati Nathibai Damodar Thackersey Women's University or *Samyit Shakti,* the original journal of the Centre for Women's Development Studies in Delhi, now known as *The Indian Journal of Women's Studies.* But there are a couple of new indicators I'd like to mention. First, with respect to Latin America, I have continued to wonder why the profile of women's studies in Latin America is not more visible, even to Latin Americans. One reason may be that there is no press, no journal that circulates through the region. On the other hand, there are new efforts, in Peru, Chile, Argentina, Mexico, to found feminist presses and even scholarly journals. In China, where women's studies began in the mid-1980s, the first major activity of Li Xiaojiang, director of the first center, was to edit and publish the *Women's Studies Series,* more than twenty volumes by and about women to be used in teaching.[18]

I want to turn now to the unfinished agenda: what are the trends that need more than naming, and not simply for their ubiquitous presence, but for other reasons?

When women's studies first began more than two decades ago in the United States, pioneers envisioned significant change in consciousness and knowledge. Women—and men—were to be reeducated in women's history. They were to rediscover the lost literature once important to various cultures. They were to rework almost a century of male-focused social science, to allow into experimental design and data the female half of the population. At the same time, since the United States is a multicultural nation, from the first, women's studies claimed that race and class, and later sexual orientation, age, and disability, also needed to be considered along with patriarchal omissions and distortions. The explosion of women's studies—both in research and teaching—was an explosion not only in consciousness and knowledge. It was as though we were following Simone de Beauvoir's message at the conclusion of *The Second Sex:* one could not change the status of women by fiat, as the Chinese or the Russians had attempted early in their separate revolutions; one had to change consciousness either first or at least at the same time.

Certainly, we seemed to have heard her message: it explained for us why, regardless of revolutionary goals, in post-revolutionary societies, women remained "the second sex." We were going to begin from the other end: changing consciousness, and more than that, producing a revolution in epistemology that some have compared to the Copernican. Feminist philosopher Elizabeth Minnich has said that one could not simply "add" the idea that the world is round to the previous idea that the world was flat; the new idea changed, indeed eradicated, the old idea—which is why it was revolutionary.[19] Similarly, the idea that women are not inferior creatures either in brain or body cannot be "added" on to the idea of women as "the second sex." Feminism displaces patriarchy—at least where it is allowed to live.

But then we come to the hard question: Where is it allowed to live? If women's studies pioneers can be faulted—and I count myself among these pioneers—it is for a failure of long-range *institutional* imagination, *strategic institutional imagination.* In the United States, we knew what *not* to do. That is, to take myself as an early strategist, I was strongly opposed to separatism, what has been called "autonomy." I knew that home economics had been a dismal failure, not only because of the limitations in its intellectual vision but also because its institutional strategy had called for separate departments, even "schools." I knew also, from a study in the 1960s of efforts to reform higher education in the United State, that separate islands of excellence called "experimental colleges," spawned by large universities themselves, had had no significant impact on the host institutions. Large, sprawling institutions were not about to "imitate" the intellectual successes of academic Edens, even when they had established these Edens in their own backyards. Further, I could see the isolation and budgetary penury suffered by Black studies departments formed as separate enclaves in response to the demands of Black students in the second half of the 1960s. And so, when I could, I recommended a very different kind of institutional model for women's studies in United States' higher education.[20]

I said, let women's studies be a strategy for change. Let women's studies form programs, not departments. Let women's studies form programs with a strong administrative center, a director, an office, a staff, a budget that will pay for faculty to teach in the program, even a budget that will pay half the salaries of faculty located half in women's studies, half in traditional departments of sociology, history, English, etc. Let women's studies expect that each year its outreach into traditional departments and into professional schools of the university will broaden and deepen until every part of the college or university has been reached and changed. Let women's studies expect also that those brave faculty within departments with a strong allegiance to women's studies will begin to transform their own discipline-based courses, and perhaps also begin to interest their colleagues in change.

Further, even as early as the middle of the 1970s, intrepid faculty members were thinking about how to change their colleagues, mostly male, mostly unacquainted with what was happening in the world of feminist scholarship. This movement, originally called "mainstreaming," gathered force in the 1980s, and has had some modest affect upon the traditional curriculum in perhaps a hundred institutions of higher education. This kind of work, slow at best, was generally paid for in the late 1970s and through the 1980s by the federal government and by private foundations, chief among them the Ford Foundation. Some of this work continues into the 1990s. But it is clear that none of it speaks to questions of long-range significant institutional change. As Cora Kaplan, formerly at Rutgers University, said at a City University of New York conference in 1994, the university has not changed at all in the twenty years we in women's studies have changed our minds and hearts. But the university in the United States has, I would add, made room for us in women's studies, and sometimes in privileged positions.[21]

Throughout the discussion of institutionalizing women's studies over the past twenty years has run the refrain of "autonomy" versus "integration." I have been one of those who claimed that neither position was tenable, that one had to have a hybrid, which I described as an interdisciplinary program inside a university, with certain ingredients—a director, an office, a budget, an approved course of study, and students earning degrees—but without the right to tenure faculty, though one might hire them either temporarily or through the cooperation of many departments in the university.[22]

What is the next step for women's studies in higher education? Or are we in the United States and elsewhere to remain as fixed in our semiautonomous/semi-integrated pattern as home economics remained as a separate department/division? And are others in the rest of the world to continue to try to change degree examinations? This question takes for granted, of course, that the male-privileged university moves forward as it always has, making room for women's studies, and that we continue to educate another generation of scholar/activists to do our work. It is certainly true that the U.S. system of higher education is uniquely suited to absorbing change from without *without* changing itself. Despite the presence of over 600 women's studies programs, the campus moves on as before, having "absorbed" or "added" women's studies along with such new areas as African studies, African-American studies, Asian studies, Asian-American studies. And in the rest of the world, where universities are organized to resist easy change from within or without, where they are structured to withstand side attacks, boring from within, or establishing enclaves inside and yet outside power structures—in such institutions, change is more difficult still.

This is a discussion not confined to the United States. European women's studies faculty raised these questions at a United Nations meeting in Vienna in October 1994. In Europe, women's studies teaching and research programs are twenty years old, or older. In some countries, especially the Nordic and the Netherlands, women's studies can be found in a variety of formations, often on the margins of universities, sometimes in well-funded, well-staffed centers, producing significant research. Yet I heard little satisfaction expressed. Rather, I heard ugly stories, painful accounts of rejections of women's studies scholars by the university "fraternity." I was somewhat surprised by these complaints, and for two reasons. First, in the United States such complaints were commonplace a decade ago. But feminist scholarship in some fields has become vanguard enough to attract male scholars, and feminist female scholars have gained positions at the most elite universities in the country. Moreover, U.S. feminists have created their own networks and institutions outside the patriarchal ones, and many of them are now able to function in both worlds.

Second, I heard nothing from the Europeans that spoke to action, to how to move their agendas forward. Indeed, the only account that I have found that prescribes institutional change is one from Australia. In a lecture on the occasion of the twentieth anniversary of the first women's studies "topic," or "paper" for a course of study, in an Australian university, Lyndall Ryan of Flinders University describes the "fragility" of women's studies in Australia, though thirty of the forty-three higher education institutions in the country offer women's studies "topics" and programs at the undergraduate or graduate level, and though there are also seven research centers. The "fragility" she describes is institutional: she describes the units as "additive," dependent on "voluntary" labor of feminist faculty she depicts in the "category of unpaid housework." She sees women's studies through university administrators' eyes as "an academic hobby with no clear long-term purpose." She depicts women's studies as "dwelling on the margins of the academy where it has ceased to be a threat to the mainstream because it uses few resources."

And not unexpectedly, her demand is for resources: the establishment of permanent, well-funded professorships and permanent, well-funded departments. The senior positions would reflect the importance of women's studies as a research area, and the "administrative coherence" would allow for the appropriate education of "the next generation of feminists."[23]

The education of the next generation of feminists is my concluding topic and my all-encompassing concern, as it is, I am sure, your own. What shall we make of the idea of "difference," wiping out "essentialism," and in some quarters of the women's studies world forbidding the very connections that made for the movement in the first place? I worry these days about "amnesia," forgetting—or never knowing about—the first twenty-five years of women's studies and, in the process, losing all that has been recovered during that period. And so I will conclude with some prescriptives for women's studies education.

First, remember and honor your foremothers, in literature and history, and in the recent period of pioneering women's studies. Whatever your specialty, teach and learn history, including the history of the past thirty years. Unless we know this history, unless we carry it with us, we will lose what we have gained, and generations long after we have gone will need to begin again.

Second, remember that women's studies has been multicultural from the start, despite its "essentialism," and that without "essentialism" we would not have had a movement. While significant differences separate women, significant characteristics connect them, not only across race and class, for example, but across nations.

Third, remember that the future of women's studies is international, which means that, beyond the women's history and culture of one's own country, one must begin to teach, to do research, and publish cross-culturally.

Fourth, remember that still largely untapped body of students, professors, and researchers who are the other half of the human race, the men some of us live with, mother, and love. How are we, in the next century, to teach them? Or will they teach themselves?

Fifth, and finally, remember and never underestimate the strength of patriarchy, that it is far more complexly entrenched ideologically and institutionally than we had imagined some thirty years ago. In the late 1960s, when some women of my generation first began to see that patriarchy controlled every aspect of women's and men's lives, we naively believed that visibility was the answer. If we could make everyone see it, we could, through vision alone, destroy it. Very simple, very wrong. It will take countless visions, innumerable sightings and namings in our lives and our books to help us see the strategies for changing the patriarchal world into one fit for humans.

But of course we have what we did not have twenty-five or thirty years ago: we have countless adherents, pioneers, and the daughters and granddaughters of pioneers on every continent, prepared for educational battle. We stand with J. P. Naik, a peaceful army of liberated women and men, with many "promises to keep."

NOTES

1. These national reports on women's studies have been published in three issues of *Women's Studies Quarterly: Women's Studies in Europe*, edited by Tobe Levin and Angelica Koster-Lossack; *Women's Studies: A World View*, edited by Florence Howe and Mariam K. Chamberlain; and *Beijing and Beyond: Toward the Twenty-first Century for Women*, edited by Florence Howe with the assistance of Mariam K. Chamberlain, Tobe Levin, and Gloria Bonder; see, respectively, *Women's Studies Quarterly* 20, nos. 3 & 4 (Fall/Winter

1992), *Women's Studies Quarterly* 22, nos. 3 & 4 (Fall/Winter 1994), and *Women's Studies Quarterly* 24, nos. 1 & 2 (Spring/Summer 1996). Also, for further information on the status of women's studies in developing countries in Asia, see Mariam K. Chamberlain and Florence Howe, "Women's Studies and Developing Countries: Focus on Asia," in *The Women and International Development Annual*, vol. 4, edited by Rita Gallin, Ann Ferguson, and Janice Harper (Boulder, Colorado: Westview Press, 1995).

2. See Alida Brill, ed., *A Rising Public Voice: Women in Politics Worldwide* (New York: The Feminist Press at The City University of New York, 1995).

3. See Committee on Women's Studies in Asia, ed., *Changing Lives: Life Stories of Asian Pioneers in Women's Studies* (New York: The Feminist Press at The City University of New York, 1995). Kali for Women published this book in 1994 in India under the title *Women's Studies, Women's Lives*.

4. Li Xiaojiang, "My Path to Womanhood," in *Changing Lives*, 114.

5. Ibid., 115.

6. See Inge K. Broverman, Donald M. Broverman, Frank E. Clarkson, Paul S. Rosenkrantz, and Susan R. Vogel, "Sex-Role Stereotypes and Clinical Judgements of Mental Health," *Journal of Consulting and Clinical Psychology* 34 (1970): 1–7.

7. Malavika Karlekar, "A Fieldworker in Women's Studies," in *Changing Lives*, 141.

8. Cho Kyoung, "To Grow with Women's Studies," in *Changing Lives*, 55.

9. See *Women's Studies Quarterly* 24, nos. 1 & 2 (Spring/Summer 1996).

10. See Anastasia Posadskaya, "Women's Studies in Russia: Prospects for a Feminist Agenda," *Women's Studies Quarterly* 22, nos. 3 & 4 (Fall/Winter 1994): 157–170.

11. See Tove Beate Pedersen, *Women's Studies Quarterly* 24, nos. 1 & 2 (Spring/Summer 1996): 343–350.

12. See Gloria Bonder, "Women's Studies in Argentina: Keeping the Feminist Spirit Alive," *Women's Studies Quarterly* 22, nos. 3 & 4 (Fall/Winter 1994): 89–102.

13. See Marjorie Mbilinyi, Ruth Meena, Athaliah Molokomme, Bolanle Awe, Nina Mba, E. Maxine Ankrah, and Peninah D. Bizimana, "Reports from Four Women's Groups in Africa," *Signs: Journal of Women in Culture and Society* 16, no. 4 (1991): 846–869.

14. See Kazuko Watanabe, "Japanese Women's Studies," *Women's Studies Quarterly* 22, nos. 3 & 4 (Fall/Winter 1994): 73–88.

15. See *Women's Studies Quarterly* 22, nos. 3 & 4 (Fall/Winter 1994).

16. The term "course" in the United States has nothing in common with the word "course" as it is used to describe an entire program of study in certain countries. A U.S. course is a small unit, one of thirty-two to forty that undergraduates need to complete their bachelor's degrees. Undergraduates take four or five such courses each semester, generally for eight semesters. Some of these might be in a "major" area of study, usually a discipline like economics or history or English or biology. Since the mid-1960s, it has also been possible at some colleges and universities in the

United States to major in an interdisciplinary area of study: Black studies, for example, or Asian studies, or women's studies, just to name a
few.

17. See Posadskaya, "Women's Studies in Russia."
18. See Li Xiaojiang, "My Path to Womanhood."
19. See Elizabeth Minnich, *Transforming Knowledge* (Philadelphia: Temple
University Press, 1990).
20. See Florence Howe, *Myths of Coeducation: Selected Essays, 1964–1983*
(Bloomington, Indiana: Indiana University Press, 1984).
21. I will add that where there once had been a handful of women college
presidents, most of them at women's colleges, there are now more than
600, some of them at major universities like Duke and the University of
Pennsylvania.
22. See Howe, *Myths of Coeducation.*
23. See Lyndall Ryan, "Women's Studies in the University Seminar," *Newsletter,*
Australian Women's Studies Association 8, no. 2 (November 1993).

*Florence Howe is director of The Feminist Press at The City University of New
York and professor of English at City College and the Graduate School and
University Center, CUNY.*

Copyright © 1997 by Florence Howe.

Women's Studies Programs—1997

Over the past twenty-five years, Women's Studies Quarterly *has maintained this list as an educational service of The Feminist Press. During this period, the listing of women's studies programs has grown more and more complexly annotated. Instead of the simple designations of minor (Min), A.A., B.A., M.A., and Ph.D. with which programs began, we include now the complexities of concentrations (Con), certificates (Cer), as well as graduate forms of these designations, along with graduate minors, or minors in M.A. or Ph.D. programs. The inclusion of credit hours or numbers of courses further complicates descriptions. At certain institutions, the designation "certificate" indicates a major; at others, a minor; at still others, something different from either.*

Analysis of this survey indicates that of the 611 programs, 79 percent (484) offer minors (eighty-eight of which are called concentrations or certificates). Forty percent (248) offer majors leading to the B.A. (or B.S. or some other form of undergraduate degree), seven of which are called concentrations or certificates. Seven percent (46) offer the master's degree; and 1 percent (7) the Ph.D. Fifteen percent offer some form of graduate minor, concentration, or certificate, some half of which are especially designated for master's or doctoral programs. In total, therefore, 22 percent of programs offer some form of graduate work.

We acknowledge the work of Elizabeth Chilton, Lakshmi Parekh, and Katja Sarkowsky in collecting and editing the information leading to the publication of this new list. All correspondence concerning this list, including corrections and additions, should be addressed to the Managing Editor, Women's Studies Quarterly, *The Feminist Press at The City University of New York, 311 East 94 Street, New York, NY 10128.*

Min **Adelphi U,** South Ave (Earle Hall Basement), Garden City, NY 11530—Women's Studies, Sally Ridgeway, Dir. Program offers a 21-cr minor.

Min **Agnes Scott C,** Decatur, GA 30030—Women's Studies, Christine Cozzens, Dir. Program offers a minor.

Cer **Akron, U of,** Leigh Hall 204, Akron, OH 44325-6218—Women's Studies, Nina Molinaro, Dir. Program offers a 19-cr certificate.

Min, BA, MA **Alabama, U of,** Box 870272, 109 Manly Hall, Tuscaloosa, AL 35487—Women's Studies, Alice A. Parker, Dir. Program offers a 21-cr minor, the BA through New College, and an MA.

Min **Alabama in Huntsville, U of, Huntsville,** Morton Hall, Huntsville, AL 35899—

Women's Studies Program Advisory Committee, Rose Norman, Dir. Program offers a 21-sem-hr minor.

Min **Alaska Anchorage, U of,** 3211 Providence Dr, Anchorage, AK 99508-8332—Women's Studies, Susan Kalina and Gretchen Legler, Codirs. Program offers an 18-cr minor.

Albion C, Albion, MI 49224—Anna H. Shaw Center for Women's Studies and Programs, Trisha Franzen, Dir.

Min **Alfred U,** Saxon Dr, Alfred, NY 14802—Women's Studies, Karen L. Porter, Dir. Program offers an 18-cr minor.

Con, Min, BA **Allegheny C,** Meadville, PA 16335—Women's Studies, Laura Quinn, Dir. Program offers a 12-hr concentration, a 20-hr minor, and a 36-hr BA.

Min **Alma C,** 614 Superior St, Alma, MI 48801—Women's Studies, Roseanne L. Hoefel, Coord. Program offers a 28-cr minor.

Min, BA **American U,** 4400 Massachusetts Ave NW, Washington, DC 20016—Women's and Gender Studies, Jo Radner, Dir. Program offers an 18-cr minor and a 39-cr BA.

BA **Amherst C,** Amherst, MA 01002—Dept of Women's and Gender Studies, Joyce Soucier, Asst to the Chair. Program offers an individualized BA. Member of the Five Colleges Consortium.

Con **Antioch C,** Yellow Springs, OH 45387—Women's Studies, E. J. LaGesse, Dir. Program offers a 48-hr concentration in the Department of Cultural and Interdisciplinary Studies.

Min, BA **Appalachian SU,** East Hall, Boone, NC 28608—Women's Studies, Melissa E. Barth, Dir. Program offers a 15-hr minor and a 37-hr BA in Interdisciplinary Studies/Women's Studies.

Min, BA, MA, Grad Con **Arizona, U of,** 102 Douglass Bldg, Tucson, AZ 85721—Women's Studies, Judy Nolte Temple, Chair. Program offers a 21-cr minor, a BA, an MA (academic and applied tracks) and graduate concentrations through Comparative Cultural and Literary Studies, English, History, and Sociology.

Cer, Min, BA, BS, MA/Min, PhD/Min **Arizona SU,** P.O. Box 871801, Tempe, AZ 85287-1801—Women's Studies, Mary Logan Rothschild, Dir. Program offers a 21-cr undergraduate certificate, an 18-cr minor, a BA, and a BS. Selected disciplines also offer graduate minors.

Min **Arkansas, U of, Little Rock,** 33 and University, Little Rock, AR 72204—Women's Studies, Frances M. Ross, Coord. Program offers an 18-cr minor.

BA **Atlantic, C of the,** Eden St, Bar Harbor, ME 04609—Women's Studies, Susan Lerner, Coord. Program offers the BA through Human Ecology.

Min **Auburn U,** c/o School of Human Sciences, 201 Spidle Hall, Auburn, AL 36849-5604—Women's Studies, Donna Sollie, Dir. Program offers a 30-qtr-hr minor.

Min **Augsburg C,** 2211 Riverside Ave, Minneapolis, MN 55454—Women's Studies, Lynne F. Lorenzen, Coord. Program offers a 5-course minor.

Min **Augustana C,** Rock Island, IL 61201—Women's Studies, Nancy Huse, Coord. Program offers an 18-cr minor.

Austin CC, Northridge Campus, 11928 Stone Hollow Dr, Austin, TX 78758—Women's Studies, Kitty Henderson, Coord.

Min **Austin Peay SU,** Clarksville, TN 37044—Women's Studies, Susan Calovini, Coord. Program offers an 18-cr minor.

Min **Avila C,** 11901 Wornall Rd, Kansas City, MO 64145—Women's Studies, Nancy Cervetti, Dir. Program offers an 18-cr minor.

Min **Ball SU,** North Quad 113, Muncie, IN 47306—Women and Gender Studies, Kim Jones-Owen, Dir. Program offers an 18-cr minor.

Con **Baltimore, U of,** 1420 N Charles St, Baltimore, MD 21201—Women's Studies, Julie Simon, Coord. Program offers a 12-hr multidisciplinary specialization in Women's Studies.

Min **Barat C,** Lake Forest, IL 60045—Committee on Women, Joan Berman, Dir. Program offers a 24-hr minor.

BA **Bard C,** Annandale-on-Hudson, NY 12504—Women's Studies, Suzanne Vromen, Coord. Program offers the BA through Interdisciplinary Studies.

BA **Barnard C,** 3009 Broadway, New York, NY 10027—Women's Studies, Natalie Kampen, Chair. Department offers a BA.

Cer, Min **Barry U,** 11300 NE 2nd Ave, Miami, FL 33161—Women's Studies, Lillian Schanfield, Dir. Program offers a certificate and a 21-cr minor.

Min, BA **Bates C,** Lewiston, ME 04240—Women's Studies, Elizabeth A. Eames, Chair. Program offers a 7-course minor in Women's Studies and a 10-course major.

Bay Path C, 588 Longmeadow St, Longmeadow, MA 01106—Women's Studies, Nancy J. Eaton, Coord.

Min **Bellevue C,** 1000 Galvin Rd S, Bellevue, NE 68005—Women's Studies Area, Roxanne L. Sullivan, Chair. Program offers an 18-sem-hr minor.

Min **Beloit C,** Beloit, WI 53511—Women's Studies, Lisa Haines Wright and Julia Sneeringer, Chairs. Program offers a 6-cr minor.

Min **Bemidji SU,** Bemidji, MN 56601—Women's Studies, Patricia A. Rosenbrock, Dir. Program offers a 30-cr minor.

Min, BA **Bennett C,** 900 E Washington St, Campus Box 25, Greensboro, NC 27401—Women's Education & Development Center, Lona D. Cobb, Dir. Program offers an 18-cr minor and a BA.

BA **Bennington C,** Office of the Dean of the College, Bennington, VT 05201— Gender-Related Studies, Henrietta Marshall, Coord. Program offers an individualized thematic BA.

Min **Bentley C,** 175 Forest St, Waltham, MA 02154—Gender Studies, Christine Williams, Coord. Program offers a minor.

Min, AA **Bergen CC,** 400 Paramus Rd, Paramus, NJ 07652—Women's Studies, Philip Dolce, Dept Head. Program offers a 12-cr minor and an AA.

Bethany C, Bethany, WV 26032—Women's Studies, Lynn Adkins, Coord.

Min **Boston C,** Chestnut Hill, MA 02167—Women's Studies, Beth Kowaleski-Wallace, Dir. Program offers an 18-cr minor. Member of the Graduate Consortium in Women's Studies at Radcliffe C.

Min, BA **Boston U,** Boston, MA 02215—Women's Studies. Program offers a 24-cr minor and an individualized BA.

Min, BA **Bowdoin C,** 24 College St, Brunswick, ME 04011—Women's Studies, Jane Knox-Voina, Dir. Program offers a 5-course minor and a 10-course BA.

Min, BA, MA/Con, PhD/Con **Bowling Green SU,** Bowling Green, OH 43403—

Women's Studies, Ellen Berry, Dir. Program offers a 21-cr minor, a BA, and graduate concentrations at the MA and PhD levels.

Min **Bradley U,** Bradley Hall 129, Peoria, IL 61625—Women's Studies, Stacey Robertson, Dir. Program offers a 15-cr minor.

Min, MA **Brandeis U,** Rabb 120, Waltham, MA 02254—Women's Studies, Shulamit Reinharz, Chair. Program offers a 20-cr minor and a joint MA with 10 departments. Member of the Graduate Consortium in Women's Studies at Radcliffe C.

Con **Brenau U,** Washington and Boulevard, Gainesville, GA 30501—Women's Studies (c/o Dept of Humanities), Leslie Jones, Coord. Program offers a specialization in women's leadership.

Min **Brescia C,** 717 Frederica St, Owensboro, KY 42301—Contemporary Woman Program, Rebecca White, Dir. Program offers a 21-cr minor.

Min **Bridgewater SC,** Bridgewater, MA 02325—Women's Studies, Francine Quaglio, Coord. Program offers an 18-cr minor.

Min **Brigham Young U,** 970 SWKT, Provo, UT 84602—Women's Research Institute, Bonnie Ballif-Spanvill, Dir. Program offers a 19-hr minor.

BA **Brown U,** Providence, RI 02912—Pembroke Center for Teaching and Research on Women, Ellen Rooney, Dir. Program offers a BA.

Con, Min, BA **Bryn Mawr C,** Bryn Mawr, PA 19010—Feminist and Gender Studies, Anne Dalke, Coord. Program offers a concentration, a 6-course minor jointly with Haverford C, and an individualized BA.

Min, BA **Bucknell U,** Race/Gender Resource Center, Lewisburg, PA 17837—Women's Studies, Catherine Blair and Karen Dugger, Coords. Program offers a 20-cr minor and a BA.

Con, BA **Burlington C,** 95 North Ave, Burlington, VT 05401—Feminist Studies, Catharine Andrecos, Dir. Program offers a concentration and a BA.

Cabrillo C, 6500 Soquel Dr, Aptos, CA 95003—Women's Studies, Rosemary Brogan, Coord.

Min **Cabrini C,** King of Prussia and Eagle Rds, Radnor, PA 19087—Women's Studies, Kathleen Daley, Coord. Program offers a minor.

Cer **Caldwell C,** 9 Ryerson Ave, Caldwell, NJ 07006—Women's Studies, Marie Hudson, Coord. Program offers an 18-cr certificate.

Min, BA, PhD/Con **California, Berkeley, U of,** 2241 College, #1070, Berkeley, CA 94720—Women's Studies, Carol Stack, Chair. Department offers a minor and a BA. A "designated emphasis" in Women, Gender, and Sexuality is offered at the graduate level for students enrolled in doctoral programs.

Min, BA, Grad Con **California, Davis, U of,** 2201 Hart Hall, Davis, CA 95616—Women's Studies, Judith Newton, Dir. Program offers a minor, a BA, and a graduate emphasis.

Min, BA, Grad Con **California, Irvine, U of,** 201 B HTC 140, Irvine, CA 92717—Women's Studies, Elizabeth Guthrie, Dir. Program offers a 28-cr minor, a 52-cr BA, and a graduate emphasis.

Min, BA **California, Los Angeles, U of,** Box 1453, Los Angeles, CA 90095—Women's Studies, Christine Littleton, Chair. Program offers a 32-unit minor and a 56-unit BA.

Min, BA **California, Riverside, U of,** 990 University Ave, Riverside, CA 92521—

Women's Studies, Marguerite Waller, Chair. Department offers a minor and a BA.

Min, BA **California, San Diego, U of,** La Jolla, CA 92093—Women's Studies. Program offers a 24-unit minor and a 60-unit BA.

PhD/Con **California, San Francisco, U of,** Box 0612, N-631-N, San Francisco, CA 94143—Women, Health, and Healing Program (c/o Dept of Social and Behavioral Sciences), Virginia Olesen and Adele Clarke, Dirs. Program offers a concentration in the PhD program in Sociology.

BA, PhD/Con **California, Santa Cruz, U of, Kresge C,** Santa Cruz, CA 95064—Women's Studies, Emily Honig, Chair. Program offers a BA and a "Notation" on the PhD in Sociology, Anthropology, History, History of Consciousness, and Literature.

Min **California Lutheran U,** 60 Olsen Rd, Thousand Oaks, CA 91360—Women's Programs, Kathryn A. Swanson, Dir. Program offers a 16-cr interdisciplinary minor.

AA, BA, MA **California, New C of,** 50 Fell St, San Francisco, CA 94102—Gender Studies, Ani Mander, Coord. Program offers the AA and BA through Humanities, and an MA in Women's Spirituality through the California Institute of Integral Studies (CIIS), Rose Frances, Dir. 9 Peter Yorke, San Francisco, CA 94110.

Min **California Polytechnic SU,** San Luis Obispo, CA 93407—Women's Studies, Carolyn J. Stefanco, Dir. Program offers a 28-unit minor.

Min **California S Polytechnic U,** 3801 West Temple Ave, Pomona, CA 91768— Ethnic and Women's Studies, Patricia Lin, Dir. Department offers a 36-unit minor, and a BA in gender, ethnicity, and multicultural studies is forthcoming.

Min **California SU, Bakersfield,** 9001 Stockdale Hwy, Bakersfield, CA 93309— Women's Studies, Jane Granskog, Chair. Program offers a 12-cr minor.

Min **California SU, Chico,** Chico, CA 95929—Ethnic and Women's Studies, Gayle Kimball, Coord. Program offers a 20-unit minor.

Min **California SU, Dominguez Hills,** 1000 E Victoria St, Carson, CA 90747— Women's Studies, Judson A. Grenier, Coord. Program offers a 15-sem-unit minor.

Min **California SU, Fresno,** Fresno, CA 93740—Women's Studies, Judith Gonzalez-Caluo, Coord. Program offers a 21-cr minor.

Min **California SU, Fullerton,** Fullerton, CA 92634—Women's Studies, Shari Starrett, Coord. Program offers a 23-unit minor.

Min, BA **California SU, Hayward,** Hayward, CA 94542—Women's Studies, Roxanne D. Ortiz, Dir. Program offers a 24-cr minor and an individualized BA.

Min, BA, MA **California SU, Long Beach,** Bellflower Blvd, Long Beach, CA 90840— Women's Studies, Norma S. Chinchilla, Dir. Program offers a 24-cr minor, a BA, and an individualized MA.

Min **California SU, Los Angeles,** 5151 State University Dr, Los Angeles, CA 90032— Women's Studies, C. E. Martin, Coord. Program offers a minor.

Min, BA, MA **California SU, Northridge,** 18111 Nordhoff St, Northridge, CA 91330-8251—Women's Studies, Julia Watson, Chair. Program offers a 21-cr minor, a BA Special Major (concentration in Women's Studies), and an Interdisciplinary Studies MA (concentration in Women's Studies).

Min, BA, MA **California SU, Sacramento,** 6000 J St, Sacramento, CA 95819— Women's Studies, Bethania Gonzalez, Coord. Program offers a 21-cr minor, a 36-cr BA, and a 30-cr MA.

Cer, Min **California SU, San Bernardino,** San Bernardino, CA 92407—Women's Studies, Nancy Rose, Coord. Program offers a certificate and a 28-qtr-unit minor.

Con, Min, BA **California SU, Stanislaus,** 801 W Monte Vista Ave, Turlock, CA 95380—Ethnic and Women's Studies, J. J. Hendricks, Chair. Program offers a concentration, a 22-cr minor, and a BA.

AA **Canada C,** 4200 Farm Hill Blvd, Redwood City, CA 94061—Women's Reentry Program, Jane Weidman, Coord. Program offers an AA.

Cer **Canisius C,** 2001 Main St, Buffalo, NY 14208—Women's Studies, Ellen Conley, Dean. Program offers a certificate.

Min, BA **Carleton C,** Northfield, MN 55057—Women's Studies, Dana Strand, Coord. Program offers a 36-cr interdisciplinary concentration and a specialized BA.

Min, BA **Carlow C,** 3333 Fifth Ave, Pittsburgh, PA 15213—Women's Studies, Suzanne M. Steiner, Chair. Program offers a 15-cr minor and an individualized BA.

Min **Carroll C,** 100 N East Ave, Waukesha, WI 53186—Women's Studies, Lori Duin Kelly, Dir. Program offers a 20-cr minor.

Min, MA/Con, PhD/Con **Case Western Reserve U,** Cleveland, OH 44106-7125— Women's Studies, Barbara Krasner, Undergrad Adviser; Janis A. Jenkins, Dir. Program offers a minor and concentrations in the MA and PhD programs in Arts and Sciences, including Anthropology, English, History, and Psychology. Program also offers courses in collaboration with the professional schools of Case Western Reserve U, including Medicine, Nursing, and Law.

AA **Casper C,** 125 College Dr, Casper, WY 82601—Women's Studies, Carolyn Logan, Coord. Program offers the AA through Liberal Arts.

Min, BA **Cedar Crest C,** Hamilton and Cedar Crest Blvds, Allentown, PA 18104— Women's Studies, Ann Hill-Beuf, Coord. Program offers a minor and an individualized BA.

Min **Centenary C,** Women's Center, 400 Jefferson St, Hackettstown, NJ 07840— Women's Studies, Angela Elliott, Coord. Program offers a minor.

Min **Central Connecticut SU,** 1615 Stanley St, New Britain, CT 06050—Women's Studies, Cindy White and Heather Munro Prescott, Co-Coords. Program offers an 18-cr minor.

Min **Central Michigan U,** 132 Sloan Hall, Mt Pleasant, MI 48859—Women's Studies, Brigitte Bechtold, Dir. Program offers a 24-cr minor.

Min, BA **Central Missouri SU,** Warrensburg, MO 64093—Women's Studies, Renee T. Betz, Coord. Program offers a 21–22-cr minor and the possibility of a constructed major.

Min, BA **Central Washington U,** Ellensburg, WA 98926-7578—Women's Studies, Bang-Soon Yoon, Dir. Program offers a 25-cr minor and a BA.

Chaminade U of Honolulu, 3140 Waialae Ave, Honolulu, HI 96816—Women's Programs.

Cer **Charles S. Mott CC,** 1401 E Court St, Flint, MI 48503—Women's Studies, Gail Knapp, Coord. Program offers a 12-cr certificate.

Min **Charleston, C of,** 66 George St, Charleston, SC 29424—Women's Studies, Marsha Hass, Dir. Program offers an 18-hr interdisciplinary minor.

Min, BA **Chatham C,** Woodland Road, Pittsburgh, PA 15232—Women's Studies, Patricia Montley, Coord. Program offers a 6-course minor and a 12-course BA.

AA **Chemeketa CC,** PO Box 14007, Salem, OR 97309—Women's Studies, Egon Bodtker, Dir. Program offers the AA through General Studies.

Cer, MA/Cer, MA, PhD/Cer, JD **Cincinnati, U of,** Center for Women's Studies, 151-155 McMicken, Cincinnati, OH 45221—Women's Studies, Robin Sheets, Dir. Program offers a 30-cr undergraduate certificate, an 18-cr certificate for the MA and PhD degrees, a two-year interdisciplinary MA, and a four-year joint degree with the College of Law leading to a JD and an MA.

Clackamas CC, 19600 S Molalla Ave, Oregon City, OR 97045—Women's Special Programs, Karen Lever, Coord.

Claremont McKenna C, Steele 108, Claremont, CA 91711—Women's Studies, Audrey Bilger, Coord. Member of the Claremont Colleges Consortium.

MA, PhD **Clark Atlanta U,** 223 James P. Brawley Dr SW, Atlanta, GA 30314—Africana Women's Studies, Jacqueline Howard-Matthews, Chair. Program offers an MA and a PhD.

Clark C, 1800 E McLoughlin Blvd, Vancouver, WA 98663—Women's Studies, Harriet K. Levi, Coord.

Min, BA, MA, PhD **Clark U,** Main St, Worcester, MA 01610—Women's Studies, Marcia Butzel and Sarah Deutsch, Co-Dirs. Program offers a 12-cr minor, an individualized BA, the MA through International Development, and a free-standing PhD.

Min **Clemson U,** Strode Tower, Clemson, SC 29634—Women's Studies (c/o Dept of Languages), Judith M. Melton, Coord. Program offers a minor.

Min, BA **Cleveland SU,** 1983 E 24 St, University Center #363, Cleveland, OH 44115—Women's Comprehensive Program, Marey Joyce Green, Dir. Program offers a 24-cr minor and a personally designed major.

Min, BA **Colby C,** Mayflower Hill Dr, Waterville, ME 04901—Women's Studies, Cheshire Calhoun, Dir. Program offers a minor and a BA.

Min **Colby-Sawyer C,** Main St, New London, NH 03257—Women's Studies, Nancy Jay Crumbine, Coord. Program offers an 18-cr minor.

Min, BA **Colgate U,** Hamilton, NY 13346—Women's Studies, Joan D. Mandle, Dir. Program offers a minor and a BA.

Min, BA **Colorado C,** Colorado Springs, CO 80903—Women's Studies, Margaret Duncombe, Coord. Program offers a 22-cr minor and the BA through Interdisciplinary Studies.

Min, BA **Colorado, U of, Boulder,** Cottage #1, Campus Box 246, Boulder, CO 80309—Women Studies, Alison Jaggar, Dir. Program offers a 21-hr minor and a 36-hr BA.

Min **Colorado, U of, Colorado Springs,** 1420 Austin Bluffs Pkwy, PO Box 7150, Colorado Springs, CO 80933—Philosophy Center for Women's Studies, Teresa Jillson, Int. Dir. Program offers an 18-cr minor.

Cer, Grad Cer **Colorado SU,** 112 Student Services, Fort Collins, CO 80523—Women's Studies, Karen J. Wedge, Dir. Program offers a 21-cr undergraduate certificate and a 12-cr graduate certificate.

Columbia C, Columbia College Dr, Columbia, SC 29203—Women's Studies, Miriam Rawly, Coord.

AA, AAS **Columbia Greene CC,** Box 1000, Hudson, NY 12534—Women's Studies,

Mary Davidson, Coord. Program offers the AA in Social Sciences and the AAS in Human Services.

BA, PhD/Min **Columbia U,** 763 Schermerhorn Ext, New York, NY 10027—Women's Studies, Martha Howell, Dir. Program offers a BA and a minor at the PhD level.

Min, BA **Connecticut C,** New London, CT 06320—Gender and Women's Studies, Linda Herr, Acting Dir. Program offers a minor and an individualized BA.

Cer, BA, Grad Cer **Connecticut, U of,** U-181, Storrs, CT 06269—Women's Studies, Susan Porter Benson, Dir. Program offers an undergraduate certificate, a BA, and a graduate certificate.

Contra Costa C, 2600 Mission Bell Dr, San Pablo, CA 94806—Women's Studies, Marjorie Lasky, Coord.

Con, Min, BA **Cornell C,** Mt Vernon, IA 52314—Women's Studies, John Gruber-Miller and Amy Ihlen, Chairs. Program offers a concentration, a 5-course minor, and a BA.

Con, BA, Grad Min **Cornell U,** 391 Uris Hall, Ithaca, NY 14853—Women's Studies, Sally McConnell-Ginet, Dir. Program offers a concentration, a BA, and a graduate minor.

Cer, Min, BA **Curry C,** Milton, MA 02186—Women's Studies, Marlene Samuelson, Coord. Program offers a 15-cr certificate, a 15-cr minor, and an individualized BA.

Cer, Min, BA **Dartmouth C,** 6038 Carpenter Hall Rm 2, Hanover, NH 03755-3570—Women's Studies, Anne Brooks, Coord. Program offers a certificate, a minor, and a BA.

Min **Dayton, U of,** 300 College Park, Dayton, OH 45469-1492—Women's Studies, Linda C. Majka, Dir. Program offers a 13-cr minor.

Min, BA **Delaware, U of,** 333 Smith Hall, Newark, DE 19716—Women's Studies Interdisciplinary Program, Kate Conway-Turner, Dir. Program offers an 18-cr minor and a 30-cr BA.

Con **Delaware SC,** Dover, DE 19901—Women's Studies, Wyatt Watson, Coord. Program offers an emphasis in black women's studies.

Min, BA **Denison U,** Granville, OH 43023—Women's Studies, Eloise Buker, Dir. Program offers a 24-cr minor and a BA.

Min, BA **Denver, U of,** 2040 S Race St, GCB 338-339, Denver, CO 80208—Women's Studies, Sieglinde Lug, Dir. Program offers a 20-cr minor and a 40-cr major.

Min, BA, MA/Con, Grad Cer **DePaul U,** 802 W Belden, Chicago, IL 60614—Women's Studies, Carol Klimick Cyganowski, Dir. Program offers a 6-course minor, a 12-course BA, a graduate concentration for the MA in Liberal Studies, and a 4-course graduate certificate.

Min, BA **DePauw U,** 109 Asbury Hall, Greencastle, IN 46135—Women's Studies, Meryl Altman, Coord. Program offers a minor and a BA.

Cer **Detroit, U of,** 4001 W McNichols, PO Box 19900, Detroit, MI 48219—Women's Studies, Claire Crabtree, Dir. Program offers an 18-cr certificate.

AA **Diablo Valley C,** 321 Golf Club Rd, Pleasant Hill, CA 94523—Women's Programs, Sandra Holman, Coord. Program offers the AA in Women's Services.

Cer **Dickinson C,** Carlisle, PA 17013—Women's Studies, Stephanie Greco Larson, Coord. Program offers an 8-cr certificate.

Con **Drake U,** 2507 University Ave, Des Moines, IA 50311—Women's Studies,

Vibeke Rutzou Petersen, Dir. Program offers an interdisciplinary concentration.
Min, BA **Drew U,** SW Bowne Hall, Madison, NJ 07940—Women's Studies, Wendy
Kolmar, Dir. Program offers an 18-cr minor and a specialized BA.

Min, BA, Grad Cer **Duke U,** 210 E Duke Bldg, Durham, NC 27708—Women's
Studies, Jean O'Barr, Dir. Program offers a 5-cr minor, a 10-cr BA, a 9-cr graduate certificate and a society of scholars for advanced graduate students.

BA **Earlham C,** National Rd W, Richmond, IN 47374—Women's Studies, Barbara
Caruso, Coord. Program offers a BA.

Min, BA, Grad Min **East Carolina U,** 128-A Ragsdale , College of Arts and Sciences,
Greenville, NC 27858—Women's Studies, Linda J. Allred, Dir. Program offers a
24-sem-hr undergraduate minor, a 36-sem-hr undergraduate major, and a 9-sem-
hr graduate minor.

Min **Eastern Connecticut SU,** Willimantic, CT 06226—Women's Studies, Marcia
Phillips McGowan, Dir. Program offers a 15-cr minor.

Min **Eastern Illinois U,** Charleston, IL 61920—Women's Studies, Ivy Glennon,
Chair. Program offers an 18-sem-hr minor.

Min, MA **Eastern Michigan U,** 720 Pray-Harrold, Ypsilanti, MI 48197—Women's
Studies, Rebecca Martusewicz, Dir. Program offers a 21-cr minor and the MA
through Liberal Studies.

Eastern Montana C, 1500 N 30, Billings, MT 59101—Women's Studies, Sue Hart, Dir.

Cer, Min **Eastern New Mexico U,** Station 19, Portales, NM 88130—Women's
Studies, Margaret Moore Willen, Chair. Program offers a 15-cr certificate and
an 18-cr minor.

Min, BA **Eastern Washington U,** 114 Monroe Hall, Cheney, WA 99004—Women's
Studies, Lee Swedberg, Dir. Program offers a 22-cr minor and the BA through
Liberal Studies.

Min, BA **Eckerd C,** 34 St S, St Petersburg, FL 33733—Women's and Gender Studies,
Carolyn Johnston, Coord. Program offers a minor and a BA.

Min **Edgewood C,** 855 Woodrow St, Madison, WI 53711—Women's Studies, Susan
Rustick, Coord. Program offers a 20-cr minor jointly with U of Wisconsin.

Min **Elon C,** Campus Box 2172, Elon College, NC 27244—Women's Studies/Gender
Studies, Seena Granowsky, Coord. Program offers a 20-cr minor.

Min **Emmanuel C,** 400 The Fenway, Boston, MA 02115—Women's Studies, Ann
Wetherilt, Dir. Program offers a minor.

Min, BA, Grad Cer, PhD **Emory U,** Atlanta, GA 30322—Institute for Women's
Studies, Robyn Fivush, Dir. Program offers a 20-cr minor, a 32-cr BA, a 14-cr
graduate certificate, and the PhD.

BA **Evergreen SC,** Olympia, WA 98505—Women's Studies, Stephanie Coontz,
Coord. Program offers the BA through Liberal or Interdisciplinary Studies.

Min **Fairleigh Dickinson U, Teaneck Campus,** River Rd, Teaneck, NJ 07666—
Women's Studies, Doris Auerbach, Coord. Program offers a 12-cr minor.

**Five Colleges Women's Studies Research Center (Amherst C, Hampshire C, Mt
Holyoke C, U of Massachusetts at Amherst, and Smith C),** Dickinson House,
Mount Holyoke C, S. Hadley, MA 01075—Women's Studies Steering
Committee, Gail A. Hornstein, Dir. See individual listings.

Cer **Florida Atlantic U,** Humanities 158, Boca Raton, FL 33431—Women's Studies,

Dorothy Leland, Dir. Program offers a 18-cr interdisciplinary certificate.

Cer, BA, Grad Con **Florida International U,** University Park Campus, Miami, FL 33199—Women's Studies Center, Marilyn Hoder-Salmon, Dir. Program offers an 18-cr undergraduate certificate and a BA major requiring 30 cr of interdisciplinary course work. Graduate concentrations in International Studies, Comparative Sociology, and Religious Studies are also offered.

Min, Grad Con, MA/Min, PhD/Min **Florida SU,** Tallahassee, FL 32306—Women's Studies (2029), Jean G. Bryant, Dir. Program offers a 15-cr undergraduate minor, a graduate concentration, a 9-hr MA minor, and a 12-hr PhD minor.

Min, BA, Grad Cer **Florida, U of,** 115 Anderson Hall, Gainesville, FL 32611—Center for Women's Studies and Gender Research, Sue Rosser, Dir. Program offers a 15-cr minor, an individualized BA through Liberal Arts and Sciences, and a 12-cr graduate certificate.

AA **Foothill C,** 12345 El Monte Rd, Los Altos Hill, CA 94022—Women's Studies, Peggy A. Moore, Coord. Program offers the AA.

Min, BA **Fordham U,** Lincoln Center Campus, 113 W. 60th St, New York, NY 10023; Rose Hill Campus, Bronx, NY 10458—Women's Studies, Janis Barry-Figueroa and Madeleine Boucher, Co-Dirs. Program offers a 6-course minor, a 10-course BA, and a double major (8 courses and a major in another discipline).

Franklin C of Indiana, 501 E Monroe St, Franklin, IN 46131—Women's Studies, Jill M. Bystydzienski, Dir.

Franklin Pierce C, PO Box 60, Rindge, NH 03461—Women's Studies, Margaret Madden, Coord.

Fresno City C, 1101 E University Ave, Fresno, CA 93741—Women's Studies, Joan Newcomb, Coord.

Min **Frostburg SU,** Frostburg, MD 21532—Women's Studies, Geri Dino, Coord. Program offers an 18-cr minor.

Min **George Mason U,** 4400 University Dr, Fairfax, VA 22030—Women's Studies, Karen Rosenblum, Coord. Program offers a 21-cr minor.

Min, MA/Con, MA, PhD/Con **George Washington U,** 2201 G St NW, Funger Hall 506-I, Washington, DC 20052—Women's Studies, Barbara D. Miller, Dir. Program offers an 18-cr minor, a 36-cr MA in Public Policy with a concentration in Women's Studies, a 36-cr MA in Women's Studies, and a concentration in the PhD program in Human Sciences.

Min, BA **Georgetown U,** 86 Intercultural Center, Washington, DC 20057—Women's Studies, C. Margaret Hall, Coord. Program offers an 18-cr minor and the BA through Interdisciplinary Studies.

Min **Georgia C,** Milledgeville, GA 31061—Women's Studies, Rosemary Begemann and Sarah Gordon, Coords. Program offers a 25-qtr-hr minor.

Min, BA, MA **Georgia SU,** University Plaza, Atlanta, GA 30303—Women's Studies, Diane Fowlkes, Dir. Program offers a minor, a Bachelor of Interdisciplinary Studies, and an MA in Women's Studies.

Cer, Min, BA, Grad Cer **Georgia, U of, Athens,** 230K Main Library, Athens, GA 30602—Women's Studies, Patricia Del Rey, Dir. Program offers a 30-qtr-unit certificate, a 20-qtr-unit minor, an interdisciplinary BA, and a 25-qtr-unit graduate certificate.

Min **Georgian Court C,** Lakewood, NJ 08701—Women's Studies, Judith Beck, Coord. Program offers an 18-cr minor.

Min, BA **Gettysburg C,** Box 2450, Gettysburg, PA 17325—Women's Studies, Jean Potuchek, Coord. Program offers a minor and a major.

BA, MA **Goddard C,** Plainfield, VT 05667—Feminist Studies, Nicola Morris, Coord. Program offers a BA and an MA.

Con **Gonzaga U,** Spokane, WA 99258—Women's Studies, Rose Mary Volbrecht, Dir. Program offers a 21-cr concentration.

Min **Goshen C,** Goshen, IN 46526—Women's Studies, Anna Bowman, Dir. Program offers an 18-cr-hr minor.

BA **Goucher C,** Towson, MD 21204—Women's Studies, Marianne Githers, Dir. Program offers a BA.

Governors SU, University Park, IL 60466—Women's Studies, Harriet Gross, Coord.

Graduate Consortium in Women's Studies at Radcliffe C, Fay House, 10 Garden St, Cambridge, MA 02138—Renee Fall, Coord. Program offers team-taught, interdisciplinary graduate level seminars to students at Boston C, Brandeis U, Harvard Divinity School, Harvard U, Harvard Graduate School of Education, Massachusetts Inst of Technology, Northeastern U, and Tufts U. Cr transfers to home university degree program. See individual listings.

Graduate Theological Union, 2400 Ridge Rd, Berkeley, CA 94709—Center for Women and Religion, Pamela Cooper-White, Dir.

Min **Grand Valley SU,** 1 Campus Dr, Allendale, MI 49401—Women's Studies, Doris Rucks, Coord. Program offers a 21-cr minor.

Con, BA **Grinnell C,** Harry Hopkins House, Grinnell, IA 50112—Gender and Women's Studies, Louise Noun Chair, Adviser. Program offers a 24-cr-hr interdisciplinary concentration and an individualized BA.

Min, BA **Guilford C,** W Friendly Ave, Greensboro, NC 27410—Women's Studies, Carol Stoneburner, Coord. Program offers a 20-cr minor and the BA through Humanistic Studies.

Min **Gustavus Adolphus C,** St Peter, MN 56082—Women's Studies, Carolyn O'Grady and Mariangela Maguire, Coords. Program offers a 5-course minor.

Con, Min **Hamilton C,** 198 College Hill Rd, Clinton, NY 13323—Women's Studies, Margaret Gentry, Dir. Program offers a 9-course concentration and a 5-course minor.

Min, BA **Hamline U,** St Paul, MN 55104—Women's Studies, Karyn Z. Sproles, Dir. Program offers a 6-course minor and a consortium-based BA.

BA **Hampshire C,** Amherst, MA 01002—Feminist Studies, Margaret Cerullo, Dir. Program offers an individualized interdisciplinary BA. Member of the Five Colleges Consortium.

AA **Harold Washington C,** 30 E Lake St, Chicago, IL 60601—Women's Studies, Robin Herndobler, Dir. Program offers an AA.

Min, BA **Hartford C for Women, U of Hartford,** 1265 Asylum Ave, Hartford, CT 06105—Women's Studies, Jane M. Barstow, Chair. Program offers an 18-cr minor and a 36-cr BA.

Min **Hartwick C,** Oneonta, NY 13820—Women's Studies, Katherine O'Donnell, Coord. Program offers a 5-course minor.

MA/Con, ThD **Harvard Divinity School, Harvard U,** 45 Francis Ave, Cambridge, MA 02138—Women's Studies in Religion, Constance Buchanan, Dir. Program offers yearly visiting scholars appointments, graduate concentration at Master's level, and a ThD in Religion, Gender, and Culture. Founding member of the Graduate Consortium in Women's Studies at Radcliffe C.

Con, MA/Con **Harvard Extension School,** 51 Brattle St, Cambridge, MA 02138—Women's Studies, Suzanne Spreadbury, Coord. Program offers concentrations in the BA and MA programs.

Min, BA **Harvard U,** 34 Kirkland St, Cambridge, MA 02138—Committee on Degrees in Women's Studies, Alice Jardine, Chair. Member of the Graduate Consortium in Women's Studies at Radcliffe C.

Min **Harvey Mudd C,** Platt Campus Ctr, Claremont, CA 91711—Women's Studies, Regina E. Mooney, Coord. Program offers a minor. Member of the Claremont Colleges Consortium.

Min **Haverford C,** Lancaster Ave, Haverford, PA 19041—Feminist and Gender Studies, Rajeswari Mohan, Coord. Program offers a 6-course minor jointly with Bryn Mawr C.

Cer, BA **Hawaii, U of, at Manoa,** 2424 Maile Way, Porteus 722, Honolulu, HI 96822—Women's Studies, Ruth Dawson, Dir. Program offers a 15-cr certificate and an interdisciplinary BA.

Con **Henry Ford CC,** 5101 Evergreen Rd, Dearborn, MI 48128—Focus on Women Program, Grace Stewart, Dir. Program offers a concentration.

Min **Hiram C,** Rt 700, Hiram, OH 44234—Gender Studies (Hiram Women's Center), Sandra Parker, Dir. Program offers a 30-cr minor.

BA **Hobart and William Smith C,** Geneva, NY 14456—Women's Studies, Toni Flores, Coord. Program offers an individualized BA.

Cer, Min, BA, MA **Hofstra U,** 1000 Fulton Ave, Hempstead, NY 11550—Women's Studies, Linda Longmire, Dir. Program offers an 18-cr certificate, an 18-cr minor, and the BA and MA through Interdisciplinary Studies at New College.

Min **Holy Cross C,** Worcester, MA 01610—Women's Studies, Theresa McBride, Dir. Program offers a minor.

Honolulu CC, 874 Dillingham Blvd, Honolulu, HI 96817—Women's Studies, Marcia Roberts-Deutsch, Coord.

Min, BA **Hood C,** Frederick, MD 21701—Women's Studies, Carolyn Knight, Chair. Program offers a minor and a BA.

Con, MA/Con **Houston, U of, Clear Lake,** Box 326, 2700 Bay Area Blvd, Houston, TX 77058—Women's Studies Committee, Susan Turell, Convener. Program offers a 9–12-cr concentration applicable to several BA, BS, and MA degrees, and a special Women's Studies track for the MA in Humanities.

Min **Houston, U of,** Houston, TX 77204-3784—Women's Studies, Elizabeth Gregory, Dir. Program offers a minor.

Cer, Min, BA **Humboldt SU,** Arcata, CA 95521—Women's Studies, Valerie Budig-Markin, Dir. Program offers a 21-cr certificate, a 15-cr minor, and a specialized BA through Interdisciplinary Studies.

Min **Illinois SU,** 604 S Main St, Campus Box 4260, Normal, IL 61790-4260—Women's Studies Center, Valerie M. Moghadam, Dir. Program offers a 21-cr minor.

Min, BA, Grad Con **Illinois, U of, at Chicago,** m/c 360, 1022 Behavorial Sciences Bldg, 1007 W Harrison St, Chicago, IL 60607-7137—Women's Studies, Stephanie Riger, Dir. Program offers a 15-sem-hr minor, an individualized BA, and a graduate concentration in conjunction with 18 departments.

Min, BA, MA **Illinois, U of, at Springfield,** Springfield, IL 62794—Women's Studies, Annette Van Dyke, Dir. Program offers a 16-hr minor, a self-designed 60-hr BA through Liberal Studies, and a 42-hr MA through the Individual Option Program.

Min, BA, Grad Min **Illinois, U of, Urbana-Champaign,** 911 S Sixth St, Champaign, IL 61820—Women's Studies, Sonya Michel, Dir. Program offers an interdisciplinary minor and the BA through Individual Plans of Study, and an interdisciplinary graduate minor.

Min **Indiana SU,** Terre Haute, IN 47809—Women's Studies, Darlene M. Hantzis, Dir. Program offers a minor.

Cer, Min, PhD/Min **Indiana U, Bloomington,** Memorial Hall East 131, Bloomington, IN 47405—Women's Studies. Program offers a 24-cr certificate, a 15-cr minor, and a 12-cr PhD minor.

Min **Indiana U Northwest,** 3400 Broadway, Gary, IN 46408—Women's Studies, Patricia Lorimer Lundberg, Dir. Program offers a 15-cr minor.

Min **Indiana U of Pennsylvania,** 352 Sutton Hall, Indiana, PA 15705—Women's Studies, Maureen C. McHugh, Dir. Program offers a 15-cr minor.

Min, BA **Indiana U-Purdue U, Fort Wayne,** 2101 Coliseum Blvd E, Fort Wayne, IN 46805—Women's Studies, Linda C. Fox, Dir. Program offers a 15-cr minor and a 30-cr BA.

Min **Indiana U-Purdue U, Indianapolis,** 425 University Blvd, CA 001C, Indianapolis, IN 46202—Women's Studies, Amanda Porterfield, Dir. Program offers a 16-cr minor.

Min **Indiana U, South Bend,** 1700 Mishawaka Ave, South Bend, IN 46634—Women's Studies, Pat McNeal, Coord. Program offers a 15-cr minor.

Cer, Min **Indiana U Southeast,** 4201 Grant Line Rd, New Albany, IN 47150—Women's Studies, Diane E. Wille, Coord. Program offers a 24-cr certificate and a 15-cr minor.

Intercollegiate Women's Studies (Claremont McKenna C, Harvey Mudd C, Pitzer C, Pomona C, Scripps C, Claremont Grad School), 1030 Columbia Avenue, Claremont, CA 91711, Jane O'Donnell, Coord. See individual school listings.

Min **Iona C,** New Rochelle, NY 10801—Women's Studies, Elaine Del Vecchio, Coord. Program offers a minor.

Min, BA, BS **Iowa SU,** 349 Carrie Chapman Catt Hall, Ames, IA 50011—Women's Studies, Linda Galyon, Chair. Program offers a 15-cr minor and a 36-cr interdisciplinary BA or BS.

Min, BA, PhD **Iowa, U of,** 202 Jefferson Bldg, Iowa City, IA 52242—Women's Studies, Florence Babb, Chair. Program offers a 15-cr minor, a BA through Interdepartmental Studies, and the PhD through the Graduate College Interdisciplinary Program.

Jefferson C, PO Box 1000, Hillsboro, MO 63050—Women's Studies, Trish Loomis, Coord.

Min **Jersey City SC,** Jersey City, NJ 07305—Women's Studies, Doris Friedensohn, Coord. Program offers an 18-cr minor.

Min **John Carroll U,** Cleveland, OH 44118—Men and Women. Perspectives on Sex and Gender, Marian J. Morton, Coord. Program offers an 18-cr minor.

Min **Johns Hopkins U,** 3400 N Charles St, 300 Jenkins Hall, Baltimore, MD 21218—Women's Studies, Judith R. Walkowitz, Dir. Program offers an 18-cr minor.

Johnson and Wales U, 8 Abbott Park Place, Providence, RI 02903—Women's Studies, Nancy Jackson, Coord.

Con **Kalamazoo C,** Kalamazoo, MI 49006—Women's Studies, Gail Griffin, Coord. Program offers a 7-course concentration.

BA, Grad Cer **Kansas SU,** Leasure 3, Manhattan, KS 66506—Women's Studies, Bonnie Nelson, Interim Dir. Program offers a 24-cr secondary major, a BA and the BS. A 9-cr graduate certificate will be offered beginning Spring 1997.

Min, BA **Kansas, U of,** 2120 Wescoe Hall, Lawrence, KS 66045—Women's Studies, Sandra L. Albrecht, Chair. Program offers a BA, BGS (Bachelor of General Studies), and a minor.

Min, BA **Kean C of New Jersey,** Morris Ave, Union, NJ 07083—Women's Studies, Sylvia Strauss, Dir. Program offers a 6-course minor and an individualized BA.

Min **Keene SC,** 229 Main St, Keene, NH 03431—Women's Studies, Anne-Marie Mallon, Coord. Program offers a 21-cr minor.

Min **Kennesaw SC,** Box 444, Marietta, GA 30061—Women's Studies (c/o Dept of History), Ann W. Ellis, Coord. Program offers a 20-cr minor.

Min **Kent SU,** 308 Bowman Hall, Kent, OH 44242—Women's Studies, Stephane Booth, Acting Dir. Program offers a 21-cr minor.

Min **Kent SU, Salem Campus,** 2491 St Rt 45 S, Salem, OH 44460—Women's Studies, Stephanie Booth, Dir. Program offers a 21-cr minor.

Kentucky SU, Frankfort, KY 40601—Women's Studies, N. D. Lundberg, Coord.

Min, BA, Grad Cer **Kentucky, U of,** Arts & Sciences, 915 Patterson Office Tower, Lexington, KY 40506—Women's Studies, Patricia Cooper, Dir. Program offers an 18-cr minor, an individualized BA, and a Graduate Certificate.

Con, BA **Kenyon C,** Gambier, OH 43022—Women's and Gender Studies, Harry Brod, Coord. Program offers a concentration and an individualized BA.

BA **Knox C,** Galesburg, IL 61401—Women's Studies, Brenda Fineberg, Chair. Program offers a 10-cr BA.

La Roche C, 9000 Babcock Blvd, Pittsburgh, PA 15237—Women's Studies, Mary C. Stuart, Dir.

Min **La Salle U,** 1900 West Olney Ave, Philadelphia, PA 19141—Women's Studies, Elizabeth A. Paulin, Dir. Program offers an 18-cr minor.

Min **Lafayette C,** Easton, PA 18042—Women's Studies, Deborah Byrd, Coord. Program offers an 18-cr minor.

BA **Lake Erie C,** 391 Washington Ave, Painesville, OH 44077—Women's Studies, Caroline Zilboorg, Coord. Program offers an individualized BA.

Cer **Lake Forest C,** Lake Forest, IL 60045—Women's Studies Committee, Abba Lessing, Jennifer Wallace, and Bunny Vignocchi, Coords. Program offers a 15-cr certificate.

Lake Tahoe CC, Box 14445, S Lake Tahoe, CA 95702—Women's Program, Cindy Smith, Coord.

Lakeland C, Box 359, Sheboygan, WI 53082—Women's Studies, Patricia Bonnet-Brunnich, Coord.

Lakeland CC, Kirtland, OH 44094—Women's Center, Meredith Ring, Dir.

Lane CC, 4000 E 30th Ave, Eugene, OR 97405—Women's Studies, Patricia Raney.

Laney C, 900 Fallon St, Oakland, CA 94607—Women's Reentry Programs, Sondra Smith-Saterfield, Dir.

Min, BA **Lawrence U,** Appleton, WI 54912—Gender Studies, Martha Hemwall and Eilene Hoft-March, Co-Coords. Program offers an interdisciplinary minor certification and a specialized BA.

Min **Lehigh U,** 15 University Dr, Bethlehem, PA 18105—Women's Studies (c/o Dept of Philosophy), Robin Dillon, Dir. Program offers an 18-cr minor.

Lehigh Valley Association of Independent Colleges, 119 West Greenwich St, Bethlehem, PA 18018, Carol Shiner Wilson, Coord. Coordinates programs at six independent colleges.

Min, BA **Lewis and Clark C,** Portland, OR 97219—Gender Studies, Jean Ward, Coord. Program offers a minor and a BA.

Lewis U, Rt 53, Romeoville, IL 60446—Women's Program, Shirley McFaul, Dir. Program offers coursework in women's and gender issues.

Min **Long Island U,** Brookville, NY 11548—Women's Studies, Alice Scourby, Coord. Program offers a 24-cr minor.

Con, BA **Long Island U, Southampton Campus,** Southampton, NY 11968—Friends World Program, Linda Yarr, Coord. Program offers a concentration in global women's studies and the BA through Interdisciplinary Studies.

Min **Longwood C,** 201 High St, Farmville, VA 23909—Women's Studies (c/o Dept of English), Kathleen Flanagan, Dir. Program offers an 18-cr minor.

Los Angeles Harbor C, 1111 Figueroa Pl, Wilmington, CA 90744—Women's Studies, June Burlingame Smith, Coord.

Min, BA, Grad Con **Louisiana SU,** Baton Rouge, LA 70803-3510—Women's and Gender Studies, Margaret Parker, Dir. Program offers an 18-cr minor, a BA, and a graduate concentration in the English program.

Min, BA **Louisville, U of,** Louisville, KY 40292—Women's Studies, Nancy Theriot, Chair. Program offers an 18-hr minor and a 33-hr BA.

Cer, Min **Lourdes C,** 6832 Convent Blvd, Sylvania, OH 43560—Women's Studies, Martha M. Mewhort, Dir. Program offers a certificate and a 5-course minor.

Min **Loyola Marymount U,** 7101 Loyola Blvd, Los Angeles, CA 90045—Women's Studies, Nancy Jabbra, Dir. Program offers an 18-cr minor.

Min **Loyola U Chicago,** 6525 N Sheridan Rd, Chicago, IL 60626—Women's Studies, Susan Mezey, Dir. Program offers a 15-cr minor.

Con **Luther C,** Decorah, IA 52101—Women's Studies, Jacqueline Wilkie, Coord. Program offers a 18–24-cr-hr (7-course) concentration.

Min **Lycoming C,** Williamsport, PA 17701—Women's Studies, Kathryn M. Ryan, Coord. Program offers a 20-cr minor.

Con **Lynchburg C,** Lynchburg, VA 24501—Women's Studies Advisory Committee, William Young, Chair. Program offers a women's studies theme.

BA, Min **Macalester C,** 1600 Grand Ave, St Paul, MN 55105—Women's and Gender Studies, Anna Miegs, Dir. Program offers a 12-course (48-cr) major and a 6-course (24-cr) minor.

Con, Min **Maine, U of,** 5728 Fernald, Orono, ME 04469-5728—Women in the Curriculum and Women's Studies, Ann K. Schonberger, Dir. Program offers an 18-cr-hr interdisciplinary concentration. Major focus on women's studies can be arranged through the Bachelor of University Studies Program. A BA in Women's Studies should be available by Spring 1998

Min, BA, MA **Manhattanville C,** Purchase, NY 10577—Women's Studies, Nancy S. Harris, Coord. Program offers a 12-cr minor, and the BA and MA through Liberal Studies.

Min, BS, MS **Mankato SU,** Box 64, Mankato, MN 56002—Women's Studies, Carol Perkins, Chair. Program offers a 30-qtr-unit minor, a BS, and an MS.

Min **Mansfield U,** Mansfield, PA 16933—Women's Studies, Andrea L. Harris and Lynn Pifer, Dirs. Program offers an 18-cr minor.

Min **Marietta C,** Marietta, OH 45750—Gender Studies (c/o Dept of Philosophy and Sociology), Sara Shute, Coord. Program offers a minor.

Marist C, North Rd, Poughkeepsie, NY 12601—Women's Studies, Nadine Foley, Coord.

Min, BA **Marquette U,** 1217 W Wisconsin Ave, Milwaukee, WI 53233—Women's Studies (c/o English, Coughlin Hall), Diane Long Hoeveler, Coord. Program offers a minor and an individualized BA.

Marshall U, Huntington, WV 25755—Women's Programs, Donnalee Cockrille, Dean of Students.

Min, BA **Mary Baldwin C,** Staunton, VA 24401—Women's Studies, Molsie Petty, Coord. Program offers a 21-cr minor and an individualized BA.

Mary, U of, Apple Crook Rd, Bismarck, ND 58501—Women's Studies, Beverly Sondag, Coord.

Min, BA **Maryland, U of, Baltimore County,** 1000 Hilltop Circle, Baltimore, MD 21228-5398—Women's Studies, Joan Korenman, Dir. Program offers an 18-cr minor and the BA through Interdisciplinary Studies.

Cer, BA, Grad Cer **Maryland, U of, College Park,** College Park, MD 20742—Women's Studies. Program offers a 21-cr undergraduate certificate, a 39-cr BA, and an 18-cr graduate certificate.

Cer **Maryland, U of, European Division,** Unit 29216, APO AE 09102—Women's Studies, LeAnn Cragun, Coord. Program offers a 30-cr certificate.

AA **Marymount C,** Palos Verdes Dr E, Rancho Palos Verdes, CA 90274—Women's Studies, Ruth Currie McDaniel, Coord. Program offers the AA.

Min **Marymount C,** Tarrytown, NY 10591—Women's Studies, Nikki Lee Manos, Coord. Program offers a 21-cr minor.

Maryville U, 13550 Conway Rd, St Louis, MO 63141—Women's Studies, Ann Campion Riley, Coord.

Min, BA **Massachusetts Dartmouth, U of,** N Dartmouth, MA 02747—Women's Studies, Barbara Jacobskind, Dir. Program offers an 18-cr minor and the BA through Multidisciplinary Studies.

Con, Min, BA **Massachusetts Inst of Technology,** 14E-316, 77 Massachusetts Ave,

Cambridge, MA 02139-4307—Women's Studies (14E-316). Program offers a concentration, a minor, and a BA. Member of the Graduate Consortium in Women's Studies at Radcliffe C.

Min, BA **Massachusetts, U of, Amherst,** 208 Bartlett Hall, Amherst, MA 01003—Women's Studies, Ann Ferguson, Dir. Program offers an 18-cr minor and a 36-cr BA. Member of the Five Colleges Consortium.

Min, BA **Massachusetts, U of, Boston,** 100 Morrissey Blvd, Boston, MA 02125-3393—Women's Studies, Jean Humez, Dir. Program offers an 18-cr minor and a 30-cr major.

Min, BA **Memphis SU,** Memphis, TN 38152—Women's Studies, Kell Mitchell, Dir. Program offers an 18-cr minor and a BA.

Mercer County CC, PO Box B, Trenton, NJ 08690—Women's Studies, Angela McGlynn, Coord.

Mercer U, 1400 Coleman Ave, Macon, GA 31207—Women's and Gender Studies (c/o Dept of Interdisciplinary Studies), Tiina A. Kirss, Dir.

Min **Mercy C,** 555 Broadway, Dobbs Ferry, NY 10522—Women's Studies, Margaret Morris, Coord. Program offers a minor.

Merrimack C, Turnpike Rd, North Andover, MA 01845—Women's Studies, Marguerite P. Kane, Dir.

Min, BA **Metropolitan SC of Denver,** Campus Box 36, PO Box 173362, Denver, CO 80217—Institute for Women's Studies and Services, Jodi Wetzel, Dir. Program offers a 24-cr minor and a BA.

BA **Metropolitan SU,** 730 Hennepin Ave, St Paul, MN 55106—Women's Studies, Kathleen Laughlin, Coord. Program offers an individualized BA.

Min **Miami U,** Oxford, OH 45056—Women's Studies, Susan Jarratt, Dir. Program offers an 18-cr minor.

Min **Miami, U of, Coral Gables,** 1252 Memorial Dr, 421 Ashe Bldg, P.O. Box 248265, Coral Gables, FL 33124-4640—Women's Studies, Barbara Woshinsky, Dir. Program offers a 15-cr minor.

BA **Michigan SU,** 301 Linton Hall, E Lansing, MI 48824—Women's Studies, Joyce R. Ladenson, Dir. Program offers a 30-cr BA.

BA, MA/Cer, PhD/Cer, PhD **Michigan, U of,** 234 W Hall Bldg, Ann Arbor, MI 48109-1092—Women's Studies, S. Smith, Dir. Program offers a BA, an 18-cr graduate certificate, and an interdisciplinary PhD in Women's Studies and English or Women's Studies and Psychology.

Min **Michigan, U of, Dearborn,** College of Arts, Sciences, and Letters (CASL), 2100 Mall, Dearborn, MI 48128—Women's Studies, Rotating Director. Program offers an 18-hr minor.

Min **Michigan, U of, Flint,** 280 UCEN, Flint, MI 48502—Women's and Gender Studies, Peggy Kahn, Contact. Program offers a 21-cr minor.

Min **Middle Tennessee SU,** Box 498 MTSU, Murfreesboro, TN 37132—Women's Studies, Nancy Rupprecht, Dir. Program offers an 18-cr minor.

Con, BA **Middlebury C,** Middlebury, VT 05753—Women's Studies, Diana Henderson and Tamar Mayer, Chairs. Program offers a 4-course concentration and a BA.

BA **Mills C,** Oakland, CA 94613—Women's Studies, Elizabeth Potter, Coord. Program offers a BA.

Con **Millsaps C,** 1701 N State St, Jackson, MS 39210—Women's Studies, Ann MacMaster, Coord. Program offers a concentration.

AA **Minneapolis CC,** 1501 Hennepin Ave, Minneapolis, MN 55403—Women's Upward Bound, Carol A. Hogard, Coord. Program offers the AA through Liberal Studies.

Min, BA **Minnesota, U of, Duluth,** 10 University Dr, Duluth, MN 55812—Women's Studies, Tineke Ritmeester, Chair. Program offers a 28-cr minor and a 54-cr BA.

Min, BA, MA/Min, PhD/Min **Minnesota, U of, Minneapolis,** 224 Church St SE, Minneapolis, MN 55455—Women's Studies (489 Ford Hall), Jacquelyn Zita, Chair. Program offers a 27-cr minor, a 56-cr major, a BA, and a graduate minor through the Center for Advanced Feminist Studies.

Min **Minnesota, U of, Morris,** Morris, MN 56267—Women's Studies, Mariam Darce Frenier, Coord. Program offers a 35-cr minor.

Cer **Mississippi SU,** PO Box C, Mississippi State, MS 39762—Women's Studies (c/o Dept of Sociology and Anthropology), Ellen S. Bryant, Adviser. Program offers a 15-cr certificate.

Mississippi U for Women, Box W-1634, Columbus, MS 39701—Women's Studies. Bridget Pieschel, Coord.

Mississippi, U of, University, MS 38677—Sarah Isom Center for Women's Studies, Joanne V. Hawks, Dir.

Min, BA **Missouri, U of, Columbia,** 309 Switzler Hall, Columbia, MO 65211-0011— Women Studies, Magdalena Garcia-Pinto, Dir. Program offers a 15-hr minor and a 30-hr BA.

Min **Missouri, U of, Kansas City,** Kansas City, MO 64110—Women's Studies, Kristin Esterberg, Dir. Program offers an 18-cr minor.

Cer, Grad Cer **Missouri, U of, St Louis,** 8001 Natural Bridge Rd, St Louis, MO 63121—Institute for Women's and Gender Studies, Frances Hoffmann, Dir. Program offers 18-cr-hr undergraduate and graduate certificates.

Min **Molloy C,** Wilbur Arts Center, Rockville Center, NY 11570—Women's Studies, Lillian Bozak-DeLeo, Dir. Program offers an 18-cr minor.

Min **Monmouth U,** W Long Branch, NJ 07764—Women's Studies, Karen Schmelzkopf, Coord. Program offers an interdisciplinary minor.

Min **Montana SU,** College of Letters and Science, Bozeman, MT 59717—Women's Studies, Diane Cuttrell, Program Coordinator. Program offers a 21-cr interdisciplinary minor.

Con **Montana, U of,** Missoula, MT 59812—Women's Studies (c/o Liberal Studies Program), Kay Unger, Dir. Program offers a 32-sem-hr emphasis in Liberal Studies.

Min **Montclair SU,** Upper Montclair, NJ 07043—Women's Studies, Linda Gould Levine, Dir. Program offers an 18-cr minor.

AA **Monterey Peninsula C,** 980 Fremont St, Monterey, CA 93940—Women's Studies, Phyllis Peet, Dir. Program offers a 60-unit AA which includes 18 in women's studies.

Con **Montgomery C, Rockville Campus,** 51 Mannakee St, Rockville, MD 20850— Women's Studies, Brianne Friel, Coord. Program offers a letter of recognition (core course plus 9 cr.)

Min, BA **Moorhead SU,** Moorhead, MN 56560—Women's Studies, Mary Ellen Schneider, Coord. Program offers a 24-cr minor and an individualized BA through Humanities.

Moorpark C, 7075 Campus Rd, Moorpark, CA 93021—Women's Studies, Carole Ginet, Dir.

Min **Moravian C,** Bethlehem, PA 18018—Women's Studies, Stacey Zaremba, Dir.

Min, BA **Mt Holyoke C,** South Hadley, MA 01075—Women's Studies, Asoka Bandarage, Chair. Program offers a minor and a BA. Member of the Five Colleges Consortium.

Min, BA **Mt St Joseph, C of,** Cincinnati, OH 45233—Women's Studies, Judith Sauerbrey, Dir. Program offers an 18-cr interdisciplinary minor and a 33-cr interdisciplinary BA.

Min **Muhlenberg C,** Chew St, Allentown, PA 18104—Women's Studies. Patrice DiQuinzio, Director. Program offers a 7-course minor.

Con **Nazareth C,** 4245 East Ave, Rochester, NY 14618—Women's Studies, Deborah Dooley, Dir. Program offers an 18-cr concentration.

Min **Nebraska, U of, Kearney,** Kearney, NE 68849—Women's Studies, Carol Lilly, Dir. Program offers a 24-cr-hr minor.

Min, BA **Nebraska, U of, Lincoln,** 337 Andrews Hall, Lincoln, NE 68588-0303—Women's Studies, Barbara DiBernard, Dir. Program offers an 18-cr minor and a BA.

Min **Nebraska, U of, Omaha,** Omaha, NE 68182—Women's Studies, Sandra Squires, Coord. Program offers an 18-cr minor.

Min **Neumann C,** Aston, PA 19014—Gender Studies, Martha Boston, Coord. Program offers an 18-cr minor.

Min, BA **Nevada, U of, Las Vegas,** 4505 Maryland Pkwy, Las Vegas, NV 89154-5055—Women's Studies, Ellen Cronan Rose, Dir. Program offers a 19-cr minor and a 43-cr BA.

Min **Nevada, U of, Reno,** Reno, NV 89557—Women's Studies, Jennifer Ring, Dir. Program offers an 18-cr minor.

Min **New England C,** Henniker, NH 03242—Women's Studies, Doris Birmingham, Dir. Program offers a minor.

New England, U of, 11 Hills Beach Rd, Biddeford, ME 04005—Women's Studies, Roxie B. Hamlin, Coord.

Min, BA **New Hampshire, U of,** 307A Dimond Library, Durham, NH 03824—Women's Studies, Mara Witzling and Barbara White, Coords. Program offers a 20-cr minor and a 40-cr BA. Honors in major available.

Min **New Jersey, C of,** Hillwood Lakes CN 4700, Bray Hill 131, Ewing, NJ 08650—Women's Studies, Ellen G. Friedman, Coord. Program offers an 18-cr minor.

Min, BA, Grad Min **New Mexico SU,** Box 30001, 3 WSP, Las Cruces, NM 88003—Women's Studies, Cookie White Stephan, Coord. Program offers an 18-cr undergraduate minor, a 24-cr supplementary major, and a 9-cr graduate minor.

Min **New Mexico, U of,** 2132 Mesa Vista Hall, Albuquerque, NM 87131—Women's Studies, Karen Foss, Dir. Program offers a 24-cr-hr minor.

Min **New Orleans, U of,** New Orleans, LA 70148—Women's Studies, Joyce Zonana, Dir. Program offers a 6-course minor through Liberal Arts.

Min, BA **New Rochelle, C of,** New Rochelle, NY 10805—Women's Studies, Susan Canning, Dir. Program offers an 18-cr minor and an interdisciplinary BA.

New School for Social Research, 66 W 12th St, New York, NY 10011—Vera List Center, Sondra Farganis, Dir.

BA **New York, CU of, Brooklyn C,** 2900 Bedford Ave and Ave H, Brooklyn, NY 11210—Women's Studies, Patricia Antoniello, Coord. Program offers a BA as a co-major.

Min, BA **New York, CU of, City C,** Convent Ave at 138th St, New York, NY 10031—Women's Studies, M. A. Samad-Matias, Dir. Program offers a 12–15-cr minor and the BA through Interdisciplinary Studies.

MA, PhD/Cer **New York, CU of, Graduate School and U Center,** 33 W 42nd St, New York, NY 10036—Women's Studies, Joyce Gelb, Coord. Program offers an MA in Liberal Studies with a concentration in Women's Studies. A 12–18-cr graduate certificate is also offered in conjunction with the PhD. Rachel Brownstein, Coord.

Min, BA **New York, CU of, Herbert H. Lehman C,** Bedford Park Blvd W, Bronx, NY 10468—Women's Studies, Anna Diz, Dir. Program offers a 12-cr minor and an 18-cr dual major.

BA **New York, CU of, Hunter C,** 695 Park Ave, Box 366, New York, NY 10021—Women's Studies, Marnia Lazreg, Coord. Program offers a collateral major.

New York, CU of, LaGuardia CC, 31-10 Thomson Ave, Long Island City, NY 11101—Family Institute, Sandra M. Watson, Dir.

New York, CU of, Medgar Evers C, 1150 Carroll St, Brooklyn, NY 11225—Women's Studies, Andree Nicola McLaughlin, Coord.

Min, BA **New York, CU of, Queens C,** Flushing, NY 11367—Women's Studies, Hester Eisenstein, Dir. Program offers a 21-cr minor and a 36-cr BA.

Min, BA **New York, CU of, Staten Island,** Staten Island, NY 10301—Women's Studies, Jo Gillikin, Dir. Program offers a minor and a major.

Con **New York, CU of, York C,** Jamaica, NY 11451—Women's Studies, Gloria Waldman, Coord. Program offers a concentration.

Min, BA, MA/Con, DA/Con, Grad Cer **New York, SU of, Albany,** 1400 Washington Ave, Albany, NY 12222—Women's Studies, Vivien Ng, Chair. Program offers an 18-cr minor, a BA, concentrations in the MA in Liberal Studies and the DA in Humanistic Studies programs, and a Women and Public Policy graduate certificate.

Min, BA, Grad Con, MA, PhD **New York, SU of, Binghamton,** Binghamton, NY 13902—Women's Studies, Dara Silberstein, Interim Dir. Program offers a minor, the BA through the Innovational Projects Board, graduate concentrations, and the MA and PhD through the History Department.

Min, BA, MA, PhD **New York, SU of, Buffalo,** 1010 Clemens Hall, Buffalo, NY 14260—Women's Studies, Ruth Meyerowitz, Coord. Program offers an 18-hr minor, 22-hr joint major, 32-hr BA major, and the MA and PhD through American Studies.

Min, BA, MA/Con **New York, SU of, New Paltz,** Guest House, New Paltz, NY 12561—Women's Studies, Susan Lehrer, Coord. Program offers a 19-cr minor, a 31-cr major with Women's Studies/Elementary Education, a 34-cr BA, and a concentration in the MA (Master's of Professional Studies) program in Humanistic Education.

Min, Grad Cer **New York, SU of, Stony Brook,** Stony Brook, NY 11794—Women's Studies, Adrienne Munich, Dir. Program offers a 21-cr minor and a 15-cr graduate certificate.

Min, BA, MA **New York, SU of, C at Brockport,** 176 FOB, Brockport, NY 14420—Women's Studies, Jennifer M. Lloyd, Dir. Program offers an 18-cr minor, an individualized BA through Liberal Arts, and the MA through Liberal Studies.

Min **New York, SU of, C at Cortland,** Cortland, NY 13045—Women's Studies (c/o Library), Gretchen Herrmann, Coord. Program offers an 18-cr interdisciplinary minor.

Min **New York, SU of, C at Geneseo,** Geneseo, NY 14454—Women's Studies, Julia M. Walker, Coord. Program currently offers an 18-cr minor; new 21-hr minor being phased in, to be official fall 1998.

Min, BA **New York, SU of, C at Old Westbury,** Box 210, Old Westbury, NY 11568—Women's Studies, Rosalyn Baxandall, Coord. Program offers a 20-cr minor and the BA through American Studies or Media and Communications.

Min **New York, SU of, C at Oneonta,** Oneonta, NY 13820—Women's Studies, Kathleen O'Mara, Chair. Department offers an 18–21-cr minor.

Min **New York, SU of, C at Oswego,** Oswego, NY 13126—Women's Studies, Geraldine Forbes, Dir. Program offers a 21-cr minor.

Min, BA **New York, SU of, C at Plattsburgh,** 101 Broad St, Plattsburgh, NY 12901—Women's Studies, Jennifer Scanlon, Dir. Program offers an 18-cr minor and the BA through Individualized Studies.

Min **New York, SU of, C at Potsdam,** Department of Politics, Potsdam, NY 13676—Women's Studies, Liliana Trevizian, Dir. Program offers an 18-cr minor.

Min **New York, SU of, Buffalo SC,** HB 113, Buffalo, NY 14222—Women's Studies, Rafika Merini, Coord. Program offers an 18-cr minor.

AA, BA, MA **New York, SU of, Empire SC,** 2 Union Ave, Saratoga Springs, NY 12866—Women's Studies, Meredith Brown, Convener. Program offers the AA and the BA through Interdisciplinary Studies, and the MA through Social Policy and through Liberal Studies.

BA **New York, SU of, Purchase C,** Social Science Bldg, Purchase, NY 10577—Women's Studies, Esther Newton, Coord. Program offers an individualized BA through Liberal Arts.

Min, BA **New York U,** 10 Washington Pl, 5th Fl, New York, NY 10003—Women's Studies, Carol Sternhell, Dir. Program offers a minor and a 40–48-cr BA with a disciplinary specialization.

Min **North Adams SC,** Church St, North Adams, MA 01247—Women's Studies (c/o Dept of Interdisciplinary Studies), Mary Ellen Cohane, Sumi Colligan, and Michele Ethier, Dirs. Program offers a 15-cr minor.

Min **North Carolina, U of, at Charlotte,** 301 Kennedy, Charlotte, NC 28223—Women's Studies, Laura Duhan Kaplan, Coord. Program offers a 21-cr minor.

North Carolina, U of, at Wilmington, 601 S College Rd, Wilmington, NC 28403—Women's Studies, K. Berkeley and B. Waxman, Coords.

Min, BA, Grad Min **North Carolina, U of, Chapel Hill,** 207D Caldwell Hall, CB#

3135, Chapel Hill, NC 27599—Women's Studies, Barbara J. Harris, Chair. Curriculum offers an undergraduate minor, a BA, and a graduate minor.

Min, BA **North Carolina, U of, Greensboro,** 200 Foust, Greensboro, NC 27412— Women's Studies, Katherine W. Mille, Dir. Curriculum offers an 18-cr minor and a 30–36-cr interdisciplinary BA.

Min, BA, Grad Min, MA/Con **North Carolina SU,** Box 7107, Raleigh, NC 27695- 7107—Women's and Gender Studies, Laura Severin, Dir. Program offers a 15- cr minor, the BA through Multidisciplinary Studies, a 9-cr graduate minor, and an MA specialization.

Min, Grad Con **North Dakota SU,** 1301 12 Ave N, 320 Minard Hall, Fargo, ND 58105—Women's Studies, Ines Senna Shaw, Coord. Program offers an 18-cr minor and a graduate concentration.

Min **North Dakota, U of,** PO Box 7113, University Station, Grand Forks, ND 58202—Women Studies, Sandra Donaldson, Dir. Program offers a minor.

Min **North Florida, U of,** 4567 St John's Bluff Rd S, Jacksonville, FL 32224—Women's Studies, Christine Rasche, Dir. Program offers an interdisciplinary 15-hr minor.

North Hennepin CC, 7411 85th Ave N, Brooklyn Park, MN 55445—Women's Studies, Sandra Stanley, Coord.

North Seattle CC, 9600 College Way N, Seattle, WA 98103—Women's Learning Center, Cecile Andrews, Dir.

Min, MA **North Texas, U of,** PO Box 13827, NT Station, Denton, TX 76203— Women's Studies, Barbara Rodman, Coord. Program offers an 18-cr minor and an interdisciplinary MA.

Min, BA **Northeastern Illinois U,** 5500 N St Louis, Chicago, IL 60625—Women's Studies, Irene Campos Carr, Coord. Program offers a 21-cr minor and an individualized BA.

Min, Grad Cer **Northeastern U,** 360 Huntington Ave (524 Holmes Hall), Boston, MA 02115—Women's Studies, Christine Gailey, Coord. Program offers a 7- course minor and a graduate certificate. Member of the Graduate Consortium in Women's Studies at Radcliffe C.

Min **Northern Arizona U,** Box 5695, Flagstaff, AZ 86011—Women's Studies, Joseph Boles, Dir. Program offers an 18-cr minor.

Min, BA, Grad Con, MA/Min, EdD/Min **Northern Colorado, U of,** Candelaria 12, Greeley, CO 80639—Women's Studies, Pamela Hewitt, Coord. Program offers an 18-cr minor, the BA through Interdisciplinary Studies, an individually developed graduate emphasis, and MA and EdD minors through the Graduate Interdisciplinary Degree Program.

Con **Northern Essex CC,** Elliott Way, Haverhill, MA 01830—Women's Studies, Priscilla B. Bellairs, Coord. Program offers an 18-cr option through the Liberal Arts degree.

Min, BA, Grad Con **Northern Illinois U,** Reavis Hall 103, DeKalb, IL 60115— Women's Studies, Amy K. Levin, Dir. Program offers an 18-cr minor, an individualized BA, and a 12-cr graduate concentration.

Min, MA **Northern Iowa, U of,** Cedar Falls, IA 50614-0509—Women's Studies, Victoria DeFrancisco and Martha J. Reineke, Dirs. Program offers a 21-cr minor and a 34-cr-hr MA.

Min **Northern Kentucky U,** Louie B. Nunn Dr, Highland Heights, KY 41099—Women's Studies, Judith A. Bechtel, Dir. Program offers a 21-cr minor.

Cer, BA, Grad Con **Northwestern U,** 2000 Sheridan Rd, Evanston, IL 60208—Women's Studies, Arlene Kaplan Daniels, Dir. Program offers a 9-cr certificate, a self-designed BA, and a graduate concentration.

Cer **Notre Dame, U of,** 104 O'Shaughnessy Hall, Notre Dame, IN 46556—Gender Studies, Jennifer Glass, Dir. Program offers a 15-hr certificate.

Con **Oakland U,** 517 Wilson, Rochester, MI 48063—Women's Studies, Susan Hawkins, Coord. Program offers a concentration.

Min, BA **Oberlin C,** Oberlin, OH 44074—Women's Studies, Edith Swan, Dir. Program offers a minor and a BA.

Min, BA **Occidental C,** 1600 Campus Rd, Los Angeles, CA 90041—Women's Studies, Mary Weismantel, Chair. Program offers a 5-course minor and an 11-course BA.

Min, BA, MA, PhD **Ohio SU,** 286 Univ Hall, 230 N Oval Mall, Columbus, OH 43210—Center for Women's Studies, Sally L. Kitch, Dir. Program offers a 25-qtr-hr minor, a BA, a 50-qtr-hr MA, and an independent PhD.

Ohio SU, Newark Campus, 1179 University Dr, Newark, OH 43055—Women's Studies, Judith Johnson, Coord.

Cer, Grad Cer, MA, PhD **Ohio U,** 001 Academic Center, President St, Athens, OH 45701—Women's Studies, Arleen Hall, Dir. Program offers a 30-qtr-hr undergraduate certificate, a 17–20-qtr-hr graduate certificate, and an interdisciplinary MA and PhD.

Min, BA **Ohio Wesleyan U,** Delaware, OH 43015—Women's Studies, Laurie Churchill, Coord. Program offers an 18-cr minor and a BA.

Ohlone C, 43600 Mission Blvd, Fremont, CA 94539—Women's Studies, Alison Kuehner, Coord.

Oklahoma SU, Stillwater, OK 74078—Women's Curriculum Committee, Becky Johnson, Coord.

Min, BA, MA, PhD **Oklahoma, U of,** Rm. 528, PHSC, 601 Elm St, Norman, OK 73019-0315—Women's Studies, Betty J. Harris, Dir. Program offers an 18-cr minor; a 36-cr BA; an interdisciplinary MA through History, English, Human Relations, and Sociology; and an interdisciplinary PhD by petition.

Min, BA, BS, Grad Cer, MA **Old Dominion U,** College of Arts & Letters, Norfolk, VA 23529—Women's Studies, Anita Clair Fellman, Dir. Program offers a 15-cr minor, a BA/BS, a graduate certificate, and the MA through the Institute of Humanities.

Min, AA **Onondaga CC,** Syracuse, NY 13215—Women's Studies, Mary Bogin, Coord. Program offers a 12-cr minor and the AA through Interdisciplinary Studies.

BA/Cer, MA/Min, MA, EdD/Min, PhD/Min **Oregon SU,** Corvallis, OR 97331—Women's Studies, Janet Lee, Dir. Program offers a 30-cr certificate, graduate minors in MA, EdD, and PhD programs, and the MA in Interdisciplinary Studies.

Min, Grad Cer **Oregon, U of,** Eugene, OR 97403—Women's Studies, Sarah Marie Harvey, Dir. Program offers a 24-cr minor and a graduate certificate.

Oxford C of Emory U, Oxford, GA 30267—Southern Institute of Gender Studies, Theodore Davis, Coord.

Pace U, 41 Park Row Room 1502, New York, NY 10038—Women's Studies, Karla Jay, Dir.

Min **Pacific Lutheran U,** Tacoma, WA 98447—Women's Studies, Nancy R. Howell, Chair. Program offers a 20-hr minor.

Con **Pacific, U of the,** 3601 N Pacific Ave, Stockton, CA 95211—Women's Studies, Sally M. Miller, Coord. Program offers a 20-unit concentration through the Center for Integrated Studies.

AA/Con **Parkland C,** 2400 W Bradley, Champaign, IL 61821—Office of Women's Programs and Services, Pauline E. Kayes, Dir. Program offers a 9-hr concentration for an AA degree in Liberal Arts.

Min, BA, Grad Min **Pennsylvania SU,** 13 Sparks Bldg, University Park, PA 16802—Women's Studies, Stephanie Shields, Dir. Program offers an 18-cr minor, a 124-cr BA (Lib Arts) and a 15-cr graduate minor.

Cer, Min **Pennsylvania SU, Erie,** The Behrend College, Station Road, Erie, PA 16563-0500—Women/Gender Studies Program, Yesho Atil, Dir. Program offers a certificate and an 18-cr minor.

Min **Pennsylvania SU, McKeesport,** University Dr, McKeesport, PA 15132—Women's Studies, Margaret L. Signorella. Program offers a minor.

Min, BA, Grad Cer **Pennsylvania, U of,** 3440 Market St, Suite 590, Philadelphia, PA 19104—Women's Studies, Demie Kurz, Dir. Program offers a 6-cr minor, a BA, and a graduate certificate.

BA **Pine Manor C,** 400 Heath St, Chestnut Hill, MA 02167—Women's Studies, Melinda Ponder, Coord. Program offers an individualized BA.

Cer **Pittsburg SU,** Grubbs Hall, Pittsburg, KS 66762—Women's Studies, Kathleen Nichols, Coord. Program offers a 15-cr certificate.

Cer, BA, MA/Cer, PhD/Cer **Pittsburgh, U of,** 2632 Cathedral of Learning, Pittsburgh, PA 15260—Women's Studies, Kathleen Blee, Dir. Program offers an 18-cr certificate at the BA level, an individualized BA, a 4-course Master's level certificate, and a 6-course doctoral level certificate.

Cer **Pittsburgh, U of, Greensburg Campus,** 1150 Mt Pleasant Rd, Greensburg, PA 15601—Gender Studies, Diane Marsh. Program offers a certificate.

BA **Pitzer C,** 1050 N Mills Ave, Claremont, CA 91711—Gender and Feminist Studies, Ann Stromberg, Dir. Program offers a BA. Member of the Claremont Colleges Consortium.

Min **Plymouth SC,** Plymouth, NH 03264—Women's Studies, Stacey G. Yap, Chair. Program offers an 18-cr minor.

BA **Pomona C,** Claremont, CA 91711—Women's Studies, Elizabeth Crighton, Coord. Program offers a BA. Member of the Claremont Colleges Consortium.

Min, BA/Cer **Portland SU,** PO Box 751, Portland, OR 97207—Women's Studies, Johanna Brenner, Coord. Program offers a 28-cr minor and a 34-cr certificate.

Portland, U of, 5000 N Willamette Blvd, Portland, OR 97203—Women's Studies, Loretta Zimmerman, Coord.

ThM/Con, MDiv/Con **Princeton Theological Seminary,** PO 821, Princeton, NJ 08542—Women's Studies, Carol Lakey Hess, Adv. Emphasis on Women's Studies designed for ThM candidates and as a specialization area for MDiv candidates—students can work interdepartmentally on concerns of women in relation to ministry. Courses in Princeton University's Women's Studies program may be taken under the Seminary's Inter-Institutional Arrangements.

Cer **Princeton U,** 113 Dickinson Hall, Princeton, NJ 08544—Program in Women's Studies, Deborah Nord, Dir. Program offers a certificate.

Providence C, Providence, RI 02918—Women's Studies (c/o Dept of Sociology), Charlotte O'Kelly, Coord.

Min **Puget Sound, U of,** Tacoma, WA 98416—Women's Studies, Florence Sandler, Coord. Program offers a 15-cr minor.

Min, MA/Min, PhD/Min **Purdue U,** 1361 Liberal Arts and Education Bldg, Rm 2258, West Lafayette, IN 47907—Women's Studies, Berenice A. Carroll, Dir. Program offers a 15-cr undergraduate minor and a graduate minor requiring 9 hrs for an MA and 12 hrs for the PhD.

Min, AA **Purdue U, Calumet,** Hammond, IN 46323—Women's Studies, Colette Morrow, Coord. Program offers a 15-cr minor and the AA.

Min, BA **Quinnipiac C,** Box 119, Hamden, CT 06518—Women's Studies, Michele Hoffnung, Dir. Program offers an 18-cr minor and the BA through Interdisciplinary Studies.

Quinsigamond CC, 670 W Boylston St, Worcester, MA 01606—Women's Center, Annie Dubois.

Radcliffe C, Fay House, 10 Garden St, Cambridge, MA 02138—Graduate Consortium in Women's Studies, Renee Fall, Coord.

Min **Ramapo C of NJ,** School of Social Science and Human Services, Mahwah, NJ 07430—Women's Studies, Yolanda Prieto, Coord. Program offers an 18-cr minor.

AA **Rancho Santiago CC,** 8045 E. Chapman Ave, Orange, CA 92669-4512—Women's Studies, Georgia Summers, Chair.

Min, BA **Randolph-Macon C,** PO Box 5005, Ashland, VA 23005—Women's Studies, Donna Serniak, Dir. Program offers a 15-cr minor and a 30-cr BA.

Randolph-Macon Woman's C, 2500 Rivermont Ave, Lynchburg, VA 24503—Women's Studies, Janice Hullum, Coord.

Min, BA **Redlands, U of,** PO Box 3080, Redlands, CA 92373—Women's Studies, Emily Culpepper, Dir. Program offers a 20-unit minor and the BA through the Johnston Center for Integrative Studies.

Regis C, 235 Wellesley St, Weston, MA 02193—Women's Studies, Mary Bryan, Coord.

Min, BA, MA **Rhode Island C,** 600 Mt Pleasant Ave, Providence 02908—Women's Studies, Maureen Reddy, Dir. Program offers an 18-cr minor, a 30-cr BA, and an independent MA.

Min, BA, MA/Con, PhD/Con **Rhode Island, U of,** 315 Roosevelt Hall, Kingston, RI 02881—Women's Studies, Mary Ellen Reilly, Coord. Program offers an 18-cr minor, a 30-cr BA, and concentrations in the MA and PhD programs.

BA **Rice U,** PO Box 1892, Houston, TX 77251—Women's Studies, Helena Michie, Coord. Program offers a BA.

Min, BA **The Richard Stockton C of New Jersey,** Jim Leeds Rd, Pomona, NJ

08240—Women's Studies. Program offers a minor and an individualized BA through Liberal Arts.

Min, BA **Richmond, U of,** Ryland Hall, Richmond, VA 23173—Women's Studies, Elisabeth Gruner, Coord. Program offers an 18-cr minor and a 30-cr BA.

Cer, Min **Rider U,** 2083 Lawrenceville Rd, Lawrenceville, NJ 08648—Women's Studies, Virginia Cyrus, Dir. Program offers a certificate and a minor.

Min **Ripon C,** 300 Seward St, Ripon, WI 54971—Women's Studies, Robin Woods, Dir. Program offers an 18-cr minor.

Rivier C, 420 S Main St, Nashua, NH 03060—Women's Studies, Annick Durand, Dir.

Rochester CC, 851 30th Ave SE, Rochester, MN 55904—Women's Studies, Arlouene Olson, Dir.

Min, BA, Grad Cer **Rochester, U of,** Susan B. Anthony Inst for Women's Studies, Lattimore 538, Rochester, NY 14627—Women's Studies, Rosemary Kegl, Dir. Program offers a minor, major, double major, BA, and graduate certificate.

Min **Rollins C,** Winter Park, FL 32789—Women's Studies, Rosemary Curb, Coord. Program offers a 21-cr minor.

Min, BA, MA **Roosevelt U,** 430 S Michigan Ave, Chicago, IL 60605 and 1651 McConnor Parkway, Schaumburg, IL 60173—Women's Studies, Susan Weininger, Dir. Program offers an 18-sem-hr minor in the College of Arts and Sciences, BGS (Bachelor of General Studies) and MGS (Master of General Studies) concentrations in Women's Studies, and a 33-sem-hr MA in the College of Arts and Sciences.

Rose SC, 6420 SE 15, Midwest City, OK 73110—Women's Programs, Gwen Atkinson, Coord.

Min **Rowan C of New Jersey,** Triad Building, Glassboro, NJ 08028—Women's Studies, Janet Lindman, Coord. Program offers an 18-cr minor.

Min, BA **Rutgers, SU of New Jersey, Newark,** 360 Martin Luther King Blvd, Newark, NJ 07102—Women's Studies, Frances Bartkowski, Dir. Program offers a 21-cr minor and a 36-cr major.

Min, BA, Grad Cer, MA **Rutgers, SU of New Jersey,** Voorhees Chapel-Lower Level, Room 8, Douglass Campus, New Brunswick, NJ 08903—Women's Studies, Harriet Davidson, Dir. Program offers an 18-cr minor, a BA, a 9-cr graduate certificate, and a MA.

Min **Rutgers, SU of New Jersey, Camden College of Arts and Sciences,** Camden, NJ 08102—Women's Studies (c/o Dept of Sociology), Sheila Cosminsky, Dir. Program offers an 18-cr minor.

Min **St Ambrose U,** 518 W Locust, Davenport, IA 52803—Women's Studies, Beatrice Jacobson, Dir. Program offers an 18-cr minor.

Min **St Benedict, C of,** St Joseph, MN 56374—Gender and Women's Studies, Linda Lierheimer, Dir. Program offers a minor.

Min, BA **St Catherine, C of,** PO Box 4150, 2004 Randolph Ave, St Paul, MN 55105—Abigail Quigley McCarthy Center for Women's Research, Resources, and Scholarship, Sharon Doherty, Coord. Program offers a minor and a consortial BA.

St Clair County CC, 323 Erie St, PO Box 5015, Port Huron, MI 48061—Women's Studies, Linda E. Flickinger, Coord.

Min **St Cloud SU,** 720 S 4th Ave, Ed Bldg, B120, St Cloud, MN 56301—Women's Studies, Pat Samuel, Dir. Program offers a 24–36-cr minor.

St Elizabeth, C of, 2 Convent Road, Morristownship, NJ 07960—Women's Studies.

St Francis, C of, 500 Wilcox, Joliet, IL 60435—Women's Studies, Rosemary Small, Coord.

Min **St John's U,** Collegeville, MN 56321—Gender and Women's Studies, Linda Lierheimer, Dir. Dept located at C of St Benedict. Program offers a minor.

Min, BA **St Joseph C,** 1678 Asylum Ave, West Hartford, CT 06117—Women's Studies, Barbara Lacey, Coord. Program offers an 18-cr minor and a BA.

Min **St Joseph's U,** 5600 City Ave, Philadelphia, PA 19131—Gender Studies, Julie McDonald, Dir. Program offers a 6-course minor.

Cer **St Louis U,** 221 N Grand Blvd, St Louis, MO 63103—Women's Studies, Judith Gibbons, Dir. Program offers an 18-cr certificate.

Min, BA **St Mary's C,** Notre Dame, IN 46556—Women's Studies, Susan Alexander, Coord. Program offers a 15-cr minor and a 30-hr self-designed major.

Con, BA **St Olaf C,** 1520 St. Olaf Ave, Northfield, MN 55057—Women's Studies, Judy Kutulas, Dir. Program offers a 5-cr concentration and a BA.

Min **St Scholastica, C of,** 1200 Kenwood Ave, Duluth, MN 55811—Women's Studies, Nancy Fitzgerald, Coord. Program offers a 28-cr minor.

AA **Sacramento City C,** 3835 Freeport Blvd, Sacramento, CA 95822—Women's Studies (Social Sciences Division), Angela Curiale, Coord. Program offers the AA.

AA **Saddleback C,** 28000 Marguerite Pkwy, Mission Viejo, CA 92692—Women's Studies, Program offers a 20-unit AA.

Con, AA **Sage Junior C of Albany,** 140 New Scotland Ave, Albany, NY 12208—Women's Studies, Sydney Pressman and Charlotte A. Newman, Coords. Program offers a 12-cr concentration and the AA through Liberal Studies.

Min **Salem C,** Main Hall, Old Salem, Winston-Salem, NC 27108—Women's Studies, Gary Ljungquist, Coord. Program offers an 18-cr minor.

Min **Salem SC,** Salem, MA 01970—Women's Studies, Pat Gozemba, Coord. Program offers an 18-cr minor.

Min, BA, MA **San Diego SU,** San Diego, CA 92182-0437—Women's Studies, Bonnie Zimmerman, Chair. Program offers an 18-cr minor, a 33-unit BA, and an MA.

Min **San Diego, U of,** Alcala Park, San Diego, CA 92110—Gender Studies, Linda A.M. Perry and Cecilia Ruiz, Coords. Program offers a minor.

AA **San Francisco, City C of,** 50 Phelan Ave, San Francisco, CA 94112—Women's Studies, Susan Evans, Coord. Program offers an AA.

BA, MA **San Francisco SU,** 1600 Holloway Ave, San Francisco, CA 94132—Women's Studies, Susan Sung, Chair. Program offers a BA and an MA.

San Joaquin Delta C, 5151 Pacific Ave, Stockton, CA 95207—Women's Program, Naomi Fitch, Coord.

Min, BA, MA **San Jose SU,** One Washington Square, San Jose, CA 95192—Women's Studies, Lois Rita Helmbold, Coord. Program offers a 15-cr minor, and the BA and MA through Social Science.

San Mateo C, 1700 W Hillsdale Blvd, San Mateo, CA 94402—Women's Studies, Marci Manhood, Coord.

Min, BA, MA **Sangamon SU,** Springfield, IL 62794—Women's Studies, Mattilow

Catchpole, Dir. Program offers a 16-hr minor, and a self-designed 60-hr BA and 42-hr MA through the Individual Option Program.

Santa Barbara City C, 721 Cliff Dr, Santa Barbara, CA 93109—Women's Studies.

Con **Santa Clara U,** Santa Clara, CA 95053—Women's Studies, Alma M. Garcia, Dir. Program offers a 6-course special emphasis.

Santa Monica C, 1900 Pico Blvd, Santa Monica, CA 90405—Women's Program, Mary Staton, Dir.

BA, MA **Sarah Lawrence C,** Bronxville, NY 10708—Women's History, Elisabeth Israels Perry, Dir. Program offers an interdisciplinary BA and an MA in Women's History.

BA **Scripps C,** 1030 Columbia Ave, Claremont, CA 91711—Women's Studies, Judy LeMaster, Coord. Program offers an individualized BA. Member of the Claremont Colleges Consortium.

Min **Seton Hill C,** Greensburg, PA 15601—Women's Studies, Frances M. Leap, Coord. Program offers an 18-cr minor.

Min **Shippensburg U of Pennsylvania,** Shippensburg, PA 17257—Women's Studies, Cynthia Drenovsky, Coord. Program offers an 18-hr minor.

Shoreline CC, 16101 Greenwood Ave N, Seattle, WA 98133—Women's Program, Dianne Dailey, Dir.

Sierra C, 5000 Rocklin Rd, Rocklin, CA 95677—Women's Studies, Mary Moon, Coord.

BA, MA **Simmons C,** 300 The Fenway, Boston, MA 02115—Women's Studies, Pamela Bromberg, Coord. Program offers a BA and the MA through Liberal Studies.

BA **Simon's Rock C of Bard,** Alford Road, Great Barrington, MA 01230—Women's Studies. Program offers a 45–50-cr BA.

Simpson C, 701 North C St, Indianola, IA 50125—Women's Studies, Katharina Tumpek-Kjellmark, Chair.

Skagit Valley C, 2405 College Way, Mt Vernon, WA 98273—Women's Program, Sharon Johnson, Dir.

Min, BA **Skidmore C,** Saratoga Springs, NY 12866—Women's Studies, Mary Stange, Dir. Program offers an 18-cr minor and a 30-cr BA.

Cer, Min **Slippery Rock U,** Slippery Rock, PA 16057—Women's Studies, Jace Condravy, Dir. Program offers a 12-cr certificate and a 15-cr minor.

Min, BA **Smith C,** Northampton, MA 01063—Women's Studies, Susan Van Dyne, Dir. Program offers a 24-cr minor and a 40-cr interdepartmental BA. A sem or year long Junior Year in Women's Studies is offered to qualified visiting students. Member of the Five Colleges Consortium.

Min, BA, MA **Sonoma SU,** Rohnert Park, CA 94928—Women's and Gender Studies, E. Kay Trimberger, Coord. Program offers a 16-unit minor, a 20-unit minor in Women's Health, the BA in Gender Studies, and the MA through Interdisciplinary Studies.

Min, BA, Grad Cer **South Carolina, U of,** 1710 College St, Columbia, SC 29208—Women's Studies, Sue Rosser, Dir (Mary Crawford, Grad Cer Dir). Program offers an 18-cr minor, the BA through Interdisciplinary Studies, and an interdisciplinary 18-cr graduate certificate.

Min **South Dakota SU,** Scobey 325, Brookings, SD 57007—Women's Studies, Virginia Norris, Coord. Program offers an 18-cr minor.

Min, MA **South Dakota, U of,** University Exchange, Dakota Hall 209, Vermillion, SD 57069—Women's Studies, Alice T. Gasque, Coord. Program offers an 18-cr minor and an MSS through Interdisciplinary Studies.

Cer, Min, BA **South Florida, U of,** 4202 E Fowler Ave, Tampa, FL 33620—Women's Studies (HMS 413), Linda L. McAlister, Chair. Department offers a 15-cr certificate on women of color, an 18-cr minor, and a 36-hr BA.

Min **Southeast Missouri SU,** Cape Girardeau, MO 63701—Women's Studies, Pamela Hearn, Coord. Program offers a 15-cr minor.

Min, BA, Grad Cer **Southern California, U of,** Safety Systems Management Bldg, Rm 116, Los Angeles, CA 90089-0036—Program for the Study of Women and Men in Society, Judith Grant, Chair. Program offers a minor, a BA, and a graduate certificate.

Min **Southern Colorado, U of,** 2200 Bonforte Blvd, Pueblo, CO 81001—Women's Studies, Penny Green, Coord. Program offers a 21-cr minor.

Min, Grad Con **Southern Connecticut SU,** 501 Crescent St, New Haven, CT 06515—Women's Studies, Vara Neverow and Rosalyn Amenta, Coords. Program offers an 18-cr minor and graduate concentrations in English and History.

Min, BA, Grad Con **Southern Illinois U, Carbondale,** 806 Chautauqua, Carbondale, IL 62901—Women's Studies, Beverly Stitt, Coord. Program offers an 18-cr minor, the BA through Interdisciplinary Studies, and a graduate concentration.

Min **Southern Illinois U, Edwardsville,** Box 1350, Edwardsville, IL 62026—Women's Studies, Barbara Q. Schmidt, Coord. Program offers a 15-cr minor.

Min, BA **Southern Maine, U of,** 96 Falmouth St, Portland, ME 04103—Women's Studies, Nancy K. Gish, Dir. Program offers a 21-cr minor and a 42-cr BA.

Min **Southern Methodist U,** Dallas, TX 75275—Women's Studies, Carolyn Sargent, Coord. Program offers a 15-cr minor and an individualized major for students with GPA 3.5 and above.

Min, BA/Cer, Grad Min **Southern Oregon SC,** Siskiyou Blvd, Ashland, OR 97520—Women's Studies, Shelley J. Eriksen, Dir. Program offers a certificate, a 24-cr undergraduate minor, and an interdisciplinary graduate minor.

Southern Utah SC, Cedar City, UT 84720—Women's Resource Committee, Betty Kingsford, Coord.

Min **Southwest Texas SU,** San Marcos, TX 78666—Center for Multicultural and Gender Studies (c/o Dept of English), Leticia Garza-Falcón-Sánchez, Dir. Program offers an 18-cr-hr minor.

Min, BA **Southwestern U,** PO Box 770, Georgetown, TX 78626—Women's Studies, Helene Meyers, Dir. Program offers an 18-hr minor and a 30-hr BA.

Min **Spelman C,** Box 115, 350 Spelman Ln NW, Atlanta, GA 30314—Women's Research and Resource Center, Beverly Guy-Sheftall, Dir. Program offers an 18-cr minor.

BA **Stanford U,** Stanford, CA 94305-8640—Feminist Studies, Estelle Freedman, Dir. Program offers a BA and an interdisciplinary graduate program.

Min, BA **Stephens C,** Columbia, MO 65215—Women's Studies (Box 2013), Carol O. Perkins, Dir. Program offers a 5-course minor and an individualized BA.

Min **Stetson U,** DeLand, FL 32720—Women and Gender Studies, Karen Kaivola, Dir. Program offers an 18-cr minor.

AA **Suffolk County CC,** 533 College Rd, Selden, NY 11784—Women's Studies, Alice Goode-Elman, Dept Head. Program offers the 12-cr AA through Liberal Arts and Sciences.

Min **Suffolk U, Beacon Hill,** 41 Temple St, Boston, MA 02114—Women's Studies, Krisanne Bursik, Dir. Program offers an interdisciplinary minor.

Con **Swarthmore C,** 500 College Ave, Swarthmore, PA 19081-1397—Women's Studies, Lisa Smulyan, Coord. Program offers an undergraduate concentration requiring at least five courses in Women's Studies.

Min, BA **Sweet Briar C,** Sweet Briar, VA 24595—Women and Gender Studies, Jody Bart, Dir. Program offers an 18-cr minor and may be constructed as a self-designed major.

Con, Min, BA, PhD/Con, Grad Cer **Syracuse U,** 109 Heroy, Geology Building, Syracuse, NY 13244—Women's Studies, Diane Lyden Murphy, Dir. Program offers an 18-cr concentration, an 18-cr minor, a 30-cr BA, dissertation recognition, and a 12-cr graduate certificate.

Min, BA, MA, Grad Cer **Temple U,** Broad St and Montgomery Ave, 616 Gladfelter Hall 025-28, Philadelphia, PA 19122—Women's Studies, Sonia Sanchez, Dir. Program offers a 21-cr minor, a BA, the MA through the Interdisciplinary Master of Liberal Arts Program, and a graduate certificate.

Min, BA **Tennessee, U of,** 1912 Terrace Ave, Knoxville, TN 37996-3556—Women's Studies, Nancy Moore Gosley, Chair. Program offers an 18-sem-hr minor and a 30-sem-hr interdisciplinary BA.

Min **Texas A&M U,** College Station, 77843-4351—Women's Studies, (306 Academic Bldg), Pamela R. Matthews, Dir. Program offers an 18-cr minor.

Min, MA **Texas Tech U,** PO Box 41162, Lubbock, TX 79409—Women's Studies, Gwendolyn T. Sorell, Coord. Program offers an 18-cr minor and an interdisciplinary MA.

Min **Texas, U of, at Arlington,** Box 19599, Arlington, TX 76019—Women's Studies, Dana Dunn, Dir. Program offers an 18-hr minor.

Con, Min **Texas, U of, Austin,** Austin, TX 78712—Women's Studies, Lucia Albino Gilbert, Dir. Program offers an 18-cr concentration and a 12-cr-hr minor.

Con, Grad Con **Texas, U of, Dallas,** Box 830608, Richardson, TX 75083-0688—Women's Studies, Deborah Stott, Coord. Program offers graduate and undergraduate concentrations.

Min **Texas, U of, El Paso,** Liberal Arts 402, El Paso, TX 79968—Women's Studies, Sandra Beyer, Dir. Program offers an 18-cr minor.

Min **Texas Woman's U,** PO Box 425887, Denton, TX 76204-5887—Dept of Sociology and Social Work, Joyce Williams, Chair. Program offers an 18-cr-hr minor.

Min, BA, PhD/Min **Toledo, U of,** 2801 W Bancroft, Toledo, OH 43606—Women's Studies, Harriet F. Adams, Dir. Program offers a 22-cr minor, a 31-cr major, and a PhD minor.

AA **Tompkins-Cortland CC,** 170 North St, PO Box 139, Dryden, NY 13053—Women's Studies, Sandra Pollack, Contact. Program offers a 21-cr AS.

Min, BA **Towson SU,** Towson, MD 21204—Women's Studies, Jo-Ann Pilardi, Coord. Program offers an 18-cr minor and a 30-cr independent BA.

Min, BA **Trinity C,** Colchester Ave, Burlington, VT 05401—Women's Studies, Linda Rodd, Dir. Program offers an 18-cr minor and the BA through Special Studies.

Min, BA **Trinity C,** 300 Summit St, Hartford, CT 06106—Women's Studies, Joan D. Hedrick, Dir. Program offers a minor and a BA.

Con **Trinity C,** Michigan Ave and Franklin St NE, Washington, DC 20017—Women's Studies, Roxana Moayedi, Coord. Program offers an 18-cr interdepartmental concentration.

Con, Min **Tufts U,** Medford, MA 02155—Women's Studies, Soheir Morsy, Dir. Program offers a concentration through American Studies and a 5-cr minor with a senior project. Member of the Graduate Consortium in Women's Studies at Radcliffe C.

Min, BA **Tulane U, Newcomb College Center for Research on Women,** New Orleans, LA 70118—Women's Studies, Beth Willinger, Dir. Program offers an 18-unit minor and a 33-unit BA.

Cer **Tulsa, U of,** 600 S College Ave, Tulsa, OK 74104—Women's Studies, Charlotte Stewart, Coord. Program offers an 18-hr certificate.

Min, BA **Union C,** Reamer College Center, Rm 302, Schenectady, NY 12308—Women's Studies, Sharon Gmelch, Dir; Karen Brison (Acting Director 1996-97). Program offers a 6-course minor and a 12-course BA.

Min **Ursinus C,** Collegeville, PA 19426—Women's Studies (c/o Dept of Modern Languages), Eileen M. England, Coord. Program offers a 16-cr minor.

Min, Cer **Utah SU,** Logan, UT 84322-0730—Women's Studies Committee, Pam Riley, Chair. Program offers a 36-qtr-hr certificate through Interdisciplinary Studies and an 18-qtr-hr minor.

Min, BA **Utah, U of,** 217 Bldg #44, Salt Lake City, UT 84112—Women's Studies, Christina Gringer, Dir. Program offers a 30-hr minor and a 50-hr major.

BA **Valparaiso U,** Valparaiso, IN 46383—Women's Studies, D. Nuechterlein, Contact. Program offers an individualized BA.

Min **Vanderbilt U,** Nashville, TN 37235—Women's Studies, Nancy A. Walker, Dir. Program offers an 18-hr minor.

Con, BA **Vassar C,** Poughkeepsie, NY 12601—Women's Studies, Colleen Cohen, Dir. Program offers a correlate sequence (a 6-unit series with a transcript notation) and a BA.

Ventura C, 4667 Telegraph Rd, Ventura, CA 93003—Women's Studies, Lyn MacConnaire, Dir.

Vermont C of Norwich U, Montpelier, VT 05602—Women's Studies, Rhoda Carroll, Coord.

Min, BA **Vermont, U of,** Old Mill, Burlington, VT 05405—Women's Studies, Robyn R. Warhol, Dir. Program offers an 18-cr minor and a BA.

BA **Villanova U,** 209 Vasey Hall, Villanova, PA 19085—Women's Studies, June W. Lytel, Dir. Program offers the BA through Interdisciplinary Studies.

Min **Virginia Commonwealth U,** 923 W. Franklin, Box 843060, Richmond, VA 23284—Women's Studies, Diana Scully, Dir. Program offers an 18-cr minor.

Con **Virginia Polytechnic Inst & SU,** 10 Sandy Hall, Blacksburg, VA 24061—
Women's Studies, Ann Kilkelly, Dir. Program offers an 18-cr concentration.
Con, BA, MA/Cer **Virginia, U of,** 227 Minor Hall,Charlottesville, VA 22903—
Women's Studies, Ann J. Lane, Program Dir; Rita Felski, Grad Cer Dir. Program
offers a 21-cr concentration, a BA, and a 27-cr graduate certificate with the MA
in English.

Min **Viterbo C,** 815 S 9th St, La Crosse, WI 54601—Women's Studies, Apryl Ferris.
Program offers a minor.

Min **Wake Forest U,** PO Box 7365, Reynolda Station, Winston-Salem, NC 27109—
Women's Studies, Mary DeShazer, Coord. Program offers a 24-cr minor.

Min **Wartburg C,** 222 9th St NW, Waverly, IA 50677—Women's Studies, Cheryl
Jacobsen, Coord. Program offers a 21-cr-hr minor.

Con, Min **Washington SU,** Pullman, WA 99164-4007—Women Studies, Deborah J.
Haynes, Dir. Program offers a concentration and a 16-cr minor.

Min, BA, Grad Con **Washington U,** St Louis, MO 63130—Women's Studies, Helen
Power, Coord. Program offers an 18-cr minor, a 27-cr BA, and a graduate core
curriculum.

BA, Grad Cer **Washington, U of,** Box 354345, Seattle, WA 98195-4345—Women's
Studies, Shirley Yee, Acting Dir. Program offers a 70-cr BA and a 20-cr graduate
certificate.

Washtenaw CC, 4800 E Huron River Dr, PO Box D-1, Ann Arbor, MI 48106—
Women's Studies, Judith Swan, Coord.

Wayne County CC, 801 W Fort St, Detroit, MI 48226—Women's Studies, Kathryn
Irons, Coord.

Min, BA **Wayne SU,** 51 W Warren, Detroit, MI 48202—Women's Studies. Program
offers an 18-cr minor and a 32-cr BA.

Min **Weber SU,** Ogden, UT 84408-1217—Women's Studies, Gloria Z. Wurt, Coord.
Program offers a 28-cr-hr minor.

Min **Webster U,** 470 E Lockwood, St Louis, MO 63119—Women's Studies, Monica
Moore, Coord. Program offers an 18-cr minor.

BA **Wellesley C,** Wellesley, MA 02181—Women's Studies, Lidwien Kapteijns, Chair.
Program offers a BA.

Min, BA **Wells C,** Aurora, NY 13206—Women's Studies, Diane Koester, Coord.
Program offers an 18-cr minor and a 35—40-sem-hr BA.

BA **Wesleyan U,** 287 High St, Middletown, CT 06457—Women's Studies, Christina
Crosby, Chair. Program offers a BA.

Min, BA, MA/Con **West Chester U,** Main 211, West Chester, PA 19383—Women's
Studies, Stacey Schlau, Coord. Program offers an 18-cr minor, the BA in
Counseling Women through Liberal Studies, and a Leadership for Women con-
centration at the MA level.

Min **West Florida, U of,** 11000 University Parkway, Pensacola, FL 32514—Women's
Studies (c/o Dept of Sociology), Mary F. Rogers, Coord. Program offers a minor.

AA **West Valley C,** 14000 Fruitvale Ave, Saratoga, CA 95070—Women's Studies, Julie
Maia, Coord. Program offers the AA.

Cer, Min, MA **West Virginia U,** 218 Eiesland Hall, Box 6450, Morgantown, WV

26506-6450—Center for Women's Studies, Helen M. Bannan, Dir. Program offers a 19-cr certificate, a 19-hr undergraduate minor in the College of Arts and Sciences, and the MA through Liberal Studies.

Min **Western Connecticut SU,** 181 White St, Danbury, CT 06810—Women's Studies, Mary Friel and Jerry Bannister, Coords. Program offers an 18-cr interdisciplinary minor.

Min **Western Illinois U,** 410 Morgan, Macomb, IL 61455—Women's Studies (c/o Dept of Sociology), Polly Radosh, Dir. Program offers a minor.

Min **Western Maryland C,** Westminster, MD 21157—Women's Studies, Tim Weinfeld, Coord. Program offers a 6-course minor.

Min, BA **Western Michigan U,** Kalamazoo, MI 49008—Institute for Women's Studies, Gwen Raaberg, Dir. Program offers a 16-hr minor and a 24-hr BA.

Min, BA **Western Washington U,** Bellingham, WA 98225—Women's Studies, Rosanne Kanhai, Dir. Program offers a 30-qtr-unit minor and an individualized BA.

Min **Westfield SC,** Westfield, MA 01086—Women's Studies (c/o Liberal Studies Program), Brooks Robards, Adviser. Program offers an 18-cr minor.

Min, BA **Wheaton C,** Norton, MA 02766—Women's Studies, Kersti Yllo and Frinde Maher, Coords. Program offers a 20-cr minor and an individualized BA.

Min **Whitman C,** Walla Walla, WA 99362—Gender Studies, Naomi Abrahams, Dana Burgess, and Andrea Dobson, Advisers. Program offers a 20-cr minor.

Min, BA, MA/Con **Wichita SU,** Box 82, Wichita, KS 67260-0082—Center for Women's Studies, Dorothy C. Miller, Chair. Program offers a 15-cr minor, a BA, and an MA concentration through Liberal Studies.

Min, BA/Con **William & Mary, C of,** Williamsburg, VA 23185—Women's Studies, Nancy Gray, Dir. Program offers a 32-cr concentration through Interdisciplinary Studies and a 19-hr minor.

Min **William Paterson C of New Jersey,** 300 Pompton Rd, Wayne, NJ 07470—Women's Studies, Barbara Sandberg, Dir. Program offers an 18-cr minor.

Con **Williams C,** Stetson Hall, Williamstown, MA 01267—Women's Studies, Jana Sawicki, Chair. Program offers a 5-course concentration.

Min, BA **Wilson C,** Philadelphia Ave, Chambersburg, PA 17201—Women's Studies, Beverly Ayers-Nachamkin, Coord. Program offers a 6-course minor and a 14-course special BA.

Windward CC, 45-720 Keaahala Rd, Kaneohe, HI 96744—Women's Studies, Janice Nuckols, Coord.

Min **Winthrop U,** Rock Hill, SC 29733—Women's Studies (c/o College of Arts and Sciences), April Gordon, Coord. Program offers an 18-hr minor.

Min **Wisconsin, U of, Eau Claire,** Eau Claire, WI 54702-4004—Women's Studies, Sarah Harder, Coord. Program offers a 24-cr minor.

Con, Min, BA **Wisconsin, U of, Green Bay,** 2420 Nicolet Dr, Green Bay, WI 54311—Women's Studies, Joanne Stohs, Chair. Program offers an area of emphasis, a 21-cr minor, and an individualized BA.

Min **Wisconsin, U of, La Crosse,** La Crosse, WI 54601—Women's Studies, 336 North Hall, Sandra Krajewski, Chair. Program offers a 24-cr minor.

Cer, BA, Grad Min, MA, PhD **Wisconsin, U of, Madison,** 110 Ingraham, 1155

Observatory Dr, Madison, WI 53706—Women's Studies, Mariamne Whatley, Chair. Program offers a 15-cr certificate, a BA, and a 12-cr graduate minor; History Dept also offers the MA and PhD in women's history.

Cer, BA, Grad Cer **Wisconsin, U of, Milwaukee,** PO Box 413, Milwaukee, WI 53201—Center for Women's Studies, Susan Burgess, Dir. Program offers an 18-cr undergraduate certificate, the BA through the Undergraduate Interdisciplinary Program, and a 12-cr graduate certificate.

Min **Wisconsin, U of, Oshkosh,** 314 A/C Bldg, Oshkosh, WI 54901—Women's Studies, Randi Warne, Dir. Program offers a minor.

Min **Wisconsin, U of, Parkside,** PO Box 2000, Kenosha, WI 53141—Women's Studies, Fran Kavenik, Dir. Program offers an 18-cr minor.

Cer, Min **Wisconsin, U of, Platteville,** 446 Gardner Hall, One University Plaza, Platteville, WI 53818—Women's Studies, Kathryn Winz, Dir. Program offers a 15-cr certificate and a 24-cr minor.

Min **Wisconsin, U of, River Falls,** River Falls, WI 54022—Women's Studies, Kathy Tomlinson, Coord. Program offers a minor.

Min **Wisconsin, U of, Stevens Point,** Stevens Point, WI 54481—Women's Studies, Nancy Bayne, Coord. Program offers a 22-cr minor.

Min **Wisconsin, U of, Stout,** Menomonie, WI 54751—Women's Studies, Sheri Nero, Coord. Program offers a 22-cr minor.

Min **Wisconsin, U of, Superior,** Superior, WI 54880—Women's Studies, Michael Ball, Coord. Program offers a 22-cr minor.

Cer, Min, BA **Wisconsin, U of, Whitewater,** 800 W Main St, 338 Salisbury, Whitewater, WI 53190—Women's Studies, Star Olderman, Chair. Program offers a 15-cr certificate, a 21-cr minor, and a 33-cr BA.

Min **Wittenberg U,** Springfield, OH 45501—Women's Studies, Robin Inboden, Dir. Program offers a 24-cr minor.

Min, BA **Wooster, C of,** Wooster, OH 44691—Women's Studies, Carolyn Durham, Chair. Program offers an 18-cr minor and a 42-cr BA.

Worcester SC, 486 Chandler St, Worcester, MA 01602—Women's Studies, Helena Semerjian, Coord.

Wright SU, Dayton, OH 45435—Women's Studies, Anne Sisson Runyan, Dir.

Min, BA **Wyoming, U of,** Laramie, WY 82071—Women's Studies, Janice H. Harris, Chair. Program offers an 18-cr minor and a 36-cr BA.

Min **Xavier U,** 3800 Victory Pkwy, Cincinnati, OH 45207—Women's Studies, Kandi M. Stinson. Program offers a minor.

Min **Yakima Valley CC,** PO Box 1647, Yakima, WA 98902—Women's Programs, Kathryn Calvert, Coord. Program offers a 17-cr minor.

BA **Yale U,** Box 5046, 315 WLH, P.O. Box 208319, New Haven, CT 06520-8319—Women's Studies. Program offers a BA.

Min, BA **Youngstown SU,** DeBartolo Hall 355, Youngstown, OH 44555—Center for Women's Studies, Linda Strom, Dir. Program offers a 21-hr minor and a major through an individualized curriculum program.

AA **Yuba CC,** 2088 N Beale Rd, Marysville, CA 95901—Women's Studies, Lynn Ireland, Coord. Program offers a 62-cr AA.

Newsbriefs

ACTIVISM

STITCH, a national network of women in the United States that seeks to support Guatemalan women workers, is attempting to link U.S. women's groups with women in Guatemalan union and community groups who are organizing around economic issues. STITCH is mobilizing a U.S. support effort against the multinational corporation Phillips-Van Heusen, where Guatemalan women workers are attempting to unionize and protest poverty-level wages and violations of basic human rights. For more information about the campaign, contact Hannah Frisch at US/GLEP, 773-262-6502.

CALLS FOR PAPERS

The *Asian Journal of Women's Studies* has issued a call for articles, book reviews, and commentaries from international sources that address women's issues, including sexuality, labor, and cultural and political issues, especially in the Asian context. Simultaneous submissions and previously published materials are not considered. Manuscripts should be in English, double spaced on single-sided paper, and no more than 30 pages; please send hard copy and 3.5" disk in MS Word or WordPerfect 5.1. Submission deadline for the winter 1997 issue is 30 September 1997. Send to Editor, *Asian Journal of Women's Studies,* Asian Center for Women's Studies, Ewha Womans University, Seoul 120-750, Republic of Korea or e-mail to acwsewha@nownuri.nowcom.co.kr.

The editorial collective of *Feminist Teacher* seeks articles, syllabi, and bibliographies from a variety of feminist viewpoints. For manuscript guidelines, write to *Feminist Teacher,* Wheaton College, Norton, MA 02766.

Frontiers: A Journal of Women's Studies invites submissions for a special 1998 issue on women's oral history. Oral history practitioner's articles should describe and analyze visual as well as oral and prose histories. Creative responses from fiction writers, poets, artists, and photographers are welcome. For submission guidelines, write to Sue Armitage, Editor, *Frontiers: A Journal of Women Studies,* Wilson 12, Washington State University, Pullman, WA 99164-4007; tel: 509-335-7268; e-mail: frontier@wsu.edu.

The *Journal of Visual Impairment and Blindness* seeks submissions for a 1998 special issue on gender and blindness and also an issue slated for publication in 2000 tentatively entitled "Measuring Outcomes." To discuss article ideas on these or related topics or to request contributor guidelines, please contact a JVIB editor; phone: 212-502-7648/9, e-mail: dbrookshire@afb.org; web site: http://www.afb.org/afb/.

The *Journal of Women's History* seeks submissions for a special 1999 issue on women and the politics of religion. The issue will focus on the history and rise of "fundamentalist" movements within diverse religious traditions. Submission deadline is 1 September 1997. For submission guidelines, write to Fundamentalism Issue, *Journal of Women's History,* c/o Dept of History, Ohio State University, 230 W 17th Ave, Columbus, OH 43210.

Signs: *Journal of Women in Culture and Society* seeks submissions for the summer 1999 issue, on "Institutions, Regulation, and Social Control." Interdisciplinary and collaborative submissions are welcomed. Submit 5 copies of articles no later than 31 October 1997 to *Signs,* Institutions, Regulation, and Social Control, Box 354345, University of Washington, Seattle, WA 98195-4345.

CONFERENCES

The second **Centre for the Study of Southern African Literature and Languages Conference** will be held 24–27 September 1997 in Durban, South Africa. Proposals addressing the conference topic, "Body, Identity, Sub-Cultures, and Repression in Texts From Africa," should be submitted before 31 August 1997. For more information contact CSSALL, University of Durban-Westville, Private Bag X54001, Durban 4001, South Africa; phone/fax: 82-02245; e-mail: cssal@pixie.udw.ac.za.

The Women's Environment and Development Organization (WEDO) of New York and The Kingston Breast Cancer Conference Committee of Kingston have joined together to host the **First World Conference on Breast Cancer,** 13–17 July 1997, in Kingston, Ontario, Canada. To register, write to World Conference on Breast Cancer Registration Office, P.O. Box 1570, 190 Railway Street, Kingston, Ontario, Canada K71 5C8; phone: 613-531-9210; fax: 613-531-0626; e-mail: event@adan. kingston.net. For more information, write to WEDO, 355 Lexington Avenue, 3rd floor, New York, NY 10017, USA; phone: 212-973-0325; fax: 212-973-0335; e-mail: wedo@igc.apc.org; http://www.wedo.org.

The **Institute for Women's Policy Research** welcomes proposals for its 12–13 June 1998 conference discussing women's progress in the areas of labor market and employment, family and work, poverty and welfare, and health care policy. Proposals must be postmarked by 17 October 1997. For details call 202-785-5100; e-mail: iwpr@www.iwpr.org; http://www.iwpr.org.

The **Oral History Association** invites proposals for presentations and papers for its 1998 annual meeting, "Crossing the Boundary, Crossing the Line: Oral History on

the Border," 15–18 October 1998, Buffalo, NY. The deadline for proposals is 15
December 1997. For further information, contact Debra Bernhardt, Robert F.
Wagner Labor Archives, 70 Washington Square South, New York, NY 10012; phone:
212-998-2640; fax: 212-995-4070; e-mail (queries only): bernhrdt@elmer1.
bobst.nyu.edu.

Cornell University will host **Reviewing the 'Woman's Era': A Conference on the
Literary and Cultural Work of Turn-of-the-Century African American Women,**
26–28 September 1997. Inquiries should be addressed to "Woman's Era"
Conference, Professor Lois Lamphere Brown, Dept of English, 342 Rockefeller
Hall, Cornell University, Ithaca, NY 14853.

FELLOWSHIPS

The **University of Michigan Center for the Education of Women Visiting Scholar
Program** invites inquiries and applications from scholars and practitioners interested in residence at CEW for a period of 1–12 months. Areas of particular interest include women in leadership; women in science, mathematics, and
engineering; women, education, and public policy (local, state, federal); women
in academia; and women and careers. For more information, contact Carol
Hollenshead, Director, Center for the Education of Women, University of Michigan,
330 E. Liberty Street, Ann Arbor, MI 48104-2289; e-mail: chollens@umich.edu.

The **Women's Research and Education Institute** is accepting applications from
graduate students for the **1997–1998 Congressional Fellowships on Women and
Public Policy.** The fellowship program places students in congressional offices and
on strategic committee staffs to work as legislative aides on policy issues affecting
women. For applications, send an SASE to WREI, 1750 New York Ave NW, Ste 350,
Washington, DC 20006; phone: 202-628-0444.

PUBLICATIONS

The **International Gay and Lesbian Human Rights Commission** recently compiled
and published a work entitled *Unspoken Rules: Sexual Orientation and Women's Rights*
as part of an effort to raise awareness of human rights violations against women
because of their sexual orientation. Contact IGLHRC, 1360 Mission St, Ste 200,
San Francisco, CA 94103; phone: 415-255-8680.

The **Institute of International Education,** working to "strengthen the international
competence of U.S. citizens," recently released a publication entitled *Increasing
Women's Participation in International Scholarship Programs: An Analysis of Nine Case
Studies* by Rona Kluger. Contact the Institute of International Education, 809
United Nations Plaza, New York, NY 10017-3580.

Issues Quarterly, a publication of The National Council for Research on Women, announces the release of a special issue on Beijing conference follow-up, entitled *IQ: Beyond Beijing: Who's Doing What to Turn Words Into Action?* Issues are $5.00 each; bulk discounts are available. Contact NCRW, 530 Broadway, 10th Fl, New York, NY 10012-3920.

The **National Center for Curriculum Transformation Resources on Women** has recently issued its catalog of publications, Women in the Curriculum. The publications consist of directories, manuals, and essays covering the primary information needed by educators to incorporate scholarship on women into the curriculum. Tables of contents and sample passages are available on http://www.towson.edu/ncctrw/. For information, write to the National Center for Curriculum Transformation Resources on Women, LLT 317, Towson State University, 8000 York Road, Baltimore, MD 21252; phone: 410-830-3944; e-mail: ncctrw@towson.edu. To place orders call 800-847-9922.

The only international women's news service, **Women's Feature Service,** founded in 1978, produced 400 feature stories during the past year. E-mail and bimonthly subscriptions are available. Write to wfs@igc.apc.org or to Women's Feature Service, 20 W 20th St, Ste 1103, New York, NY 10011.

The **World Health Organization** recently issued its annual 1997 report entitled *Conquering Suffering, Enriching Humanity,* which focuses on chronic diseases. For further information write Thomson Prentice, Health Communications and Public Relations WHO, Geneva, Switzerland; phone: 41-22-791-4224; e-mail: prenticet@who.ch.

AJWS

Asian Journal of Women's Studies

Asian Center for Women's Studies
Ewha Womans University Press

AJWS is an interdisciplinary journal, publishing articles pertaining to women's issues in Asia from a feminist perspective. The journal offers articles with a theoretical focus, country reports providing valuable information on specific subject and countries, and booknotes containing more information on recent publication on women in Asia.

The first edition of the jounal was published in 1995 in commemoration of opening the **Asian Center for Women's Studies** at Ewha Womans University in Seoul, Korea. As of 1997 the journal is to be published four times a year.

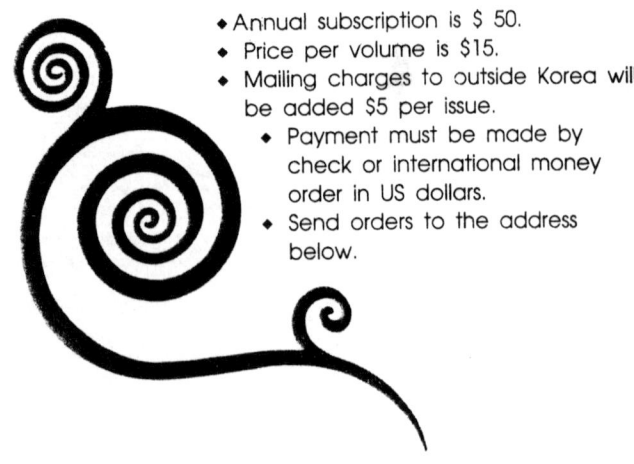

- ◆ Annual subscription is $ 50.
- ◆ Price per volume is $15.
- ◆ Mailing charges to outside Korea will be added $5 per issue.
  - ◆ Payment must be made by check or international money order in US dollars.
  - ◆ Send orders to the address below.

Asian Center for Women's Studies
Ewha Womans University
Seoul (120-750), Korea
Tel : (82-2) 360-2150   Fax : (82-2) 360-2577
E-mail : acwsewha@nownuri.net